Tahitians

S0-BTA-112

Robert I. Levy

Illustrated by Pierre Heyman

Tahitians

Mind and Experience in the Society Islands

University of Chicago Press
Chicago and London

The University of Chicago Press, Chicago 60637
The University of Chicago Press, Ltd., London

© 1973 by The University of Chicago
All rights reserved. Published 1973
Printed in the United States of America
International Standard Book Number: 0-226-47605-7
Library of Congress Catalog Card Number: 73-77136
80 79 78 77 76 98765432

Robert I. Levy is professor of anthropology at the University of California at San Diego. He is a specialist in clinical psychiatry, social psychiatry, and psychological and cultural anthropology. His earlier experiences have included private practice in psychiatry.

Pierre Heyman, the illustrator of this work, was born in Paris in 1908. He began studying painting with André Lhote in 1926. In 1934 he went to Tahiti and has lived there ever since. He is now the foremost contemporary illustrator of Tahitian people and life.

1973

To Gregory Bateson

Rabbi Baruch once said,

"What a good and bright world this is if we

do not lose our hearts to it,

but what a dark world if we do!"

Martin Buber, *Tales of the Hasidim*

Contents

Acknowledgments

This is a first book and I am much indebted. First, for essential things learned, to Rabbi Harold Sapirstein, Théophile Kahn, Leon Kaplan, Dina Goldstein, John Frosch, Clara Thompson, Jane and Felix Posen, and to my parents Nathan and Miriam Levy.

The work in Tahiti required the support and faith of many people. Alexander Simon and Stanley Bateman of the School of Medicine of the University of California at San Francisco encouraged and helped me during the planning and pilot study periods. At Tahiti, Aurora Natua, Bengt and Marie-Thérèse Danielsson, Alan Tyree, and Roruhama Hira shared with me their deep understanding of Tahitian life and history.

I have a special debt to Ralph Gardner White of Punaauia, Tahiti. His profound studies of the Tahitian language greatly facilitated my task. The copious marginalia that he wrote on the typed transcriptions he made of tape-recorded interviews clarified many problems and prevented some foolishness.

Officials, scientists, missionaries, and people in commerce in Tahiti and the Leeward Islands were consistently helpful and generous to me, provided much information, and facilitated my work in many ways. I am particularly indebted to the social scientists of the Office de la recherche scientifique et technique Outre-Mer — Michel Julien, Michel Panoff, Paul Ottino, and Claude Robineau — for a multitude of kindnesses and instructions.

The book will attest to what I owe the people of Piri and Roto. They will understand that I am writing about myself as well as about them. And when, soon, they begin to wonder how they look to *pōpa'a* eyes, perhaps this work will help.

The National Institute of Mental Health supported my pilot study, and the National Science Foundation supported my subsequent research. Albert Spaulding and Richard Lieban of the National Science Foundation were repeatedly helpful during the years of the grant.

I was able to begin to digest and report on the fieldwork thanks to some years of relative peace and quiet in Hawaii, first as a senior fellow at the Center for Cultural and Technical Interchange between East and West, and then as an associate of the Social Science Research Institute at the University of Hawaii. Much kindness, support, and stimulation came from Arthur Feraru, then director of the Fellows program at the center, and William Lebra, then director of the institute.

Several colleagues have read earlier versions of some sections of the book. I am grateful to Ronald Gallimore, James Ritchie, Lee Sechrest, Roy D'Andrade, Melford Spiro, and Sam Nelken for useful agreements and disagreements.

Helen Takeuchi and Judith Wolf typed, edited, did research, corrected grammar, and actively and with great skill helped make the book.

There are four persons who are intimately involved with the ideas and images in this book, and to whom I owe affectionate gratitude. Alan Howard and I have had a continuing dialogue about Polynesian matters; and we are not sure who thought of what first. My cousin, Roy Rappaport, and I have been instructing each other since childhood and many of our conversations are in this book. Douglas Oliver invited me into this study, let me read his unpublished manuscripts and field notes, and helped me find my way toward significant questions. Gregory Bateson, to whom this book is dedicated, through his friendship, teaching, and writing has helped me think about what I have seen.

And, finally, Jehanne Teilhet has shared and has helped me keep a sense of proportion throughout much of this.

Several sections of the book contain material which I have published elsewhere in more or less similar form. The publishers have kindly given permission for use of passages from the following articles and chapters:

Ma'ohi drinking patterns in the Society Islands. *Journal of the Polynesian Society* 75 (1966).

Tahiti observed: Early European impressions of Tahitian personal style. *Journal of the Polynesian Society* 77 (1968).

Tahitian folk psychotherapy. *International Mental Health Research Newsletter* 9 (1967).

Child management structure and its implications in a Tahitian family. In *A modern introduction to the family*, ed. Ezra Vogel and Norman Bell. New York: Free Press, 1968.

On getting angry in the Society Islands. In *Mental health research in Asia and the Pacific*, ed. William Caudill and Tsung-Yi Lin. Honolulu: East-West Center Press, 1969.

Tahitian adoption as a psychological message. In *Adoption in Eastern Oceania*, ed. Vern Carroll. Honolulu: University of Hawaii Press, 1970.

Tahitian Protestantism: Personal forms and meanings. *Journal de la Société des Océanistes* 25 (1969).

The community function of Tahitian male transvestitism: A hypothesis. *Anthropological Quarterly* 44 (1971).

Tahiti, sin, and the question of integration between personality and sociocultural systems. In *The psychoanalytic study of society*, vol. 5, ed. Warner Muensterberger and Aaron Esman. New York: International Universities Press.

Introduction

Between 1954 and 1963 Professor Douglas Oliver and several of his students made a number of studies in the Society Islands of French Polynesia. Their major concern was the social dynamics of life in eight Tahitian-speaking communities. These communities are in a group of islands which had been culturally and socially integrated until their discovery by Europeans. Language, religion, political forms, and life-style were, with only a little variation, common to the area, which was united by alliances, by frequent visits, and by institutional forms spanning the entire group and holding them in a loose interaction that stopped short, however, of formal political unification.

The first European landing in the group that now constitutes the Society Islands[1] was on Tahiti, and within a very few years after the discovery of Tahiti, writers started designating the language and characteristics of the Society Island group as "Tahitian."[2]

"Tahitian" is used today by the islanders themselves, as well as by the westerners living there, to refer to indigenous aspects of Society Island life. "Tahitian" is not used to designate the other Polynesian cultures of French Polynesia — the peoples, languages, and customs of the Marquesas, Tuamotus, and Australs. "Tahitian" is also used to designate some aspects of life on the island

1. The present Society Islands were first named by Cook as two groups — the Georgian Islands and the Society Islands.
2. "As I shall frequently mention the inhabitants of Tahiti and of the Society Islands, in comparison with other islanders, it will be proper to observe that since the natives both of Tahiti and of the Society Islands are perfectly alike in most respects, I shall indifferently call a custom Tahitian, or usual at the Society Islands, which is common to them both. Therefore, unless I expressly put these terms in contradistinction to each other, I wish to have them understood in general as synonymous" (G. Forster 1777; 1: 424).

of Tahiti itself — in contrast to one of the other Society Island communities — in contexts where this limited meaning is clear.

Samuel Wallis, who discovered the island of Tahiti to the west, sailed into Matavai Bay on the north coast of Tahiti on 19 June 1767. Matavai Bay is a large, sheltered harbor, one of the best on the island, and it became the first port of call for most of the European vessels that quickly followed Wallis. Throughout the succeeding years most of the western influences on the Society Islands — political, religious, economic, and the everyday man-to-man or man-to-woman encounter of values and styles — entered the Society Islands through Papeete, the town which grew up near Matavai Bay. As the chiefs of the district in which Papeete was situated became, with European help, paramount chiefs or "kings" of increasing extents of the islands, Papeete became their seat. It became the principal port of call for whalers and traders, the center for burgeoning missionary enterprises, and later the political and administrative center.

Through the years the modern world — warships, schools, hospitals, breweries, cinemas, newspapers, electrification, hotels, and tourism — came first to Papeete. Until very recently much of it stayed there, passing beyond only in very diluted doses. The distant villages and islands still maintained much of their old technology, much of their ability to live off the land and sea; they underwent, however, a slowly increasing involvement in market economy based on vanilla, copra, and, most recently, food crops for the markets of Papeete. Involvement with western forms and enterprises has increased in recent years; but, in general, the farther a village is from the town of Papeete and the more difficult it is to reach it from that town, the less involvement it has had with the variety of western-introduced forms. By studying villages at various distances and difficulty of access from Papeete, one has an opportunity to see what effects, if any, these variations in degree of involvement with "the West" have had on traditional life.

In order to exploit these comparative features, Douglas Oliver, Paul Kay, Ben Finney, and Anthony Hooper, the members of the research group most concerned with village social organization, each worked in two communities, selected to provide contrast in accessibility and intensity of interaction with Papeete. Complementing this village research were studies by Richard Moench on the Chinese community in the Society Islands and by Roger Green, by means of archaeological techniques, on the settlement patterns in the islands before European contact.

In 1960 Douglas Oliver invited me to participate in the study. The work of the anthropologists involved those aspects of village life which had to do primarily with the systematic organization of social relationships and the performance of village and group tasks, particularly economic enterprises. They were interested in the public aspects of behavior, those aspects that were most evidently related to the maintenance of organized village life. My task was to try to find out something about the more private, personal aspects of behavior and how such aspects were related to the public world which was of concern to the anthropologists. This book is a report of my study. It is an attempt to describe and to reflect upon some aspects of Tahitian experience.

In keeping with the project's emphasis on comparison, I selected two communities for this study. One of them, which will be given the pseudonym Piri, is[3] relatively rural, traditional, and isolated. The other community is an enclave in the town of Papeete; it is in the social center of the islands and thus much closer in numerous ways to the outside world. It will be called Roto. These communities had previously been worked in, respectively, by Douglas Oliver and Paul Kay. I was thus able to enter the communities with detailed information on censuses, household membership, kin relationships, and community economics.

I worked in the Society Islands for twenty-six months, first during a pilot study in July and August 1961, then during the two-year period between July 1962 and June 1964. Most of my

---

3. In all studies of changing communities written up after some time has passed, one must choose the tense in which the community is to be described. The present tense will be used for conditions during the period of the study. As the postscript, based on another visit to the communities some nine years after the beginning of the study, indicates, much is changing.

time was spent in Piri, which was the major setting for my work, with Roto being used secondarily for comparison.

In the months before and after the first field period I made a number of preparations for the study. I hoped to base my study on psychiatric skills of observation and interviewing. Such interviewing directed to private worlds requires, ideally, an almost native competence in language and nonlinguistic communication. I approached this by two years of preliminary study with native Tahitian speakers in the United States and by deferring intensive life history and "psychodynamic" interviews until the end of the first year of fieldwork. One helpful entrée into the "psychological vocabulary" was the use of John Davies's *Tahitian and English Dictionary* (1851), which includes some eleven thousand terms collected by the English missionaries working in the islands in the early years of the nineteenth century. Almost sixteen hundred terms of psychological relevance were found in this dictionary and were employed as a checklist for modern Tahitian vocabulary and usage in relation to psychological description. There will be frequent reference to the Davies "missionary" dictionary throughout the book.

In addition to language it was necessary to learn as much as possible about the public culture; for psychological judgments, if they are to be more than ethnocentric fantasies, have to begin with a thorough knowledge of traditional, more or less conventional, aspects of behavior — of "culture." I approached this in part through a study of the extensive descriptive literature on the Society Islands, which began on the day of European discovery. The European explorers, sea captains, naturalists, sailors, missionaries, and commercial men — encountering the Society Islands at a time when description of the inhabitants of new worlds was of intense interest to the people of Europe — produced copious descriptions of Tahitian institutions and of everyday Tahitian life. The many descriptions of "small interactions" — of drinking, of responses to threats, of attitudes during religious rites, of sexual behavior — gave some clues to what I am here calling "private behavior" during the first years of western contact. These forms, seen in the light of my own field observations and in comparison with description of the behavior of culturally related Polynesian peoples, provide the basis for some speculations about traditional aspects of psychological forms. Similarly, later descriptions of Tahitian life provide clues to stability and change in these forms. Historical materials are used throughout the book to illuminate contemporary life and processes of stability and change.

The two contrasting emphases, "private" and "public," which guided my first questions and observations are not at all isomorphic with such higher abstractions as "personality" and "culture." But the two pairs are intimately related. A knowledge of private reactions is a necessary first step for thinking about an individual's "internal psychological organization."

By "private" I mean those aspects of an individual's experience which are related to his body, his feelings, his sense of self, his needs for personal definition and integration, his understanding of what is going on around him as it involves himself. "Public" includes those aspects of his behavior most related to, most influenced by, the systematic relationships and formal arenas of community life. The village chief acting as chief is public; the fears and pleasures of the man acting the role are private. One must not overemphasize these distinctions. There are varying degrees of publicness and of privacy, but no pure cases. There is personality and psychology in the most public behavior and culture in the most private.

The plan of presentation in the book generally follows the sequence of observation and understanding, of abstraction, involved during my work. There is first a sketch of the setting and community life, then an introduction to some individual lives, and finally a survey of some of the general, shared, or prevalent qualities of private life. The book begins concretely and descriptively. As it proceeds there is a shift toward a consideration of more general aspects of psychological organization, and the discussion becomes more abstract and further from observed behavior.

The book is directed to two audiences, and what is written for one is sometimes irrelevant for the other. One audience is those who are interested in the natural history of this sample of Polynesian life; the other is those concerned with problems of psychological anthropology and of personality theory. I ask the forbearance of both groups as I slip back and forth from one audience to the other.

The description of some of the general aspects of community life which begins the book was based on community observation, including the observation of life in some households, and on the use of people as "informants" ("Tell me about life in Piri") rather than as "cases," subjects of study in themselves.

In the last year of the study, when I felt that I had sufficient competence in the language and knowledge of the general organization of community life, I began "psychodynamic interviewing." This differed from traditional psychoanalytic interviewing in many significant aspects and more closely resembles "psychodiagnostic interviewing." Some remarks on the form and limits of this kind of interviewing are necessary here.

Alex Inkeles and Daniel Levinson (1954) pointed out that one of the several difficulties in national character studies was that workers had tended to organize their data in such a way that the studies were not comparable; each author had studied those "psychological elements" which seemed significant to him, and there was, for example, no way of telling if the slighting of a topic was a sign of its unimportance among the people studied or a matter of neglect. For comparative studies some sort of standard check sheet of significant categories would have to be used. But which categories, at what level of organization? The problem was the a priori imposition of western categories on nonwestern data versus the search for possible new categories relevant to the inquiry, with the latter involving the problem of noncomparability.

My own thinking was influenced by Freudian models of personality organization, by neo-Freudian criticisms and developments of psychoanalytic concepts, and by more recent aspects of behavioral and cognitive theory, particularly the work of Gregory Bateson. To try to make the topics chosen for inquiry comparable with those of standard psychodynamic concern, I used a check sheet of psychodynamic constructs developed by the Institute for Human Development at the University of California at Berkeley. This was used to supplement psychological constructs suggested by various writers, by my own interests, and by the pilot field study. These various constructs (e.g., "identification," "pathology," "internalized behavioral controls") guided me in constructing a questionnaire, or more properly check sheet, based in part on suggestions from a question schedule used by the Institute for Human Development. This comprised a minimal set of topics to be covered in the open-ended psychodynamic interviews given during the latter part of the fieldwork. Discussion was guided into certain areas, and items on the check sheet which had not been spontaneously discussed were systematically brought up. The check sheet is reproduced in Appendix 1.

The psychodynamic interviews were recorded on tape and then transcribed in typescript on an exact phonemic basis, first by myself and then by Ralph White, a linguist specializing in the Tahitian language. Appendix 2 gives a sample of the transcription, with a literal translation of a passage which is used in free translation in chapter 11. All direct quotations given in this book are translations of tape-recorded statements. In these transcripts my statements to the subject are in parentheses, and my comments on the transcript are in brackets. Dashes indicate pauses, and ellipsis points denote the omission of some transcribed material. All the tape recordings were eventually checked with Tahitian informants from other communities to help in interpreting idiomatic and idiosyncratic usages and in interpreting paralinguistic clues on the tape — involving such information as anxiety, irony, impatience, and so on — essential additions to the verbal statements.[4]

4. In a study of paralinguistic behavior, *The first five minutes* by Robert Pittenger, Charles Hockett, and John Danehy (1960), the authors assert that paralinguistic habits "show variation from culture to culture and from region to region. They are as much the product of experience as are one's language habits" (p. 185). Actually, after the semantic and syntactical conventions of Tahitian were learned, most of the paralinguistic aspects of utterances immediately became clear to me, as validated by contexts, later

Tape-recorded interviews were done with twenty persons in Piri and Roto; of these, nine (seven men and two women) in Piri and three (two men and one woman) in Roto were chosen, according to criteria which will be noted later, for detailed, generalized interviews. The number of tape-recorded interviews per person ranged from two to eight; the interviews lasted from one to two hours each and produced typed transcripts totaling some twenty-nine hundred pages. These interviews were done after I had had many months of acquaintance with the people involved and often after a great deal of life-history material had been gathered through systematic, relatively formal interviewing which was not tape-recorded. The tape-recorded interviews were not primarily life-history interviews, but an attempt to elicit individuals' *responses* to that history and to their present life.

In both Piri and Roto I had a work house separated from other houses where people could talk in a privacy which was for most of them a unique experience.

The relatively open interview, the invitation to talk about such subjects as death, anger, and childhood as they wished, with prods and queries from me ("Why did you put it like that?" "What did you feel when that happened?" "You don't seem to like to talk about that subject") led to the kind of personally organized statements — clumping of themes, slips of the tongue, obvious defensive maneuvers, evidence of emotion, fantasy, and speculative thinking — which is the stuff of psychodynamic model-building.

The tape recordings were of great usefulness to me here. Many of these formal characteristics of the interviews were not ap-

---

information, and the consensus of Tahitian hearers. This was to be expected of those forms connected with body state — symptoms of, say, anxiety or anger — but it also was true of such varied messages about messages as "insincerity," "direct quotation," "uncertainty," "reference to the uncanny." There are a limited number of logical variations on a conventional speech pattern, and they seem to have a strong *analogical* relation (hesitation, lack of expected resolution, rushing, and combination of such elements) to the message which is directly cross-culturally understandable in a way that the local word for "tree" is not.

parent to me until I had listened to the tape recordings or studied the typed transcripts of the interviews. I was then able to follow up clues from the tapes in further interviews. The use of recordings makes it possible, in cross-cultural interviewing, to discern formal characteristics which might have required many more hours of ongoing interviews before they became obvious or which might never have been discovered.

Anyone familiar with psychoanalytic interviewing technique will have perceived that a number of field conditions strongly modify the technique and its possibilities. It was impossible to give a fully nonstructured interview to busy villagers. They had no reason (in contrast with symptom-laden "patients" expecting relief) to tell me at length "anything that comes into your head." Furthermore, they had good reason *not* to tell me some private things. I lived in the village, participated in its social life. They had little motivation to "give away" any thought or memory which might cause too much present discomfort or create an apparent threat to status or self-respect. It was surprising to me, nevertheless, how frankly they did talk. In part this was perhaps because for most people the interviews provided a unique chance to explore and share their private worlds, in contrast to the very public, psychologically superficial interpersonal styles and pressures of Tahitian community life. The series of interviews became, I believe, for most of the subjects their first chance to try to articulate and communicate seriously their private thoughts and feelings. Most of them were reluctant to end the interview series, asking me, when we would meet, "Isn't there something else you would like to know about?"

Another major contrast was the status of "transference," the subject's complex of tendencies to interpret and respond to our relationship, presumably based on generalizations of various early developmental experiences. For the subject and I had real and complex relationships before and outside of the interview series; and I could only make fairly obscure guesses about the transference and countertransference aspects of the interviews.

There is a further difference from standard psychoanalytic method. The goal of the latter is to a large degree to understand the unique mix and organization of psychological elements in an individual; one expects now to find few new elements (e.g., a previously undescribed defense mechanism). But I was looking for more or less generalized village patterns of experience and personal organization or major variations and contrasts in those patterns. This is a different observational task from attempting to define the unique qualities of an individual. It is, in fact, logically prior to it. It has to be done first.

Just as one must have some understanding of cultural generalities, of conventional forms, before one can understand personal relationships to those forms, so one must understand something about shared or prevalent psychological qualities before one can study and understand variations, whether those variations designate a *type* of person (e.g., innovator, leader, deviant) or a unique individual.

I have included sketches of individuals and notes on some aspects of variation of interest for social analysis. But I am not concerned here with the more idiosyncratic components of an individual's personality, those components presumably determined by the fine details of his constitution and his developmental adventures, by his responses to the unique reality of his experience. The markedly different stylistic, ethical, and psychological qualities of my respondents, their colorful individualities, are background, as is their evident common humanity, the first basis of our relationships and of my understanding of them. I am interested here in their *experience as Tahitians.* I believe that my methods revealed much of this. But it must be kept in mind that these methods and my interest in *Tahitian* qualities produce a partial portrait.

Consideration of Tahitian experience implies a contrast or a comparison with the experience and modalities of other *groups* — primarily the western patients, college sophomores, and nursery-school children on whom so much observation rests — and it involves the sense of normality of western psychological practitioners and theorists. This orientation to a large degree determines the questions one asks and the observations one makes in exotic places ("Why are the Tahitians so unaggressive?"). The fact that psychodynamic data are fundamentally relational makes things complicated, but this seems to be a condition of much, and perhaps the most interesting, human knowledge.

It follows that Tahitians would be described differently by, say, an Eskimo anthropologist, an event which would extend, not controvert, other descriptions, excepting error or autism.

It also follows that if one were to shift one's emphasis from "Tahitian experience" to the contrasting experiences of individual Tahitians, both as perceived by themselves and as progressively clarified to an outside observer, the dimensions of contrast and of interesting observation would probably differ in many ways from those characterizing Tahitian experience in comparison with some sample of non-Tahitians.

I will generally proceed to report on and discuss my findings as though they were absolute and not relational. It is difficult to proceed otherwise. The old Jewish joke is appropriate here:

Sam to Harry: "How is your wife?"

Harry: "Compared to what?"

It will also be apparent that my information on the specially male aspects of experience (e.g., supercision, male sexual experience) is more extensive than that on the uniquely feminine aspects of experience (e.g., menstruation, female sexual experience). There were barriers of propriety in talking about some areas of experience with many women, even though women were generally open and frank. Nevertheless, deeper understanding of specifically female experience requires studies by a woman. There are also some possible methodological reasons for a relative emphasis on male experience in a study of this kind. I will return to this in chapter 15.

During the summer of 1961 and in the first few months of my fieldwork in 1962 to 1964 I lived in the household of Teri'i Tui in Piri. My observations there gave me some suggestions about patterns of household interaction, particularly in regard to the socialization of children, and helped me formulate questions for others about household patterns. After moving into my own house in Piri, I continued to take my meals with the Teri'i Tui family during the whole period of my fieldwork and thus had a

chance to watch events in the family, including shifts in the behavior of the growing children over a three-year period.

Toward the end of the work period, many of the people of
Piri had gone to Papeete to seek work, owing to markedly changing economic conditions in the territory; I did some of my interviewing of them in Papeete. Contrary to the original plan of
working equally in the two communities, work in Piri became
my main concern, and Roto was used mostly for comparison.
This was reflected in the division of my time, in the number of
interviews in each place, in the method of finding material for
comparison (usually a question or observation would arise in Piri
and then would be checked for in Roto), and in the general organization of this book.

Whereas my study of Piri consisted of household observations
and participation in village life, in addition to various kinds of
interviews, my study of Roto was largely limited to interviews.

Piri was a relatively organized, bounded community; Roto was
little more than a line drawn around a grouping of houses, containing a sample of city dwellers. Piri seemed to offer a chance
to understand the relation of tradition, community, and historically measurable pressures for change to aspects of private lives
and to psychological behavior in a way that the fragmentation
of Roto did not. I was interested primarily in understanding aspects of being Tahitian and only secondarily in problems of
modernization. If my concerns had been reversed, then the study
of Roto, with Piri for comparison, would have been the appropriate emphasis.

It is necessary to use Tahitian terms where an English gloss
would be misleading or awkward. Important terms introduced
in the text are listed in the glossary. The Tahitian language has
nine consonants, transcribed as *f, h, m, n, p, r, t, v*; the glottal
stop ' (indicated here by an apostrophe); and five vowels, transcribed *a, e, i, o, u*, which may be long or short. The glottal stop
represents a "cutting off" of sound, as in *Hawai'i.* Long vowels
are designated by a macron, as in *ā*. As an approximate guide to
pronunciation, *a* is pronounced something like the *a* in "fat"
(but shorter), *e* as the *a* in "fate," *i* as the *e* in "equal," *o* as the
o in "over," and *u* as the *u* in "flute."

I will use the same Tahitian term for singular and plural forms (as is done in noninflected Tahitian) rather than to add *s* to the Tahitian form. No attempt has been made to standardize the spelling of Tahitian terms in quotations from other authors. Such terms are not italicized.

I Orientations

1

The Setting

It is necessary to present a sketch of the setting and the community life and culture which serve as a context and background for the concerns of this study. Additional details are added throughout the book as they bear on special themes, but this chapter will serve as an orientation. The setting is described, using the present tense, as it was in the early 1960s.

French Polynesia consists of some 130 islands with a combined surface area of 1,520 square miles, scattered throughout 1,544,400 square miles of the South Pacific Ocean from 7° south latitude to 29° south latitude and from 131° west longitude to 156° west longitude.

It is an Overseas Territory of France and, like other such units, has a Territorial Assembly elected by universal suffrage and a Government Council nominated by the assembly. The chief executive is the governor of the territory, who represents France and is appointed by the French government. As French citizens, the nonalien inhabitants of the territory may participate in elections for a deputy and senator to represent them in the metropolitan French National Assembly and Senate. The senator is chosen indirectly. Voters choose municipal councilors, who in turn elect a senator.

The early European influences on Tahiti and the surrounding islands were English. After the discovery by Wallis in 1767 there were French and Spanish landings, but most of the ships were English. The various landings of the *Bounty* (after the mutiny some members of the crew returned to Tahiti to live) provided some of the first prolonged Tahitian-European contacts, and the coming of the English missionaries in 1797 initiated a systematic and forceful period of education. One result of this English period, aside from a coloring of puritanism, is a large number of

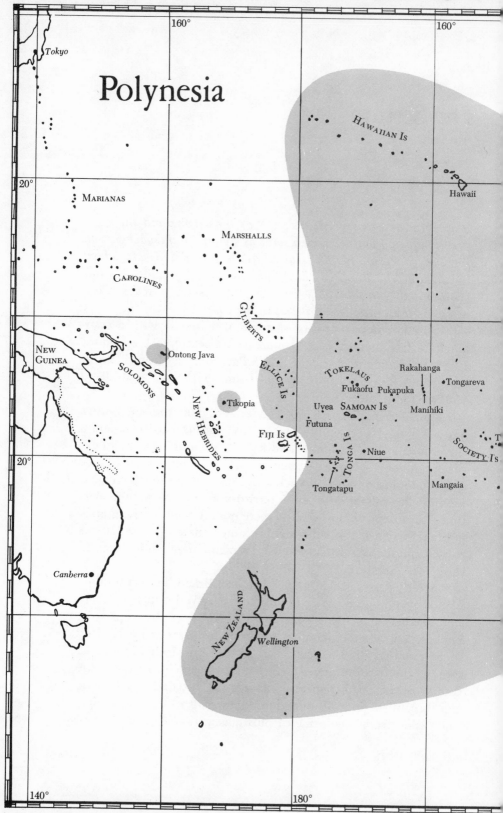

Polynesia

Tokyo

MARIANAS

MARSHALLS

CAROLINES

HAWAIIAN IS

Hawaii

GILBERTS

NEW
GUINEA

SOLOMONS

Ontong Java

NEW HEBRIDES

Tikopia

ELLICE IS

TOKELAUS

Fukaofu   Pukapuka

Rakahanga

Tongareva

Uvea   SAMOAN IS

Manihiki

Futuna

FIJI IS

TONGA IS

Niue

SOCIETY IS

T

Tongatapu

Mangaia

Canberra

NEW ZEALAND

Wellington

20°

20°

160°   160°

140°   180°

From Irving Goldman, *Ancient Polynesian Society* (Chicago: University of Chicago Press, 1970)

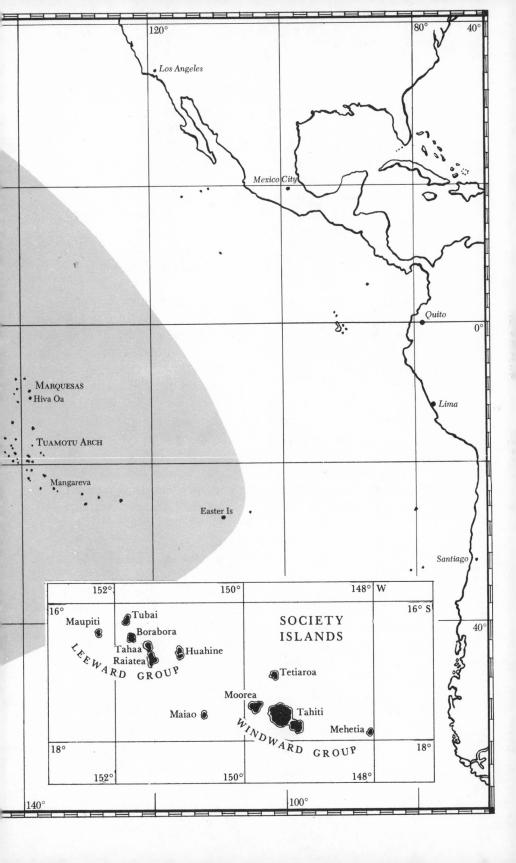

Los Angeles

120°   80°   40°

Mexico City

Quito   0°

Lima

MARQUESAS
Hiva Oa

TUAMOTU ARCH

Mangareva

Easter Is

Santiago

152°   150°   148° W

16°   Tubai   SOCIETY   16° S
Maupiti   ISLANDS   40°
Borabora
Tahaa   Huahine
Raiatea
LEEWARD GROUP   Tetiaroa

Moorea
Maiao   Tahiti
WINDWARD GROUP   Mehetia

18°   18°

152°   150°   148°

140°   100°

words for introduced items based on English. Thus "boat" is
poti in Tahitian, "match" is *mati*, "time" is *taime*, and so on
through hundreds of words.

French influence began to grow starting in the 1830s, and
after some very complicated events Tahiti and the adjoining islands became a French protectorate during the 1840s. Huahine
and the other Leeward Islands remained independent until 1888.
The attempt to extend French control was met with armed resistance by the natives of Huahine and other Leeward Islands,
and it was not until 1897 that the French regime finally was
peaceably established.

The islands are mostly clustered into a number of archipelagoes, the principal ones being the Tuamotus, the Gambiers, the
Marquesas, the Australs, and the Society Islands. The Society
Islands are divided into two geographical and administrative
clusters, the windward group and the leeward group, respectively
up- and downwind in relation to the prevailing southeasterly
trade winds. Each of the major archipelagoes tends to have its
own cultural and linguistic features, and the dialects spoken in
many of the groups are partly unintelligible to people from
other groups. Tahitian serves as an areal lingua franca. With all
the local variations, however, the subcultures of the various
archipelagoes are all members of the Polynesian family of cultures, found throughout the vast triangular area in the Pacific
from New Zealand in the west to Easter Island in the east and
the Hawaiian Islands in the north.

The two communities which are the settings for this study lie
within the Society Islands group — one within the windward
subgroup and one within the leeward subgroup. The islands
within each subgroup are in sight of one another, and the short-
est distances between the two groups are less than one hundred
miles, in contrast to the three hundred miles which separate
Tahiti from the Australs, the nine hundred miles which separate
it from the Gambiers, and the seven hundred miles which separate it from the Marquesas.

The Society Islands have a relatively mild tropical climate, Tahiti having an average temperature of some seventy-seven degrees

fahrenheit, with annual variations of from sixty-nine degrees to ninety-four degrees. The leeward group has slightly higher temperatures.

There is a relatively warm, rainy season from November to April and a cooler and relatively dry season from May to October. The town of Papeete has an average annual rainfall of about seventy inches. Because of the prevailing southeast trade winds there is a good deal of variation in rainfall on the windward and leeward sides of the high mountainous islands, and such high islands have a variety of microclimates, varying from valley to valley. (For the physical and economic geography and demography of French Polynesia see Doumenge [1966], Freeman [1951], McArthur [1968], and the issues of the *Bulletin de statistique*.)

According to the official census made in 1962 there were 84,500 persons in French Polynesia, of whom 68,245 lived in the Society Islands. Of these, 52,068 lived in the Windward Islands and 16,177 in the Leeward Islands.

PIRI

The village of Piri is on the island of Huahine in the leeward group of the Society Islands. The leeward group consists of five "high" islands, volcanic cones varying in height to a maximum of thirty-four hundred feet, and four "low" islands, coral limestone formations anchored on submerged volcanic peaks. The high islands are Huahine,[1] Raiatea, Tahaa, Bora Bora, and Maupiti; the atolls are Tubai, Mopihaa, Fenua Ura, and Motu One.

The Leeward Islands are an administrative unit, or *circonscription*, of French Polynesia. The unit's administrative center is in the town of Uturoa, on the island of Raiatea. Uturoa is the seat of the district administrator and is a port and secondary communications and commercial center through which communication and trade with Papeete and the Leeward Island group are

1. I will not usually attempt to use vowel-length notations and glottal stops in place names, but will follow the conventional spellings. Thus Bora Bora, more consistently Pora Pora, is a product of an early attempt at transcription.

funneled. A large proportion of the town's population are Chinese, who are occupied with shipping and island trade and with a multitude of small retail stores and services. Commercial and legal affairs and serious illness (there is a government hospital at Uturoa) require many of the inhabitants of the surrounding islands to make occasional trips to Raiatea.

The island of Huahine, the most easterly of the Leeward Islands, lies about one hundred miles northwest of Tahiti. It is a high island, a weathered, broken-down volcanic cone whose highest peaks do not exceed fifteen hundred feet, indented with bays and surrounded by an almost complete barrier reef, which separates a wide lagoon from the encircling ocean. The reef is broken by a wide pass on the northeast side of the island, providing an entrance into a natural harbor. The island's major town, the harbor town of Fare, has grown up here. The island as a whole is elliptical, about 8 1/3 miles long and 5 1/3 miles wide at its longest axis, comprising about twenty-nine square miles of base area. Scattered around the island littoral are thirteen villages situated at the edge of the lagoon and a number of isolated households and small household groups. There are a few households in some of the valleys, but most of the people live along the coast, although they may have houses for occasional shelter on valley garden land. For administrative purposes, the thirteen villages are sorted into seven districts.

In 1962, 3,214 persons lived on Huahine. For the purposes of the territorial census of that year, they were identified as 16 Europeans, 251 Chinese, 137 *demis*, and the remainder as Polynesian. Most of the Europeans were in Huahine for visits or short-term work projects at the time of the census. Thirteen of them were living at Fare or the adjoining community of Maeva, a few minutes away by road. *Demis* were those people who identified themselves or were identified to the census takers by the "head of the household" as belonging to a vaguely bounded cultural and social category of "Europeanized Tahitians."

A shallow inlet splits Huahine into two halves, Huahine Nui, or Great Huahine, to the north, and Huahine Iti, or Small Huahine, to the south. Piri is on the southwest coast of Huahine Iti and is reached by motor launch, a ride of six miles, which takes from forty-five minutes to an hour, depending on what calls the launch makes at the villages on the way.

Piri is on the shore of a bay, which is about a mile long and a quarter of a mile wide through much of its extent, running generally north and south. Its long axis is perpendicular to the barrier reef, which is more than a mile across the lagoon from most parts of the village. The village of Piri occupies the entire western shore of the bay. Although there are a few households on the north and east shores and on the southern coast facing the lagoon, most of the inhabitants of these households have little to do with the people on the western shore. Although they are included in government censuses of the village, we can follow the usage of the people themselves, a usage reflected in interaction patterns, and consider the western strip as the village of Piri.

Piri lies on the long, narrow strip of littoral between the steep slopes of the mountainside and the bay. There is a dirt path running parallel to the bay and spanning the length of the village, and houses are built in two rows along the sides of the path; two-thirds of the houses are on the bay side. Some of these are built partially over the shallow edge of the bay on wooden piles to exploit better the narrow flat littoral strip. The people of the village sometimes commented on its spatial properties as being *piri* ("narrow or confined"). I have taken that characterization as the pseudonym for the village.

The path has, in local description, two sides and two directions. There is the side toward the mountain, *pae i mou'a*, and the side toward the shore, *pae i tātahi*. The directions, in characteristic Polynesian fashion, are the inland direction, *uta*, and the lagoon direction, *tai* (for Piri, north and south, respectively).

In the fall of 1962 Piri's 284 persons lived in 54 houses. The inland-seaward directions of the length of the path tended to separate the villagers in terms of their economic or political status in the village. The more important people generally lived toward the seaward end of the village, whereas the humbler, ordinary people lived toward the inland end.

Village architecture has been in constant transition as various western building materials have replaced traditional ones at rates determined by the erratic course of the village's mixed economy. Most of the houses have thatched roofs and board floors and board or composition-board walls. Some of the simpler houses have bamboo matting walls on their less exposed, leeward sides. The typical house has one large room separated by partitions into two or three sleeping areas, with an adjacent wooden shed serving as an eating and cooking house. A few houses, most impressively those of Teri'i Tui, of Tano, the Protestant pastor, and of Teiva, a dissident deacon who had led a church schismatic movement, plus two or three more rudimentary samples, are cement-walled and tin-roofed — damp and hot in the wet season, but coveted signs of advancement.

Home furnishings have changed markedly since the childhood of the older and middle-aged men in the village. Beds, chairs, tables, a few dishes, pots and pans, chests or wardrobes, oil lamps, hurricane lanterns, and primus stoves are essential furnishings found everywhere. Most houses have battery-operated radios (awkward pretransistor affairs in the early 1960s) with which to listen to the Tahitian-language broadcasts of Radio Tahiti. Clocks of various shapes and sizes, condition, and setting are frequent. Houses are decorated with photos of relatives and, particularly on Sundays and special occasions, with patchwork bedspreads and pillowcases, made in the village from scraps of cloth, a craft introduced by the wives of the first missionaries at the beginning of the nineteenth century. In some houses artificial flowers are displayed.

The village is clean. Flowering plants are grown and tended along the village path and in some of the yards. The smells of flowers and of vanilla and copra being dried are the more prominent odors of the village, supplemented during the rainy season by the smell of mud. Chickens, a few dogs, and small pigs wander in the village. Large pigs used to be kept in the village, but since they occasionally broke away and caused damage, they are now kept out of the village on the garden lands. Land crabs, the *tupa*, have their burrows everywhere and help keep the village clean by dragging fallen leaves, pieces of paper, and refuse of various kinds into their underground burrows. Rats live in the brush and in the coconut trees. Small lizards are everywhere, inside of the houses and out. There are a few annoying insects, mosquitoes, centipedes, millepedes, mildly venomous scorpions, and a recently introduced sandfly.

The health of the villagers is excellent. There is plenty of nutritious food, and aside from filariasis[2] there are no serious tropical diseases.

Piri has a few nonresidential buildings. These are the schoolhouse, the Protestant church building, two meeting houses for church groups, and two "Chinese stores." At the inland end of the village is a field where the adolescent boys and young men of the village sometimes play soccer and practice for occasional intervillage or interisland competitions. These are typical rural Society Island village features, but in 1962 Piri also had an unusual building, a small Mormon meeting house at the inland end of the village; this structure was replaced before the end of 1964 by a modern, elaborate Mormon church building.

The economic life of Piri is a mixture of subsistence and marketing activities. The balance between these two types of activities varies from month to month with the conditions of the market at Papeete. But the general trend throughout recent years, with some violent fluctuations, has been toward using work time to produce cash crops and the purchasing of food and materials. The principal cash crops had been vanilla and copra. By the early 1960s, with an increase in the population of the town of Papeete, it had also become profitable to export various food crops, particularly taro, from Huahine to Tahiti.

Until recently little food was bought. The lagoon and reef provide fish, shellfish, and crustaceans. People cultivated taro, sweet potatoes, *taruā* (*Xanthosoma sagittifolium*), and other root crops; manioc, bananas, plantain, breadfruit, coconuts, pineapple, man-

2. Filariasis is a nonfatal mosquito-transmitted disease, causing acute fever and chills and, if untreated and chronic, occasionally permanent swelling, or elephantiasis, most usually of the lower extremities and male genitalia.

goes, and a variety of other less frequently used fruits and vegetables. The rivers provide eels and freshwater shrimp, the latter
an important ingredient in a favorite fermented coconut sauce.
Local husbandry provides chickens, pigs, and occasionally dogs.
To these foods some store-bought foods are added. When I first
arrived Piri had two Chinese stores, parts of a territorialwide network of economic activities run by local Chinese (Moench 1963;
Coppenrath 1967).

From these stores and from the larger and better-equipped
Chinese stores at Fare, the people of Piri buy bread, twisted
doughnuts, rice, flour, sugar, canned milk for babies, canned
corned beef, sardines, apricot jam, kerosene lamps and wicks,
needles, thread, and buttons, flashlights and batteries, guitar
strings, baby bottles and nipples, soft drinks, fishhooks, and
other inexpensive goods. At the biggest stores in Fare they can
also buy pots and pans, bush knives and other tools, primus
stoves, hurricane lamps, lumber, cement, guitars, Algerian red
wine, Tahitian beer, and candy and cookies. For certain goods
like an outboard motor or a battery-operated phonograph it
might be necessary to take the weekly schooner into Papeete or
Uturoa.

Throughout the lifetime of the older members of the village
there has been a progressive replacement of locally made products with store-bought western products. Even though one still
has some choice on whether to use coconut or pandanus thatching or tin sheets for roofing, bamboo matting or store-bought
lumber for a leeward wall, a dugout canoe and paddle or a boat
with an outboard motor, there is a continuous wearing away of
the remnants of old traditional know-how and a continuing increase in the use of goods and techniques which have to be paid
for. The older men remember living in houses of largely native
construction, sitting on the floor and eating from leaf plates and
drinking from coconut-shell bowls. They remember being able
to make fire with the traditional fire plough if they had to, or
being able to strike a fire off a flint stone.

Most of the adult men in the village have vegetable gardens on
either their own or their wives' family lands. In some cases both

a man and his wife have land in the area. Others rent a parcel of land belonging to somebody else, usually for a very small sum, or work the land of an absent friend or relative. Much of the garden work is done by the head of the family, by himself or with the help of a small family group — his wife, his elder sons perhaps, his elder daughters and their husbands, depending on the seasonal demands of the vanilla or taro crop.[3] When a large area of land is to be cleared or a large number of crops are to be planted, the land's proprietor may employ a men's work group from the village to help him. The groups work sometimes for hire, being fed and paid by the contractor, and sometimes on a reciprocal basis, with each member of a group having a claim on the group's time for his own needs, which might include house repair or construction as well as garden work. A few men in the village who either have little or no land of their own or who have not developed their land adequately work at times for others on an individual basis, helping out with various aspects of gardening,[4] climbing kapok trees to gather the pods (a hazardous and specialized skill), making canoes, or doing some carpentry. This exchange of services or products between households in the village, although substantial, is, in comparison with independent, household-based activities, a minor aspect of the economy. Each household largely manages its own economic affairs.

Previously the lagoon was an important source of food. It was fished by hook and line and by net, and fish were speared both from the surface and by diving. Shellfish were gathered on the reef. With the increasing importance of cash crops, fishing has

3. Vanilla, the most important cash crop, was introduced into Tahiti in 1848, and is now widely cultivated throughout the Society Islands. The plants flower from June through late October, with a peak in August and a secondary peak in October. The flowers have to be fertilized by hand during this period. The resulting beans, appearing several months later, are dried and exported. Taro may be planted throughout the year, and matures throughout the year depending on the planting. The best season for planting, however, is at the end of October toward the beginning of the wet season.

4. I will follow the convention of calling Tahitian horticultural activity "gardening" and the worked lands "gardens."

become somewhat more of a sport and an activity of adolescents, and it has become more common to buy fish from commercial fishermen who go from village to village in motor launches selling tuna or other fish caught in the open sea beyond the reef. For a special feast or for the copious Sunday dinner, families may spend an afternoon or evening fishing; but during the week, except for the poorer families, the meat or fish is likely to be in a can, bought at the Chinese store, or fresh fish bought from a commercial fisherman. Fresh meat, for Sundays and important meals, comes from pigs, chickens, and, rarely, dogs.

The island of Huahine is administered by a French gendarme, the *chef de poste*, with the help of a native assistant. His functions are to exchange information with the Leeward Islands' administrative center on Raiatea, to supervise shipping to and from Huahine, and to help maintain law and order. This latter task is mostly done for him by individual district "chiefs" (*chefs de village*) who use appeal to the gendarme as a threat (which is seldom carried out) if the authority of the individual chief and village policeman is not obeyed.

Each district has a native policeman, the *muto'i*, who is appointed by the administrator of the Leeward Island group, of which Huahine is a part. The *muto'i* is always a native of the district to which he is appointed. The mission of the *muto'i* is to keep the peace and to report any infractions of French law to the *chef de poste* at Fare. In practice the good *muto'i*, like the good chief (good in the evaluation of both the people of the village and the French administration), are those who manage the largest possible number of incidents within the confines of the village without bringing them to the attention of the French authorities.

The chief, or *tāvana* as he is called (*tāvana* being a Tahitian version of the English "governor"), is elected by the adult members of the village for a period of six years. (The system of electing village chiefs dates from 1945; before that they were appointed, usually by the previous chief with the agreement of the *chef de poste*.) The *tāvana*'s salary is paid by the French administration, and he has some official duties under French law. He keeps, usually with the help of the village schoolmaster, the vital records of the village, *l'état civil*, the records of birth, death, and marriage. He reports on needs for repairs and construction of roads, wharves, and water supply. He receives and welcomes visiting officials and arranges and guides meetings between the village as a political unit and those officials. He is responsible for carrying out policies and decisions transmitted to him from higher levels. He supervises the electoral proceedings of the village, including those related to territorial and metropolitan elections. He also meets occasionally with the village council, made up of an "assistant chief," *tāvana piti*, and six other members to discuss village affairs.

For important matters in Piri the village males meet as a whole, usually in an open field toward the center of the village, with a number of politically concerned women in the background listening carefully to the discussion. The *tāvana* presents the issue to be discussed. After he has finished there is silence. The men, sitting on chairs and boxes or leaning against trees, look off into space in various directions. After three or four minutes somebody will start to speak and offer his opinion in a semiconventionalized oratorical rhetoric. He looks at nobody; nobody looks at him. When he is finished, the *tāvana* grunts and says, "That is well thought out," which does not signify approval or disapproval of the content of the thought. There are further silences followed by further performances. Some of the oratory is impassioned, some of it is joking and burlesque. After several people have spoken, the village Protestant pastor gives his opinion. His followers support his argument, his enemies object. The *tāvana* listens, and when everyone who wants to has spoken he announces what appears to be the consensus of most of the members. The dissident members, having spoken their piece and been heard, are now supposedly bound by the majority.

According to the 1962 census of French Polynesia, the leeward group of the Society Islands (within which Piri is situated) had in that year 12,847 Protestants and 930 Catholics out of a population of 16,177. The others were listed as "dissidents" (Protestants adhering to a "nonofficial" branch of local origin),

111; Seventh-Day Adventists, 733; Jehovah's Witnesses, 20; Mormons, 552; "Sanitos" (the Reorganized Church of Jesus Christ of the Latter-Day Saints), 24; "ancestor worshipers" (members of the Chinese population), 70; "without religion" (including Chinese and Europeans who may or may not be atheists and Tahitians, mainly believers but without a formal church membership), 790; and a residual category of "other religions," 83; and "nondeclared," 17.

Piri's population in that year reflected the Leeward Islands' Protestant/non-Protestant ratio. Of the 140 villagers over the age of fifteen, 116 were Protestants, 15 were Mormons, and 2 were Jehovah's Witnesses. The 4 Chinese in the village described themselves as having "no religion." Only 2 persons in the village were Catholics — the schoolteacher who was on assignment there and who came from the island of Tahiti and a young woman, also from Tahiti and living with one of the young men of the village. The schoolteacher's wife, who was born in another district on Huahine, was a Seventh-Day Adventist.

In the early 1960s there had been a schism in the village Protestant church. At this time about half the village families, led by one of the deacons, Teiva, formed an independent congregation. It was during the disunity of this period that Mormon missionaries had the opportunity to convert a few village families to Mormonism. The schism was against a background of traditional Tahitian village Protestantism.

Thirty years after the discovery of Tahiti (in 1767) a group of British evangelical Protestant missionaries arrived, sent out by the newly formed London Missionary Society. There followed a series of vicissitudes famous in Tahitian and mission history; but by 1815, after the conversion of some of the principal chiefs and "pagan" priests of Tahiti, mass conversion began, and by 1830 Tahiti and the Society Islands were largely Protestant. When in the early 1840s Tahiti became a French protectorate, the position of the Protestant pastors and of Protestantism was in doubt for some time, but in 1863 the French Protestant *Société des missions évangéliques de Paris* took over the maintenance and encouragement of Tahitian Protestantism, which flourishes today throughout the Society Islands.[5]

The London Missionary Society, as W. N. Gunson has written in a valuable study of the background and values of the missionaries,

> stemmed directly from the great Evangelical or "Methodist" movement of the eighteenth century. The great missionary societies were the direct outcome of the preaching of the revivalists, Whitefield and Wesley. There were also certain definite doctrinal and methodistical characteristics associated with Evangelicalism, which were to be found in these missionary societies. First and foremost there was the preaching of the Atonement, the doctrine of the cross; there was an emphasis on the eternal peril of the soul; and there was an emphasis on the propagation of the Bible. . . . In most respects, Evangelical doctrine is essentially a Puritan doctrine. (Gunson 1959; pp. v-vi)

Even the most casual observation of Piri and of rural village life elsewhere in the Society Islands indicates that Christianity has become, in some sense at least, of central importance in the life of the village. The Protestant church building, along with the schoolhouse and the Chinese store, is one of the obvious physical reference points in the village. Churchgoing and church-related formal activities organize much of the nonworking time of the villagers, preempting Sunday mornings and often one or two weekday evenings. The Protestant pastor, usually a native of the village in which he works, shares with the village chief the political decision-making focus of the village. He conducts the Sunday school, teaches the Bible, and presides over weddings and funerals. Assisted by his elected deacons, he presides over the communicants — the *'etaretia*, the "elect" of the village — village couples who have rejected the life of frivolity of the "fun-loving youth,"

5. A detailed technical study of the dynamics of the introduction of Protestantism by members of the London Missionary Society into Rarotonga and Aitutaki, which had many cultural similarities to the Society Islands, is E. Beaglehole (1957). For accounts of the introduction of Protestantism into the Society Islands, see Ellis (1830), Wilson (1799), Newbury (1961), and Wright and Fry (1936).

the *taure'are'a*, and have legitimatized their unions by legal marriage and are entitled to take the communion bread and wine at the monthly service for communion Sunday, *tāpati 'ōroa.*

The pastor, the *'orometua a'o*, preaches a morality of family stability. He opposes heavy drinking, adultery, gambling, and irresponsibility of any kind that would interfere with the maintenance of the household. Churchgoing and the eventual acceptance of an individual into the group of communicants is a sign of a minimal probity necessary for salvation of the soul, and the pastor thus has considerable authority. The transplantation of English dissenting Protestantism would seem to have been successful. But this simulacrum of a Calvinistic community is misleading, as we shall see, for example, when we consider the quality of religious belief and the personal meanings involved. But here I am sketching what are, from the viewpoint of private experience, surfaces.

In traditional neo-Tahitian[6] villages, the Protestant pastor and the *tāvana* were allied figures of equal importance. The *tāvana* was usually a deacon in the church, and the pastor was an important influence in village leadership and political decision-making. Churchgoing and church affairs provided, after economic activity, the major concern of village life and the major setting, in terms of sheer frequency, in which the members of the village came into face-to-face contact and shared the same tasks. These included cleaning and repairing the church or the pastor's home; raising money for some Protestant cause in some other part of the territory; preparing a feast for visiting church dignitaries; and the more usual weekly tasks of learning hymns or getting together for the traditional *tūāro'i* session, a formal discussion of the meaning of various Bible passages, interspersed with hymn singing (with music based on both western and traditional Polynesian musical forms), an activity which would often last far into the night.

6. Neo-Tahitian is a useful term to indicate the rather stable and integrated sociocultural patterns that have developed in the rural Society Islands after the successful incorporation of certain western elements, especially Christianity, in the early nineteenth century.

This was the situation in Piri until three years before my first visit. At that time a part of the congregation, under the leadership of one of the deacons, Teiva, had walked out of the Protestant church and established itself as a separate congregation. The precipitating events were a variety of tensions and hostilities which had arisen over assessments for the building of a meeting house for the congregation. Added to this was resentment over the official position taken by the Protestant church in the territory, and expressed by the pastor in his official capacity, toward an emotionally laden plebiscite which was to take place at that time to determine whether or not French Polynesia was to stay within the French community. The issue had narrowed to a matter of support or rejection of Pouvana'a A O'opa, a political leader who had been born in Huahine. Pouvana'a had recommended rejecting continued membership in the French community, whereas the church leadership in Papeete was urging support of continued membership. After weeks of tension Teiva, encouraged by a prophetic dream, demanded the removal of the pastor. Unable to obtain support for this action from the church authorities in Uturoa and Papeete, he led an exodus of more than half of the members of the congregation. A number of other members took this opportunity of a break in the unity of the church to stop all churchgoing. The Teiva sect considered themselves a legitimate congregation who were temporarily at odds with the current pastor. Soon after the break a number of people in Teiva's group dropped out. A few returned to the old church, a few stayed home, and a few became involved with the Mormon group which was beginning to establish itself in the village, particularly among some of those who had rejected both church groups after the split.

Before the church split Mormon proselytizing in Piri had been unsuccessful. There had been two Mormon villagers; one, a man, had come from the Tuamotu Archipelago from a family which had been Mormon for some generations and had married into one of the large Piri families. The Mormons had little success in their early attempts in Piri. The young male missionaries, marked by the clean white shirts and dark neckties they wore even in the hottest weather and by the fact that they were always in pairs,[7] had made only one convert — a young married woman, Rahera, whose husband, Taere, chose to remain with the Protestants. At the time of the breakup of the pastor's church, a number of people at the inland, "humble" end of the village began to express interest in the Mormons, and by 1961 the Mormons had a congregation of seven families and Rahera. Because of this first breakthrough in tightly Protestant Huahine, the Mormon authorities decided to construct a church building in Piri. A Mormon community in Oregon raised, reportedly, thirty thousand dollars toward this project. During 1962 an imposing church was erected on a hillside just next to the village path, complete with movable walls for varying the size of meeting rooms, an electric generator, electric tools, a small organ, and flush toilets — all innovations for Piri.

After 1958 all three groups — the Protestants, the dissidents, and the Mormons — began holding church services and conducting religious education for children and a variety of secondary prayer meetings and discussion meetings. The organized religious life in Piri had become rather complicated.[8]

In addition to the Mormon church, the Protestant church and meeting house, and the two Chinese stores, the one other specialized building in Piri is the schoolhouse, a one-story cement structure divided into three rooms, situated toward the seaward end of the village. In 1962 eighty-five children attend this school. Forty-seven of them are in the two sections of the elementary group, taught in one room by an affiliate teacher, a nineteen-year-old Tahitian girl from Raiatea. These are the beginning pupils, from six to eight years old, and a number of backward pupils, some as old as twelve, who are not considered ready to move into the advanced section. The advanced section consists of five classes, all conducted at more or less the same time by a *demi*, a teacher of mixed Polynesian (Tahitian and Tuamotu)

7. These pairs were at first only Americans or Canadians; by 1962 one member of the pair which visited Piri was Tahitian.

8. By 1970, as is noted in the Postscript, the Mormon enterprise in Piri seemed to have collapsed.

and French cultural background. Of the fifteen students in the most advanced section, eight are in a terminal course and seven, five girls and two boys, are in the section preparing for the possibility of more advanced study. The advanced study would require going to schools in Uturoa or Papeete. It is possible at Papeete to go as far as the baccalaureate examination, but only a handful of pupils from Piri have ever left the village to advance their education, and none has ever achieved the baccalaureate degree.

There has been some kind of a schoolroom and teacher in Piri ever since 1937 or 1938, although at first very sporadically, with long periods without any teacher and with frequent replacements. It was not until 1946 that the present schoolhouse was completed. Before 1937 the only older villagers with some schooling were those few who had spent some of their childhood in Tahiti or in one of the Leeward Island port towns where there might have been a small school. Some, who had relatives in Fare, had been sent there to go to school. For most of the adults who did have some French education before 1937, the exposure was brief, usually only a few months, and the effects seem to have been superficial and fleeting. The French which was used as the teaching language was not used outside of school and was often quickly forgotten. Many of the teachers were poorly educated themselves.

In later years the quality of the teaching improved and later students speak somewhat better French and have a better knowledge of the outside world. In Piri French tends to be used only at school, and the students speak mostly Tahitian with one another and with their parents.

Whether or not they attended French schools, most people in Piri went at one time or another to classes given by the Protestant pastor. These classes, in addition to religious and Bible subjects, taught the reading and writing of the Tahitian language. Learning to read Tahitian is fairly simple, since the system, devised by the early English missionaries for transcribing this previously unwritten language, is relatively phonemic, with a one-to-one correspondence of letters and sounds. Conventional transcription, however, generally does not differentiate long and short vowels, or place the glottal stop.

Some indication of the Tahitian literacy rate for the older and middle generations in Piri is given by a 1962 household census. Taking "heads of households" and their spouses as a sample, sixty-six reported that they could read and write Tahitian with ease; nineteen said that they could do so with some difficulty.

In the 1820s the missionary William Ellis, writing of the pagan, pre-Christian society of the recently converted Tahitians and of the various events that had attended their conversion, noted in a chapter on music and amusements that

freed, in a great degree, so far as the means of subsistence were concerned, from anxiety and labour, the islanders were greatly devoted to amusements: war, pagan worship, and pleasure appear to have engaged their attention and occupied the principal portion of their time. Their games were numerous and diversified, and were often affairs of national importance. (Ellis 1830; 1:287)[9]

Games and sports then included boxing, wrestling, foot racing, javelin throwing, archery, mock battles, a variety of ball games, dances, cockfights, and surf-riding, and for the children such things as stilt-walking, games resembling blindman's buff and jacks, kite flying, and building and sailing toy boats. Ellis concludes the chapter,

These are only some of the principal games, or amusements, of the natives; others might be added, but these are sufficient to show that they were not destitute of sources of entertainment, either in their juvenile or more advanced periods of life. With the exception of one or two, they have all, however, been discontinued, especially among the adults; and the number of those followed by the children is greatly diminished. This is, on no account, matter of regret. When we consider the debasing tendency of many, and the inutility of others, we shall rather rejoice that much of the time of the adults is passed in more rational

9. In eighteenth- and early nineteenth-century quotations spelling and punctuation have been modernized.

and beneficial pursuits. Few, if any of them, are so sedentary in their habits as to need these amusements as a means of exercise; and they are not accustomed to apply so closely to any of their avocations as to require them merely for relaxation. (Ellis 1830; 1:310)

Henry Adams had written from Christian Tahiti in February 1891:

To me the atmosphere is more than tinged by a South Sea melancholy, a little sense of hopelessness and premature decay. The natives are not the gay, big, animal creatures of Samoa who sang and danced because their whole natures were overstocked with life; they are still, silent, rather sad in expression, like the Hawaiians, and they are fearfully few in number. . . . Except in the remoter places, the poor natives are all more or less diseased. They are allowed all the rum they want, and they drink wildly. They are forbidden to dance or to keep any of their old warlike habits. They have no amusements, and they have *gens d'armes.* . . . I never saw a people that seemed so hopelessly bored as the Tahitians. . . . If they have amusements or pleasures, they conceal them. Neither dance nor game have I seen or heard of; nor surf-swimming nor ball playing nor anything but the stupid mechanical himene. They do not even move with spirit. (Adams 1930; pp. 466-67, 476)

Adams was being curiously insensitive to the *himene* — chants and religious songs of both western and traditional form, often of considerable beauty and complexity. But his description is in striking contrast to descriptions of some of the first visitors to the pre-Christian islands such as John Forster, who, having visited Tahiti with Captain Cook in 1773 and 1774, wrote: "The natives of these isles are generally of a lively, brisk temper, great lovers of mirth and laughter, and of an open, easy, benevolent character" (J. Forster 1778; p. 231).

The demoralization indicated in Adams's letters reflected a general breakdown of meanings and purposes, which to different degrees and at differing tempos throughout the islands was recovered from as meaningful ways of life were reconstructed around some of the newly introduced forms. But the long shadow of the Puritan position on games and amusements still falls on Piri and other rural villages. A number of children's games have survived missionary criticism and new ones have been introduced, and young men and adolescents now play soccer; but adults find themselves with a very limited repertory of amusements. Some of the old dances persist and are encouraged by the government — at least for the yearly folklore festival held each July to commemorate Bastille Day — although it is doubtful how long these dances (not to mention such archaic festival activities as javelin throwing, canoe racing, and fire walking) would survive without the stimulus of the yearly festival and the considerable state financial support it is given.[10] By and large the village adults have accepted the missionary doctrine that fun, games, and amusements are for young people — if for anybody — and one of the defining characteristics of somebody who has entered the life stage of "maturity" is that he does not engage in amusements, except in special and limited circumstances. Formally defined amusements for adults, mea ha'uti noa ("things for playfulness" — the contrast is with "seriousness," not with work), include an occasional movie brought from village to village by boat and projected against a bedsheet; visits to the port town of Fare, usually on the weekly ship days; occasional visits to other districts in Huahine; and (very rarely, before 1964) visits to Papeete motivated or excused by bringing some produce personally to the Papeete market; and, for many adults, drinking. Aside from the sparse formal amusements, politics and churchgoing, group work activities, fishing and food gathering in the lagoon and on the reef (in contrast to working on the lands, which is felt to be more tedious), and gossip and tales of village events and of the supernatural give village life some liveliness and adventure.

Marriages, funerals, birthday parties for one-year-old children, visitors and villagers arriving and departing, occasional unexpected visits of yachts at the village wharf, and for a few of the

10. Some kinds of more or less traditional dance have been elaborated for tourists and hotel shows, but this does not affect Huahine.

more liberal households an occasional "party" involving some drinking, singing, and perhaps dancing all break the routine quiet of the village at infrequent and irregular intervals.

Two important yearly festivals divide the year. During the summer Bastille Day festival in July most of the population of Piri goes to the town of Fare for several days of drinking, dancing, races, and contests and for a chance to visit with people from villages around the island of Huahine. The other major holiday time of the year is the week or two following New Year's Day. At this time people from Piri who have gone to live in Tahiti or in some other island try to return to Piri. For a week or ten days there are continual parties. It is a time of feasting and drinking, of decking the houses out in the best linens and quilts, of visiting from house to house, and of trying to patch up old quarrels.

Those activities which are considered proper or natural in an individual are, to a large degree, related to the named life stage in which he is. The infant is called an *'aiū* (literally, "milk eater"). At some point between the ages of one year and perhaps three or four years, the *'aiū* begins to be defined more and more as a *tamāri'i* (a "child"). Instead of being addressed as *'aiū* or *pēpē* ("baby"), he or she is called by name and referred to as *tamāri'i* ("child"), *tamāroa* ("boy child"), or *tamāhine* ("girl child"). As the child approaches puberty, he or she begins to be designated as a *taure'are'a* (meaning literally "the time or period of pleasure"). For boys, entrance to this stage is associated with the operation of supercision of the foreskin of the penis, a survival of pre-Christian rites of passage. Sometime between his mid-twenties and early thirties the *taure'are'a* becomes, ideally, a *ta'ata pa'ari* (a "wise or mature person"). The *ta'ata pa'ari* ends up becoming *rū'au* ("old"), and if he passes into senility, *'aru'aru* ("weak and helpless"), a description also applied to very young infants.

Much of the life of Piri centers in the household, which tends to a considerable degree to be sealed off from the larger village life. Adults meet at the variety of public village occasions already indicated, but there is very little informal visiting among houses of non-kin, and the kin involved are usually very closely related (brother and sister, parent and child).

The traditional Tahitian kinship nomenclature, technically a "Hawaiian" type of nomenclature, although still known in Piri, has been somewhat collapsed and simplified in recent usage. For an individual of either sex, his parents, and their generation of brothers, sisters, and cousins are *metua*, the males being *metua tāne* ("male parent") and the females *metua vahine* ("female parent") — the last terms being frequently replaced by the more informal "papa" or "mama." Finer distinctions can be made, as in other kin classes, by qualifying the term; for example, *ta'u papa fana'u* ("my biological father," "the father who caused me to be born"). Ascendant ancestors preceding the parents' generation are all classed as *tupuna* ("ancestors"), although the generation of the parents' parents and their siblings and cousins are often designated as *mama* or *papa rū'au* ("old mother or father") and sometimes by the same terms as the parental generation. Kin of the same generation are traditionally designated according to whether a male or female is speaking. For a man his older brothers and male cousins are *tua'ana*, his younger brothers and male cousins are *teina*, and his sisters and female cousins are all *tuahine*. For a female speaker, her older sisters and female cousins are *tua'ana*, her younger sisters and female cousins are *teina*, and her brothers and male cousins are all *tū'āne*. Some simplification is tending to take place in these terms referring to one's own generation; and the French *soeur* and *frère*, *cousin* and *cousine* are used now in preference to the traditional terms, although *soeur* and *frère* may be used for the same range of kin as *tuahine*, and so forth.

I will employ the convention of using an English relational term without quotation marks (e.g., grandfather, aunt) if it is equivalent to its English sense and using it with quotation marks if it is being used in the Tahitian fashion to indicate the extended sense (e.g., a "sister," a "father" — in this case the "sister" might be either a sister or a cousin in our nomenclature).

For descendants, traditional terms are still used. A man's or woman's children, and the children of their brothers, sisters, and cousins are their *tamāri'i*, a "son" is a *tamaiti*, a "daughter" is a *tamāhine* (which is the same as the word for female child, in contrast to the differentiated words for "son" and "male child"). Second-generation descendants are *hina*, third are *hina rere*. These and subsequent generations are *hua'ai* ("descendants").

A man's heterosexual partner, spanning transient through settled relationships, is his *vahine* (literally "woman"), and a woman's partner is her *tāne* ("man").

This is not a complete list of relational terms (I have, for example, neglected marriage-created terms such as "son-in-law"), but it will serve as an introduction.

An important aspect of family life in Piri, as elsewhere in Polynesia, is the prevalent practice of adoption. Twenty-five percent of the children in Piri do not live in the household of a biological parent, and twenty-five of Piri's fifty-four households include adopted children. The ordinary term for adoption is *fa'a'amu* ("to feed"). People may have both adopted (*fa'a'amu*) and biological children, and adopting parents (also *fa'a'amu*) and biological parents.

Among the threads of their identity the people of Piri consider themselves to be Tahitians, *ta'ata tahiti* ("Tahitian people"). They contrast themselves in various ways with white foreigners (*pōpa'a*), Chinese (*Tinito*), black foreigners (*ta'ata 'ere'ere*, "black people"), and the class of French-Tahitian cultural amalgamation known as *demi* in French or *'āfa* ("half") in Tahitian.

They call their more traditional villagers and customs, the true, old manner of life as they understand it, *mā'ohi*.

Introduction to a Household

When I first arrived in Piri in July 1961, the launch from Fare left me off at the village wharf. No one knew that I was coming, who I was, or why I was there. I stood on the wharf with my suitcase and typewriter, anxiously wondering how the village would deal with the problem. It was midmorning, and many of the villagers were away on their garden lands. I explained to the small, curious crowd of strangers around me that I wanted to stay in the village for a while and that I was a friend of Douglas

Oliver, who had been there the year before. A young man picked up my suitcase, and I followed him to a house, that of Teri'i Tui. Teri'i had plenty of space and was accustomed to entertaining the foreigners who occasionally came to the village and stayed for a few days or weeks. I lived in Teri'i's house during the first summer and, on my return to Piri one year later, spent several weeks more. When I moved out, finally, into my own house, I continued to take my meals with Teri'i and his family. The household provided my first and, for such things as patterns of household interaction, some of my most detailed views of the intimate aspects of life in Piri.

On an August day in 1961 the house and household looked like this:

Teri'i Tui's house is cement-walled and tin-roofed; it is on the bay side of the village path toward the seaward end of the village. The cement house is attached to an older wooden house which was the Tui family's home in the days before Teri'i had saved enough money from his vanilla and copra profits to build a fancier one. In front of it, separated from the path by a wire mesh fence, is a dirt yard, riddled by the burrows of land crabs and containing a variety of flowering plants in half-buried tin cans.

The cement-block house, facing on the path, has a large front room in which there are some rattan chairs, a round table, two narrow beds, and a portable commode containing bed covers and sheets. This front room is used for formal occasions. To the left of the large room are three small bedrooms, separated from it by a wall. Each of these rooms has two beds and a chest for linen and clothes. The doorways to the large room are screened by cloth curtains. In one of the bedrooms is a foot-operated sewing machine; in another is a tile sink which Teri'i bought on one of his trips to Papeete. The sink is connected to nothing and stands as an ornament in the room.

The three bedrooms are separated from one another by walls which do not reach the flat composition-board ceiling underneath the slanted tin roof. This gives an effect similar to the incomplete partitioning of rooms in the more traditional village houses of thatch and wood. At the back of the large front room, separated by walls about five feet high, is the washing area. There is a basin of water and a drain in the floor.

The back door of the big room opens into the wooden house, which has one large room to which two sheds are attached. One shed is used for sorting and drying vanilla (for that part of the drying process which has to take place out of the sun), and the other shed is used as a cookhouse. Piles of firewood and dry coconut husks are stored here, and stalks of various kinds of bananas and bunches of taro are tied to the rafters. Fire is often kept smoldering in the coconut husks, in the ancient style; when a usable fire is desired, sticks of firewood are ignited from the husks. When the fire is burning a thick acrid, eye-irritating smoke fills the shed and finds its way out of various openings. Some of the cooking is done over the fire in pots and pans. Frequently, stones are heated over the fire, and food wrapped in leaves is placed on them to cook. Often another layer of leaves is placed over the bundles of food to help concentrate the heat. This system is a modification of the traditional Polynesian earth oven.

Meals are usually eaten in the main room of the wooden house, and most informal meetings take place there. For rare events like a visit of an important official or a birthday party for a small child, which in recent years has become the excuse for an occasional semiformal party, the front room is used as a dining room or meeting room. But most of the life of the household takes place in this back room, which was the entire house of the Tui family in the years before the new part was built. The main furnishings in this room are a long rectangular table, which can easily seat twelve or fourteen, some wooden upright chairs, and a bedstead. There are shelves holding dishes, pots, and curios of various sorts, and a screened box serving as a food safe to protect food from ants, rats, and flying insects. In the food safe there is some cold fish, an open tin of butter, part of a loaf of bread, some sugar, and some cooked taro root. There is also a kerosene-run refrigerator which functions intermittently and which contains several bottles of water and several large bottles of beer.

The back of the wooden house opens toward the bay. A yard surfaced with crushed coral is full of chickens, some dogs, and a few small pigs, all of which will eventually be eaten. At one side of the rear yard is a large flat platform for drying chunks of coconut and the pods of vanilla beans. Next to the platform are stacked sheets of roofing tin which are to be used to protect the copra or vanilla if a shower seems imminent.

A narrow and somewhat unsteady plank leads to an outhouse built over the water. This outhouse has a wooden seat with a round hole in it, and feces and urine drop directly into the lagoon. Most of the outhouses in Piri are similarly placed, an excellent system from a public health point of view, protecting soil and drinking water from pollution. Near the outhouse is a small shed in the water where Teri'i Tui keeps a boat for which he has an outboard motor. Beached on the shore are two outrigger canoes which were built in the village.

Teri'i Tui is sixty years old in 1961. The composition of his household varies somewhat from month to month, but in the summer of 1961 it consists of his wife, Mari, forty-nine; their daughters, Romana, seventeen, Rui, fifteen, Tara, nine, and Ari, seven; a foster child, Etienne, four (the son of Teri'i Tui's daughter by a previous marriage); and Romana's *tāne*, Tino, about nineteen. Once or twice a week Teri'i's household is joined by thirty-year-old Toni, a son from his previous marriage, who brings his *vahine* Nui, twenty-five, and their infant son Little Toni with him. During the rest of the week Toni and his family stay in a small house on one of Teri'i Tui's lands at the far end of the bay.

In Teri'i Tui's home, as in most homes in Piri, the household begins to stir shortly after 6:00 in the morning. On this morning, a day when Toni and his family are not there, Teri'i, Mari, Romana, and Tino are up, washed, and dressed by 6:30. At 7:00 Mari is busy grating coconuts for a coconut sauce, and Rui is grinding coffee in an ancient grinder, using coffee beans which were grown on the hillside and roasted in a frying pan over the cookhouse fire. Romana is cooking a pancake made of flour, sugar, and coconut milk. Tino and Teri'i are placing copra chunks from a burlap bag onto the sun-drying shelf. The smaller children, Tara, Ari, and Etienne, are still sleeping. By 7:20 Etienne is up, looking a little stunned, and five minutes later Tara is awake. Ari continues to sleep. Now Teri'i and Tino are test-running the outboard motor in a barrel full of water. Mari has fed the pigs. Romana is still cooking pancakes which will be eaten warm for breakfast and served cold for other meals. The village seems silent except for two or three small children passing on the village path. One man, leaving the nearby Chinese store with a bag of sugar, can be seen from Teri'i Tui's front door.

By 7:45 the family is at the table for a breakfast of pancakes, coffee, some cold reef snails with a fermented coconut sauce, and apricot preserves from the Chinese store. Before sitting down to breakfast everybody washes his hands in a basin of water which has been placed on the far end of the table, the water getting dirtier and dirtier as each one uses it.[11] At 7:50 Mari sends Tara to wake Ari, who makes her way into the washing room with a dazed look on her face and splashes some water around. Face and hands suitably washed, she comes to the table. Tino has left and is outside sharpening a bush knife for clearing some overgrown land. Teri'i Tui leaves the table, washes, plays a few notes on his harmonica, and then returns to the table for a few minutes. An animated joking conversation goes on. At a few minutes after 8:00, Teri'i Tui and Ari leave in one canoe, Tino and Romana in another. They are going to nearby family lands to pollinate vanilla. The motorboat is saved for more distant trips. A few minutes later the table has been cleared and Mari is busy washing the dishes. The children help with the household chores. If it were not school vacation they would spend the day in the schoolhouse a few yards down the path. But now they help clean the house and yard, and in the late morning they go out on the village path to play.

11. One aspect of this washing is that people eat with their hands, serving themselves from common bowls. However, "European style food" — rice or canned peas, for example — is eaten with fork and spoon.

At 1:00 or 2:00 the canoes return. Lunch is some fried fish, taro, and cooked plantains; and for Teri'i Tui, joined by Mari and Tino, a glass or two of imported Algerian red wine. Teri'i sleeps for an hour after lunch, then he looks after his vanilla and copra, spread out drying in the sun, and sorts and bundles the vanilla beans that are ready for marketing. In the late afternoon he braids some rope and makes some repairs on a canoe. He then bathes, puts on a casual *pareu*, a cloth wrapped around his waist, and walks up to the Chinese store for conversation with some of the other village men who have started to gather there. It is 5:00 in the afternoon.

Meanwhile, Tino and Romana have gone out in one of the canoes. Tino has a mask and a spring-operated fish gun, and he dives for fish while Romana waits in the canoe. The young children go to play along the village path in a variety of highly energetic, joyful games. By 6:00 the coffeepot is over the fire, and people return to the household.

After supper Teri'i Tui listens to the Tahitian-language broadcast from Tahiti on his battery-operated radio. Mari and Romana are making a dress from some cotton cloth. If there were unattached adolescent boys in the household they would have bathed, anointed themselves with perfumed coconut oil or cheap store-bought perfume, and gone strolling after dark on the village path. Once or twice a week Teri'i Tui takes a lantern and goes out, sometimes with Toni, Tino, or Mari, to spear fish in the shallows of the lagoon or to search for shellfish on the reef, crabs in the shallow part of the bay, or shrimp in the freshwater rivers. On such nights he does not return until after midnight. Tonight he is asleep by 9:00. The younger children fall asleep at the dinner table (during school season, over their schoolwork) and are carried or chased off to bed. By 10:00 the others have followed.

Roto

Papeete, on the island of Tahiti, is in all respects the center of French Polynesia and, more particularly, of the Society Islands.

Territorial politics, commerce, communications, and tourism begin there and spread first to the farther districts of Tahiti, then to the other Tahitian-speaking islands, and finally to the other archipelagoes. Papeete has had a rapidly growing population, and in 1962 19,903 of the territory's people lived there. It is a town of considerable sociological complexity and flux (see, for example, Jullien 1963).

The urban neighborhood, here called Roto, from the Tahitian word for "within," contrasts in many ways with the village of Piri. Embedded deeply within the town of Papeete, it is not a community. It is a mixed neighborhood of about two hundred persons, living in forty-eight households;[12] and although some of its people do interact closely, many have as many (or often more) relationships with people elsewhere in Papeete as they have within Roto. Roto was chosen for study in an earlier phase of the Society Islands project by Paul Kay, as a sample of urban life containing a high percentage of inhabitants of Society Island origin, in contrast to many other Papeete areas with their mainly Chinese, European, or non-Tahitian Polynesian populations.

Roto does have some Chinese, Europeans, and islanders from the Marquesas and Tuamotus living among the Tahitian population. The Tahitian population of Roto is itself differentiated by the very salient Papeete classification of "Europeanized" Tahitian versus "traditional" Tahitian. It was the "traditional" Tahitians of Roto who concerned me in this study.

For both the "Europeanized" and the "traditional" Tahitians of Roto, although in different degrees, one dimension of life is derived from the western-influenced Tahitian past and another from the currents of modernization[13] flowing around them.

12. These figures are based on censuses made by Paul Kay. They do not include Chinese households.

13. It seems empirically useful to make some distinction among externally introduced influences toward change. One may distinguish the general impact of various western and Chinese forms and ideas (e.g., missionary Christianity), which may be called "acculturation," from a specific set of structural changes which one may call "modernization." Modernization consists of "successive shifts from partial subsistence economies to market and finally, wage economies; of progressive urbanization of centrally lo-

The life of a distant village such as Piri helps clarify aspects of Roto's past. Many elements are still common to both settings, as we shall see. What is unique in settings like Roto is, I must repeat, not one of the major concerns of this book.

Paul Kay observed the daily life of Roto, and it was against the background of his observations that I interviewed some of the people who lived there. I will borrow an extensive passage from him for a sketch of the setting, in which I have substituted my own pseudonymous community name.

Roto is the name of a loosely defined geographical area in Papeete. It comprises most of the interior of a large city block and does not include any of the houses facing on the paved city streets. The houses face lanes, footpaths, or merely open court, and the majority are not accessible by automobile in wet weather. . . .

Measuring from its closest boundary, Roto is about 350 meters from the Papeete produce market. It is thus one of the closest residential areas to the town center. Roto is in no sense a social unit. I shall refer to it as a neighborhood, but even this term may connote more of a social unity than in fact exists there. . . .

The city block in which Roto is situated contains roughly 80,000 square meters of ground of which one half to two thirds may be thought of as belonging in Roto proper. . . . Although a considerable amount of the land area is not covered by houses, none of it is gardened, with the exception of two plots cultivated by men who live in other neighborhoods of Papeete. Grass grows in a number of spots, but the greater part of the terrain is bare earth, tending to become mud with the advent of the rains. A large number of trees throughout the neighborhood cast the greater part of it in shade. By far the most important of these from an economic point of view are breadfruit trees, which furnish a significant part of the diet of many of the resident

cated island towns with the creation of hinterlands and of peasant conditions; of the development of an active labor market and the creation of a town proletariat; and of the development of widespread, low-cost communication networks, on the one hand bringing in masses of [foreigners and] tourists, and on the other allowing opportunities for the islanders to travel and to seek work in various 'developed' countries" (Levy 1969; pp. 7-8).

households during the appropriate seasons. Also there are some avocado trees and two families plant a few bananas.

Roto is essentially a residential neighborhood. Typically for Papeete, there are Chinese-owned retail stores at most of the points of egress from the neighborhood, where the interior lanes connect with the city streets. However, within the neighborhood proper, there are a number of commercial installations of varying degrees of importance. . . . The neighborhood [also] contains a Protestant meeting house.

Houses differ considerably with respect to construction materials and the types and location of cooking, toilet, and washing facilities. The major materials used are cement, imported milled lumber, galvanized iron sheets, poles cut from local trees, and siding and roofing sheets made from dried and braided coconut-palm leaves (*ni'au*). Generally speaking, houses may be classified as made of cement (with galvanized iron roofs and cement floors), wood (galvanized iron roofs and wooden floors raised on wooden piles or cement blocks), or *ni'au* (walls and roof of *ni'au* attached to a framework of locally cut poles with a packed earth floor). . . . To the latter, least expensive and least prestigious, category one may add a marginal group of shacks built largely out of odds and ends, boards, *ni'au*, old pieces of sheet iron, etc. . . .

Most households have outbuildings — privies, wash-sheds and cook-sheds — separate from the sleeping house. Only the most expensive cement houses contain indoor kitchens and flush toilets. Among the remaining houses there is considerable variation in the location and ownership of and use-rights to outbuildings. Some outbuildings are erected and consequently owned by landlords, some by tenants, the latter being the more frequent case. In some cases cook-sheds are attached to the back of the sleeping quarters, in others they stand as separate structures. Outbuildings are built of poles, boards, *ni'au*, and galvanized iron sheets, the latter two materials being used mainly as roofing. . . .

Almost all sleeping houses in Roto are wired for electricity. All households have access to the city water supply in one way or another. However, due to the irregular placement of houses throughout the area and the city ordinance requiring that the householder (or landlord) run his own pipe from the main water line to his house or cookhouse, there is considerable variation in the distance that wash and cook-sheds are located from the various sleeping houses. In some cases, a single unsheltered spigot furnishes water to several households which are tenants of the same multihousehold dwelling.

The day's activities begin soon after sun-up in Roto. The morning meal usually consists of coffee and bread, perhaps including some left-overs from the previous day. Poor people, who cannot afford coffee every day, may have tea or hot water and sugar. Coffee is much more often bought from a Chinese store than made at home. Frequently a child is sent with the pot to fetch the morning coffee.

The central produce market opens at about 5:00 A.M. It may be visited any time during the morning. From 6:00 to 7:00 A.M. most men and some women leave for work and children for school. Throughout most of the morning, the neighborhood is empty of all but very old men and perhaps a few who are between jobs or on their day off. Women are occupied in minding pre-school children, washing, hanging out and ironing clothes, preparing the noon meal, and visiting and gossiping. The few able bodied men around are occupied in building, improving or repairing the house or household equipment or just lounging.

The big meal of the day comes at noon. About 11:30, men start arriving home from work, often to help their wives with the preparation of the meal. Men are particularly likely to help if the earth oven . . . is to be made that noon. There are a number of modern variations of the traditional earth oven used in Roto, such as substituting a section of a fifty gallon oil drum for the traditional hole in the ground. There is a good deal of cooking in metal pots on primus and other kinds of stoves as well [as] buying of prepared meals from the Chinese stores. In general, men in Roto always return home for the noon meal unless their job, e.g., working on the road in another district, prevents it.

After the meal many people sleep for an hour or two, attend to some household chore, or merely sit around. At 1:00 people are beginning to leave for work again, and by 2:00 the neighborhood has taken on again its empty aspect of the morning.

The afternoon in Roto passes much like the morning. Perhaps on the average less work and more visiting and gossiping are done by the women, but this is largely an individual matter.

Toward six o'clock men begin returning to the neighborhood. Some have stopped at the afternoon market or Chinese store and picked up something for the evening meal, but mostly supper is much like breakfast with a bit more in the way of leftovers from the noon meal and perhaps a can of meat, *pâté* or fish from the Chinese store. After supper, people sit around and talk, listen to the radio and perform minor indoor chores by the light of small, bare, electric bulbs. By nine o'clock few lights are showing.

Sundays are not very different from weekdays in Roto; people leave, not for work, but for various distractions such as football [soccer] matches or to visit relatives and acquaintances in other neighborhoods. Some receive visitors at home. Organized religion occupies little time for most Roto residents. There is a strong tendency in Papeete for people to devote either the vast majority or virtually none of their leisure time to religious activities. The latter pattern is by far the most common with the result that the churches are a highly dominant influence in the lives of a small segment of the population and of very little importance to the majority. (Kay 1963; pp. 1-8)

2

Some Actors

The principal dramatis personae of my presentation of Piri and Roto are members of Teri'i Tui's household and those people who were given the recorded psychodynamic interviews. The latter were chosen, for Piri, in order to represent a variety of "types" of social actors. In contrast, the three persons who were interviewed in Roto were chosen more at hazard, largely because they were accessible in a community which tended to guard its privacy. They considered themselves "real Tahitians" and had been born and lived most of their lives in Papeete, and that was enough for my limited comparative purposes.

Of the people I wished to interview in Piri, only two declined. One was a part-Chinese man who lived at the "humble" end of the village and was a convert to the Mormon church. The other was a nineteen-year-old man who was the village *māhū*, or transvestite. He came for two interviews, but when I began to probe about his personal life, he found a series of excuses not to continue.

A number of other people were interviewed in more focused and limited ways for specific types of psychological or social information; for example, the *māhū* in Roto and a prominent *tahu'a* ("spirit doctor") in Tahiti. But those people who agreed to be interviewed intensively are a special group. They provide the most sustained, open, and intimate self-reporting I was able to get. I was interested not only in what they had to say about the experience of their lives but in how they said it — the interplay of content and form.

In this chapter I will introduce each of them. I have used pseudonyms. After my interviews with "Teiva," he said to me one day that he was concerned that I would write about what he had told me in a book and that one of his children might buy the book in Papeete someday, which would be embarrassing. I promised him that I would use false names. Many of the names I have chosen as pseudonyms are not real Tahitian names; they are Tahitian descriptive adjectives — "poor," "morally correct," and so on — fantasied nicknames. I will refer to each of these interviewees throughout the book. Their statements will be dissolved and distributed for evidence for some generality on "feelings," "defense mechanisms," and so on.

In these introductions I have also used individuals to introduce or underline themes — aspects of experience which expand or add new elements to some of the background remarks of the last chapter and which will concern us in later chapters.

PIRI

Poria, the Anthropologist's Friend

Fieldworkers in exotic communities seem often to find on entering the community that there is somebody who is eager and not too busy to help them. He may be called the "anthropologist's friend." The fieldworker looks on him with a cautious eye. The very fact that he has free time and is anxious to explain the community to the stranger makes it likely that he is not part of the village "establishment," which has reason to be busier and more cautious with strangers. He must be "interesting" in order to maintain his helper's role — but his effort to be interesting and the exaggerations this may entail make for a useful dialectic with the often cautious conventionality of more important villagers. In Piri the anthropologist's friend was Poria.

Poria is thirty-seven years old at the time of the interviews. He is dark-skinned with a strongly Polynesian face, in a village which, like most Society Island villages, has a great range of facial features, body builds, and skin colors, owing to a considerable European and Chinese genetic admixture. Poria, muscular but somewhat obese, gives an impression of innocent and bemused sweetness. Although most of the other villagers seem more or less actively involved in the social changes and stirrings of modernization which are washing up in Piri, Poria refuses to strive. He lives in his simple thatched board house, fishing a little and occasionally working for others when they need help on their lands. He stays away from church and is only an onlooker and not taken seriously in village decision-making. He is, by general consensus, one of the five or six "grown-up adolescents" (*taure'are'a pa'ari*) in the village and the constant member of a group of them who meet in the evening once every ten days or so to drink beer or homemade fermented fruit juice and to talk, joke, and argue. He is described by other villagers as being *mā'ohi* ("traditional," "truly Tahitian"). There are several concepts of what truly Tahitian really is. Living by old and rigid missionary community standards is one version, but Poria, in the simplicity of his way of life, represents another. As applied to him, the word *mā'ohi* is used ambivalently in a slightly pejorative fashion, implying a combination of pastoral simplicity and bumpkinism. Poria has simplified his life to the point of deviance. He is one of the two individuals in the village who live alone, the other being a young man who is a spastic. All other men in the village, after leaving their childhood homes in late adolescence, live with a *vahine* and eventually with children or else, if they are widowed or unable to hold a woman, with relatives.

Poria was born in Piri and was delivered at his grandmother's house. His mother was a *taure'are'a*, still in her teens at the time of his birth and living with her parents, but in Poria's phrase, "slept everywhere." Poria was her first child, and, as often happens in such cases, she left the baby's care to her parents. Poria is not sure who his biological father is, although he was told when he was a young adolescent that his father was perhaps "a relative of the Vehia family — but I am not sure."

As he remembers it, his mother was around the house until he was about six or seven, but it was his grandmother, for the most part, who was responsible for looking after him. When he was about six his mother left to live with a new *tāne* in another district of Huahine. He saw her infrequently after that, when she occasionally visited Piri; and when he was about thirteen she died.

His grandfather's one-room house did not have chairs, tables, or western-style beds. A variety of grass was used as a floor covering. They ate sitting on the floor, using both "French" dishes, cups, and glasses and native equivalents — leaves for plates and half coconut shells as cups. They slept on mats and kapok-stuffed mattress sacks. As was common in Piri, the household size and composition during Poria's childhood varied greatly from one period to another. Various uncles and aunts came and went with their spouses and children. Thus when he was ten years old there were nine other children and six adults living in the house; when he was fifteen there were fourteen children and four adults.

When Poria was a child there was no school or schoolteacher in the village. When he was thirteen a Frenchman came to the village as schoolteacher. The Frenchman stayed three or four months and then left and was replaced by another who also stayed only three or four months. There followed a long period without a teacher, and these six or eight months were the sum of Poria's French schooling. Aside from being able to count and knowing a few other words, Poria does not understand French. He does read and write Tahitian and thus can write letters and read the Bible — this he learned at the pastor's Sunday school.

When Poria was about ten his grandmother died, and the household was broken up. The children she was taking care of went to live with their biological parents or various other relatives, and Poria and his grandfather moved in with one of the grandfather's settled children. The grandfather was irritable, stubborn, and hard to get along with, and a series of arguments with his children kept him moving from one household to another, with Poria always following.

As a child he played with the village children, both boys and girls. When he was nine or ten he would go to play and sleep in the house of one of his near relatives as often as two or three times a week. At eleven or twelve he began to play only with boys; there were six boys in the village of approximately his age, who became special friends, *hoa*. At twelve he and four others of these *hoa* decided that the time had come to become super-

cised. The older adolescent boys had started to mock them because of their unsupercised penises. They asked a man in the village who knew how to do it to operate on them. They all went
on the same day to be cut. Poria recalls the details of the events
surrounding the operation with sentimental pleasure.

For Poria, as for all others, his transition from childhood to
taure'are'a was a gradual one. The supercision was only one of
the episodes involved in the transition. It was not until he was
fifteen that he considered himself to be fully a *taure'are'a*. For
him, as for other boys in the village, adolescence was a time of
considerable freedom; he considers it the best period of his life.
In childhood, he says, one is too much under the control of
others, and in adulthood one has too many responsibilities; but
in adolescence one is free to live as one wants to.

His years from fifteen to eighteen centered on *taure'are'a* activities. The high point of the day was the evening, after supper,
when, washed and perfumed, Poria and his friends would go
strolling along the village path. They would talk and joke and
sometimes sit on the village wharf, singing and playing the guitar
and ukulele. (In Poria's adolescence the guitar had already been
introduced into Piri. For the generation before him the harmonica and the accordion were the popular instruments.) Later in
the night Poria and his friends would try, usually unsuccessfully,
by "night crawling" secretly into a house when everyone was
asleep or by some prearranged tryst in the brush, to find a girl
for sexual intercourse. In the morning Poria would often sleep
late. Sometimes he would help his grandfather or one of his
uncles in their work in the gardens, or more likely he would go
fishing.

When he was eighteen or nineteen Poria and his grandfather
set up a household together. Only the two of them lived there.
As his grandfather grew older and less able to work, Poria took
more and more care of the household.

In his early twenties he traveled to the "Phosphate Island" of
Makatea in the Tuamotu Archipelago to "dig in the dirt," and a
year or two later he spent a year in the army, during which he
was sent off for eight months to the town of Noumea in New

Caledonia. On both occasions he spent all his time with Tahitians, mostly men from Huahine. He then returned to Piri and lived with his grandfather until he died in his eighties in 1961. After the grandfather's death Poria lived alone.

When he was twelve he had sexual intercourse for the first time, with a girl about his own age. He was with this girl only once. When he was thirteen he lived with a girl for the first time; she was twelve. He brought her to the house of the uncle he and his grandfather were living with at the time. They stayed together three months, then broke up because "there was trouble" between them. "She was jealous of some other girls. We would all go to dance the western-style dance, to have a good time. Then there would be fighting when we got back to the house. She thought I was flirting with some other girl. I said to her, 'That's not true.' But she didn't listen. Because of that, we fought all the time; we had trouble, then we separated. She went to another house to stay. And after three nights I went and fetched her again, and we went back to our house. But then we went out again to have a good time. And there was trouble again. Finally I didn't go and fetch her anymore. I said, 'That's it. Go, if you want,' and so she went."

He did not live with another girl until he was twenty. The second relationship lasted about six months. He had one other relatively long relationship with a *vahine*, when he was in his late twenties. The woman had been the *vahine* of Ah Kui, the China-born proprietor of one of the Chinese stores, and for a number of years she moved back and forth between Poria and Ah Kui. She finally left both of them and returned to the nearby island she had come from. Poria was left with only his grandfather, and when his grandfather died, he found himself alone.

Tāvana, the "Chief" of Piri

The chief, or *tāvana*, of Piri was called simply Tāvana, and the younger members of the village did not know him by any other name. I will follow village convention and refer to both him and his job as Tāvana. Ideally, people say, a *tāvana* must be someone who loves the villagers, and he must not be proud or ambitious, but must be kind and gentle. The schoolteacher, with an outsider's view of the village, noted that in addition to these qualities a *tāvana* in the Society Islands has to be a Protestant, a friend of the pastor, preferably a deacon, and of "good morals," which the teacher explained by saying that, for example, he should never have been in jail.

The *tāvana* of Piri has all these qualifications. In 1945 he became the first elected *tāvana* in Piri. (For many years before 1945 the village *tāvana* had been appointed.) And he has been reelected every five years since then. From all evidence he manages the subtle responsibilities of the *tāvana* role with a delicate and lighthanded virtuosity. For the thirteen or fourteen years before becoming *tāvana*, Tāvana had been the village policeman, the *muto'i*. During the years of being *muto'i*, which at that time required two tedious three-hour canoe trips between Piri and Fare every week, he never reported a breach of Piri order to the gendarme, but, in cooperation with the various *tāvana* of the time, managed to resolve problems within the village.

Tāvana is a fine-featured man, gray haired and somewhat fragile with age. Like Poria he has a sweet face, but Tāvana also conveys an impression of dignity and intelligence. He was born in 1902 in the village of Maroe on the northeast side of Huahine Iti. Maroe, which is connected with Piri by a path through the hills (about an hour's walk), is more closely related to Piri than any of the other villages on Huahine. Marriages between the two villages are frequent, and a number of people move from one village to the other. His mother, who was born in Piri, went to Maroe to stay with a *tāne*. Tāvana was her sixth child. Shortly after birth he was given up for adoption, in his explanation because "that woman [the adoptive mother] wanted to, because she was a relative. So she took me and carried me off to be an adopted child." Tāvana lived with his adoptive mother and her *tāne* (he calls her "my mother," and the man "her *tāne*") in Maroe until he was about two. He was the only child in the house, since all her children were grown and had left home. When he was about two they went to the nearby island of Tahaa to live. Soon afterward his adoptive father went off to the Tuamotu

Islands to dive for pearl oysters and returned paralyzed as a result of brain damage caused by diving. He was no longer treated as a member of the family, but lived literally "under the house," the house being built on wooden piles. He died shortly afterward.

When Tāvana was about six his adoptive mother was invited to visit a friend, who was married to a pastor in one of the rural districts of the island of Tahiti. She went to Tahiti and brought Tāvana with her. They spent two years in the district, where Tāvana went to school. On returning to Tahaa two years later he continued going to school.

He left school at fourteen, typically, because he was "beginning to start my *taure'are'a* activities." He began to go out at night, to watch the older *taure'are'a* enjoying themselves. A year or two later he began to shift from being a spectator to being an actor. While he was still going to school, at thirteen, he decided to become supercised. He and a group of his friends had all decided to have it done, and over a period of a week or two they went in small groups for the operation. Tāvana, however, went by himself.

His mother died of influenza during the disastrous epidemic which spread throughout the islands after the First World War. Shortly after her death he "settled down" with a *vahine* of his own age in Tahaa. They stayed together only a few months, then he stayed with a second *vahine*, also for a few months, and finally settled with a third, who bore him a child. Tāvana was then sixteen. This *vahine*'s mother did not approve of their staying together and, therefore, according to Tāvana, they broke up. His *vahine* took the baby boy with her, but she soon began to wander again (*ori*, to "stroll" or "wander," is the standard term for the *taure'are'a*'s shifting attachments), and her mother took the child and brought it up. The child is, says Tāvana in a matter-of-fact way, a *tamāri'i fa'atūri* (a "child of fornication") and is now a Protestant pastor on Tahaa.

After he left his *vahine* Tāvana stayed with three or four more for short periods of time until, at the age of seventeen, he met the girl whom he eventually married and who became Tāvana

Vahine ("Tāvana's wife," a semititle). Tāvana had gone for a visit to Huahine, and on his return he saw a girl on the boat. "We were on the same boat. I tried to meet her, she permitted it. When we arrived there in Tahaa, I asked her [if she would stay with him], she permitted it. And that was that. Just like that. She agreed to come to me in my house."

After beginning to stay with Tāvana Vahine, he started to think about gardening and "improving his life." He began working on family lands in Tahaa, but there were not enough lands, and so eventually he and Tāvana Vahine moved to Maroe. He worked there for about two years on lands belonging to his family, but there was a great deal of family argument about the exact ownership of the lands and the sharing of profits, and he left them to go first to another village, Fitii, in Huahine and finally, when he was about twenty-six, to Piri. In Fitii he worked lands he rented from a Chinese. "The Chinese had said to me, 'Go on that land and stay, and divide the profits with me.'" After he had been in Fitii about two years, the mother of his *vahine* died, and in a settlement of her lands, some lands in Piri became available to his *vahine*. So they came to Piri to work their own land.

His *vahine* had one child by a previous *tāne*. She and Tāvana lived together in Piri for several years. When they had five children they decided, as a next step into full adult status in the village, to get married in the Protestant church, and under French law. Of the nine children they had in their union, they raised only three; the others were given out for adoption.

After his marriage he and his wife became communicants in the church at Piri, and some years later he became a deacon. His commitment to working his lands, his interest in village affairs, his marriage, and his entrance into the communicants indicated to himself and to others that Tāvana, then in his forties, had become a full "adult" member of the community, a ta'ata pa'ari.

By missionary standards he had faults. He had been a relatively heavy drinker throughout his years as *muto'i* and in his first years as *tāvana*. He had once deserted his wife, some years after their marriage, and gone off briefly to Tahiti with the wife of another man in the village. For Piri such human failings better fitted him for his role as *tāvana*. He was not too "high," too "swollen."

Early in my stay in Piri, before my interviews with Tāvana, Tāvana Vahine died. A year later he married Veve Vahine, who will also be introduced here.

Tano, the Pastor of Piri

In 1963, at the time of the interviews, Tano was forty-five years old and had been the Protestant pastor of Piri for twenty years. Fleshy, slightly potbellied, he is somber, reserved, troubled, and hard-working. Tano has accumulated more money from his vanilla planting and taro garden than anybody else in the village. Some others worked almost as hard, but men like Teri'i Tui worked to make money to spend for enjoyment. Tano saved.

Tano was born in Piri in 1918. Like all other homes in Piri at the time, his was a thatched-roof house. When this house was blown down in one of the islands' rare hurricanes in 1926, his father replaced it with a tin-roofed house, the first built in Piri. Tano was the third of seven children. He had two sisters — one five years older and the other two years older than he. A year after his birth another boy was born, then two more male children. When he was three or four, Tano was adopted by a *"soeur,"* a classificatory sister, of his mother. Tano does not know why he was given for adoption at this time. His explanation, typically, refers to the adopting parents and is that "probably I was taken because they wanted to have me." When he first went to these new parents, he was the only young child in the household, though there were a large number of older adolescents and their *tāne* or *vahine* staying there. These adolescents were biological or adoptive children of his new parents. He remembers that at least twelve persons stayed in the household, all in one undivided room. Soon the household was supplemented by infants as his adoptive mother took her "grandchildren," infants of these *taure'are'a* "children," into her care. During the next four years Tano stayed mostly with his adoptive mother and father but occasionally went to visit and eat at his biological parents' house. When he was eight, one of the young couples living in the household took Tano to Tahiti with them, where he lived until he was eighteen, when he returned to Piri.

In his childhood there was still no school or schoolteacher at Piri, the nearest school being in Fare. Tano started school in Tahiti in the district of Punaauia, where his new family was living. He went for four years and then stopped because he was "fed up." "*Taure'are'a* thoughts had come." Even though he was getting ready to prepare for his "certificate" of completion of secondary studies, he had "lost the desire" to go on. That was that. He stopped.

Like many people, Tano looks back on his childhood as an unhappy period. Whereas others explain their unhappiness in terms of having too many people give them orders and not being free to do what they wanted, contrasting this with the subsequent freedom of being a *taure'are'a*, Tano explains his unhappiness in childhood as being due to shortages. They were poor, and there was not enough to eat. Tano is heavy now and was, he says, a fat child. But he remembers not getting food when he wanted it, and often, particularly in his first years in Piri, having to wait from breakfast until late in the evening for his second meal. Of his life in Tahiti, he complains of being hungry, of having to walk long distances to school, and of being disliked by his new adoptive mother, who now had a family of her own biological children and did not treat him like one of them.

Tano went to be supercised with four other friends when he was only eleven and still at school. He was a relatively restrained *taure'are'a*. "I didn't like to drink. . . . I drank in the beginning, but I never got drunk. One glass; that was enough. I didn't want any more . . . to enjoy myself, sing, that was enough. That's what I like. . . . In my *taure'are'a* time, I didn't waste my money, I saved it, even though it wasn't very much. But what I liked was to get together with some friends and play the guitar and sing. I had a lovely voice for singing in those days. Now, though, I don't do those kinds of things anymore — I've cast them away."

When he quit school he found various ways of making money. He went into the deep valleys in Tahiti to gather oranges to sell. He worked for various people in the rural district where he lived, clearing the brush on the coconut plantations, helping prepare copra, working on gardens and vanilla plantations. When he returned to Piri he continued working for others at first but then "I didn't want any longer to work for others, I wanted to work in my own lands. My father gave me some land, and I began to cultivate it. There was some vanilla already on it but not much when he gave it to me. I planted new vanilla. Even when I went to Papeete to the pastor's school I did some gardening in the fields at the school." He continued to develop his lands when he finally returned to Piri as pastor. In addition to vanilla he planted food crops, melons, manioc, taro, and *taruā*, and he raised pigs and cows.

Between fifteen and eighteen Tano lived, he says, with eight different girls. At eighteen, much earlier than most of his contemporaries, he decided to get married, and he married a girl from Piri.

When Tano was nineteen the pastor of Piri died. The people of the parish decided that Tano should replace him. "The people in Piri saw that there was no one else besides myself to be chosen to do it."

At twenty-three he and his wife went to Papeete, and he entered the school for Protestant pastors there. After three years of training he returned to Piri to take up his job as pastor.

His work as pastor and with his crops and animals occupied his life. When he evaluates his life, he has some difficulty in breathing, as several people in Piri seem to do when they are troubled. He says, "I am not happy . . . my life is now exhausting . . . even though I have enough food and my life is flourishing, it is not a happy life to my way of thinking. My life comes out of my exhaustion, from the work of my hands and my body. If my life were good, I wouldn't be exhausted, then I would be happy. . . . And who knows, anyway, what the future will bring, there is no way of telling that we will get what we want out of

life, and anyway I am going to die and it will all be wasted."
Tano is caught between two worlds.

Teiva, a Dissident Leader

When in late 1958 a part of Tano's congregation, for a tangle of
ostensible reasons, walked out of his church and established
their own church across the pathway at Teri'i Tui's house, their
leader was one of Tano's deacons, Teiva.

The older people of Piri had conflicting images and evaluations of the Piri of their childhood and early youths. For Teri'i
Tui it was a time when people still knew how to sing and dance
and drink and enjoy themselves. For some old women it was a
time when people still lived by the rules of the church, religious
activities flourished, and girls were well behaved. For many others it was a time of pastoral simplicity, a time when the oranges
flourished, when you could grow your crops with a minimum of
work, and when money had not become an important and troubling factor in people's lives. But for Teiva it was a time of primitiveness and shame. Although other people had in certain moods
some criticism of the old days — rare and mixed with a certain
self-irony — Teiva was alone in the intensity and obsessiveness
of his point of view. "When I was a child, the village was dirty
and disgusting. There was no water in the village. People had to
bring water in buckets from a spring far inland. There was no
money. People sat on the floor and ate and slept on the floor.
The houses were jammed right next to each other and they were
dirty. Everything was filthy. The people were thieves, always
stealing chickens and pigs. There was trouble and hard feelings
all the time. They were disgusting days."

One day while sawing wood, surrounded by a group of young
men, Teiva tells a story. When the white men first came to Huahine, they had tools the natives had never seen before. The natives particularly desired to have a saw. So they stole one and
took it to a sacred prayer site and buried it in the ground so that
it might grow and produce more saws. Teiva laughs bitterly. The
young men around him, not sure whether they should be proud
or ashamed of the old days, seem embarrassed.

Teiva is forty-six at the time of the interviews. His biological mother and father were both of mixed Polynesian and Caucasian descent, and Teiva, thin and light-skinned, looks very European. But he was brought up by a China-born Chinese "father," and villagers in critical moods refer to Teiva as a "Chinese type." By this they mean first that he often eats Chinese food at home, that he eats with chopsticks, and that he speaks a few words of Chinese. But also he works too hard and plans too much to be an ordinary Tahitian. It is because, they say, he is used to Chinese ways.

Teiva built himself a modern tin-roofed house that was full of innovations for Piri. It has louvered windows and a back yard shaped and extended with coral fill. He was the first man in Piri to learn to dry and sort his own vanilla beans rather than passing the green beans on to Ah Kui at the Chinese store for further processing. He is like Tano in his economic activities — a kind of "modern man." But he is not of the village in the same way that Tano is. He insists on placing himself in contrast to Tahitian things. "The Chinese," says Teiva, comparing his upbringing with that of the other villagers, "teach their children how to work. The Tahitians are lazy — they just let their children alone, let them play most of the time. But the Chinese teach their children how to cook, how to grow foods. They teach you to be energetic about getting wealth. Tahitians are different; they are lazy about life. They can't help it — it is because of the way they were brought up."

Teiva was born in the town of Fare. His mother had been married but had separated from her husband, and she went to live with another man in Fare, Teiva's biological father. Shortly before Teiva was born this man left Teiva's mother. Teiva never saw him, although he was told that he was a "man from Papeete," that he was part *pōpa'a* or "European." A few weeks after Teiva was born, he was taken by a "grandmother" of his mother. She shared his care with a close relative of hers, Nani, who was also related "closely" [the emphasis is Teiva's] to his biological mother. As a very young child Teiva spent part of his time with Nani in Piri and part with one adoptive mother in

Fare. But then, when he "was very small," he was taken to Piri to stay with Nani, who had no biological children of her own. She lived with Ah You, a *tāne* born in China, who worked in Piri as a farmer and as a carpenter. Teiva was their only adopted child, and there were no other members in the household until he was about seven, at which time they adopted an infant girl. This completed the unusually small household. When he was thirteen he was sent to Fare to stay with relatives and to begin school. He continued at school for about three years, returning to Piri for vacations. The teacher in Fare at the time did not speak French, and the school was conducted in Tahitian.

Teiva went with a group of friends to be supercised when he was fourteen. He had had intercourse for the first time some months before his supercision. He stayed with a *vahine* for the first time when he was fifteen. They remained together for two years, until she died in childbirth. During the next three years he had, he says, many girls. He settled with his present *vahine* when he was about twenty. During their adolescence, most boys of his generation and later generations made close friendships with a small group of boys about their own age and spent most of their time with them. They later looked back on these friendships with considerable sentimentality. These boys would make an occasional foray into a group of *vahine* for a transient sexual relationship, or would stay with a girl for a few weeks or months, only to leave her and return to the group of boys again; the eventual decision to stay more seriously with a *vahine* represented a more or less painful rupture with their male friends. For Teiva the situation was reversed. He avoided close male friends as an adolescent, because he felt that this interfered with his relations with girls, which were more important to him. For one thing, as he says, the sisters of one's close friends became like sisters to you and thus had to be sexually avoided; and therefore close male friends were a disadvantage. For another, members of bands of close friends had a way of interfering with one another's sexual successes.

The first *vahine* he lived with was beautiful, he says. Both his relatives and hers did not want them to stay together because

they were distantly related. But, as he says, the lightning was
there, and they were attracted to each other. And so in spite of
the displeasure of the relatives they settled down. But when,
after two years, his *vahine* was ready to deliver their first baby,
her adoptive father, angry about the incest violation and being
skilled as a spirit doctor, or *tahu'a*, cursed her, and therefore
both Teiva's *vahine* and their baby died in childbirth. Teiva
mourned his wife, but he neither publicly accused nor "was
angry at" his *vahine*'s adoptive father. "It was not for *me* to do
anything. . . . Within two years after my *vahine*'s death, the
father was dead."

Teiva had a casual affair with his second *vahine* for several
months, sneaking into her house through a window late at night
when others were asleep and sometimes meeting her in a secluded place outside the house, but after several months her
father caught him in the house. He didn't want her to have trouble. "I couldn't just get rid of her. She had been without trouble
in her own house. Now suddenly there were all kinds of difficulties, I couldn't just cast her off. So I went to fetch her and bring
her to my house." They lived in this house with his adoptive
father and mother until Ah You died, when Teiva was twenty.
Shortly after Ah You's death, Teiva married his *vahine*. By 1963
they had had thirteen children, of whom ten are still living. They
gave four children away to others, including their first three surviving children.

After his marriage, Teiva and his *vahine* became communicants
of the church. He began to work his lands, finding ways of improving their value; he began to make and save money; and he
began to build his tin-roofed house. He was made a deacon of
the church in 1950.

When tensions and ill-feeling began to grow in Tano's congregation in the late 1950s, it was natural for some of the congregation to turn to Teiva for leadership because, he says, "I was a
deacon." He provided stern and uncompromising criticism of
Tano (including a criticism of Tano's interest in worldly goods
and in making money) and of the Protestant church's political
stand. When Tano, in a fit of irritation at the criticism directed

toward him, refused to conduct a church service and had the church locked, Teiva offered to give a service elsewhere, and a large part of the congregation followed him. Soon passions began to cool, and people began to talk about rejoining Tano. Teiva refused — the others could do as they wished. Many then decided to stay with Teiva. According to critics of Teiva it was "only his stubbornness" which kept the village split.

Uta, a Mormon Convert

It might be possible to walk from one end of the village path to the other in about ten minutes at a comfortable strolling pace. But one's walk is always interrupted by encounters with people coming the other way along the path or sitting in front of their houses. The conventional greeting is "Where are you going?" The correct answer, if one is going in an inland direction, is "Inland"; and if one is going in a seaward direction, "Seaward." If the encounter involves more than a minimally polite exchange, then commonly the next question, from people living in the inland part of the village, is "What is new at the seaward end?" — and vice versa from those at the other end of the village. In social space the two ends of the village are farther away than a ten-minute walk. A line drawn about two-thirds of the way up the path toward inland would divide the village into two subcommunities. The seaward people are the principal actors in village affairs — the bigger landowners, the tāvana, the muto'i, the village council, the deacons, the pastor, and the former and probable future holders of these roles. Beyond the line were the "other people who lived in the village," the common people, ta'ata ha'eha'a, the audience for official village happenings.

When the schism occurred in Tano's church, many of the people in this end of the village walked out; but, instead of joining Teiva's group, some of them gave up churchgoing, and a number accepted the teachings of the two Mormon missionaries who had been working with little success in Huahine. One of the converts was Uta.

Uta is twenty-nine at the time of the interviews. He is muscular and benign-looking, with a somewhat dull, bemused expression. He was born in Piri and his biological mother and father are still living in the village. He was the second child, some two and a half years younger than an older brother. One year later another boy was born, and a year after that his last sibling, a girl.

While Uta's mother was pregnant with him, she began to have abdominal pain. It took her seven days to deliver him, he says, and he was a rather sickly infant. The elders in the family said that he should be taken out of his father's household, and so he was taken by "grandparents" to be raised.

His "grandparents" were "already old" at the time they took him to their house on their garden lands near Maroe in an isolated area outside of that village. When he was two or three they adopted another child from Piri (Rahera, daughter of Teri'i Tui and the *vahine* of Taere), whom they took as an infant. When he was about three his "grandmother" died and his "grandfather," his "sister," and he lived in relative isolation, the "grandfather" taking the children with him as he went out to do his garden work. When Uta was six he began school. At that time the school closest to Maroe was in Piri, and he and some other children walked to school every day and came back again at night. He brought food with him from his grandfather's house to eat during the day and only rarely went to his biological parents' house in Piri to eat or to visit. A year or two later, when he was seven or eight, his "grandfather" returned to Piri to live with another one of his "daughters." Uta did not want to live with this woman, who was a stern disciplinarian. "I didn't want her to direct me because it wasn't she who had adopted me. It was better for me to return to the parents who had given birth to me — I decided it was right for them to direct me."

He quit school when he was thirteen and one-half because he didn't feel enthusiastic about going. He began to work alongside his father in his father's gardening.

Uta had a peculiar adolescence, for Piri. He was supercised at sixteen not because of his decision that he wanted it, but in response to his "grandfather," who was the village superciser at the time and who came and urged him to be cut. He accepted, because "it was a law that all the *taure'are'a* be supercised, a law written in the Bible and thus it was proper that one be cut." Uta went alone, and only his grandfather and another adult helper were present for the operation. Even after his supercision, Uta did not join in the evenings with the other *taure'are'a* boys when they went to sing or to talk and joke, nor did he, like Teiva, isolate himself in order to be more efficient in the pursuit of girls. His life centered around his parents' household. He remained a virgin until he was twenty-one.

According to Uta, his *taure'are'a* period really started at twenty-one. Before this he worked on his father's lands and went to church and to the pastor's "evangelical class" for adolescents, mostly girls, who were assumed to be leading chaste lives.

When Uta was twenty-one he went to the island of Raiatea with a soccer team from Piri to play against a local Raiatean team. It was the first time he met the girl who is his present wife. He met her and they began to talk and become *mātau*, "accustomed" or "unembarrassed" with each other. "I asked her to go with me to Piri, but she didn't agree, but asked me to stay there in Raiatea. So I stayed there." He stayed with the girl at her adoptive parents' house for four years and helped her parents with their garden work and fishing. Their first child was born in Raiatea. After four years he and his wife and baby went back to Piri for a "visit" with his parents. "We came back to visit with them and then we didn't go back to Raiatea again, we stayed here." They had not planned to change their residence, at least not verbally and overtly; it just happened. His *vahine* had their second child in Piri. They had, as of 1963, seven children, of which six survive. They gave one to his father, and they keep five children in the household.

When he was twenty Uta got drunk for the first time, at the occasion of the finishing of the soccer field at the inland end of Piri. Being drunk frightened him, and he did not try alcohol again for a year. When he returned to Piri with his *vahine* he began to drink frequently. "I was changed a little when I got drunk. It was as if bad things came along out of the drunkenness. I would go and *motoro* [crawl into a house at night when the family was sleeping to try to have intercourse with one of the girls in the house]. I would steal other people's food during the night, things like that." He drank when he had to go into Fare; and he drank in the village, making his own orange beer, or at "parties" when a work group of which he was a member was paid by food and beer or wine. He continued to drink frequently until he entered the Mormon church.

Several months after Uta returned to Piri, his father, annoyed by his drinking and by his affairs with other *vahine*, sent Uta's *vahine* and their youngest child back to Raiatea. Uta did not want her to leave, and, he says, his *vahine* did not want to go, but "because my father said 'go,' she went. She was put on a boat, and my father went with her to take her to Raiatea. There was no way she could stay." Uta, twenty-four at the time, did not see her leave because he had gone inland to hide. She was in Raiatea for a year and eight months, and delivered a third child a few months after her return there. "The desire came to me to go and see the child. So I went to see him and I also met her. The thought came to me that we should return [to Piri] again." So they went back to Piri. He kept up his drinking, but, he says, he then stopped pursuing other women.

Before the split in Tano's church, Uta had been an infrequent churchgoer; so "when the time of the trouble came along I didn't go to either church, I stayed in the house. And then the Mormon missionaries came and I went to see how they did things, went to have a look at their teachings. I began to understand a little of the teachings and the organization of the Mormons and that stirred up my thoughts to enter among the Mormons." He felt interested, he says, from the first day the Mormon missionaries arrived in Piri. The missionaries held several meetings in a house at the inland end of the village and Uta and others attended. He approved of their teachings and felt attracted to them. He and others at that end of the village asked what they had to do to become baptized. He was told that he would first have to get married and then would have to renounce smoking, drinking, and adultery. He eagerly arranged to marry his *vahine*, stopped smoking and drinking, and was soon accepted into the Mormon congregation. He had been living his new life for three years at the time of the interview. During 1963 the Mormons' new church building was completed in Piri, and Uta became caretaker of the building, for which he received a small salary; this, with a little subsistence gardening, enabled him to live comfortably. He has become an important person at the inland end of the village.

Veve Vahine, a Poor Old Woman

In the three years during which I knew the life of Piri there were, of course, some changes in people's status. The most dramatic change in terms of the physical space of the village happened to Veve Vahine, a frail, wizened woman, who, when I first came to the village, was a widow living in a shack at the far inland end, with only a boy of eleven or twelve to help her. The two of them cooked, cleaned, repaired, gathered firewood, and tended her garden plots and seemed to have little to do with village affairs, except for rigorous attendance at all of Tano's church activities. During the summer of 1961 Tāvana's wife died. A little more than a year later Veve Vahine married Tāvana and was living with him in his tin-roofed house at the far seaward end of the village. She worked just as hard as she had inland, cleaning and repairing Tāvana's clothes, cleaning the house and yard, caring for the chickens, and cooking — she was busy all day long. Most of the women in the village, particularly Tāvana's daughters and their allies, resisted accepting her as the new Tāvana Vahine, and still referred to her as Veve Vahine ("Mrs. Veve") after her first husband.

Veve Vahine was born in Piri in 1907. Her mother had also been born in Piri. Her father came from the island of Maiao in the windward group of the Society Islands and had come to Piri in his childhood or early adolescence. Her parents had married before they had any children; Veve Vahine was the firstborn. She was followed by two boys, both of whom died as infants — one at four months, still "a little tiny thing"; the other at about one year — "He was able to talk a little bit." After the death of the boys, her parents adopted two other children, first a girl, now a woman still living in Piri and the one close friend of Veve Vahine, and then a boy. When Veve Vahine was eleven her mother died, and the household consisted of her, her father, and her two adoptive siblings; ten years later her father married again.

Her family was relatively poor, since they did not have land in Piri. "My father had land in Maiao; he used to say we would go back to Maiao, but we never did." But he had some land to work and by "twisting and turning" they managed to get by. "Even though we were poor we were energetic about managing things." The problems of getting by were simple. It was mostly a question of food; they did not need much money. It was still the days before there were many tables, chairs, or other western-bought items in Piri, and, in contrast to Tano, she looks back on the days of mild hardship with pleasure, as the time of family solidarity and purpose. "When I was young we ate on the floor." She laughs. "It was good and it was pleasant. Do you think it was something to be ashamed of?" She laughs again.

And in contrast to Teiva, she remembers Piri in her youth as being cleaner than it is in the 1960s. "In the beginning this was a number one land when it came to cleanliness, and for everything. The houses were clean and decorated with quilts. And there wasn't trouble between the people over church affairs."

As a child in Piri, Veve Vahine played with friends, helped around the house, took care of the younger household members, and went to the pastor's Sunday school. There was no French school at the time, and she learned to read and write Tahitian at the pastor's school. When she reached adolescence her life was not much changed from childhood. She continued to live at home and help out in the household. Since her mother had died, this was particularly her responsibility. Most of the adolescent girls in the village stayed at home helping out with the household tasks, their life being a relative continuum from childhood to adolescence and into early adulthood, in contrast to the boys, with their marked change from childhood into *taure'are'a*, and from *taure'are'a* into adulthood. "Things have changed very much for the worse now for girls," she says. "They begin strolling on the village path when they are only thirteen, and begin to stay with a *tāne*," she says with disapproval. In her day, girls stayed at home until they were in their twenties, staying with a *tāne* only if the relationship was serious, and if it had been arranged by the relatives or if the *tāne* had asked the girl's parents for permission. Veve Vahine lived in one of the several historical Piris, all of which existed at the same time and which became separated and purified in different memories.

For Veve Vahine the period of adolescent *taure'are'a* was not a biological phase; it was an activity, and she and her girl friends avoided it. She describes what she did during the years: "I wove hats, I washed clothes, I ironed clothes, I cleared the brush on the vanilla plantations, I studied the Bible." Although some of the other girls in the village went during the festivals at Fare or Papeete to dance Tahitian group dances, she and her close friends did not join in; but they did sing the *himene*, the old traditional chants about the islands and the districts, their physical beauty and their ancient heroes. The main reason she gives for avoiding *taure'are'a* dancing and flirting activities is not their wrongness, but rather fear. *Taure'are'a* activities involved, she says, drinking, trouble, anger, and fighting. It was better to stay away from them.

When she was twenty-two she married Veve and lived with him until his death twenty-six years later. They lived with her parents at first, then built a house in the inland end of the village where she was still living before her marriage to Tāvana. She had three children, of whom only one, a boy, survived infancy. Veve had only a very small amount of land in Piri. Shortly after their marriage, they went to Papeete, where Veve worked for a while, but they soon returned to settle down in Piri.

For the first five years of their marriage Veve Vahine was, she says, happy. But then Teri'i Tui taught Veve to drink, and this was the source of much trouble for them. She hated him to drink "even if he was well behaved" when drunk, and nagged him continually over it. Occasionally he would hit her for her nagging. Three times she ran away to Raiatea, but after a few weeks she always returned. She had to put up with Veve's drinking until his death.

After their marriage she and Veve entered the pastor's class for religious study, preparatory to entering the communicants, and after a month of study they were accepted. Churchgoing, hymn singing, Bible reading, and explaining and discussing the meaning of Bible verses during *tūāro'i* meetings were always a central passion in her life. "I have been crazy about those things from the beginning until now." ("Crazy about" is a Tahitian as well as an English idiom.) In talking about her love for the church, she seems to be intrigued mainly by the activities, the busyness, the game of preparing, memorizing, and delivering commentaries on Bible verses.

Veve Vahine is a good woman, in terms of Piri ideals and on a more universal scale. When Tano began to urge the widowed Tāvana that he should not live alone and that he should marry again, it was Veve Vahine he recommended. Tāvana, needing a companion and a helper, followed Tano's advice. And Veve Vahine, after a period of embarrassment, consulted at some length with her "daughters" and her son, got their permission, and finally accepted.

Pua, a Young Married Woman

Just to the seaward side of Teri'i Tui's house is a simple thatched and wood house. It has one large room, partially divided by partitions into a larger and a smaller section. In the smaller section a sixty-year-old woman, an adoptive sister of Veve Vahine, lives with her eleven-year-old adopted son. This woman was the adoptive mother of Maote, the twenty-eight-year-old head of the household.

Pua, twenty-four at the time of the interviews, is his *vahine*. They have with them in the house three young daughters, two, six, and seven years of age. (Pua was pregnant at the time of the interviews and delivered another daughter some months later.) She is gay and sweet-looking. Her prettiness is beginning to fade.

Like most of the women of the village who are seriously settled with a *tāne*, she is busy all day — cleaning, cooking, repairing, watching children, helping sometimes with garden work or fishing. Many of her evenings and much of each Sunday are taken up with church activities.

Pua was born in Piri in her parents' house, which still stands toward the middle of the village. She was the eighth of nine children. Only one of the children was given for adoption. The house was thatched and, in her childhood, was furnished with chairs, tables, beds, dishes — "just as we have now."

She started school in Piri when she was six years old and continued until she was twelve. Neither she nor the other children of the time, she says, earned the certificate attesting completion of intermediate studies, because "the teacher herself was ignorant in those days." The teacher, a young woman, was a *demi*. Pua learned some French but, she says, she doesn't understand it very well anymore. From the ages of eight to fifteen Pua went to Tano's Sunday morning class, where she learned to read and write Tahitian and studied the Bible. At fifteen she was ejected from the pastor's school for "some *taure'are'a* behavior."

Pua was twelve when she began to menstruate. She was disturbed because she didn't know what was happening to her. She asked some of the older women in the village about it, adding "I did not tell my mother about it at first." She was frightened: "I thought it was a serious illness." The woman she spoke to told her mother. Both her mother and her father scolded her for not telling them; they both together proceeded to prepare warm water and cloths for her. Her periods were not painful until she was fourteen, at which time she began to have stomach pain. She was given an herbal remedy which cleared up the pain within an hour. And by the time she was fifteen the pains had disappeared. During menstruation as an adolescent and a young woman she went about her ordinary everyday activities, even though she was told that if she became chilled during menstruation she might become ill, a caution she ignored, and that if she touched plants or fish they would spoil, which she considers to be simply lies handed down by the old people. Although many other women in the village believed in the harmful effects of touching plants or fish, she says, "I've always gone [while menstruating] to fertilize the vanilla blossoms, to plant food crops; I've gone fishing — nothing bad ever happened. The vanilla flourishes all the time. There are plenty of flowers around the house. I go and pick them and I don't tell people I am menstruating. I just go and pick them. Did the flowers die? It's all lies."

During her adolescence Pua continued to live with her parents. She did not, she says, live with any man before Maote. It was already a violation of Piri's expectations about the relationships between men and young women settled with a *tāne* for me to be interviewing Pua alone in her house. It was impossible for me to ask her about any sexual experiences outside of her relationship with Maote. She would have had to deny them and would have been disturbed at the question.

When Pua was fifteen a cargo schooner tied up one day at Piri's wharf. The captain of the schooner flirted with her and asked her to come aboard. She and some other of her girl friends went aboard. "Nothing happened. He kept flirting with me but I didn't pay any attention to him." When her relatives heard that she had gone aboard they became angry with her and told Tano that she should be dropped from the Sunday school class, which he agreed to.

According to Pua, she did not "stroll on the village path," but stayed with her parents until Maote came to ask for her. Other boys had come first to the house to ask that she go to stay with them, but neither she nor her father accepted this. Maote, who was in his early twenties, had had another *vahine* who had died in childbirth. According to Pua, she had died voluntarily because of her anger with Maote — she had not wanted either herself or the baby to live. After her death Maote had lived for some months with his adoptive mother. It was this adoptive mother who came to ask Pua's father if she would go to live with Maote. Pua's father did not answer, but said he would talk it over with his daughter. Pua said to him, "It is not for me to say. It's up to you; you tell me what the decision is." If she had not wanted to go to Maote, she would have told her father that she would not accept him; so, in fact, this was her way of accepting. There were formal family discussions and hesitations over the next two or three weeks, but it was finally agreed that she would go. One of her uncles was angry that they were to stay together without getting married first. But Pua preferred it that way. "We would stay together first, and if it worked out well, then we could get married."

She went to stay with Maote at his house. During the first years of their staying together there was, typically for the village, a good deal of trouble. "I was jealous of Maote about the girls he knew and Maote was jealous about the group of boys I knew. We had all kinds of trouble in the beginning. He would talk about my boyfriends, I would say to him 'That kind of thing has all stopped, that's an ancient story now. Let's think about our new life.'" Jealousy and arguments continued for two or three years, but then began to disappear. "We don't have that kind of trouble anymore; trouble at the house and running the house, yes, but not that kind of *taure'are'a* trouble."

After they had been together three years and had two children, Tano came to them and asked if they wished to be married. They accepted. Pua dates the ending of their *"taure'are'a* trouble," of their jealousy, from their decision to get married.

Pua had her babies at home, helped by her mother and some female relatives. For the first baby, they attached a rope to one of the house beams so that she could deliver her baby sitting up and holding onto the rope in the old Tahitian fashion. She refused and insisted on lying down during delivery, and that was the way she had all her babies. Instead of getting up two or three days after delivery and starting to help again in the care of the baby and the house as was customary, Pua, encouraged by her mother, who came to the house to help during these periods, spent two weeks after delivery mostly lying down and being taken care of. "My mother didn't allow me to stand up, she threatened to hit me with a switch if I did." Her mother, says Pua, had always spoiled her. Thus, when she was a child of seven years, and her mother was still nursing Pua's youngest brother, Pua would come home from school and her mother would nurse her also. Pua recounts this with peals of laughter.

Shortly after their marriage, Pua and Maote were admitted into the communicants, and they stayed loyal to Tano when the church split.

Pua is interested in the politics of the village and, more unusual for a village woman, the politics of the territory. She is
one of the few villagers who has some faith that the people of
French Polynesia might be able someday to cope with the problems of ruling themselves.

TRANSITION TO TAHITI

The stories and life histories of villagers are full of references to
people who left Piri. They left to stay with a *tāne* or *vahine* in
some other village or island, because of inadequate land or for
adventure. They left to work in the phosphate mine of Makatea
or to join the army. They left because they did not like Piri.
Many stayed away for a year or two and then returned. These
villagers returned (including the village *muto'i*, who came back
after six years in France and Southeast Asia as a French para-
trooper) apparently little changed by their adventures. There
were perhaps two basic types of emigration. The majority, even
though they had moved to another place, were still part of the
interlocking series of rural communities of which Piri was, for
them, the center. Even when these people moved to Papeete
they lived in "rural" Papeete, in neighborhoods and in activities
which kept them in close contact with Leeward Island affairs
and visitors, and from which they could easily return to Piri,
having seen the big city life very much from the outside. For a
small minority of others, emigration from Piri was an attempt
to escape the whole system. For these, the schools, movies, and
bars of Papeete provided a chance to enter or approach the life
of the *demis*. A few others falling between the two worlds became drifters and vagrants.

Both sorts of emigration (the first balanced by people who
moved *into* Piri, where they had a spouse or family lands) were
evidently useful to Piri and to the individuals involved. The first
represented an equilibrium; the second, a way for potentially
dissident individuals to escape the village and its wider relationships.

This was the situation during most of the time I was at Piri. In the last few months I was there, many men, with their *vahine* and children, totaling a full third of the population of the village, left Piri for Papeete; they were attracted by an enormous increase in jobs in Papeete caused by the arrival of several thousand French engineers, construction workers, and soldiers to build facilities for French nuclear tests. The men who left were not men like Tano, Teiva, Tāvana, or Uta, men who had important things to do in the life of Piri; nor were they, at first, men like Poria and his cronies, who were happy with the remnants of traditional subsistence, *taure'are'a* life. They were men from a nondescript in-between position, neither successful nor, perhaps, comfortable in the village.

But this book concerns Piri before the exodus.[1] Two of the men I interviewed had already emigrated from Piri to Papeete. One of them, Oro, had in fact gone to live in Roto.

Taere, an Emigrant

Henpecked, shy, cramped, humorless, and apparently not very bright, Taere could be characterized in Piri by his lack of color, or of any special quality in the dramatics of village life. There was only one Tano, one Teiva, one Tāvana in Piri, but there were many Taeres.

I first interviewed him in Piri in the spring of 1963, when he was twenty-nine years old, and a year later I interviewed him again in Papeete, where he had been living for eight months. There was a difference. In our interviews in Papeete he seems less constricted and less depressed than he seemed in Piri. He looks happier and says he is happier. In Piri he was a poor, landless, low-status villager. In Papeete he is one of the new wage workers. He is among equals, and the new life is interesting. He plans to stay in Papeete for a year or two and save money. Then, he says, he will return to Piri and build a house with the money he has saved. Then, he feels, he will be comfortable in Piri. He

1. Poria and most of his friends did eventually leave Piri. For some impressions of the situation in Piri in 1970 see the Postscript.

will have a good house and will be able to use the small earnings from his work in Piri for food and clothes. (As of 1970 he had not returned to Piri. He had gone with his wife and children to Noumea in Melanesian New Caledonia and was working there.)

Taere and his wife Rahera (adoptive sister of Uta and daughter of Teri'i Tui) and their six children live in a simple one-room house on the banks of the Fa'ataua River, which flows through the outskirts of Papeete. The house is surrounded by a large number of similar ones, mostly inhabited by people from Huahine. It costs him a rent of five hundred oceanic francs a month (at the time the exchange rate was eighty-eight oceanic francs to one American dollar).

It was Rahera who first came to Papeete, for medical examination in the Central Hospital for pains in her abdomen. She was in the hospital for about a month. Two or three weeks after she left Piri, Taere left the children with another village family and went to Papeete to see how Rahera was, and while he was there he took temporary work. When Rahera left the hospital a week or two later, Taere continued working for some weeks and finally decided that it would be "proper" for them to stay in Papeete. They went back to Piri to get the children and then returned to Papeete. Taere, who is skilled in carpentry, having been one of the village canoe makers, got a job as a carpenter's assistant, working on the enlargement of one of the major stores. He is paid by the day and earns nine thousand francs in an average month, working six and a half days a week. Rahera also works two days a week — washing and ironing for a *demi* family and making two thousand francs a month, which she is saving for her own purposes, namely, to buy a set of false teeth, since her own, like many young Tahitians', are badly decayed.

Taere was born in Piri. His father, who had come to Piri from Raiatea at the age of sixteen, had had two children by a previous *vahine* who had died, while Taere's mother had had one child by a previous *tāne*. His mother and father settled down together in Piri and had four children, boys, of whom Taere was the first. The other boys came two years, four years, and ten years later. Taere's siblings spanned a twenty-four-year period. Taere lived in Piri until he was five; and then until he was nineteen he and his family alternated between two houses — one in Piri and one in Maroe. From Tuesday to Friday the family would stay in Maroe, where they had garden lands, and on Friday or Saturday they would return to Piri to spend the weekend and go to church. On these weekends others of Taere's father's relatives would come and stay with them at the house in Piri. The house was thatched, with one large room and a terraced area adjoining the house, covered by an extension of the roof. In Maroe his father grew food for their own use and for sale — vanilla, taro, *taruā*, coconuts, pineapple, and melons. Taere went to school from the ages of seven to fourteen. As Uta had done, since there was no school in Maroe, he walked with a group of other children over the path from Maroe to Piri. The school then had two half-day sessions. The Maroe children would arrive for the session beginning at 8:00 and leave at 11:00.

As a child Taere was relatively isolated. He played by himself, he says, more frequently than the other children did — spearing small fish, swimming, playing in the brush. He had only one close friend as a child, not the gang of friends that many other people reported. This boy, he remembers with pleasure, was a "bad boy." He would stand up to the older boys, and he had courage. But Taere as a child was often bullied by the other children; they would twist his ear, chase him, tease him.

When he was fourteen he was supercised. He went with two other boys. There were ten other boys in the village about the same age or a year older. They were all, he says, supercised that year and they made up his "generation" (*u'i*) of *taure'are'a*. Whereas the other informants consider either their period of *taure'are'a* or their adulthood the happiest and best time of life, Taere considers his childhood happier than his *taure'are'a* period. "In childhood there is no work, you eat and when you are full, then you play. Being a *taure'are'a* is good sometimes, but other times, when you don't have any money, then you are not happy." As an adolescent he had one close friend, a year older than he. He remarks that although when he had a little money he would help his friend, when the friend had money, he would not in turn buy things for Taere. Taere was apparently an awkward and peripheral *taure'are'a.*

He was sixteen at the time of his first sexual intercourse, with a girl of his own age. He had approached two or three young *taure'are'a* girls before, but they had said no because of "fear of their parents." During the years from sixteen to twenty-one, when he was married, he had relations with four girls. Two of these, like the first girl, were casual and secret contacts — it was important to him that neither the other *taure'are'a* nor the girls' relatives know what was happening — but he lived openly with the other two; the first, when he was seventeen, for a period of three months, and the second a year later for only two weeks. With both of these there were "troubles and arguments," and Taere left.

He had no particular interest in Rahera, who had not had any special relationship with him other than as a casual village acquaintance. Her adoptive father approached Taere's father to try to arrange a marriage between Rahera and Taere. His father told him of the request and Taere did not answer at all for three days. "I didn't answer and he was angry at me. I didn't answer because I wasn't yet tired of enjoying myself." His father threatened to hit him for not answering. Taere decided he wasn't sure whether it would be a good thing or a bad thing but that he would go ahead and try it. So they were married in a formal church service, with Rahera in a white dress and a white veil, signifying her virginity. Taere has not much to say about their subsequent relationship, but from village gossip it seems a notable case of a shrewish housewife and a passive, unprotesting husband.

Although all the other families who joined the Mormons joined together, with the husband usually taking the first official steps, Rahera joined the Mormons on her own. Taere, who had left the pastor's church, went for a while to Teiva's group and then quit altogether, staying at home on Sundays and occasionally reading his Bible.

Aside from a small amount of subsistence gardening, Taere did not work lands in Piri. He worked for others, helping them put up or repair houses, and worked with work groups on others' lands. He was a specialist in making outrigger canoes, and he had made and sold many of them in the village. The length of time he spent and the price he charged depended on size and on the kind of wood the canoe was made of. An "average" size canoe (holding three or four persons) of breadfruit wood, considered a good wood, took about a month to make and sold for five thousand oceanic francs. Less durable ones, made of the wood of the kapok tree, took half the time and cost half the money. Outrigger canoes, particularly the larger ones, were slowly being replaced by motorboats, which added to Taere's economic problems.

Rahera and Taere were peripheral in Piri. After a series of more or less accidental events they found themselves living away from the village.

Oro, a Taure'are'a

I interviewed Oro in Roto about six months after he arrived there from Piri. He is not quite seventeen years old. In Piri Oro was the leader of one of the two groups of *taure'are'a* boys in the village. His coming to Roto was precipitated by trouble with Teiva, for whom he had been working. He went to Papeete because "it would be easier to make money," meaning, it became clear, that he thought he would be freer there. He is renting a room in a house in Roto, sharing it with a nineteen-year-old *taure'are'a* friend and that friend's seventeen-year-old *vahine.*

When Oro first arrived in Tahiti he went to work for a cousin who had left Piri years before and was now a house builder. He quit after four months because of problems with his cousin's wife, who was acting as paymaster on the job, and got a job as a stevedore on the Papeete docks. He worked loading and unloading two or three ships a month. Each ship required only two or three days' work. The work was exhausting, lasting through much of the day, but was well paid at fifteen hundred to two thousand francs a day. Between ships, however, he did not work.

Before coming to Tahiti, Oro had only been out of Huahine briefly on two occasions. When he was thirteen he had gone to

Raiatea for three or four days with a brother who had gone there to be examined for his school "certificate of studies." And in 1962 he had come to Tahiti for the first time for one week as a substitute on a Huahine soccer team. He had, in fact, seldom been out of the district of Piri before his move to Papeete.

Oro was born in Piri. He was the second of three children, all boys. His brothers were two years older and two years younger than he. Several months after the younger brother was born, Oro's mother died. According to Teiva, who is an adoptive brother of Oro's mother, she died a magical death through her involvement with a spirit lover. Oro says that she died of a natural illness.

Shortly after Oro's mother's death, Oro's father left the three boys with Nani, who had also been Teiva's foster mother, and went to another village on Huahine, where he stayed with a new *vahine*, whom he subsequently married and with whom he had four children. Nani, whose *tāne* had died, at this time had one other adoptive child living with her, a daughter of Teiva's, who was four years older than Oro. All four children grew up together at Nani's. The house, consisting of a single large room, was of board, with a thatched roof. Although it was furnished with table and chairs and a bed, when the children were young they and Nani ate sitting on the floor and slept on mattress sacks on the floor.

Oro went to school in Piri from the ages of six to fifteen and quit after getting a "certificate of studies." He had thought of going on for a higher certificate, but since he was not doing very well in school "because he was not paying attention," he decided not to go on. He regrets that decision, which would have required going to Uturoa or Papeete, because, he says, it is hard to find a good job in Papeete with only a "certificate of studies." During his school years, when he was not at school or helping around the house he played with the other children, both boys and girls. They swam, played local versions of cat and mouse, hide and seek, and tag, jumped rope, spun tops, and played a variety of other games. As he approached his *taure'are'a* period he stopped playing with girls. "The boys began to 'wander' in the night. It was friends together. But the girl children — they didn't take part."

At fifteen Oro went with three other friends of the same age to be supercised. He relates the start of his *taure'are'a* period more closely to his supercision than others did. For him and his friends this period started when the supercision wound healed and they began to "play" (*ha'uti*) with the girls. *Ha'uti* is the same word used for children's play, and it means here all the contacts, conversation, joking, teasing, flirting, and seduction which might lead to the girls' acceptance of intercourse. But even if not successful, it is valuable and pleasant in itself. As a group they joked about approaching girls, discussed how it was done, while younger boys listened, and bragged afterward about their successes, often lying. Actual attempts to succeed with girls had to be done slyly without the other *taure'are'a* boys' knowing about it, or they would "as a joke" interfere. They would, for example, throw stones at the side of a house one of their members had entered late at night in order to wake the girl's parents. If one of their members was relatively serious about a girl, he would be particularly careful not to tell the others about it, because by gossip and lies to the girl or to the boy himself, the other *taure'are'a* boys would try to stir up jealousy and break up the affair.

In spite of much talk, they seldom engaged in heterosexual activities and spent most of their evenings in talk, in singing and joking, in throwing stones at people's houses to frighten them and disturb them, and in entering houses as if to approach a girl but making so much noise that the family would get upset, chase them, and be angry at the girl. Rarely, they traveled together to another district to visit and see the sights.

Oro and his *taure'are'a* friends, like other *taure'are'a* boys, when together were usually in close physical contact with one another. They walked along the village path holding hands or with arms around one another's shoulders. They would lie in a heap on the deck of the launch going into Fare with their arms, legs, and heads intertwined, sprawled on one another's bodies. I saw them several times in the shadows at the edge of the dance shed during the New Year's festival in Piri, dancing western style with each other, one of them pretending to be a girl. Some of the post-*taure'are'a* young men who tended to tell exaggerated and fanciful stories about the *taure'are'a* sexual behavior said that Oro and the other *taure'are'a* of his generation engaged in group masturbation. Oro, who had no hesitation in talking about homoerotic or overtly homosexual activity, denies this.

In his several months as a *taure'are'a* at Piri before coming to Roto, Oro says he had intercourse with three girls. Two of these were about his own age. He had intercourse with the first one twice and with the second one five times, he says. The other was the assistant schoolteacher who had come to Piri from Raiatea. She was about two years older than Oro. He says that he had relations with her almost every night over a period of some two months. Most of the other boys in his *taure'are'a* group had remained virgins because "so many of the girls in Piri were their relatives and thus forbidden to them."

After coming to Roto Oro only had two or three sexual contacts with girls. He also had relations with two male homosexuals (*māhū*), twice with one and once with the other. The contact consisted of the *māhū*'s performing fellatio on him. It is, he says, the same thing as being with a *vahine*, although, he adds in a matter-of-fact way, the pleasure is stronger with a *māhū*.

Oro had started drinking the year before in Piri. He made him feel better, made him feel less shy, made it easier for him to approach women. He has kept up his drinking in Roto. The life of Roto frightens him. He is afraid to walk in the streets at night for fear that somebody will attack him, a fear not justified by the actual violence in the town.

Many of his *taure'are'a* friends in Roto are committed thieves, stealing food, watches, and motorbikes. Stealing, which was a *taure'are'a* game in Piri, is a much more serious affair in Roto, and Oro is afraid he might get involved in this somehow.

He plans to stay in Papeete. He hopes, he says, to go back to Piri to visit from time to time, but he does not want to live there. "There is not enough money there."

ROTO

The role tags — chief, pastor, even "poor old woman" — given to people in Piri indicate something of an individual's relation to the social system of the village. One cannot do the same sort of thing for Roto. Roto is not much of a community, and so one cannot sort people simply by the kind of interacting roles they play in any integrated local system. Most of the people living there are role players in a score of systems — churches, businesses, Chinese and European communities, various trades, various political groups — most of which have their centers elsewhere, systems whose interacting personnel are made up of people of various other neighborhoods. The social typology of Roto, therefore, is of another order from that of Piri and is hardly comparable.

But there is, as I have noted, a certain segment of Roto's population who consider themselves "true Tahitians," in contrast to the *demis*, Chinese, and Europeans of the area. Many of them have been born and have grown up in Roto or in nearby districts. They have thus spent their lives in the "most native" of the various Papeete environments. Three of them will be introduced here.

Manu

Being poor in Papeete is quite a different thing from being poor in a village like Piri. The concept of "poorness" seems to predate the European arrival. The first missionary dictionary, our best indication of pre-European usages, has the currently used word for poverty, *veve*, which, illuminatingly, was defined as "poor . . . to be in want . . . having no property." Papeete in the early 1960s had none of the abject poverty of so much of the rest of the world. There were no beggars, no one was starving. There was always some kind of work for those who needed it, although if one wanted to limit oneself to a skilled or semiskilled trade there were sometimes difficult periods, as for Manu. There were government social services to help mothers and children, and for many city people there was a network of relationships with family, as well as lands on other islands to support them and to provide a place to return to if the going got too difficult. But whereas the "poor" person in Piri usually had his fish, breadfruit, taro, chicken, and so on like anyone else and had, if not a tin-roofed house, a comfortable thatched house, the poor Tahitian in Papeete had to eat more beans and low-grade "Chinese food" than he liked and might have to live in a shack, which, although adequate for the subtropical temperatures of the territory, *looks* like a shack, both because of its city setting and because of its contrast with the much fancier houses and ways of life surrounding it. Movies, large hotels, tourists, and rich and successful Chinese and *demis* living in Papeete all make up a context in which the poorer city Tahitian looks, to himself and to others, considerably poorer than his rural equivalent. He is somewhat poorer than his rural counterpart by material measure, but very much poorer in contrast to his social context.

Manu is poor. He is fifty-one when I interviewed him, living with an unkempt, shriveled, heavy-drinking *vahine*, several years older than he, in a tiny one-room shack right in the center of Roto. A bed, a couple of chairs, a small table, a cabinet, and a small kerosene cookstove are crowded into the shack. Chickens flutter in and out, spattering the furniture with droppings. Manu's *vahine*, Tetua, gives the place a perfunctory cleaning in the morning and then spends much of the rest of the day in gossiping with neighbors, particularly the neighborhood *māhū*, who is a close friend, and in drinking beer. As Manu says, he never saves any money. He gives his money to Tetua and she "wastes it on drink. She drinks," he says, "every day, sometimes as much as ten bottles of beer a day." When asked why he gives his money to her, he says, "Well, she manages the house and buys all the food. I am trying to teach her that she must set some money aside for our old age, but I haven't had any results so far."

Manu is short and grizzled, with strongly negroid features inherited from his biological father. He has worked at various unskilled jobs. For the nine years before our interview he worked principally as a mason's helper, mostly on building construction.

The demand for masons' helpers varies greatly depending upon how many large stone buildings are being built in Papeete, and Manu has gone through several unemployed periods. When he has work he bicycles off early in the morning and, unless the building he is working on is very close to Roto (in which case he comes home for lunch), he does not return until evening, when Tetua is supposed to have supper ready.

It was because of their poverty that I got to know Manu and Tetua. A stranger walking through the paths of Roto was not welcomed, as he would have been in Piri, with questions and the formal greeting, "Come and eat!" People in Roto were suspicious of strangers. Why were they strolling around, looking, asking questions? Were they potential thieves? Were they spies either for the government or for another country? The "true Tahitians" still put some value on hospitality and conversational openness once their suspicions were overcome, but a stranger walking through the quarter was not a presumptive guest as he was in Piri.

It became apparent that if I were to work in Roto it had to be on a "business" basis. Tetua was happy to rent me a corner of their hut as a work area and when, later, I had found a separated workhouse where I could interview people in private, Manu was equally happy to hire himself out as an informant. He became, as Poria had in Piri, the "anthropologist's friend." Like Poria's, Manu's motives presumably and apparently changed as we got into the details of his life history, his reminiscences of Roto, and his responses to and evaluations of his life and life around him. But his initial motive was money.

Manu was born in Roto and was delivered at home, in the house of his mother's adoptive father. This man had become his mother's mother's *tāne*, and had "taken" Manu's mother and "become a father for her." The house, now the site of a church meeting house, was just adjacent to the property on which Manu's small shack now stands. Manu's mother died three months after his birth, as a result, he says, of complications following his delivery. She was seventeen at the time of her death. She had had no previous children.

His biological father was, he says, an American Negro who had made several trips to Tahiti as a sailor on an American ship and who had then settled down there working as a sailor on the local copra schooners until his death. His name, says Manu, was "Mr. Ford." He was much older than Manu's mother, and Manu estimates that he was in his fifties at the time of Manu's birth. Mr. Ford lived on in Tahiti until he was in his seventies. As a boy Manu saw him occasionally. He lived alone between his voyages, Manu's mother's pregnancy having come out of a casual relationship. Mr. Ford helped out Manu's foster "father" (or "grandfather") occasionally with money, and once, Manu remembers, brought him a pig. It was his mother's foster father, his "grandfather," who raised Manu, and the two of them lived alone during Manu's infancy and childhood. The old man, from what Manu had been told, prepared his bottle, fed him, and took care of him as an infant. He was in his sixties and stayed at home most of the time to take care of Manu. Occasionally, when his "grandfather" left for the market an aunt, an older sister of his mother's who lived nearby, came to take care of him. His "grandfather" lived by renting the other room in his house to two "wandering" *vahine* who were seldom at home and who did not have anything to do with Manu's household. Manu and his "grandfather" shared a room, with Manu sleeping on the bed (protected from bed-wetting by an oilcloth) and his "grandfather" sleeping on a mat on the floor.

When Manu was six, his "grandfather" died in the influenza plague which had reached Tahiti and was devastating the islands. Manu was taken to stay with his aunt, but the first night he got up and sneaked out of her house and went back to sleep next to his "grandfather's" body. The next morning they came to get him again. In later years he learned that his "grandfather's" body had been burned, as were those of many of the influenza victims, and this still troubles him, as does the fact that his "grandfather" did not live long enough that Manu might have "served him" in gratitude for his early care.

His aunt and uncle became his new adoptive parents. Their home was a three-room tin-roofed house. Manu, the only child, shared a room with his adoptive parents, and the other two rooms in the house were rented — one by a *tāne* and his *vahine* and the other by a single woman. They all cooked and took their meals together. His new parents spent many evenings outside the house, drinking and "enjoying themselves." Manu stayed at home, frightened and often hungry.

Manu never went to French school. He went to a religious school for two months but never learned to read or write Tahitian, except for his name and a very few words.

When he was seven he was taken by his adoptive father and mother to Flint Island, one of the British Line Islands lying to the north of Tahiti. His parents went to work on the coconut plantations there, and Manu spent the next nine years on that small atoll, some three miles long by half a mile wide, with some thirty or forty other Tahitian workers and their children.

He remembers Roto in his youth as being different in a number of ways from what it is at the time of the interviews. As he recalls it, Roto then had only a few houses and very few people, less than a hundred scattered throughout the area. There were more fruit trees and food gardens than there are now, and people grew much of what they ate, buying relatively few things, such as fish, sugar, and flour. Women wore ankle-length dresses with long sleeves and high necklines. The men wore long-sleeved shirts and pants or sometimes a *pareu.* Men worked at the docks and in the few Papeete stores, which were "mostly owned by Europeans and not yet by Chinese." They seemed to spend much more time in the quarter and to work less. There were, he recalls, parties in the district, at which people would get together to drink, sing and play music, and dance Tahitian dances. One of the changes in the quarter is that there are no more neighborhood parties. People now go to the many bars in Papeete to drink. Instead of the drinking's involving everyone together and lasting for circumscribed periods of time, people go off to drink by themselves or with a few close friends, and many men, says Manu, now drink all the time whenever they have some money to waste.

He remembers that people had their big meal in the late morning instead of in the evening and that they cooked the food in an earth oven. When you walked through Roto in those days, people would call out the traditional village greeting, *Haere mai tama'a*, "Come and eat." Nobody does this anymore.[2]

In those days people often slept after the noonday meal "because Tahitian food made you sleepy," he jokes. It is now very rare that people sleep during the day. In those days it was natural; now if people see you sleeping, they make fun of you.

In his childhood and early youth, he thinks, *tāne* and *vahine* did not settle down until they were at least in their early twenties. Now boys and girls of thirteen or fourteen stay together. He also recalls the religious life of that time as being more unified. Everyone was Protestant and went to the same church. Now outsiders have brought in other religions, the old unified Protestantism has split, and the Tahitians are divided among the various new religions.

The epidemic of 1918 killed many of the people in Roto, and later new people, mostly relatives of the dead householders, moved into their houses. In later years, as Papeete grew, Polynesians from the Marquesas and the Tuamotus who came to Papeete to work began to move into the district, as did a number of Chinese and *demis*.

When he was thirteen Manu began to work on Flint Island. He helped prepare copra, gathering and husking coconuts, splitting the shells, prying out the dried meat, arranging it on the sunning racks, and, when it was properly dried, putting the copra chunks into burlap bags. When he was eighteen or nineteen he returned to Tahiti with only seven hundred francs saved from his years of work, equivalent at the time to perhaps one month's wages for unskilled labor. The reason he had saved so little, says Manu, was that even though the pay at Flint was not bad, the prices

2. This formal invitation, even though it was not taken seriously as an invitation to a meal, was an invitation to conversation and personal encounter. Its disappearance is an important change.

for clothes and store goods were so high that it was difficult to save.

He returned to Tahiti alone and went back to Roto to live in his adoptive parents' house. Two years later they returned from Flint Island and joined him there. On his return he worked for various Europeans, doing house and yard maintenance and repairs, and he did this sort of thing for about ten years, continuing after he began to live with Tetua at the age of twenty-three. When he was thirty he started working for a *demi* who had a small jewelry manufacturing business. Manu learned how to make rings, earrings, and jewelry for the local shops and for the tourist trade. He worked at this for thirteen years until his boss died and the business broke up. Manu then found a job as a mason's assistant, and, except for a short period as a trucker's helper, this has continued to be his trade.

Although Manu has a claim on a small parcel of his family's land in Roto, the rights to this land have been tied up in court battles for at least a decade. Without land Manu is at the mercy of the Papeete labor market. When nobody needs a mason's helper, he has to run up bills at the Chinese store, simplify his already simple menu, and try to hustle up a temporary job. His capital is his bodily strength, and he worries a good deal about getting old. "Who will feed me when I have become weak through age?"

Manu was the only boy of his age on Flint Island. When Manu was ten his adoptive father suggested that he should be supercised, and it was his "father" who performed the operation. There were no unattached girls on Flint and only three or four older boys who were *taure'are'a*. Manu says that his *taure'are'a* period did not begin until he returned to Tahiti. He was a virgin when he came back to Roto at the age of nineteen and says that he was shy and still "like a child." When girls would tease or flirt with him he was embarrassed and silent. When he was twenty-three he had intercourse for the first time, and it was then that his *taure'are'a* period began. Before that he used to return to the house in Roto each evening after work, but his friends eventually pushed him into going with them to the Papeete town bars, and it was there that he began to meet *vahine*. He did not drink or dance, but he specialized, he says, in getting the *vahine*. He would find a *vahine* every three or four days, bring her to the house, sleep with her, and then let her go the next day. Even after he began to live with Tetua he had secret sexual relations, usually during the day, with other women. These affairs and going to the bars with Tetua, even though he did not drink, were "*taure'are'a* life." His *taure'are'a* life continued, he says, for five or six years after he began to live with Tetua. He met her when he was twenty-four years old. She was about six years older than he and had been legally married and then separated. When he met Tetua they stayed together in his room for two or three days. He recounts that during this time she washed and cleaned his clothes for him. He was impressed by this and thought that perhaps it would be better to stay with her and to begin to save money because he would "not be spending so much on other women" and because she would be able to help him around the house. He thought this over for about a month and finally decided to settle with her. They had lived together for twenty-seven years at the time of the interview. They had no children of their own, nor did they adopt any.

They consider themselves Protestants but do not go to church. Their life consists of work, gossip, a very rare visit from or to relatives, beer drinking for Tetua, and apparently little else.

Flora

The "girls of Tahiti" have surely been the central element in Tahiti's image in the rest of the world since the time of European discovery. Their latest avatars, at least for the casual short-stay tourists as well as for the French soldiers and sailors stationed at Tahiti, are the girls who frequent the combined bar-dance halls of Papeete, particularly the long-established Quinn's. It is the center for girls who have come to Papeete from small villages in the outer islands, who are looking for adventure, and who are willing to tolerate the mild stigma of being a "Quinn's girl." Quinn's girls lead a life in many ways similar to that of *taure'are'a* boys in the villages. They are a tight band of close friends, involved in amusing themselves, drinking, dancing, and storytelling. Their sexual contacts with men involve brief, superficial encounters with a variety of men, which do not interfere for long with their allegiance and return to the other girls. Although some girls stay on, the turnover is very rapid, and life at Quinn's is for most a temporary period of perhaps one to three years, after which the girls might return to their home islands or enter into Papeete life in a variety of ways.

For girls of Papeete itself, if they come from a family with European standards or pretensions or with serious religious commitments, frequenting Quinn's is considered lower class and a bad thing to do. But for many of the more *mā'ohi* girls, it is a natural place to go for adventure at some time during their *taure'are'a* period.

Flora, who is twenty-five at the time of the interviews, lives with her widowed father and her three-year-old son Eric in a two-room wood-framed house toward the center of Roto, on property which has been in her mother's family "from the days of the Tahitian royalty." She has lived her entire life in Roto, has never been off the island of Tahiti, and in fact has seldom been out of Papeete and its immediately adjoining districts. She frequented Quinn's from the age of twenty to twenty-two, and these years made an interlude between the time of her "childhood occupations" and the time she settled down to take care of her newborn baby and her father's house. Flora is an unattractive young woman with an abnormally prominent forehead and a mild stammer. She has watched more attractive and ambitious sisters and girl friends leave Roto for other strata of Tahiti society or even for France and America. She stays behind, apparently contentedly, remaining an observer and a commentator.

Flora's parents met and were married at Flint Island, where it was the regulation that all couples who wished to live together had to marry. Her father had gone out to work on the coconut plantations; her mother had gone there with her parents. Flora's parents had six children, the first three born at Flint. The family then returned to live in Roto on property which had belonged to Flora's mother's great-grandmother. Three more children were born there, Flora being the youngest — twenty-two years younger than her eldest sister. Flora was delivered at the maternity hospital at Papeete. When she was a young child all her sisters and brothers were at home, but she was taken care of primarily by a sister fourteen years older than she and by an adoptive sister ten years older. According to Flora, she nursed from her mother's breast until well after she started going to school, estimating that she was nine years old before she stopped, which was only, she says, after her mother smeared her breasts with the juice of hot peppers.

Flora went to school in Papeete from the age of five to seventeen. She quit at sixteen without taking her certificate, shortly after her mother's death. She learned to speak the slightly simplified and idiosyncratic Tahitian version of the French language and often used French with her playmates, but she speaks mostly Tahitian at home.

Flora's father worked at the shipyards as a ship caulker. The older children worked at various jobs and contributed some money to the household. School, some household chores, and play, mostly within the boundaries of Roto with the boys and girls of the quarter, were, she says, the occupations of her childhood and youth. She continued playing ball games and tag and climbing trees until she was eighteen and occasionally did so afterward. They were not, she says, like children of this new generation, occupied with flirting and sexual play. She and her girl friends frequently went to one of the Papeete cinemas. When she was about eighteen they began to gather in one or another house in the quarter and played music on ukuleles and guitars and listened to phonograph records. They began to learn the *'ori pōpa'a*, the western-style dance, from slightly older friends. When she was twenty the group went together to Quinn's for the first time. She went at first to watch, but soon went for dancing and "fun," *'ārearea*. They usually went on the nights when a foreign ship was in port, when the sailors and crew would be at Quinn's. She enjoyed the dancing, the excitement, the gossip and joking, and particularly the *tōtōa* ("pranks") they played. These (equivalent to Oro's throwing stones against houses where people were sleeping in Piri during the night) included getting sailors to spend their money and then disappearing, overturning trash cans in the streets and hiding to watch the annoyance of the policeman when he discovered the mess, and stealing small objects from Chinese shops. All this was part of the fun and excitement of her *taure'are'a* period. Flora did not drink, and took only lemonade at Quinn's; this, she says, was because on the one occasion when she tried to drink she vomited after the first glass of beer. During her first year at Quinn's her relationship with men there did not go beyond dancing, joking, and *tōtōa*.

Flora had her first menstrual period at the age of thirteen. Like Pua, she was unprepared for it. The bleeding began one day when she had been climbing a tree, and she thought she had injured herself in climbing. She thought she had cut her thigh. She went home and told her mother, "I have cut my leg and my pants are bloody." Her mother said, "Crazy girl, no, that is a disease which women get." She was told to bathe in warm water, and her mother told her how to clean herself and how to prepare a napkin. She did not tell her friends what was wrong with her for fear they would make fun of her. But she says that with later menstrual periods she was no longer ashamed and went and played with her friends. She had no pain or feeling of illness during her periods. Her mother told her to avoid getting chilled or eating cold things for fear she might get the *ma'i fa'a'i* (the "filled sickness"), an illness caused by menstrual blood's accumulating in one's body and eventually choking a girl or causing her to become crazy. The *ma'i fa'a'i* could also be caused by prolonged virginity.

When she started to go to Quinn's Flora was still a virgin. After she had been going to Quinn's for about one year, she met a young man, a *demi*. His name was Hans, but his Quinn's nickname was *'otu'u* ("heron") because of his long neck. Hans came to talk to her, and they discovered that they had known each other at school. He returned to his group of male friends at their table but came over several times during the evening to ask her to dance.

Here is the story of the remainder of the courtship. "When the music played, he came and touched me to dance and it went on like that until closing time at midnight. I said to him, 'I am going back to the house.' He said he would accompany me. He accompanied me as far as Ah Kiau's [a Chinese store at the edge of Roto]. We stopped, and I said to him, 'You have to go. I am going to Esther's house to sleep.' He said, 'Tomorrow night can I come and get you?' I said, 'Where?' 'Here, at Ah Kiau's.' 'Okay.' I didn't think he'd come, I thought he was playing. Early the next morning I went to Ah Kiau's to get some bread. There he was, drinking lemonade. I didn't pay any attention because I didn't know that it was he. That evening I went again to get some bread. As I was leaving, he grabbed me. I said, 'I didn't recognize you.' He laughed. He asked, 'Tonight where are you all going?' I said, 'I don't know. Perhaps we are going to the movies.' He said, 'I'll go and get the tickets.' He went and got four tickets. One for him, one for me, and two for my girl friends." After the movies he went with them to Quinn's, but Flora was beginning to get bored with him. She started dancing with other men. "He pinched my behind and said, 'Don't dance with different men, it should be just us.' I said, 'Go and get another girl for you. Girls are pig feed [a dime a dozen] at Quinn's.'" She continued to dance with sailors from a Chilean ship that was in port. Hans drank "to get himself drunk" and then came over to the table and hit Flora on the head with a beer bottle.

The next morning Flora had pain in her head and went to a doctor. There was a piece of glass in her scalp. "For two weeks I didn't speak to him. I was mad at him because he hit me on the head with the beer bottle." He kept coming to talk to her at Quinn's and came to the house where she was sleeping. She chased him, then hit him with a stick, but he didn't leave. He slept on the cement in front of the house. "There was nothing I could do," she says; "I was obliged to stay with him." She felt unable to resist this demonstration of willpower. Hans lived with her for nine or ten months.

According to Flora, Hans was also a virgin when they began to stay together. The first time they tried to have intercourse Flora fainted, and Hans had to call a doctor. Their intercourse was infrequent, perhaps once a week. Although she liked foreplay, particularly kissing, she did not like intercourse itself, and she would find excuses to avoid it. For example, she would encourage him to drink and then tell him that she would not have intercourse with him because he was drunk. She found intercourse exhausting, and it made her weak. She got pregnant after their first few weeks together. She was not happy staying with him because of "the trouble of having to cook for him and clean his clothes"; and after her relatives objected to their staying together because "I was Protestant and he was Catholic," she accepted their objections and told Hans he would have to leave. He stayed on, however, until shortly after the birth of their baby, a boy. He comes to visit from time to time, and he continues to send some money to help Flora with the expense of the baby. On some visits Hans sleeps at the house; Flora places the baby between them.

Flora has given up Quinn's and stays at home cleaning the house, reading, and taking care of and playing with the baby, whom she adores. One baby, she says, is enough. She doesn't want to have any more, but she is glad that she has this one. She has no plans for the future, but she is sure that her days at Quinn's are over.

Hiro

Hiro, thirty-four at the time of our interviews, spent his life in Papeete and has lived in Roto for sixteen years. It is with strong emotion that he labels his way of life "Tahitian," in contrast to those who live *demi* lives and who have *demi* mannerisms. He speaks of the *demi* with irony and hostility. "They are always acting disgusted. They don't like things associated with dirt. If a begrimed man comes, they don't want to have anything to do with him. If their own relative has Tahitian customs they are ashamed of him. The *demi* are bad people and liars. They prefer *pōpa'a* customs and don't like Tahitian food. They pretend to be disgusted by everything and don't know anymore where they came from."

In contrast to them, Hiro calls himself a true Tahitian. But his Tahitianness has a peculiar quality of verbal overtness and self-consciousness which goes well beyond that of the other people interviewed. He says such things as, "A basic problem for Tahitians is that they are divided between their desire for liberty and their desire for security," using *liberté* and *securité* for the abstractions in his otherwise Tahitian sentence. His interest in contemporary Tahiti is to some degree theoretical. His interest in the Tahitian past is to some degree antiquarian. He has become an intellectual.

Hiro was born at the then newly established maternity section of the government hospital in Papeete. His family lived in a rented house in the Tipaerui Valley in the southeastern part of Papeete. In Hiro's youth the valley was relatively unsettled and rural in appearance, but it was only a short distance from the more urbanized parts of the town. The house was made of boards with a tin roof. There were two sleeping rooms, an eating room, a porch, and a separate shed for cooking in an earth oven. The house was scantily furnished, according to Hiro, since they were "poor," but had a dining table, some beds, benches, and chairs, and a cabinet for clothes. They ate, he emphasizes, Tahitian-style food. Hiro lived in this house until he settled with a *vahine* in Roto when he was twenty-one.

Both his parents came from the neighboring island of Moorea. In contrast to the people of Piri, who seldom talked about, and in fact knew very little about, "ancestors" whom they had not known personally, Hiro talks with pride about his ancestors in Moorea. He knows of a paternal great-grandfather who was a pastor there and of a great-grandmother who came from Raiatea and married into the Moorea family. One of his mother's grandfathers was a *tāvana* of the district. His father's father and an uncle of his mother were pastors.

Hiro had seven siblings, two girls and four boys older than he and one sister younger. His parents were married in Moorea, and all his older siblings were born there. Hiro's father had worked family lands in Moorea. He was called to Papeete for a period of service in the army shortly before Hiro's birth. His mother, Hiro says, decided to take advantage of this change by taking all her children and accompanying her husband to Papeete so that the children could go to school there. After his short period of army service, Hiro's father worked at various handyman and helper jobs. He also fished a good deal and sold part of his catch at the town market. Hiro's mother worked as a maid and a laundress, mostly for other Tahitians who were better off than they were. Neither his mother nor his father had gone to school.

As a child Hiro was taken care of by his mother, his older sister, and sometimes one of several aunts from Moorea who came from time to time for visits. Often, when his father did not have work and his mother did, his father took care of the younger children.

Hiro describes his mother as being "somewhat different from other women." She was good to those of her children she liked, but she liked only her girls and one of her boys, and she did not "like very well" her other boys, including Hiro; and, he says, she was often irritable and nagging with them. Hiro was a favorite of his father, whom he describes as silent and dominated by his mother, and he would follow after him and go fishing with him whenever he could.

At six Hiro started school at one of the two public schools which existed in Papeete at the time. He continued until he was fourteen, and he had started to prepare for his examination for his "certificate of studies"; but, he explains, because some of his older brothers had left home for the army and navy and as an older sister had married, he decided to quit school in order to work to help the family.

His first work was helping his father and brothers net fish in the lagoon to sell at the market. At fifteen or sixteen he began to work for the municipal public works department, painting public buildings. After three years of this he took a job with a private builder, as an unskilled worker carrying equipment and helping out carpenters and masons. At twenty he was called into the army and sent to New Caledonia, but after three months he became ill and was returned to Tahiti and discharged. Then at twenty-one he found a job in a shop which specialized in repairing utensils and equipment of various sorts and continued to work there without any interruption — the last several years as a lathe operator. At the time of the interviews he has been working for this same employer for sixteen years. He works five days a week, eight hours a day.

Between the ages of nine and fourteen, after school and on school holidays, Hiro had, he says, played with a group of from ten to twenty children of about his own age from the district of Tipaerui. His descriptions of the play emphasize *tōtōa* ("pranks" or perhaps better here, "dirty tricks") which they played on one another and, more frequently, on outsiders — Chinese, policemen, and gangs of boys from other districts. He describes stealing fruit and vegetables from Chinese truck farms; hunting for birds with slingshots; looking for wasp's nests on hillsides so that during the game of sliding down a muddy slope after a rain they could direct their friends to a "good slide" which would end up in a wasp's nest; provoking fights with other gangs; and smearing spit on the lock and handle of the doors of the Chinese shops just before opening time and then hiding to watch the annoyance of the Chinese proprietor trying to get into his store. "We did not consider playing marbles a good time," he says. "It was only after we had played a trick on someone that we said to ourselves, 'That was really a good time.'" The roughness he describes differed greatly from the very mild pranks of the Piri children and *taure'are'a*, in intensity and in the availability of a large number of outsiders against whom the Tipaerui boys could direct their aggressive pranks. At fourteen, when Hiro began to define himself as a *taure'are'a*, the play group broke up and he, like the others, began to work and to seek girls.

When he was twelve he went with eight of his friends to be supercised. They did not tell their parents, but made the arrangements themselves. In describing the events of the day and the days following, Hiro passes briefly over the cutting itself and emphasizes at length the pleasure the boys took in sharing experiences and the detailed methods for healing and curing the cut foreskin. At fourteen Hiro began to spend the evenings with his friends in Papeete. They would walk around and talk and joke with the young girls they knew, or go to the movies, or stand outside the bars and dance halls and look in. He did not have intercourse for the first time until he was sixteen, because before that "in our time we didn't try to have intercourse with children [girls his own age] still going to school." Before sixteen they would talk and go to the movies together. After his first sexual experience at sixteen, with a girl from one of the districts of Tahiti whom he met in Papeete, he found it easy to find girls for intercourse, and this became one of his major interests. He changed frequently. Sometimes he saw the same *vahine* continually for a couple of weeks, but then he would change again, and he never lived with any of them.

When Hiro was twenty-one, shortly after he had come back from New Caledonia, he met Meri, a foster sister of Flora's. He saw her occasionally during a year's time and gradually decided that she would be a good woman to settle with because "she was energetic about working and knew how to save money." He settled down with her in a house in Roto, deciding that he would see whether it worked out. They continued to live together, never marrying, and had four children, all girls, and all with French names (Meri and Hiro speak French to their children in order to prepare them for French at school). About a year after settling down Hiro began to drink. He usually drank four or five bottles of beer or a bottle of wine at supper each evening on weekdays. He drank more on Saturday nights, and on Sunday mornings he drank beer to help get rid of his hangover. When he drank he would, as he describes it, want to be by himself, and he would become irritated and hostile if people talked to him or disturbed him. By himself, he says, he would think about the various bad things he had done and, instead of being disturbed by them, think that they weren't so bad after all.

And he thought about a good many other things — about God and religion, about diseases and the physiology of the body, about the nature and motives of the French, about the economic and political situation of the Tahitians.

II Shared Privacy

The chapters which follow continue the attempt to describe some of the culturally influenced aspects of private experience in Piri and Roto. Now the emphasis is on prevalent or common aspects of private experience and on culturally influenced, more or less regular variations in that experience. It is against this background that one may ask how the experiences of, say, Poria, have been influenced by his life in that temporal-spatial sample of Tahitian historical experience that envelops him.

A mixture of data of various kinds underlies these descriptions: the content and form of the intensive interviews; observation of the community behavior of the subjects of those interviews; interviews with and observations of many other people inside and outside the two communities; and various reports, historical and contemporary, bearing on Society Island life.

I have sliced up behavior, or rather abstractions at varying distances from behavior (generalities about "cleanliness" are less abstract than generalities about "moral controls"), into gross categories — "bodies," "souls," "feelings," "thinking" — purposely naive categories which are natural for me. Within these gross categories there are finer ones which take some account of native categories.

However one organizes description and analysis, one must do violence to experiences which in reality are unified. Sexuality, for example, is related to body function, to interpersonal relationships, to identity, to fantasy, and so forth. I have coped with the problem in two unsatisfactory ways. Sometimes an experiential unit, such as sexuality, is dissected and considered in relation to various other topics; sometimes the introduction of a topic leads to a general and tangential discussion of that topic.

The first chapters are relatively descriptive, although they begin to introduce some of the more abstract themes and speculations that will be considered in later chapters.

Because I am also interested in what has been stable within a sample of historical experience and in what has changed or is changing, and because I find previous patterns useful in understanding present forms, these chapters also contain fragments of historical description.

3

Style, Integrations, and Surfaces

The general impression one person or group forms of another person or group in the course of their first contacts is of considerable interest in terms of how it is formed and what its effects are. It is impossible to approach Tahiti free of its myth.

If one turns to writings about Tahiti by the first westerners to see it, one can see the myth in its first stages. It was an utterly interactional product — Tahitians reacting to and interpreted by Europeans, who are reacting to Tahitians and being interpreted by them — but one can guess something about the Tahitians from these writings. The Europeans were reacting in part to styles, surfaces, integrations, and presentations of self. Some fragments of their writings will indicate the nature of their response.

James Morrison of the *Bounty*, who spent two years ashore in Tahiti from 1789 to 1791, was one of the closest and most dependable of the first European observers of Tahiti. "The people in general," he wrote, "are of the common size of Europeans . . . their gait easy and genteel and their countenance free, open, and lively, never sullied by a sullen or suspicious look — their motions are vigorous, active and graceful and their behavior to strangers is such as declare at first sight their humane disposition, which is as candid as their countenances seem to indicate, and their courteous, affable and friendly behavior to each other shows that they have no tincture of barbarity, cruelty, suspicion or revenge. They are ever of an even unruffled temper, slow to anger and soon appeased and as they have no suspicion so they ought not to be suspected, and an hour's acquaintance is sufficient to repose an entire confidence in them" (Morrison 1935; p. 170).

The naturalist John Forster, with Cook on his second voyage in 1773 and 1774, had written of the Tahitians, "In short their character is as amiable as that of any nation that ever came un-improved out of the hands of nature." He described them, as I have already noted, as being of an "open, easy, benevolent character" (J. Forster 1778; p. 231). His son, George Forster, also on the voyage, mused on the "character of the Tahitians . . . their gentleness, their generosity, their affectionate friendship, their tenderness, their pity" (G. Forster 1777; 2:133).

Captain Cook, showing his famous common sense, put it more interactionally: "Three things made them our fast friends: their own good natured and benevolent disposition, gentle treatment on our part, and the dread of our fire arms" (Cook 1955-67; 2:398).

The appendix concerning the inhabitants of Otaheite in the London Missionary Society's report of the first missionary expedition to Tahiti, which arrived there in 1797, sums up: "their manners are affable and engaging; their step easy, firm, and graceful; their behavior free and unguarded; always boundless in generosity to each other, and to strangers; their tempers mild, gentle, and unaffected; slow to take offense, easily pacified, and seldom retaining resentment or revenge, whatever provocation they may have received" (Wilson 1799; p. 327).

In these and many similar reports the Europeans seemed to be responding to several aspects of the Tahitians' behavior. There are descriptions indicating integration and energy — vigorous, active, graceful motions, an easy, firm, and graceful step. We are also told that the Tahitians are courteous, affable, friendly, slow to anger and soon appeased, benevolent, gentle, generous, affectionate, tender, mild, compassionate, tractable. The apparent mildness and lack of overt aggression, indicated in these reports and widely reported throughout Polynesia and Micronesia, are here being described from the first period of European contact. The traits that the first Europeans read as "gentleness" determined much of Tahiti's subsequent history; they apparently helped the London Missionary Society decide to choose Tahiti for its first mission field. As one of the founders of the society, the Reverend Mr. Haweis, put it: "On frequent reflection upon all the circumstances of these islands, ever since their discovery,

I have been persuaded, that no other part of the heathen world affords so promising a field for a Christian mission: Where the temper of the people, the climate, the abundance of food, and early collection of a number together for instruction, bespeak the fields ripe for harvest" (Newbury 1961; p. xxix).

Not only were they gentle, but the Tahitians were engaging and attractive and evoked warm feelings in most of the Europeans. They seemed expressive, open, easy to read. Joseph Banks, on Cook's first voyage, remarked, "few faces have I seen which have more expression in them than those of these people" (J. Beaglehole 1962; 1:256). Lively, clear, engaging expressiveness struck the Europeans from the very first contacts. The sailors of the *Dolphin*, the discoverers of Tahiti, found themselves confronted with women who "came down and stripped themselves naked and made all the alluring gestures they could to entice them onshore." The sailors were ordered to refuse the offer, and did so again the next day. When they put off, "they were pelted with apples and bananas by the women, who made great halloing" (Wallis 1766-67; 21 and 22 June 1767). And gestures of friendship, of "lively compassion," of sorrow at parting, of mourning, and of sexuality were clear and compelling.

Or so they seemed at first. But the Europeans soon found that perfectly convincing gestures could sometimes be used for deception. The meaning and the "sincerity" of the Tahitians' emotional expressiveness puzzled some observers. When Cook left Huahine in the Leeward Islands during his second voyage, "The chief, his wife and daughter, but especially the two latter, hardly ever ceased weeping. I will not pretend to say whether it was real or feigned grief they showed on this occasion. Perhaps it was a mixture of both; but was I to abide by my own opinion only, I should believe it was real" (Cook 1955-67; 2:428).

For the Europeans the willful production of dramatic, expressive behavior was noteworthy. Cook describes a wrestling match: "The conqueror never exulted over the conquered, neither did the conquered ever repine at his ill luck, but the whole was carried on with great good humor. Notwithstanding, during the combat their countenances appeared to express as much fury as if they had been really in earnest" (Cook 1955-67; 1:91).

William Bligh, in the journal of his stay in Tahiti before the mutiny on the *Bounty*, noted passing by the mother of a dead child who was "in a violent degree of distress." He approached the mourner and was startled to find that "we no sooner came in sight than the mourner burst into a fit of laughter at seeing me. . . . Several young women were with her, but they all resumed a degree of cheerfulness, and the tears were immediately dried up." Bligh told the district chief who was with him that "the woman had no sorrow for her child, as her grief could not so easily have subsided if it was the case she regretted the loss of it — when with some humor he told her to cry again; however, we left her without any visible marks of its return" (Bligh 1937; 2:15).

To the western mind this separation of surface emotional display from the inner "truth" was to be a particular problem; it confronted the evangelical missionaries who appeared in strength in the early nineteenth century, looking for salvation for the inner man. They were first taken in by the "depth" of the conversions they had effected, then later were discouraged. When the Reverend John Davies collected almost eleven thousand words for his *Tahitian and English Dictionary* in the first decades of the nineteenth century, he found some twenty-six Tahitian terms having to do with a separation of personal action or qualities from some inner correspondence. He gave them such glosses as "fair and deceptive, as the speech of a hypocrite," "great in appearance only," "empty sympathy," "a fair exterior and that the only good quality," "to pretend faith or obedience in order to gain some end."

The Europeans were also struck by the "casualness" of Tahitian behavior, in contrast to European ideals which, if not always practiced, called for seriousness. Some of this was related to religious behavior. The Europeans apparently expected that uncivilized people, or "savages" as the evolutionary terminology of the day had it, would be deeply and fearfully involved in their religions, in some preenlightenment fashion. Although the missionaries gathered all the descriptions of "pagan rites" they could, Tahitian religious behavior seemed somehow casual and low-key. As William Bligh noted in his journal: "I should have reasoned that people strongly impressed with superstitious notions or ideas would be equally affected at the same rites attending them, but it is powerfully the reverse here; laughing, ridiculous questions, and the strongest proofs of inattention in all the ceremonies I have met with, convince me to the contrary, and I do believe that whatever their sacred ceremonies are, they are followed up with very little reverential awe and with no respect" (Bligh 1937; 2:14).

Another variety of casualness, of some importance for Tahitian history and of great importance for the legend of Tahiti in the West, was in regard to sexual behavior. It seemed to the Europeans shame free, easily available, and either freely given or given as a simple, uncomplicated quid pro quo.

In short, the early Europeans perceived a Tahitian personal style and a Tahitian presentation of self which they found graceful, gentle, expressive, superficial, casual, and sometimes deceptive.

These were images growing out of the interaction of two greatly different cultures. They were a murky mixture of the special perceptions of the Europeans, the special situations involved in Tahitian-European contact,[1] and of Tahitian personal

---

1. The problem in reflexivity, the special response of the Tahitians to altered circumstances, is noted by James Morrison: "Here it may not be improper to remark that the idea formed of this society and of the inhabitants of this island in general by former voyagers could not possibly extend much further than their own opinion, none having remained a sufficient length of time to know the manner in which they live, and, as their whole system was overturned by the arrival of a ship, their manners were then as much altered from their common course as those of our own country are at a fair, which might as well be given for a specimen of the method of living in England" (Morrison 1935; p. 235).

The willingness to believe anything about Tahiti is splendidly illustrated in an extract from the journal of a member of the first missionary expedition to Tahiti in 1797: "A fact was reported to us this day which, if true, was shocking. In one of Captain Cook's visits he left a great monkey, who was made a chief at Attahooroo; he had a wife and thirty servants, and

style and integration. The deductions the Europeans made from their images helped determine the meaning and interpretation of the Tahitians for the Europeans and helped determine their plans for dealing with the Tahitians. The images were reflected back to the Tahitians themselves, entered into their self-interpretations, and are still important in the identity of contemporary Tahitians.

I will add my own impressions of the style of the people of Piri and of the "true Tahitians" of Roto. These impressions were clearest at the beginning of my stay, before details and variations began to obscure them. This is the way it looked to me toward the end of the second month of my first visit to Piri. Much echoes the reports, quoted above, of almost two hundred years earlier. I knew those reports at the time, and they influenced me, but they seemed to be describing something persistent.

My overall first impressions were of gentleness, softness, and a formal, conventionalized openness, with considerable underlying reserve. These qualities were demonstrated not only in people's relations to me but in their relations with one another.

People seemed active, energetic, but unhurried. Their movements were graceful and coordinated. They seemed self-centered and composed rather than expansive and out-flowing. There was less of a contrast in patterns of movement and expression between the men and the women than I was accustomed to in American and European cultures, so that at times the men seemed a little feminine and the women a little masculine.

In certain settings people showed extremely abrupt transitions between active, lively, happy-looking, and engaged states and passive, reserved, withdrawn-appearing ones. The happy-looking states were manifest during specific, culturally defined periods

---

abundance of everything. They called him Taata ooree harrai, the great man dog. One day the woman seeing him catch the flies and eat them, which they abominate, she ran away into the mountains; the monkey and his toutous [servants] pursued, but being met by Temarre, who was jealous of his authority, he knocked him down with a club and killed him" (Wilson 1799; p. 172).

for gaiety, and this contrasted with the general background of quiet reserve.[2]

When the people of Piri and people from other villages of Huahine were joined in a crowd, as, for example, during the Bastille Day festival at Fare, they moved discreetly, rarely touching and never jostling one another. Sometimes, however, when there was something that they had to crowd tightly together to see — a lottery wheel turning at a festival booth for a big prize, or a cockfight — the onlookers would put their arms about one another's shoulders, and body would seem to blend with body. But when the attraction was over, the mass would fall apart, and people would again keep their distance.

An exception to this interpersonal separation was found among adolescents of the same sex, particularly boys. As I noted in the sketch of Oro, boys of thirteen or fourteen would walk along the village path arm in arm or holding hands, or lie on the deck of a boat or relax on the ground with their arms, legs, and heads on each other's bodies. Adolescent girls also went arm in arm or hand in hand in the village, although it was less common to see this.

People could sit sometimes with little motion or activity, for example, when they were waiting at the port for a ship to come in, or sitting on a boat during a passage between islands, or waiting for a meeting to start. People sat quietly, impassively. Rarely, one of these idling sitters would demonstrate some disquiet in a rapidly tapping foot motion or ticlike eye-closing. But most people were able to sit almost motionless.

Sometimes someone would tell the story of some interesting event. In his voice and in the expression of his eyes and face, the dramatic, lively, emotional aspects of the story were conveyed

2. It was particularly striking, for example, in the rural districts of the island of Tahiti to watch people before, during, and after a dance rehearsal or performance. During the dance there was the famous archetypal South Sea Island Tahitian — smiling, face full of expression, of happiness, and flirtatiousness. But before the onset of the dance, or the moment it was over, there was something abruptly different — some sense of quiet, sadness, and isolation.

with vividness. In a story of the uncanny, one could hear the awe in the storyteller's voice, see the amazement in his eyes; likewise for stories of anger, sadness, and comedy. The tale teller made less use of his hands or his body to convey expression. The body seemed relatively impassive around an expressive face and voice.

Soft, gentle, reserved, controlled but not cramped, able to reach out from the reserve in certain clear-cut situations to touch, to express joy, to exhibit themselves and then to pull back quickly — these were, to my aesthetic judgment, some of the stylistic aspects of people in Piri and, when I knew them later, of many of Roto's "traditional Tahitians."

4

Bodies

Cleanliness

Most of the early visitors to the Society Islands who left written records were impressed by the cleanliness of the people, particularly as it compared with some of their other ports of call and with the prevailing standards in late eighteenth-century and early nineteenth-century Europe. George Forster remarked on the natives' frequent washing and commented that "the cleanliness which results from this custom . . . has the further advantage of making these people enjoy the comforts of society in a higher degree than those savages who seem to shun the water, and become indifferent to each other, and loathsome to strangers by their squalid appearance, and fetid exhalations" (G. Forster 1777; 1:339). (His father, John Forster, in his account of Tahiti, thought the relative whiteness of the Tahitians compared with other islanders might be due to their frequent washing.)

George Forster noted that he had been told "that there are at Taheitee no less than fourteen different sorts of plants employed for perfuming, which shows how remarkably fond those people are of fine smells" (G. Forster 1777; 2:83).

Joseph Banks, who was with Cook on his first voyage, called the Tahitians "as cleanly a people as any under the sun." He also noted, "Both sexes eradicate every hair from under their armpits and they look upon it as a great mark of uncleanliness in us that we did not do the same" (J. Beaglehole 1962; 1:335-37).

Much of the emphasis on cleanliness was associated with eating and, sometimes in connection with eating, sometimes independently of it, with ritual contamination. Morrison had noted, "They always wash themselves before and after they eat, and should a dead lizard, mouse, or rat touch them they would wash before they handled any food, and should they happen to find one in or near their oven or touch any of their culinary utensils, they would use them no more" (Morrison 1935; p. 184).

Moerenhout, a Belgian active in the early commercial life of the Society Islands, added in the 1830s, "In all operations of their cookery as well as eating they are very cleanly, always washing their hands before they touch anything" (Moerenhout 1837; 2:89).

Morrison had noted some causes and responses to contamination: "If any person touches a dead body, except of those killed by war or for sacrifice [he] is rendered unclean and can touch no provisions with their [*sic*] hands for one month, during which time they must be fed by another. If the man killed in war be touched by a relation they must undergo the like but otherwise washing is sufficient. If any person have a running sore or large ulcers they are touched by no person else and if they die the house wherein they lived is burnt with every thing belonging to it" (Morrison 1935; p. 184).

Some reports indicated that the personal cleanliness did not apply to houses. Bligh noted: "In all operations of their cookery as well as eating they are very cleanly, always washing their hands before they touch anything, and they are not less so in their persons which they bathe and clean twice a day, so that among these people in ever so great a crowd you feel no offensive smells among them. They are nevertheless filthy about their dwellings, and so much so, that it is really surprising such could be the case among a set of people as cleanly in every other respect" (Bligh 1937; 2:9).

A discrepancy between filthy dwelling places and personal cleanliness was noted again by Moerenhout, who had commented on the culinary cleanliness of the Tahitians. He had a somewhat romantic image of the pre-European Tahitian, thought the dirtiness of the houses was recent, and blamed it on the evident demoralization of the Papeete of his day:

The most disagreeable thing is their entire neglect of the cleanliness of their dwellings. . . . At Papeete, most of the Indians are badly housed. Most of them . . . live in shacks, well roofed, but small and badly kept up. They eat there, drink there, sleep there, and infect them by spreading around their slops and the remains of their meals; habits which, coming from the abolition of the tabus must be regarded as one of the reasons of their illnesses. The only good habit which they have conserved, is that of maintaining the cleanliness of their bodies by bathing several times a day, and through the games of children, women, and men in the water, which happily no one was able to forbid — these alone give a little life to these islands and help very much, I think, to conserve for the people the little good health which remains to them." (Moerenhout 1837; 1:229-30)

Personal cleanliness is still a very salient and general characteristic of the people of both Piri and Roto. People bathe at least once a day, sometimes more often. As Forster and Bligh had noted, a crowd of dancers, or workers, or spectators on a hot day smell only of soap or flowers. In contrast, some villagers comment that Europeans have a "strong" body smell. People in the village often wear old and tattered clothes, but those clothes are almost always very clean. Washing clothes is one of the important household occupations. Being dirty or wearing dirty clothes is a matter of shame and is considered a sign of considerable deviance.

Piri is a clean village. The village path and the yards around the houses are clear of rubbish, and the dirt house yards are usually swept each day to clear and smooth the surfaces. The insides of houses in the village range from moderate cleanliness to immaculate, scrubbed cleanliness.

To anticipate later arguments, cleanliness seems among Tahitians to be associated with the presentation of the self in social groupings and in sexual contact, with covert "oral" orientations and with key dimensions of internal behavioral controls, of conscience. Freudian theory holds that stress on cleanliness is often related to conflicts about defecation and feces. There is no indication for any marked conflicts or stresses related to excretion, at least in any of the more overt aspects of life in Piri. As we shall see, excretion training seems rather casual and is begun at a time when considerable motor development may be presumed to have taken place in the child. Urination and defecation are not particularly hidden or shameful. Members of a family or friends (even if they are of mixed sexes) may urinate in sight of one another if on a road out of the village, for example, and occasionally in groups of the same sex people will defecate within potential sight of one another. It is, however, good manners for others not to look at the defecating or urinating person. Usually people will go off at a distance to defecate, but according to informants it is not a cause of more than mild embarrassment if one is seen by others. When people are asked to list shocking words and to rank them by shock value, words related to excretion, such as *tutae* ("feces"), *titi'o* ("defecation"), *tiho* ("anus"), or *'ōmaha* ("urine" or "urinate") are not included, nor are there any "vulgar" and shocking synonyms for these words, as there are for words for other body functions and parts. (The word *'ohure* [roughly "buttocks"] is shocking when it is used for the female, but not when it is used for the male. For the female, the word designates an area which includes also the vagina.)

Eating

Much of the ancient Tahitian tabu[1] system of avoidances and prohibitions was involved with the act of eating. Eating prohibitions were related to attitudes about evident dirtiness and direct contamination (as by flies) and to more subtle and symbolic contamination. The report of the first missionary voyage notes: "If a man eats in a house with a woman, he takes one end, and she the other, and they sleep in the middle. If a woman has a child, the provisions for it must not come in at the same door with the mother's, but there is an opening like a window, through which they are received, and it would be reckoned beastly in the highest degree for her to eat while she is suckling her child. When they travel, their provisions must be carried in separate canoes" (Wilson 1799; p. 351).

1. The word is Polynesian; in Tahitian it is *tapu*.

The most evident eating tabu to the Europeans was the prohibition on men and women eating together, a tabu which seemed to concern the men and their anxieties more than the women. Joseph Banks commented:

What can be the motive for so unsocial a custom I cannot in any shape guess, especially as they are a people in every other instance fond of society and very much so of their women. I have often asked the reason of them but they have as often evaded the question or given me no other answer but that they did it because it was right, and expressed much disgust when I told them that in England men and women eat together and the same victuals; they however constantly affirm that it does not proceed from any superstitious motive. Eatua [a god] they say has nothing to do with it. But whatever the motive may be, it certainly affects their outward manners more than their principles. In the tents, for instance, we never saw an instance of the women partaking of our victuals at our table, but we have several [times] seen them go 5 or 6 together into the servants' apartment and there eat very heartily of whatever they could find. . . . When a woman was alone [with us], she would often eat even in our company, but always took care to extort a strong promise that we should not let her country people know what she had done. (J. Beaglehole 1962; 1:348)

The diary of Maximo Rodriguez, who took part in an abortive Spanish attempt to establish a foothold in Tahiti in the years 1772 to 1774, provides a possible and intriguing clue to the personal motives associated with the eating separation: "All that I told them [about European customs] met with approval in their sight, except that women should eat with the men; for they are imbued with the superstition that by getting food for the woman and eating in company with her, the men would be struck blind or crippled" (Corney 1913-19; 3:111).

Reports of pre-Christian Tahiti indicate that another symbolic and anciently realistic aspect of eating was the question of being eaten oneself. The Tahitians were not cannibals at the time of European discovery, but their neighbors in the Tuamotus and the Marquesas were, and some aspects of their rites (e.g., the offering of the eye of a sacrificed man to a chief, which he pretended to swallow) and their traditions indicated that they had been at some time in the past. A vocabulary of cannibalism persisted. The missionary Ellis noted as examples of insults, "mayst thou be baked as food for thy mother" and "take out your eyeball and give it to your mother to eat" (Ellis 1830; 1:222), which recall Rodriguez's note on men's fear of being blinded if they were to eat with women. One of the phrases designating incest was, and still is, *'amu ta'ata* or *'ai ta'ata*, both meaning "to eat people," which was also the term for cannibalism.

There are at least three early references to being eaten as a purifying rather than a destructive fate. Morrison says, "When anyone dies they say their soul is fled, and that it flies to the deity who, as they express it, eats it — that it then comes out through him and partaking of his divinity is sent to take care of some other mortal who may be born at the same time, or suffer to roam at large through the heavenly mansions where it wants for nothing" (Morrison 1935; p. 177). The surgeon Anderson, on Cook's third voyage, notes that "they expect no permanent punishment hereafter for crimes committed upon earth, the souls of good and bad men being indiscriminately eaten by the deity. But they consider this coalition as a kind of necessary purification before they enter the regions of bliss" (Cook 1784; 2:103).

A note in the journal of the missionaries Charles Wilson and James Elder for 5 July 1803 also has this theme, with a specific familial reference. The Tahitians had been arguing with the missionaries against the doctrine of the resurrection of the body:

They [men after death] are rotten and become dirt. Therefore, they affirm, it is impossible. . . . They strengthen their unbelief in the resurrection by their own traditions. They say that it was through the first woman, whom they call Hina, that the moon, apples, tumeric, etc. was put into that state, to die and live again in their season, and if she had got her will, man would have been so too. But the first man, whose name was Ti, would not agree to her proposal, and therefore man will never live again. They say that at death the soul leaves the body and goes into the other world, and is ate by one or [an]other of the gods. It comes through him again, among his excrements, is raised to life again, washed, turned into a god, rendered immortal and never liable to any more suffering. Those spirits which have been eaten, eat other spirits, at the death of the body. If the parent is dead before his children, it is his prerogative to eat their spirits. And if the children die before their parents they [nevertheless] do not escape eating. In this account of theirs, there is a punishment after death . . . that of being eaten, there is a resurrection of the spirit after being eaten; . . . but they will not allow of the possibility of a resurrection of the body, after it is once rotten. (London Missionary Society Archives)

As we will see, the idea of the spirit being eaten persists in contemporary Tahiti — but it only happens to occasional spirits, it is an "accident," it leads to extermination, not purification of the spirit, and it is not a god or a parental spirit who does the eating, but an "evil spirit."

The doctrine of purification through being ingested and absorbed relates to the symbolism of cannibalism. Morrison, for example, had asked about the ceremonial offering of the eye of a human sacrifice to a chief. He was told, "The king [chief] is the head of the people for which reason the head is sacred. The eye being the most valuable part is the fittest to be offered, and the reason that the king sits with his mouth open is to let the soul of the sacrifice enter into his soul, that he may be strengthened thereby, or that he may receive more strength of discernment from it" (Morrison 1935; p. 117).

Eating in quantity and, more particularly, being fed by others was a sign of status. George Forster has a lucid description of this, which creates a strong image of infantile beatitude. He had been walking and came upon "a neat house, where a very fat man, who seemed to be a chief of the district, was lolling on his wooden pillow. . . . A woman who sat down near him crammed down his throat by handfuls the remains of a large baked fish, and several bread-fruits, which he swallowed with a voracious appetite. His countenance was the picture of phlegmatic insensibility, and seemed to witness that all his thoughts centered in the care of his paunch. He scarce deigned to look at us, and a few monosyllables which he uttered were only directed to remind his feeders of their duty when we attracted their attention" (G. Forster 1777; 1:295-96).

According to the report of the Spanish expedition, "The arii [chiefs] . . . are all stout, some of them to ungainliness, so that they have two Indians constantly kneading their legs and even then are scarcely able to stand upright" (Corney 1913-19; 2:55).

It seems that in pre-Christian Tahiti eating bore a heavy symbolic and communicative load, in some contrast with sexual relations, which seemed to the Europeans to be loose and perverse or else bucolic, depending on the European's point of view.

Eating now still has evident social meanings. The people who eat together regularly, the "household," constitute, particularly in Piri, the essential, core interactional group. Feasts of traditional Tahitian foods on Sundays and a variety of special occasions and preferences for certain foods and styles of eating are among the major markers of Tahitianness — a salient sign of a demi is said to be that he does not like or pretends not to like Tahitian food.

There are some contemporary status indicators in eating. Men and women tend to sit at different ends of a table, with men seated at the front (path side) of the house and women toward the back. Better foods (e.g., the freshly cooked rather than cold fish) are given to the adult men and guests first.

At Sunday meals and at the various feasts, in contrast to the adequate but not copious amounts of food during ordinary meals, much more food is served than can be eaten. For some demis this "wasting" of food is an important characteristic of village Tahitians.

Fatness is very unusual in Piri and Roto; the one really fat person in Piri is called Mama Pori, a corruption of the designation "Fat Mama." The class of optionally idle ari'i has long since disappeared.

Verbally "palatability" (as indicated by the negative idea "disgusting") is a salient evaluative description. The word faufau, which means nauseated and also refers to objects which induce nausea, is applied to certain kinds of disapproved behavior. Disgust is indicated in conventionalized expressions of disapproval in which there is an apparent mimicry of mild retching expressions.

Exposure

In Piri young children play in the village without clothes, girls going naked until two or three, boys sometimes until four. It is said that fifteen or twenty years ago boys played without clothes until they were six or seven but that girls had always been clothed earlier. Captain Cook noted of the Tahiti of 1769 that "the children . . . go quite naked — the boys until they are six or seven years of age and the girls until three or four; at these ages they begin to cover what nature teaches them to hide" (Cook 1955-67; 1:126).

It is said to be shameful for people past early childhood to expose the genitals, particularly to a person of another sex, but it is most shameful if a female's genitals are exposed in front of males. Related to this is a relatively greater shock value of most terms for female genitals than those for male genitalia. Men and women living together are said to tend to keep their genitals covered except during the act of intercourse.

Young adolescent girls and older women sometimes leave their breasts exposed in public settings, usually when they are working. Women from fifteen until the late thirties usually keep their breasts covered in public settings, except to nurse children. Rarely, some young Piri woman would bathe, washing herself from one of the pathside water taps, with breasts exposed and a cloth around her hips. She would do this at a moment of the day when few people were using the path, but if a man approached and had to pass her on the path he would look fixedly ahead as if the young woman were not there.

Traditional reports indicate that after childhood people kept their genitals covered, except during certain dances.[2]

2. There are several descriptions in the early literature of the ceremonial presentation of tapa cloth, in which a young woman was wrapped in the cloth and then was stripped naked and the cloth presented. But according to Rodriguez, the women wore loincloths under the presentation tapa (Corney 1913-19; 3:43).

Morrison describes exposure of women as part of a game-dance.

After they have played at this for some hours, they kick the ball to one side and both parties strike up together, when each, to draw the spectators to their exhibition produce two or three young wantons, who stripping off their lower garments cover themselves with a loose piece of cloth, and at particular parts of the song they throw open their cloth and dance with their fore-part naked to the company, making many lewd gestures. However these are not merely the effects of wantonness but custom, and those who perform thus in public are shy and bashful in private, and seldom suffer any freedom to be taken by the men on that account. The single young men have also dances wherein they show many indecent gestures which would be reproachable among themselves at any other time but at the dance, it being deemed shameful for either sex to expose themselves naked even to each other, and they are more remarkable for hiding their nakedness in bathing than many Europeans, always supplying the place of cloths with leaves at going in and coming out of the water, and the women never uncover their breasts at any other time. (Morrison 1935; p. 225)

Bligh describes exposure and genital tricks performed by male members of the 'arioi, a religious and performing group in pre-Christian Tahiti, during a public entertainment:

The men now began their performance, which of all things that was ever beheld I imagine was the most uncommon and detestable. They suddenly took off what clothing they had about their hips and appeared quite naked. One of the men was prepared for his part, for the whole business now became the power and capability of distorting the penis and testicles, making at the same time wanton and lascivious motions. The person who was ready to begin had his penis swelled and distorted out into an erection by having a severe twine ligature close up to the os pubis applied so tight that the penis was apparently almost cut through. The second brought his stones to the head of his penis and with a small cloth bandage he wrapped them round and round, up towards the belly, stretching them at the same time very violently until they were near a foot in length which the bandage kept them erect at, the stones and head of the penis being like three small balls at the extremity. The third person was more horrible than the other two, for with both hands seizing the extremity of the scrotum, he pulled it out with such force that the penis went in totally out of sight and the scrotum became shockingly distended. In this manner they danced about the ring for a few minutes when I desired them to desist and the Heivah ended. It however afforded much laughter among the spectators. (Bligh 1937; 2:35)

The context-influenced exhibition/shyness contrast noted by Morrison has modern correspondences. In most settings people of all age grades are restrained. Attention-getting, noisy, showing-off behavior is usually considered shameful or "crazy." But there are a number of situations (parties, festivals, dances, some kinds of formal church activity) when people are suddenly performing. When the episode is finished they return abruptly to their usual reserve.

Morrison's observation about the women's keeping their breasts covered is modified by other observers. The Spanish reports, for example, note that although women's costumes generally cover their breasts, "There are many amongst the women, however, who go entirely nude from the waist upwards, which is attributed to their individual poverty" (Corney 1913-19; 1:331). Moerenhout notes that when he arrived in Tahiti in 1829, "we were surrounded by people, especially girls, the most of them naked to the waist" (Moerenhout 1837; 1:218).

Masturbation

The missionaries, ever sensitive to the vices of the Tahitians, noted masturbation. "The men that are not wealthy in cloth, hogs or English articles, wherewith to purchase a wife, must go without one; and this leads them to practice the great crime of onanism to an excessive degree, and renders them unfit to co-habit with women; but all their vices of this nature are too shocking to be related" (Wilson 1799; p. 192).

Morrison, in the context of a general discussion of sexual practices, has a statement which seems to refer to children's sexual behavior, possibly including masturbation. "They lay no restraint on their children, because they are the head of the family and therefore do as they please; having no law nor custom to prevent them, they have a number of amusements which would not suit the idea of Europeans, which however are dropped as they grow up, when they become ashamed of these childish sports, but are not compelled unless they think proper themselves" (Morrison 1935; p. 236).

The subject of masturbation now has several special features. Uta, talking about masturbation, remarks that his children do it. "My [boy] children — I see it these days, the very little ones." ("How old?") "Three years old, perhaps." I ask how long they continue as they grow older, and he answers: "I don't know. But when I see one [do it], I slap his hand." ("Are you angry? How do you feel?") "I'm not angry, but it isn't proper if people see it, it is dirty."

Uta also masturbated as a child. "I was young, too . . . perhaps four years old, like that. . . ." ("When did you stop?") "As a child? When my grandfather saw me, I got hit, my hand got slapped. [I stopped] at six, perhaps." He says that he never masturbated again, either in childhood or in adolescence, although he was a virgin until his early twenties. He did have frequent nocturnal emissions during his adolescence, "perhaps once a week."

Poria, who, like Uta and most other men, laughs when asked about masturbation, says, "That is a habit of children"; he says he started at four or five, stopped at five or six, and never masturbated again.

The word for masturbation, tīto'ito'i is derived by duplication from the word tīto'i. Tīto'i means to retract the foreskin of the penis, and the duplicated form would mean grammatically to do this repeatedly. Tīto'i implies that the penis is unsupercised, that the foreskin is intact, and it is, as are other terms referring to unsupercised penises, among the strongest, most shocking Tahitian terms. Tīto'ito'i is a less shocking word, although men using the term will laugh and sometimes lower their voices. Its apparent grammatical origin indicates that it may once have referred primarily to prepubertal male masturbation. The term now is also used for postsupercision masturbation and, more or less tentatively and somewhat dubiously by some, to refer to female masturbation.

The emphasis on prepubertal male masturbation is striking. Although several male informants say that they masturbated as children, only one, the adolescent Oro, says that he masturbated as an adolescent. (And Oro claims that he had *not* masturbated before adolescence.) As Poria notes, it is "a habit of [pre-*taure'are'a*] boys." There is some indication that there was previously more leniency toward preadolescent boys' masturbation. One man in his sixties says that in his youth parents did not slap their children; they laughed sometimes — but they scolded all the same. The reason he gives for the scolding is echoed in some of the meanings associated with the supercision operation. He states that parents disapproved because as the foreskin had not been cut yet and as the foreskin was tight around the head of the penis, parents were afraid that children might hurt themselves by injuring the foreskin.

Similar themes are expressed in the interviews of those men who deny masturbating as children. Hiro, who has many anxieties about his bodily health, says that he objects to presupercised boys masturbating because the foreskin might get torn or split. Teiva, in a unique hypothesis, says that young boys masturbated in the hope that the foreskin would split so that they would not have to submit to the supercision. (This is a thematic reversal. For the others, supercision is most overtly an enabling, freeing operation. Teiva, significantly, conceives of it here as a danger to be privately avoided.)

Both Manu and Teiva express the relationship of *tīto'ito'i* and supercision in the flow of their ideas. Manu, describing his resistance when other boys urged him to masturbate, says, "I didn't want that sort of thing, and that is the way it went until I was ten. That was the time I got supercised." He then goes on to describe the supercision. Teiva thinks that he did not masturbate as a child because of his fear of being hit by his Chinese father. "That is why that fear remained, right to my growing up. Right up to the time I got supercised, he didn't have to hit me for that kind of thing."

As I have noted, people say that there was previously (perhaps twenty or more years ago) less hiding of and less reaction to children's masturbation. Toni and other young men state that one often saw both boys and girls rubbing their thighs together or playing with their genitals, but now, because everyone is more enlightened, children are ashamed to be seen. As Uta says, "It isn't proper if people see it."

Masturbation by postsupercision boys is considered shameful, but the emphasis is different. It is a sign that the boy is unable to get a girl, and it has a tinge of "unmasculine" to it. For some it is a *māhū* type of behavior.

Oro believes that the older informants who uniformly deny masturbating as adolescents are lying, adding, in a satiric comment on their generations, "There were people in those days who had intercourse with horses." But Oro's contemporary generation of village *taure'are'a* boys seems childish and unmanly to many of the older village males. It may be that frequent male adolescent masturbation is new, an autistic shift, and, like middle-age masturbation in western communities, related to loneliness and breakdown in sexual meanings and opportunities, particularly in those meanings and opportunities associated with the *taure'are'a* period, which has been a critical period for Tahitian personal growth.

Oro freely admits masturbating, as often as once a day, when he does not have a *vahine*. For him it is a substitute activity, like his contacts with *māhū*. He says that all his *taure'are'a* male friends masturbate when they do not have *vahine*.

In contrast with presupercision masturbation, people deny any ill effects of adolescent masturbation. There is no lore of the body being weakened or harmed. For Oro it was "the same thing as having intercourse with a *vahine*." And he expresses no overt shame or fear about it.

Although some young men say, as a kind of semijoke, that postpubertal girls masturbate, with one exception female informants, including those who apparently spoke quite freely on sexual matters, deny knowing anything about this. Flora, asked about girls' masturbation, says it seems "crazy" to her; after all,

"Why were *tāne* provided?" She saw one episode, however, which disturbed her — a girl of ten or twelve masturbating with a tree branch in a shed. Flora assumes that she must have done this because she had seen an act of intercourse and was aroused.

Whatever the situation is regarding actual behavior, in terms of reports and cultural visibility preadolescent male masturbation is salient, whereas preadolescent female masturbation is not.

Supercision

The rite of passage of supercision,[3] a longitudinal dorsal cutting of the foreskin of the penis, like all such rites, condenses a variety of meanings, functions, and historical residues. I will discuss it here in regard to its more overtly sexual emphases. I will return to it again in later sections to consider its meaning more fully in relation to a variety of aspects of psychological organization.

Somewhere between the ages of eleven and fourteen the child gradually begins to be considered and to consider himself more and more as an "adolescent" or *taure'are'a*. "*Taure'are'a*" is a complex reference, made up of several aspects including body appearance and various types of role behavior. The onset and meaning of the *taure'are'a* period differs for boys and girls. Girls are physically *taure'are'a* after the onset of menstruation and the development of secondary sexual characteristics. Their *taure'are'a* role behavior does not usually involve marked discontinuities from their preadolescent household life.

For boys the period is felt to be in contrast with childhood on the one hand and the later assumption of adult life on the other. The boy gradually enters his *taure'are'a* period. It is marked by shifts in "desires" and activities. Supercision is one of the elements in the shift — but was never conceived of as *the* point of transition. Usually men describe their supercision as preceding their full *taure'are'a* life by a year or two. It usually precedes the first experience of sexual intercourse, but there are some

3. "Supercision" seems semantically more fit than "superincision." I am following the usage of Douglas Oliver here.

young men who brag that they had intercourse before being supercised, a matter for bragging precisely because it is a breaking of a rule.

It is noteworthy that supercision has persisted, whereas most other pre-Christian rites have disappeared. Supercision has in part been supported because it has a biblical charter, and many contemporary Tahitians believe that it was introduced by the missionaries as a Christian innovation. It stands out from the usual subdued style and course of village life as being "violent" and "unnatural" — as representing a sudden change. Historically it seems a last remnant of some of the ancient, more violent themes such as tattoo, warfare, infanticide, self-wounding during mourning, and human sacrifice, which counterpointed the generally easygoing and benign aspects of the old culture.

Older adolescents who have already undergone supercision mock the younger ones who have not, and dislike of being mocked is one of the standard answers to "Why did you decide to become supercised at that time?" The older adolescents would call out *taioro* or, more rarely, *ure hore*. *Taioro* is a white fermented coconut sauce and here, as an insult, refers to the white smegma which accumulates under the uncut foreskin. This smegma, also called *huahua*, is considered dirty and disgusting. One of the common explanations given for the supercision is that it eliminates smegma. *Ure hore* means a penis with the foreskin stripped back and refers to the unsupercised male's ability to do this. It is, curiously, one of the two or three most shocking "dirty" phrases in Tahitian.

Girls are said to disapprove of the unsupercised penis, and there is supposedly some shame involved for a man in having intercourse before the cutting. Some say that the girl might tell and it would be the older male adolescents who would mock. But intercourse before supercision does occur and, as I have noted, some men boast of having done it. The girl's objection may also relate to fear of being teased by others and to the total Tahitian context, as well as specific responses to an unsupercised penis. Some of the same girls who object to having intercourse with an unsupercised Tahitian have no objection to having intercourse with uncircumcised Europeans. (One common derogatory term for Frenchmen, however, is *taioro*.)

Although the standard answer to questions about the purpose of the operation is cleanliness, a few adults add that the operation increases sexual pleasure for both participants — for the woman because the cutting of the foreskin is supposed to allow a greater expansion of the head of the penis, and for the man because the foreskin no longer acts as an insulating membrane between the head of the penis and the vagina. An unsupercised man is supposed to have a quick and ungratifying orgasm. This is said to be a "skin orgasm."

As we saw in connection with pre-*taure'are'a* masturbation, it is felt that sexual activity might split an uncut foreskin, and the removal of this danger is occasionally given as an explanation. But the most common overt explanation for the operation is to produce "cleanliness."

Usually boys go to be supercised with a group of friends of the same age. They decide that the time has come to have it done and, usually without their parents' knowledge, ask the man in the village who knows best how to do it to operate on them. He will do the operation as a friendly service; there are no payments or gifts involved. The expert usually asks another man to help him. He and his helper meet the boys in a secluded place.

The boys go to be cut one at a time, while the others wait at a distance. The boy sits. The operator places a small piece of coconut shell between the dorsum of the glans penis and the foreskin and spreads the foreskin tightly over the shell. Meanwhile his assistant stands behind the boy and presses firmly on the boy's ears. As he presses, the operator, using a razor blade (formerly a sharp sliver of bamboo), makes a sudden longitudinal cut. The boy then goes into the sea to wash. The other boys are cut. Then the cuts are treated with herbal medicines. A fire is made, and leaves are placed on it. The boys, in a group, hold their penises over the vapor from the leaves, then bandage them with cloth. There are variations on the treatment phase, a number of ways and sequences of curing the cuts. In its core aspects the procedure seems little changed from its pre-Christian form.

It is characteristic of the description and recall of the actual events of the day of supercision that an informant quickly passes over the actual operation, usually mentioning that there was little pain, and then goes into a lengthy discussion of the techniques and procedures for treating the wound. Most of the men reporting on the operation stress that there was really no danger, although one young man said that if the dorsal vein of the penis was cut during the operation, impotence might follow. But the only complications usually stressed are that occasionally a young man might faint or have several days of pain while the wound is healing. Several times in discussing supercision men play with the words *tehe* and *pātehe* in a joking manner, saying, "Don't get them mixed up." *Tehe* means the cutting which produced the supercision and *pātehe* means to castrate, as was traditionally done, for example, to pigs. *Tehe* is considered a somewhat shocking word and is often replaced in polite speech by *piritome*, which was introduced by the missionaries. (The original form was *peritome*, a translation of the biblical "circumcision," from the Greek for "cut around.")

A slight excursion bearing on the symbolism of the custom is useful here. Although contemporary Tahitian usage separates *tehe* as supercision and *pātehe* as castration, the Davies missionary dictionary of terms collected in the early nineteenth century gives *both* "castration" and "superincision" for *tehe*; *pātehe*, however, is given only the meaning "to castrate." The *Dictionary of Some Tuamotuan Dialects of the Polynesian Language* by Stimson and Marshall gives both "to superincise" and "to castrate" for *tehe* in some Tuamotuan dialects and also gives the definition "the penis with the glans bared." Apropos of this latter definition, Bruce Biggs notes for the Polynesian New Zealand Maori, "Male modesty was even more narrowly [than the female's modesty concerning her genitalia] centered in the *glans penis*. Circumcision was not practised, and on occasion men danced stark naked, but with a cord tied round the foreskin to prevent exposure of the *glans*. The word *tehe*, signifying an exposed *glans*, was a term of ridicule and insult. . . . To the Maori all aspects of nature were either male or female. The positive male element represented force and ritual well-being and effectiveness. In the human male this force was centred in the penis. The protective rites against witchcraft involved retraction of the prepuce and exposure of the usually concealed *glans*" (Biggs 1960; pp. 15-20).

The man who does the cutting in Tahiti now has no special status. In Piri he is one of the more undistinguished and unimportant members of the village. There are no religious or magical ceremonies or beliefs related to supercision, the emphasis being matter-of-fact casualness, and there were none at the time of first western contact.

The close similarity of contemporary practices to the first-described forms is striking. Thus John Forster notes in 1773 and 1774 that supercision "is performed merely from principles of cleanliness, by the priest, though there is not any religion or religious ceremony mixed with the custom, for which reason it is not performed on a certain day after the birth of the child, nor at any certain age, but when the child is capable of attending to it" (J. Forster 1778; p. 556). Forster indicates that the age when a child was "capable of attending to it" was at least twelve.

Anderson, the surgeon on Cook's third voyage in 1777, gives a description which would hold today, except that it is not usually the father who initiates the action and the shark's tooth has been replaced by a bamboo sliver or razor blade.

From a notion of cleanliness, the cutting of the foreskin is a practice adopted among them; and they bestow a reproachful epithet upon those who neglect that operation. When five or six lads in a neighborhood are pretty well grown up, it is made known to a tahoua ["expert practitioner"] by the father of one of them. The tahoua, attended by a servant, conducts the lads to the top of the hills, and after seating one of them in a proper manner, places a piece of wood beneath the foreskin, at the same time amusing him, by desiring him to look aside at something which he pretends to see. The young man's attention being thus engaged, he immediately cuts through the skin with a shark's tooth, and separates the divided parts; then, after putting on a bandage, he performs the same operation on the other lads who attend him" (Cook 1784; 2:100).

A few adolescent boys, eight or ten a year, in the island of Huahine (according to the nurse) go to the male nurse at Fare, who does a circumcision, not a supercision. But the great majority still have supercisions in the village. In Roto most of the *mā'ohi* boys are operated on by someone in the neighborhood, not in the hospital.

After the operation the young man reports a sense of pleasure, of accomplishment and pride. He will often exaggerate the awkwardness of his gait to be sure that the other young people in the village know immediately that he has just had an operation.

Although women participate in and discuss most of the aspects of life in Piri, the details of the act of supercision are not told to them, and many of them seem ignorant of the details of the operation. This is one of the few things that were strictly the men's affairs.

Sexual Intercourse

Most adolescents in Piri are said to begin sexual intercourse between the ages of thirteen and sixteen. Some individuals report having played at sexual intercourse from the age of nine. Some few girls, now and in recent generations, remained virgins until later ages, as have some boys in the current generation of adolescents. This latter is said to be mostly because there are not enough available girls in Piri. (One reason for this shortage was that more adolescent girls than boys have moved to Papeete.) Previously it was the custom for groups of adolescents to travel around the island from one district to another for adventure and in the hope of meeting sexual partners. This is less frequent now and is part of the general shift in *taure'are'a* conditions in what seems to older men a more "childlike" direction. Some boys in older generations remained virgins to young manhood through timidity or apparent lack of drive, as had Uta. This was apparently rather exceptional.

Sexual relationships between young adolescents are usually transient and secretive, although a boy might boast of it to a trusted friend and, after it was over, to a larger circle of male adolescents.

A traditional practice, *motoro*, still exists, although it seems to be getting less frequent. The young adolescent boy, after summoning up his courage and making sure none of his peers know what he is up to, waits until everybody is asleep in the household of a girl who attracts him. He will then sneak through an unlocked window or door and, trying not to wake anyone, go to the girl's sleeping area and lie down beside her. Most often they talk in whispers for a short time and the boy leaves, relieved to have escaped unscathed. When he next meets his friends, if he does not plan to go back again to the same girl, he will tell the story of his deed, perhaps adding an untrue ending of sexual consummation. If the boy is serious, he is much less likely to tell his friends. He may next enter the girl's room several times on subsequent nights, and if she approves of him they may have intercourse there. Most likely he will ask her to leave the house and meet him somewhere. After he has left through the window she may get up and, if her parents wake, tell them she is leaving the house to go to the outhouse, and then meet the boy for a brief act of intercourse. This is silent and quick, and, in the reminiscences of some mature women, often of interest to the young girl mostly as an adventure, not as a sensual experience.

After some time, rarely within months of their first transient sexual experiences and usually not until some years have gone by, individuals will begin to move into a series of more and more stable unions of longer and longer duration. These involve overt living together instead of clandestine meetings and also involve shifts in the qualities of the sexual act.

The male is supposed to initiate the various sequences which might lead up to intercourse. For couples who are not "settled down" and if it is not a matter of *motoro*, this may start in an encounter on the village path. If there is anybody around, a boy is particularly careful not to look at or show any reaction to a girl in whom he is interested; but if there is no one around he may begin teasing her or joking with her. And at some point he will propose overtly that the girl find a way of meeting him somewhere out of the village or in some village house which may be momentarily unoccupied. Boys also ask other boys, sometimes a relative of the girl, to serve as go-betweens. A woman can always say no and that is the end of it. Rape, *haru*, even though people say it existed in previous days and even though villagers suppose it to be the common method of initiating intercourse among the young people in such barbaric distant islands as the Tuamotus, is considered shocking and a bad thing in contemporary Piri. There are no cases of violent rape in recent years known to the *chef de poste* at Huahine.

In a stable relationship the woman often more or less covertly initiates the sexual act by signaling her receptivity through her attitude and, perhaps, dress.[4] Living in Teri'i Tui's household, I could predict the evening before by Romana's shift in attitude toward her *tāne*, Tino, whom she usually treated with cool casualness, that they would have intercourse during the night. The rest of the family apparently slept soundly through the muffled sounds.

There are cultural encouragements for beginning intercourse. It is believed that if the onset of menstruation is not followed within the next very few years by at least one act of intercourse, a girl will suffer from *ma'i fa'a'ī* ("filled-up sickness"). This is an illness assumed to be caused by the blockage of the adequate flow of menstrual blood, which instead of flowing completely outside, fills up the body. The blood will eventually cause choking sensations in the throat and may lead to insanity and death.[5] Continual intercourse was not needed to prevent *ma'i fa'a'ī*, but at least one act of intercourse was necessary to insure good menstruation. (In spite of this belief, some girls in the village did re-

4. Teiva notes that for many years during his thirties and early forties he had intercourse with his wife only once or twice a month. Nevertheless, she had several children during this period. There is no evidence of village gossip that she was unfaithful. It is of interest to speculate about a possible relationship of female control of the timing of intercourse to conception and to birth rates.

5. Resemblance of these symptoms and their explanation to the old European idea of female hysteria is striking. In hysteria, in which the sensation of choking or difficulty in swallowing, *globus hystericus*, was the classical symptom, it was thought that this symptom and others were caused by the migration of the uterus into the upper part of the body.

main virgins.) Virginity was only one cause of *ma'i fa'a'i*. Blockage could also be caused by becoming chilled during menstruation and by a late menarche.

Young male *taure'are'a* were urged toward attempting intercourse by teasing by their friends and were rewarded by peer-group approbation for reports of exploits, as well as by the considerable, although slightly disguised, pride that their fathers, older male relatives, and other village men took in the reports of the boys' sexual accomplishments which reached them occasionally. The external pushes for initiating sexuality had some analogues in village festivals and certain household festivities, kinds of activities which were labeled as having the goal of *'ārearea* ("fun"), in which the *tāvana* or some other official or, in the household, the host would repeatedly urge the shy, uncomfortable, or bored-looking participants to "enjoy yourselves and have a good time." The pushes helped to overcome timidity and perhaps some weakness of conscious "drive." Uta, for example, states that he never felt any sense of strong sexual desire until he began to have intercourse. After he started, it was difficult for him to stop — he lived with one girl and also had frequent outside contacts at the same time. Several women, including Flora, say they felt little sexual pleasure or desire in their first acts of intercourse. It took them months or years before they began to feel sexual passion or desire. The beginning of this type of more intense sexual feeling for both men and women is often the reason for establishing a more permanent union and is a standard explanation for it.

Adult males reporting on themselves and speculating on others, say that in the first year or two of a permanent union a couple has intercourse daily, sometimes two or three times a night; after a year or two there are intervals of days or a week without intercourse; and after several years the frequency goes down to once every two or three weeks or once a month. It is agreed that if a man got a new *vahine* the frequency would go up again.

Intercourse continues during pregnancy until two or three weeks before delivery and begins again, depending on the healing of the woman's genitalia, in one or two months. Intercourse does not usually go on during menstruation; menstrual blood is considered dangerous for the male. (An exception is that intercourse toward the end of the menstrual flow is believed to be one way of overcoming sterility.) It is assumed that people continue to have sexual desire and active intercourse until advanced old age.

From the moment of European discovery the overtness of sexual behavior in various aspects of the life of Tahiti made a strong impression on all foreign observers. George Robertson, the master of the *Dolphin*, which had discovered Tahiti five days earlier, notes in his journal for 24 June 1767, "At sun rise about three hundred canoes came off and lay round the ship. As many as could conveniently lay alongside traded very fair, and took nails and toys for their hogs, fowls and fruit. By eight o'clock there was upwards of five hundred canoes round the ship, and at a moderate computation there was near four thousand men. The most of the trading canoes which lay round the ship and dealt with our people had a fair young girl in each canoe, who played a great many droll wanton tricks." The purpose of the girls was to distract the discoverers, and shortly "all our decks was full of great and small stones, and several of our men cut and bruised" (Robertson 1948; p. 154).

After the Tahitians discovered that stones were no match for guns and cannons, women were still presented to the Europeans in quantity. Wallis, the captain of the *Dolphin*, noted in his journal, "The women in general are very handsome, some really great beauties, yet their virtue is not proof against a nail — for they would prostitute themselves for a nail — the lower sort for a small one, and the nail must be larger in proportion to the lady's beauty. Even the fathers and mothers and brothers brought them to the people [the ship's company] and showed sticks proportioned to the nail they were to give" (Wallis 1766-68; 27 July 1767).

Bougainville, who rediscovered Tahiti ten months after Wallis had visited there, was so struck by the erotic aspects of Tahiti that he named it *La Nouvelle Cythère*, after the island where Aphrodite, in some versions of her history, first appeared from the sea. According to Bougainville, "Each day our men walked in the country without arms, alone or in small groups. They were invited into the houses and fed; but it was not a light snack to which the civility of the host is limited here. They offered them their daughters. The hut filled instantly with a curious crowd of men and women who made a circle around the guest and the young victim of duty to hospitality. The ground was covered with leaves and flowers and musicians sang, to the harmonies of the flute, a hymn of joy. Venus is here the goddess of hospitality, her worship does not admit of mysteries, and each joy is a celebration for the nation. They were suprised at the embarrassment that they witnessed. Our customs have tended to forbid that kind of publicity" (Bougainville 1958; p. 128).

Many dances and games involved sexual gestures and, as we have noted, exposure of the genitalia. Cook noted, "The young girls, whenever they can collect eight or ten together, dance a very indecent dance which they call Timorodee, singing most indecent songs and using most indecent actions in the practice of which they are brought up from their earliest childhood" (Cook 1955-67; 1:127).

As to the variety of sexual techniques, Bligh, after describing male transvestite homosexuals and their sexual relations with other males, remarks, "It is strange that in so prolific a country as this men should be led into such sensual and beastly acts of gratification, but perhaps no place in the world are they so common or so extraordinary as in this island. Even the mouths of women are not exempt from the pollution, and many other as uncommon ways have they of gratifying their beastly inclinations" (Bligh 1937; 2:17).

Under missionary pressures the Tahitians lost most of their repertory of amusements, sports, and entertainments. As to sexual practices, it is difficult to know which aspects were lost, which continued sheltered from the scrutiny of missionaries and pastors, and which things were introduced or reintroduced as Puritan pressures loosened.

Kissing was introduced by the Europeans. The traditional Tahitian "kiss" was the *ho'i*, which involves bringing the noses together in a combined nuzzling and sniffing. Kissing on the mouth is still considered as a mild perversion, but it is done during foreplay. One woman in Piri remembers twenty years ago hearing a woman insult her husband during a public fight by saying that when he was drunk he would try to kiss her. According to the young men now, kissing, fondling the woman's breasts, and occasionally cunnilingus, mouth-vaginal contact, are the types of foreplay they practice. Fellatio, mouth-penis contact, was reportedly not done in village heterosexual intercourse and was considered a perversion limited to "bad girls" in Papeete. This was in spite of the fact that fellatio was the activity performed by the *māhū*, the traditional male homosexual, with whom some of the village men had contact.

Some men claim they spend half an hour at foreplay; some say the period of caressing is a matter of five minutes or so; and others report that they begin intercourse immediately. In Piri the sexual positions reported are with the girl on her back and the man on top, or with the couple side by side. They deny using other positions, though some heard that in Papeete "as a result of French influence" other positions are used. Estimates of the duration of intercourse are from three or four minutes to ten to fifteen. Much of the timing is regulated by the woman's orgasm. Most male informants stress the importance of bringing a woman to orgasm. It is said that a woman may leave or shame a man if he does not satisfy her, but this is considered extremely unusual. The overt, public opinion expressed by young men is that it is not difficult to satisfy a woman sexually.

The clitoris is named, *teo* (it also has several metaphorical names based on its shape), and its function as providing a special source of pleasure to the woman and its erectile nature are generally known.

An aspect of women's sexual performance, talked about by men and said to be a rather unusual skill, is the ability of certain women to *'ami'ami*, that is, to voluntarily and intermittently contract and relax the paravaginal muscles in a "milking" fashion. The term is also used in the Tuamotu dialects and may represent a remnant of traditional, more elaborate sexual craft.

The woman's sexual responsiveness is related to the type of relationship. There is an old tradition (as indicated by the Wallis quotation) of women's using the sexual act in a direct and open marketing exchange for goods or services. This is the case in many of the sexual relations between Polynesian women and Europeans, for example, although it also exists in the village setting where some girls will have intercourse with men they do not find attractive in exchange for money or presents. Reports of the women's response in these kinds of relationships often note considerable passivity and lack of responsiveness.

There are no reports of frigidity among adult women, although as noted there are reports of relative lack of feeling during early sexual experiences. Men deny experiencing or having heard about impotence except as a result of physical illness or, more commonly, as a result of severe chilling after diving for fish. This lack of reported impotence is partially due to the concept of the interrelation of the "self" and the sexual act. In a casual relationship, if a man starts to caress a woman and finds that he does not have an erection, he will decide that the woman is not attractive to him and make some excuse to avoid proceeding. This is not considered a failure, nor is it considered that in spite of this desire for intercourse he cannot perform. He simply concludes that he does not want to have intercourse.

Both men and women report nocturnal sexual dreams, often accompanied by orgasm. These are always felt to be the result of some spirit activity and are felt to be dangerous.

The various statements about attributes desirable for a sexual partner — which are not, of course, the only traits that are desirable in a spouse — stress such things as cleanliness, attractive smell, pleasant face, smooth skin and hair; that is to say, qualities of softness, blandness, and pleasant surfaces. These are ideals. Most partners seem to take what they can get, whatever turns up, and there seems to be a considerable sense of interchangeability, a feeling that one partner is as good as another for transient and casual relationships. Another consideration enters more permanent unions. This is a mutual sexual attractiveness

said to be peculiar to the specific combination of the partners'
bodies, a "properness" of interaction. It is independent of the
other qualities mentioned. In Papeete, at least among the more
western-oriented Tahitians, there is said to be more stress on the
visual beauty of the partner, partially in terms of the public impression this will make.

In Piri most partners either for casual sex or for unions are
close in age. In Papeete there is more spread, the man often being considerably older than the woman. This is partially due to
the relative importance of money in Papeete and the chance
that an older man will have more.

Homosexuality

The earlier visitors to Tahiti were struck by the presence of
males who played female roles. Morrison noted for his 1789 to
1791 stay,

They have a set of men called Mahoo [*māhū*]. These men are in
some respects like the Eunichs in India but are not castrated.
They never cohabit with women but live as they do. They pick
their beards out and dress as women, dance and sing with them
and are as effeminate in their voice. They are generally excellent
hands at making and painting of cloth, making mats and every
other woman's employment. They are esteemed valuable friends
in that way and it is said, though I never saw an instance of it,
that they converse with men as familiar as women do — this,
however, I do not aver as a fact as I never found any who did
not detest the thought. (Morrison 1935; p. 238)

That the *māhū* did "converse with men as familiar as women
do" was attested by other observers. Morrison's captain on the
Bounty, William Bligh, wrote,

On my visit this morning to Tynah and his wife, I found with
her a person, who although I was certain was a man, had great
marks of effeminacy about him and created in me certain notions which I wished to find out if there were any foundations
for. On asking Iddeeah who he was, she without any hesitation

told me he was a friend of hers, and of a class of people common in Otaheite called Mahoo, that the men had frequent connections with him and that he lived, observed the same ceremonies, and ate as the women did. The effeminacy of this person's speech induced me to think he had suffered castration, and that other unnatural and shocking things were done by him, and particularly as I had myself some idea that it was common in this sea. I was however mistaken in all my conjectures except that things equally disgusting were committed. Determined as I was either to clear these people of such crimes being committed among them, or to prove that they were so, I requested Tynah to inform me, which as soon as I had requested it, a dozen people and even the person himself answered all my questions without reserve, and gave me this account of the Mahoos. These people, says Tynah, are particularly selected when boys and kept with the women solely for the caresses of the men, here the young man took his Hahow or mantle off which he had about him to show me the connection. He had the appearance of a woman, his yard and testicles being so drawn in under him, having the art from custom of keeping them in this position. Those who are connected with him have their beastly pleasures gratified between his thighs, but are no farther sodomites as they all positively deny the crime. On examining his privacies I found them both very small and the testicles remarkable so, being not larger than a boy's five or six years old, and very soft as if in a state of decay or a total incapacity of being larger, so that in either case he appeared to me as effectually a Eunuch as if his stones were away. The women treat him as one of their sex, and he observed every restriction that they do, and is equally respected and esteemed. (Bligh 1937; 2:16-17)

John Turnbull, who had voyaged to Tahiti in 1804, through the editor of the *London Review* in 1806 (who was answering a letter asking for details on the sexual behavior of the *māhū*, the *Review* having discussed some of the results of Turnbull's observations in an earlier number) gave some details in Latin, the translation running, "They put the penis into the unfortunate's mouth, and go on to emit the semen, which the wretch eagerly swallows down as if it were the vigor and force of the other; thinking no doubt thus to restore to himself greater strength."[6]

Most of the early descriptions indicate that the *māhū* played the feminine role and was sexually receptive, but there is ambiguity about the active and passive role in fellatio. One account of the non*māhū* partner as active is in a letter of a member of the London Missionary Society working in Tahiti in 1801 to the London office, which noted that the

chief of Hapy-ano was detected committing an act of bestiality with another man, which perhaps had no existence even in Sodom and Gomorrha. . . . The chief [had] laid himself down in the room upon one of his attendant's cloth as if to sleep. . . . We went out . . . [and] not long after, having occasion to go back for something, and entering, suddenly he [another missionary] saw sufficient to assure him a most singular and horrible species of beastiality was committing . . . the chief having in his mouth the others . . . [original ellipsis]. . . . The most unnatural lusts are indulged by the Otaheiteans perhaps to as great an excess as in any nation under the sun. Satan has them in his arms in a very awful manner, and the planting of the gospel on this island must evince the power of the grace of God in saving sinners very conspicuously. (London Missionary Society Archives)

There were an adolescent young man in Piri and a fifty-eight-year-old man in Roto, both designated as *māhū*. People speak of "the *māhū*" of a village or district, and say that most villages have a *māhū* (even if they do not know who it is). A tape-recorded fragment illustrates this. Toni, in Teri'i Tui's household, asked about *māhū* in the various districts of Huahine, said that there is never more than one "because when one dies then another substitutes. . . . God arranges it like that. It isn't allowed . . . two *māhū* in one place. I've traveled around Huahine and I haven't seen two *māhū* in one place. I never saw it. Only one *māhū* . . . and when that one dies, then he is replaced."

The word *māhū* refers generally to a particular type of masculine role. There is some disagreement and confusion about the

6. This correspondence is quoted by M. L. J. Bouge, in a note in the *Journal de la Société des Océanistes* 11 (December 1955): 147.

proper terminology to be applied to other types of male homosexual behavior or to female homosexual behavior in general. A
few people apply the term *māhū* to these kinds of behavior with
qualifications, but most use special forms to distinguish them
from the *māhū* proper. These problems of classification and
terminology come up for the most part in Papeete. For Piri,
aside from hearsay, there is only one type of homosexual, and
that is the traditional *māhū*.

In Piri an effeminate man can be described as *huru māhū* or
*māhū*ish, but he nevertheless is assumed to be in general an "ordinary" kind of man, involved in standard male activity and, if
not engaged in normal heterosexual practices (although most are
assumed to be), certainly *not* engaged in the *māhū's* type of
homosexual behavior. Either one is a *māhū* or one is not. One
can discontinue being a *māhū* as one can discontinue being chief.
There is a case in the village of a young man who in his early
adolescence dressed from time to time in girl's clothes and was
thus a *māhū* and who in his early twenties rejected (*fa'aru'e*,
"cast off") the role. It is assumed in the village that this is the
end of it and that he is leading an ordinary masculine life. This
man later left the village for Papeete. His dress, motility, and
manner of speaking in Papeete were "masculine."

Being a *māhū* does not now usually entail actually dressing as
a woman. A *māhū* from Raiatea, who once visited the village,
had long hair and dressed as a woman. He was a source of much
comment and surprise in Piri.

The *māhū* in Piri (who left for Papeete in 1963) is sixteen
years old in 1962. Although there are pictures of him in a girl's
dancing costume complete with brassiere prominently displayed
in a frame in the house of one of his foster mothers, most of the
time in the village he wears either the neutral *pareu* or ordinary
male dress. His speech and manner are somewhat feminine, like
those of other rural *māhū*, resembling feminine mannerisms
rather than mocking or exaggerating them. But his feminine
role-taking is demonstrated for the villagers because he performs
women's household activities. He helps clean the house, takes
care of babies, braids coconut palm leaves into thatching plaits.

His associations are with the village girl adolescents and he visits with them and gossips with them. He is sometimes to be seen walking with his arm interlocked with an adolescent girl's, behavior otherwise seen only among young people of the same sex.

The relation of overt sexual activity to the *māhū* role is equivocal. Many people in the village say that homosexual activity is not necessarily part of a *māhū*'s behavior, and some of the men in the village say that most *māhū* do not engage in sexual activities. Others, mostly the younger men in Piri, state that all *māhū* engage in sexual activities with other males, although they may be discreet and secret about it. This is also the opinion of the *māhū* in Roto. Some of the young men claim that in Piri the *māhū* had sexual relationships with most of the young male *taure'are'a*, but these men tended generally to exaggerate *taure-'are'a* sexual behavior.

It is stated that there is nothing abnormal about this as far as the male *taure'are'a* are concerned. Some adults in the village found the idea of homosexual relations with the *māhū* "disgusting." But they did not seriously stigmatize those males who engaged in them. Sexual contact with the *māhū* tends to be treated in conversation as a standard kind of sexual activity, which is often justified as due to a lack of available women. A *māhū* is seen as a substitute female. The sexual activity which the *māhū* is held always to perform is *'ote moa* (literally, "penis sucking"). Anal sodomy is categorically denied as a *māhū* activity, as Bligh's informants denied it, but is said by some to have been introduced in Papeete as a European custom. Intercourse between the thighs is said not to be done.[7]

A common joke among the young men is that the *māhū* swallows the semen after his partner's ejaculation. According to Toni, "They really believe that is first class food for them. Because of

7. In 1962 the first case of sodomy which had ever come to the attention of the authorities at Huahine was under investigation in the port town of Fare in Huahine. It involved a seventeen-year-old boy who had not been considered to be a *māhū* in his community, who had allegedly performed sodomy on six young boys from seven to twelve years of age.

that *māhū* are strong and powerful. The seminal fluid goes throughout his body. It's like the doctors say about vitamins. I have seen many *māhū* and I've seen that they are very strong."

Males describing their relationships with *māhū* tend to stress their passive participation in the relationship and the lack of symmetry, as the following quotation from Toni suggests. "I was 'done' by a *māhū* in Papeete. . . . He 'ate' my penis.[8] He asked me to suck his. I did not suck it. . . . I said he would get hit by me. He offered me money. I said [again] I would hit him. I did not want that sort of thing, it is disgusting." Toni then goes on to explain that the reason he went with the *māhū* was that he was drinking and had not gotten a girl. He recounts this as an amusing story, without any hesitation and in the same manner that he recounts his other sexual adventures.

Oro, as has been noted, mentioned that he had relations with two *māhū* in Papeete. He states that this was a shameful matter, not for himself but for the *māhū*. He says that he had one contact with one of the *māhū* and two with the other. "It's just like doing it with a woman, but his way of doing it is better than with a woman, as you just take it easy while he does it to you. . . . He doesn't let go quickly and it makes you very limp. When you go to a woman, it's not always satisfactory. When you go to the *māhū* it's more satisfactory. The sexual pleasure is very great. You can't stand it any more, because of that you try to push his head away." Asked again if there is any shame in this for the non*māhū* male, Oro goes on, "No, you're not ashamed. You don't put any value on it. It's like feeding the *māhū* with the penis. You're better off [i.e., get more pleasure out of it] than they do, and they don't have the same thing done to them by other *māhū*. For you it's just the same thing as if you were having intercourse with a woman. You don't take it seriously."

Whatever the sets of personal meanings about *māhū* behavior may be to those non*māhū* males who have relations with *māhū* — and to the community at large (which will be considered in later

8. Babies are sometimes said to eat (*'amu*) the breast. Cunnilingus is sometimes called "eating the vagina." Babies also suck (*'ōte*) the breast.

chapters) — there is, of course, the meaning and use of the *māhū*
role to the man who plays it. Attempts were made to interview
the *māhū* of Piri after he moved to Papeete in 1963. He is one
of the very few Piri informants who is evasive in his answers, and
he discontinued the interviews after the second one, before the
subject of his *māhū* behavior was approached. The *māhū* in
Roto, Timi, is not hesitant about being interviewed or talking
about his specifically *māhū* activities. In 1964 Timi is a fragile,
graying man of fifty-eight with a slightly feminine manner in his
voice and movements, but these are not greatly exaggerated or
caricatured. Following are some rather staccato notes on an interview with him.

He was born in a small village in Raiatea. In 1964 he is working for a Chinese family in Roto as a maid, washing clothes and
helping occasionally with simple cooking for the morning meal.
He is friendly with some of the women in the neighborhood, including Manu's *vahine*, and when his work is done he drops in
and drinks beer and gossips with them.

He was the oldest of six children and as an infant was taken
as a foster child by his father's biological father. There was no
one else in his household except him and his foster father, since
his foster father's *vahine* had died before he was born. The house
they lived in was roofed with coconut thatching and had walls
of woven bamboo, and in his early childhood they sat and slept
on the floor and ate out of coconut bowls. Only later, when he
was ten or so, did they begin to acquire some western-style
chairs and tables.

There were no other children near him, since the house was on
a farm some distance from the village in the district. He mostly
played by himself or followed after his foster father. He remembers that he liked to sweep and clean the house and prepare
food for his grandfather. At seven or eight he began to go into
the village to school. It was about this time he began to wear
girl's clothes. He says that he wanted to dress like this, and that
his grandfather asked some of their relatives to make the clothes
for him. This began before he knew that *māhū* existed, and it
was some years later that he saw an adult *māhū* for the first time.

When he wore the girl's clothes to school, the other children would sometimes mock him. He would then go off and hide. At the age of fourteen or fifteen he was brought to Tahiti to work for a French couple who had met him in Raiatea. He worked for them washing clothes, which was the kind of work he did during most of his subsequent life. When he left Raiatea for Tahiti he stopped wearing girl's clothes and never wore them again.

His first sexual experience was when he was fourteen and still at school in Raiatea, with a "non*māhū*" boy of fifteen or sixteen. The older boy had initiated this, and "stirred up his desire," and asked Timi to suck his penis. He says that he was frightened the first time he had relations with this boy, but on the one subsequent time with him and in his relations with other males he did not have any fear. Through the years following this he had a series of relationships with men and only one brief relationship with a woman, lasting two months, during which he performed three or four successful acts of intercourse with her.

Timi believed, he says, that all *māhū* engaged in sexual activities with *taure'are'a* males. He says, however, that most *taure'are'a* males do not engage in relations with *māhū*, only a small proportion. He has no desire, he says, to have sexual relations with other *māhū*, but he likes to be with them to talk and joke. His usual sexual activity is sucking the penis of the non-*māhū* partner. Although sodomy exists in the island of Tahiti, it is much rarer than fellatio. When he first came to Tahiti it was not done, he says, and it is only recently that it is being done. He thinks that it is a "non-Tahitian" practice which was brought in by the French. When he occasionally engages in sodomy, he is the passive recipient. But it is he who sucks the penis of the partner and not vice versa. He does not swallow the semen, but spits it out. He would vomit if he swallowed it. Asked if he knows about other *māhū* swallowing the semen, he says that he does not, but adds that they never talk about things like that. During the sexual act he does not have an erection. When the partner ejaculates, that is the end of the act.

He often wishes he had a woman's body. In recent years he has frequently dreamed that he had a woman's body and that a man, usually a European, had intercourse with him. In this dream he has a vagina, and the intercourse is ordinary genital intercourse.

In his single brief contact with a woman, it was she who asked that they stay together. He talks about this with a faint disgust. He says that it didn't work out as "our bodies were not proper for each other." (These are the same terms in which a hetero-sexual couple explains why they have or do not have strong sex-ual feelings about each other.) He did have erections during this relationship. He states that as a young man he would occasion-ally wake up in the night with erections which he explained as caused "perhaps by the desire to urinate." He says that he and other *māhū* of his generation were supercised.

A younger *māhū* at Papeete, in his early twenties, says that he and the *māhū* he knew, mostly of his age, were not supercised. They became *māhū* in the first place because their penises were very short. Therefore they were unable to have intercourse with women, and so had not wanted to be supercised. Apparently the avoiding of supercision by *māhū* is modern, but I have no evi-dence about this from the literature concerning traditional Ta-hiti, aside from the fact that I have found no statement that they were *not* supercised. Informants in Piri believe that *māhū* are supercised.

Timi says that a male who engages as a partner with a *māhū* is not at all a *māhū* himself, nor in any way an abnormal man. As to his feelings about being a *māhū*, "That's the way it is, that's what I am." He says, however, that he has felt some shame about washing clothes and doing a woman's work in the house, but not about his sexual behavior. This is probably connected with the fact that the external woman's role performance of the *māhū* is supported in Piri but is much less supported in Roto, where the *māhū* is exposed to much more mockery and to much more overt hostility from males than he seems to be in more traditional settings.

The attitudes in Piri about *māhū* are complex. There is gen-eral consensus among men and women that the *māhū*'s perform-ance of a woman's household tasks is an amusing, interesting, and even admirable phenomenon. As was noted, many informants, particularly some of the older, more distinguished men in the village, say that the Piri *māhū* does not involve himself in sexual activity. They feel that *māhū* homosexual behavior is unusual and disgusting. Their acceptance of the *māhū* is in relation to his nonsexual activities. Even though some men, such as Oro, talk of the superior pleasure involved, there are no reports of any men for whom sexual relations with a *māhū* is a constant or even a frequent behavior. Probably only a minority of men in the village have engaged in this kind of activity, and no one is reported to have had contact with a *māhū* more than a few times.

When people are asked to evaluate *māhū*, they usually say in Piri that they are "natural," and that therefore moral evaluations don't apply. There is no consensus about how the *māhū* gets to be a *māhū*, since this is not an issue for "natural" things, but the explanations tend to be in terms of something which has no connection with the *māhū*'s will or moral worth. Some people say he is born like that, and that the tendency to be somewhat effeminate runs in families and may take its full form in one member of the family after birth. Other people say that it is due to adults' amusing themselves with the child by dressing him in girl's clothes, and that this establishes the habit.

Boys and girls are sometimes teased by adults by being called *māhū*. Sometimes, as in the case of Marita, an eleven-year-old girl in Piri who wore boy's clothing, this was often a fairly bitter teasing. This kind of teasing or mocking is directed against the behavior. Sometimes the term *māhū* is used with timid preadolescent or early adolescent boys as a mild goad to get them to be more daring or courageous.

Tetua, the *vahine* of Manu at Roto, used to refer constantly to Flora's three-year-old son as *māhū* when she was talking to him, for no reason obvious in the boy's behavior. Flora accepted this with apparent amusement. In this case I had the vague feeling that Tetua was trying to coach the boy into being a *māhū* rather than to tease him out of being one. Tetua, by the way, was the best friend of the Roto *māhū*. A series of pushes from the child and pulls from some members of the community may well be involved in the filling of the *māhū* role.

Although allowing the child to dress in the clothes of the opposite sex may be seen as a sign of encouragement of role development by the parents, or at least as a sign of passive complicity, this is not the only factor in the parents' compliance. In certain of its aspects the will of the child is considered to be irresistible. A child who demands forcefully enough to wear clothes of the other sex, as Timi did, might be allowed to do this even if the parents disapproved.

In recent years a new word has been introduced to refer to homosexuals, *raerae*. Its origin is unknown, although Timi thinks it may have been the nickname of a particular *māhū* which then became used as a general term. The word apparently was introduced in Papeete. For most people in Piri it is known as a slang equivalent for *māhū*, but some people in Papeete use it to differentiate nontraditional types of homosexuality from the more traditional *māhū*. *Raerae* refers to inverted overt physical sexual behavior of either males or females. Thus a man who lives a female role in the village and who does not engage in sexual activity would be a *māhū* but not *raerae*, whereas somebody who does not perform a female's village role and who dresses and acts like a man, but who indulges in exclusive or preferred sexual behavior with other men would be *raerae* but not a *māhū*. There is no agreement on this usage, nor, similarly, is there full agreement about the proper terminology for female homosexual behavior.

In Piri a female who is in some way like a man in terms of action or dress is a rare and mostly hearsay phenomenon in comparison with the highly visible male *māhū*. Women dressing and living somewhat as men and playing western-type lesbian roles have been known in the island of Tahiti for some generations at least, but there is no mention of this anywhere in the earliest historical descriptions of Tahiti. The Davies missionary dictionary has a word, *pa'i'a*, which is defined as "sodomy." This word means the rubbing together of genitals without penetration and is now used to refer to one of the types of female homosexual behavior. *Māhū* is considered by many to be misused for describing female homosexuals, and the term given is *vahine pa'i'a*. The existence of this word in the Davies dictionary is a vague indication that the practice of female homosexual contact may have been named, although there is no evidence for a full female homosexual role corresponding to the *māhū*. There are no reports of female homosexual behavior in Piri. In Papeete, on the other hand, transient homosexual contacts between women are said to be frequent. These are said to involve mutual mouth-genital contact or mutual masturbation. These contacts are not considered particularly abnormal or signs of altered sexuality. They involve women who also engage in ordinary heterosexual behavior.

According to the chief of the territorial gendarmerie there has, in the four or five years before 1964, been a marked increase in the number of mannish-looking female homosexuals in evidence at Papeete. He considers that this had been very rare before.

I will return to the question of the *māhū* and homosexuality later, in the context of more information about villagers' sense of sexual identity.

Conception, Pregnancy, and Childbirth

The verbal forms and some of the doctrine surrounding conception and childbirth stress the shared male and female participation in these events. It is said at Piri that the seminal fluid of the male, *pape* ("water") or *tātea* ("seminal fluid"), affects the blood in the uterus, which would ordinarily flow as menstrual blood, to form the fetus. Some people think that the woman contributes a fluid which is a result of her orgasm and which is necessary also for the conception. Conception requires the proper balance between the fluid of the male and the fluid and blood of the female. One act of intercourse can lead to conception, but it is felt that several acts of intercourse with the same man lead to a greater chance of conception; and there are some fragments of the old Polynesian belief that frequent changing of partners may decrease the possibility of a woman's becoming pregnant.

There are a variety of speculations, particularly among the young men, about what might prevent pregnancy. Such contraceptive possibilities as the woman's not having an orgasm, the woman's urinating after intercourse, the woman's washing her vagina after intercourse, a man's withdrawing before orgasm, and a variety of contradictory ideas about relations of timing of intercourse to the menstrual cycle are speculated about.

In Piri there is little emphasis on contraception. It is stated that when conception occurs and the child is not wanted an abortion can be done later, and it is claimed that there are traditional remedies which are absolutely dependable abortifacients. There are said to be medicines for inducing abortion which cannot fail if taken early enough, before the fourth month. If this does not work, it is said that various parts of plants can be introduced into the *vaira'a tamari'i* ("the uterus" — literally, "the child's place") through the vagina.[9] The general faith in the efficacy of herbal abortifacients in the face of probable evidence to the contrary is a public doctrine which seems to alleviate anxieties about unwanted pregnancies as a consequence of intercourse. It is said that abortion occurs occasionally in Piri among young girls who are still staying with their families and among unfaithful wives who are afraid that the baby's face will reveal that the father is not the man she is living with. But in fact in Piri, apparently, most pregnancies are allowed to continue, although in Roto and Tahiti in general there are reportedly many abortions.[10]

9. The missionaries, as usual, are good recorders of such things. In a letter of 11 November 1799 they noted, "the abominable sins [they] are guilty of, viz, murdering of infants both in the womb, and after they are born, the sin of Sodom and the offering of human sacrifice. Natives have a most dreadful custom of which they are often guilty, viz, the killing the infant in the womb, which they do by taking a grass stalk having a hard white stem which they cause to pass to the embryo which kills it. This they say they can do if the woman is not gone above four months. If she exceeds four months it is fairly sure to kill her. Some have expired through it" (London Missionary Society Archives).

10. In pre-Christian Tahiti abortion and (mostly female) infanticide, overtly directed toward population control, were widely practiced.

Although most girls in rural areas are said to begin having intercourse by the time they are sixteen, there appear to be relatively few pregnancies among girls of this age, which seems to be due in part to the relative sterility of early adolescence.

It is said by the older women and men that most girls are happy to be pregnant and that pregnancy is usually easy. Casual observation in the village tends to confirm this. The doctrine that "most girls are happy to be pregnant" and that "pregnancy is usually easy" in itself may have some influence on producing these states. It may also be, as will be discussed, part of a general male doctrine belittling male-female differences and special female disabilities. The same considerations may apply to the "ease of childbirth."

Intercourse continues during pregnancy, and the woman goes on with her ordinary household and field tasks until shortly before term. Women are said to acquire tastes for special foods such as unripe mangoes, and some women are said to have a desire to taste such things as soap or gasoline. The Davies dictionary has a term, *'ai'ai'fa'a*, which is defined "to eat improper things, as pregnant women do." This indicates that this was probably a precontact phenomenon.

Verbal forms for childbirth allow some male equality. The word used for "to deliver a child" is *fānau*. Some idea of its range of usage can be given by glossing it "to bring children forth." Thus a woman at childbirth is said to be in the process of *fānau*ing. A male will say "we *fānau*ed" so many children. Or he will say "I *fānau*ed that child by means of that woman." Or he may simply say "*I fānau*ed" so many children. It combines the English distinctions "to give birth to" and "to sire" or "to father." There is no term which applies solely to the woman's special role. Both men and women say that there is little danger in childbirth and that the pain is brief. Women claim that they have little anxiety before delivery. There are well-known histories in the village of death in childbirth or of extremely painful deliveries, but the doctrine of lack of danger exists in spite of this. However, extremely difficult childbirth or death of the mother or child during childbirth is attributed either to some supernatural evil influence or to a perverse will to die or not to give birth on the mother's part. Both of these evils are felt to be avoidable.

Almost all deliveries in Piri take place in the household, although an occasional difficult birth may now be concluded at the clinic at Fare. Within the last several years the old Polynesian practice of delivering sitting up has mostly been replaced by delivering in a lying-down position, which is felt to be more modern. Most of the women of the village past forty delivered by the old method. A rope is tied to the crossbeam of the house, and the woman sits holding onto the rope with her hands above her head and her knees drawn up. One helper sits to one side or behind her to massage her stomach, another in front of her to help take the baby as it appears. The helpers exhort the woman to bear down, and as the baby appears the helpers ease its delivery. During an ordinary delivery the woman will not cry out during labor. (This is related to response to pain in general, which will be discussed subsequently.) The helpers are usually female relatives, but often, for example if the delivery takes place on an out-of-the-way farm, it is the husband who helps his wife deliver.

When the placenta is delivered, the umbilical cord having first been tied and cut, it is given to the woman's *tāne*, who takes it and buries it underneath the house. Nobody knows now any reason for this except that it is an ancient custom and it is the right thing to do. It is said that it is buried in a safe place under the house because if it were placed somewhere else and someone should happen to build a fire over it, anyone approaching the fire would become blind. This is the only overt vestige of the supernatural that is connected with childbirth. Although Piri has plenty of magic beliefs and practices, they are not tied up with such things as childbirth or supercision.

Within one or two days, unless it has been a particularly wearing delivery, the woman will be up and helping to wash the baby linen and perform other child care. It will be some weeks before she returns to full work.

Menstruation

Menstruation is said to start usually at twelve or thirteen. A variety of reactions are reported. Girls are sometimes frightened, sometimes embarrassed, and sometimes happy. According to one woman, they are happy because they have heard that if they do not begin menstruating the blood will go to their heads and may kill them. This is a variety of *ma'i fa'a'i* mentioned previously in connection with the initiation of intercourse. The same *ma'i fa'a'i* can also occur if a woman is badly chilled during one of her menstrual periods. According to some older women, girls usually know something about menstruation before it starts. They hear something from their mothers, sisters, or older girl friends. But this knowledge seems to be very limited, and there were some girls, including Pua and Flora, who knew virtually nothing about menstruation; for them the onset of menstruation was shocking and surprising; it was only afterward that their mothers began to reassure them.

Menstruation is referred to as female sickness, *ma'i vahine*, or monthly sickness, *ma'i āva'e*. Menstrual blood is properly referred to as *vari*, a word which also means "mud." There is no term for menstruation which does not have a reference of sickness. Menarche, or the beginning of menstruation, is simply called "the beginning of the female illness," and menopause is "the ending of the female illness." During menstrual periods women say there are a few cases of cramps or backache, and occasionally a woman or girl will lie down because of the pain, but this is considered very rare. Mostly the women go about their housework, wearing napkins of folded cloth to block the flow. It is said that there are native medicines for menstrual pain which "always work." Pua says she had no pain when she started to menstruate, but three years later when she was about fifteen she began to have some pain. "Each time I began I had pain. I drank some medicine, that was that. There was no more pain." An hour after she drank the herbal medicine, she says, the pain went away. As she grew older the pain during her menstrual periods disappeared.

Although they work around the house during menstrual periods, some women avoid washing clothes or getting near cold water for fear of inducing the *ma'i fa'a'i*. Women in Piri avoid going to the garden lands or picking fruits or flowers during their menstrual periods. It is believed that if they touch plants it will cause an illness of the plant, a spoiling of the fruit, or a wilting of the flowers. This has nothing to do with a direct physical contamination with the menstrual blood, and washing in no way prevents this effect, which is a direct effect of the touch of the menstruating woman. Some women also avoid going fishing, for it is believed that if a menstruating woman touches the fish, this will somehow spoil it. Men refrain from intercourse with menstruating women because this might make a man sick; he might develop swelling of his testicles, or crab lice, for example. The danger is to the man, not to the woman.

The avoidance of intercourse during menstruation is ignored, as has been mentioned, in some cases where it is felt that sterility could be overcome by having intercourse during the last phase of the menstrual flow.

It is not said that menopause is a difficult period. Veve Vahine, stating that she began to stop having her periods in her early forties, mentions that she had headaches and aches throughout her body but that these had gradually disappeared. Pua states that the only thing that she knows some women are troubled about during the early stages of menopause is the fear that they might be pregnant, which would be shameful for a woman of such an age.

Women show no overt evidence of shame or anxiety in talking about various aspects of the menstrual cycle or in their overt behavior in regard to it.

5

Souls

It has been useful in psychological anthropology, following the cultural analysis of Freud, to categorize certain aspects of culture as *projective systems*, socially shared fantasies which express aspects of individual psychology, usually thought to be conflicted and unconscious. The projective systems — myth, religion, magic, and art — are situated in those aspects of group life which are felt to be minimally determined by economic, ecological, and social restraints and in which fantasy has the greatest chance of free expression.

Few people would now argue that a simple dichotomy of projective and nonprojective areas of culture is tenable. The commonsense aspects of everyday life are profoundly affected by aspects of expression, defense, and maintenance of the structures of individuals' private worlds, while, on the other hand, myth, religion, magic, and art have many formal determinants and functions aside from expressive ones. But with these evident qualifications the classical projective areas of culture are clearly essential sources of psychological analysis.

If one may speak of an "area" of group life that is practical, everyday, commonsense, and ordinary and contrast this to another "area," the "nonordinary," in which, for example, art and the supernatural might be placed (we are admittedly starting here from western preconceptions), then one may argue that the "nonordinary" plays a very limited role in contemporary Tahitian life compared with many other cultures.

The people of Piri live largely in a cool, commonsense world. They have forgotten their traditional myths and arts in large part, but the superordinary still exists in Piri and Roto in dreams, magic, and religion. Dreams will be considered elsewhere. Here I wish to consider those aspects of life which take the western gloss "supernatural." In this discussion I will separate "traditional supernaturalism" from "Tahitian Christianity." This distinction is less arbitrary than it may sound. Although there is some overlap and interpenetration, the distinctions between the psychological and social aspects of traditional supernaturalism and Tahitian Christianity are striking. They represent two realms, not only historically but within the experience of the Tahitian. This is not only because Christianity represents an introduced form, which is in some way competing with more ancient forms, but is also because it represents the continuation, apparently, of a pre-Christian distinction. Christianity has absorbed or, better, mixed with the old "high" religion of Tahiti, the religion of cosmological principles, social organization, territorial integration, and group identity.[1] "Traditional supernaturalism" continues the "low" religion, the religion of immediate personal concern to the individual and the household, the area of spirits, demons, and personal orientation and power.

We will consider the forms of belief and practice, and their personal usages for the two supernatural realms.

Traditional Supernaturalism

To refer to the "supernatural" raises the question whether there is for the Tahitians a "natural" world which is in some juxtaposition with a supernatural one. Some early writers had suggested that this dichotomy is a western rationalistic distinction. They argue that the "primitive" has a type of "mentality" or world view which is essentially magical in its logic and characterizations and that his "world" is pervasively magical. I will consider this unfashionable proposition later in connection with Tahitian thinking. Whatever "magical" elements there may be in their ordinary thinking, the Tahitians go to some length to separate an ordinary world from what we would call a supernatural one; and they had, and have, a marked tendency to try to keep that supernatural world in its place.

---

1. Although, as we shall see, Christianity also encompasses some "low" religious elements.

The physical day of the Tahitians is divided verbally into the period of daylight, the *ao*, and the period of darkness, the *pō*. By metaphorical extension the *pō* is said to be the home of the ghosts and spirits. Ralph White has very well epitomized this: "Pō, the night world, is the complement of ao, day, daytime, day world. An understanding of these two terms is very necessary to an understanding of the Polynesian ethos. Pō is the land of spirits, gods, souls of the dead, etc.; ao is the land of human beings and material things. There is, of course, some degree of contact between the two. Both pō and ao exist all the time; they are not restricted to night and day as the primary meanings might indicate. White man psychology might define pō as the world of the subconscious mind and ao as the world of the conscious mind. To the Polynesian mind the two are of equal reality" (White 1948).

They are of equal reality, but they represent *different* realities — different in terms of conception and different in terms of the feeling engendered by experiences in the two worlds.

The early explorers' reports of Tahiti presented it as sunny, non-demon-ridden, secular, lacking the "wild, superstitious, demonic rites" that some, at least, of the early explorers and missionaries had expected to find among savages. Recall Bligh's reaction to Tahitian religious behavior: "I should have reasoned that people strongly impressed with superstitious notions or ideas would be equally affected at the same rites attending them, but it is powerfully the reverse here; laughing, ridiculous questions and the strongest proofs of inattention in all the ceremonies I have met with, convince me to the contrary, and I do believe that whatever their sacred ceremonies are, they are followed up with very little reverential awe and with no respect" (Bligh 1937; 2:14).

Bligh's interpretation was that the Tahitians felt that they could deal with their gods through ritual means, "as a Roman Catholic would do to a confessor," and that their behavior outside the essential ritual was of no consequence. This is consonant with many aspects of present-day behavior. It also implies that the gods have their place and can usually be kept there.

We may consider two questions here. Under what circumstances do people in Piri and Roto encounter and make use of the supernatural world? What are the persisting beliefs about the inhabitants of the *pō* and their relations with "the day world"?

Whatever the possible personal meanings and usages which might be potentially represented in the body of beliefs available to a group, the way these beliefs are used by particular people at a particular time in the group's history is a different problem. We are not inclined to take an American's "God bless you!" in response to a sneeze as a serious incantation. We are aware of the usage and meaning to which he is putting this supernatural fragment.

One must make the same distinctions for Tahiti. Pua, for example, uses vividly described ghosts on family garden land to explain why she is afraid to go and help with the brush clearing there. She tells me, with peals of laughter, that she is lying, because she much prefers to work around the house in the village, and that this is a perfectly effective excuse. For other villagers, however, she is adding evidence for their ghost beliefs.

Related to the problem of usages of available beliefs is the danger that in describing supernatural experience and belief they will come to seem more prevalent, more experientially salient than they are. They are important background phenomena, possibilities which are alive. But as direct experience the supernatural is only occasionally encountered. An individual in Piri might encounter the supernatural personally (except for dreaming) perhaps two or three times a year. He may witness someone else's supernatural illness and, perhaps, healing somewhat more frequently. Most frequently, perhaps weekly or biweekly, he may hear about some supernaturally tinged event. This is different, for example, from the situation of western psychotic individuals who are said to be constantly inhabiting magical, supernatural worlds.

It is indeed a problem to understand why, with so much magical doctrine available, it is so *little* used by the people of Roto and Piri.

Supernatural Sensations

In the Tahitian classification of feeling states, there is a kind of fear-related feeling which is clearly separated from "ordinary" fear in terminology, in the kind of sensation involved, and in the setting in which it occurs. It is generally called *mehameha*, which may be glossed as "uncanny feelings."

Tano describes it: "There are times when you go into the bush and suddenly your head begins to swell, and your body feels changed, and you hear something, a rustling, a noise. When you hear those things, the head begins to swell. You get gooseflesh, and you think 'there is a spirit'. . . . it starts when you hear something. If you know that someone has died here in Piri and you go into the brush, you are disturbed and your head swells because you think about him and your body is different and [so is] your head and you get gooseflesh. . . . I would say at that time, that is *mehameha*. You are in an altered state, you feel *mehameha*."

I ask Tano whether if he knew the noises he heard were made by an animal he would still feel *mehameha*. He answers, "If you don't know what is causing the noise, you are *mehameha*; but if you do know, it disappears." Everyone describes the sensation of a swollen, enlarged head, hair standing on end, and gooseflesh as the body reaction of *mehameha*. Oro, who is particularly susceptible to the state, also describes sensations of heaviness in his head and body. All these sensations are said to be different from the sensations of ordinary fear in which, for example, one's heart beats fast and one has unpleasant feelings in the abdomen.

According to Teiva, *mehameha* and fear (*ri'ari'a*) are similar because they both arise inside the body. But "one becomes *mehameha* because there is something *strange*. In the case of fear, the reason you become afraid is because you think you might die."

Mehameha, then, is recognized as a specific type of feeling in a specific context, the context of the "unknown." But it is the unknown in a special sense. If the unknown, such as an unfamiliar mountain trail or a first ride in an airplane, involves "physical" dangers, one suffers from ordinary fear.

Jerome Bruner has written:

Categorizing is the means *by which the objects of the world about us are identified.* The act of identifying some thing or some event is an act of "placing" it in a class. Identification implies that we are able to say either "There is thingumbob again" or "There is another thingumbob." While these identifications may vary in the richness of their elaboration, they are never absent. A certain sound may be heard simply as "that sound which comes from outdoors late at night." Or it may be heard as "those porcupines chewing on that old tree stump." When an event cannot be thus categorized and identified, we experience terror in the face of the uncanny. And indeed, "the uncanny" is itself a category, even if only a residual one. (Bruner, Goodnow, and Austin 1956; p. 12)

It is the residual category of things that go bump in the night.

Not all difficulties in categorization, certainly, lead to a sense of the uncanny. It seems to be particularly a quality of difficulty in making those categorizations which help anchor us in "commonsense" reality — in familiar time, space, size, causal, and logical contexts. (It is not that I cannot tell a nickel from a dime which gives me the sense of the uncanny, but that I may have entered a state or "world" of which it is a quality not to be able to tell nickels from dimes.)

The sense of *mehameha* does seem to arise in situations of possible contextual confusion. It also is facilitated in these contexts by expectations of such feelings. As Tano notes, "You know that some one has died here in Piri, and you go into the brush."

Sensations of *mehameha* typically occur when one is out of the village — particularly in an uncultivated, uncleared, overgrown area — or walking in the village after dark. They frequently occur at twilight. They almost always occur when a person is alone. That is, they occur in "sensory deprivation" contexts. Often men will take a young boy with them if they have to walk through the brush because being with somebody else, no matter who, prevents the feeling of *mehameha*. Oro got feelings of *mehameha* if he walked on the village path after dark. Therefore,

"Whenever I used to go out to walk through Piri I would take another *taure'are'a* to go with me. Otherwise I wouldn't go."

The fear of being alone and its relation to uncanny feelings and the supernatural is an old and pervasive Tahitian theme. William Ellis noted in the early nineteenth century, "I have sometimes entered the large houses in Huahine, soon after our arrival there, and have seen, I think, forty, fifty, or sixty sleeping places of this kind in one house. . . . One of the reasons which they gave why so many slept in a house was their constant apprehensions of evil spirits, which were supposed to wander about at night and grasp or strangle those who were objects of their displeasure and whom they might find alone. Great numbers passing the night under the same roof removed this fear and inspired a confidence of security from the attacks their idolatrous absurdities led them to expect" (Ellis 1830; 2:67).

One of the terms for the unpleasant feelings caused by being alone is *mo'emo'e*. The term most commonly designates a feeling combining "loneliness" and "a sense of the uncanny."

The sense of *mehameha* is taken as immediate and strong evidence that one is in the presence of the supernatural. It is almost a *perception* of the supernatural, as warmth is a perception of heat. One may be mistaken, have an illusion — "It was only a rat" — but usually it directly indicates the presence of a supernatural situation.

The Supernatural as a Mode of Classification and Explanation

There are other experiences which are interpreted as indicating the supernatural. Some of them may have a tinge of *mehameha*; others, sexual dreams, for example, do not. These are experiences which are "unusual," "strange," *huru ē* (literally "of a different kind"). Here one is faced not so immediately with a sense of the uncanny, but with a set of more intellectual problems in classification. A variety of personal experiences, illnesses, misfortunes, and phenomena of nature may be included here.

These strange events are thought to involve the spirit world. Examples of the *direct* effect of individuals on the physical world — such as the harmful effects of a menstruating women on plants or the helpful effect of medicinal plants which derive their power from the *mana*[2] of the particular person who prepares them — are not strange. They are natural phenomena of the *ao* world and are "supernatural" or "magical" only by non-Tahitian analysis.

Personal experiences indicating the supernatural include hypnoid hallucinations, nocturnal sexual dreams, certain aspects of ordinary dreaming, and a variety of rare psychopathological states, such as possession states and hallucinations.

Hypnoid hallucinations are very common.[3] They occur as a person is drifting off to sleep. Typically, although his eyes are closed he can see that there is something vague in the room. He is frightened but is unable to move or to call out. The thing in the room, a spirit, approaches him and begins to squeeze his throat or to press against his chest. The person struggles to move or cry out. Finally he is able to mobilize himself. He recovers, knowing that he has been in the presence of a spirit.

Another experience thought to be clearly supernatural is the nocturnal sexual dream, usually accompanied by orgasm, of both men and women. The strong experience of reality of the dreams, as well as the orgasm, is a sign that a phantom lover has come to visit the individual.

Ordinary dreams have a status not quite natural and not quite supernatural. There is a lack of agreement about the proper explanation of dreaming. For some people it is simply the same sort of thing as thinking or imagining. But for others dreaming occurs because the soul has left the body and is wandering around in the *pō* encountering the souls of others. There are thought to be two types of dreams — ordinary dreaming, which usually occurs early in the night, and rare, prophetic dreaming, which usually occurs just before awakening. These prophetic dreams involve messages from spirits, usually ancestor ghosts. Prophetic dreams are for all, even for those who deny the wan-

2. *Mana* will be discussed later.
3. They will be discussed further in chapter 12.

dering soul theory of ordinary dreams, an experience of the supernatural, a visit to or message out of the *pō*.

The supernatural is also used to explain certain kinds of personal illness or misfortune. It is part of the realm of folk medicine and of the native healer and will be discussed in connection with the latter. It may be noted here that the supernatural, however, is by no means used to explain all misfortune or illness, but only those which have a particularly severe or bizarre quality. Thus a woman and her husband may accept her first two miscarriages as natural occurrences and only after her third miscarriage begin to wonder if somebody is cursing her. Mental illness and hysterical phenomena are usually explained supernaturally, but some mental illness is explained naturally, as a result, for example, of diving for oysters or sitting too long in the sun. It is usually the bizarre or dramatic psychosis or neurosis which is considered primarily a matter of supernatural influence.

The use of supernatural explanation for nonpersonal phenomena — that is, something not directly involved with an individual's body, psychological state, or the fate of his loved ones — is very unusual. It is applied to a few unusual phenomena of nature. Ball lightning is always, and a shooting star is sometimes, interpreted as a powerful spirit flying through the sky. Phosphorescent light, occasionally associated with rotting organic material, is also interpreted as a sign of the presence of a spirit.

Sometimes phenomena which are usually explained naturalistically are explained supernaturally if they occur in connection with some disturbing personal event. Thus a rain following the death of an individual is considered a special type of rain which is a response to that death. After the death of Tāvana's first wife, a boat sent to fetch one of Tāvana's sons approached the pier. It was raining to the right and to the left of the boat, but the boat was in a dry corridor. This was explained as a sign of Tāvana Vahine's death. At another time Toni and I were discussing his belief in the devil, while walking through the bush. Suddenly the wind which was blowing died down and it became quiet. Toni said that this indicated that the spirits had heard our conversation.

What, if anything, unifies these experiences so that they become relegated to the supernatural world, become cases exem-
plifying supernatural doctrine? In part they represent a violation
of the usual boundaries between private worlds of mental and
interpersonal events and the "natural world." In some cases nature suddenly signals clearly its response and concern; it stops
going about its usual lawful business. In others an individual becomes extended beyond his ordinary limits and conventional
order.

The Supernatural as a Human Instrument

I have considered the encounter with the supernatural through
uncanny feelings and as a principle of explanation for some
kinds of intellectually "strange" experiences. The supernatural
is also used and encountered in matters and modes having to do
with power and interpersonal manipulation. This use of the
supernatural in contemporary Tahiti is a vestige of the pre-
Christian situation in which principles of *mana* and *tapu* (tabu)
were important dimensions of social control. The nature and use
of these concepts in traditional Polynesian societies were complex and not entirely clear. (See, for example, Firth [1940],
Handy [1927], and Monberg [1966].)

Mana is related to the idea of power and efficacy, as an immanent principle in people, spirits, and objects which explains and
legitimizes that power. *Tapu* combines the idea of the sacred
(one of its contrasts is with *noa*, "ordinary") and of prohibition — and sometimes one or the other idea is predominant in
the usage of the term. *Mana* and *tapu* are related in that the
magical or political principle which legitimizes and enforces
the *tapu* is based on *mana*.

In traditional Tahiti *tapu* and *mana* were elaborated into a
system of political and social controls. The terms are still used,
and the traditional sense of their meanings still adheres to them.

Mana is sometimes used now to designate personal authority
or power. It may signify secular power, like the *mana* of the territorial governor, or it may be a supernaturally related power.
Tano, the pastor, for example, says that he has acquired *mana*

by becoming a pastor, and therefore spirits will not bother him. Tama, the *tahu'a*, believes that he has *mana* which allows him to influence spirits. This *mana* represents an influence over people or humanlike spirits.

Reports of traditional *mana* beliefs emphasized its impersonal "force of nature" quality which produced harmful results from improper contact with it. In western analyses a metaphor of electricity was frequently used: "When flow from superior positive to inferior negative occurred under improper circumstances, as when a common person came in contact with a high-born chief, there were two resultant effects: the superior was to some extent drained of potential energy; and the inferior, unsuited as a transmitter or container, was subject to various injurious effects as a result of the overload or surcharge. Hence the necessity for insulation of the transmitter and reservoir (the sacred chief or priest, for example) for his own protection and that of the higher mediums with which he was in contact (the gods), and for the protection of others, by means of tapu designed to prevent direct contact, or indirect contact through the medium of food, clothing, or other conductors" (Handy 1927; p. 28).

Handy believed that "*mana* was thought to come into individuals or objects only through the medium of gods or spirits" (Handy 1927; p. 28); and Firth found such a belief in traditional Tikopia. But once it had entered an individual or object, it then (according to these accounts of beliefs) acted directly.

Whatever the traditional Tahitian belief may have been, there is little presentation now of the belief in the harmful effects of contamination, of violation of a prohibition, or of curses as being the direct, unmediated effect of *mana*. The *mana* of a person or an object almost always is said to cause ill effects by its relation to intervening spirits with minds and wills of their own, who are the ultimate effective agents.

There are a very few examples of a doctrine of direct effect. One person, the wife of Tano, told me she thought that the bad effects of displacing a boundary marker between two properties were due simply to its *mana*. (Such markers are prayed over by the pastor, so that they might become invested with *mana*.) But

Tano himself and all other informants believe that the efficacy of such markers and the ill effects (illness, misfortune) following violation of ancient sacred places, of disturbing old stone spirit images, and so forth, were caused by God, the ghosts of ancestors, or spirits who concern themselves with such objects. The *direct* effects of *mana* or of contaminating forces (e.g., the effects of menstrual contamination) seem to be considered mainly as aspects of the natural world, of day world cause and effect. The true supernatural is, for the most part, peopled.

Supernatural sanctions bearing on violation of boundaries and rules and the lese majesty of inadequate respect for sacred matters persist in beliefs about the dangers of disturbing formerly sacred places and objects and in some beliefs about Christian matters which I will consider later in this chapter. In those aspects of daily life which are not specifically involved with Christianity and the church the supernatural as an instrument is mostly a matter of curses and of healing practices.

Informants in Piri and Roto make a distinction between the curse of an ordinary individual who happens to have some *mana*, usually owing to a powerful guardian ancestor spirit, and the curse of a specialist in magic, the *tahu'a*. Ordinary curses are a type of *tāho'o*, a word which means in general "dirty trick" but which also has in certain usages the meaning "to get even." They are said to be brought about almost entirely by women and are usually directed toward people with whom the women have intense personal relationships, particularly their husbands. The *tāho'o* curse usually follows a serious argument in which the wife, enraged, says, "You will see what will happen to you now." Many men receiving such a threat will not go fishing or do any dangerous work until they have made up with their wives. One man, in the inland part of Piri, did rashly go fishing after such a curse and, he reports, fell out of his canoe and was bitten by a shark. (The wound and scars subsequently miraculously healed.) What has happened in such cases is that the spirit of a powerful ancestor of the woman has overheard her angry words and arranges the calamity. A woman who can make such curses effectively is said to have a "poisonous mouth." Such curses are said to be very uncommon and an indication that the woman feels overwhelmed and unable to deal with her husband. Women purposely try not to express their anger in the form of a threat in *words*[4] (angry feelings alone will not cause a curse) for fear of a serious result. This is particularly true if a woman is angry with a daughter or daughter-in-law who is pregnant or who has young children. She does not want to be responsible for any calamities. She is also constrained by the belief that a curse may be turned back on the curser through the agency of some other spirit and that it is thus dangerous for an ordinary individual to initiate a curse.

Serious curses, curses with life-threatening effects (the result of the *tāho'o* curse is usually, though not necessarily, some relatively lighter discomfort) are thought to come from individuals with special skills and with special types of relationships to the spirit world. These are a special class of *tahu'a* ("expert"), those who deal with spirits. In the Tuamotus and the Marquesas there are believed to be evil *tahu'a* who specialize in destructive curses and black magic. They are called *tahu'a pīfa'o* (*pīfa'o* means "curse"),[5] and they often use exuvia magic, gathering sand on which an intended victim has walked, or spittle, urine, nasal mucus, or cuttings of hair from the victim. (According to a Marquesan informant, even with the use of exuvia a spell is effective only because of the aid of spirits.) Although these Marquesan and Tuamotuan customs are well known to the people of Piri and Roto, there are not believed to be any specialized evil-doing Tahitian *tahu'a* of the type of the *tahu'a pīfa'o*, nor is there any exuvia magic whatsoever.[6] There is, instead, thought to be only

4. Or in articulated thought. The reasons for this will be discussed later.

5. Its root meaning is "a barbed hook," and its use as "curse" is metaphorical. As Ellis noted, *pīfa'o* "is indicative of the condition of those under the visitation of evil spirits who were holding them in agony as severe as if transfixed by a barbed spear or hook" (Ellis 1830; 2:227).

6. Exuvia sorcery existed in pre-Christian Tahiti, and its absence now in Piri and Roto is of particular interest. Ellis, for example, writing on Tahitian sorcery, noted: "It was necessary to secure something connected with the body of the object of vengeance. The parings of the nails, a lock of the hair, the saliva from the mouth, or other secretions from the body, or else a portion of the food which the person was to eat" (Ellis 1830; 2:228).

one kind of public practitioner, called simply the *tahu'a*, who is primarily a healer but who, if he should be angry at someone, can curse him effectively through the help of his spirit servants. The *tahu'a* who are known to the people of the two communities are real people, who for the most part perform a *tahu'a* role. The helping *tahu'a* occupies a genuine village status which is perceived in rather similar terms by the occupant, his clients, and the villagers in general. The hurting activities of *tahu'a* seem to be more of a fantasy. Nobody has ever seen such activities, nor does anyone know a person who has confessed to such cursing.

Hurting *tahu'a* are said to be sometimes relatives who have *tahu'a*like skills and sometimes nonrelated *tahu'a* who have some personal grudge against someone or who are, rarely, acting for a client. Relatives with *tahu'a* skills often are in an intermediate position between the poison-mouth family curser, aided by a family ancestor, and the fully committed *tahu'a*, such as Tama, who will be described later. That is, they are thought to control various spirits and to have achieved more power than the person using a family-powered curse. They *want* to use supernatural power and may strive to increase it. They differ from the *tahu'a pīfa'o* in that they are considered much less evil and operate within their own family. Their jealousy or disapproval of a family affair is often said to have some legitimacy, even though their methods are unpleasant. As opposed to the helping *tahu'a* and the "poison-mouth" curser, they seem to be a largely imaginary category.

The supernatural in its relation to action, to control, and to magic appears now in infrequent curses related to family dynamics and controls, in some sanctions involving the church and land, in vestigial ancient sanctions (disturbance of shrines and stone images), and in healing.

The supernatural is *not* used, as far as I was able to find out, in positive magic — that is, in charms or incantations for good luck in, say, fishing or love.[7] Magic now is believed to be used either harmfully or else curatively after a problem has occurred.

---

7. Villagers who had worked in Melanesian New Caledonia were impressed and surprised by the use of positive magic there.

Some Elaborations of
Traditional Supernatural Beliefs

There is a Tahitian word, *piri*, which designates a curious or wondrous occurrence. *Piri* include riddles ("Hard hat on top, food inside; what am I?" — "A reef snail"), legends of the remarkable accomplishments of traditional heroes such as Maui, and curiously shaped holes in mountain rocks where some ancient hero flung his javelin. Within the range of *piri* are the set of curious and remarkable occurrences which have to do with the spirit world. Such an occurrence is often said to be a *peu*, something involving a creature or influence from the *pō*, or dark world. As I have noted, there is thought to be a realm of being for the disembodied intelligent forces, the *pō*, which is, however, in contact with the everyday world, the world of the "day," the *ao*. For religious purposes, as we shall see, the *ao* is contrasted as "this world," *ao nei* — the world of everyday life *plus* the spirit world — and *ao rā*, "that world," the world of God and the angels and of the Christian afterlife.

The traditional Tahitian pantheon of supernatural beings, as was generally true throughout Polynesia, was divided into rather distant high gods — representing cosmological explanatory principles, some acting as patron gods of a district or larger political unit — and a host of local and familial tutelary and mischievous spirits of considerable concern in the day-to-day life of individuals. Although Christianity has generally replaced the high gods, the local, lower-level spirits have persisted, although modified as *peu*. Some of these beliefs were supported by biblical demonology (and later by such movies as *Dracula*, a great favorite in Papeete and Uturoa movie houses) and by the tendency of the missionaries to accept the reality of Tahitian spirits. Ellis, one of the most thoughtful of the early missionaries, evaluated the question. He notes that "sorcerers pretended to be able to inflict the most painful maladies, and to deprive of life the victims of their mysterious rites." He then goes on,

It is unnecessary now to inquire whether satanic agency affects the bodies of men. We know this was the fact at the time our Saviour appeared on earth. Many of the natives of these islands are firmly persuaded that while they were idolaters their bodies were subject to most excruciating sufferings from the direct operation of satanic power. In this opinion they might be mistaken, and that which they regarded as the effect of super-human agency, might be only the influence of imagination or the result of poison. But considering the undisputed exercise of such an influence, recognized in the declarations and miracles of our Lord and of his apostles, existing not only in heathen, but Jewish society, and considering in connection with this, the undisputed dominion, moral and intellectual, which the powers of darkness held over those that were entirely devoted to the god of this world, it does not appear impossible, or inconsistent with the supreme government of God, that these subordinate powers should be permitted to exert an influence over their persons, and that communities, so wholly given to idolatry of the most murderous and diabolical kinds, should be considered corporeally, as well as spiritually to be lying "in the wicked one" . . . some of the early Missionaries are disposed to think this was the fact. (Ellis 1830; 2:225-26)

The inhabitants of the spirit world now are generally of two kinds. The ordinary ones which gather around the village and are most frequently encountered as *peu* are *tūpapa'u*, or ghosts of formerly living people. According to the late eighteenth-century and early nineteenth-century reports, *tūpapa'u* originally meant corpse. Its shift in meaning to ghost accompanies a general simplification and condensation of the supernatural categories of the old culture. A *tūpapa'u* is the postdeath state of the *vārua*[8] ("soul") of a living person. The *vārua* inhabits the body during life, although it may wander during dreaming. Death and unconsciousness, which are both named *pohe*, are caused when the *vārua* leaves the body. If the *vārua* returns to the body, it is only a temporary death; if it leaves the body for good, it is a permanent death.

There are complications in the theory of the *vārua*, probably caused by the introduction of Christian theory. In ordinary discourse the *vārua* is assumed to become a *tūpapa'u*. But in the

8. *Vārua* is also used for "spirits" in general.

more restricted context of Christian discussion the soul is assumed to go to God's right hand to await Judgment Day. When people are confronted with the apparent contradiction in these two theories of the soul, different answers are given. Tano's answer is, "What is the use of speculating on these things? There is no profit in it. We have no way of knowing." For most others the explanation is a theory of two separate souls: the explanation is that at death a "true soul," the *vārua mau*, goes to God's world, while a second soul or spirit inhabiting the body, sometimes called the *vārua toto*, which seems to have no other existence except to solve this problem, becomes a *tūpapa'u*. *Toto* means blood, and this designation is sometimes explained in terms of the blood which a powerful evil spirit spits out if he eats a *tūpapa'u* and sometimes in terms of the fact that dead people have no liquid blood in their veins and it is thus the blood which has been transformed into the *tūpapa'u*.

There are two other explanations for the double theory on the fate of the soul. One is that the transformation into a *tūpapa'u* has nothing to do with a spirit, but needs no continuing substance. Others, more specifically influenced by biblical demonology, such as the deacon, Teiva, say that the spirits of the dead are really demons who were created at the beginning of the world and who take the form of dead people. But these same people, out of the context of Christian theoretical discussion, deal with the *tūpapa'u* as though they were some kind of direct essential extension of a former living person and not a masquerading demon.

A *vārua* turned into a *tūpapa'u* will wander endlessly around the village, with occasional long trips to other places in the world, in a relatively bland and pleasant existence. The only danger that might befall it is to be eaten by some rare malevolent spirit, a *vārua 'ino*, which will then spit out the blood of the *tūpapa'u* onto the ground or onto a housetop, the *tūpapa'u* having been annihilated in the process[9] — an accidental fate which

9. This is in contrast with the traditional beliefs in being eaten as an act of "purification," which were noted in connection with the symbolism of eating.

has nothing to do with an individual's behavior or qualities before death. A few people look forward with some anticipation to becoming a *tūpapa'u*, as it will be interesting and give them an opportunity to see new things; but most seem not to think very much about it in terms of their own future transformation, although they are interested in *tūpapa'u* in general.

Tūpapa'u have the same moral characteristics as the living person from whom they were derived, although the transformation makes them uncanny and distinctly unhuman and no longer objects of affection. Good people make benign *tūpapa'u*, and bad people make mischievous and moderately evil *tūpapa'u*. Thus it is felt that the ghosts of the dead of many generations ago are more disturbing to living people than the ghosts of those recently dead, because the ghosts of the recently dead are spirits of people who were more enlightened and less barbaric in their ways of life and thought. In general, even bad *tūpapa'u* are not particularly troublesome, and an insult or an attitude of indifference can render them harmless. Occasionally a very evil person, dying full of hatred and feelings of vengeance, can be transformed into a particularly effective and malevolent form of *tūpapa'u*, a process called *'aiaru*. This kind of transformation, which can cause sickness and death to members of the family and to other villagers, must be quickly dealt with by digging up the body and turning it on its face or sometimes by cutting its throat or burning it.

In addition to the ordinary ghosts of the dead, there is another set of powerful and active spirits. These include the ghosts of ancient heroes or men of eminence, *'aito*, who act as guardian spirits over their descendents. They protect sacred places and come to the aid of individuals when called upon in times of need. These are the spirits who effect the *tāho'o* curses. There is also a set of now ill-defined powerful spirits which were never the souls of living people. These are vaguely suspected of being evil and of being dangerous to living people and to ordinary *tūpapa'u*. They manifest themselves as glowing lights and strange atmospheric phenomena such as ball lightning or, more rarely, as human forms of peculiar and frightening size and appearance.

They are considered to be much more rarely confronted, and of considerably more power than *tūpapa'u*. The heroes' spirits and the never-alive spirits are sometimes grouped as *vārua 'ino* ("bad spirits"), although when this term is used for the district or ancestral *'aito*, it does not seem to have any clear negative connotation, and such a spirit is talked of positively as being a good and helpful phenomenon. Some people refer to such a spirit as a *vārua maita'i* ("good spirit"), but this designation is usually used for the Christian "Holy Ghost."

Spirits and ghosts are mostly encountered, as I have noted, as presences in wild, uncultivated places after dark or around graveyards or old sacred ruins. Most encounters can be easily dealt with. One leaves the ruin or grave to stop disturbing the spirit. A chance encounter with a spirit or an encounter with a spirit who has some evil intention, who has entered one's room at night as a strangler or as a sexual seducer, can be dealt with by a method which is understood and considered effective by all informants. First one must prevent oneself, as much as possible, from feeling fear. The average spirit is effective only to the degree that the person he confronts is "weak" and fearful of him. If in one's consciously organized thoughts one can state that one is not afraid, one is relatively invulnerable. One must also swear at the spirit and insult him. One must call him a "stinking dog" or a "pig." He will feel ashamed and go away.[10]

Thus the spirits which are ordinarily encountered are not particularly powerful or dangerous if one is careful not to become emotionally concerned (*ti'aturi*) with them or to allow oneself to think fearful thoughts and if one shames them.

The spirits and ghosts who are not so easily managed are much rarer. Although it is sometimes said to be a matter of chance encounter, for the most part the unmanageable spirits are thought to be guided by *tahu'a*-instigated activity. As such activity is usu-

---

10. Note the European parallels in Luther's dictum: "The best way to drive out the devil, if he will not yield to texts of Scripture, is to jeer and flout him, for he cannot bear scorn." And Thomas More's, "The devil . . . the proud spirit . . . cannot endure to be mocked" (quoted in C. S. Lewis, *The screwtape letters* [1961], epigraph).

ally motivated by some social breach — arousing somebody's jealousy by bragging or becoming too visibly rich or powerful, by violating an incest tabu, or by stealing somebody's property or usurping his land — much of this kind of spirit encounter can be avoided simply by behaving properly in these regards.

In these more serious cases, one must go to a *tahu'a* for help. One cannot entirely avoid this kind of trouble, because occasionally one does anger somebody without realizing it, and also there is a small but definite chance of simple random bad luck or evil befalling someone. He may accidentally uncover a buried stone spirit image. Or he may go to a *tahu'a* for help in another problem and be chosen by the *tahu'a* as payment to the *tahu'a*'s helping spirits. He will sicken and die so that his *vārua* may be eaten by those spirits.

Spirits and ghosts can take the form of living people or animals, but more important from the point of view of personal anxiety, they can enter into people or animals and possess them. The approach of a spirit, or his attempt to strangle someone, is frightening but not very serious. It is when the spirit enters into the body that he is able to cause illness or death. Spirits, however, can also cause accidents in some ill-defined way — by causing a canoe to tip over or causing someone to fall out of a tree or to slip while using an ax.

The *tahu'a* can perform his healing or harming functions only with the aid of spirits and ghosts. They offer to help him in a kind of contractual arrangement, as we shall see. He is not effective without these helpers. And they, on the other hand, are ordinarily not particularly effective or dangerous without the direction and control of the *tahu'a*.

The Tahu'a

There is no *tahu'a* in Piri now, and it is said that there has not been for the last twenty years. There are two or three well-known ones on the island of Huahine, all of whom are well-regarded, important men in their villages. Two are deacons, and one is the *tāvana* of a nearby district. These are all men, and are healing *tahu'a*. Most healing *tahu'a* are said to be men. Tama, the *tahu'a* I interviewed, estimated that the ratio was about two men to one woman. The much vaguer category of the *tahu'a* who are assumed to have caused curses are in the reports in Piri and Roto mostly thought to be women, and often, as I have noted, are closely related to the recipient of the curse.

When somebody in Piri or Roto feels he has a disorder or problem which requires action beyond ordinary daily coping measures, he has a number of choices, which requires that he make a preliminary diagnosis of what kind of trouble he has and to whom he should go for treatment. He can use medicines, either generally known Tahitian herbal remedies or store-bought western ones. He can go to a "natural" medical expert, either a Tahitian herb expert or a western-trained doctor. Or, sometimes along with these "natural" treatments, he may seek some kind of supernatural help. He may pray to God or, rarely, ask the Protestant pastor to pray for him. If he feels either that the nature of his problem is unclear or that it is a serious supernatural problem, he goes to consult a *tahu'a*. An act of diagnosis, then, must be done by the affected individual or his family before the *tahu'a* is consulted. Later, we will consider the diagnostic schema used by the *tahu'a* himself, which will suggest some of the dimensions of the individual self-diagnosis.

People in Piri went to one of the other districts to consult a *tahu'a* if they thought it was necessary, or one was sent for Sometimes they went to Tahiti itself. The best-known *tahu'a* in Tahiti at the time was a man I shall call Tama. The following sketch is a summary of interviews with Tama and an observation of some of his healing sessions, supplemented by generalities based on statements about *tahu'a* by people in Piri and Roto.

The word *tahu'a* meant, in old Tahitian, "expert craftsman." Thus the "herb doctor" is called *tahu'a ra'au* (*ra'au* means "plants"); the full-time sorcerer who is supposed to originate curses but who is not essentially a healer (and who is said no longer to exist in Tahiti) is called *tahu'a pīfa'o*; and the person who can become inspired or possessed, and through whom one can communicate with the dead, is called *tahu'a fa'aura* (*fa'aura* means "possessed").

The unqualified word *tahu'a* refers to the spirit doctor. He is considered *the* healer. The possessed *tahu'a fa'aura* is very rare compared with the *tahu'a* and is only rarely referred to or made use of. He is considered to be a bizarre and anxiety-provoking phenomenon, whose principal interest is as a curiosity.

Men who become *tahu'a* are often quite successful people by village standards. There are, as was true for Huahine, *tahu'a* who are village chiefs or deacons or pastors in the village Protestant church. Others, in the more modernized setting of the island of Tahiti, have been successful entrepreneurs.

Each *tahu'a* has to decide on his techniques more or less for himself on the basis of tales he has heard about others' practices or on the basis of treatments he may have witnessed. There is no formal training for the role. Nevertheless, there apparently are considerable similarities in concepts and techniques used.

Tama, a man of about forty-five at the time of my study, is a highly regarded *tahu'a*. He successfully cultivates his own garden lands and is a skillful businessman. He manages a cooperative for the production and sale of art objects, maintains a store as an outlet for these goods, runs a bar and dance hall at the yearly two-week Bastille Day folk festival in Tahiti, and is active in territorial politics.

He gave no special thought to healing or to the supernatural until twelve years before our interviews, when he had a vision in his sleep. A cloud appeared to him in this vision, and a voice came out of the cloud saying, "Heal the sick. Cure the people." Similar dreams are said to mark the onset of most *tahu'a* careers. They signify a "contract" with supernatural forces which gives an individual the power to cure supernatural illnesses. They also signify that the *tahu'a* does not seek his power, but is approached in spite of himself.

Most people talking about *tahu'a* say that their contacts are with spirits and that they must pay the spirits by occasionally letting them eat the soul of an innocent client and by having them eat their own souls when they die. Tama says this is true for other *tahu'a*, but that he himself uses only Christian spirits such as angels. He heals, he says, through Jesus Christ, "the greatest *tahu'a* of them all."

The day after his vision he discussed it with his pastor, who said that perhaps this was a message from God and that he should try healing. A few weeks afterward he was speaking with a man who had a swelling in his neck. Suddenly the idea "came into his head" that certain plants would be helpful for treating it. The man tried the plants, and soon the swelling disappeared. Similar attempts followed, with success, and he began to see more and more people and to work with more difficult illnesses, spirit illnesses. His fame as a *tahu'a* began to spread.

Tama is sent for by the client or his relatives if the client is very sick, or else the client and relatives will go to Tama's house. He leaves his door open, as most *tahu'a* are said to do, so that people passing by can see what is going on — that it is not anything evil or harmful. While the client is being worked with, relatives, friends, and neighbors sit in the same room, watching but also gossiping and joking about unrelated subjects, seeming to pay close attention only during the more striking parts of the process.

Tama's patients are more often women than men. Most of the people who come to see him have spirit-caused illness. Women are more vulnerable to this because they have weaker wills and less self-control, and the average spirit, as I have noted, can only affect someone who is concerned with it, who worries about it and shows his fear of it. Someone who is strong enough to say, "I will not take you seriously; go away," is relatively invulnerable. But children are also infrequent patients, and most of his clients are over fifteen. This requires a little more sophistry in the explanation: children are less vulnerable to spirits because they also do not concern themselves much with spirits or worry about them; it is not strength of character that counts for children, but lack of anxious concern.

When he first sees the client, Tama asks him to tell his story; from the history and from observing the client during the first few minutes, Tama determines the nature of his trouble.

A rough approximation of Tahitian major classes of disorder is in terms of proximate causes. Thus there are natural disorders, *mai'i mau* (e.g., sunstroke, falling from a tree, measles) which, however, may or may not have had some supernatural distal cause leading the individual to become involved with the natural sequence. But, regardless of the distal cause, natural disorders can be cured by natural means. Next there are those illnesses which are caused directly by spirits, *ma'i tāpiri*. Finally, there is a vague and rare group of illness caused most directly by some serious affront to God or the natural order.

Tama's first problem, then, is to find out which category of illness he is dealing with. The diagnosis is made by the circumstances in which the illness occurred, by its nature, and by the observed behavior of the client.

Usually the circumstances under which the disease occurred are a minor part of the diagnosis. If the form indicates a *ma'i tāpiri*, then the *tahu'a* searches for a plausible explanation for it in the client's experiences. But certain circumstances are independent evidence — sickness following the death of a close relative, an incestual liaison, a serious argument between spouses or between a person and his parents are strongly suspected of being *ma'i tāpiri*, even if their form may resemble *ma'i mau*. (These circumstances are, of course, presumptively strongly stressful, and just those in which we would expect psychological components in any subsequent illness.)

Tama also looks for certain features in the description of the disorder which indicate its spirit nature. For example, the illness may be or be associated with a sleep disturbance. The client may have recurrent bad dreams of being chased or being hurt. Often he may wake and find himself unable to move. He may see some figure in the room which approaches and tries to choke him. He tries to call out and cannot.

The nature of pain felt aids Tama in diagnosis. Pain in *ma'i mau* stays in one place; pain in *ma'i tāpiri* shifts from one part of the body to another. Women often complain of shifting feelings within their abdomens. Frequently the client has had feelings of being chilled without any fever. Fever is rare in *ma'i tāpiri*.

Visions, involuntary movements, weakness, loss of interest in life, anxiety, and phobias all indicate supernatural illness to Tama.

Another much rarer type of supernatural illness is chronic wasting and disfiguring illnesses which, particularly if they have some bizarre quality (such as an unusual skin disease), are interpreted as spirit-caused.[11]

Having heard the history from the client and his family, Tama then gets further clues from watching the client lying before him. If the client has a spirit illness he may resist lying down. He will suddenly sit up or try to run away. This is because the spirit which possesses him fears the treatment. As he lies still, his arms and legs may begin to move "by themselves." Sometimes he begins to speak with an altered voice, as though some person or an animal were speaking through him. His pain may shift from one place to another as he lies on the mat. Sometimes he seems to have difficulty breathing.

On the basis of the story and of the client's behavior, Tama will get a feeling about the kind of illness involved, even if the signs are not entirely clear. Suddenly the understanding of the case "jumps into his head." He is now certain about its nature.

If he decides that the case is a nonspirit illness, a *ma'i mau*, he may prescribe an herbal medicine; or if he believes that western medicine can better deal with this kind of case, he tells the client to go to the western hospital or to a western physician.

When he prescribes herbal medicines, even though this is not primarily a supernatural matter (although the potency of the remedy does have some supernatural aspects), Tama's special powers may give him insight about the best remedy. He has collected and written down hundreds of detailed herbal recipes in his trips around the islands. They give in minute detail the exact amounts of the eight or ten herbs and plants which may be used in one concoction, how to prepare them and mix them, exactly how much to take and at what intervals. Whatever the degree to which the actual contents of the remedy are active, preparing

11. Tama, if he is unsuccessful with such illness, will urge the client to go to a western physician. A generally pragmatic attitude toward trying what will work independently of the theory behind it eventually causes many people with unsuccessfully treated spirit illnesses of this nature to seek western treatment.

them is a time-consuming and presumably anxiety-absorbing act.

Another remedy for *ma'i mau* is vigorous deep muscle massage. This, like herbs, may well have been tried before the client comes to see Tama, but he may recommend more of it. It will be done by a member of the family or someone in the village skilled in massage.

Illnesses may be a mixture of *ma'i mau* and *ma'i tāpiri*, in which case herbs and massage or referral to a western practitioner may be combined with procedures directed toward the spirit aspects of the illness.

If the client has a *ma'i tāpiri*, this indicates to Tama that a spirit has entered the client's body in an attempt to harm him. There are many reasons why this may have happened. Someone may have been angry with him and asked the spirits of dead ancestors to curse him; the client may have wished to die and prayed to an ancestor's spirit to help him do so; he may have mourned too intensely for a recently dead loved one, thus giving the dead person's spirit power over him; he may have gotten involved with an ancient stone idol, inadvertently digging it up or kicking it in the brush; or he may have offended an evil *tahu'a*.

If it is suspected that the illness arises out of an injury done to someone else, the *tahu'a* may ask the client to name the people he has offended and describe the wrongs he has done them. This is in front of the audience of family and curious villagers. Sometimes he may be requested to go and ask the injured person's pardon and then return for treatment if it is still necessary.

The diagnostic-treatment session begins with a prayer by Tama, who then asks the client to tell his story. The client lies supine on the mat, with Tama sitting behind him with his fingers pressed lightly above the client's eyes. Tama keeps him like this for ten or fifteen minutes, watching him. Tama has put some perfumed coconut oil on the client's fingers and toes. This is to ease the exit of the possessing spirit, if he turns out to have a *ma'i tāpiri*. He asks the patient to let his mouth gape.

Now the patient with *ma'i tāpiri* may begin to move. His arms and legs may twist or rise in the air. He may begin to moan. Sometimes he talks incoherently or grimaces.

Tama, sure of his diagnosis, now explains the possession and its cause to the client and the onlookers. Then he sits quietly watching the client's behavior and concentrates on God.

He may touch, rub, or tap different parts of the client's body, especially the extremities. If the client begins to become too active, he stops the session by saying quietly, "That is enough." The theory is that a violent spirit must be treated over several sessions, or else the patient will die; too much excitement is dangerous.

If the session is considered incomplete, either because Tama feels the strength of the possessing spirit requires more treatment or because, even though he has seen no "strange" motility, he still believes it may be a case of *ma'i tāpiri*, he asks the client to come back another time. He rarely sees anyone more than two or three times, and often one session is enough.

Usually, after watching the expressive "possessed" behavior of the client, Tama chases the spirit out with words and with the help of tapping or massaging the extremities. He then says to the client, "All right, it is finished." The client stops moaning or writhing or, if he has shown no expressive behavior, simply gets up. This is the end of the treatment. The client goes away, presumably feeling better.

The Tahu'a *as Healer, and Some Preliminary Psychological Abstractions*

If such procedures are helpful, then one may ask why. To speculate on the question of *why* in connection with any of the phenomena I have been describing requires a shift in discourse. In these first sections of the book I have tried to minimize theoretical speculation in favor of description, albeit a description often influenced by covert theory. I will now begin to mix speculation with description, speculation toward developing a model which may to some degree explain and unify some of the described patterns. Much of this speculation will involve generalizations based on material scattered throughout the book, often, unfortunately, in sections subsequent to particular discussions. These are necessary problems of slicing impressions and observations into books.

To approach the question of *tahu'a* effectiveness one may note some qualities of the *tahu'a* role and of the treatment session and its context. I have indicated that the *tahu'a* is a successful, competent, this-worldly man. He represents a priestlike model of control; he is not a model of discharge, of the uncanny, of the other world, or of repressed motives, feelings, and images. He is, that is, symmetrical with what I shall argue to be ideal attributes of Tahitian identity, rather than being complementary and representing forbidden or suppressed aspects. The symmetry extends to the details of his role. Tahitians of Roto and Piri admire skill, restraint, and casual, low-key mastery. They fear naked power, which is considered dangerous to both its possessor and others. Thus the *tahu'a* must have his powers thrust on him, without really having been ambitious for them. He must use them casually for no pay or apparent reward and must not brag about them.

The Tahitian distrust of power explains in part the suspicion that very possibly the *tahu'a* is at the core in some way bad or dangerous and will suffer an unpleasant fate. Tama, for example, is *more* effective in general than a Tahitian should be — and thus runs the risk of supernatural sanctions himself, not to mention envy and gossip.[12] People's ambivalence toward *tahu'a* does not prevent them from having personal relationships with them and from making use of them as therapists. But it does mean that they will use them as an unpleasant necessity and will separate themselves from them as soon as possible.[13]

12. Note that to some degree the idea that his effectiveness results from his *mana* makes it more tolerable to his neighbors than ordinary "inflatedness" would be.

13. Inversely, people often *continue* to have "normal" relations with people they suspect of having instigated curses. Thus in Piri curses were thought to be due to the *tahu'a*like skills of the mother of the wife of the village schoolteacher who, disapproving of her daughter's marriage, caused her to have a series of miscarriages; and to Teiva's first *fa'aea vahine*'s father, who, also disapproving of the relationship and being angry at her, caused her to die in childbirth. After the schoolteacher's wife's miscarriages she went to her mother's house to recuperate. Similarly Teiva kept on good terms with his father-in-law. The explanation given by Teiva and the school-

The *tahu'a* is not subject to possession, hallucinations, or bizarre actions. He has had the minimum of supernatural experience necessary to validate his profession. The limited loss of control, regression, and catharsis which occur for the *client* during the session are in the context of a protective, controlling figure and not in imitation of an expressive, discharging one.

Not only is the *tahu'a* a person who is in control of disruptive forces, but he himself is under considerable informal control from the client's relatives and the community at large. His open door and community visibility and the presence of curious neighbors during sessions indicate his responsiveness to community ideals and shame sanctions.

The relatives of the client and the client himself also have some control over the procedure. The *tahu'a* discusses his opinions with them. He asks their permission to try exorcism if he feels that it is necessary. Village discussions of *tahu'a* healing procedures usually stress that he is acting as an agent for the family.

Treatment is a triadic — client, *tahu'a*, community — rather than a diadic process. And in it, in keeping with the public participation, intrapsychic and intimate *private* interpersonal elements are generally disguised and supressed, while *public*, group-related ones are emphasized.

In the course of his discussion with the *tahu'a* the client's situation is interpreted to him in two different ways. Insofar as there are distal social causes of his discomfort, particularly the disturbance of some relationship, these are labeled clearly; and occasionally he is advised to take action to heal the disturbance. The proximate explanation for the disorder is spirit possession. This explains and interprets immediate body sensations and functional changes. Such explanations deflect attention from personal emotional response and shift the locus of attention to

---

teacher's wife were similar. "Well, we cannot be really sure that they are responsible; and anyhow, what is the use of having any further trouble?" And finally, if they had really done evil they would ultimately be automatically punished.

the public world, to socially motivated spirits and their human evokers. Social disorder is interpreted clearly, and personal disorder (e.g., depression) is masked by being explained supernaturally.

Although during the session there is some expression of impulse and conflict in various motor forms, there is little expression of any direct, integrated emotion. The expression of the symbolic, dissociated affect and ideation is encouraged only enough to be encountered, labeled as supernatural, and then turned off.

The *tahu'a* sees his client only a very few times. It is a short "touch and withdraw" therapy, and no long-term relationship is set up. Chronic dependency is not encouraged. The client does not learn a new role, for example, that of the long-term patient or that of the apprentice sanctified healer.

The treatment sequence, rather, with some minor transient gratifications of dependency, of needs for attention and for self-dramatization, essentially urges the client, through the model of the *tahu'a*, through the involvement of relatives and neighbors, and through the theory of illness applied to him, back toward social reintegration at a casual, semi-impersonal level.

I must here anticipate later arguments to suggest what is happening. In traditional Tahitian culture, the socialization of children and other developmental forces tend to produce individuals who have conflicts about affiliation, dependency, interpersonal cooperation, and trust. People solve this by participating in relationships in a relatively casual and uninvolved way. Conflicts and symptoms often occur, from the opposition of poorly recognized feelings of loneliness, needs for intimacy, and feelings of deprivation and anger to dominant needs to be casual, independent and free of the domination of one's own emotions, and independent of other people. From a social point of view and ultimately from that of the individuals embedded in the system, the main danger in this conflict is a withdrawal from participation with others at least at some level. The burden of many cultural customs is, in the face of only weak internalized personal thrusts toward interpersonal and community integration and solidarity, to encourage such behavior and the return to the public world. This seems to be the theme of the *tahu'a* procedure, and in the context of the problems and meanings of his community it seems to be effective.

Tahitian Protestantism: Private Aspects

In chapter 1 I introduced Tahitian Protestantism and aspects of church membership in Piri. Here I will consider something of the quality of Protestant belief in its private shapes and meanings. As elsewhere, I am concerned with prevalent private meanings, not idiosyncratic ones. I suspect that these interpretations and usages of God and Christianity may well hold for the relatively small Society Islands rural Catholic population, but not necessarily for the converts to the millennial religions, Seventh-Day Adventists and Jehovah's Witnesses, who seem to represent some of the more uprooted and marginal people of the territory. These new religions apparently are serving for individuals a different purpose from the now traditional Protestantism, Catholicism, and (in some of the other archipelagoes) Mormonism[14] of the territory.

For the people of Piri and our segment of Roto "Protestantism" is the form in which Christianity concerns them.

The formal aspect of church activities, the kind of morality preached by the pastor, and the importance of the community of church communicants in the village noted in chapter 1 give a superficial impression that the transplantation of English dissenting Protestantism into Piri and into the church-concerned segment of Roto has been "successful."

All informants in Piri and Roto believe in God in one form or another. According to some of the older men in Huahine, it was the fashion some forty years ago for some of the more daring adults to deny the existence of God — some eddy, perhaps, of

14. As has been noted, there are two long-established churches derived from the teachings of Joseph Smith represented in French Polynesia: the Church of Jesus Christ of the Latter-Day Saints and the Reorganized Church of Jesus Christ of the Latter-Day Saints.

fashionable European atheism having reached the islands.[15] But frank atheism in the rural communities of Huahine seems virtually nonexistent now. The men who report having heard atheistic statements in their youth say that increasing "enlightenment" and better church education have overcome such sentiments now.

There was only one Tahitian on the island of Huahine, as far as I could find out — certainly the only one known to the villagers of Piri — who had completely and openly renounced all religious activities. This man, a resident of the port town, did not read the Bible or go to church, nor did he refrain from working on Sunday. He did not believe in the truth of the Bible or the existence of heaven or hell, but he believed that a distant, impersonal God did exist. He differed from other less radical skeptics specifically in disbelieving that God interferes in the affairs of this world and that one had therefore better maintain at least some essential religious behavior. This man received, as did many of the more commonly found skeptics in the more modernized island of Tahiti, the final impetus to skepticism from the conflicting claims of the active new millennial cults struggling for converts among the established Christians. After hearing a proselytizer for the Jehovah's Witnesses say that the Tahitian Protestant belief that burning a Bible would bring personal disaster was not true, but that cursing God would bring immediate disaster, he began to think that perhaps if one was not dangerous neither was the other. And he began gradually to discard the Tahitian Protestant rules and tabus. As Manu in Roto said, expressing skepticism about the existence of paradise, "Paradise and hell are only a doctrine of the pastors, and there are so many kinds of pastors." He listed seven Christian sects and concluded, "We can't trust that the truth exists in that crowd of pastors."

This response to the conflicting theories of the sects, that perhaps they are all wrong, rather than an attempt to find which one among them has the authentic truth, expresses, I think, a

15. But an atheism which, in the villages at least, was probably associated with a strong commitment to traditional supernatural forms.

general hesitancy, shared by less radically skeptical villagers, to accept the authority of others as a basis for interpreting reality unless the authority's propositions coincide very closely with an individual's own perceptions and common sense. (This skeptical attitude to "authoritative doctrine" is also related to some people's mixing acceptable bits of various religions into their private system.) Neither the statements of the village pastor nor the Bible itself were taken as absolute truths by most of my informants, but were considered the quite fallible interpretations of men; and Tano, the pastor, himself expressed considerable doubt on many biblical propositions.

If one rejects authority in Christian doctrinal matters, it seems that a belief is held because it seems intrinsically plausible or natural, because there is evidence for it, or for both reasons. Informants talking, for example, about the power of prayer which induces God to help out in personal affairs, usually give examples of successful prayers, and these examples are presented as evidence for the belief. Those parts of Christian doctrine which seem neither intrinsically plausible on the basis of Tahitian experience nor open to evidence provide, naturally enough, the parts of Christian belief accepted with the most disagreement, skepticism, and confusion.

One way of making a sketch map of the quality and usages of belief is to consider aspects of the meaning of God. I have suggested that the current realm of Christianity echoes the traditional realm of high gods who represented cosmological explanatory principles and served as patrons of districts or large political units. The patron gods of the political divisions were dealt with with a certain pragmatism. The report of Cook's third voyage noted, "As different parts of the island and the other neighboring islands have different gods, the respective inhabitants imagine they have chosen the most emminent, or the one who is, at least, sufficiently powerful to protect them and to supply their necessities. If he should not give them satisfaction they think it no impiety to change" (Cook 1784; 2:101).

Such attitudes certainly facilitated the substitution of Jehovah for the traditional gods. But the dichotomy of a high god versus environing spirits is somewhat blurred, for God now has several aspects, some very much of the realm of spirits.

We may first isolate the area of churchgoing and church activities. It is here that the social processes and social order of the village are most clearly reflected and that social and personal motives of the most diverse sort are condensed. But churchgoing, insofar as it represents membership in the "official" village church, is only very tenuously connected with the kinds of personal supernaturalism I am considering here. The established church is not seen as the only path to whatever religious goals individuals may hold. The motives and pressures to belong are largely social, in the serious sense that many village dynamics are symbolized and acted out in church forms, but there is no confidence that membership or exclusion from the Protestant congregation (or from the schismatic congregation or from the Mormon church) has anything essential to do with religious reward or punishment. Membership in one or another group may be conceived as strengthening the possibilities of religious effectiveness, but it is neither a necessary nor a sufficient activity.

There are three aspects of God with which people are involved or toward which they have to take a stand. The first is God in relation to the affairs of this world,[16] the second is God in relation to cosmological order, and the third is God in relation to the fate of the soul in heaven and hell.

God in this world has several subaspects. First there is the parochial God who is the patron spirit overseeing his special worldly realm of the church. This is the God who punishes (through bad luck or illness) people who work on Sundays or who swear falsely on the Bible. Most people, whatever their other doubts, tend to believe in this, but with a peculiar qualification. The violation of a church form is punished not because this is a violation of some natural law but because an individual has made a sort of contractual commitment to the particular rule by becoming "psychologically involved," *ti'aturi*, in it. The

16. As I have noted, there is a terminological division of "this world," *ao nei*, and "that world," *ao rā*. The latter is the realm of Christian other-world events, particularly heaven and hell.

law then becomes operational for him; it has *mana* and a subsequent violation of it involves punishment. Communicants who try to drink the communion wine but who have violated the communion Sabbath by some hostile behavior (which might have been acceptable on any other day of the week) are unable to drink the wine without spilling it. People who ignore the Sabbath day of rest and *who previously honored it* will have bad luck. Thus Protestant villagers expect that God will punish Mormons and Catholics who violate *their* (Mormon and Catholic) rules.

In this manifestation God protects his church in the same way an ancestor spirit protects his descendants.

In addition to enforcing whatever particular form of religious behavior has become sanctified for a particular individual, God also takes a limited role in the active protection of individuals in this world. This is the realm of prayer. In response to prayers God will occasionally heal a sick child or protect an individual from evil spirits. This has nothing to do with the moral worth of the supplicant. All informants believe in the efficacy of prayer for producing results for themselves in this world, even those who are firmly convinced that they will go to hell and those who do not believe in an afterlife. The prayers, which are used sparingly, are conceived as a direct manipulation of God which he accepts because you have become "involved" with him, an involvement, which as noted, gives the supplicant certain extra responsibilities and vulnerabilities in his relationship with God. In this matter of personal protection, as in parochial guardianship, God is a kind of primus inter pares among spirits. Ancestor spirits and ghosts in general can also, if entreated or prayed to, help protect an individual.

God in this world has one other special concern. Whereas ancestral spirits may help protect family interests and influence disputes between and within families, God becomes active occasionally when a certain kind of *general* order, either "natural" or "social," is breached. It is God who punishes violations of the natural limits, which for the villagers and many urban Tahitians means in particular acts involving ambition, striving, or pride. The man who wants too much, who strives too much, who is too ambitious about accumulating wealth or developing his lands, the man who is not humble enough, who is too aggressively self-confident, will be punished by God in this world. He will become ill and lose the fruits of his striving. The tribulations of Job are, for some villagers, the natural response of God to a man who has too much. The news from Europe and America of satellites and rockets and of attempts to get to the moon disturb many village Tahitians as being a violation of God's order, and they believe that hurricanes and volcanic eruptions will be caused by these violations. This God of ecological and social balance is one of the many examples of how the "Protestant ethic" was not transmitted to Tahiti along with Protestantism.

The other aspect of God that is generally accepted is God as the cosmological creator and organizer. The *tāvana* of Piri, who does not believe in heaven or hell or a personal soul (but who does believe in *tūpapa'u* as created spirits), says that he derived his belief in God from the crafted order of things. "I became certain there was a God. I saw all the things up in the sky, and that's how I came to understand. The stars, the moon, all those things – I looked, nothing fell, they kept burning, nothing changed. Then I believed that there is, indeed, a person to look after all those things."

It is in relation to God as the gatekeeper of heaven and hell, as the judge of Judgment Day, that the most disagreement and variation among informants occurs. Although a very few disbelieve in heaven and hell, most people seem to accept them. Most of those who believe in heaven and hell seem to believe that the vast majority of the *other* villagers, at least, will end up in hell. They estimate that perhaps one in a hundred or one in a thousand will be saved. They say that God's law cannot be borne by man and that most people violate it.

Although doctrinally everyone agrees that it is not only people's actions but what is in people's hearts that counts for salvation, there is a considerable difference in emphasis among individuals between the relative importance of proper acts and of a proper "inner state." Although most people interviewed agree on the difficulty of others' getting into heaven, there is a division of belief about an individual's assessment of his own fate. In general the simpler, more traditionally oriented people in the village who accept the traditional emphasis on the importance of formal, surface behavior believe that they will be saved. But the more striving, innovative, "modern" people, including Tano and Teiva, believe that they personally will probably go to hell. They emphasize that damnation is dependent upon the inner "heart," or more properly intestines, *'ā'au*, the seat of the emotions. They emphasize that no matter what people might do in terms of external behavior, most people will not change internally — they are "stubborn." God is never pictured as genuinely forgiving or understanding; and it is noteworthy that Jesus is virtually never mentioned in discussions of personal theological beliefs, except as the judge of Judgment Day.

The external rules, God's law or *ture*, which one must obey to get to heaven, are not, for those who accept external behavior as sufficient, really very complicated. People must obey what they call the "don'ts," the *eiahā*, which are the Ten Commandments. Many villagers have violated the commandments concerning stealing, adultery, and honoring one's parents. But for those who accept action as a guarantee of salvation, the goal is to have put oneself in some sort of conformity with the Ten Commandments before dying. This is a matter of reading the Bible frequently, legitimatizing one's relationship with one's spouse, establishing some household stability, and, if one is within the church, becoming a communicant. This takes care of the "true soul" while the perhaps more important part of one's personality prepares to be transformed into an earthbound ghost. But the people whom I have designated as more "modern" are not so sure that this strategy will work, and they do not seem to have any other strategy to replace it. One part of them, at least, will eventually be punished because of some given uncontrollable quality in their nature, and there doesn't seem to be anything they can do about it. The people who believe they will go to hell nevertheless believe that God will aid them in this world in response to prayers. The two matters are entirely separate.

God in this world and God as the cosmic craftsman not only is anthropomorphic, but seems to be conceived of as relatively close to human status. He is not talked about or referred to with any particular awe (nor with affection). He is sometimes referred to as a person, a *ta'ata*, and people will sometimes explain their theological opinions by saying, "Now suppose that you were God and I prayed to you." God is neither loving nor interfering. He takes action in this world only when one violates some fairly clear boundary of acceptable behavior or when one specifically asks him for help. He is a craftsman who is able to take care of this world and the people in it because he made it all, and one of the expressed motives for prayer is to thank him for having made everything.

People's overt expressed motives for their involvement with religion or with God depend upon which aspect of religion they are referring to. People stress the pleasure and entertainment value of church activities, particularly the hymn singing and the long formal discussions on the meaning of Bible verses that take place at special evening meetings, the *tūāro'i*. Most people say they first began to attend church meetings as children and young adolescents because of various kinds of social pressure from their family and other villagers, but they often state that by thirteen or fourteen they began to find reading the Bible intrinsically interesting. They stress the pleasure of stories such as those of Cain and Abel and the resurrection of Lazarus. The Bible serves them as a source of fantasy in an impoverished culture long deprived of much of its art, myths, and folktales. Others state that they had a feeling that there was perhaps some meaning in the Bible that might explain something about life. Still others read the Bible expressly so that they could perform well in the *tūāro'i* sessions.

Another expressed motive for the involvement in religion is "protection from one's own impulses to bad behavior." Teiva, for example, says that all villagers are religious (although not enough to save themselves from hell) because they remember the savage pagan behavior of their ancestors, the wars and cannibalism (matters which missionary teachings constantly emphasized when they portrayed the salvation from savagery brought by religion), and being afraid of backsliding, use religion to protect themselves from doing evil. Several informants, including the pastor, state that a rigid devotion to God's commandments is the only thing that protects them from wrongdoing, such as irresponsibility to their households, drinking, and adultery. These people believe that devotion to God's law helps inform their otherwise undependable personal judgment about how to act.

Tahitian Protestantism is a recognizable variant of Judeo-Christianity. It has, however, become "Tahitianized"; that is, congruent with the ethos and style of surviving Tahitian culture and consonant with prevalent forms of perception, cognition, and motivation of Tahitian individuals.

God in this world, for example, is conceived of and acted toward as an emotionally bland and neutral, nonintrusive, disinterested individual who becomes "actualized" if one of his rules is broken, or if he is called upon. Obeying his rules is a matter of conforming to rather simple overt behavior and of not violating social and ecological balance by being prideful and personally ambitious or too visible. He does not care about your inner states, your "real feelings" or "true emotions," but is interested in your minimally correct behavior. He has some commitment to you because he made you, but mostly he is committed to you because you have involved yourself with him through prayer and Bible reading. He will reward you essentially by leaving you alone (people can get along without any special help from God in ordinary activities), by not punishing you, and by helping out rarely in an emergency. In all this, he demonstrates the qualities Tahitian parents manifest in caring for and educating their children. He is the Tahitian parent-child relationship written large. And this is also reflected in the familiar traditional western attributes that are *missing* — the sense of a deep and abiding personal concern on God's part; his knowledge of the inner man; his capacity for compassion and forgiveness; the concept of grace, of unmerited salvation.

It is God of the next world, the judge, the potential savior, which has been the most difficult for villagers and urban Tahitians to deal with and to make meaningful. For those who can maintain a belief that God's judgment is based upon one's ability to perform some defined, definite behavior there is no problem. Such a belief allows the more traditional Tahitian to be optimistic. He knows what the rules are and can stick to them, although the doctrine of damnation does give him a chance to express usually muted village hostility in his opinions about the eventual unpleasant fate of his neighbors. Some few villagers who believe that rule-obeying behavior is the key to salvation feel that the proper behavior requires such enormous care and application, since even small errors are fatal, that they are uneasy about their ability to "carry the burden of God's law." This anxiety, as I have noted, seems to occur among the more striving, western-affected individuals who feel out of balance with the traditional present-oriented, noncompetitive Tahitian world — who feel that their striving is in itself a violation of God's laws.

But the people who have the most severe difficulties with the concept of judgment are those who have come to believe that inner feelings, the state of the *'ā'au*, are the key to salvation. The relative form and definition of Tahitians' "inner" and "outer" selves differ markedly from western personality ideals and actualities. Tahitian socialization and group process produce, as I will argue, an individual who is willing to modify his social behavior under group pressure, who feels responsible for his public actions and afraid and ashamed if his observed actions are improper. He has learned to inhibit his passions, particularly anger and possessive love, so that he will not be uncontrollably and passionately motivated toward violations of socially approved action. But it is action which counts, which defines the man. This action includes not only visible social behavior, including speech, but also formulated discursive thought. This articulation of fragmentary feelings and ideas is a process called *feruri*. (Compare chapter 8, "Thinking.") Hatred, as I have mentioned, when it is formulated, but not before, may automatically turn into a curse and hurt someone; the formulated fear of a ghost makes one more vulnerable to that ghost, and so one must "think" and act as if one were not afraid; the formulated wish to die may make one die, or the formulated wish not to die can, in non-violent deaths, prevent one from dying. That is, if you do not articulate the feelings and the fragments of thought, even though you may be well aware of them, they are relatively harmless. Impulses, desires, fragments of thoughts are nothing to worry about. The "inner self" is part of the natural givenness of things, for which the individual has no responsibility. These feelings and impulses arise in one's *'ā'au*. In the head *feruri* begins; this is willful, and it is at this point that responsibility commences. Thus, traditionally, the condition of the *'ā'au*, the inner "psychological" man, is not stressed as the important locus of the self or as a basis for reward and punishment, lovableness, or social approval. Furthermore, there is little feeling that this aspect of the self is controllable in itself, although its transformation into action is controllable.

What is a Tahitian to make of a theory of salvation in terms of the quality of, or his ability to change and improve, his inner self? He is helpless and lost, unless he believes in God's grace. But grace, as loving forgiveness, is also entirely alien to his experience of reality. The idea of a close, intense love, troubled by moral or behavioral imperfections, cool for a while, and then ready from its own will to welcome one back to a state of unconditional acceptance, has little precursive basis in experience. Tahitian parents do not commonly use the withdrawal and manipulation of love as a way of influencing children. After the child reaches three or four years of age, parents tend to become relatively cool and detached. A child is reacted to in terms of its superficial disturbing or cooperative behavior and of the moods of the parents, siblings, and relatives who are involved in its upbringing. Intense concern, educational withdrawal of love, forgiveness and understanding, intensive protective relatedness with its intimations of paradise, all this is minimized; and with it is lost an important experiential foundation for the understanding of the concept of grace and of forgiveness.[17]

17. The question of "sin" and "repentance" will be considered in chapter 10.

On a more general level Christianity provides for people in Piri and Roto, as religion does everywhere for religious men, a sense of regularity and order in the physical and social universe, a sense of ultimate meaning. They have particularized Christianity, however, in their own way, although some aspects of the doctrine resist taming. Uta, who changed from Protestantism to Mormonism, gives an excellent example of pragmatic syncretism in action: "I have discarded the teachings of Protestantism. But there are truths in the Protestant faith, some parts of it, so I have held onto them. The parts that weren't good, I have rejected. The correct elements, those I have taken and joined to the Mormon religion. I still have, of course, my faith in God."

6

Aspects of Personal Relationships

This chapter considers aspects of heterosexual, friendly, and authority relationships. The emphasis, as usual, is on the personal aspects of these relationships rather than on those aspects systematically related to social dynamics. I will discuss other elements of relatedness elsewhere (for example, love and hate in relation to "feelings"); the emphasis here is on action and on recurring forms of relationships between individuals.

Heterosexual Relationships

In chapter 4 I discussed physical sexuality. In later chapters I will discuss some "intrapsychic" aspects of sexuality, such as sexual identity. Here I wish to discuss some forms and qualities of heterosexual relationships.

The patterns I sketch here refer to Piri as it was at the time of my study and to the various Society Island settings of my respondents' youth. They were also, apparently, more or less representative of Roto and other traditional segments of urban Tahiti through perhaps the mid-1950s. The contemporary aspects of heterosexual relationships among adolescents and young adults in Roto seem to be undergoing considerable change and are not considered here.

As children boys and girls play together at the same games. In their games and activities on the village paths, on the wharfs, and in the fields at the edges of the village they are a common band. When they reach "preadolescence," between perhaps ten and twelve, they begin to separate into same-sex groups, and by fifteen or sixteen the separation is complete. The preadolescent boys begin to hang around the older *taure'are'a* boys, whereas the girls begin to become more active and responsible in household activities and to spend more of their time in the household.

Girls sometimes belong to a small group of girls of their own age, who are often related to them, but their friendships are closely tied to the household or, perhaps, to some church activity and do not resemble the male *taure'are'a* "gang."

The same-sex relationships of the adolescents are close, sentimental, and clearly manifested in public behavior. An individual will designate a close relationship within the same-sex group as a *hoa* (a "friend"). The word *hoa* is sometimes used to refer to a heterosexual partner in an established relationship; so used it has the flavor of a church-derived terminology and seems to have the stilted and formal sense of "my helpmate." In general for a man *hoa* designates a male friend, and *vahine* (or "woman") designates a partner in physical heterosexual relationships from the most casual to the most settled. Qualifying terms added to the word *vahine* can designate special kinds of relationships. Thus *vahine fa'aea* means literally a *vahine* with whom one is staying (living in the same household). *Vahine fa'a'ipo'ipo*[1] means a *vahine* to whom one is formally married. And *vahine metua* (*metua* meaning "parent") indicates a *vahine* with whom one is setting up a stable household, with the implication that raising children will be a part of the business of the household.[2] The same terminology, substituting *tāne* for *vahine*, is used by women.

As was noted in chapter 4 and in the biographical sketches, sexual intercourse often begins as early as thirteen or fourteen and is furtive and transient. For the male it involves, in a sense, furtive raids from out of the comfort and security of the male *taure'are'a* group. It is looked upon by members of the group with mixed feelings. Sexual intercourse represents a daring accomplishment, on the one hand, but on the other hand it is a

1. *Fa'aea* means "to stay, to remain" and also "to discontinue." *'Ipo* means something like "darling" or "cherished one." And *fa'a'ipo'ipo* means "to make somebody one's darling." This romantic term may have been a missionary adoption for Christian marriage.

2. It also implies that the spouse is "parent" to the household in a more general sense. It is of interest that in pre-Christian New Zealand Maori polygamous marriages of chiefs, the principal wife was called the *wahine maatua* (*vahine metua*) (Biggs 1960; p. 57).

threat to the solidarity of the group, and there is a considerable attempt on the part of the *taure'are'a* group to prevent these relationships from becoming "serious."

Most frequently a boy will have relations with a specific girl only a very few times; a young adolescent boy will tend to have relationships with several girls in the village, and a girl with several boys. After a while the boy may find himself more interested in one particular girl. Rarely a man or woman will report that he or she felt greatly obsessed or excited by the thought of the partner: this is a state called *ma'ama'a hia* (literally "having become crazy over the partner"); it is considered funny and mildly shameful. It is reported less often than the state of being "interested," usually expressed as "my thoughts became involved with her."

Except in those very rare cases where the first *fa'aea* relationship is initiated as an arranged marriage, the early "staying togethers" are considered simply that and have no implication of a long-term commitment. According to some village informants, the decision to stay together is often initiated by the girl, and there is some reason to believe that she is more hopeful for a permanent household role than is the man in some of these early *fa'aea*.

In Piri a number of very short-term *fa'aea* relationships preceding a more permanent relationship are very common, whereas in Roto it is more likely that the first *fa'aea* relationship has somewhat "more serious" motives and is expected to be long-term. There are a number of evident economic and social influences on this. In terms of expressed motives, a man in Piri tends to explain his early *fa'aea* relationships by saying that "our bodies were suitable for each other," indicating thus that they were "physically attracted" to each other. To this, men in Piri often add that the girl was good-natured and not a scold. In contrast, the explanation for the more permanent early *fa'aea* relationships in Roto, illustrated by Manu and Hiro, is a desire to begin to give up *taure'are'a* activity, to save money, to avoid waste, and to have a neat and orderly household. Men in Roto are much more likely to be either living by themselves or else living in their parents' household in a much more detached manner (working out of Roto and coming home mostly to sleep) than the men in Piri. Men in Piri, that is, are still closely tied in to their parental households at the time of their first *fa'aea* relationships.

For Piri the first *fa'aea* relationships last a matter of days, weeks, or occasionally a month or two, and then break up, often following arguments and expressions of jealousy. People reporting such episodes note that when they became uncomfortable or unhappy with the relationship, they would "seek some trouble." This trouble would provide an excuse for breaking up the relationship, would dramatize its failure, and would be a way of getting rid of the partner which would be more difficult to do if they were getting along in ostensible peace. So one or another partner would stage some small event in order to make the other jealous, or he would begin to accuse the other partner of an unfaithfulness about which he did not have any deep conviction. When the relationship was otherwise satisfactory, both partners would make some effort not to express feelings of jealousy. As Uta and others state, it is a bad thing to express ideas about jealousy, because if it is only your imagination, your *vahine* would then be tempted to do the very things you are imagining.

Most of the early *fa'aea* relationships break up quickly, but occasionally they move into a more lasting relationship. When asked why one of these early *fa'aea* relationships does *not* break up, why it has persisted, a frequent explanation is the physical one, "their bodies fit." The nature of this "fitting" is a not-uncommon subject of male conversation. Men, speculating on young couples who seem to be becoming established, comment on the relative disproportion of physical beauty between the two of them — one or the other may be considerably more attractive than the other — and one hears the comment by the people involved and by outsiders that the "fitting," the *au*, is not simply a matter of the beauty of the face, body, skin, or smell, all of which are agreed-upon elements of sexual attractiveness. The core of the sexual *au* or "fittingness" has something to do with the act of intercourse. Teri'i Tui, for example, notes that many girls who did not particularly enjoy the casual sexual relationships before *fa'aea* began to have their first sexual feelings during a *fa'aea* relationship. Teri'i Tui says cynically that they have come to believe that it is only this particular *tāne* who can produce these feelings and that this provides a bond between them. The fittingness seems to refer to all the elements which make up a satisfactory psychosexual relationship. If their "body fit" is good, people will maintain their relationships a long time even if there is considerable bickering, lack of agreement, and interpersonal tension, and even if the man, for example, feels that the woman is not a particularly adequate household keeper.

Prolonging a *fa'aea* relationship for a year or two by no means guarantees a permanent relationship. Relationships of from two to several years sometimes break up. Teri'i Tui went through three or four such relationships before he settled down with Mari. Teri'i's son Tihoni lived with a girl on her father's property on a nearby island for three years, and after the birth of their second child he left her to return to his parents' household. The first two or three years of *fa'aea* relationship are particularly brittle. There is liable to be a considerable amount of fighting and arguing and a considerable amount of anxiety on the part of one or the other partner that the other one has not yet "given up their *taure'are'a* thoughts." The free life of the *taure'are'a* and of sexual adventure is obviously a threat to the early settled couple, and any contact of either partner with *taure'are'a* friends may well be the basis for an argument and for jealousy, a jealousy that is related to a very real threat. The basic question for a man is whether he was *fiu* ("fed up") with his *taure'are'a* — whether he had enough of it. Hiro and others state that if somebody did not have enough varied sexual experience before settling down, it is less likely that he will be faithful to his *vahine*.

The coming of the first pregnancy does not necessarily cause a commitment to the relationship. Here the complex institution of adoption plays a role. There is some chance that the first child or two may be taken from them whether the parents want to give it up or not. If the relationship seems to be going in a stormy manner, somebody will ask for the child, or the mother can arrange in more or less covert ways that the child pass into somebody else's care. It is really when people begin to *keep* their children that a first commitment to a lasting spouse relationship seems to begin.

A number of the young couples in Piri have gotten married[3] some months after their first child was born as a way of sealing their commitment, but until recently marriage, which has been necessary for full status as a church member and as an "adult," was often put off until a couple had several children and seemed reasonably sure that neither would want to break off the relationship.

Generally, then, people tend to drift into long-term relationships. They have opportunities to test and to escape before they become seriously engaged.

An exception to this pattern, very rare now in Piri, is the parentally arranged marriage of a young couple. Such a marriage, which must have been much more common in earlier missionary Tahiti, involves a couple who may have had little previous relationship. It entails a considerable commitment of money and gifts by relatives (kindreds) of both spouses and a large and public church wedding. There was only one such wedding while I was in Piri and only one of the interview subjects, Taere, had had one. My impression from the histories of villagers and village opinion was that such marriages are often particularly stressful and frequently fail. In contrast, formal marriages which occur, as in the case of Pua, after a couple has been living together three or four years, often after a child has been kept, are a public affirmation and reinforcement of a relationship that is settled and likely to be successful. As I have noted, most marriages take place after a couple has been living together for many years and the people are ready to become *ta'ata pa'ari*, adults. These are small affairs, often involving only the pastor and the household. And some couples, Manu and his *vahine* are examples, never marry. They say sometimes that after all the years of living to-

---

3. "Marriage" includes a church ceremony and legal commitment under French law.

gether they would be embarrassed to be formally married. They are willing to take their chances about damnation.

Even without the ceremony of marriage most people establish permanent heterosexual relationships and households. Not counting the ,widowed, who often, like Veve Vahine, reestablish a household even in their old ages, only three men in Piri live without a *vahine*. Poria and Manoi, a spastic, live in small houses of their own, and another man, Pana, in his fifties, who "had never been able to find a woman because he was always a *taure'are'a*," lives in the household of relatives. (A fourth single man, a hostile and somewhat bizarre-acting man in his fifties whose wife deserted him many years previously, left the village shortly after my arrival.) All these people are considered strange in one way or another. At the very least, they are said to be "unable to find or hold a woman," and this seems to be considered a mild stigma. At another level, the fact that they are, with the exception of Pana, living alone (in considerable vulnerability to ghosts and spirits at night) gives them an aura of strangeness.

Marrying, as I have noted, is necessary for full church membership and is one of the things one should do before dying to avoid damnation. For those younger couples who choose to marry, it makes it somewhat harder for them to backslide into *taure'are'a*, household-threatening lives. Not only is their relationship officially sanctioned, but they become heavily involved in church activities, which further separates them from the unmarried youths.

The reason given for avoiding marriage, even by those who have been living together for many years with established households and many children, is, in addition to the embarrassment noted above, often that they are not sure about the relationship. They often say that marriage involves a promise to God. If they made this promise and then changed their minds and broke up the marriage, the consequences — that is, the supernatural retributions — might be very serious.

The question of adultery or liaisons outside the settled relationship, either *fa'aea* or married, presents somewhat different aspects in Roto and in Piri. A major variable is a matter of the increased possibility for secrecy in Roto with the environing city of Papeete at hand. Both Hiro and Manu, with considerable caution and anxiousness, admitted (in response to my probing) that they had had a number of brief and transient sexual contacts through the years following their settling down. In alluding to this they both urged me to secrecy, saying that there would be great trouble if their *vahine* found out about this.

Nobody in Piri admits to adultery with other people in the village,[4] although adultery is one of the things men say they want to do when asked whether they "have any wishes they are afraid or ashamed to act on." It seems, however, more or less taken for granted that when a man goes by himself into Papeete he may try to find a woman with whom to have sexual intercourse, and a number of men who deny any relationships in the village brag about conquests in Papeete. In both Piri and Roto it is said that adultery was more common in past generations, the generations of people's parents and grandparents, than it is now.

A serious settling down, even a relatively limited settling down, means, particularly for the man, a difficult and conflict-laden transition. At the very least it represents a movement from the "irresponsible" *taure'are'a* period toward an adulthood which is generally seen both by *taure'are'a* themselves and by adults as being wearying and less pleasant than the *taure'are'a* period. A major effect of the breakdown of the traditional culture was to deprive the male's adult role of its aspects of power, ceremony, wisdom, and adventure which had compensated for the loss of youth. The impoverishment of the life of the adult male Tahitian compared with pre-Christian times is infinitely greater than the impoverishment in the life of children, adolescents, or household-managing women. In addition to whatever symbolic problems and conflicts there are in shifting from *taure'are'a* to the

---

4. It is difficult to evaluate such reports, because people who are frank about much of their behavior are very guarded about discussing actions which would cause disturbances in present village relationships. Nevertheless, if there were adulterous relationships between people in settled households in Piri, they must have been unusual and very discreetly managed.

early household stages of being *pa'ari* is added the problem that the rewards for growing up seem fairly thin.

As sixteen-year-old Oro sees it, "*Taure'are'a* only want to enjoy themselves. But not an adult [*ta'ata pa'ari*]. His thought each morning is work. He thinks about his livelihood, [how to take care of] his flock of children. The *taure'are'a*, he doesn't trouble himself. He goes and gets drunk for days on end if he wants, and goes back to his [parents'] household to eat. That is all he has to think about."

I ask him how adults feel about their life. "Your thoughts turn to youth. You have longing thoughts. But you are adult, and work and feed your flock of children. You cannot go and have a life of enjoyment. Your *vahine* would die of hunger. You work. A new group of *taure'are'a* has come along. You see their fun, and remember, 'I was like that in my youth.' But there is nothing you can do about it. You have become an adult. You must begin again [after your longing thoughts] to work. It is a life of fatigue."

"Aren't you anxious," I ask him, "to become an adult?" "No. If only a person could stay young, it would be splendid." Many men looking back, wistfully agreed.

Settling with a *vahine*, moving tentatively toward *pa'ari* status, begins to move a man from *taure'are'a* life[5] and thus deprive him. But it also protects him from what are seen with some anxiety as wasteful and irresponsible aspects of *taure'are'a* life.

Manu, describing his decision to settle with a *vahine* because she would wash the clothes, take care of the house, and have food ready for him, says, "One decides to get hold of oneself, to stop a little bit the 'wandering life.' My life changed in that time; it was as if it went a bit back to the way it was in the beginning when I was a child." That is, for Manu and for others, settling down represents the reestablishment of the "ordered" household of their childhood. The man is giving up freedom and

---

5. Although still in his *taure'are'a* period, the man who settles down tentatively is radically removing himself from the *taure'are'a* male peer group for the time being. He may, however, return to it.

playfulness to have an "orderly life," which has some private meaning of security. At the same time, it involves responsibilities to "seek a good life," that is, to make a living. Most informants stress the ordering of their life that was involved in settling down.

Both partners tend to bring to heterosexual relationships a number of expectations, interpretations, and conflicts which make the transition into a permanent state fragile and vulnerable. But the problems get solved, in that most people establish long-lasting, generally comfortable and effective relationships; they bring up children[6] and cooperate in the necessary variety of household economic and managerial tasks.

The "order and security" of childhood has its cost. Most informants look back on childhood as a burdensome period from which they were glad to escape into the *taure'are'a* period. It is, as we shall see, an experience of considerable household pressure, of often moody caretaking (both by members of the parental generation and especially by older siblings), of severe disappointment of dependency-seeking behavior. One is taught in many ways that the way to have a successful relationship with somebody is to keep cool, not become too deeply involved, not be vulnerable. The tentative and often lengthy easing oneself into a spouse relationship reflects, I think, anxieties about being bound into a household and to a close relationship, as well as anxieties about relinquishing *taure'are'a* freedom.

Both men and women value their independence, that is, being left alone and not nagged by their partners. An ideal partner as a spouse is "kind" and "soft." Since pre-Christian times the political, social, and household power of women has been, compared with many other societies, close to the power and authority of men, and this situation still obtains. Although there are

---

6. To some degree the fact that they have had and reared children together is an overt basis for a spouse relationship. Veve Vahine, for example, refers sometimes to her first *tāne* affectionately as "the father of my [son] Pū'ātoro." She explains her feeling of lack of authority in her marriage to Tāvana in relation to his children and other kin as being because she has not had any children by him.

some pieties about women properly deferring to men, in action and assumptions about "how things really are" there is little of this, and women are actively involved not only in household management but in most village affairs; and they are involved as independent thinkers. This also adds to the tentativeness of relationships, as patterns of decision-making have to be negotiated by each couple.

Most households ultimately seem to proceed in peace. Couples work together. Arguments and yelling occur when there has been some failure — a meal not ready when a hungry husband returns from the fields, a piece of equipment lost, a husband who drinks "too much." Mostly, however, one sees in settled households respect, equality, and cooperative working together.

Friends and Acquaintances

In Piri, as I have noted, children play in groups of boys and girls. Occasionally, but rarely, a child is seen involved in some solitary activity or playing with just one other child, often a family member. These are often the very young children. As the children get older they begin to associate in larger bands. Adults sometimes refer to the members of the childhood group as *hoa* or frequently *hoa tamāri'i* ("childhood friends"). But the unmodified and unqualified word *hoa* (particularly in Piri; it is being modified in a European direction in Roto) refers to a special type of relationship, characteristically of the *taure'are'a* period. As a matter of fact, saying of an adult man in Piri that he has many *hoa* or that he spends a good deal of time with his *hoa* tends to designate him as an overaged *taure'are'a*.

Hoa is usually used to apply to those of one's own sex with whom one feels a particularly close bond during the *taure'are'a* period. For a boy they are often the group of boys with whom he goes to be supercised. The older and younger members of the *taure'are'a* generation are not generally considered to be *hoa*, though there are some exceptions. Taere, for example, as was noted in his biographical sketch, had an asymmetrical relationship with a *taure'are'a* two or three years his senior and considered him a *hoa*. *Hoa* are not siblings (as the narrow age set tends to guarantee), and from the evidence of the life histories and of contemporary Piri they are not close relatives or *feti'i*.[7] (People talking about close associates group *feti'i* and *hoa* separately.) In Piri, where most intimate activities, activities related to the household or having much personal emotion attached to them, involve either cognatic or affinal kin, the close relationships and shared activities of non-kin-related *hoa* are particularly striking.

In pre-Christian Tahiti, there were various terms for "friend," *tau'a*, *taiō*, and *hoa*. The first two of these, at least, designated a formal relationship, a "bond-friend," which involved a mar- riagelike ceremony, an exchange of names, and the establishment of a fictive kin relationship involving many of the rights and re- strictions of sibling kin relationships. Whether these first two terms also applied to some kind of nonritualized relationship and whether *hoa* also referred traditionally to a formal bond- friendship is unclear.[8]

The ceremony of bond-friendship still exists, but apparently it is now very rare in the Society Islands. According to Ben Fin- ney, both *hoa* and *tau'a* are currently used to designate ceremo- nial bond-friends, although, he says, *tau'a* seems to be the more specific term, and *hoa* is a more general term for friend or mate (Finney 1964). As I noted in the previous section, the use of *hoa* for "mate" has a highly restricted meaning and probably re- flects western, missionary ideals for the spouse as "friend." But in Piri *hoa* in its common same-sex meaning retains (among the qualities which differentiate it from the western term "friend") some of the elements of "fictive kinship," even though there is no formal name-exchanging ceremony involved in its inception.

The clearest indication of the sense of kinship involved in the *hoa* relationship in Piri is that *taure'are'a* avoid sexual approaches to the classificatory sisters of their *hoa* friends. Teiva made it quite overt. He differs from other informants in that the hetero-

7. *Feti'i* (literally "tie or bind together," e.g., as a bundle of sticks) re- fers to all people who have some kind of cognatic or adoptive kinship rela- tion to an individual or household.
8. Douglas Oliver (forthcoming) discusses the evidence relating to social forms of friendship in pre-Christian Tahiti.

sexual activities of his mid-*taure'are'a* period seem much more important to him than the activities and relationships with *taure'are'a* boys. Asked about his association with other *taure'are'a* of his youth, he says, "There isn't any value in becoming a *hoa* with them, because afterward there are going to be difficulties. You will have a sexual desire for some girl who is a *feti'i* of that *hoa*. Because you have become a *hoa* with him and that girl is his 'sister,' what can you possibly do? . . . When somebody has been made a *hoa*, she becomes as a *feti'i* for you and therefore you cannot [try to seduce the girl]." ("Would it be like 'incest'?") "No, it isn't incest [*'amu ta'āta*], but it is a matter of shame because you have become a *hoa*, that is the same thing as if she were a *feti'i* for you."

Adolescent *hoa* may go fishing together, will travel into the port town together, and go walking together after dark on the village path. Sometimes they go to eat at and may sleep at each other's houses. If they are not close *feti'i*, people in Piri rarely enter each other's houses unless there is a special, formal occasion requiring the grouping of people in a household. The accessibility of each other's household is another *feti'i*like aspect of the smaller *hoa* groups within the *taure'are'a* generation. *Hoa* will also give each other gifts of food occasionally,[9] and one will sometimes buy a sweet such as a twisted doughnut or a bottle of syrupy soda for the other at the village store.

I will later return to the *taure'are'a* period in its relation to personal psychological development. The period — its activities and the friendships made during it — provides some essential contrasts and corrections of the effects of childhood experience. Here we may note that the friendships are intimate, sensual, sentimental, and in alliance against the older and younger generations.

The great majority of men "cast off" or "throw away" their *taure'are'a* period over a period of time as they begin to settle into serious heterosexual relations. As we have seen, the *taure'are'a* period and lasting heterosexual relations are thought to be, and are, incompatible.

9. Particularly fish, the spearing of which is a *taure'are'a* specialty.

Some men, "grown-up *taure'are'a*" (*taure'are'a pa'ari*, an ironic term), continue, like Poria, a life with cronies. But for most the end of the *taure'are'a* period means the end of their *hoa* relations, except for rare parties, usually accompanied by drinking, where some of the joking and affection is sentimentally and briefly revived.

"Friendship" for adults committed to a household in Piri or Roto is very much limited and quite different from the *taure'are'a* model. In nonfestival times most of a man's nonworking time is spent within his household, except for formally organized church activities, funerals, parties for work groups, weddings, and other semiformal occasions. At twilight men wander down to the front of the village store to talk and joke, and occasionally a group of men may meet in the evening in front of somebody's house to talk. But for the most part after dark everyone is in his own house.

Those visits that do take place are virtually always of *feti'i*, kin, and almost always very close *feti'i*, usually a son or a daughter who has just left the household to set up a separate household somewhere in the village and who has come back with his wife and children to eat or perhaps to sleep for a day or a few days. Except for an emergency or a structured, relatively formal occasion, adults in Piri who are not close relatives never visit the interior of one another's houses. Visits may take place in the front yard, and they are often short and for the purpose of exchanging important information. Jokes and pleasantries are exchanged between a person standing in his doorway and a villager passing on the village path, but nonrelatives rarely enter.

There are a number of terms for special kinds of interactional relationships which adult people in households may have with outsiders. They may be "acquaintances," *ta'ata mātau* (literally "people who are accustomed to each other"), a designation which is used more commonly to describe relationships in Roto. They may be related as "neighbors," *ta'ata tupu*, who live in the same segment of the village.

Beyond the household are kin of various kinds and distances. Most people have many kin living in the village and scattered throughout Huahine and the other islands. In terms of ordinary experience the kin are a latent category made real by a wedding or funeral. Those of the kin group who are "close," particularly an adult's "brothers" and "sisters" who grew up with him in his childhood household, remain in interaction. These are the people who might visit one another and who would be most likely to help out in house building or some field work requiring extra hands. One is supposed to make use of such relatives in times of need.

Most people would prefer not to have to depend on such *feti'i* unless it is a matter of necessity. "If they help you, they will brag about it . . . make you feel small." "They interfere with household decisions, such as mate selection." "There are arguments when *feti'i* must work together." "It is better that the household do things by itself if possible." These are frequent sentiments. *Feti'i* are an ambivalently employed resource.

Vertical Relationships: Authority and Respect

The relationships we have been considering so far are "lateral relationships," relationships between people whose power or authority is not the main organizing feature of the relationship. In "vertical relationships," on the other hand, authority, power, subordination, and respect are of central importance. Contemporary Society Island villages are characterized by a marked absence of vertical relationships. This is in contrast to the strongly hierarchical organization of pre-Christian Tahiti.

Life in Piri has a markedly egalitarian cast. There is minimal formal "respect behavior" — toward the *tāvana*, village officials, heads of households, elders. Where differences of power or authority do exist, they are veiled. Power is somewhat more in evidence in Roto, for there people work for bosses and have many more confrontations with colonial bureaucracy.

The egalitarian cast of villages like Piri is in part the result of the peculiarities of Tahitian history after western contact. In pre-Christian Tahitian society, a number of hereditary chiefs led political units, which were for the most part confined to a valley. There were alliances and a hierarchy of statuses among chiefs of the various districts, which in a sense united all the Society Islands. But it appears that the superdistrict political organization did not usually have much bearing on the life of the district itself. The chiefs of various districts, through a series of shifting alliances, maintained a balance of power between districts (cf. Adams 1947).

There is also considerable indication that the power of chiefs within their districts was limited. Early observers noted the peculiarities of the system to European eyes. On the one hand the chiefs had the powers involved with *mana* and *tapu*. But there were limits. Chiefs were satirized in sacred satirical theatrical performances (*heiva*). Their authority was limited by the opinion of other high-status people of the district. And it was limited by the system of *tapu* itself.

George Forster believed that the Society Islanders were "in general . . . extremely fond of their chiefs. In return, their [the chiefs'] behavior to everybody was so affable and kind, that it commanded a general good will" (G. Forster 1777; 2:97). And, "the affection of the Tahitians for their chiefs, which they never failed to express upon all occasions, gave us great room to suppose that they consider themselves as one family, and respect their eldest born in the persons of their chiefs. . . . The lowest man in the nation speaks as freely with his king as with his equal, and has the pleasure of seeing him as often as he likes" (G. Forster 1777; 1:366).

Whatever the forms and limits of hierarchical power and authority,[10] colonial events completely destroyed both the authority and even most of the genealogical identity of chiefly lines. The structured *tapu* system collapsed and no longer served as possible sanction for status or decision.

Under missionary influence people in districts became grouped into villages. After a period of missionary control, with the waning of missionary power, the villages became secular, self-sufficient units. For generations they were administered by chiefs

10. For the major attempt to reconstruct pre-Christian Tahitian society, see Oliver (forthcoming).

appointed by and backed up, if necessary, by the more or less distant central French government. Then in the mid-1940s the system of elected village chiefs began. Before this time the central government was willing to enforce decisions of the chief by jail sentences — so that someone who declined to work on village repairs or a new wharf could be so sanctioned. With the coming of elections villagers were subject only to the same laws as the French themselves. Some very few people looked back on the old laws as orderly and Christian, but most villagers welcomed the freedom of the new polity.

A common theme of most interviews is the wish for autonomy — to make one's own decisions, to not yield to the will of others. This does not mean usually confronting or struggling with others, but it means the search for autonomy in more subtle ways. In situations requiring decisions people tend to involve the smallest number of people whose consensus is deemed necessary (family, kin segment, village), but they resist the overt and autonomous decision-making authority of an elder, an "expert," or the *tāvana*.[11]

People are resentful of overt power. Many group activities in the village (e.g., work groups) often have different leaders for different activities. But in those situations in which there are fixed leaders (e.g., the *tāvana* or the island gendarme) leadership should have certain qualities. Ideally, a leader should not tell people what they should do; he should help them find out. He should help them come to a consensus and get things done by "helping them find their own way."

---

11. For exploratory purposes I gave a somewhat modified Kluckhohn Value Schedule to four informants: Manu, Hiro, Taere, and another man from Piri, Marahiti. On the items supposedly testing collateral, individual, and lineal (i.e., hierarchical) orientations, they all reject the lineal ones and hesitate between collateral (help from family and peers) and individual. Their preference is for individual, but there are secondary reasons for choosing collateral in some cases. Thus, it is better to have the village as a whole decide where to place a well — because if they all have a vote, no one can argue about the decision later. Collaterality is seen as a way of coercing the intransigent individuality of others. See Kluckhohn and Strodtbeck (1961).

Such a leader may fail in two directions, according to the frequent discussions in Piri about various *tāvana* and gendarmes. A leader may be too willful, intrusive, or controlling. Tāvana's predecessor, appointed under the "old" law (people say that he never would have been chosen by the people themselves), was a leader of this intrusive sort. But, it is said, it is also possible to be too easy. A *tāvana* or a gendarme may be too easygoing, too much involved in just enjoying himself instead of seeing that "people get on with each other." The *tāvana* of Piri is considered by most people to be an excellent leader. He is there when important things are going on. He listens. He encourages people to formulate their thoughts and say what they think. He helps people discover what the other people in the village are thinking. But he is not proud and he does not put on airs. He does not push his own ideas. He loves the people. This kind of leadership is a very delicate job. It might be noted here that the qualities which make for good village leadership — unintrusiveness, sensitivity to group consensus, humility and the lack of any obvious ambition, a desire for harmony — are by no means the virtues for political leadership or for a political representative at the *territorial* level, let alone at the metropolitan level in France. At both these levels partisanship, aggressiveness, and the ability to represent one's people against the interests of other legislators or executives seem to be necessary virtues. But these are the very characteristics the people of Piri find suspect, unpleasant, un-Tahitian, and dangerous in a leader. This has been one of the factors hindering the development of supervillage leadership in the Society Islands.

The ideals people have for the *tāvana* are those by which they evaluate the islands' administrative gendarme. Gendarmes and other colonial administrators are rated as good men or bad men, depending on the villagers' perception of their intrusiveness and their proper nonauthoritarian stance.

The Tahitian language has many words indicating "stuck-up," "putting on airs," proud, making oneself high. The administrator, the *tāvana*, and the villager should avoid such behavior. The lack of such tendencies is considered to be one of the characteristics of a *mā'ohi,* and one of the frequent descriptions of an *'āfa* is that he is becoming "proud and inflated."

Village officials such as *tāvana* and the *muto'i,* the village policeman, must use indirect devices of coercion. One of these is the clarification and subtle manipulation of village consensus so that "visibility controls" (see chapter 9) are established and clarified. Another is to play on the villagers' sense of *arōfa* ("empathy and pity") in the hope that this will cause villagers to avoid doing things that will be too troubling to the officials. A poignant illustration of this occurred at a gathering of the *taure-'are'a* at a dance shed which they had just completed for the New Year festival. The *tāvana* and the *muto'i* went down to inspect the shed. The *muto'i,* who, after spending some years in the French paratroop corps, had returned to Piri where he had been born, made a speech saying that he hoped that everybody would enjoy himself during the festival. He hoped there would not be any trouble, that people would behave themselves and not fight. If there was any trouble, he went on, as he was responsible for peace in Piri, the French gendarme at Fare would blame him and be angry at him. He then began to cry and was unable to go on with his speech.

Contemporary Piri also has extremely little formal respect behavior. The Tahitian language has no special honorific forms. There are, however, polite forms, such as attenuated imperatives. There are many occasions for polite and courteous forms of behavior, involving guests, visitors, and formal occasions. But this courteous behavior, which is used sometimes in exaggerated form to entertain visiting (and powerful) French officials, is not related primarily to the marking of relatively permanent superordinate and subordinate positions.

There are no special verbal or social forms for dealing with parents, for old people, or for role holders like the *tāvana,* the pastor, or the *muto'i.* One hears statements that people should treat their parents with respect or that one should respect the pastor. But in practice the *tāvana* and the pastor, parents and old people are treated largely in terms of how they act as people rather than in terms of special qualities of their role definition.

This means, in fact, that old people are largely ignored and given minimal subsistence support by their children. When they become nuisances, they are treated as nuisances. People in interviews, reflecting on dead parents, will sometimes say, "I wish they were alive now and I would treat them better than I did. I would serve them." But people's actual behavior toward older relatives seems to be a matter of a number of situational factors, such as how pleasant they are, how useful they can still make themselves, and a certain amount of community and *feti'i* pressure. People in Piri and Roto cannot count on "natural respect" due to the aged to insure comfortable treatment (let alone high-status treatment) in their old age.

Nor is any special emphasis given to "wisdom," the accumulated understanding of the elderly plus the knowledge of the old times they have lived through. Special craft and skills in canoe making or gardening are valued, as is knowledge of medicinal herbs and curative *tahu'a* magic practices. But there is no special regard for the knowledge of the old days, the ancestors, the lineage.

III Psychological Abstractions

Continuing the mixture of description and generalization of the previous sections, I will begin to organize the description around more psychological abstractions: "the self," "thinking," "feeling," "conscience." These abstractions become elements in the even more abstract matter of "psychological organization," which will be the concern of the next section.

7

Self and Identity

What can be said about the sense of the "I," of the "self," of people in Piri and Roto?

The word *vau* or "I," the first person singular pronoun, is often used in contexts indicating the total individual in a physical sense. Such English sentences as "I returned to the house," "I became ill" have Tahitian formal equivalents. But *vau*, again as in English, is frequently used to indicate an aspect of the speaker which is considerably less than his total body and considerably less than his total experience of internal psychological events. Manu, for example, talking about anger, discusses his experience of it in a quite typical way. "In my youth [it was] a powerful thing. A powerful thing, very powerful, very powerful 'it'[1] was, when it came, and I tried to hold it down. . . . There was something that was not right. That was the cause of a lot of bad anger inside one. But I tried to endure, because I knew [if I did not] then my leg would start to go, my arm would start to go — that kind of behavior [i.e., he would start to fight]. But I was also powerful in holding down that anger. And after a time, that was that . . . that thing [the anger], 'it' would go away. Then I would again think good thoughts."

In describing parts of his body,[2] a person is most likely to use a possessive form, "my tooth hurts," although he occasionally may say "the tooth hurts."

1. "It" translates as *'ōna*, the third person singular, which seems to have a strong quality of personification when used as "it." Thus the phrase has some of the quality of "very powerful he/she was."

2. The possessive form associated with parts of the body involves an interesting Tahitian linguistic feature, which is characteristic of many Polynesian languages. There are two classes of possessive forms marked by the use of *a* and *o*. These forms indicate the possessor's logical relationship to the thing possessed in ways that have not been fully worked out in psycho-

A number of verbal forms seem to depersonalize parts of the body, verbally at least, beyond western practice. Thus people will frequently say "my eye saw such and such a thing," or "my ear heard such and such a report," rather than the grammatically available alternative "I saw it" or "I heard it." Another common "depersonalizing" verbal form is used in regard to the sense of drive or emotion. People will say "my intestines [the seat of the emotions] desired that" or "my intestines were angry." The differential use of these forms[3] suggests that this is sometimes more than a conventional verbal form, but may indicate a situation with which the responsible "I" has some difficulty coping.

Vau then frequently indicates a subaspect of an experiencing person, an "I" within a larger self.

Let us note some of the matters indicated by such glosses as "I," "self," and "identity" in Poria, noting some similarities and contrasts with others.

Like all the other people interviewed, Poria considers himself different from the other people in the community. "They and I, we are not of the same measurements [literally, *faito*, "measurement" or "weight"]. Their kind [*huru*, "kind, nature, essence"], the way they do their work, their thinking, their calculations [*feruri*], the decisions they make, these are different from mine."

------

linguistic analysis. In general, the *o* possessive relationship, which is used in relation to parts of the body, may be said to characterize those relationships in which there is an intimate and "blending" relation of the subject to the thing possessed. Thus not only are parts of the body *o* relationships, but a person's clothes, house, and canoe, which he in a sense is intimately surrounded by, are *o* relationships; and his parents, ancestors, siblings, and *hoa* (which, as noted, have a special quality of kin intimacy about them) are all *o* relations. That is, all cognatic and fictive cognatic kin of the same or *ascending* generation are *o* relations. On the other hand, possessions to which an individual has a less intimate and enveloping relationship, such as his chickens, the paddle of his canoe, or his tools, are of the *a* class of relationships. Interestingly enough, a person's spouse and his children are *a* relationships. They are verbally categorized, at least, as less closely and essentially related to him than his canoe.

3. Compare the section on distancing mechanisms in chapter 13.

Poria labels himself, includes himself in, or contrasts himself with different groups depending on shifting contingencies, on shifting contexts for self-labeling. Because of the great genetic mixture in Piri and Roto, Tahitian social acceptance of such mixture, and the lack of correlation between racially influenced physical appearance and social status, the question "What are you?" always has two possible answers — one's *peu* or "customs" and one's *toto* or "blood." The unqualified question "*Eaha 'oe?*" ("What are you?") usually gets an answer having something to do with behavior, association, loyalties. *Toto* is used to explain a person's appearance or indicate his descent and is often used in a joking manner. Flora teasingly refers to Manu as a *marīte 'ere'ere*, "a black American," referring to his appearance and his biological father. But *toto* is (with the exception of a nascent use which I will return to) a minor element in the labeling of oneself and others. It is very much overweighed by *peu*, behavioral labels. Thus Teiva, who has very Caucasian features, is commonly labeled "Chinese" by Piri villagers because of his eating and working habits. Flora calls herself "Tahitian" and her sisters and cousins *demi* because of differences in their way of life. Pouvana'a, a political leader, very much more Caucasian in appearance and ancestry than many of the more Europeanized political leaders, is called *mā'ohi* ("traditional Tahitian"), and the latter are referred to as *demi* or *'āfa* ("Europeanized Tahitians").

Throughout the course of his interviews Poria defines himself in various ways in terms of *peu*. In terms of his living and eating habits in Piri he considers himself, and is considered by others, a *mā'ohi*. In his youth there were people whose eating habits and lives seemed to him unpleasantly sloppy, wild, savage. He describes them, borrowing the missionary vocabulary and values which stigmatized them, as *'ētene* ("heathen customs"). He is more proper, "genteel" than this. He differentiates himself from the more Europeanized household styles of others in the village, calling them *'āfa*.

Others, including Teiva, Tāvana, and Tano, contrasting the ways of life of people like Poria with their own, call him *mā'ohi* but do not call their own ways of life *'āfa*, a term which tends to be pejorative. They simply call them "Tahitian styles," *peu ta'ata tahiti*, the customs of Tahitian people. Similarly, Flora, Hiro, and Manu, much more concerned with differentiating themselves from the *'āfa* in Papeete, refer to themselves as *ta'ata tahiti*. When they use *mā'ohi* it may be in a sentimental way to refer to the old-time customs. It often has a touch of the derogatory flavor that Poria expressed in *'ētene* and has the quality of "rural" or "hick" custom; but it sometimes is used to label a valued old custom, such as being kind to strangers. In this, Hiro, for example, calls himself *mā'ohi*.

When Poria is contrasting himself with the Chinese or the French, he calls himself a Tahitian, *ta'ata tahiti*. In this he includes the *'āfa*. This use of Tahitian to contrast with the Chinese and French is shared by all informants. *Mā'ohi/'āfa* differentiations disappear in this usage. This is the political classification and represents primarily the identification of all "natives" against the French, a new sentiment for most people which was beginning to grow rapidly in the years just preceding my study. (In some contexts territorial-born Chinese are included in the reference of *ta'ata tahiti*.)

It was in this contrast, the political one, that *toto* was occasionally used in a new way. Thus Poria, in a discussion of the French in general, as contrasted with all the Polynesians of the territory, says of the French, "They have a different blood," to explain their strange behavioral characteristics. "Blood" then has a tentative usefulness for Poria and others as a mark for a maximal differentiation of territorial ingroups and outgroups. The origin of this use of "blood" is not clear, but the idea of genealogically determined behavior is salient and presumably ancient.

When Poria goes to Papeete, or when he went to the island of Makatea to work in the phosphate mines, he finds himself grouped sometimes with others from the Leeward Islands, which he calls *Ra'iātea ma* ("Raiatea and the associated islands") after the major island in the Leeward Island group. He distinguishes this group, or sometimes the "Tahitians," in these settings from the Polynesian people of the other island groups, the Tuamotuans or the *Hiva'oa*, the people from the Marquesas.

The ground, however, of Poria's orientation is Piri itself; that is what he usually refers to when he says "here," "this or that happened here." Events occurring in Huahine elsewhere than Piri are sometimes referred to as having taken place "outside."

Poria seldom goes "outside" of Piri. In Piri he is simply Poria, a unique individual with his own ways of getting on with others and of organizing his life. He is one of a large number of different kinds of individuals in the world of Piri, and he feels himself to be not "of the same measurements" as the others. People in Roto have, perhaps, more occasion to identify themselves as "types," Tahitians, in contrast with the many non-Tahitians surrounding them, or to solidify themselves with others on the *mā'ohi/'āfa* question. This may explain in part Hiro's self-conscious and thoughtful identification of himself as a Tahitian and his special attempts to understand something of the Tahitian past.

The development of a conscious, intellectual, often folklorist and antiquarian interest in the "old culture" represents a certain amount of alienation from it. It is still rare in Tahiti, although there are a very few Tahitians who might be called intellectuals about Tahitian culture. It is much more common, for example, among some New Zealand Maori and Polynesian Hawaiians. In a psychological study of Maori individuals, John Williams (1960) found two types of Maoriness. One, unselfconscious, "natural" Maoriness deriving from growing up embedded in Maori culture, he called "Maoriness by enculturation." The other, a willful and conscious, intellectual identification with and awareness of Maori culture he called "Maoriness by cognitive choice." Poria and, with the possible transitional exception of Hiro, all the other subjects of this study represent "Tahitian identity by enculturation."

In both Piri and Roto, people's sense of uniqueness seems to be increased by a general disinclination to explore and discuss private feelings and perceptions. Conversation is mostly in the public sphere — gossiping and joking, work and rumors, politics

218 Psychological Abstractions

and weather. Private stories may be told if they are very dramatic, particularly if they have a dimension of the supernatural.
But Poria, like others, does not really know much about those
thoughts and feelings of others related to their private concerns.
Most people, asked about others' values, beliefs, and so forth,
answered, "I don't know, you will have to ask them." Part of
this is a caution about gossip, part a genuine lack of knowledge.
(This lack of communication about feelings and personal orientations seems also to be characteristic of the *taure'are'a* stage, in
spite of its general same-sex intimacy.)

Poria's sense of individuality has much to do with his relationship to his family. His lineage, his ancestors, mean little to him.
Like all the interviewees (with the sole exception of Hiro) and
like almost all the people of Piri, Poria has lost track of his ancestors above the generation of his grandparents.[4] He knows in
a general way who his relatives or *feti'i* are, although, like other
young men, during his *taure'are'a* period he was sometimes surprised that a girl he was interested in was forbidden to him because she was "some kind" of a *feti'i*. He would hear this from
an uncle or a grandparent. But exactly how his *feti'i* are related
is sometimes confusing to him. Whatever knowledge he has, however, is entirely limited to present relationships and to vague
genealogical statements such as "their grandmothers were 'sisters.'" But he and others have no idea who these related people
were. He also knows that some of his *feti'i* came from a distant
island called "Harorai" but where that was or why or when they
left he does not know. In all this he is entirely representative.
He knows nothing about his ancestors and he has no fantasies
or images about what they might have been like.

Like many others, however, Poria believes that his larger family group, the *feti'i ta'ata*, has some characteristics in common
and that he shares these characteristics. He notes as an example
of this a tendency to cry when he gets upset, and he mentions
two other members of his *feti'i ta'ata* who do the same thing.
The ascription of some characteristic such as high energy or ef-

4. Some informants know one or another great-grandparent.

feminacy to a group of relatives is common in village description.

Although people for the most part do not know much about their own ancestors, they have many, although vague, ideas about "the ancestors," *tupuna*, in general. These ancestors are the old Tahitians of the "beginning." The "beginning" refers to the pre-Christian state of heathenism, and people are not sure when it existed.

Pua talks about "the ancestors." "I have heard . . . some of the women were telling me — the ancestors in the beginning, the people in the beginning — killing people, that was their custom in the beginning. Killing them and cooking [in the earth oven] the people. Not here but over there in ____ [she names a nearby village]. . . . There are old people here — they saw it — they saw it with their own eyes."

Others also thought that practices of cannibalism, which were already discarded in the Society Islands at the time of discovery in 1767, still existed in their grandparents' or great-grandparents' time. People are ambivalent about these collective ancestors. On the one hand they are ashamed of the primitiveness and heathenism of their past, from which Christianity had rescued them, as generations of pastors have reminded them. Thus Teiva once showed my copy of Lévi-Strauss's *Tristes Tropiques* to his wife, saying, "Look at these pictures [of mostly naked South American Indians]. This is what your ancestors were like."

But the ancestors are also admired for their power. Much of the most important magical power is mediated by ancestors from the pre-Christian days, ancestors who were warriors, high-status men, and men of skill. One hears that the people in the old days were much taller and more skillful in many ways than people are now, and the ruins of the old *marae* (sanctified meeting places), which often involved the placement of very large stones and slabs of rock, are looked upon as technically remarkable and beyond the capability of present Tahitians. There have been gains in enlightenment, losses in power.

Poria, like most others, was brought up by a large number of adoptive parents, uncles and aunts, and older children. He was

educated, as we will see in a later chapter, by a system that dif-
fused authority and put a considerable amount of distance between parents and children. When Poria is asked how he learned
things as a child and an adolescent, he says that "he learned
things for himself." He would watch other people doing things
and he would think about them. "Nobody taught me, I just used
to look." Like all the informants except Teiva, whose father was
Chinese and did actively teach him, Poria has the idea that he
achieved his various skills by himself, in his own way, by watching and choosing what to do and when to do it. He did it in his
own time and his own way. He is a self-made man.

When people are asked if they resemble one or another person
in their childhood households, they often list some traits in
which they think they resemble or, more rarely, differ from an
individual. This is usually one of the older individuals of the
same sex who took care of them, usually a "mother" or a "father." Thus Poria contrasts himself with the grandfather who
raised him, in terms of sternness and irritability. But Poria's tendency to withdraw and to be relatively isolated is, he says, similar to his grandfather's. Manu was like his first adoptive father
in "being gentle, and in giving things to people in need"; Tano
was like his biological father (who had little to do with raising
him) in his emphasis on getting money and saving; Hiro was
"shy" like his father; Teiva was similar to his adoptive father in
planning and thinking through his work. He differs from his
father in his "seriousness about religion," and in this he resembles his adoptive mother. Pua thinks she is like her mother
in the way she manages her household affairs, "but I would
have to ask someone else to compare them," she says; she isn't
sure.

For all except Veve Vahine these conscious resemblances are
limited to a few traits, elicited by direct questions. Veve Vahine,
however, constantly and spontaneously compared herself with
her mother: they had the same number of children, were married the same number of years, had the same attitudes about
drinking and about religion, and managed their households in
the same way.

Except for Veve Vahine, no one describes himself or portrays himself indirectly as being generally similar to a family member.

Related, perhaps, to this was a general denial of having any childhood "hero" or admired model for behavior. Most informants remember people in the village who had possessions, a good house or motorboat, that as children they wanted to have someday. But no one recalls wanting to be like anyone else in terms of actions or characteristics.

There were, however, people in the village who provided negative models, whose drunkenness, "heathen" behavior (e.g., rough eating manners), or failure to care for their families disturbed informants. They hoped *not* to be like such people when they grew up.

The emphasis on uniqueness is somewhat limited in that much of an individual's behavior, values, and ways of thinking is thought to be typical not so much of his particular orientations as of the life stage he is in. Fighting and jealousy of heterosexual *fa'aea* partners, for example, are considered to be natural *taure-'are'a* behavior. The explanatory principles, "I acted that way because I was a child; children are like that" or "I acted like that because I was a *taure'are'a*" are very common in people's explanations of their past behavior. A fairly large number of their developmental experiences, at least those they choose to talk about, are explained as the characteristics not of themselves particularly, but of the life stage through which they were passing. Similar stances are taken about the behavior of others. These ascriptions of behavior to a life stage are almost always limited to childhood and the *taure'are'a* period. They are, in a sense, excuses. They explain and justify behavior which would not be acceptable in adults.

Previously people might change their names several times during the course of their lives, after important events — marriage; the birth of a child; the illness, death, or recovery of a child; the accession to a position of power; the establishment of a formal bond-friend. In Piri now such name-changing, with whatever implications it may have for identity, is limited mostly to formal marriages of young couples. Here, in one of the important events separating the *taure'are'a* period from adulthood, the man frequently takes a marriage name, and this name is used to refer to him and to address him, the old name disappearing. If he has changed his "first" name (*i'oa pi'i*, literally, the "name by which one is called"), say from Timi to Ta'aroa, his *vahine* will be called Ta'aroa Vahine but addressed informally by her old given name. That is, the discontinuity indicated by name change is greater for the man.

Let us return to Poria. I have noted the distinctions he makes in his social identity and suggested that he feels, in spite of the shared memberships implied in these distinctions, unique in Piri. So do all the other informants. What does Poria think about his unique self?

When Poria is asked whether he likes himself, he laughs and says that he does. Most of the interviewees find the question surprising and amusing. All except Teiva and Tano indicate that they approve of themselves; and there was little in any of the interview or day-to-day behavior to belie this assertion. People in Piri and Roto pretty much accept and approve of themselves as they are — as their forefathers did, much to the irritation of the missionaries.

The self is conceptually not something one can change: it is what it is. There are changes from one life stage to another. Oro confidently expects that he will stop drinking and "wasting" his money and will settle down to responsible family life. But even such changes are partially an expectation of a growth of part of the self (one becomes wiser, *pa'ari*) and largely a hope that the *desire* to drink, to waste, will change.

When Tāvana is asked about changing himself and his way of life, he remarks, "How can I change — kill myself?" Oro, asked the same thing, answers, "Nothing, there isn't one quality I want to do away with." In these responses speculation about change involves the idea of giving up something, of loss.

Both Teiva and Tano differ from the others in their assumptions about the need to struggle with the world. Asked about their evaluations of themselves and their lives, they express not direct self-disapproval, but anxiety and weariness.

Teiva is eloquent about it. "I am not happy. I am not happy. Myself here and now, here I am. . . . I am not happy. It would be better — it would be better if only I didn't exist. As I reflect on it, trouble is great in this world. Don't you agree? Trouble is great. You see illness, you see hunger. You go and work, you are exhausted . . . soon you have children, your wife gets sick, your children get sick . . . you are surrounded by trouble. Even the trouble of someone dying. Your trouble is great. Therefore, I have come to believe that it would be better if only I didn't exist. It would be good. But there is nothing to be done about it. My parents brought me here. There is nothing to do. If only it hadn't been, it would have been better. . . ." Asked about suicide, Teiva says that he has thought about it, but this would be a bad thing to do to his children. They would be ashamed.

Tano, although he answers my question by saying he does approve of himself, shows at other times that he has considerable doubts whether he is doing the right thing in struggling to make the most money possible out of his lands and to control the events in his parish. During my first visit to Piri he asked me what was the use of concerning oneself about these things, since one must die anyway. One should really pay attention to one's soul. Teiva's thought of suicide and Tano's concern with death as negating the value of his life's work are unique preoccupations.[5] Their discomforts about their "being in the world" are in marked contrast to others' self-comfort and acceptance.

No one expresses a wish for changes in such things as skillfulness, competence, understanding, or moral qualities. But Tāvana and some of the other older people want to have more energy. Energy, strength, enthusiasm, weakness, laziness — feelings and qualities having to do with the sense of "push" — have a salient prominence in Tahitian discussions of action.

Aspects of this are noteworthy for the problem of the image of the self. Poria, after laughing at the question about self-

5. Oro and Poria had each had at least one suicidal plan as *children*. They had both climbed trees with the intention of killing themselves by jumping off, and then changed their minds.

approval and saying he is happy with himself, goes on to say that he would like to be thinner, "but nothing can be done about it — there is a strong desire to eat my food, to eat a great deal." Elsewhere he lists goals he wanted to achieve — a good house, a boat. But, he says matter-of-factly, "There was no way, I was weak about seeking money; if only there was forcefulness [in me] like some other grown-up men. . . ." Uta attributes his ignorance to his weakness in studying. The contexts in which these explanations are given suggest that they are simply conditions of the psyche, for which one is not responsible.

The quality of the relation of impulse to self is suggested in answers to questions about sexual impotence. With one exception, discussions about impotence have this form: "There was never any time I could not have an erection, but there were times I did not have an erection and then I knew that I did not desire that woman at that time." (The exception to this is Oro's statement that after prolonged diving in cold water, even if he wanted to have intercourse, he could not.)

Energy, desire, and anger are self-actors. One hopes they are manageable and expects that they will be. As in so many other things the Tahitians are here optimistic fatalists. One cannot do much to change these forces, but things will be all right.

Related to the self as natural and given are answers to questions about self-anger. When Poria is asked if there are times when he is angry at himself, he answers in almost the same way as everyone else: he is angry at himself when he is working and does something wrong, has forgotten a tool, or does something in the wrong way. Examples people give of self-anger are connected with technical mistakes in relation to their work. There are some few examples, during the life histories, of people expressing limited anger at themselves in relation to some interpersonal error. But statements about self-anger concern errors in technique and not some postulated, more essential quality of the self.

Although Poria made a suicidal gesture in his childhood, he, like everyone else except Teiva, denies any fantasies or impulses toward suicide. As Manu put it, "What is the use of killing yourself? When the time comes for you to die, you will die anyhow; there is no use trying to hurry it." Not only is suicide a sign of self-disapproval and an uncharacteristic attempt to manipulate the natural world, it is also interpreted by all informants as a form of outward-directed hostility. It therefore comes under the web of controls involved in the expression of hostility and aggression, which I will consider presently.

Later presentation of the personal phenomena associated with anger and violence, of the functions of drinking for people in Piri and Roto, and of shame and embarrassment will indicate the prevalence of a certain sense of fear and of weakness vis-à-vis others. As Poria, who is large, powerful, and oxlike, remarks, "When I am sober then I am afraid of big men. . . . Even the young *taure'are'a* — I am afraid of them when it comes to fighting." The percept of others' being bigger and stronger than oneself (contrary to my impressions of the case) is common and is part of the general Tahitian gentleness. This seems related, among other things, to techniques of child socialization which are explicitly designed to produce a generalized fear, to limit children's will to make trouble.[6]

Death and the Self

In chapter 5, "Souls," I described the theory of transformation after death; I will consider the reaction to the deaths of others in a later chapter. Here we may consider reactions to one's own death. Let us turn to statements from the interviews.

Uta told me that he was not afraid of death. I then asked him a peculiar question, "Why not?" "Well, the reason is because one dies of course. People die. Because of that, it isn't anything very frightening." He goes on: "One dies, one cannot just keep

6. As I noted in the sections on the supernatural, people by themselves feel particularly anxious and vulnerable to the uncanny. It is enough to be with another person, even a child, to feel less vulnerable to such dangers and anxieties. Does this have something to do with the mass of others in relation to whom Tahitian children usually grow up and to the extreme rarity of their being alone as young children? Is susceptibility to uncanny feelings when alone related to special qualities of self?

living, one dies. It is the arrangement of things that people die. Therefore it is not frightening. Because you do not know the time that you will die, therefore it is not frightening when it comes." ("If you knew when you would die, would that be frightening?") "Yes, that would be frightening." ("Why?") "Because you know that your death is near. And you don't know what it is going to be like, will it be painful or not." ("What will be painful?") "Your body, if you die." ("After you die, or at the time you die?") "At the time you die."

Manu says that he seldom thinks about death. "It is seldom, because I know in the life of man, indeed, man cannot live continuously without an end. Myself, I don't concern myself with the nature of my death. If I am working, and if I die, well, that's it. If tomorrow I die, that's the day that I will die." ("Are you afraid?") "I am not afraid because I have realized that, even though I were afraid — I will die; and even though I were not afraid, I will also die. Therefore, it is the same thing. If you think, 'I don't want to die soon,' you would still die. Therefore, there isn't any value in calculating, in being afraid of death, or even in not dreading death — you wait till the time you die; that's it, it's finished."

Poria is somewhat less philosophical. He says he is afraid of death. "I don't want to die soon. I don't want to die when I am young, only when I am old." ("Why are you afraid of death?") "I am not sure. I am afraid of death." ("Is it a strong fear sometimes?") "Yes. There was one time that I climbed up a tree, then I had a strong fear of death. Because I fell from the tree. And I was dead at that time. When I came back to life, I was afraid. I was full of pain. Full of pain. Ah, therefore, dying is a fearful thing. Yes, I fell from a tree. I was dead. Afterward I came back to life." ("That kind of 'death' like that — is that the same thing as being 'very dead?'") "The same thing. If only I didn't come back to life, I would have been very dead. But, it is only ordinary 'death,' it isn't a very bad kind."

Poria goes on to say that the fact that he will die sometime in the future does not frighten him: "When you are old, death is a good thing. What's the use of living anymore?" He goes on to say that he is worried about death in the near future but that he is not worried about his eventual death. I then ask him what happens when he dies. "When I have finally come to die? It is a painful thing." ("Why?") "Yes, death is a painful thing, people say it is very painful. You don't want to live anymore — [you think] that you should be dead. You don't want to live anymore. You want to be 'very dead.' You want to be 'very dead' and buried."

Although Uta and Manu are philosophical, Poria is anxious about dying soon. Death also preoccupies the *taure'are'a* Oro. But he also is worried about dying *soon*, with death representing either a punishment or an attack on him. Oro and Poria are worried not about nonexistence or about change of state, but about either the pain or the prematurity of death. They are worried not so much about death as about dying. (As Alan Howard and Robert Scott [1965-66] have pointed out, the fear of dying seems to be universal, whereas the fear of death varies depending on its culturally influenced significance.)

Poria's remarks indicate that the words I have glossed "death," *pohe*, and "life," *ora*, span some of the use of the English terms, "unconsciousness" and "consciousness." *Pohe* spans a range including being ill, loss of consciousness, and an irreversible state, death. It is only in the very late stages of this continuum that the process is irreversible. Although one must die, one has often some choice of *when* to die, in ordinary illnesses. In doctrine, the soul of severely ill people, which at this time still has much of the thought and personality of the living individual, hesitates between leaving and remaining in the body and may make some temporary excursions and return again. One of the reasons for stressing the pain, as Poria did, is that it is only when the soul has decided that the body is in such great pain or has become so weak and ugly that it no longer *wants* to stay in it that ordinary death[7] will occur. Therefore, mixed with the fatalism about dying, that "all men must die," there is also a theme that dying is

7. I say "ordinary death" because in magically induced death, and in the equivocal category of accidents, external forces overwhelm an individual's will, and he dies, so to speak, in spite of himself.

essentially an act of the will, that it happens when one is fully ready to die. One can also will to die. This was said of Pua's *tāne*'s first *vahine*, for example. There are many tales about willed deaths.

I was at Tāvana's house when his first wife was dying. A large number of relatives and their children were at the house waiting for her to die. During this time they kept up a lively, joking, loud conversation about everyday matters. It was not until she actually died that the audience quieted down, and one of her daughters began to wail over her. I asked later about the light-heartedness and joking, which seemed to me even more than at ordinary family gatherings. One of her daughter's husbands told me, "We always joke like that, because if the person who is dying sees that we are grieving and unhappy, it makes it harder for his soul to leave his body."

Even after someone has allowed himself to die, the "consciousness," now referred to as the *vārua*, has still not permanently left the body. According to some, even while the coffin is being carried out to the burying ground, one still may recognize signs of a struggle because the *vārua* has not entirely decided to leave the body. But for the most part the decision is made.

For most people there seems to be, as we have noted, little thought about the postdeath state, when many believe that they will be transformed into an earthbound *tūpapa'u*. Although one or two women in the village talk about their postdeath *tūpapa'u* as a direct extension of themselves and say they would like to travel and see the world at that time, most other people say they have no idea what it would be like to be a *tūpapa'u*; they seem to assume that it would have little connection with their present selves. Many people, as we have also noted, are also concerned with the state of their Christian souls in relation to heaven or hell, and some people have considerable anxiety about what might happen to them in that form. But attitudes about death seem to be independent to a certain degree of beliefs about post-death conditions.

Teiva shares some of the traditional attitudes about dying, but with additional emphases. When asked whether there are times when he thinks about death, he answers, "Yes, sometimes. When one makes a mistake in one's work [he is referring to carelessness in potentially dangerous activities], ah, then you think, if it goes on like that I shall die." His first response about death is tied in with consequences of mistakes, over which he should have some control. Here death becomes a punishment for error and a goad to careful performance. He says that he usually does not think about death, but when he does, it is frightening. ("Why?") "Because . . . you don't know what it is about. We don't know what it is like. Will you die in your sleep or will death follow something painful?" Asked what is fearful or bad about death, he replies: "It is because . . . I am used to it here. . . . I am accustomed to this world. Therefore, it is a fearful thing for me . . . to go into the dirt." He laughs and goes on. "Because when one gets buried, that produces uncanny fear [*mehameha*]. Soon one will rot. You aren't resplendent [*'una-'una*, a poetic term] anymore. You start smelling bad." ("And therefore?") "It is frightening."

Death seems more threatening for Teiva than for the others I have mentioned. There is also a question of time involved. Although Poria does not want himself obliterated in the near future, he supposes that he will accept this eventually. Teiva's concern involves longer lasting integrity. But even Teiva does not express concern about the radical loss of his present self. He is concerned about dying and body changes.

The hard-working, future-oriented, money-saving pastor Tano has a unique reaction to death. I have touched on it. He claims that he is not afraid of it, that he welcomes it because he will have no more trouble or weariness or hard work after he dies. He says, however, that he worries that he will die before he has been able to get all the things he wants. Then, shifting again, he asks, "What is the use anyhow?" All the things he has tried to get in life will be wasted because they will be lost when he dies.

Death seems to threaten the validity of his passion for accumulation. In talking about this, Tano tends to use the Bible as an argument for traditional values, for the values of balance. "There are those things told in the Bible . . . the things that are gathered and done in this world have no value. They have no value. They are only bad things and perishable things . . . therefore those thoughts entered into me. What is the value [of trying to "improve" your way of life]? Even though one gathers together all kinds of things, they are not suitable. It is stated that the only good thing is faith in God." A moment later he continues, "Thoughts about death are not frightening . . . not frightening, but one is in this world only one time, and it is wasted . . . if you are a man with a lot of money and now you are dead and you have exhausted yourself from morning to night, from morning to night, and you have gathered money — now it's all finished . . . now you are in a new place again. You are now dead. What was the value of what you had done before?"

For Tano death is a threat to the strategy of security in accumulation. Tano was unique in recalling his childhood as unpleasant because he was poor and hungry. He believes that by his work he can somehow make things all right. He has considerably sacrificed his friendly relationships with other people in the village in order to do this, working much longer than they do and being much more austere about sharing. He has also violated a basic village caution, that he who strives too much will cause a dislocation in the nature of things which will end up by the striver's being punished. Death, for him, involves special kinds of fears.

Tāvana provides other contrasts in his response to death. He has a number of conclusions about the way things are which differ from most of the other villagers' and which he usually keeps to himself. Tāvana does not believe in any kind of personal persistence after death, either as a *tūpapa'u* or as a Christian soul. He believes in God and in spirits as part of the created world, but he believes that man does not have a soul, simply breath which was given to him by God. God blew breath into Adam, and that was how life came to the first man. The dead are "finished" and do not have any awareness or consciousness. As part of his argument Tāvana says that if *tūpapa'u* were really the souls of people who had died in Piri, considering how many must have lived in the district and died there since it was founded, there would be so many ghosts around the village and on the village path at night that nobody would be able to walk around without bumping into them.

Tāvana, who was brought up in close relationship to a foster mother in a household which contained no other adults and who had a different upbringing from most others in this respect, mourned the death of his first wife well beyond what the village considered proper. For him the idea of a soul or a *tūpapa'u* would have been a consolation. If, he says, he believed that *tūpapa'u* and souls existed, he would not have been so upset about his wife's death, since she would be able to come and stay by him as a spirit.

In an earlier interview he says that he does not fear death. "I am not afraid about death because all people die. There is nothing to be done about it. There is no use in saying I don't want to die. You will only die anyway, and go into the earth, the same dwelling place as others. I am not afraid." He then adds, "I am afraid that I might die, for example, when one climbs up into a tree and then one may fall. But just staying in the house, and then dying, that doesn't trouble me."

In a later interview he modifies this stoicism. He says he is afraid. First he repeats Poria's preoccupation. "It is fearful that one might die. People don't want to die soon." ("Why?") "They haven't yet lost their desire. They aren't yet tired of living." He laughs. "Nobody wants to die. It is very frightening." I remind him that he is not afraid of going to hell, which he doesn't believe in, and ask him why he is afraid. He gives a short nervous laugh. "Because, the reason you are afraid about dying — when you are dead, you don't know anything anymore, you are by yourself, there is nothing anymore. It is you by yourself who goes into the earth. Therefore, nobody wants to die." I ask him whether dead people have any awareness, and he answers that they are not aware of anything. "When you are dead, that's it, it is the end." ("When you think on this ending, that you will not exist anymore, that is frightening for you?") "That one dies is very frightening. Because you will not come back to life, you are dead, and it is only you alone. Only you, only you in the hole." Tāvana's fear of death, recognizably modern, is the fear of separation: separation from others and the kind of separation from his own self which is nonbeing.

Sexual Identity

Let us now consider some dimensions of sexual identity, those aspects of the self which are partially defined in their contrast with qualities of "the other sex."

Henry Adams wrote home from Tahiti in the 1890s that "the Polynesian woman seems to me too much like the Polynesian man; the difference is not great enough to admit of sentiment, only of physical divergence" (Adams 1930; p. 484). And Paul Gauguin, writing of Tahiti of the same period, described a Tahitian man as "androgynous," adding that "there is something virile in the women and something feminine in the men" (Gauguin 1957; p. 47).

Adams and Gauguin referred to qualities, apparently, of personal style and motility as well as to some aspects of body build. Gauguin, for example, notes that he was walking in the woods behind a person whom he took to be a woman but who turned out to be a man, occasioning the remarks just quoted. I believe these impressions, heightened by a contrast with late nineteenth century Euro-American styles and ideals of sexual contrast, are significant. Let us first note some cultural forms bearing on sexual role contrasts.

The Tahitian language does not express gender grammatically. Pronouns do not reflect the gender of the speaker or of the object, and gender does not affect any other aspect of grammar. It is possible to listen to a person describe an interaction with someone else for a long time without knowing whether that person is male or female.

Although the related New Zealand Maoris, for example, are said, in myths at least, to have classified many nonsexual items of their environment into male and female (Biggs 1960; p. 12), there is nothing of this in contemporary Tahiti. Those things which have a natural, evident biological male/female division are, when necessary, designated by adding the words *tāne* or *vahine* (classically *otāne* and *ovahine*) to the base word. There are a few other words that can be added to the name of an animal (e.g., *oni*, "male"; *ūfa*, "female") which also indicate gender, and a very limited number of specific sexually differentiating terms for animals. Usually, unless there is a specific sexually related context (e.g., the specification of a nursing sow), the animal is referred to nonsexually, as we say "dog" or "horse," and in contrast to a designation such as "cow" or "bull."

The great majority of traditional Tahitian proper names can be applied equally well to a male or a female, although the many European or biblical proper names now used do have discrete sexual reference. There are a few names which are applied preferentially to boys or girls. Some of these refer to mythic figures of a particular sex, and some of them are specifically masculine or feminine terms like Tuahine (a man's "sister"), but even these names can sometimes be given to someone of the inappropriate sex, and some people in Piri have male relatives who are called Tuahine or Tamāhine ("daughter").

A great many activities in Piri are done by either men or women, but there are many specialized tasks. Men do the tree climbing, most of the garden work (with the help of women in the busy times), and much of the fishing and house construction. Women plait the coconut fronds used for roofing material, clean the house, and supervise the younger children. Both share the cooking tasks, particularly for the more important meals. Men take a leading part in festive and traditional cooking when the earth oven is used; women do most of the "ordinary" non-festive cooking. In times of need there is some crossover of tasks. If a man is sick, his *vahine* will do some of the essential gardening and firewood gathering, whereas the man may stay home and watch over the infant children if there are no older children around to take care of them. There is usually, however, as noted, some differentiation in work, with the woman oriented to household tasks and the man to food production and house building and repairs. Men are also in the forefront of village political activity, with the women as an interested and vocal background.

Ideally, whereas women gossip and act as part of the day-by-day "conscience" of the village, men are supposed to be above such activities. Role task differentiation exists, then, but is not dramatically differentiated or rigid.

In pre-Christian Tahitian society there was more differentiation. For example, it was, as we have noted, tabu for women to eat with men, and a woman could not enter the important sacred centers, the *marae*. Nevertheless the early descriptions tend to support John Forster's remark that, compared with the other South Sea islands, "in O-Taheitee [Tahiti], the Society, the Friendly Isles and the Marquesas, the fair sex is already raised to a greater equality with the men. . . . We find the women esteemed at O-Taheitee and its neighborhood; they mix in all societies, and are allowed to converse freely with everybody without restriction" (J. Forster 1778; pp. 421-22). The early observers took note of women chiefs with effective political power, of women participating in sports (sometimes wrestling with men), of upper-class women dominating and sometimes beating their husbands, and of many women who were curious, active, independent, and seemingly very little under submission to their men. For purposes of political power, descent was reckoned in both the maternal and paternal lines, and, as indicated by the mention of female chiefs, a woman could sometimes find herself, because of her genealogical superiority and abilities, in a position of power.

A western observer still forms an impression of relative equality between the sexes in contemporary Piri. This is in part because some of the dimensions which, ideally, are supposed to characterize male/female differences in the West are not strongly marked. Men, for example, are not particularly more aggressive than women. Women do not seem to be much "softer" or more "maternal" than men; both men and women exhibit a certain coolness toward their children and their mates.

But within the differences that do exist, there are, in the minutiae of behavior, kinds of crossing over, particularly on the part of men, which are surprising to a westerner who tends to expect some anxiety to arise if male/female categories are blurred.

I noticed some *taure'are'a* young men dancing together in close body contact (a "western-style dance"), and I ask Teiva about it. He explains, "There aren't enough *vahine*. The *vahine* are taken up [by others]. Now, I wish [he is explaining by example] that we press close together and dance. Because there isn't a *vahine*. . . . If there were a *vahine*, I wouldn't press close to you. I take the place of a *vahine*, because it is nice to have a *vahine* to dance with."

Poria described *taure'are'a* dancing together in his youth. "*Vahine* with *vahine*. *Tāne* with *tāne*. Some *tāne* would dance like a *vahine*. He would make himself like a *vahine*. . . . I would make myself like a *vahine*. You are the *tāne*. You would have me dance." I asked him later whether they had erections when dancing like that. He laughs, "We would laugh because our penises became stiff."

For those men who have sexual contact with a *māhū*, such as Oro, the standard explanation, as I have noted, is that the *māhū* is simply a substitute woman, and it is no threat to the definition of a man's masculinity if he utilizes this substitution.

There are many other examples of minute crossovers in role playing by men. Teri'i Tui, for example, demonstrated the traditional method of giving birth to me and to his youngest children by pretending he was pregnant and sitting down on the floor in the proper position. He then asked his oldest sons to pretend to help him with the delivery. Other men, when talking about the nursing of a baby, showed how it was done by holding an imaginary baby to their own breasts.

A very common kind of verbal blurring or blending occurred during the course of interviews of male speakers. That is, in things having to do with women and with women's relationships with men, the speaker would illustrate something by saying, "Suppose you are the man and I am the woman, and we have an argument." Sometimes in an example he would make me the woman and himself the man.

Fantasy also provides examples of sexual blending or lack of sexual discrimination. People are sometimes not sure of the bovine creature that frequently chases them in their dreams. Was it a cow or a bull? As Poria once remarked, "I didn't have time to look." Similarly they are not always sure of the sex of the spirit which approaches them at night to strangle them or enter their body in the common hypnagogic hallucinations.

In my observations these crossover and blending behaviors in Piri are mostly male behaviors. The reportedly prevalent female episodic homosexuality among "Quinn's girls" (see Flora's life sketch) may indicate a potential not brought out in other settings.

When informants are asked specifically about differences between men and women — in character, thoughts, moral characteristics, difficulty of their lives, or happiness — most answer that there are no general differences; some women are better, some worse than men, and so for the quality of their lives. For Piri, if differences were noted, they were minor. Tāvana, in the middle of a passage indicating that it all depends on the particular *tāne* or *vahine*, adds a minor differentiation. "But as to thinking about work [getting tasks done] men are better. The women are a little below. But as to studying there are some women who are full of knowledge, they have powerful understanding. Some men, they are a little below." This mild passage stands out among all the repeated assertions in Piri about the equality of men and women.

Such assertions reflect partially a general disinclination to generalize about the quality of individuals based on their membership in a class. But there is also indication of a "doctrine of sexual equality" working against generalizations about differences. I will return to this shortly.

Hiro and Manu both express something I did not hear in Piri. The life of the woman is happier because it is easier. Hiro even reports joking with his wife about his wish to be a woman and have an easier life — the only example in the interviews (except for the *māhū*) of a reported overt wish to change sex. Both equate women's and men's qualities generally, although Manu remarks that women are better in managing household affairs, particularly in making money go as far as possible in buying food.

But they both say women have happier lives, and their arguments are similar. Manu puts it, "As for women, even if she doesn't work, she can clothe herself, enjoy herself, get what she wants. But the man, it is very difficult. He needs money . . . and if he doesn't go and work, he doesn't have any money. . . . But women can go [and enjoy themselves] out of themselves alone. . . . She can find a man with a lot of money. . . ."

And Hiro: "The woman is luckier than the man. Because she is a woman. All she has to do is go along, and her money comes. But a man, for him it's difficult. If the woman goes along she gets money, she gets a man. The man, if he just goes along he doesn't get a woman. It needs money in the pockets. Then he gets a woman. The woman even though she has no money she still gets a man . . . and she gets money." He laughs and then adds, switching from Tahitian to French, *"Quelle différence!"*

Papeete's work economy, with the special stresses this puts on men as providers, and the urban importance of a woman's granting sex as a commodity have dislocated the sense of balance and equality striven for in places like Piri. Hiro jokes with his wife, "If only I were a woman, it would be better. And you, you would go and work for us. I would look after the household and cook." He does this to tease her, he says. But he thinks she has an easier life. He strives, she receives.

This, I have asserted, is in contrast to Piri. In Piri not only are special advantages or qualities of either sex denied, but there even seems to be a tendency of men to play down special experiences of women which are related to reproduction. Men in Piri claim that childbirth is not painful or dangerous unless some special situation, a curse, or a woman's angry desire not to have the baby complicates it. They claim that menstruation is not any problem for women, and may involve themselves in it. (Pua and other girls in the village remark that their fathers had aided their mothers in cleaning them up and taking care of them at the time of their early menstruation.) Women, men say, do not have an easier life than men, but neither do they have a more difficult one.

A verbal example of biological equality is in the terminology for "giving birth." A woman's giving birth to a child is named *fānau*. A man using the same word will say "we gave birth" to that child or "I gave birth to that child through her."

In spite of the doctrine of equality, there is certainly evidence in cultural forms that women are seen as having special characteristics which must be compensated for. Thus, as has been noted, one of the few residual tabus in Tahitian life concerns menstruating women, whose state can harm plants and fish by direct contagion. It is also of interest that now, as in traditional times, whereas a little boy might run naked in the village until the age of six or so, girls cover their genitalia at an earlier age. (As I have noted in the section "Exposure" in chapter 4, girls' earlier genital covering was remarked on as early as 1769.)

Although there are several neutral terms referring to a penis, which exist alongside the more shocking terms, there are no neutral terms to refer specifically to a vagina. The common neutral terms in use are either euphemisms, like *mea* ("the thing"), or most commonly two words, *hua* and *'ohure*, which are not specific for vagina. *Hua* refers to both male and female genitalia, and *'ohure* refers to the buttocks of both sexes; but it includes the vagina in the female while excluding the penis and scrotum in the male. Such items suggest that the doctrines stressing women's similarity to men, their lack of any special basic qualities setting them off from men, involve denial by men of anxiety-producing aspects of women.

As has been noted, except for Manu and Hiro none of the informants expresses any overt envy of the role of the opposite sex. If everything is equal, there is no rational ground for envy or for feelings of superiority. In the context of questions about the comparison between the natures and lives of men and women, I asked each person whether he had ever had any desires or fantasies about being of the other sex. Manu gives the typical answer. "But — I can't think like that, because my having been made as a man is a done [finished, committed] thing. . . . Sometimes I look and I say, Ah, the life of women is better than that of men. . . . But to become a woman, no, one can't, because one is indeed a man." Flora, who has heard some of her girl friends at Quinn's say that they wished they were men, says that she doesn't think like that. "Here I am created as a woman, and a woman is what I am." For all the others, including Hiro, the answer is a matter-of-fact no, sometimes with a laugh.

The self is a naturally given thing, not easily changeable. The fantasy of being something else, of creating in fantasy something different from the given world, is, as we shall consider, restrained in various ways. But perhaps this "lack of a conscious wish to change one's sex" is simply lying. It does not seem likely. People are frank about a range of socially forbidden wishes, as we shall see in the section on moral behavior. Whatever the deeper currents might be, consciously people accept their sexual roles.

In the background to discussions of sexual identity is the *māhū*, the man who plays a woman's role in the village. My questions to men about wanting to be a *māhū* were also greeted with laughter or with a stern reply to the effect that God creates the *māhū* and that is the way it is.

The *māhū* and the supercision rite both clearly have bearing on the question of sexual identity. So do various aspects of the developmental experience of children and *taure'are'a*. I will return to these questions after considering other aspects of psychological organization.

8

Thinking

The people of Tahiti and the Society Islands, John Forster felt it important to record, "have ideas of many things which never occurred to other nations of the South Seas. Their intellectual faculties, enlarged by instruction and exercise, are capable of comprehending, retaining, reproducing, and combining ideas" (J. Forster 1778; pp. 346-47).

In the 1830s, reflecting on his considerable knowledge of the people of the Society Islands and Samoa, the missionary John Williams deftly presented the case.

It is a remarkable fact, that almost every race thinks itself the wisest. While, in the pride of mental superiority, civilized nations look upon barbarous tribes as almost destitute of intellect, these cherish the same sentiments towards them; and even Britons have not been exempted from degrading representations. So far back as the time of Cicero, we find evidence of the low estimate in which *we* [original italics] have been held. In one of his epistles to his friend Atticus, the Roman orator recommends him not to obtain his slaves from Britain, because "they are so stupid, and utterly incapable of being taught, that they are unfit to form a part of the household of Atticus." At the present day, the Chinese do not form a much higher opinion of our capacities; and even with the South Sea islanders, it is common to say, when they see a person exceedingly awkward, "How stupid you are; perhaps you are an Englishman."

It will depend, however, upon the standard by which we measure intellectual capacity, whether we pronounce the South Sea islanders inferior to other races. If depth of thought, and profundity of research be the only satisfactory evidences of superior minds, I shall yield the point at once. But if wit, ingenuity, quickness of perception, a tenacious memory, a thirst for knowledge when its value is perceived, a clear discernment and high appreciation of the useful; readiness in acquiring new and valuable arts; great precision and force in the expression of their thoughts, and occasional bursts of eloquence of a high order, be evidence of intellect, I hesitate not to affirm, that, in these, the South Sea islander does not rank below the European; and that many of them would, if they possessed equal advantages, rise to the same eminence as the literary and scientific men of our own land." (Williams 1837; pp. 513-14)

An attempt to consider the "intellectual faculties" of the latter-day South Sea islanders living in Piri and Roto involves a variety of peculiar difficulties — the most troubling being the question of just what one should consider when approaching "thinking" in these communities for some understanding of its specific qualities as contrasted with "western thinking." These difficulties in deciding what to emphasize in a chapter on thinking have led me to spend a disproportionate amount of space on problems of background. And because the special intellectual qualities, such as they are, of the thought of the people studied are often illustrated in rarely expressed and experientially trivial aspects of their behavior, I am departing from my method of the other chapters, where salient and prevalent behaviors are emphasized.

If we take a textbook definition of "thinking" — for example, Ernest Hilgard's "*Thinking* is any behavior that uses *ideas*, that is, *representational* or *symbolic* processes" (Hilgard 1962; p. 336) — then much of the subject matter of this book has bearing on it. We are everywhere concerned with Tahitian ideas, their history, their genesis in individuals, their consequences in behavior, the ways they are used.

But one can consider "thinking" in various special ways. There are, for example, the multitude of special assumptions which, insofar as they are held by particular individuals, are the internal representation of Tahitian culture. These assumptions include definitions and rules. ("Menstruating women are dangerous in certain specific ways." "If you have frequent nightmares, consult a *tahu'a*.") Some of these assumptions are cultural doctrines, overtly phrased and taught. Others are repeatedly generated by individuals from prevalent patterns of experience.

Cultural doctrines and their implications are considered throughout this study. The question of assumptions generated from patterns of experience, particularly from those patterns influencing the earlier phases of the psychological development of individuals, are relevant not only to thinking, but to such matters as "values" and "character." This aspect of thinking will be considered in later chapters.

Here I am interested not in particular ideas, rules, and definitions, nor in those characteristically Tahitian shapes given to thoughts, values, and personal characteristics, shapes which have something to do with Tahitian style and cultural identity — with Tahitian *ethos*. I am concerned here with qualities of thinking which may have something to do with the generic situation of the people of Piri and Roto as "primitives," that is, as subjects of traditional anthropological investigation and discourse.

Such a concern will involve us in some antique issues. We may begin with the problem of separating "mental process" from "mental content." There have been strong historical (and polemical) forces in traditional anthropology urging this separation, and an identification of "thinking" with "process."

Although it might seem easy to separate "mental content" and "mental form" for polemic purposes, it is extremely difficult, often impossible, in actual studies. Is the belief that when a baby dies the sky rains in physiognomically expressive pity an indication of a certain process of thinking, or is it an "idea" embedded in unremarkable logical processes? Not only is such a discrimination difficult, but "content" and "process" are not really distinct, in that "contents" profoundly influence "processes."

Questions about cultural differences in thought "processes" have had an evolutionary and "parallelistic"[1] cast in early anthropological theory.

1. This approach considers "parallelisms" based on analogues of system complexity, so that in some characteristics thinking in simple societies is considered to relate to thinking in complex societies as thinking of children

Evolution-oriented discussions of the thought of people in "primitive cultures" have generally turned about two partially related topics: the question of magical (mystical, etc.) thought, and the capacity for a kind of thought suggested by Williams's "depth of thought and profundity of research," which we may designate tentatively as "protoscientific." Echoes of these questions about "primitive thought" continued to haunt me during my experience in Piri and Roto. I was embarrassed to be so haunted, because I considered them to be residues of outworn ideologies. Yet there seemed to be something in the style and organization of people's thinking that somehow seemed natural to the very simplicity (in some sense) of life in Piri and Roto, something that distinguished that thinking from the thinking of urban, middle-class people I had known (including those I had known as "patients" in interview situations somewhat similar to the ones in Piri and Roto).

In this chapter I will discuss some of the matters which gave me this impression, as well as some few additional miscellaneous fragments related to "thinking" in Piri and Roto.

Let us consider some issues influenced by evolutionary considerations about "mind." The question of the comparison of thinking in different cultures involves, as John Williams knew, passions, confusions, and entrenched positions. In the development of anthropology as a discipline many conceptual and ideological battles took place over the relationship of "primitive behavior" to "primitive mind," a relationship central to issues of racism, liberalism, relativism, the culture concept, and so on (see, for example, Stocking 1968).

I will quote at some length from the first (1911) edition of Franz Boas's *Mind of Primitive Man*, because it clearly indicates assumptions about the relationship of "organization of mind" and biological (racial) competence which Boas assumed to be logically valid and to which he was ideologically opposed, as well as the solution he proposed. These assumptions about the

---

does to that of adults, of brain-injured people to people with intact brains, of psychotics to nonpsychotics, and so forth.

validity of the problem and its solution became part of common sense in American anthropology.

Thus we recognize that there are two possible explanations of the different manifestations of the mind of man. It may be that the minds of different races show differences of organization; that is to say, the laws of mental activity may not be the same for all minds. But it may also be that the organization of mind is practically identical among all races of man; that mental activity follows the same laws everywhere, but that its manifestations depend upon the character of individual experience that is subjected to the action of these laws.

It is quite evident that the activities of the human mind depend upon these two elements. The organization of the mind may be defined as the group of laws which determine the modes of thought and of action, irrespective of the subject-matter of mental activity. Subject to such laws are the manner of discrimination between perceptions, the manner in which perceptions associate themselves with previous perceptions, the manner in which a stimulus leads to action, and the emotions produced by stimuli. These laws determine to a great extent the manifestations of the mind. In these we recognize hereditary causes.

But, on the other hand, the influence of individual experience can easily be shown to be very great. The bulk of the experience of man is gained from oft-repeated impressions. It is one of the fundamental laws of psychology that the repetition of mental processes increases the facility with which these processes are performed, and decreases the degree of consciousness that accompanies them. This law expresses the well-known phenomena of habit. When a certain perception is frequently associated with another previous perception, the one will habitually call forth the other. When a certain stimulus frequently results in a certain action, it will tend to call forth habitually the same action. If a stimulus has often produced a certain emotion, it will tend to reproduce it every time. These belong to the group of environmental causes.

The explanation of the activity of the mind of man, therefore, requires the discussion of two distinct problems. The first bears upon the question of unity or diversity of organization of the mind, while the second bears upon the diversity produced by the variety of contents of the mind as found in the various social and geographical environments. (Boas 1911; pp. 102-4)

Boas in 1911 accepted the assumption of the racial theorists that such "mental characteristics" as "inhibition of impulses," "power of attention," and "power of original thought," would be "hereditary" if they were somehow qualities of the psychological *organization* of individual thinkers. As an alternative he explained them cogently as generally human responses to different sociocultural situations: "The proper way to compare the fickleness of the savage and that of the white is to compare their behavior in undertakings which are equally important to each" (Boas 1911; p. 107). This was a powerful corrective to the ethnocentric foolishness of his opponents but established a climate in which *any* statements about differences of the "organization of the mind" seemed regressive.

The idea of differences in "organization of primitive mind" persisted in continental European work, particularly in the work done or influenced by Lévy-Bruhl, Heinz Werner, Lévi-Strauss, and Piaget.[2]

The arguments for organizational difference in such work do not require racial or biological explanations. Modern learning and developmental theory can provide plausible nonbiogenetic hypotheses for many of the posited comparative forms. There is, however, a residual ideological discomfort for some social scientists that "differences in mental organization" imply, if not something vaguely racist, at least negative evaluation, a charter

2. Many of the ideas on differences in organization of primitive mind, organized on the concept of parallelisms in psychological development, are summarized in Heinz Werner's *Comparative Psychology of Mental Development* (1948). Lévi-Strauss's work, in spite of his demurrers, implies special qualities of organization of "primitive mind," which represents to him a system of logic not transformed by civilized accretions.

The application of Piaget's concepts and methods to nonwestern peoples, as, for example, in the work of Bruner and his associates, has been held to indicate differences in cognitive organization. Thus, "With respect to the growth of representation, what turns out to be virtually impossible for the unschooled Wolofs are cognitive accomplishments that can be carried out only by symbolic means, for instance, nominal equivalence and superordinate language structures" (Bruner, Olver, and Greenfield 1966; p. 318).

for specific politics, and a suggestion of a depth of difference of cognitive organization which, they feel, is not justified by the behavior studied.

Let us now consider some aspects of thinking in Piri and Roto. I must first echo John Williams in emphasizing the evident qualities of wit, ingenuity, quickness of perception, and so on which characterize the intelligence of many of the people I worked with. Furthermore, although we will become involved in some exotic bits of thought and culture, the vast majority of examples of Tahitian thinking, as indicated in verbal statements involving plans, explanations, and justifications and as illustrated in various actions, is ordinary and intelligent by western standards of good thinking. Its limits and stylistic features are not strange in the way that, for example, the thought of a "schizophrenic" may seem strange.

Tahitian Theory of Thought

We may consider first how informants in Piri and Roto think that they think. One may begin with two key terms, *mana'o* and *feruri*. *Mana'o* may be glossed as "a thought" or as "the process of thinking" in its most general aspects. But *mana'o* also is used to contrast with *feruri*. *Feruri* indicates "to work out a thought," "to think something over carefully," "to prepare one's thoughts for responsible social presentation." *Mana'o* is used both for a process and a product, while *feruri* is used for a process; a "worked out" thought is referred to as a *mana'o feruri*. When, during a village meeting, someone is called upon to express his opinion, he will remain silent, often for a long full minute or two before answering. He is said to be *feruri*ing his *mana'o* during this time.

Now let us consider Poria as he is asked to think about thinking. ("When someone thinks [*mana'o*] ...") "Yes..." ("...what is the nature [*huru*, "nature, kind, essence, quality"] of that thought?") [Poria laughs, and I repeat.] ("What is the nature of that thought?") "The working out [*feruri*] of the thought [*mana'o*]?" ("What is it like, *mana'o*, *feruri*, things like that?") "That's a little difficult to figure out [*feruri*]." ("That's true, but try.") [A three-second pause.] "[Suppose there is] some difficult task. You think [*mana'o*] inside of yourself. A task. You think [*mana'o*] about that task. At this time I figure out [*feruri*], 'I will do that thing.'" ("Where does the *mana'o* come from?") "It originates in my body, my thought [does]. My head." ("Your . . .?") "My head. My brain,[3] it does the *feruri* of tasks. By it [head, brain] is done the *feruri* of that thought [*mana'o*] and that thought and that thought. This night one *feruri*s, 'Tomorrow morning I will go and clear the brush.'"

Tāvana, characteristically, has his ideas better organized. He also laughs when asked how thinking takes place but goes ahead to try to work it out. "*Feruri* goes on by means of the head but if, for example, the eye sees something this starts off the *feruri*. Perhaps the eye sees something that is not proper, or perhaps something that is especially proper, then the head begins to *feruri*. The *feruri* is inside of the head but it comes from the 'heart.' [Heart is a biblical substitution for the traditional notion of the intestines or gut as the seat of the emotions, and when Tāvana talks about the "heart" he points to his abdomen.] Things start in the 'heart' and the *feruri* goes on inside of the head. The *mana'o* goes into the head, for the purpose of being *feruri*ed, for the working out of the *feruri*."

Later Tāvana, talking of fear, says, "When your eye sees something fearful, then your intestines [here he uses the traditional word] feel altered. Things are different inside the intestines. The eye sees something frightening, and the intestines are altered." He goes on to say that shame and anger, for example, start in the intestines.

3. All informants identify the head with *feruri*, and some add specifically the brain. I do not know whether the identification of the head or brain or both as related to thinking precedes western influence; but the relation of head injuries to confusion, the head as the center of seeing and hearing, the localized sense of strain during concentration or difficult problem-solving, the attention to partially controlled facial expressions as the indicator of a person's "psychological" state, all would make plausible a traditional identification of the head (and indirectly the brain) as an important center of conscious calculation.

All informants, with only minor variations, use the same schema to explain thinking. There are three references: outside events, the abdomen or the intestines, and the head. Outside events are "seen by the eye" or "heard by the ear." They tend to stir up a reaction in the body, particularly in the abdomen. This is a mixture of feeling and of the first stages of thinking. The reaction can lead immediately to action — running away or angry action — but more frequently the thought/feeling is worked over by the head, in order to come to a rational, planned decision. Outside stimulation is not necessary. The thought process may begin as some feeling, such as desire or anger, in the abdomen and may be passed on to the head for *feruri*. Or the process of *feruri* in the head may give rise to an emotion in the abdomen.

Much of this mechanical and depersonalized description of thought is produced by the question, "How does thinking work?" In ordinary contexts people will simply say, "I am angry" or "I am *feruri*ing."

Tahitian vocabulary includes a variety of terms for aspects of thinking — remembering and forgetting, error and stupidity, confusion, certainty, truth and lies, belief and doubt, wisdom and being well informed. It is a vocabulary full of subtle semantic contrasts.

Tahitians are well aware that the internal and external worlds are not always immediately given to the understanding. There are occasions when one must think about things.

Ordinary Thinking and Magic Thinking

Evolutionary considerations of primitive thought emphasized "magic thinking," something which was progressively left behind, it was thought, as mankind developed. A gross error was made in considerations of magic and primitive thinking. It was assumed that aspects of thought involved with special areas of cultural activity (e.g., religion, ritual, the supernatural) were *generally* characteristic of the thought of individuals in the group. The unwarranted assumption was also made that one could directly deduce the kind of thought inherent in culturally influenced behavior. This is the error of taking the "God bless you!" after a sneeze as a serious incantation implying an individual's commitment to verbal magic.

The first error has some justification. That is, a potential resource, a way of thinking, may have its implications for areas in which it is not ordinarily used. The "common sense" of someone for whom religion, say, is deeply real, albeit perhaps in its own realm, may differ from that of someone for whom religious thought is not developed.

The second error, the problem of cultural form and its meaning to the individual, is relevant to most of the concerns of this study. There are various ways of trying to pry self from role and individual from cultural cliché (easily accomplished, for example, when Pua says she only pretends to believe in some kinds of ghosts). Sometimes the stereotypicality of some sample of apparent thought may be suggested by contextual factors and tested by studying thinking in relation to new problems, to see how solutions are generated. It is important to note that I am not suggesting that "culture" is not involved when private thinking and problem-solving are operating. But it is involved from the point of view of an individual in a much different way than if he is only repeating and adhering to a given cultural doctrine.

By using Tahitian distinctions, we may separate specially magical realms from ordinary realms and thus consider ordinary, everyday thinking. In an earlier chapter I noted the tendency of Tahitians in Piri and Roto to segregate the supernatural and the uncanny into a "nighttime world" of the *pō* which was separated from the "daytime world" of the *ao*. Within the *ao* is the commonsense, workaday, everyday world. It is the world of ordinary personal relationships, of ordinary pleasures and disappointments, of making a living; and it makes up the vast majority of the activity, and to all indications, the fantasies of the people. When people are asked what they think about when they are alone or quietly musing, the usual answer is that they think about the day's activities, about what they have to do the next day, or about short-term projects like immediate improvements or changes in the house or the farm. Most musing is reported to be on the happenings of everyday life or on those things which can be easily changed. There is very little "fantasy." (I will return to the question of fantasy in chapter 11.)

Questions requiring someone to imagine himself in an action or setting much different from those of his everyday life usually produce uneasiness and constricted responses. Thus, when asked what would they change in their lives, people answer, "Well, I am doing what I can. I can't change things." If they do suggest a change, it is of the order of "I wish I could plant more vanilla and then be able to hire somebody to help me with my work."

Occasionally there are more fanciful answers. Poria wanted to save some money (he had no idea by what means) and then rebuild his house so that the back of the house would be toward the village path (an unheard-of innovation) and the front facing on the lagoon. He wanted to hire a personal servant and to build a small swimming pool in what would become his front yard. He seemed quite serious about the possibility of accomplishing all this. Ropae, a *taure'are'a* son of Tāvana, told me when I first came to the village that what he would like to do was build a raft and drift until he came to an island or to a new land. He would then walk around and see the sights. He would leave the raft there and take a boat back to Huahine and tell the people about what he had seen. Then after a while he would take the boat back to the place where he had left the raft, get on the raft again, and then drift until he came to a new place, return to Huahine again, and so forth.

But reports of such acts of imagination are exceedingly rare. Mostly, judging from what people reported to me, people's imaginations are tightly and concretely bound up in a fixed, everyday, mundane reality. On those rare occasions when they find themselves involved with the magic world, it tends to present itself to them in its own conventionalized, limited, and defined forms.

In general the world with which people in Piri and Roto are involved is a world which comes to them through the senses, a world they can see and hear and smell and understand directly. Although people, particularly in Piri, are often credulous about rumors, especially about political events affecting the territory, in general they are skeptical about things they have not personally experienced. They will qualify such reports by saying, "It isn't certain. It is only something I heard. My eyes did not see it."

An orientation to direct, perceived experience, uncorrected by culturally provided information, may best explain an illusion which was prevalent in both communities. I asked each subject whether there was any change in his sense of the speed with which time passed when he contrasted his adult condition with memories of childhood. Everyone reported that time had speeded up for him. However, this sense of the speeding up of time is often given a particular interpretation.

Poria leads off. "Now it is very rapid . . . the month goes very fast. A month is a very short thing. In the old days, people thought it was a very long thing — a month. People got tired waiting for the end of the month to come. Now one isn't weary of it when the month is over — now it doesn't take long, and suddenly the end of the year is here." ("What do you think is the reason for that?") "Well, we have now a fast epoch. This epoch — these years — these months — are rapid now." ("Do you think they are rapid for everybody here — for children also?") "Yes, they are rapid. These days children are very small when they are fourteen years old. In the beginning, in the old days they were big at fourteen or fifteen years old." ("Why is that?") "I am not sure why, but time goes rapidly now. And children are very small when they are fourteen."

In a later interview I returned to this and asked Poria to explain to me again why the children are small now. He says, "I am not exactly certain, but I think it is because the years go so quickly now and that is why the children are so small." Time has speeded up, and therefore children simply do not have much time to grow. Poria is combining two impressions — time has speeded up, and children seem smaller than he remembered them as being in his youth — and he takes them both to be objectively changed aspects of reality.

In Roto Manu makes a similar connection. "In the old days, in my childhood, when I would look at it, the going along of the month was a gradual thing, the counting-off [*tai'o*, the enumeration of items in a series] of the month was slow, and the counting-off of the years was slow. In these days, from my own observations, and indeed this is what I hear other people say, this is a very fast period. The counting-off of the days now, the counting-off of the weeks, the counting-off of the months and of the years — it isn't long. It isn't long, and day becomes night. It isn't long and the week is over. It isn't long and the month is over. And it isn't long and the new year is reached. The old days, it was a rather slow period. Now the counting-off of the days goes quickly." ("Why is that?") "In people's calculations [*feruri*] — people see the way children are now. In the beginning children — children went on slowly, they didn't grow up quickly. Now, it isn't long and children of twelve years, of thirteen — you look at them, they have the appearance of adults. And similarly, the counting-off of the days, of the months, of the years goes quickly. Therefore people grow rapidly now." ("People grow rapidly now?") "People grow rapidly now — I mean the way they get big. When I look at all the people now — when they are twenty years old, or twenty-five they have started to have white hair. And they quickly become old. When they are forty, or fifty, their hair is very white . . . even though they are young when you look at their bodies." ("Was it different in the beginning?") "It was different in the beginning, different in the beginning. People in the beginning [i.e., Manu's youth] when they were thirty or forty years old you didn't yet see gray in their hair." ("Why do you think things have changed?") "Ah, people say it is because of the shortness [quickness] of the period we are in." ("What do you think?") "Ah, to my thinking, the period goes very rapidly now. Therefore it is not long and the year is gone — it is not long and the month is gone. That is the sign [the indication that time is speeding up]. The quickness of the counting-off the days, and the quickness also of the growing of people, because our period goes quickly." ("Is this true for everyone?") "Yes, all the same." ("Children also?") "Yes, all, all."

I then ask him what things were like in the life of his grandfather. "From his childhood and until his old age, things were slow. They were not fast. . . . Things were different in my grand-father's day. . . . When he was fifty he was still full of energy. . . . At sixty-seven he started to be weak, but he could work. If only he didn't die in 1918 [of influenza] he could have worked until he was seventy." And so forth.

For both Poria and Manu their sense of speeding up of time indicates an "objective" situation. Other people also comment on the general speeding up of the world, adding such observations as that food ripens faster and various food crops are not as big as they used to be. But not everyone interprets his sense of time speeding up as a simple objective change.

Thus Tano, asked about any change in the speed with which time passes, answers immediately, "It is only the thought [*mana'o*] inside of people, as I calculate [*feruri*] it. People's thoughts make this period changed, make them say that the year goes much quicker now, and that the year went slowly in their day. As I work it out [*feruri*] it only comes out of people's thought. When I think it over, it has been the same since the beginning, nothing has probably changed, I think. Myself, I can say that time runs easily [and thus quickly], it is very rapid. The year is very rapid now. When I figure out the basic [*tumu*, from "trunk"] thought, the certain thought, the year isn't changed now. It is the same from the beginning and up until this time. Concerning the nature of the hour, the day, everything — nothing has changed. Twenty-four hours in the day, [it has gone on] like that. I think nothing has probably changed. But the thought of people, ah, that has changed a little. 'It is not long and it is night. It is not long and it is day.' They talk like that."

But the immediately following sequence indicates that the apparent epistemological contrast between Tano on the one hand and Poria and Manu on the other is limited. The creation of "objective" public reality is piecemeal.

I start to ask Tano in a fumbling way if children now still think time goes slowly. But he uses the question to go on to the question of change in size of children. "In the beginning, children were big. I saw them. Children were big. As each age was reached they were rather big. People were big while they had few years [were chronologically young]. Now people are small and they have many years. . . . Now children are small, with many years on them. . . . In the beginning the person was big, the years were few." He goes on to explain this, with illustrations from animal breeding, as owing to changes in the "blood" of the people.

Like Tano, Tāvana believes that the change in the sense of time is caused by thought processes and not by a change in reality. Tāvana ascribes it to the "enlightenment."[4] "It is because when the *feruri* was not enlightened about how the day went, the people did not know how to count off the days properly [i.e., by means of the calendar], then time went slowly. But now, people pay attention to those things [counting the days], and all the houses have calendars and that is why the time goes quickly. [Tāvana refers to calendar both as *tārēna*, phonetic for the English "calendar," and also as *tāpura'a mahāna*, literally "the thing which cuts the days."] Therefore I think because of that, that the day does not go faster; it is the same as it was in the beginning. But, to my thought, because of the enlightenment now, we have come to think that it goes rapidly.

When Tāvana is asked about the thought of children at this time, he does exactly what Tano did and goes on to the changes in their size. But he reverses Tano's emphasis and says that children are bigger now at a given age than they used to be, and that this, perhaps, has something to do with the amount of food they eat now. That is, he corrects fully for his private memory of the size of children in his youth and adds the objectively warranted increase in size. But he then goes on to say that people do grow up much more quickly now and that they become mature and then older much more quickly than they used to. And when asked again about contemporary children's sense of the passing of time, Tāvana says that he believes that it probably does pass quickly for them, and that this is because they, like the adults

4. The term is *māramārama*, literally "enlightenment," a concept introduced by the missionaries to designate the bringing of Christian knowledge, and now applied to nontraditional introduced knowledge in general.

now, are enlightened and learn at school to calculate and attend to the passing of time.

In these examples, presumably of fairly original thinking, changes in the perceived duration of a unit of time, in the size of children and fruit and vegetables, in the rate of aging of one-self and one's contemporaries, are taken to be objective qualities of a real world. For these items, at least, the people quoted are in a more "subjectively" interpreted world than our ideal westerner.

The extent of such "subjectivity" varies with the individuals interviewed. Tano, for example, shows less "subjective" thought in these quotations (and in general) than Poria or Manu. Yet Tano, after presenting a less subjective, more differentiated view of time (he deduces an objective time, with which he corrects his personal experience of duration), presents a relatively personal and undifferentiated view of size. That children looked comparatively bigger to him as a child is used to indicate an objectively changed aspect of the world.

It is possible that Tano has arrived at a new principle concerning the relation between experience and public reality, a new epistemology, and Manu has not — that Tano's thinking has become "reorganized." In this case, he has simply failed to apply the principle to the matter of children's sizes. But if the principle is stated as *not all personal impressions represent public knowledge*, then Manu and all the other informants are well aware of it. Tahitians must, like competent members of any culture, attend to the question, "What is truth?" and the related question of personal versus public truth. If there is a difference between Manu and Tano or Poria and Tano, it is a question of how often, how pervasively, in what areas, under what circumstances "subjective" or "objective" thought is used.

There are some areas of the culture of Piri and Roto where everyone thinks "subjectively," magically — in the supposed presence of a *tūpapa'u*, for example. I have suggested in chapter 5 some of the various circumstances under which the culturally provided magic and supernatural worlds are encountered and used. Almost all cases of such encounters which came to my attention entailed considerable emotional involvement with the supernatural and acceptance of cultural explanations by the individuals involved.

Every informant and, as far as I could tell, every Tahitian member of the two communities believed and had personal experience of realms in which magical and supernatural wonders took place. Roti, the young woman who was the assistant school-teacher in Piri, watched me do a sleight-of-hand trick one evening as I made an apparently cut piece of rope rejoin, meanwhile incanting "abracadabra." Roti asked me afterward if it were necessary to say "abracadabra" to make the trick work. Tivini, the senior village teacher, who is widely read and informed on matters beyond the limits of the territory, believed in a mixed bag of wonders — ghosts, curses, magically effected fire walking, and levitation (the latter not a Tahitian wonder, but something he had read about in French magazines). Not that many of the French inhabitants of Tahiti do not believe in the same list; but Tivini is the most critical, rationalistic, skeptical thinker in Piri.

Although we may find a mixture of styles of thought both in a given individual and in a community, a significant question is the available range and limit. For Piri as a community, Tivini represents the limit reached in the direction of a certain ideal of western skeptical rationality.

Magic thought has been characterized in a number of ways. The most general assumption seems to be that thinking tends to have intrinsic tendencies (most clearly expressed in dreams, art, psychosis, myth, the thinking of infants, and the like), but that something in the hard and slowly discovered nature of the external world requires and imposes other logics and "schemas." Qualities of thought related to these first tendencies are "magical" ("mystical," "dereistic," "autistic," "primary process," "paralogical," and so on). Magical thinking "blurs fantasy and reality," "makes thought and wish omnipotent," is "free of the constraints of space and time," is "egocentric," and so forth.

"Nonmagical thought" or "objective thought" makes sharp distinctions between an inner world of private mental events, an interpersonal world of social communication and experience, and a nonsocial, natural world. An attribution of qualities of the inner world to the interpersonal world, or an attribution of qualities of either the inner world or the interpersonal world to the natural world (e.g., words affect social processes and are therefore assumed to affect natural processes) is a central feature of magical thinking.

Everyone in Piri and Roto thinks magically in the proper circumstances. But people do not live constantly in a magic world, in the sense that infants and some psychotics may. They do not even enter very frequently into such a world, in comparison with, say, a dedicated mystic. They do not inhabit the diffusely magical world that some romantic writers had ascribed to "primitives," nor, from all evidence, did their pre-Christian forebears.

Although the supernatural world, with its special assumptions and logics, is distinguished from the everyday world, there are assumptions within the everyday world about how the supernatural world is evoked — what one must do to actualize it. These assumptions, bearing on the borderline between the two realities, have in themselves a magical quality.

I have noted that there is a verbal separation of "worked out thoughts" (*feruri*) from fragmentary thoughts, and that "worked out thoughts," like speech, may have consequences in the external world. Several informants generalize this. According to Uta, "Tahitians believe that if you are concerned about something — for example, the death of someone — it will occur. Tahitians believe that through their thought something will happen." He then asks me what Americans think about this. (Note that this is a problematic belief for him.) Manu, talking about curses which come true, says, "That is the nature of Tahitians. Their mouth speaks, and that matter [that they refer to] comes about." And Taere, remarking that he does not think about his own death, says, "If I were to think about my own death, I would die." I ask him what he does if thoughts about death come into his head in spite of this. "I make them go away. One must not have weak thoughts; one must have energetic thoughts."

A key idea in discussions of the effects of thoughts on the world is *ti'aturi*, which I have glossed as "concern" in the quo-

tation from Uta. *Ti'aturi* means to believe in the truth or existence of something, but essentially to believe with feelings of
trust or confidence that the matter is so. *Ti'aturi* means literally
to "lean against," and thus figuratively to trust someone or
something. People say that ancestor spirits are disappearing because people don't *ti'aturi* them anymore. Their very existence
depends on it. Similarly, as we have noted, *tūpapa'u* have power
to harm in proportion to the amount of *ti'aturi*, belief and concern, that people have in them.

Here on the boundary between the ordinary and supernatural
worlds one must be careful to control certain mental processes,
or they will actualize the spirit world.[5] We have here a classic
element of magic theory, that some psychological or social operation will affect the nonsocial world directly. But there are
limitations. Not all wishes and fears and thoughts affect the nonsocial world. Furthermore, the theory about how that world
might be affected is based on a social model — the forces are
mostly personified, and, except for the rare powerful evil spirits
(whose power is independent of one's amount of *ti'aturi*), they
are rule-bound. If these are dreams, they are ordered and tamed.

Ordinary Thinking: The Question of "Concreteness"

A frequent characterization of the thinking of "primitive" and
in fact various distinctly nonprimitive, nonwestern peoples is
that it is "concrete." Sometimes this is presented as a preferred
style of thinking, sometimes as a deficit, a "low capacity for
abstraction" or a "lack of abstract intelligence."

Such labels are as imprecise and subject to polemic as other
comparative characterizations of thinking, but their frequency
in description suggests that they refer to something of possible
importance. "Concreteness" seems to be used to refer to two
different qualities of thinking, qualities which have different implications. The first is a style of understanding, calculation, and
communication which emphasizes the rich and complex pheno-

---

5. I have noted in chapter 5 that the belief in the *direct*, not spirit-
mediated, effect of thought and words on the nonpersonal world, which
was apparently more developed in pre-Christian Tahiti, is now greatly diminished.

menological attributes of whatever is being considered.[6] This usage corresponds to the dictionary definition of concrete as "pertaining to realities or actual instances." "Concreteness" in this first meaning has an "opposite," a style of understanding ("theoretical") which emphasizes a very limited number of attributes of the matter being considered.

The second meaning given to "concreteness" emphasizes something different from an attention to "complex phenomenological attributes." Now the emphasis is on a deficit, a limit, a rigidity of thinking. Seymour Sarason states it clearly in his discussion of an analysis of Rorschach records of Trukese. "Concreteness of thinking is found in almost all of the cases. By concreteness is meant the inability to respond to a stimulus in more than one way — to be unable to assume, so to speak, that a stimulus may have various significances or meanings. . . . A concrete response is not in itself a 'poor' way of responding — everyone at some

6. Compare these remarks on a nonprimitive population, the "Great Russians," by Alex Inkeles and his associates. In an analysis of the Great Russians' "modes of cognitive functioning," they write, "In discussing people, the Russians show a keen *awareness of the 'other'* as a distinct entity as well as a rich and diversified recognition of his special characteristics. Other people are usually perceived by them not as social types but as concrete individuals with a variety of attributes distinctly their own. . . . In reacting to the interpersonal relations 'problems' presented by one of the psychological tests they more fully elaborated the situation, cited more relevant incidents from folklore or their own experience, and offered many more illustrations of a point. In contrast, the Americans tended more to describe the formal, external, characteristics of people, apparently being less perceptive of the individual's motivational characteristics. The Americans also tended to discuss interpersonal problems on a rather generalized and abstract level."

Even though they are talking of "modes of cognitive function," Inkeles and his coauthors indicate that such modes may be restricted to specific subject areas. They go on to state, "With regard to most other types of situation, however, especially problems involving social organization, the pattern was somewhat reversed. Russians tended to take a rather broad, sweeping view of the situation, *generalizing* at the expense of detail, about which they were often extremely vague and poorly informed" (Inkeles, Hanfmann, and Beier 1958; p. 11).

But note that "generalizing at the expense of detail," which may be due to lack of information, is not necessarily the same thing as attending to "formal, external, characteristics," which may be a preferred cognitive strategy.

time or other responds in this way — but when it becomes a characteristic way of responding its limiting effect on the individual becomes apparent" (Gladwin and Sarason 1953; p. 225).

A similar idea is expressed in Ernest Beaglehole's study of Polynesian children on Aitutaki in the Cook Islands. "[A] characteristic aspect of Aitutaki thinking is the fact that it functions mainly at a perceptual, rarely at an abstract, level. . . . [For example] the children of Aitutaki have plenty of experience of coloured objects or variously shaped objects, but their culture teaches them to be interested mainly in the objects and not in their abstracted shapes, colours and patterns. Therefore the quality of their thinking will reflect this perceptual orientation, and imaginative thinking either of a controlled or a free fantasy type will be rare" (Beaglehole 1957; pp. 222-23).

Here the emphasis is on being "bound" by stimuli, on being unable to separate or having difficulty in separating objects or attributes from the contexts and frames of reference from which they ordinarily take their meaning. This kind of concreteness does not entail attending to a variety of attributes of an object. One may "abstract" some very few index factors to identify or categorize an object or event. But the indexes are chosen for the purpose of placing it in its familiar contexts.

Concreteness in this sense implies "literalness." The "opposite" cognitive style is suggested by terms such as "imagination," "innovation," "abstract science." Insofar as theoretical science requires both a search for simplified index qualities of events *and* the relating of those index factors to a theory — that is, a newly invented frame or context which differs from the commonsense context — both kinds of concreteness are antithetical to a scientific, or a protoscientific, style of thinking.

The kinds of behavior that have suggested "concreteness" in both these senses to observers viewing nonwestern thinking from the contrast of suppositions and ideals concerning western thinking are evident in Piri and Roto. Thus the limitation of individual fantasy and the various ways of generalizing personal perceptions of shifting duration and size are the sorts of behaviors which have some bearing on "concreteness" in the sense of be-

ing bound to commonsense contexts. I will briefly consider
other matters bearing on "concreteness" in one or another sense,
deferring until the final section of the chapter my understanding
of their significance.

I noted in chapter 7 some of the categories people use in shifting ways to identify themselves and others. These categories
certainly entail many evaluations. In hearing descriptions by villagers of, say, "Frenchmen" or "Chinese" there are clearly shared
impressions of the power, moral qualities, and attractiveness of
these "classes" of people. But informants generally deny that
these attributes characterize any particular Chinese or Frenchman who happens to be the subject of discussion. One has to
know much more about his actions and his life.

Questions calling for evaluation and summary ("What were
your parents like?" or, for town dwellers, "How was the
movie?") tend to produce one of two kinds of response: either
a brief, very banal response, "They were good"; "It was fun,"
or a very detailed description. These options are what one might
expect in attempted transcultural communication between myself and Tahitians, but they also seem to characterize an option
in Tahitian communication — either an informationally shallow
generalized response or a detailed, often dramatic recreation of
the events which will provide a basis in the hearer for evaluation
and understanding.[7]

The details in the latter case, and in the recounting of a movie,
dream, or adventure simply for entertainment value, seem often
to approach "total recall." There is usually no way of knowing
if the details are being consciously or unconsciously made up
for the sake of the story, but in the cases where I knew the
event, particularly in the reporting of a movie, the recall of detail seemed remarkable to me.

7. The "concrete style" is well illustrated in the way a term is often defined for a non-Tahitian. For example, when Poria is asked the meaning of
the word *hoa*, which we may gloss as "friend," he says: "A *hoa* — we love
each other — I come and get you to go to my house so that we might eat
together. Sometimes we go and stroll together on the path. Sometimes I
go to your house to eat. Sometimes I want you to help me with my work.
Sometimes I go to help you. Sometimes we go to joke with the girls."

Qualities of certain classifications indicate concreteness in the sense of the marked significance of context for the meaning of a term. In my first naive attempts to get a "cultural map" of Roto and Piri, I asked such questions as "When does the *taure-'are'a* period begin?"; "In what life stage is X?"; "How far is it to Y village?" These were for me intuitively unproblematic questions — which turned out to be full of problems when stated in such form. The *taure'are'a* period does not begin at any particular point. It develops gradually, and a variety of factors are weighted together to indicate the probability of someone's being so labeled. Similarly the life stage X is said to be in depends on who is talking, how old he is, how he feels about X, what kinds of activities he is using to judge X's status (political, religious, sexual), variables which are in turn related to the context of the conversation in which the question arose. How far it is to Y village depends on how you go there.

One is dealing with a calculus in which terms are understood on the basis of a large number of contextual factors.[8] This is no problem in communication to villagers, who know the factors involved and can allow for them.

There are familiar western analogues. The statements "I was awake last *night* until 5 A.M." and "I woke up at 4 A.M. this *morning* to go fishing" provide no problem, although they might to a naive Martian anthropologist. Nor are there difficulties in understanding the sixty-year-old's comment that his colleague who died in his mid-fifties was "such a young man." Again it is a matter of extent. The emphasis on contexts and cases, a familiar attribute of conversations among intimates, seemed to me to characterize much of village behavior having to do with personal and social description.

---

8. The ordinary term to designate the *meaning* of a word or situation is *au ra'a*. *Au*, as we will see in several contexts, means the "fitting together of matters," "the relationship of things"; sometimes it implies a relationship which is fitting, comfortable, pleasant to the speaker. *Ra'a* indicates a process. *Au ra'a* used for kin designates their kin relationship. Thus the word for *meaning* designates the object's relationships, its contexts.

Ordinary Thinking: Culturally Provided Abstractions

In contrast to such relatively personal, context-dependent modes of thought and communication, we may place the *absolute* terms of a public world, in which terms have meaning independent of the special qualities of the participants and situation. That is, in contrast to such context-defined terms as "warm" or "slow," consider terms such as "forty degrees centigrade," "6 A.M.," "five miles," "twelve years old." These terms refer to features of things which can be understood free of contextual contingencies. The Tahitian language, as used by people in Piri and Roto, has many such terms.[9] But the language gives a faint indication of some limiting features.

Let us consider the vocabulary of logical terms. As various translations of segments from the interviews indicate, the Tahitian language provides a wide range of forms for logical discrimination. Conjunction, negation, exclusion, implication, contingency,[10] various degrees of certainty and probability, can all be clearly expressed, usually through specific particles. There are terms for making causal propositions[11] and for indicating nuances of temporal and spatial relationships and qualities.[12]

9. Terms for all objects (cow, house) are absolute or context-free in the sense given here. It is in the realm of relationships and processes that there seem to be limits.

10. There are two forms for "if," one indicating a simple possibility, the other something that might have been possible, but is, in fact, contrary to the actual situations. "If I had a boat [but I don't], I would lend it to you."

11. Explanatory forms are separated grammatically into two types. There are those which refer to relatively root explanations. These are indicated by use of the particle *nō*. In relation to a journey, *nō* indicates the starting point of the journey, and for a causal explanation indicates analogously a starting point or origin for the matter being explained. In contrast are forms using the particle *nā*, which indicates the route along which a journey proceeds and, analogously, influencing and shaping causes. Another way of indicating "basic" causes is by the use of the word for tree trunk, *tumu*, indicating the "trunk" or "root" cause. In ordinary speech the *nō* and *tumu* forms are much more frequently used than *nā*. The *nō* and *tumu* forms do not imply exclusive cause. There may be several *nō* causes.

12. It may be noted here that Tahitian, like English, uses the greater of pairs of contrasting measurement terms to indicate the quality being meas-

There are certain forms, however, which do not exist in Tahitian. Thus, Tahitian provides words indicating the propriety, urgency, value, and correctness of an action or state of affairs, but none for the idea of its simple necessity.[13] For this idea a French form, *il faut*, Tahitianized as *i fō*, has been introduced.

If we consider *il faut*, "it is necessary," as an "absolute term," indicating a condition without exceptions or qualifications, we may note that there are peculiarities in what seem to be absolute terms in Tahitian. That is, there are a number of Tahitian terms that are customarily glossed in English or French translations as if they were absolute: for example, "never," "always," "all," "every," "nothing." These terms have some interesting features. In contrast to the elementary particles for logical operations referred to previously (*rā*, "but"; *'ē*, "and"; *paha*, "perhaps"; *nō*, "because"; and so on), they are all compound terms, or more properly, short phrases. Thus "always" is *'aita e 'ore*, literally, "not stopping"; "all" is *pau roa*, literally, "very much consumed/emptied/used up." When one has become used to translating these terms as absolute, one is occasionally surprised by their usage in contexts which imply that they in fact indicate extreme tendencies but do not exclude exceptions. They are highly probabilistic but not categorical. Thus, for example, Teiva talking about his death says, "It is rare that I think about it; *pau roa* of the time I don't think about it." *Pau roa* is the strongest available term, and is, as we noted, usually glossed "all"; but here it has to be translated as "most."

Such linguistic features may be related speculatively to the question of the firm embeddedness of ideas in commonsense contexts. I will return to this later.

We have discussed aspects of private time. Cultures provide classifications of time and space and various other "categories

---

ured; e.g., "short" is *poto*, "long" is *roa*, "length" is *roa ra'a*. Similarly for length of time, size, or weight one asks, as in English, "How *long ago* was it?" "How *large* is it?" "How *heavy* is it?"

13. It also seems impossible in Tahitian to say "opposite," in the sense that "up" is the opposite of "down," "up" taking its meaning from "down" by opposition and exclusion.

of the understanding" which have something to do with facili-
tating individuals' movement into less private worlds — through
the encounter with and learning of the classifications.[14] Such
classifications may be more or less determined by contexts, more
or less closely related to the natural world.

Thus there are Tahitian terms for direction relative to an individual or object — terms indicating right, left, in front, behind,
above, below. There are also terms relating to island directions —
inland, seaward. And there are terms having to do with the most
abstract directions — toward the setting or rising sun, and upwind
or downwind in relation to the ordinary path (southeast) of the
trade winds. By far the most commonly used directional terms
in both Piri and Roto are those relating to island directions.
These are complicated (and made more concrete), in that the
directions used in relation to any path or route are based on the
eventual destination of the route. Thus on a winding route a position actually closer to the sea than another might be described
as "more inland" if the route passed them both and the second
position were farther along on its eventually inland direction.

There were traditional Tahitian systems for dividing up the
solar year and for marking divisions of the day. The traditional
system calculated lunar months, daily cycles of the moon, and
seasons based on the lunar calendar, on dry and wet periods,
and "on the rising and setting of the Pleiades."[15] Sidereal calculations were apparently skillfully done and were one of the bases
for navigation. The day was divided into light and dark and
subdivided primarily in terms of positions of the sun.

The calculation of years, seasons, months, and days shifted to
the western system, with its more mechanical "counting-off" of
the days. We have seen that this shift is still a source of concern
to some people. They are responding not to the introduction of
the system, which long antedated their births, but to its increasing importance in the coordination of their lives.

14. These are among the cultural forms which Bruner calls "[cultural]
amplifiers of human ratiocinative capacities" (Bruner, Rose, and Greenfield
1966; p. 56).

15. Some indication of traditional time systems is given by Henry (1928).

Clock time was not very important in Piri in the early 1960s,[16] although it was soon to change with the introduction of transistor radios (causing clocks to be coordinated and providing exactly scheduled Tahitian-language broadcasts). Time was based on sectors of the day designated by the height of the sun, a system which was used with some contextual variations (e.g., "It was still dark night, *pō*, this morning, *po'ipo'i* [usually the period after dawn], when I woke up").

The Question of Truth

However people in Piri and Roto may proceed to their understanding of the world, they are, of course, aware of the possibility of lies and errors. The ordinary word for "a lie" or "to lie" is *ha'avare*, which is the causative form of *vare*, "to be deceived," meaning therefore "that which causes one to be deceived" or "to cause to be deceived." *Ha'avare* is always used to indicate an intentional falsehood. There are also in Tahitian a number of words which mean "to be mistaken or incorrect" and words indicating correctness or accuracy. Such words apply to technical and moral behavior as well as to thought.

Words for "correctness" are used in opposition to words for "error." The word or phrase most frequently used in opposition to *ha'avare*, or "lie," is *parau mau*, or more rarely *mea mau*. *Parau* means "speech," and *mea* means "thing"; and used in conjunction with *mau* they signify "true speech" or "true thing" or "idea." *Mau* in this usage seems to be related to other meanings of *mau* which signify "caught," "fixed," or "unchanging." A canoe tied up to a stake or a post firmly fixed in the ground is *mau*. Another verbal way of indicating the truth of something is by the strongest word in the series of probability terms, *pāpū*, indicating "extremely likely."

---

16. The meanings of these new, relatively context-free, time schemas are not entirely unproblematical. Teiva, one day, was complaining about the present-day *taure'are'a*, who seemed to him to be much more restless, unsettled, and unsure of what to do than the *taure'are'a* of his own youth: "First they do this thing, and then they do that. They are always changing — like a clock."

There are assertions which are qualified as not being *parau mau* or *pāpū*, because they are *mana'o noa*, "only [my] thought." Others are qualified as only rumor, "something which has been told to me" or "something my ear has heard." The word for "knowledge" or "understanding" is *'ite*, which is also the word for "to see." Visual perception seems thus associated with knowledge, auditory perception with hearsay.

Parau mau, as "truth," seems to imply something which is both clearly known to the individual speaking and fixed as truth in community consensus.

There is another way of evaluating assertions besides "correct" or "true." This is an evaluation, independent of experiential and community truth, which has to do with human fitness. It involves things which are *au*. An idea, an event, or a prospect which is *au* is something the speaker regards as being pleasant, as fitting in with his needs and hopes in an attractive way. Things which are *au* fit and facilitate rather than restrain or guide. Thus people will sometimes explicitly accept a doctrine knowing that it may not be *parau mau*, but saying that they find it *au* to accept it.

"Primitive Thought" in Piri

I have sketched some miscellaneous behaviors and cultural forms which were selected not because they were necessarily particularly important for understanding the day-to-day thinking of individuals in Piri and Roto, but because they have some bearing on the question whether life in relatively simple and traditional communities such as Piri entails in itself, independently of special cultural traditions, some influence on ways of thinking. I have followed long-established preoccupations in the discussion of "primitive thought" by emphasizing matters having to do with "magic thinking" and with "concreteness" in its various senses.

I have indicated, with qualifications, that there do seem to be some qualities of thinking of the people in Piri and of the *mā'ohi* people of Roto which, I think, are implications of the "simplicity" of the cultural system in which they are involved. I have portrayed a style of thought which seems closely involved with the world as presented through the senses. People do not move far in world-altering fantasy, nor do they engage in much logical and intellectual play with the data of that world. In this sense they justify John Williams's qualification that the otherwise obvious intelligence of the South Sea islanders was not manifested in "depth of thought and profundity of research."

Private perceptions are brought into encounter with public classifications which are in themselves for the most part context-determined and not "absolute." I have given examples of private perceptions in some realms taken as aspects of the public world; we may take this as an indication of some limitation of the public culture's ability to "coerce" objectivity. Where objective public understanding is reached, people understand one another to a considerable degree through a calculus which takes the context (i.e., "what is going on") into account in interpreting key terms of discourse and classification. When they describe those portions of their world having to do with people and with events, there is a tendency to make use of a large variety of data, including the position of the observer. Oriented to richness of detail for understanding, people will try to portray an unfamiliar event to others by such a detailed description. On the other hand, because of the mass of shared information and experience, familiar events can be indicated by a few suggested details.

In Piri the contexts in which one's experiences take place are all within a fixed and unified set based on the same underlying cultural postulates. There are no contrasts or exceptions to these postulates. They are not seen from the outside, nor as special cases among other possible cultural systems.

To be concrete: when some people in Athens and Sparta become deeply aware that the way people are punished for wrongdoing, and the kinds of wrongdoing for which they are punished, vary in the two cities, they may begin to ask, "What is Justice?"; "What are Morals?" The knowledge of alternative systems will sharpen the question of which behaviors or relationships are necessary in both (or any) systems, as opposed to which are proper only within the contingencies of one or the other city. We may note that terms such as "much," "frequent," "little," and "very probable" characterize a directly experienced world. But "always," "never," and "necessary," as formally absolute terms, are never illustrated in the finite experience of that world. They require a standing outside, a reflection on that world from the vantage point of another "system." Intimate knowledge of two sociocultural systems is one way of getting outside.

The thinking of people in Piri is *embedded* in its contexts and operates, often wisely and intelligently, within them, but does not challenge the context itself. In this sense it is not theoretical and not conducive to science nor to any of the other intellectual games which require the awareness, challenging, and reconstituting of contexts from which events take their meaning.

It is perhaps only in a world of rigorous, context-independent laws of cause and effect that magic begins to be banished, for the magic world is experientially true. The people of Piri and Roto, lacking the possibility of banishing the world of magic and the supernatural by convincing themselves that it is only illusory, must take other precautions — must place it in its own realm and issue directions for minimizing encounters.

But people in Piri and Roto have lived in contact with radically different systems for two hundred years. That has not been enough to make intellectuals of them (with the exception of Hiro). Rooted in their old culture, with its successful digestion of Christianity, the assumptions of the other cultures are very distant from them, and their experience of unified, commonsense reality is, except in fleeting moments, not quite yet under serious challenge.

The intellectual sets indicated are probably strongly influenced by patterned aspects of child development, which we will consider in later chapters. For cultural complexity to affect the "organization of thought" of a traditional community it must both enter into the set of culturally transmitted assumptions, those serving as "amplifiers of human ratiocinative capacities," and also cause shifts in conditions of the intellectual development of individuals. It is not enough for the contrasting cultural postulates to be somewhere along the margins of a community —

they must intimately affect and transform the experience of individuals to cause a reorganization of their way of thinking.

The *mā'ohi* of Roto illustrate this most poignantly. Living in constant daily contact with Chinese, Europeans, and *demis*, having their community shrunken almost to their own households, they live in a cultural cocoon which makes them think much more like the far-off people of Piri than like their neighbors of Papeete. They still show qualities of thought which make sense in Piri and a multitude of places like it, but which make them seem "simple," in the patronizing phrase of their *demi* neighbors and the anthropological observer.

9

Feeling

This chapter considers a variety of matters which have some unity, in that one of their main references is to bodily sensations. I am excluding here feelings associated with shame and guilt, with sexual experience, and with "pathological states," all of which are considered elsewhere.

By "feeling" I mean something more than "emotion" — I have thus included some remarks on pain and on the feelings related to "drive." "Emotion" seems, in western usage, to indicate a vaguely bounded subset of feeling. Emotions seem to be feelings which convey and represent information about one's *mode of relationship as a total individual* to the social and nonsocial environment; and they seem to involve sensations with essential autonomic nervous system components.

As I indicated in the discussion of the theory of thinking of informants in Piri and Roto, people say that such matters as "anger," "desire," and "fear" arise in the *'ā'au*, or intestines. This is the traditional seat of such feelings in Tahiti. Some people say that these states could also "enter into the heart." This is in part an introduced biblical form for the seat of the emotions, but it may also involve the perception of visceral emotional responses in the chest as well as in the abdomen.

"Anger," "desire," and "fear" can arise spontaneously in the *'ā'au*, or else they may be stirred up by some thought from the head, or by something "seen by the eyes," or "heard by the ears." Pain arises in the affected part; feelings of "energy" invest the whole body. In a crude way those feelings which do involve the *'ā'au* or "heart" indicate the category of "emotions." There are possible exceptions; "uncanny emotions," as we have seen, are localized in the skin and head. There is no Tahitian term for either "feelings" or "emotion."

271

In ordinary speech, even as people discard the theory of thought to say "I think . . . ," so they discard theories of feeling (which more precisely are generated by questions of the kind, "What is the nature of anger?"), and say something like "*'Ua riri vau,*" "I am angry" or "I have become angry." They refer to themselves in an undifferentiated way.

The class of "feelings" and particularly the "emotions" have to do with sensations which are intimately and importantly connected with interpretation and labels. That is, Tahitian interpretations of feeling have an influence on the action connected with the perceived body state which is far more significant than, for example, the influence Tahitian ideas *about* thinking have on the act of thinking itself. Interpretations (and less intellectual precipitates of learning) influence both the production of the feeling and its consequences.

It is even possible to classify something which to an observer seems to be an "emotion" as some other kind of feeling. This is what happens when Tahitians classify feelings consequent upon the loss of someone whom they love as "illness." Now instead of having direct conscious knowledge about a quality or change in their "mode of relationship to the social and nonsocial environment," they become concerned with the feeling as disordered body function, as illness. (We have noted how the *tahu'a* in his healing practice labels emotions as nonemotional symptoms of spirit activity.)

In the chapter on "style" I suggested some stylistic features of the display of emotion. I noted that emotion is often displayed clearly — indicated in a lively way through qualities of the voice and face, particularly the eyes.[1] I noted that in comparison the expressive use of the rest of the body is relatively muted.

Generally, people were serious and concerned during their interviews with me. While recounting past events they often dram-

---

1. Paul Ekman and Wallace Friesen have argued that the emotion expressed by the face is closest to conscious control; it is most easily self-monitored. The face is also the focus of interpersonal attention. Less controlled and conscious emotional states are expressed through the trunk and extremities (Ekman and Friesen 1969).

atized the accounts, simulating various kinds of emotion to add to the color of the story. The nonsimulated demonstration of a strong emotion during the interviews was very rare and stood out in contrast to the usual expression of feeling. Tāvana, for example, in talking of his dead first wife, had his eyes full of tears. There were few such episodes.

I will argue that the people of Piri and Roto distrust strong emotions. Strong passions force one out of control, make one do things one does not want to do. One needs some control, some freedom from these passions. Willful dramatization is a way of controlling emotions as well as expressing them.

Unfriendly Feelings and Actions

In chapter 3 I noted some of the early descriptions of the inhabitants of Tahiti and the neighboring islands, which emphasized the gentleness and friendliness of the people. Morrison epitomized it: "Their courteous, affable and friendly behavior to each other shows that they have no tincture of barbarity, cruelty, suspicion or revenge. They are ever of an even, unruffled temper, slow to anger and soon appeased and as they have no suspicion so they ought not to be suspected, and an hour's acquaintance is sufficient to repose an entire confidence in them" (Morrison 1935; p. 170).

The Reverend William Ellis, writing in the years from 1817 to 1824, noted that the Tahitians, now Christians, of the time "are, generally speaking, careful not to give offense to each other. . . . There are . . . few domestic broils; and were fifty natives taken promiscuously from any town or village, to be placed in a neighbourhood or house — where *they* would disagree once, fifty Englishmen, selected in the same way, and placed under similar circumstances, would quarrel perhaps twenty times. They do not appear to delight in provoking one another, but are far more accustomed to jesting, mirth, and humour, than irritating or reproachful language" (Ellis 1830; 2:24).

There were some fights and disorders reported by the early observers, although often with some indication that they seemed somehow unusual. Thus John Forster remarked, "Nor are the inhabitants of the islands in the South Sea [he is talking about Tahiti and the Society Islands] quite free from a coarseness of manners, even to indelicacy in many respects, especially among the lower class of people; which appears from the disputes of many of them, wherein they fall to beating one another with the fist, and pulling one another's hair" (J. Forster 1778; p. 409). And Morrison later noted, "Private disputes between men relative to themselves only seldom produce a blow" (Morrison 1935; p. 163).

There were, in fact, extremely few reports of angry behavior. The ship's doctor on Cook's third voyage, during which four months were spent in the Society Islands, reacting perhaps to the French tales of Tahiti as the *nouvelle cythère*, the Isle of Love, inhabited by noble savages, remarked, "As the women, in such a life, must contribute greatly to its happiness, it is surprising that they should not only suffer the most humiliating restraints with regard to food, but should be often treated with a degree of brutality, which one would suppose a man must be incapable of towards an object for whom he had the least affection or esteem. It is, however, extremely common to see the men beat them most unmercifully" (Cook 1784; 2:99). If this was "extremely common" it is not reported as such by other observers, but occasional wife-beating, and even husband-beating by wives, was noted.

There was community-sanctioned violence in such things as human sacrifice and war, but the details of these institutions do not make them appear unnecessarily brutal. John Turnbull, who had visited Tahiti in the first years of the nineteenth century, wrote, "They certainly live amongst each other in more harmony than is usual amongst Europeans. During the whole time I was amongst them, I never saw such a thing as a battle; and though they are excellent wrestlers, and in their contests give each other many a hard fall, the contest is no sooner concluded, than they are as good friends as ever. Their frequent wars must be imputed to the ambition of their chiefs; and were it not for the restless disposition of these men, I am persuaded that war would be almost unknown amongst them" (Turnbull 1812; p.

372). Turnbull generalized, "Their dispositions are gentle to an extreme. [With two exceptions] I never saw an Otaheitan out of temper the whole time I was in Otaheite" (Turnbull 1812; p. 339).

Morrison, who had noted that the Tahitians were "slow to anger and soon appeased," has a passage in his journal bearing on the rapid appeasement. He records in his journal of March 1790 the murder of one of the *Bounty* mutineers, Thompson, in revenge for the murder of another mutineer, Churchill. Churchill had been made the "blood brother" of a chief of a small district, thus gaining some chiefly status, and some of the natives of the district felt they had to avenge Churchill's death.

The manner was this. Patirre . . . being sorry for his friend's death was determined to be revenged on Thompson, and having got five or six more (who when they knew the cause were equally enraged), they went to Thompson's house and saluted him . . . and told him that he was now chief, and such like flattering stories till Patirre got between him and his arms, and being a stout man, knocked him down. The others whipped a short plank (which happened to be at hand) across his breast, and placed one on each end, while Patirre ran for a large stone, with which he dashed his skull to pieces. They then cut off his head and buried the body [cutting off the head was for ritual purposes]. . . . I asked him why they had not brought him to us at Matavai, when he replied, "The distance is too great, and our anger would be gone before we could get there; and we should have let him escape when we were cooled and our anger gone so that he would not have been punished at all and the blood of the chief would have been on our heads." (Morrison 1935; p. 95)

Out of the copious reports of the early visitors to Tahiti one gets the impression that acute, explosive, hostile behavior was rare in relation to European expectations and that prolonged, intense bad temper, grudge-holding, and vengefulness were even rarer. Many examples are given of individuals' avoiding giving and taking provocations to anger and being quick to seek ways to make peace with one another as well as with the powerful Europeans.

In the early years of the attempts to convert the people to Christianity, a time of political instability before the establishment of hegemony by a missionary-supported chief, there was, according to the missionary Ellis, some violent drunkenness. This was hearsay evidence; it had taken place some years before Ellis arrived in Tahiti.

He wrote, "Under the unrestrained influence of their intoxicating draught, in their appearance and actions they resembled demons more than human beings. Sometimes, in a deserted stillhouse might be seen the fragments of the rude boiler and the other appendages of the still, scattered in confusion on the ground; and among them the dead and mangled bodies of those who had been murdered with axes or billets of wood in the quarrels that had terminated their dissipation. It was not only among themselves that their unbridled passions led to such enormities. One or two European vessels were seized and the crews inhumanely murdered" (Ellis 1830; 1:231).

Whatever the objectivity of Ellis's report on the effects of drinking in 1814 and on murders of the time, later reports of drinking, which continued to be widespread, presented it as nonviolent. And Jacques Moerenhout noted in the early 1830s that there had been no case of murder in the Islands since 1814 (Moerenhout 1837; 1:256).

"Gentleness," defined negatively as behavior in which manifest hostility or violence is unusual, is still very saliently characteristic of Tahitians of French Polynesia. The gendarme who administered Huahine in the early 1960s had worked in Indochina, French Guinea, Algiers, and Morocco. For him the people of Huahine are "lambs." He contrasts them with the people of Morocco, who were "hot-tempered, easily angered, thieves, murderers, and rapists." Huahine, he says, is "the other end of the world." What surprised him, he says, echoing the early reports, is the lack of a vengeful spirit. Even though people are occasionally cheated or insulted by a visitor or merchant, they do not seem to show any anger over this, or any need to get even. There is, he says, no serious crime in Huahine, no violence, no "forced" theft. There are only very occasional and minor disturbances connected with drinking, and these are usually easily controlled by a few stern words.

The records for Huahine between 1940 and 1962 showed only one serious crime, a murder, in 1953.[2] For the period before 1940 there is only one other serious crime known to the older people in Huahine. This had taken place in 1928 and involved a man who, angry with his wife, had beaten and then drowned her.

Comparative crime rates are notoriously difficult to interpret. Official reports and available statistics for French Polynesia as a whole suggest, however, low *total crime* rates as reflected in cases coming to the attention of the authorities.[3]

2. "Serious crime" here is used for the French legal designation *crime*, generally equivalent to "felony." These are serious offenses which require adjudication at a special criminal court, the *assise*, and which entail at least five years' imprisonment.

The 1953 crime was a very violent, and probably impulsive, murder, although there was some question about the amount of premeditation involved. It concerned an eighteen-year-old man, a native of Huahine, who, after an argument with a Chinese farmer, killed him by stabbing him and hacking at his body with a bush knife. They had had previous arguments and had exchanged insults and threats.

3. The Gendarmerie nationale at Papeete has published statistics for the territory for selected sample years. Table 1 shows the number of cases of murder and total *crime* in sample years between 1900 and 1959. These are *crimes* committed and not the number of criminals involved. *Crimes* recorded are artificially somewhat low, as for various reasons some offenses which would be handled as *crimes* in metropolitan France are handled as *délits* (misdemeanors) in the territory. On the other hand, there is no indication of which of the *crimes* were committed by Tahitians rather than Chinese or Europeans.

A supplementary report (Bouvet 1962) gives total *crime* totals for 1960 and 1961 as only two and one, respectively.

The murder rates for 1930 and 1959 are not "low" in terms of comparisons with other countries. Ceylon, for example, which is said by Arthur L. Wood to have a high homicide rate, had a homicide rate of 5.9/100,000 in 1957. But such rates were typical for each year reported for Ceylon between 1939 and 1957 and were not occasional findings. The more remarkable comparative aspect of these figures is the "total crime rate." Thus Ceylon in 1957, in addition to the homicide cases, had rates of "attempted homicide," 2.6/100,000; "grievous hurt," 25.7/100,000; and "hurt by knife," 38.4/100,000. These figures total a rate for *crime against persons* of 72.6/100,000. Adding *crimes against property*, *sex crimes*, and miscel-

TABLE 1

MURDERS AND TOTAL *Crimes* IN SAMPLE YEARS, FRENCH POLYNESIA

Year	Total Population	Murders	Total Crime
1900	28,960	0	0
1910	31,770	0	2
1920	34,910	0	2
1930	39,480	4	8
1940	49,770	0	0
1950	61,270	2	5
1953	67,280	0	3
1956	73,201	0	0
1959	Approx. 80,000	5	8

SOURCE: Bouvet and Iorsch 1960.

As we shall see, informants sometimes designate suicide as a form of angry behavior. Some indication of the frequency of suicide may be given here. Informants remembered three suicides in Huahine since 1945. Two were natives of the island, and one was an official from Tahiti, a *demi* who was temporarily assigned to Huahine.

One of the resident cases involved a man who had been having intercourse with his fifteen-year-old daughter. The village policemen had found out about it and had decided to tell the gendarme at Fare. On the day that the village policemen went to report, the man hung himself.

The other resident case involved a girl of fifteen. According to the tale, her adoptive father, a Chinese, had died, and her adoptive mother, a Tahitian, took a new *tāne* who was much younger than the mother. The girl was unhappy about this. The mother one morning had become angry with her over something or other, had threatened her, and then had hit her. The girl said to

_____

laneous other crimes, a certain percentage of which are equivalent to French *crime*, the total Ceylon figures for "grave crime" for 1957 were 213.0/100,000. (Figures from the Ceylon Police Service, quoted in Wood 1961; p. 54.)

her mother as the mother was leaving the house, "You will never see me again." Then she laid out her white clothes (those used in important church ceremonies, at funerals, and to be buried in) and hung herself.

Officials believe that suicide in the territory as a whole is relatively common among Chinese, rare among Tahitians. Between 1958 and 1962, figures for the territory,[4] exclusive of the Leeward Island group, which kept separate records, showed nine suicides. Of these only two were Tahitians, four were Chinese, one was Vietnamese, one was French, and one was a tourist of unspecified origin.[5] The two Tahitian cases were men, both living on the island of Tahiti.

Even if one has adequate rates for some types of violent behavior, there is always the question of what, if anything, the comparatively high or low frequencies of behavior making up the rates have to do with the ordinary behavior of others in the population. In the Tahitian case the apparently low amounts of "crime" seem to be related to a pervasive lack of violence in everyday life.

Let us consider violence and anger in Piri. My first impressions of life in Piri were, as I have noted, of interpersonal restraint and a lack of hostile aggressiveness. As I learned more about the community, it was clear that the effective hostility, both in terms of discharge and in terms of hurting effect, mediated in "small" acts such as gossip, teasing, coolness, was more important that I had been able to judge at first.

There were very few physical fights in Piri, and those that did occur were not particularly violent. I saw only one physical fight there (which I will describe shortly) and none in my visits to Fare, the port town in Huahine; my visits there included the period of the July festival, when villagers from all of Huahine went

---

4. From the records of the Gendarmerie nationale and from the records of the Palais de justice at Papeete.

5. The relevant population base for the reporting area in 1962 was 68,373, of which approximately 7,800 were "Chinese or part Chinese"; 44,453 were "Tahitians"; and 7,197 were *"demis."* The remainder were "Europeans."

to Fare for several days of sports, dancing, and drinking. Three other fights reportedly did take place at Piri during the time I was there. These all were among the same group of drinking companions and mostly involved quickly terminated pushing and shoving.

In Piri lack of fighting is particularly striking among children in public settings. Groups of children usually play near the schoolhouse, on the wharf, or in the fields near the village. Play of children in these groups is highly energetic and involves a good deal of joking and, in same-sex play, body contact, and often mock aggression, such as pushing or a tug of a girl's pigtail. The mock aggression does not usually turn into more serious forms. Occasionally during a game a critical or irritated remark is made, and the recipient will simply ignore it or, rarely, withdraw crying. He disengages.

When things get more serious in children's conflicts (I saw only two such episodes), the fashion of expressing a threat is carefully ineffectual. An offended boy chases his tormentor but never catches him, while other children look on with serious expressions. Then, giving up, the boy throws a small piece of dry coconut husk at his antagonist but carefully misses. Children are excellent marksmen in other kinds of throwing.

The village school in Piri had eighty-five children in 1963. The head schoolteacher says that in his two years at Piri he has never seen a fight among the older schoolchildren (from eight to fifteen years of age) in the schoolyard. The children come to play there before and after school and also have regular play periods during the day. He says that younger children (six to eight) occasionally cry angrily or throw pebbles at each other over some disagreement but that this is very rare.

Another teacher, who has worked in Piri and in other villages in Huahine for nine years, contrasts the behavior of children in Huahine with behavior in Anaa in the Tuamotu archipelago, an island group in the territory with marked linguistic and cultural differences from the Society Islands. At Huahine, she says, the children do not fight much, and it is rare to have a bad child in class. In the Tuamotus the children "are wicked. They fight and throw stones at each other, and sometimes threaten the teacher. When they play, it is not to have fun but often to hurt each other. In their language, they are vulgar and dirty, as are their parents. In Huahine it is very rare to hear dirty language even among the adults, and very unusual among the children."

Public hostile behavior (i.e., that which takes place in out-of-the-house village areas or within a house when there are visitors) was often characterized by a restraint of physically hurting action, by the dependence on and playing to an audience, by anxiety of the audience, and by a later exaggeration in reporting the incident to others.

Some of the quality of village violent behavior is illustrated in this incident:

During the New Year's festival at Piri in 1963, which lasted eight days and involved a considerable amount of drinking, there was only one episode which might have been described as violent. This involved a deviant man in the village named Tore, who lived by himself in a small house in the far inland part of the village. Tore stayed out of most village activities. He was regarded sometimes as a clown and sometimes as mildly frightening, and he seemed to encourage and enjoy generating anxiousness. He usually wore sunglasses and a unique knotted handkerchief cap and affected dramatic mannerisms. The New Year's festival had started with church services, to be followed for most people by an all-night prayer, hymn singing, and a Bible discussion session. Everyone was dressed in his best clothes — the older men and women in white, the women wearing broad-brimmed cloth hats, many of which were trimmed with lace for such special occasions. The only one who was not dressed up was Tore. He made a point of walking through the groups of people assembled outside the various church meeting houses, wearing only shorts, an old shirt, his handkerchief cap, and his sunglasses.

On the second day of the festival Tore appeared at a dance shed which had been set up for the occasion. There were food and jugs of wine at the shed. Tore rapidly drank three or four water glasses of wine, one after another. It was generally said that Tore was troublesome and bad when he drank. Immediately after having finished off the four tumblers, he began to stagger around in exaggerated discoordination. Onlookers looked mildly anxious. He began to try to pick arguments with people, who ignored him. After an hour or so of such attempts, the village policeman, who was also somewhat drunk, took hold of Tore, who made little resistance, and tied him up to a tree. He was left tied to the tree for about two hours. Many people ignored him; others commented that it really had not been necessary to tie him up. It began to rain, and Pae, a neighbor of Tore, came and untied him. Some time later he entered the dance shed again. Tamu, one of Piri's "heavy drinkers" who was slightly drunk, accused Tore somewhat angrily of "frightening people." They began to hit each other lightly. Tamu finally pushed Tore, who fell down. Then Tamu picked up the chastened Tore and, aided by Tetuanui Vahine, a sister of Tore, walked Tore, his arms about their shoulders, off to his house inland, where he went to sleep.

The next day Tore claimed that he did not remember anything of the previous afternoon after his first drinks. He said that he had been drunk, and that he had done wrong, and that he was through drinking for the rest of the New Year's festival. This was an accurate prediction. During the rest of the festival he was occasionally to be seen sitting at the edge of the dance floor and quietly watching the dancing.

This was a typical "blowup," in that it was rather dramatic and relatively harmless, both immediately and in terms of any relatively long-term, unresolved consequences. Drinking (which will be considered in chapter 12) seemed necessary for Tore's expressive behavior, but his "drunken" behavior was in itself restrained.

There are two salient types of hostile-appearing behavior in Piri which do not involve physical hurting. First are activities such as gossip and teasing — the usual daily hostile activities. They are widely used in socialization and village social control. Second are those episodes in which a dramatic expression of destructive action is carefully limited in its effectiveness. Thus Ropae, a son of Tāvana, furious at his *vahine*, sets fire to some coconut thatching sections lying on the ground at a safe distance from his and other houses. Or a group of men, driven to exasperation after months of administration by a crudely interfering and destructive gendarme, gather one night and throw very small stones a safe distance from his feet; when the time comes for him to leave the post, he is given an exaggeratedly elaborate farewell feast, combining regret for the action and further indirect hostility. In those fights that do take place between men they do not hit each other very hard, as in the fight between Tamu and Tore, and it is easy for the bystanders to hold them back.

The presence of bystanders, of audiences, seems necessary for these expressions. First a main object of the explosion is to bring some tension from the private into the public realm, to express a dissatisfaction or to shame an opponent. Even when the outburst is a more simple discharge of tension, the presence of the audience gives safety to the actor or actors, in that they will be controlled if the fight begins to look serious.

The lack of serious physical destructiveness is striking just because of the showy, dramatic quality of the behavior. The usual bland, quiet, "easygoing" style of life gives noisy or mildly destructive episodes a particular shock value. There seems to be an analogy of Weber's Law for perception that holds for such cases, namely, *the lower the initial stimulus level, the less an increment has to be to be perceived as an increment.*

Episodes which look relatively mild to people familiar with forms of destructiveness in other cultures are often reported later in what seem to be exaggerated terms, overstating the amount of injury sustained. People also frequently report fear of possible physical harm from other people in settings in which the fear does not seem to be objectively warranted.

They would say of themselves, "Tahitians are terrible when they get into a fight"; "Tahitians could never play American football [with tackling], they would kill each other." Some of the women stayed away from the dancing and drinking sheds in Piri during the New Year's festival because they were afraid "someone would get killed." Oro, who had said that he was afraid to walk on the dark streets in Papeete (which were objectively safe), says that the only reason he is not afraid to walk on the path in Piri after dark is that no one would try to hurt him, since everyone in the village would immediately know who had done it. The fear of the consequences of anger, of hostility, of violence — with little apparent experience of such consequences — is noteworthy.

If there is little violence under ordinary conditions, there also seems to be little under conditions of personal breakdown, including drunkenness. Drinking is common, particularly during the two yearly festivals. With the exception of a few incidents, such as the episode of Tore, people are as unhostile drunk as sober. In more private settings, drinking is associated with somewhat more violent behavior. People who drink in the house or return to the house when drunk often begin arguments and occasionally hit a spouse or child.

Interpretations of Anger

The ordinary word for anger is *riri*. It is one of the emotions which have their seat in the *'ā'au*, although it may be stirred up by thoughts or observations. It goes from the *'ā'au* to the head, where it should be thought over before action.

Extreme rage is *hae*, when, according to Poria, "The person is so extremely angry, he wants to devour you." There is another term, *'iriā*, which refers to a state of irritability, a proneness to become angry, and which is often used to refer to a type of person.

Out of a total list of 301 items in the missionary dictionary which seemed to describe various feeling states, 47 referred to angry feelings. It may be significant, and is congruent with contemporary forms, that in the list of terms for feeling terms for anger were the most numerous type, as contrasted with the number of terms in such commonsense sets as pleasure, fear, longing, "agitation of the mind," sadness, tenderness, shame, and so forth. Of these 47 items, at least 12 seem to represent trustworthy terms for anger, probably carrying different nuances of meaning. Of these 12 terms, only 3 are in use in contemporary Tahitian. In spite of the limited number of surviving terms, anger is "hypercognated" in Piri and Roto. That is, relative to some other feeling states (for example, interpersonal longing and loneliness, which, as we will see, may be interpreted as some vague "being out of sorts"), there is considerable doctrine about anger, its effects, and what to do about it.

Anger is generally portrayed as a bad thing, although it may be useful in small amounts, as Tāvana puts it, because it helps you overcome fear when someone has wronged you. But it can lead, people say, to knife fights, to injuries, and to killing. (It is noteworthy that the common word for "beat up" or "thrash," *taparahi*, also means "kill." Similarly, as I have discussed in connection with death, the word for "unconscious," *pohe*, also means "dead.")

These statements about the violent effects of anger are, as noted, in the face of little experience of such anger. They are related to a generalized and culturally valued timidity.

If anger is generally stated to be dangerous, it is also said that once one is angry the proper thing to do is to express it, preferably by angry words, so that one's anger may calm down. For, as Tāvana says, "The Tahitians say that an angry man is like a bottle. When he gets filled up he will begin to spill over." Unexpressed anger has bad effects on one's body; it may give one trouble in one's head or heart. There are people who have died from anger.

Oro, asked his thoughts about anger, describes the unpleasantness of the experience of being angry. "[Anger] isn't a good thing." ("Why?") "You think you will hold it inside of you and then a time comes when you don't feel any sense of drive [*'ana-'anatae*, to be discussed later] anymore. Because of that thing [the anger] you become weak, if you are angry at some person, [and] hold it in. If there is a time you are angry, don't hold it inside of you." ("What is a good thing to do when one gets angry?") "If you are angry at that man, don't procrastinate, go and talk to him, finish it. And afterward, things will be all right again between you, things will be finished [i.e., bad things]. If you are angry and you simply hold it in and you are annoyed with that person, it is a bad thing. It's as if your head isn't right."

If you hold it in and don't go to confront the person who makes you angry, he goes on, you will come to want to go and kill him so that "the anger will lift from you."

Flora adds that unexpressed anger will turn one's hair white.

Expressing anger implies, as Oro makes clear, an attempt to tell someone you are angry in order to correct the cause of the anger. This is not only a personal relief from unpleasant feelings but a way of trying to avoid further trouble. As Veve Vahine explains why she prefers people to tell her if they are angry with her, "If somebody doesn't tell me when he is angry at me, he'll go and tell somebody else. He'll gossip about me, and exaggerate, and then trouble will start in the village."

Shy, *māmahu*, people do not express their anger at the moment it is stirred up. Toni gave a typical characterization of such people: "They can't look you in the eye. They don't seem to get mad easily, but you have to watch out, because if they finally do get mad they are very violent."

All this is part of a general understanding that undischarged anger takes substitute forms and a clear labeling of these substitute forms as expressions of anger. A young man in Piri explains his punishing of his children one day as being because he was angry at his *vahine* but could not hit her, fearing more trouble. His anger, he says, had gone over to his children.

One of the motivational explanations given for actual or attempted suicide is anger. Poria tells of wanting to kill himself as a child because of his anger toward his grandfather, who had mistreated him. Even if suicide is not directly caused by anger, it is considered an act which shows a certain shameful loss of self-control. Teiva notes that he sometimes felt discouraged. If he had no children, he says, he might have thought of suicide. But now he wouldn't consider it, for it would make his children ashamed.

We have noted that some supernatural beliefs, particularly those involving cursing, involve the expression of anger. Ordinary curses are connected with effective threats ("something is going to happen to you"), usually by women. As Toni once remarked, "If a man gets angry he can always hit a woman, but the woman can only make [supernaturally effective] threats."

The main effect of magic beliefs about anger leading to curses is to make people wary about other people's getting mad at them. The beliefs provide a pressure for conciliation. One way to avoid becoming the victim of unpleasant magic is to avoid angering others in the village.

Anger, then, is related to a considerable amount of theorizing. The rather detailed psychological and social doctrine related to *riri* is not the case with all other affective sets. Some — anger, shame, fear — are well discriminated; others — loneliness, depression, guilt — are poorly discriminated. The high discrimination of angry behaviors combined with strong, shared evaluations and interpretations facilitates psychological and social control.

When we examine childhood experience and socialization and also various aspects of prevalent psychological organization of people studied in Piri and Roto, we will see that doctrines about *riri* are supported by, and both reflect and reinforce, various "modes of reaction." Socialization techniques and other aspects of community experience seem to produce, through sequences which will later be considered in detail, orientations which are the common sense of individuals and which are in a way prior to doctrines. Thus, for example, there is a general timidity about encounters with others, who are perceived as stronger and bigger than oneself. There is a conviction that "nature" in general, not just the offended individual, will turn against and punish someone guilty of hurtful action. There is a general sense that passions are disruptive to the self, that they must be kept at low levels.

Such intuitions about "the way things are," amplified by doctrines concerning anger and violence, lead to strategies for coping with anger: Try not to get into situations which will make you mad. Don't take things seriously, or withdraw if possible. If someone else is mad at you, try not to let it build up. If you do get angry, however, express it by talking out your anger, so that things can be corrected and you will not be holding it in. Express your anger, if possible, by verbal rather than physical means. If you use physical means try to use symbolic actions, not touching the person. If you do touch him, be careful not to hurt him.

All this seems to work, in part because of a variety of factors which minimize frustrations, situations in which anger may be generated. Life in Piri and even in Roto is meaningful, and the particular frustrations of "anomie," of social disorder, are minimal. There are, obviously, many tensions in the life of both places, those related to the organized life of small communities. But there are certain themes which seem to reduce the meaning of events as frustrations. For example, the training and doctrine against striving. Too much striving is morally bad, is unproductive, is even dangerous. If one does not strive, if one is unambitious, there is less chance of being frustrated by some particular encounter. Related to the lack of striving is an emphasis on the substitutability of goals and desired objects, which are assumed to be in adequate supply. If you lose one woman, you will get another. If you don't get fish one day, you will on another. The best way to get ahead is to take it easy.

As the end product, perhaps, of experiments in adaptation to life on small islands, the arrangements for minimizing the interpersonal effects of anger seem to work quite well.

Unpleasant Feelings

Sadness. We may take feelings, which we suppose to be engendered by the loss of someone or something one cares about, and call them "sadness," as a first approximation.

We may begin to examine such feelings in connection with the death of others. I have considered death, in chapter 7, from the aspect of the meaning of people's *own* death to themselves and have noted there (and in chapter 5) some of the doctrine and sentiments about death. But one's own death and the death of those one cares for are different matters.

Early observers recorded aspects of pre-Christian mourning behavior. I have quoted Bligh's report (Bligh 1937; 2:15) of several women, including the mother, mourning over the body of a young girl; "[the mourner] burst into a fit of laughter at seeing me. . . . They all resumed a degree of cheerfulness, and the tears were immediately dried up."

Edmond de Bovis, who studied the rapidly changing Tahitian culture of the mid-nineteenth century, has a related note. He states that ceremonies related to death were "simple private transactions where religion or government did not intervene in any regular manner" and adds: "The only thing which resembled a ceremony and which had become an indispensable formality, were the cries and signs of mourning. When someone had just given up his last breath, those of his close ones who found themselves in the house began to wail in a peculiar way. Each new relative who arrived to visit the dead one cried in like manner. . . . Most of the women and men 'criers' are not particularly sad, because one sees them in leaving the dead man's house give themselves over to their ordinary pastimes and jokes until the arrival of a new relative alerts them that it is time to begin the cries again."

He goes on, "It is bizarre that the joy of seeing each other after a long separation is demonstrated in exactly the same manner, and that the arrival of a member of a family who has been absent for a long time is celebrated by the same crying and the same tears as are associated with the burial" (de Bovis 1909; p. 60).

Joseph Banks in his journal for August 1769 comments on wailing and mentions a custom which struck most observers of pre-Christian Tahiti — self-wounding by women for expressive purposes.

Their manner of disposing of their dead as well as the ceremonies relating to their mourning for them are so remarkable that they deserve a very particular description. As soon as any one is dead, the house is immediately filled with their relations who bewail their loss with loud lamentations, especially those who are the farthest removed in blood from, or who profess the least grief for the deceased. The nearer relations and those who are really affected spend their time in more silent sorrow, while the rest join in choruses of grief at certain intervals, between which they laugh, talk and gossip as if totally unconcerned. . . .

No sooner is the corpse fixed up within the House . . . than the ceremony of mourning begins again. The women (for the men seem to think lamentations below their dignity) assemble led on by the nearest relation, who walking up to the door of the house swimming almost in tears, strikes a shark's tooth several times into the crown of her head, on which a large effusion of blood flows, which is carefully caught in their linen, and thrown under the bier. Her example is imitated by the rest of the women, and this ceremony is repeated at the interval of 2 or 3 days, as long as the women choose or can keep it up, the nearest relation thinking it her duty to continue it longer than any one else. Besides the blood which they believe to be an acceptable present to the deceased whose soul they believe to exist and hover about the place where the body lays observing the actions of the survivors, they throw in cloths wet with tears, of which all that are shed are carefully preserved for that purpose, and the younger people [i.e., women] cut off their hair either all or in part and throw that also under the bier. (J. Beaglehole 1962; 1:376-78)

While the women signaled their grief by self-mutilation, the men went through a complementary ritual.

When these ceremonies have been performed for 2 or 3 days, the men, who till now seemed to be entirely insensible of their loss, begin their part, which the nearest relations take in turns. They dress themselves in [an extraordinary] dress . . . [in which] they patrol the woods early in the morn and late at night, preceded by 2 or 3 boys who have nothing upon them but a small piece of cloth round their wrists and are smutted all over with charcoal. These sable emissaries run about their principal in all directions as if in pursuit of people on whom he may vent the rage inspired by his sorrow, which he does most unmercifully if he catches any body, cutting them with his stick the edge of which is set with sharks teeth, but this rarely or never happens, for no sooner does this figure appear than every one who see either him or his emissaries fly inspired with a sort of religious awe, fly with the utmost speed, hiding wherever they think themselves the most safe, but by all means quitting their houses if they lie even near the path of this dreadful apparition. (J. Beaglehole 1962; 1:378)

De Bovis noted that mourning behavior was duplicated when people met each other after long separations. Morrison had noted the same peculiarity.

When they meet each other after but a short absence they embrace each other as we do, but instead of kissing each other they join noses and draw in each other's breath through their nostrils. Sometimes in token of great love they almost suffocate each other by their long continuance of their embrace, this method is common to both sexes. But if they have been long absent the women weep and cut their heads with a shark tooth till the blood flows copiously, which is always the case in either excess, whether of grief or joy, to show their love. They always perform this ceremony on the slightest accident happening to their children and every woman is provided with one or two as soon as she is married, as they never cut their heads before. (Morrison 1935; p. 189)

Female self-wounding and the inverse behavior of male mourners disappeared after Christianity was introduced. Ritual wailing is still reported as occurring in rural villages, and one hears it occasionally in Piri.

Let us turn to the details of an event in Piri, the death of Tāvana's *vahine*. I had been in Piri about two weeks when, one evening, Teri'i Tui Vahine said that Tāvana Vahine was very ill. I went down to Tāvana's house at the seaward end of the village to see what was happening. Tāvana Vahine was lying on a mattress on the floor of a large shed adjoining Tāvana's uncompleted cement house. The shed enclosed a large wooden table and a number of benches and was used for eating, visiting, and working by Tāvana and his family. It was crowded with twelve adults and sixteen children and young adolescents. The adults were Tāvana Vahine's sisters and brothers, her and Tāvana's grown children, and some of these people's spouses. The children were her grandchildren.

When I approached the house there was loud, animated talking, joking, and laughter coming from it. It resembled a festive family party, and little notice was apparently being taken of Tāvana Vahine, lying off in one corner. Her "favorite" daughter, Hama Vahine, sat next to her at the head of the mat, preparing compresses of cloth soaked in cold water, which she applied to her mother's head.

Tāvana Vahine was fully alert and aware. I went over to talk
to her, and she took my hand and held onto it, looking very
frightened and anxious for help. She had been having severe
chest pains for several months, and had had several fainting
spells during the day. Now she had pain in her chest and abdomen and pain in her left arm. Her lips were blue and her legs
were swollen. She was obviously gravely ill.

During the next two or three hours the adults continued their
joking conversation. They talked about such matters as vanilla
prices and the July festival which was going on in Piri at the
time. Tāvana was very much in the conversation, joking and
laughing. The youngest children were asleep, but the elder children made a ring of quiet spectators, watching the conversation
and the dying woman.

The husband of one of Tāvana Vahine's daughters told me
that the visitors had come the night before and that they would
stay there until she died. But one of Tāvana Vahine's sons and
his *vahine* and one of her daughters and her *tāne* were not there.
They had all gone to Fare on the afternoon boat to drink and
"amuse themselves" at the *fête*. I had seen them all leave on the
afternoon boat, and they were manifestly in excellent spirits. As
the evening went on, the elder people continued their talking,
with Tāvana actively participating and seldom glancing over at
his wife.

Tāvana Vahine was clearly in great distress but showed it only
in her clenched hands and in her frightened but whispered and
controlled remarks to Hama Vahine, describing where she felt
pain and where Hama Vahine should apply the cold compresses.
From time to time one of Tāvana Vahine's other daughters, and
at one time one of her brothers, went over to her and knelt by
the mattress to massage her legs. As they did this, they participated in the general conversation, restraining most of their interaction with Tāvana Vahine to the mechanical act of massage.
Tāvana Vahine did not moan, cry out, or complain. She was dying in a restrained, low-key, matter-of-fact way. After I had
been there awhile, some of the older children withdrew into the
house, and there were sounds of laughing, running, and playing.

Their elders made no attempts to quiet them, except for one or two not very forceful or effective requests to "quiet down a little." The playing children, however, returned from time to time to the edge of the shed to see what was going on.

There was only one time that the adults seemed to react directly to Tāvana Vahine's situation. She suddenly vomited, and the men sitting around the table and the women at the sides became quiet. They looked down at the floor or off into space, avoiding looking at one another. After a few minutes when Tāvana Vahine became quiet again, they continued their conversation.

Late at night I went back to Teri'i Tui's to get some sleep. When I awoke, Teri'i Tui Vahine told me that Tāvana Vahine had died. I returned to the house. Tāvana and his daughters had reddened eyes but were otherwise composed. There was a good deal of talk about how many children and grandchildren and even great-grandchildren she and Tāvana had had and that they would be coming in from the other districts and other islands for the funeral. Now the talk was quiet and the atmosphere subdued.

Tāvana Vahine died on a Sunday morning. The split congregations had their services as usual, one congregation meeting at the church and the other at Teri'i Tui's. Both services finished at the same time. After the services the people in both congregations, joined by others who had not gone to church that morning and by some of the Mormons from the inland end of the village, began to stream up the village path toward Tāvana's house. They were dressed in their Sunday churchgoing clothes, perhaps a little more carefully than usual, the men wearing white or cream-colored shirts, some with old and tattered jackets, and the older women wearing faded print dresses and large wide-brimmed straw hats. The village moved as a whole, spread out along the path. As we approached Tāvana's house, half a dozen young men were assembling a wooden coffin. A raised concrete tomb had already been prepared in the yard some twenty feet or so to the side of Tāvana's house. Like most people in the village, Tāvana Vahine was to be entombed near the house where she lived and where her family were to continue to live.

We entered the house. Tāvana Vahine's body was on a bed toward the center of the large room of the house. She was covered with a spread except for her face. Chairs had been placed at her left and at her right. Tāvana was seated at her left and one of her daughters was seated in the chair at her right. A number of women and children of Tāvana's family were seated on mats to the right of the body.

The first villagers that entered the room were mostly members of Teiva's congregation. Mats had been placed to Tāvana Vahine's left side. Women and children visitors seated themselves on the mats, facing Tāvana and the body, while the men seated themselves in an outer circle behind the women and children.

When everyone was seated, Teiva read from the Bible and then spoke, praising Tāvana Vahine. As he began this, Tāvana's eyes were brimming with tears, and he sobbed silently. After a few minutes of this he stopped sobbing and sat quietly with his eyes closed. The eyes of all the adult villagers in the room were full of tears, and all the women and some of the men held handkerchiefs with which they would wipe their eyes. During all this nobody looked at anyone else, looking either off into space or down at the floor. Once during the service Teiva's voice broke, and he started to sob quietly. Several of the other people in the room seemed to me at this time to be making a strong effort to restrain themselves from breaking down. When Teiva had finished, Tāvana stood up and gave a quiet, formal speech of thanks. When he had finished his talk, Teiva, followed first by all the other men and then by the women, went up to Tāvana and kissed him on both cheeks[6] and then proceeded to the body of Tāvana Vahine, whom he also kissed. When Teiva got to the body he took a small bottle of perfume from his pocket and poured some of it over the body. He then left the bottle standing by her side. Four of the women had brought with them bouquets of pink, lavender, and white flowers wrapped in ferns, which they left by the body.

6. This, like kissing in general, is a European, and here (the kissing on both cheeks) specifically French, innovation.

The third woman in the line approached Tāvana Vahine's body to kiss it and suddenly began to wail. The sudden wail was a shock after the prolonged low-key emotional expression which had preceded it. There was a sudden rustle throughout the crowd, silent tears seemed to increase, and the people in the group again looked to me as though they were struggling to keep in control. The woman, a nonrelated villager, wailed for three or four minutes; she then left the body, and the next woman approached, this time crying silently.

The wail was a high-pitched, singsong sound, with much of the quality of a whine, seeming to come from deep within the woman. Several others, including some of Tāvana's daughters, wailed in a similar way at the burial the next day. I heard a very similar kind of wailing frequently during my stay in Piri and Roto. It was from children, in a particular phase of their experience of growing up, crying in a particularly controlled and turned-in-upon-themselves manner.

In the afternoon Tano's group came to pray and sing, and the morning's scene was repeated.

At supper, at Teri'i Tui's house, Toni remarked that the previous day when the boat had left for Fare, there was a pouring rain in front of the boat and behind it but that it did not rain on the boat. People on the boat took this as a sign that something was going to happen, and they were anxious. Toni said he thought that this was a sign that Tāvana Vahine was going to die.

That evening most of the people in the village went back to Tāvana's house. It was now only some sixteen hours after Tāvana Vahine's death, and the day for Tāvana and his family had been completely filled with visits from villagers. The house was full of people sitting on chairs and mats, and there were a large number of people standing and sitting in front of the house. Inside, under the leadership of Tano and Teiva, the leaders of the dissident sects united now, prayers were offered, short speeches of praise for Tāvana Vahine given, and the people joined in singing hymns. Now the climate of the crowd of people changed. There was an atmosphere of mild joking. When someone made a mistake in his entrance in the contrapuntal *himene* pattern, the participants laughed. Tano, urging the people in the house on in their singing, joked mildly, "The Huahine dance team at Papeete took first prize — see if you can do as well in your singing." The singing and joking were done by the nonfamily villagers. The family, including now some thirty or so people, listened quietly.

The entombment was to take place the following morning. People began to arrive at Tāvana's house about 8 A.M. Tāvana Vahine's body had been put in the newly made coffin, which was open at the top, and had been placed in the front room. A group of women were sitting around the coffin arranging flowers and wreaths over the body. Two of her daughters, who were said to be the closest to her, were sitting on chairs next to her. They cried, sometimes silently, but often in the whining wail.

Tano prayed for a few minutes. Then the daughters and the brother and sisters of Tāvana Vahine picked up the coffin and brought it to the small family graveyard next to the house, where it was placed in the simple concrete tomb that had been constructed the day before. More flowers were placed on the body. Hama Vahine, the "favorite daughter," knelt by the body, wailing. Most of the other people around were crying silently.

Several important visitors had come for the funeral — the gendarme from Fare and the *tāvana* of several of the other districts on the island. Flower petals were given to the gendarme and to the *tāvana* and to Tano. Tano said another prayer, and he and the important visitors slowly sprinkled the flower petals over the body. Tāvana Vahine's daughters then reached into the topless coffin and took out the plaited wreaths of flowers. The wooden planks were now placed over the top of the box and one of Tāvana Vahine's sisters reached over and placed Tāvana Vahine's best woven straw hat on the top of the coffin. With this, it seemed to me that the participants reached a kind of crescendo of sadness. The young men who had prepared the coffin and the tomb now placed a piece of roofing tin over the coffin. Tāvana Vahine's daughters put the wreaths they had taken out of the coffin on top of the tin.

Now Tāvana, who had remained composed during the entombment, made a grave and polite speech of thanks. He invited the assembled people to come and eat with him and his kin.

Tāvana left for his house. Some of the younger men began preparing concrete to close off the top of the tomb. They soon began joking and laughing. Now Tāvana, with the help of many of his kin, gave a feast for the villagers and the visitors. He was now actively the host, urging people to eat and to enjoy their food. Dish after dish of elegant traditional food reached the tables, and a buzzing, animated conversation went on among the villagers, for whom the unusual village unity and the presence of visitors from other districts and islands seemed to give the event a good deal of festive excitement.

For the next three or four weeks there was constant activity at Tāvana's house. A week after Tāvana Vahine's death, I passed by the house one morning and counted twenty-seven adults and children in sight, while the noise of others could be heard from other parts of the house. The people around the house were mostly relatives, Tāvana's children, their spouses and children, and sisters and brothers of Tāvana Vahine and their spouses and children. (Tāvana had no living brothers or sisters of his own, which partly explains the asymmetry.)

One of the very few nonrelated individuals who was frequently at Tāvana's house during those days was Veve Vahine. Although she had been a friend of Tāvana Vahine, as had several woman in the village, her presence in the days after Tāvana Vahine's death seemed unusual. A year later, at the arranging of Tano, she and Tāvana were married.

Often when I went by the house Tāvana was sitting with two or three children playing next to him. Sometimes he held a young child in his arms. The first few days after Tāvana Vahine's death both the men and the women sat at Tāvana's house during the day, but after four or five days the men started going to the fields and to fish during the days, while Tāvana and the women and children stayed at the house. Tāvana commented to me one morning that the reason he had not gone to his fields was that he was helping to watch the children.

Within a few days of the funeral, Tāvana's grandchildren had begun to play on Tāvana Vahine's tomb, sitting on the raised concrete, talking and laughing and rearranging the flowers which had been placed there. Three or four days after Tāvana Vahine's death a woman who had once taught school in Huahine and who was visiting in Piri (and who delighted in gossip) told me that Tāvana had been seen at night crying on his wife's tomb. The reason for this, she told me in French, was that he felt remorse, as he had been frequently unfaithful to her during their life together, once having even run off to Tahiti with the wife of another man in the village.

After three weeks I was told by one of Tāvana's youngest sons that Tāvana's *pe'ape'a*, his troubled feelings, had disappeared. Within a few more days the visitors had also disappeared, and Tāvana and his youngest son and the son's *taure'are'a vahine* were the only ones left at the house.

The events surrounding the death of Tāvana Vahine had some atypical qualities. Tāvana was the village chief, and his *vahine*'s death came at a time of considerable village tension and concern over the breaking up of the village religious community. People's anxieties about village division presumably heightened the significance of her death. It is, however, the behavior which I take to be more typical of bereavement that I wish to consider here.

Let us begin with the joking audience to Tāvana Vahine's dying. Villagers queried about this had two explanations. Thus, according to the *tāne* of one of Tāvana's daughters, it is "the custom" to joke in such circumstances. If a man's *vahine* is very sick, and if you can make him, and even her, laugh in such circumstances, then the man thinks for a moment that she is better. He adds that after she dies the man is very "heavy," and it is a good thing for people to joke occasionally. The bad time, he concludes, is after all the people have left, and one is finally by oneself.

The other overt explanation, which I noted in a discussion of people's thoughts about their own death, is that people were making it easier for Tāvana Vahine to die. According to the *tāne* of another of Tāvana's daughters, it is a difficult thing for the soul to leave the body. It hovers above it and reenters, deciding whether the time has come to die. It is bad to show grief while somebody is dying, as this increases his difficulty in deciding to leave this "daytime" world. This is generally accepted doctrine. Even after someone has been placed in his coffin or into his grave, his spirit may still move into and out of his body, and the body may have various kinds of consciousness. But now a transformation into the uncanny is taking place, and it has become a matter of a ghost and not the spirit of a loved one.

The lightheartedness in the face of dying reflects another theme, which becomes more important after the death. There is a general sense, which I have referred to in various contexts, that too much concern causes difficult processes (usually social and supernatural ones) to become even more difficult and unpleasant. In regard to dying, if you are too concerned about it, and in particular if you mourn too much, the transformed spirit of the dead person may gain power over you. It can make you sick or possess your body. Being casual, then, frees the dying person from you, and you from him or her.

The spirit becomes separated by passing into the *pō*. The parallel Christian doctrines about the spirit's state after death seem to be much less salient during the bereavement period. Teiva's pouring perfume on the body, which was also doused with perfume at the time of entombment, was in part to repel bad spirits who might be attracted to the body and the nearby soul/spirit of Tāvana Vahine. Similarly, people who attended *tahu'a* exorcising sessions would sometimes put on perfume in order to prevent a spirit expelled from a treated person from entering their own bodies.

The story about the rain's sparing the boat carrying villagers was also a sign that in the village an event was taking place which was no longer of the ordinary world. Tāvana Vahine was being moved out of the world of the *ao* into the world of the *pō*.

As Tāvana Vahine lay dying and children played around the edges learning how it was all to be managed, much of the style of people's behavior seemed superficially to deny that anything of importance was going on.

When she died, this changed for a while. In the two days following her death there were sadness and tears. There was emphasis on rebalance and restitution. People spoke repeatedly to Tāvana of all the children and grandchildren he and Tāvana Vahine had. Members of the extended family came to stay with and help Tāvana. The village moved together to center about him. He became responsible for giving a feast for the village, thus participating in the most significant village symbol of solidarity, eating together; and he served as host, with its further implication of head of a family. And in *giving* the feast, Tāvana was following the way village relationships are frequently established or reestablished — that is, by a gift.

In the period following the death most of the expressions of grief I saw were subdued. People controlled themselves. There was some momentary sobbing, which people struggled to control. Only the few episodes of wailing stood out against the quiet.

As I have noted, the wail, which historical reports indicated was the conventional mourning behavior of people not intimately connected with the dead person, resembles very closely the constricted, inhibited sobs of village children who are in a period when they are being pushed out of a specially intimate relationship to the elder people in the household, toward other kinds of adjustments. It is a peculiar wail, which seemed to me, in children at least, to indicate misery and anger which are somehow defeated and controlled in their expression.

Within a day or two there was little mourning to be seen. Continued mourning is considered abnormal and, as I have noted, supernaturally dangerous.

In their life histories people reported doing various things to help themselves get over mourning. Teiva, after the death of his first *vahine* in childbirth, started his *taure'are'a* life again, "searching everywhere in the night to make my thoughts about her go away." Veve Vahine, after the death of Veve, her *tāne* of many years, increased her participation in church activities. "I was thinking about Veve and our life together. It was that [church activities] which made it all stop. I became happy when I involved myself in God's work. Through all that, my troubled thoughts about him [her *tāne*] disappeared."

When Tāvana's crying on his wife's grave at night was reported to me, it was not considered natural, but had to be explained. It was said to be because he felt remorse for having wronged her. The explanation given did not involve his "loss."

In the days immediately following her death some, at least, of those of her close kin who did not, apparently, feel any particular grief did not make any pretense of it. Thus two of her biological sons, one of whom had been adopted by and brought up by somebody else in the village, continued their usual joking, *taure'are'a* styles, except for the period of the funeral itself.

Within four or five days after the funeral of Tāvana Vahine people seemed no longer anxious to talk about it. I did not hear it discussed in ordinary conversation around the village, and people tended to change the subject when I brought it up.

When, during interviews, people discussed deaths of others with whom they were closely involved, they usually talked about them in a matter-of-fact way, saying that they grieved and recovered, usually in a matter of a few weeks. There were exceptions. Tāvana, interviewed a year after Tāvana Vahine's death, had his eyes full of tears as he talked about it. Veve Vahine said that at times she still grieved for Veve, who had died several years before. Manu reported being distraught and unable to eat with any appetite for four or five months after the death of his adoptive father, when Manu was a child. Teiva was still deeply moved by the death of one of his daughters, several months before our interviews, and he avoided talking about her. But these were counterpoints to the usual emphases, especially the public ones. The public emphasis was: Don't get too upset, and get over it quickly.

One day in Piri I met Eria, a man in his twenties, who was settled with a *vahine* by whom he had four children. He was coming home from sitting up all night with the family of a female relative in another district who had lost her three-month-old baby. Instead of the usual restricted formalities of conversations when meeting on the village path, Eria was talkative. He had gone, he said, to help feed the other visitors. They sat up all night and talked and talked. When a tiny baby of one or two months dies, it is not so bad; but when the baby begins to smile, to recognize one, and then later even to say "Papa" or "Mama," then it is very bad [for the parents] when it dies. He then continued, extending the subject in a personal way. When one's *vahine* dies, it is also very bad. Usually you work all day, then you come home, there is food ready for you, and the house is in order. If your *vahine* dies, then it is all different. The children ask where she is. You say she is gone. They cry and you grieve. His eyes are swimming with tears as he describes this hypothetical case.

Eria's remarks about "a man losing his *vahine*" illustrate two matters associated with "sadness" in Piri and Roto: a tendency to react to hypothetical sad situations, which may be called "sentimentality," and a certain tendency to emphasize the disturbance caused by the lost person's not being there rather than the loss in itself.

The easy sentimentality in hypothetical situations or in circumstances where the cause for emotion seems relatively minor contrasts with the relative lack of emotional display in situations where the cause seems more important. I have noted the village policeman's crying as he told the *taure'are'a* to behave so they would not bring shame on him. People, when drinking together, would sometimes explain with tearful emotion how much they liked each other, how glad they were that past troubles were over.

I saw people's eyes full of tears on various other occasions. Toni's eyes swam with tears as he recounted a public insult he had received. A drinking companion of Teri'i Tui's was tearful as he silently watched Teri'i angrily and unjustly hitting one of his children.

Tears were particularly plentiful as villagers gathered at the wharf in Piri to say goodbye to friends and families leaving for Papeete. But always, within a few minutes of the departure, peo-

ple were joking and carrying on as usual. Such tears have, perhaps, a certain conventionalized aspect. As I prepared to leave
Piri after my first short summer's stay, one village man told me
that the people would cry for me when I left because they had
become accustomed to me.

I had the impression that death, parting, unfairness, and insult
tapped some deep well of loneliness and sadness in people which
sprang to the surface for a few moments and then, as a result of
some combination of inner and outer pressures, was quickly
sealed off again. And I recalled Rabbi Baruch's saying, "What a
good and bright world this is if we do not lose our hearts to it,
but what a dark world if we do!"

In Eria's sentimental reference to the imaginary loss of a *vahine*, he mentions first the disturbance because the house was
no longer in order, and second, the disturbance of having to
cope with the children's distress. One would think, at first, that
this could easily be translated by Eria into something like "I
love my wife and would therefore be very disturbed if anything
happened to her," but there is some indication that such an underlying statement may not be so easily accessible.

Events such as the following caught my attention. The *vahine*
of Tihoni, a son of Teri'i Tui by an early liaison, refused to return with Tihoni to Piri, after they had spent some months
working on her father's lands on another of the Leeward Islands.
They had one child, an infant son, and she kept the son with
her. Tihoni returned alone to Piri to Teri'i Tui's house. He came
to my house one day and sat and made small talk for about an
hour. Then, with evident embarrassment, he said that he had a
question. He said that he had been feeling "not good" and
"without energy" and asked me if I had any advice or maybe
medicine that would make him feel better. He then said that
another thing that bothered him is that his thoughts kept turning back to his *vahine* and his child, and he could not seem to
do anything about those thoughts; they would not go out of his
mind. For Tihoni the fact that he should be obsessed with his
loss seemed apparently to be abnormal and a problem. It was
also something that he had not discussed with others in the vil-

lage and which he brought to me, I presumed, because I was an outsider. And he interpreted his feelings about separation as some sort of vague sickness.

One day Viriamu, a villager living toward the inland end of Piri, told me a story of a curse. He was pearl diving at the island of Hikeru in the Tuamotus. His wife had delivered their first child just a few weeks before. One day his wife saw three sailors in French uniform walking quietly toward their house. She greeted them, but they did not answer and turned and walked silently away. That afternoon the baby appeared sick. They took it to the island's male nurse, who could do nothing for it. So they took the child to a *tahu'a*, who said that the child was sick because of a curse which had been caused by the mother of Viriamu's *vahine*, who disapproved of their marriage.[7] The *tahu'a* told Viriamu that he could save only his *vahine* or the baby, and that Viriamu must choose between them. He thought it over, and then, he told me, because he knew that if he chose the baby to survive, his wife's relatives would be angry at him, he chose his *vahine* to survive. That evening the baby died. The explanation for his choice did not bear on his feelings and his relationships to his *vahine* and baby, but related to "exterior" considerations.

In part such kinds of responses to situations of deprivation illustrate the "concrete" style of thinking discussed in the last chapter. But they also are typical of responses to personal loss and separation in that they seem to avoid naming and labeling what would seem to a western observer to be the emotional significance of the events. This contrasts with responses to and descriptions of angry interactions, where, as I have noted, the angry response is clearly labeled as an aspect of the action.

Public values about longing behavior are indicated in various ways. *Taure'are'a*, for example, say that it is shameful to show that you are upset if your *tāne* or *vahine* leaves you. It is said by some that if you once leave the village where you grew up,

7. His *vahine*'s mother was living in Piri at the time he told me this story, and, typically, Viriamu continued to have apparently ordinary relationships with her.

you should go back only for very brief visits, for if you stay for a longer period of time, you are liable to become sick. As we saw earlier under "Heterosexual Relationships," being romantically in love with someone, the kind of love which causes one to become jealous and to feel deeply about a person is called literally being "crazy," *ma'ama'a*, in relation to that person; and it is considered somewhat bad and abnormal.

There are aspects of Tahitian vocabulary which represent perhaps both an expression of a situation and a control over its occurrence, in the present case a lack of a specific vocabulary for the expression of mild or moderate longing emotions. There are words for severe grief and for lamentation.[8] There are, however, no unambiguous terms which represent the concepts of sadness, longing, or loneliness in the sense of "depressed or sad because of the lack of friends, companionship, and so on." People would name their condition, where I supposed that the context called for "sadness" or "depression," as "feeling troubled" (*pe'ape'a*, the generic term for disturbances, either internal or external);[9] as "not feeling a sense of inner push" (*'ana'anatae*, inner push or enthusiasm); as "feeling heavy" (*tōiaha*); as "feeling fatigued" (*haumani*); and a variety of other terms all referring to a generally troubled or subdued bodily state. These are all nonspecific terms, which had no implication of any external relational cause about them, in the sense that "angry" implies an offense or a frustration.

Fairly competent French-Tahitian bilingual speakers, such as Flora or Hiro, did not understand the meaning of *triste* in its sense of "sorrowful, mournful, sad, melancholy, dejected" and defined and used it as *haumani*, "fatigued," or *marū*, "gentle."

The common word used for the feeling that arises when one is alone is *mo'emo'e*. It is related to a word, *mo'e*, meaning "to

8. These are *mihi* and *'oto*. In old Tahitian the word *'oto* also meant the song of birds and insects and the sound of a musical instrument and thus emphasized the sounds of grief. In modern Tahitian the common word for weep or cry, *ta'i*, is still used to designate the sound of a musical instrument.

9. Thus *pe'ape'a* is also used for "guilt" and other nondifferentiated unpleasant feelings.

lose." In the first missionary dictionary *mo'emo'e* was defined as "solitary" or "lonesome." When *mo'emo'e* is used to describe the emotional state produced by being alone, the word as used in Piri indicates uncanny feelings, a state of "having the creeps." As was noted in the discussion of uncanny feelings and the supernatural in chapter 5, the presence of another person, any other person, is enough to protect an individual from having uncanny feelings, unless he and his companions are in a particularly "haunted" place. The uncanny feelings produced by being alone in a house at night or walking through the woods can be allayed by having anybody else along. The typical Tahitian question to somebody who found himself or herself alone and separated from family or villagers, or who was forced to live or travel in such a situation, was not "Weren't you lonely?" in the English sense of the word, but "Didn't you have the creeps?" For the prevention of uncanny feelings, people are interchangeable. Loneliness, as verbally complained of, is usually a matter of being separated from people, not a particular person.

The lack of specific vocabulary does not mean that these states are unexpressible. It would be perfectly possible for a man to say something like "I felt bad because my *vahine* had gone on a trip, and there was no one else in the house, and my thoughts kept turning to her." The common way, in fact, to express that one misses an absent person is to say that one "thinks"[10] about him or "thinks repeatedly" about him. It seems hard to say more than that.

The themes of loneliness and of melancholy are rare in the interviews. For one thing, most people are seldom alone. When they lose somebody through desertion or death, they soon find someone else to take his place. Even those who did live alone, as Poria does or as Veve Vahine did for a short period, though they might complain of the unshared work, of being frightened, or of uncanny feelings, did not complain of loneliness as such, or express self-pity.

10. That is, *mana'o*, and therefore one thinks in the form of images rather than plans or calculations.

Fear. As future chapters will indicate, fear is an important aspect of the goals and techniques of child rearing and a significant dimension in moral controls. I will consider it elsewhere, but here I wish to note some aspects of the cultural labeling and understanding of fearful states.

Fear, like anger and, as we shall see, shame, is a frequent theme in interviews and in village events, both as an experience and as a principle of explanation.

The two most common terms related to fear are *ri'ari'a* and *mata'u*. In their common usages *ri'ari'a* indicates a present visceral condition of fear ("I am afraid because the dog is biting me"), whereas *mata'u* indicates an apprehension of the possibility of being in a situation where *ri'ari'a* might be stirred up ("I am afraid of dogs"; "I fear the Lord").[11]

There are other words besides *mata'u* which imply the anticipation of danger and thus of feeling fear. One of them is *taiā*, which is usually used to indicate the anticipation of more mildly frightening events than *mata'u*. One may be *taiā* about having to give a speech in a public meeting. A third term, *atāta*, tends to be used for anxious anticipation of specifically physical dangers, such as climbing a tall tree. Like most Tahitian terms referring to emotions, all these terms can apply either to the situation (e.g., a "fearful" situation) or to the response.

The core feeling, *ri'ari'a*, which will be stirred up if these anxious anticipations of social or physical unpleasantness prove accurate, is, as I have noted in discussing the supernatural, differentiated from the feeling in the face of the uncanny, *mehameha*. If *mehameha* gets strong enough and one feels one is in danger, then *ri'ari'a* is added to it or supplants it.

People in Piri and Roto are timid. It is important to note here the shape of the timidity. They are not timid when it is a matter of their personal physical skill in relation to the impersonal

11. *Ri'ari'a* also has a very much less salient usage. In this usage it means a mild repulsion about certain kinds of food. If one is *ri'ari'a* about eggs, one just doesn't want to eat eggs and finds them mildly unpleasant. In this sense the term is less strong than the numerous terms that mean "disgusting" in relation to food.

world. They climb tall trees; they dive in the lagoons for fish and, if they visit the Tuamotus as pearl divers, for oyster shells; and they suffer occasional stormy boat voyages with apparent confidence. In relation to the impersonal world they are not heroic, but they are confident. They are anxious about the spirit-invested corners of the nonliving world, but this is a matter of the shadowy and unclear parts, where there is cognitive ambiguity and where the sleep of reason produces monsters.

What they tend to be timid about is people and social encounters. In an interview, talking about *tūpapa'u*, Hiro added an afterthought. "The very frightening kind of *tūpapa'u* are living people, people like us here. That's the thing that is very frightening for me — because you don't know what they're going to do to you; you may be hit by a stick, stabbed by a knife, you don't know. That's the frightening thought when you hear a rustling noise, that really makes you frightened." He then returns to his discussion of spirits.

In the interviews, as in everyday village life, manifestations of fear about other people are a very much more salient topic than fear of the supernatural. Interpersonal fear is connected with a sense of shyness and a certain kind of discomfort in the presence of others, which will concern us elsewhere.

There is no shame about being fearful; a certain social timidity is a desirable personal quality. Not only do people freely admit fear in tales of encounters with other people or the supernatural world, but they evidently often get pleasure out of telling of such experiences. One of the common subjects of village storytelling or of stories at the supper table at Teri'i Tui's was of encounters with frightening events. Sometimes these stories were told humorously and sometimes as a thrilling tale. But it was the fear of the storyteller, and not his heroism, that was the theme.

Pain. It has become apparent that pain is a complex feeling state, which involves a good deal more than elementary biological sensation.[12]

As Wolff and Wolf noted, "The ability to perceive pain depends upon the intactness of relatively simple and primitive

12. See, for example, Petrie (1967) and Sternbach (1968).

nerve connections. Reaction to pain, on the other hand, is modified by the highest cognitive functions and depends in part upon
what the sensation *means* to the individual in the light of his
past life experience. This simple distinction between perception
of pain and reaction to the experience was not at once appre-
ciated by investigators and consequently until recently confusion existed regarding the nature of pain" (Wolff and Wolf 1948;
p. 13). Subsequent work in perception has indicated that differences in meaning seem to enter into perception itself and not
only some later "reaction."

One day in Piri one of Uta's sons, eight years old, fell out of
a tree at the other end of the village from his home. His upper
arm was broken and clearly bent out of shape. Holding his fore-
arm and elbow with his other arm, the boy walked to his family's house. His mother looked at him and, showing little emotion, told him to sit outside by the house. I asked her what she
was going to do. She said that one of her brothers was good at
setting bones and that when he came back from the fields he
would take care of it. The boy sat for six hours before the uncle
came home at his usual time. He sat quietly, obviously concerned, but looking neither anguished nor greatly frightened.
When Uta himself saw the boy, he said to him, "That will serve
you right for climbing tall trees."

A few days later I asked Uta about his son. He said that they
had not been able to make the arm straight when they set it and
that it would be permanently curved. He laughed and said that
that would keep his son out of trees in the future.

Although children in Piri cry easily when they are angered,
punished, or insulted, children I saw in painful situations of various types either showed very little response to the pain or were
quiet and subdued. Six- and seven-year-old children being inoc-
ulated en masse by the visiting island nurse showed no reaction.
Children in Teri'i Tui's household and elsewhere, when they suffered from toothaches, as they frequently did, were often silent
and dazed-looking, but did not cry out.

Women, during childbirth, were said not to cry out unless it
was a terribly difficult birth, and the one time that I was nearby
during a childbirth, the woman did not make any sound.

One of the village semijokes about the Chinese was that the Chinese cry out when they have pain or an injury, whereas the Tahitians do not. This was very true, at least in Piri, for the son of the Chinese storekeeper, Ah Kiau, who cried out noisily and lustily whenever he was injured in play.

A French doctor at the hospital at Papeete said that people from rural villages (such as Piri) were more stolid in their reaction to pain than townspeople from Papeete. (He also said that, nevertheless, even the rural villagers were considerably *less* impassive about pain than village peoples whom he had worked with in Africa.)

Such behavior in relation to pain seemed curious to me because of its contrast with the social timidity and fearfulness discussed above and because of a general absence of heroic ideals.

There are two common words for pain, *māuiui* and *māmae*. The two words seem semantically equivalent (although there is some possibility that *māmae* tends to be used somewhat more for aching pains, and *māuiui* for sharper pains). The usual verbal phrasing of pain is equivalent to the English "My hand hurts" or "My head hurts." It is the affected part of the body that hurts, and this, again like English, is in contrast to the Tahitian form, *'ua ri'ari'a vau*, "I am afraid," even though the fear may be localized to a sensation in the abdomen.

Uta, discussing his wife's various deliveries, said that she never groaned or cried out in pain, except briefly during her first delivery. I asked if this was because she did not have very much pain. He said yes, childbirths are painful, but his wife bore the pain without demonstrating it.[13] I asked him if it were a matter of shame to express pain. He said no, not at all, that when one really has very severe pain, one cries out; this is not a matter of shame at all. But most pains one can bear. He went on to say that he had often twisted and sprained arms and legs, but he never moaned. Perhaps, he said, if he had had a broken leg, he might have.

13. I have noted in chapter 7 that men generally tend to play down the special differentiating characteristics of women, including any special discomforts or dangers of childbirth.

Uta emphasizes here some matters which seem widely accepted. Although a number of behaviors are doctrinally said to be a matter of shame and therefore controlled in their expression, the expression of pain was generally not said to be shameful. Two or three times I did hear a remark that it would be shameful for a woman to cry out in childbirth, and Manu in Roto said that since the expression of pain implied a certain weakness (Chinese, who cry out easily, are said to have "weak blood"), there was therefore a certain amount of shamefulness in someone who calls out too easily. But I much more frequently was given the explanation that a Tahitian does not call out "not because he is ashamed to, but because he is able to bear it." The word I have been glossing "bear" here is *fa'a'oroma'i.* The word implies to endure, more or less patiently, an unpleasant situation, and it is a salient term in Tahitian behavioral explanations. As Poria says, "There is no shame about crying out in pain, but that is the nature of Tahitians, they can *fa'a'oroma'i.*"

And according to Taere, "It is not shameful to cry out in pain; some people cry out, but others, they aren't afraid and they do not cry out."

These quotations suggest that the relative lack of expression of a response to injury and presumably painful illness is not primarily or wholly a matter of the comparatively gross behavioral inhibitions that are connected with shame. One would have to look to more subtle aspects of the control and shaping of expression, to meanings of injuries and illness, and to aspects of psychological organization for further explanations of pain behavior.

There are other reasons besides shame directed to the expressive action itself why one might not want to express feelings of pain. Uta's response to his son's falling out of the tree is part, as we shall see, of a generalized socialization technique in which injuries and misfortunes are used for educational purposes and presented to the child as some deserved punishment by "nature," a punishment justly received for some wrong action of the child's. Therefore to some degree pain, particularly in regard to injury, is understood in part as something which one may be responsible for and about which one might thus not want to make a public issue. But this socialization device makes use of only some pain-producing situations (e.g., certain types of injuries). More generally, for children who are in pain from an illness (for example, a toothache) there is a show of concern from adults and older children, and in these situations the pained state is "rewarded" rather than punished. (It is, however, important to note that in cases I observed involving pain in children, the parents and older children reacted directly to their understanding of the child's pain-inducing situation, and the child did not have to vocalize or cry out or continue crying to insure their response.)

My impression is, however, that the ability to *fa'a'oroma'i* pain is related in large degree to the quality of the experience of that pain, rather than to styles and controls of expression.

Uta's amusement about his son's injury seems at first to be cruelty and lack of empathy. One evening at Teri'i Tui's, Toni told of a child who had also fallen out of a tree and who had had a bone in his arm sticking out through the skin. The child's father had seen it and, thinking that it was a stick which had punctured the boy's arm in the fall, tried to pull it out. Toni told this as an example of the man's stupidity, and both he and his hearers laughed at the story. Similarly people in the village watch with amusement as children play with captured wild birds secured by a string attached to one of their legs. The child lets the bird fly up into the air and then pulls it down again, much to the interest and apparent pleasure of the child and bystanders. Again cruelty, or lack of empathy with the sufferings of the child or the bird, or some mixture of cruelty and diminished empathy are evident possible explanations, the episodes being particularly problematic in relation to the "gentleness" described previously as such a pervasive behavioral trait. But it is also possible that the sufferings of the child or the bird were perceived as being less severe than I, watching or listening, empathically felt them to be, and that this perception was a generalization from personal sense of the meaning of pain for the observers.

Some of the general features of psychological organization which have been found to correlate with increased "pain tolerance," defined as "the duration of time or intensity at which a person is willing to endure a stimulus beyond the point where it began to hurt" (Sternbach 1968; p. 77) are characteristic of people in Piri and Roto. In the discussion of thinking in the last chapter, I suggested contrasts in thinking styles between individuals in Piri and Roto and idealized western thinkers, entailing in Piri and Roto a more "personalized thought" which is in specific ways comparatively less differentiated. A correlate of less differentiated thought is a comparatively strong dependence on the immediately surrounding context for understanding and orientations. Sternbach, in a review of research on pain, reviews work indicating that people who have the cognitive qualities — which may be comparatively ascribed to people in Piri and Roto — of relative undifferentiation and relative field-dependence are, experimentally, more likely to show low pain reactivity (Sternbach 1968; pp. 60-61).[14]

Without going too far from verifiable behavior, I have asserted that reaction to presumably pain-inducing illnesses and injuries seems comparatively subdued and that this seems to have something to do with the quality of the felt pain rather than only with expression of pain. If one asks about aspects of symbolic meaning which might limit the troubling aspects of felt pain, this becomes even more speculative.

As we shall see when we consider "pathology," although the people interviewed had a variety of illnesses, stress symptoms, and "hysterical" symptoms, only two informants, Hiro and Oro, showed anxious concern with body symptoms. That is, there

14. Another correlate of perceptual/cognitive organization and pain reactivity is the augmentation or reduction of the estimated size, or other quantity, of a perceived object in comparison with its "objective" size. Those people who are "reducers," who consistently underestimate size under given experimental conditions, were also "significantly less able to tolerate sensory isolation," and "much more able to tolerate experimental pain from radiant heat" (Sternbach 1968; pp. 61-62). Such a clump of behaviors is suggestive in relation to Tahitian style.

was little hypochondriasis. People suffered injuries, illnesses, and tooth loss not only with little expression of pain, but with little expression of anxiety or depression about any "threat to the body." Although people worry about aging and the consequent restriction of their ability to provide for themselves, in other illnesses and injuries there seems to be little sense of the body as fragile and easily "used up." I suppose that questions of forms of conscience and fantasies of punishment, of body image, of attitudes about the body as an instrument for production and security, and of attitudes about the self in general, all enter here.

Happy Feelings

There is, when the times are right, something peculiar about happiness. If someone tells us that he is sad, anxious, angry, suffering, and the like, we are tempted to ask him why and expect that we will receive some kind of explanation. If he tells us that he feels quite well, unless we know him to have been in recent trouble or to be congenitally dyspeptic, we are less likely to wonder about him. Happiness, unless it is in some exotic form such as ecstasy, is not much of a problem for ordinary discourse.

In the differentiated vocabulary collected by the missionaries before the cultural involution attendant on western contact, I was able to find 301 terms for "ordinary" feeling states. (There were other terms which combined indications of emotion and *disorder*, as "to be in a frantic state of mind.") In this group were 27 terms for "pleasurable states." The other terms referred either to feelings which were clearly unpleasant or to feelings related to the pressures of "desire" and of ambiguous pleasantness. The pleasurable terms as defined by the missionaries seemed to fall into two groups: "peaceful feelings," glossed by terms such as "serene," "unruffled," "calm," "comforted," "at ease"; and "joyful feelings," glossed by such terms as "delighted," "cheerful," "gay," "exulting," "mirthful."

The missionary lexicon was inflated by metaphors, variants, words from neighboring dialects, and, perhaps, misunderstandings. But most of the words they noted were probably in ordinary use. Of these relatively few are known to the contemporary adult villagers of Piri.

The most salient terms used now in relation to apparently "happy states" are *'oa'oa* and *'ārearea*. *'Oa'oa* is used in ways which are similar to the English "happy." It is used in sentences like *ua 'oa'oa vau*, "I am happy," which are of the same form as sentences asserting "I am angry" or "I am afraid." One also uses *'oa'oa* about events or people to indicate, again as with anger or fear, that the event or person "caused" or was associated with a "happy" feeling in the individual. A pleasant period of life, such as childhood, may be described as *'oa'oa*, and one is *'oa'oa* to see somebody again, or because one has had a good life or recovered from an illness.

Hiro says that people who get to heaven are *'oa'oa* there. "It is an *'oa'oa* situation. You don't get fatigued. You don't get sick. You don't get angry. You are just *'oa'oa*." "Happy" or "content" seems to gloss this very well.

The common term for having a "joyful" good time is *'ārearea*. It refers to the general situation of a group of people who are doing such things as laughing, joking, dancing, and drinking. The term usually refers more to the kind of activity of the group, the "fun" of the group, than to the internal response of enjoyment, but it is used to indicate the latter also. *'Ārearea* is a matter of parties, of festivals, of special occasions which are clearly separate from activities of ordinary everyday life. Engaging in *'ārearea* activities is, however, one of the ideal aspects of the boys' and young men's *taure'are'a* period. This is suggested by the etymology of *taure'are'a*: *tau* means here a period of life, and *re'are'a* comes from a word which is no longer used in contemporary Tahitian, but which meant "joy, gaiety, or mirth." The word is still used, according to Stimson and Marshall, in the Tuamotuan word *rekareka* with, according to them, a sexual emphasis. They gloss *rekareka* as "to experience delight, ecstasy, sexual gratification, rapture, the sexual orgasm" (Stimson and Marshall 1964). This sense of *rekareka* or *re'are'a* is related to the Tahitian term, *navenave*, discussed below.

There are a few more specialized terms for pleasure. *Au*, which I have discussed in relation to the conditions in which ideas are accepted (chapter 8), conveys the idea of "nice," "fitting," "pleasant," of something which is properly related to the condition and special qualities of an individual and which therefore produces pleasant feelings. A food, a situation, a particular sexual partner may be described as *mea au roa*, a very agreeable thing.

There are a number of terms which indicate "satisfaction," in the sense of quenching a desire or calming an unpleasant passion. The ordinary word for this is *maha*. There are also a number of more specific words referring to quenching or satisfying particular desires, such as hunger or thirst.[15]

There is a word which means "sexual pleasure," *navenave*. It refers mainly to genital sensations. *Navenave* also refers to the qualities, or to the feelings engendered in the hearer, of beautiful music or singing. In another use of the term, *navenave* describes the feelings of parents about a child who is a cherished favorite. He is said to be a *navenave* thing for his parents.

As *'oa'oa* is used now, it implies quiet contentment. *'Ārearea*, defined in the missionary dictionary as "cheerful, gay, through the presence of company," is now used, as I have noted, with an external emphasis. As Teiva once said, when asked if he were *'oa'oa* during the drinking and singing of his *taure'are'a* period, "I don't know if I was *'oa'oa*, I was just concentrating on *'ārearea*." That is, "I don't know if I was happy, I was just concentrating on having fun."

There do not seem to be any words now which imply "joyful," rather than "content." The missionaries had defined *navenave* as "pleasurable and delightful" in general, and its constriction to sex and song and "cherished child"[16] may be significant.

---

15. The term now used conventionally for "thank you," *māruru* (it has several phonetic variations), was defined in the missionary dictionary as "to be calmed, eased, pacified."

16. This use for "cherished child" seems to be a cliché and a residue of older usages when a range of other relationships might have been described as delightful.

The terms which they glossed as "gay," "exulting," and the like have disappeared or become subdued in meaning. At any rate, the occasions producing joyful emotions were one of the things largely lost in the Christianizing and colonialization of the old society. The loss of traditional games, sports, and entertainments; the loss of the great events related to war, politics, and ancient religious ceremony must have brought a great diminution in occasions for joy. *Taure'are'a*, as I have noted, are concerned about becoming grown up, because the occasions for pleasure seem few.

But if there is not much exultation in Piri and Roto, there is plenty of low-key contentment.

Friendly and Loving Feelings

In discussions of feelings associated with what we may call friendly or "positive" interpersonal action, there are four prominent terms — *hīna'āro*, *mātau*, *here*, and *arōfa*. Thus in speculating on the motives for the formation and maintenance of a heterosexual union it may be explained that the couple first came together because of *hīna'āro* (desire), but as they remained together they became *mātau* (accustomed to each other) and began to feel *here* (love). They decided not to separate because of *arōfa* (compassion for the suffering of the other that a separation would entail).

Hīna'āro means to want or desire something. It appears to be the most general, nonspecific term for "desiring." (There are many special desires, e.g., *hia 'amu*, the desire for food.) When a visitor enters a house, he may be asked, "What do you *hīna-'āro*?" The use of the term encompasses the most trivial wishes, as well as long-term plans and projects and physical desires.

Statements about continuing to do something because one has become *mātau*, used to the relationship or the situation, has, as we shall see in the next chapter, a special force because of its contrast with the strong and uncomfortable feelings which most people have when they are not *mātau* in a situation, namely *ha'amā*, embarrassment or shame. The force of *ha'amā* makes *mātau* a particularly desirable, and therefore presumptively motivating, condition for maintaining relationships.

I have glossed *here* as "love." "Love" being such a problematic western construct, we must look somewhat closer at the uses of *here*.

In an interview with Manu I ask him if he and his *vahine*, Tetua, felt *here* for each other. He answers at length. "Yes, if we didn't love each other, our life [together in the household] would not be going properly." ("No?") "Yes, for example, if only I *here*ed[17] Tetua, and she did not *here* me, then she would go and do the things that she desired [without taking Manu into account]; and, if it were the case, that it was Tetua who *here*ed me, and I did not *here* Tetua, then I would not pay attention to her, I would only pay attention to the things that I wanted to. But the way it is, she *here*s and I *here*, and that's that. When things are like that, life goes properly for a couple." ("Can you try to explain to me the meaning of that word, *here*, as you understand it?") "Yes . . . the significance of talk about *here* — when you talk about *here* it is the sort of thing that, you have come to believe [*ti'aturi*, "believe, have faith, be involved in, trust"] with your body, with your calculating thoughts [*feruri*], with everything, that this is your true [*mau*, "fixed, true, relatively permanent"] *vahine*. And, for example, in all kinds of activities that you think about doing, you request your *vahine* [to do them with you]. And, for example, there comes a time when you eat your meal in some place where you have been invited, and you arrive at that meal, and now you start to eat, and now your thoughts go to your *vahine* back in the house because she is not eating that food that you're eating. And now, while you're eating, you have compassion [*arōfa*] for her. You put aside a portion to take her in the house. That is *here*. That is the basic quality of *here*. You trust and believe in [*ti'aturi*] that *vahine* of yours. It is as if she were a parent [*metua*, "mother," "father"] for your household, for your way of living. That is what it means when Tahitians say *here*."

17. By inflecting the Tahitian verbal forms with English endings it is possible to indicate the syntactical use of the term somewhat more accurately.

He pauses for a few seconds and then goes on, "Now there are some people, for example, who do not *here* their *vahine*. He only desires [*hina'āro*] that *vahine* for someone to live with, but the whole ensemble of his thoughts has not come to be directed toward that *vahine*. That is the kind of person who goes into the different amusement places. They enjoy themselves [*'ārearea*], pay attention only to their own desire [*hina'āro*], and then they don't think any more about that *vahine* in the house. Those kind of people, it is said of them, 'They don't have *here* for their *vahine*', but desire only . . . desire arising out of the body."

Pua, discussing her relation with Maote, echoes some of Manu's emphases. I ask her what she likes about Maote. She answers directly, "He has *here* for me. In the beginning — he had *here* for me from the beginning. [At the start of their staying together] we had trouble, and I left, and then, he had *here* for me, therefore he went to fetch me. And myself, I *here* him too. And therefore [*nō ria*, implying a basic cause] we have peace now. But in the beginning we constantly had trouble. But now it is gone away. Our staying together [i.e., relationship] is very good now. He has *here* for me, I have *here* for him, and therefore [*nō ria*] we are right [*'āfaro*, straight]. If only I didn't *here* him, I would think to go again and seek a new *tāne*. We would have trouble, we wouldn't be right together."

And Hiro, talking of his relation with Meri, asked if they felt *here* for each other from the beginning of their relationship, says somewhat pompously, "When we became acquainted [*mātau*], it wasn't a definite [*pāpū*] thing. But, so to say, we pursued that goal. We, so to say, pursued it so that that valuable thing would be gotten. Now, it is definite, it has been gotten, she has come to *here* me, I *here* her. . . . If she didn't *here* herself — me [he has made a slip and corrects it], I wouldn't love her. That is my nature. . . . If she didn't *here* me, there wouldn't be any value in our staying together, no use. But, as we are equal [in *here* for each other], our staying together is wonderful."

I don't know if pre-Christian Tahitians talked like this, but it is possible. There are many reports of old Tahitian heterosexual liaisons as shifting and fragile, and where such arrangements are matters of personal choice, *here* may be of particular significance.

The missionary dictionary does not give *here* in the verbal form in which it is now commonly used, but as a substantive, "a favorite," "a beloved one"; and as an adjective, "dear," "beloved," "favored." It is of interest that a homophonous old Tahitian word means "to ensnare, entrap, or catch by a noose or snare."

In the quotations given, *here* is clearly used as an explanatory principle for something that maintains a relationship. It is different from sexual desire, habit, and pity. It is illustrated or deduced, to some degree, by external behavior. (One thinks about bringing food to one's *vahine*.) It has very much the appearance of "love."

Although I have illustrated *here* in heterosexual relations, the term also applies to feelings and relations between parents and children, friends, siblings. When people describe their relations with their parents during their childhood, they often say things like "My mother loved [*here*] me, she was always good to me," or "My father loved me, he never hit me," or "I loved my mother because she was good to me." *Here*, in such statements, is ascribed to something which must come out of behavior, and not the "natural" qualities of the relationship. Such statements, and Hiro's statement about loving Meri insofar as she loves him, have to do, among other things, with the general emphasis on actions rather than a construct of intentions (chapter 10), as well as an important aspect of parent-child relationships which I will call "contingency" (chapters 13 and 14).

Manu remarked that his hypothetical man, invited to dinner without his wife, would think of her and feel *arōfa* for her.[18] Part of the meaning of *arōfa*, as in Manu's example, is "pity" or "compassion." One has *arōfa* (ideally at least) for cripples, for relatively poor and struggling people, or for people who have had some disaster strike their family.

---

18. *Arōfa* also occurs as a phonetic variant, *arōha*, but *arōfa* was the form used most frequently by my informants.

The sense of *arōfa*, as the feeling one has for somebody who is unfortunate, is used also in a weaker sense. Manu, talking about his anger at Tetua over some failure in housekeeping, said, "I tried to hold my anger inside of me." When asked why, he said, "Because she knew that I was angry at her, but I had *arōfa* toward her, when I saw that she did not understand anymore what she had done. She was afraid because she saw that I was angry, and she did not know what it was that she had done."

Oro, talking of a suicide fantasy, said he did not commit suicide because of his feelings of *arōfa* for his adoptive mother. Some people explain their reasons for avoiding stealing, for example, or avoiding trying to initiate a sexual relationship with the *vahine* of another villager as *arōfa*, the anticipation of feeling sorry for the individual if one carried out the projected act. In this form, as I will discuss in the next chapter, *arōfa* is a significant aspect of moral controls.

Arōfa is also frequently used to deal with those situations of sadness caused by separation from someone to whom one is attached. Avoiding as usual the statement, "I feel sad," people say, "I feel *arōfa* for the person who has left," and who is thus separated from them.

As Manu says, "*Arōfa*, we do not really know what is its nature. But Tahitians say that *arōfa* is like, for example, when there is a situation where you *here* your *vahine*, and she indeed, *here*s you, and there comes a time that your *vahine* has gone to a far-off land, or to some distant place. Now, at that time, you go about your affairs, you come back to the house, now it is only you there. You come back to the house, your *vahine* is not there, and now you begin to think about her in that place far away. A long time you have stayed together, and now for the first time you are separated and that is the cause for your feelings of *arōfa*." *Arōfa* is used commonly in this sense in Tahitian poems and songs.

Arōfa in its broadest sense implies "empathy," although it usually is used for "empathic suffering because of the sufferings of others." It implies caring about someone else.

Feelings as Motives for Action

As the preceding sections have indicated, different kinds of feelings in Tahitian discourse are often presented as explanations of action. There are some terms involving feeling which are narrowly related to action, feelings which have something to do with a sense of "drive" or "push."

One of the first words learned by Europeans who have serious relationships with rural Tahitians is *fiu*. They hear it as an exclamation, *"Fiu!"* or mixed into a French sentence, *"Je suis fiu,"* "I am *fiu*." The Europeans learn to pay attention to the word. It may be simply a sign of an irritated and annoyed mood, or it may signify that the speaker is getting ready to stop what he is doing, break off a relationship, or leave a job.

Fiu indicates either annoyance, or the disappearance of the felt motive for a task, or a combination of both. It is different from feelings leading a person to stop an activity because the desire which motivated it has been gratified. The common word, as we have noted, for such a feeling of "fulfilled desire" is *maha*, which indicates something like "quenched" or "calmed down." *Fiu* indicates wanting to disengage before satisfaction. The opposite, in a sense, of *fiu* is *'ana'anatae*. People will say that they are not *'ana'anatae* any longer, they are *fiu*; and then, later, they may say they are not *fiu*, they are now *'ana'anatae* again. *'Ana'anatae* indicates "enthusiasm," a sense of a pleasant state of the self in which carrying on an activity vigorously is natural. *'Ana'anatae* has other contrasts besides *fiu*, a variety of words having to do with lack of physical well-being or with exhaustion or weariness resulting from hard work or sickness.

People, particularly in Piri, very commonly explain their behavior in terms such as enthusiasm (*'ana'anatae*); strength (*pūai*) of feeling or desire; energy (*itoito*) about doing things; or of being "fed up" (*fiu*), weak (*paruparu*), weary and bored (*haumani*), or exhausted (*rohirohi*). Such terms are used to explain activity by the strength of the felt desire to do it.

Although people talk about such things a good deal, they report that they generally feel energetic, that they enjoy getting up in the morning and look forward to the day's activities — and watching them, I got the impression that they most generally did enjoy doing the day's tasks and that they did them with energy.

If one does not feel *'ana'anatae*, one stops what one is doing if possible, rests, changes the task. But a more pervasive lack of *'ana'anatae* is a problem. People then look for a way of increasing their feelings of "enthusiasm."

Oro, after going to live in Papeete, felt *haumani*, so he sought "some means to become *'ana'anatae.*" He went for walks and for rides on the trucks that provided public transportation; but most of the time this did not help, and so he just lay around his room when he was not working. In Piri people are exhorted in various ways so that they may become *'ana'anatae*. Guests at a formal celebration, who are often fairly uncomfortable and embarrassed, are urged by the host to drink and enjoy themselves and "make their thoughts [*mana'o*] *'ana'anatae.*" One of the most commonly described ways of regaining *'ana'anatae* is drinking. Drinking, as will be noted in chapter 12, is a common and important activity, particularly among village men. When asked why they drink or what changes occur when they drink, most informants say that they feel less fearful, less embarrassed, and that they have a stronger sense of *'ana'anatae*.

There is some reason to think that enthusiasm about getting things done has some particular importance in the general pattern of motivation of people in Piri and the more *mā'ohi* members of Roto. I will return to this after presenting more elements for later use in considerations of psychological organization.

Some Generalities about Feeling

Starting from the idea of "feelings" of various kinds, I have portrayed behaviors more or less connected with different kinds of feelings. I have indicated that there is an ample Tahitian vocabulary and set of cultural understandings bearing on feelings. "Feeling" becomes associated with cultural understandings which designate the cause of the feeling and what should be done about it. Feelings are halfway stations to action and are amenable to considerable cultural manipulation.

I have suggested that some sets of feelings are relatively "hypercognated," controlled, so to speak, by discrimination, whereas others are "hypocognated" and controlled by cultural invisibility or at least by difficulty of access to communication. The matter of hypocognition raises an important problem, which also is related to other aspects of the particular cultural shapings of emotions. That is, when Tihoni, feeling strange after being separated from his *vahine*, interprets his feelings as illness and in so doing accepts a pervasive cultural pattern of playing down feelings of loss, it is evident that in some way and at some level he must know that he has suffered a significant loss. That is why his separation from his *vahine* made him feel sick or strange in the first place. That is, one "feels" considerably more than cultural forms may make consciously accessible.

Ernest Schachtel clearly designated the kind of thing that seems to be involved in an essay "On Memory and Childhood Amnesia." Some of the rich and diverse understandings of childhood experience, he wrote, are filtered out by a "process [which] leaves the culturally unacceptable or unusable experiences and the memory thereof to starvation by the expedient of providing no linguistic, conceptual, and memory schemata for them and by channeling later experience into the experience schemata of the culture. As the person, in the process of education, gradually comes to live more and more exclusively within the framework of the culturally and conventionally provided experience schemata, there is less and less to remind him of the possibility of trans-schematic experience" (Schachtel 1949; p. 47).

In a later chapter we will examine some of the culturally prevalent shapings of childhood experience. Such shapings modify, I assume, generally human qualities in certain directions. We must then try to distinguish the sociocultural forms in Piri and Roto which "starve," foster, or shape these first forms.

It should also be noted here that although we have seen various special Tahitian shapes and nuances of the phenomena associated with various feelings and emotions, the central tendencies referred to by such terms as *riri* (anger), *ri'ari'a* (fear), *here* (love), *mihi* (grief), and *māuiui* (pain) are, as far as I can tell from their usages in interviews and in living as I observed it, the same as those in the words used to gloss them.

10

Moral Behavior

In part, being a Tahitian is having a "Tahitian mind," operating with assumptions and motives which have been shaped by various aspects of growing up and of everyday life in Tahitian communities. People act in a Tahitian way and "conform" to Tahitian culture because it is the natural thing for them to do.

But people also act like Tahitians, or more precisely like good Tahitians, when they are aware that they might very well like to do something else. Insofar as individuals act like Tahitians because of the very shape of their motives and thoughts, they feel free. Insofar as they "conform" because of internal and external pressures felt as being in some tension with those motives and thoughts, they are aware of coercion, of "culture" versus "man." It is this coercion which will concern us in this chapter.

The missionaries were very much concerned with "conscience." They had their own peculiar view of what a conscience should be and found it problematic in their Tahitian converts. The wife of a missionary in the culturally related Cook Islands epitomized the problem in 1827: "I am far from considering the generality of them *true Christians*, as many who make a profession want the *essentials*, which are, a sorrow for sin when committed and a hatred for it afterwards" (E. Beaglehole 1957; p. 31).

The missionaries were reacting to something about a contrast between the quality of Polynesian moral responses and their own. The natives' apparent lack of "sorrow for sin" was a problem for the missionary's wife. There have been anthropologists who also believed this lack to be a valid and important quality of the moral life of some nonwestern societies. Ruth Benedict gave it an influential phrasing. "True shame cultures rely on external sanctions for good behavior, not, as true guilt cultures do, on an *internalized conviction of sin* [my italics]. Shame is a reaction to other people's criticism. A man is shamed either by being openly ridiculed and rejected or by fantasying to himself that he has been made ridiculous. In either case it is a potent sanction. But it requires an audience or at least a man's fantasy of an audience. Guilt does not. In a nation where honor means living up to one's own picture of oneself, a man may suffer from guilt though no man knows of his misdeed and a man's feeling of guilt may actually be relieved by confessing his sin" (Benedict 1946; p. 223).

The contrast of "shame cultures" and "guilt cultures" or of "shame" and "guilt" as contrasting bases for social conformity preoccupied many social scientists for a while.[1] The simple dichotomy turned out to be full of difficulties. The anthropologist Alfred Kroeber noted, "The reputedly independent and separate verdicts of Anglo-Saxon anthropologists on Asiatic, Oceanic, native American, and African cultures, that shame is a far more influential motivation in them than sense of sin, does not really specifically characterize these cultures nearly so much as its opposite — conscious sinfulness — characterizes Anglo-Saxon and Protestant culture" (Kroeber 1948; p. 612).

And Milton Singer, surveying a literature in which "sense of sin" had become "sense of guilt," summed up, "Whether, then, we consider the criterion of internal and external sanctions, or the cross cultural psychometric data, or the psychoanalytic interpretations of cultures, we cannot find sufficient evidence to justify the theory that most cultures of the world are shame cultures. . . . What evidence there is, tends to support the conclusion that the sense of guilt *and* [original italics] the sense of shame are found in most cultures, and that the quantitative distribution of these sanctions has little to do with the 'progressive'

1. The original emphasis on a *sense of sin* as what was to be contrasted to shame became transformed in some later discussions to "guilt as a motive for social control" as contrasted with "shame as a motive for social control." An "internalized conviction of sin" as a motive for good behavior is not at all the same thing as "guilt as a motive for self-control." For a review of the problem in anthropology and psychoanalysis, see Piers and Singer (1971).

or 'backward' character of a culture" (Piers and Singer 1971; p. 99).

But the phenomena bearing on conscience and moral controls in Piri and Roto *do* have special features, and they seem to be the kind of features which troubled the missionaries. I will describe them first, and then suggest a possible explanation for the problem of the missionary's wife.

On Not Doing Wrong in Piri and Roto

I approached the problem of the more conscious and doctrinal aspects of self-control in Piri and Roto by asking people whether they had impulses or desires on which they did not act. Almost everyone said that he did. I then asked why they resisted them.

In presenting some of their answers to the question, I will leave two key terms in Tahitian: *ha'amā*, which may be glossed "shame/embarrassment," and *arōfa*, which may be glossed as "empathy/pity/compassion." *Ha'amā* will be analyzed further here; *arōfa* was introduced in the last chapter.

I say to Poria that people often wish to do things but refrain because they consider them bad: Poria grunts his understanding. I then ask him if this is true for him. He says that he does have such thoughts "inside" of him. ("What kinds of thoughts?") "One example . . . there grows up the thought to go and steal. And afterward . . . I think it out, 'Ah, do not do it. It is a bad thing to go and steal and be seen/known,[2] and be locked up in prison. Ah, that is a bad thing, so stop.' [He pauses for a moment and then goes on.] Another example, you decide to go and seduce some woman. You think about going, but there grows in you the idea, 'Don't, it is a fearful action.'" ("Why?") "If you are seen, her *tāne* would come and beat you up, or if not, he would beat up the woman and kill her. That is the way it is when bad thoughts arise."

("Do you have other bad thoughts?") "There are some thoughts . . . some bad thoughts that one thinks about doing

2. *'Ite*, as we have noted (chapter 8), means "to see" and "to know." Thus in these quotations "to be seen" also means "to be known about."

but [one says to oneself], 'Don't, it involves fear.'" ("Why?")
"It is a matter of *ha'amā* if one is seen." ("A *ha'amā* matter if
seen?") "Yes, [it is] a *ha'amā* thing if seen, bad behavior."
("Yes —") "But if one does good things, ah, it is not a matter
involving *ha'amā*."

("Now suppose that the thought to steal came to you, or the
thought to try to go and seduce [someone else's] woman, and if
you were very sure that you would not be seen . . .") [He interrupts.] ". . . *one would be seen.*" ("No, we are not talking about
the way things are, but just supposing —") "All right." ("If you
were absolutely certain that no one could see you — if a *tahu'a*
or an angel said to you nobody could see you, what would you
do?") "About stealing?" ("Stealing, that sort of thing —.") "If
the desire within me were strong, I would go and steal."

I then ask him what he would do if everyone had left the village for a day, and he answers, "I think I would go and steal."
("And as to the woman?") "There would be times when the
wish would grow, and I would indeed go and 'play around.'
There would be no way [to stop it], I would think that I should
not do it, but no, the thought would be powerful to go and lie
with her."

I then ask Poria if there are bad things he has done, which nobody had seen but about which he is nevertheless sorry.[3] He answers without hesitation. "Yes, when I go and do that sort of
thing, and no one sees me, and then I return to the house, I reflect, 'Stop.'" ("Why?") "It's a bad thing." ("Why?") "Because,
if one is seen, those things produce *ha'amā*. If you were seen
when you go to play around with some woman, it is a very
ha'amā thing when morning comes and people say, 'That man,
he went to play around with some *vahine*.' It isn't a good thing."

Still looking for longer-lasting disturbances of "conscience,"
I ask him: ("Was there something you had done that you kept
thinking about for a long time, a week, two weeks, a month?
Was there something that you'd done in your life, and afterward,
you could not forget that thing?") "That kind of activity, going

3. The term I am glossing "sorry" and "regret" is *tātara hapa*.

and playing around with a *vahine*. A long time —" ("How long?")
"— two or three months I had been playing around with that
vahine, and afterward I stopped. Then the *vahine* left the village,
she broke things off. She ran off and went far away, along with
her *tāne*." ("And then what?") "It had stopped, and then I was
sorry, because of my playing around with his *vahine*. It caused
arōfa [i.e., within Poria] afterward. That man, it was an *arōfa*-
causing thing, because he had been staying with his *vahine*, they
had been well together, and then I, I had come to play around
with his *vahine*, I was bad." He continues, "I had stopped that
activity. But then I started again, yes, I started again. After a
long time it became seen [and known], it produced great *ha'amā*.
If it hadn't been seen [and known], I would not have stopped."

Poria constantly refers to the danger of disapproved behavior
being seen and thus becoming known to others in the community. He sees this danger as not just a possibility, but as highly
probable. He expects to be visible. He controls himself out of
anxiety that he may be seen and that there will then be trouble.
The trouble includes violence, physical punishment, and, as one
element among several, being shamed. He asserts that only the
threat of being seen controls him and that otherwise he would
act on his impulses if they became strong enough to move him.

As an apparent afterthought he mentions his feelings of *arōfa*
over the pain he caused to the *tāne* of the *vahine*. After a brief
remark about *arōfa* he says that he had, in fact, continued his
affair with that *vahine* until people found out about it.

Tāvana, whose suppressed desire, like most male informants,
is to have intercourse with other women besides his *vahine*, puts
it this way: "Yes, indeed, thoughts like that arise, desire stirs up
the thought, that wish to go, to go and take some *vahine*, and
then trouble grows. It doesn't stop, when people act like that."

I ask Tāvana again why he controls his wish to seek other
women. "I don't want to go to do it, because there will be trouble, trouble will arise. Therefore, I don't go." He specifies that
he would fear trouble from his own *vahine*. Furthermore, if the
new *vahine* that he might approach had a *tāne*, there would be

very bad trouble. Her *tāne* would severely beat up "someone," and there would be "no end to it."

Teiva, whose desire also involves other women, says that some people are afraid that if they are seen in wrongdoing they will be sent to prison. He characteristically steps up the seriousness of the punishment that would occur if one were seen. Then I ask him what he would do if he were sure that nobody would see him. His answer differs from Poria's: "I still wouldn't want to do it." ("No?") "Although nobody saw one, still there is no wish to do it, because if you think within your heart you recall God." ("Yes?") "That is the person who is looking at you — you know that God is up in the sky looking at you. Therefore, you don't steal."

Teiva's emphasis on God's eye replacing the community eye is an unusual use of God in Piri. For others, such as Tano, Veve Vahine, and Uta, who talk of trying to live by God's law in everyday life, the emphasis is different. They refer not to the constant watching of God, but rather to his set of explicit rules for behavior which can be followed to prevent one from getting into community trouble as well as eschatological trouble.

Tano, heir to the missionaries, has no hesitation in talking about some, at least, of his suppressed desires. "I still have such desires, which have lasted even to this time, I tell you — thoughts about adultery."[4] ("Adultery?") "That is the truth. Yes, adultery, the desire for a new *vahine*. That thought still exists inside of me. To this day. I'm not lying to you, because that is the nature of things inside of me, as I must explain to you; but there are the rules of the pastor's profession which I have. I am protected from those things. If only I were not energetic in protecting myself about those things, then I would be in trouble. All the things that are forbidden to us, we desire — we desire to do all those things. We desire to do all those things that are forbidden to us: 'Don't do that, that, that, that, they are bad.' The

---

4. *Fa'atūri* is used now for adultery, and in old Tahitian was used for a variety of other irregular liaisons.

desire — up until these very days, the desire persists to do those things, but because of my profession as pastor, there is protection."

I ask Tano if bad desires are a sin.[5] [He pauses.] "To my thought, if you think about those things, it is of course an evil thing. It was made known in the Bible, that although you don't do [the act], although you don't eat — although you don't drink those poisonous things, but you think about going and doing the thing, you have indeed sinned. Similarly, concerning a *vahine*, you think about that *vahine*, even though you don't go and take her, even though you don't sleep with her, you have sinned."

Tano is presenting the biblical case and not, as we shall see, his own conclusions. I, not yet understanding this, ask him whether the sin in thought and the sin in action are of the same importance. He answers, "Ah, according to the way it is written, 'Even though you don't go and do the act, and if you have had the thought, you have sinned.'" ("Yes?") "It is a difficult matter, what do you think about it?"

I avoid the question, saying that I want first to record his thought, and he goes on without hesitation, "Ah, when I think, when I think my own thought —" ("Yes?") "— even though you think, there is no difficulty [i.e., wrong] in it. You think about sleeping with that *vahine*, about committing adultery with that *vahine*, but you do not commit adultery with her — there is no difficulty at all. Because the thought inside of you — all people have that thought inside of them, there is not one man without that thing inside of him. What can be done? That thought exists inside of you, because it does not stop. It is the same as some machine that keeps running inside of you, and so goes your thought." ("Yes?") "If you concern yourself with [i.e., bring into action] that thought, you have sinned, and that is a thing which will produce difficulties." ("Because, all —") [He interrupts.] "Because — you did not take that *vahine*, you cannot be punished. Because it was God who made that thing

5. Sin, *hāra*, will be discussed later.

inside of you." ("The desire?") "Yes, the desire and the thought [*mana'o*], and from those things, there is not one mark against you. If only you had taken that *vahine*, then that would have been a black mark and one could say you had sinned, and you were bad. But, if you only reflect, if you only think, and you don't do anything, one cannot [be charged with a sin]. That is my thought, what is your thought?"

I then ask him what he thinks he would do if he were not a pastor. "I would go [and commit adultery], it is certain." ("Certain?") "That's what I think. Because, there is not one law to protect me, it would have become broken, the path would be far off, there would not be one thing to protect me, not one thing to forbid me, nothing to protect me from harm. I would go, that's what I think." When asked about other suppressed desires, such as wanting to hurt someone else or to steal, Tano says that he no longer has such feelings. He then modifies this, "Indeed there does exist, there does exist that thought concerning stealing or concerning beating someone up, it is not that those things are not inside of me, they are indeed also inside of me, but they are not things that I desire all the time, every day — to steal, to go and beat up a person. No, the big thought inside of me, every day, almost every day, the thought concerning adultery, that is the biggest thought, nothing else."

The thought then is not what counts, even for Tano, the pastor. He reflects the general consensus in Piri when he says that only outer behavior is morally significant, and his freedom in describing his desires indicates that he does not consider them any threat to his respectability. He, like Poria, states that without an external form of control (e.g., possibilities of being shamed, of breaking God's law or civil law), he would go ahead with the wrong action.

Adherence to God's law is one way one can prevent oneself from acting in ways that will cause trouble. Trouble is generally related to being seen, an exception being the self-control related to *arōfa*. One, but not the sole, penalty which comes from being seen in wrongdoing is feelings of *ha'amā*. Let us examine the meaning of *ha'amā*.

Ha'amā, *Shame, Embarrassment, and Shyness*

The word *ha'amā* is very frequently used in the daily talk of Piri and Roto. I asked Teri'i Tui, "What makes people feel *ha'amā?*" He gave me some concrete situations which produce it. (1) When young people in Piri first see a stranger, they feel *ha'amā*. (2) If he, Teri'i Tui, were to enter someone's house and did not know the person, he would feel *ha'amā* at first. (3) If he were to bring me into a friend's house unannounced, and if the house were in disorder, the friend would feel *ha'amā*; however, if the friend knew we were coming beforehand and had a chance to put his house in order, he would not feel *ha'amā*.

Poria has a list of six *ha'amā*-producing items. (1) If you have to go to ask someone to give you or loan you something. (2) If you try to seduce a woman and she calls out or chases you away. (3) If you are walking along the village path all dressed up, with a wreath of flowers on your head and perfumed with perfumed oil, and people make fun of you. (4) If you have been drunk and the next day people recount what you have done. (5) If you sing but have a bad voice. And (6) (a blanketing final item), "If you do something bad."

These typical first presentations are generally not involved with evident moral behavior of a *good versus evil* type but, with the exception of Poria's vague sixth item, with two sorts of *ha'amā* situation. The first has no moral tone in itself; the second has a moral tone of proper/improper or fitting/unfitting.

The first group, the "nonmoral" *ha'amā* occasions, are all situations where an individual becomes engaged in a situation involving other people which is not ordinary, familiar, and in order. A stranger in one's house, entering the house of a stranger, having a familiar person enter one's house when it is not properly arranged, even being seen when one is more dressed up and decorated than usual, seem to share these features. When the children in Teri'i Tui's household had begun to feel comfortable with me, we would occasionally find ourselves together during a family festival at a table in a part of the house which was not usually used for eating. The children became embarrassed again. That is, in these cases the shift of the familiar frames and contexts of behavior produces *ha'amā*. We recognize this as "embarrassment."

This aspect of *ha'amā* is constantly related in Tahitian speech to the commonly used expression, *mātau*, which means to get used to or be acquainted with a person or situation. People were said to be *ha'amā* because they were not *mātau* in a situation, and becoming *mātau* was an explanation for the disappearance of the *ha'amā*. This *ha'amā*, embarrassment caused by violation of the familiar, tends to be morally neutral in relation to the acts or conditions which bring it about. *Sensitivity* to *ha'amā* is considered to be a desirable quality of character. It is a key element in people's approving separation of themselves from "brash" *demis*. It is good that one can feel *ha'amā*. In those examples of states or acts producing *ha'amā* referred to later, where the state or act is morally disapproved, the sensitivity to disapproval is, at another level of evaluation, approved; but in these first examples the situation producing *ha'amā* does not reflect negatively on the person who has the feeling. *Ha'amā*, as discomfort caused by becoming visible because of violation of the familiar, can, in fact, inhibit acts which are generally recognized as good. For example, a twelve-year-old girl in Piri told me that she wanted to give a flower wreath to the schoolteacher when he was to leave for a vacation, but she did not because the other children were not going to do the same thing, and she was afraid she would feel *ha'amā*.

The examples of *ha'amā* about a disorderly house and Poria's remark about his nonbeautiful singing voice (most people in Piri sing beautifully) are examples of a second cluster of occasions for *ha'amā* — those situations in which the body, body actions, personal skills, and the state of certain objects which intimately belong to one, such as clothes and house, are not maintained or performing adequately. These are related intimately to the approval or disapproval by others as judges.

Dirtiness and disorder are salient aspects of this kind of *ha'amā*, both in themselves and as metaphors for other types of shameworthy behavior. As we have seen (chapter 4), there is considerable emphasis on avoiding personal dirtiness of body or of clothes. Such dirtiness is not only a matter of shame, but is considered quite deviant; personal dirtiness, in fact, would suggest deviance of psychotic dimensions.

The word for clean is *mā*. One expression for the act of cleaning something is *ha'amā*, to make clean. Whether this homonymous word gives any clue to the historical etymology of *ha'amā* as "shame/embarrassment" is unclear. But it is a tempting speculation. Metaphoric terms related to dirtiness, disorder, and disgust (the latter with a strong tone of gastric rejection, the core meaning referring to a desire to vomit) are used to refer to moral *ha'amā* situations such as incest.

Dirtiness is an important metaphor for this group, but there are examples to which dirtiness does not apply. Poria's inadequate singing voice is one. Similarly, people sometimes say they feel *ha'amā* because of body defects. Adolescents who had missing teeth would cover their mouths when they laughed, and this was explained as being due to *ha'amā*. Tāvana said that he felt *ha'amā* as an adolescent because he was relatively puny. He put it, "In the time of youth, you had a little *ha'amā* because you were young and rather weak. You had *ha'amā* because people would say, 'That person is a very weak person,' and you were ashamed."

Ha'amā is also related to some sexual behaviors. Here the idea of *ha'amā*, both as a criticism and as a feeling, is particularly related to exposure of the genitalia. Whatever the complex of meanings and affects which might be involved with social disapproval of genital exposure, one strand of significance seems to involve dirtiness and contamination. Recall the contaminating qualities of menstrual blood and the marked emphasis on shame-producing dirtiness of the head of the penis as a motive for supercision.

Ha'amā is frequently invoked in criticism of incestual unions. Reported incest usually involves questionable liaisons within the extended family. Such unions are considered to be "disgusting" and "disorderly." People frequently explain the impropriety of these extended family incestual unions as because the relational designations of the people involved would become confused.

"Would she be his [classificatory] aunt or his wife?" "His son would be his own [classificatory] brother."

I have suggested that at first approach there are two kinds of situations in which *ha'amā* is felt or invoked. Both involve disorder. One cluster concerns the involvement of an individual in a situation which is not ordinary, familiar, and in order.[6] The other involves a judgment on the individual's adequacy, on his presentation of self. Here a moral tone enters, involving metaphors of "dirtiness," "defect," and "personal disorder." This meaning of *ha'amā* involves "shame."

Poria's final comment, "You feel *ha'amā* if you do something bad," suggests a residual group of occasions for *ha'amā*. Here one is ashamed because one is seen in any act which the community defines as *bad*. The emphasis shifts from "improper" and "incompetent" to "bad." "Bad" involves, as I will argue, another set of meanings and controls than "proper." But being seen and known as having done something bad has as a *secondary* implication a questioning of one's competence. Because of this, one feels *ha'amā*, or shame. But shame, which is essentially related to self-adequacy, is only a peripheral factor in the self-controls involved with "good" and "evil" in Piri.

I have been discussing the content of *ha'amā*-producing situations. Let us note some of their formal aspects. The quotations emphasize that *ha'amā* occurs when an individual perceives that he has been observed. As Uta put it, "If you are dirty or smell bad and hear someone comment on it, *then* it is a very *ha'amā*-producing matter for you." And in Poria's discussion of suppressed behavior he expresses a feeling of fear in anticipation of being seen performing a disapproved act. His fear is connected with foresight, but his *ha'amā*, in this sequence, would arise only at the moment when he realized he had been seen. This is the much emphasized "external direction" of "shame-related" behavioral controls. But, as the quotations also indicate, *ha'amā* is

6. Not all kinds of disordered situations produce *ha'amā*. In a festival the slight disorder of normal, ongoing, everyday social frames and contexts which is involved produces feelings of elation. Disorder of certain familiar *physical* contexts may produce uncanny emotions (see chapter 5).

only one of the consequences of wrong behavior which require visibility.

Reports of the temporal extension of the feeling of shame in retrospect occasionally occur. "I felt *ha'amā* the next morning, because somebody probably saw me while I was drunk." Most prospective statements, however, were like Poria's — including the sequence, "I had the impulse, I felt a sense of fear that I might act on it and then experience *ha'amā* or some other punishment." In most reports *ha'amā* is related to the moment of feedback and to actual audiences, not imagined or "internalized" ones.

If, however, *ha'amā* is limited in time, it is easily extendable in "actor space," from the self to people with whom one feels identified. People feel *ha'amā* for close friends, for their peer groups, for relatives — if the others are involved in something which would bring *ha'amā* to the self. For example, Tāvana, talking of his *taure'are'a* days in Tahiti, spoke of going with his friends to wrestle with boys from another *taure'are'a* group. Not only did he feel *ha'amā* if he lost, but, "We were a group. If one of us went to fight and if he lost, I felt *ha'amā* — we all felt *ha'amā*. I felt *ha'amā* because you lost. If I lost, you felt *ha'amā*. That is the way it was. And if it were some relative of mine and a relative of yours, and they are wrestling, and mine loses, I feel *ha'amā* very strongly."

The capacity to feel *ha'amā* for extensions of oneself varies with different individuals. Narcissistic and immature individuals (by both Tahitian and more generally human standards), such as Taere, had a narrow, sometimes self-limited sensitivity. Those more widely involved in village affairs, more trusted and respected, such as Tāvana, tended to have much wider *ha'amā* identifications.

The fear of being shamed and the dysphoria of shame/embarrassment are, judging from interviews and observations, strongly felt and easily aroused states.

There are a number of cultural patterns which reduce the oppressiveness of *ha'amā* susceptibility. Essentially judgments on adequacy are not severe or intrusive — they are directed to surface presentations. Informants have no hesitation in listing impulses, for it is only, as Tano argued, the action which is involved with *ha'amā* moral doctrine.

Moral *ha'amā* is limited by an elaborated doctrine of "natural behaviors." Drinking, aspects of sexual behavior, or adolescent shirking of household duties may be matters of *ha'amā*, but they are also natural, part of the essence of a particular life stage or of being human. They are matters which one will outgrow, which are qualities of one's family line, or which are made by God. Such deeply felt doctrines reduce both the use and the pain of shaming.

In connection with relief from the oppressiveness of visibility, it may be noted that not all audiences have the same power to shame as the village audience in Piri or "the people one knows" in Roto. People, for example, are generally expected to be freer in their drinking and sexual behavior when they visit Papeete or work on a distant island. For the *demis* and Europeans this represents hypocrisy. As Tivini, the schoolteacher, remarked, "They pretend to care so much about the behavior of their *taure'are'a* children in Piri, but they don't care what they do when they go to Papeete."

Within Piri and the *mā'ohi* segment of Roto there are restraints on looking, gossiping, and expressing curiosity. When people walk on the village path they carefully avoid looking at partially naked villagers who might be bathing in potential view of the path, or at people sitting in an outhouse whose door may have fallen off. Walkers look carefully straight ahead.

If there is an argument on the village path, "mature" people pretend not to note or, like Teri'i Tui, peek out secretly through a crack in the wall of their house, not showing themselves at the window. It is a matter of *ha'amā*, particularly for men (village gossips are mostly women) to show interest in squabbles.

In potentially embarrassing, exposed situations, people in a group avoid all eye contact. When, as I have noted, a group of men are at a village political meeting which requires them to play roles different from those of their everyday, ordinary life, although they joke and look at one another before and after the

formal part of the meeting, during the meeting itself when anybody talks no two people in the group encounter each other's
eyes or look at the speaker.

Although gossip is an important part of "shame control," the
words designating gossip have a pejorative tone, and gossiping is
said to be a bad thing to do. Ideally, the behavior which would
produce shame on becoming visible has to spontaneously force
its way into visibility; people are not supposed to search out
shameful acts. Such a searching out is in itself a *ha'amā* thing.

In spite of these restraints, community visibility and the resulting problem of privacy are experienced ambivalently. On the
one hand, they are felt to be protective — they prevent one from
doing bad things and they prevent others from doing bad things
to one. On the other hand, people who do leave the village for
urban life express relief about being away from the village eye,
although they might feel anxiety about the complementary dangers of city life, where other people are not restrained (so goes
the fantasy) by village scrutiny.

Arōfa, *Error, Guilt, and Sin*

The adolescent Oro discusses feelings of *ha'amā* at length. He
drinks to overcome *ha'amā*, here shyness and timidity, so that
he can approach girls. When he drinks too much, he feels *ha'amā*,
now indicating shame, when he recalls the foolish things he had
done in front of others. He recounts that he had stopped drinking for six months, "But then finally one sees one's friends
drinking and one starts again." ("Why had you stopped?") "My
'mother' said to me, 'Stop that sort of thing, there isn't any
profit in it,' so I stopped. Until those days when my *taure'are'a*
friends were drinking, and they came and pulled at one [i.e.,
me]. If one doesn't go and drink, one feels much *ha'amā* — so
you drink, like that, you do it more frequently, you get drunk,
and it all starts again."

Here, in order not to feel *ha'amā*, Oro violates the wishes of
his "mother." One wonders, by avoiding "shame" does he now
feel "guilt?" There are, in fact, problems about determining
this.

I ask Oro if there was any of his behavior that he had felt sorry about afterward, aside from things which produced *ha'amā*. He answers, "Indeed yes. About that thing, one goes and steals from some man. In the morning you regret. You remember that it was not through your fatigue [that the food was grown], it was through his fatigue. Ah, you think at that time, 'Stop.' But then you and your friends get together, and the thought comes to you to amuse yourselves. You go again and do some mischief to the man. And afterward you are sorry again. All the bad things I did, I regretted afterward, and then I did them all again."

I then ask him whether he thought the other *taure'are'a* boys regretted their stealing. He says, "There were perhaps some who were not sorry, who did not have *arōfa*. As for me, no, when I saw that person, the one who had suffered the bad-doing, I felt very strange [*huru ē*, literally "altered," "changed in one's nature"]. It was an old man. He couldn't go up on the mountainside anymore to gather food. [Oro's voice is now full of feeling.] It is a very *ha'amā* thing, if you had been seen." ("What?") "A very shameful thing indeed, if you were seen by the people, [that they saw] that you were the one going to steal his things."

His description shifts abruptly from indications of "internalized" compassion and guilt to *ha'amā* and the matter of being seen. The shift is perhaps in part because of the social desirability of using *ha'amā* explanations. The good citizen in Piri, and among the *mā'ohi* of Roto, is one who is sensitive to community visibility.[7] And in part it is because explanations involving "guilt" are unnatural for him.

I have suggested that feelings related to shame and embarrassment have undergone considerable cultural definition and elaboration and are significant aspects of socially important behavioral control.

7. In the same manner the proper response to tests of "moral intelligence" in the West, such as "What would you do if you found a stamped, addressed, sealed envelope?" indicate one's knowledge of the relative social desirability of various types of moral discourse.

In contrast, the feeling of guilt is *culturally* played down to the point of conceptual invisibility. The Tahitian language has no word which signifies anything like a sense of guilt. The missionaries had to resort to awkward metaphors like "pain in the intestines" or "the burden of the intestines." The ordinary Tahitian way of expressing what would seem to a western observer to be from the context "guilt feelings" is the nonspecific term *pe'ape'a*, which indicates "trouble," either as an internal sensation or as an aspect of a social or interpersonal situation.

The quotations indicate, however, a term which does contrast with *ha'amā* in discussions of motives for self-control. It is, like *ha'amā*, a highly salient motivational explanatory principle. The term is *arōfa*,[8] which, as noted, may be glossed "empathy/pity/compassion."

Thus Hiro, discussing conscious impulses on which he would not act, denied that his self-control was a question of being seen and of *ha'amā*: "Whether people saw or did not see . . . if I really wanted to do it I would do it. I am not afraid of people. It is not a matter of the person's talking about me. If I said to myself, 'Go and kill yourself,' then I would go and kill myself. If [I decided] go and get money, I would go and get money . . . but I don't want to do such things because it is forbidden to me, I am prevented from doing them because of *arōfa*." ("*Arōfa* for whom?") "*Arōfa* for the person to whom I have done a bad thing, and *arōfa* toward myself. I am jumping into a hole."

Arōfa, as Hiro uses it, has two contrasts with *ha'amā*. It is "internalized," not needing an external audience, and it refers to something other than "presentation of self" or "acceptability." One feels *arōfa* for cripples, for hungry people, for people who have undergone calamities. It indicates "pity." But it also means that one feels the suffering of these people as they feel it; thus it indicates "empathy." It is applied in discussions of self-control where, through one's feelings of empathy with some-

---

8. The Hawaiian term *aloha* is etymologically and semantically related. It is defined as "love, affection, compassion, mercy, pity, kindness, charity," as well as the more familiar "greeting" (Pukui and Elbert 1957).

one, one realizes that one *must* pity him. Why? Because he has
suffered some *harm* because of one. Thus the other and, I will
argue, significant contrast with *ha'amā* is that instead of considering behavior having to do with "competence," we are approaching behavior having to do with "harm" and with the
question of "good" and "evil." *Arōfa* is only one kind of emotion having to do with self-control over harming others. The
others are more external in their reference.

Manu emphasizes judgment and self-control as prior to considerations of visibility. He has said that he has had occasional
thoughts about stealing. But he has prevented himself from doing it. "I prevent myself from doing those kinds of things because I know — I know, I mustn't do those bad things, such as
stealing, and going to beat up somebody. I prevent myself. Because, I know, I have thought it over inside my head, I have
worked out in my thought which are the good things, and
which are the bad things. If I know that that is a bad thing, I
protect myself from doing it. And I seek again some other
means, that is, a good means. Even though I know where there
is some valuable object, like money, and I know the place, my
thought does not form that I should go and take it. No. I have
thought, inside myself, it is better for me to be energetic in
working, and earn my money, that is the good way."

At various places throughout the interviews, Manu has stressed
his self-respect, his pride in choosing good action and avoiding
bad. When I push him to explain why he avoids bad action, he
says, "Yes, it is true — the cause that I don't want to do bad
things is because, I know that they are a *hāra* [sin]. I know,
that a *hāra* — there is a law to punish it. That is the thing that
prevents you. If you do something *'ino* [bad], if you have done
a *hāra*, after the *hāra* you will be punished by the law, because
of the bad thing you have done." ("Which law?") "Two kinds
of law. Religious law and the law of the government." ("Which
law comes first in your opinion?") "The law concerned with
religion. Because it has been said by the pastors, and in the Bible, that although you do something in some secret place, and
the people don't see, nevertheless God sees you at the time you

are doing your act." ("Do you believe that?") [He has expressed doubt on many things taught by the Bible and the pastors.] "Yes, I have certain confidence in that. Those are the things that I have confidence in in order to protect myself; don't do such and such, that is the reason." I ask him what kind of a punishment he would get from the religious law. "It is the spirit that would be punished, when the time comes that you die. It is your spirit that will carry that *hāra* which you've done during your life. . . . It will go into the fiery pit and your spirit will not go to Paradise." He enlarges on that for a while and then turns to the civil law. "Sometime, if you do such acts, and there is somebody who sees you . . . and the knowledge comes to the boss who owned the thing which you have taken. Then. . . ." He goes on to a long description of how you are confronted, accused, and end up for several months in prison.

Arōfa and fear of punishment are something other than *ha-'amā*. They have something to do with "good" and "evil" rather than "proper" and "improper." But they are still far in quality from "a sorrow for sin when committed and a hatred for it afterward" as understood by the Puritan missionaries.

Although the missionaries did not find a term for feelings of guilt, they did find terms which they thought meant "repent" and "sin." The term they used to translate "repent" was *tātara hapa*. *Tātara* means "to untangle or unsnare." *Hapa* has the general sense of "error." The term means literally "to untangle oneself from the consequences of having made an error."

In the first Tahitian dictionary compiled by the missionaries in the early nineteenth century, some sixty years after the western discovery of Tahiti, *hapa* was one of three words given similar definition. *Hapa* was defined as "a deviation from a rule, a missing of a mark, an error, sin, or crime." *Hape* was defined as "an error, a mistake, a sin." The third term, *hāra*, was defined as "a sin, transgression, crime, or guilt"[9] and also as "unequal, not hitting the mark, deviating from a line or rule."

9. I.e., *guilt* as "responsibility" for a "crime," and so forth.

In contemporary Tahitian *hape* refers primarily to minor mistakes (either technical or social ones), and *hāra* to serious social transgressions, which involve probable punishment. The contemporary narrowing of reference of *hāra*, the loss of its technical reference, is probably due to Christian theological and biblical usage. *Hapa* survives now mostly in compound terms such as *tātara hapa.*

These words, with their implications of making an error or deviating from a mark, have as their antonyms in social discourse words meaning (socially) proper, which are also derived from physical correctness. Examples are *tano* which means "to hit a target or mark" and *'āfaro*, "straight, as a straight line."

The concept of *hāra* has been taken over to a large degree by Calvinistic theology to deal with the Christian idea of "sin." In pre-Christian Tahiti there were a number of punishable behaviors recorded by the first western observers. They included murder, sociosexual violations (adultery and incest), theft, failures in expected economic exchange, and violation of proper formal respect and deference toward high authorities. A variety of punishments were described — deprivation of part or all of the offender's property; banishment; killing (one form of which was ritual sacrifice) — carried out in some cases by the offended person, who was protected by ideas of justice from further retaliation for his retaliatory act, in other cases by the tribal chief or other high-status individuals.[10]

When people now are asked to list *hāra*, the list depends to some degree on whether or not the individual is a highly involved church member. Veve Vahine, very much involved in church activities, answers by listing selections from the Ten Commandments. She says these are the things you have to do to avoid going to hell. "You have to pay attention to the law. ... Do not steal, do not kill, do not thrash people, do not covet, do not commit adultery. .... If you do this then your spirit will arrive [in heaven]. If not, then it will not."

10. The material on these offenses and sanctions is collated and analyzed by Douglas Oliver (forthcoming).

She states she is not *certain* that she will avoid hell, but then she continues with confidence, ". . . if you pay careful attention, if you pay careful attention to His law . . . Do not do that thing, do not do that thing, do not do that thing, and continue like this until your end, you arrive in heaven. If however you do not — even if you pay attention sometimes and there are other times when you do not pay attention to His law, then you will go into the fire."

The need to pay continuous attention to not violating God's tabus as set forth in the Ten Commandments is common doctrine. It is all highly impersonal, mechanical, and legalistic; and, as we noted in chapter 5, neither repentence nor forgiveness — God's grace — is relevant. The emphasis, in contrast to missionary hopes, is on external behavior, not intent. And the behavior emphasized is avoidance of transgression. Repenting, *tātara hapa*, means in practice doing the mechanical things which will restore one's ritual relationship to God.

Nonreligious lists usually stress hurting behavior. Asked to list ordinary, common *hāra*, Uta says, "Hitting someone, that is the most frequent *hāra*." Asked what else, he says, "Killing someone." Pressed for others, he adds, "Insulting people." Some matters listed as causes for *ha'amā* are also listed as *hāra* — particularly adultery and stealing.

The ideas of error, of hurt, of law, of punishment are all associated with *hāra*. *Hāra* also involves justice, the proper application of a law. Injury which would be accepted if "merited" is a *hāra* if unmerited. "He hit me, but I did not know the reason. I had not done anything. Therefore it was a very bad thing." *Hāra* also entails the idea of "good" and "bad," for *hāra* are extreme cases of bad-doing.

The most general Tahitian terms for "good," *maita'i*, and "bad," *'ino*, have a wide range of uses. They apply to good and bad fish, good and bad craftsmanship, and skillful and unskillful performance. When they are applied as a moral evaluation, they imply a dimension of good/evil. Destructive spirits are *'ino*, as are a harmful and frightening man, a destructive hurricane, and dangerous sharks. The semantic structures of the terms are complex, but in their sense of good/evil (as contrasted to good/ spoiled, nice/not nice, etc.) they are the usual evaluative terms applied to harmful or helpful behavior, as *ha'amā* is applied as an epithet to the kinds of behaviors described in the previous section.

Behavioral Controls and the Integration of People into Social Systems

Starting with answers to the question, "What keeps you from doing some of the things you are aware you would like to do?", I have presented some of the Tahitian ideas which are associated with such a question. The data I have presented indicate that "shame" has a good deal to do with some behavior relating to self-control and the social evaluation of behavior in Piri, and to a lesser degree in Roto, but by no means with all of it. It would be misleading to call it a "shame culture," for shame is important only to one subset of behavior controls, those having to do with adequacy.

In order to suggest how I think behavioral controls in a place like Piri differ from "guilt controls" as understood in the West, I will embark on a short abstract and fanciful journey, which presents ideal-type models of Piri and "the West."

There seem to be two very general tendencies in the foregoing material. One involves shame, embarrassment, cleanliness, order, adequacy, fear of ridicule, fear of shame, orientation to the familiar, presentation of self. The other involves good/evil, harm, error, empathy, law, justice, retaliation, social trouble, fear of punishment. This second group, which at first sight seems to involve "guilt controls," has features which contrast with western, particularly Calvinistic, expectations. With the exception of *arōfa*, the emphasis is on being seen (even if only by God) as a necessary element for punishment, on the externality of sanctions (physical consequences rather than painful guilt feelings), on avoiding evil rather than on doing good, on action as the basis for moral evaluation rather than intention. In these latter emphases the second group has some formal resemblance to the first or "shame" group — but it is in essence quite different.

The meaning of these groupings has something to do with the way people fit into the social system of Piri and the kind of a system it is. These forms are related to the dynamics of the integration between individuals and their sociocultural system (which is what behavioral controls are concerned with) and build upon more privately organized tendencies. I consider more private aspects of fear, shame, and guilt in the next section and in other chapters. Here I am concerned with the question of psychosocial integrations.[11]

Members of any social group must be evaluated in terms of two aspects of their relationship to that society. First, are they acceptable as members of that group? Do they fit the proper definitions of what one must *be* to fit into the group? Do they have the proper control over their bodies? Do they have the proper kinds of bodies? Are they oriented to proper social behavior? Shame and embarrassment, with their relation to proper orientation to familiar contexts, to the smooth presentation of self, to body cleanliness and competence, to the fit into "culture" through the control of the disorder of private patterns of sexuality and other bodily activities — are powerful affectual mediators of this aspect of self-society integration. The emphasis is on immediate acceptability to others, on being seen by them, and on their immediate judgment. In Piri, and apparently generally in Tahitian culture, the smooth and successful presentation of the self involves powerful symbolic mediators of cleanliness, of surface attractiveness, of being palatable. When one fails in matters of acceptability, one is considered unfit, inadequate. One may be ridiculous, disgusting, laughable — but not "bad" or "evil." "Bad" or "evil" indicates failure at another kind of integration.

11. Singer, in his review of the problems of using "shame" and "guilt" to make a typology of modes of social compliance in different cultures, expressed the opinion that "psychological characterizations and comparisons of cultures . . . are of low validity because they seek to isolate 'pure' psychological categories. Their validity and fruitfulness will increase as they abandon this 'psychologism' and develop instead characterizing constructs in which the emotional emphases of a culture are integrally related to cultural values, world view, overt behavior, and features of social organization" (Piers and Singer 1971; pp. 99-100).

The second aspect of individuals' relation to their societies which must be evaluated and controlled is social and interpersonal action, the carrying out of the tasks which are entailed by one's membership in the group and which are necessary or important to its functioning, to the well-being of its members.

The problem of social and interpersonal action and its evaluation differs from the problem of acceptability and its evaluation in any given social group. In addition, the evaluation of action in a sociocultural setting such as Piri and its evaluation in the kinds of communities from which the missionaries and anthropologists come have essential differences, which we must note if we are to understand the problem of the missionary's wife.

I find it useful to introduce some elementary system theory notions which may help suggest important issues in the contrast between Tahitian and missionary conscience. In system theory language, one may assert that the main purpose of action in Piri is to maintain the *variables* of the sociocultural system and not to change its *parameters*. A quotation from Gregory Bateson will indicate the meanings of *variable* and *parameter* in my statement.

A house with a thermostatically controlled heating system is a simple self-corrective circuit. . . . A thermometer appropriately placed in the house is linked into the system to control a switch in such a way that when the temperature goes above a certain critical level the furnace is switched off. Similarly, when the temperature falls below a certain level the furnace is switched on. But the system is also governed by another circumstance, namely, the setting of the critical temperatures. By changing the position of a dial the owner of the house can alter the characteristics of the *system as a whole* by changing the critical temperatures at which the furnace will be turned on and shut off. Following Ashby [1956], I will reserve the word "variables" for those measurable circumstances which change from moment to moment as the house oscillates around some steady temperature, and shall reserve the word "parameters" for those characteristics of the system which are changed for example when the householder intervenes and changes the setting of the thermostat. I shall speak of the latter change as of higher order than changes in the variables. (Bateson 1958; p. 292)

Action in Piri goes on in a sociocultural system where the emphasis is on stability, on "steady state," and not on change. Problems of acceptability and of action have special dimensions in a steady-state sociocultural system when contrasted with the nature of such problems in a sociocultural system with strong tendencies toward "growth" or change, tendencies which involve constant alteration of the parameters and goals of the system.

Whereas questions of acceptability require scanning of the immediate situation and of the responses of others, the question of proper *action* in relation to larger system maintenance in a steady-state system requires general information about the variable state of the sociocultural system and its fixed parameters or values. How much productive work should one do? How should one distribute various kinds of resources? How much deference, cooperation, criticism, affection, or resistance is due various other people? To act, individuals must know the optima involved and where they are in relation to them. What is good behavior, what should be done to make things go along well, to avoid trouble? To the missionaries such concerns seemed a kind of "good-doing" which was pragmatic, shallow, trouble-avoiding. This kind of successful integration did not involve self-realization, rising above the crowd and the momentary situation, and the winning of a salvation-worthy individual integrity.

Questions of proper action involve law, justice, and (in comparison with acceptability considerations) sensitivity to relatively delayed feedback (e.g., a series of events culminating in trouble). Now the question of harm and hence badness becomes relevant. If an individual does not maintain system variables within proper ranges, there will be a consequence for the situations of other people in the system. The harm can come from too much or too little of the proper behavior. Now this has something to do with one's fit into the system, and therefore there are still problems of acceptability and shame; but doing harm essentially involves actions. The moral stress is on one's actions, not one's intentions. This latter will only be added, I will argue, when considerations of change and complexity become important. Violence and physical injury are only one type of harmful behavior. Stealing, violation of orderly incest rules, lese majesty, and underperformance (for example, so that one's family goes hungry) are all harmful in relation to maintenance of the sociocultural system.

In matters of action in a steady-state society, guilt has a very different status than it does in a change society. In a steady-state society one can to a considerable degree avoid major transgressions of the rules. One activates the controls associated with the rules by behavior which approaches deviance, and one feels their effect in the form of trouble caused, of disapproval from others, of covert feelings of guilt represented as "being troubled," and of empathic suffering with the injury one may cause to others. By attending to such clues that one is beginning to do something wrong, and because the rules generating them are fairly clear, one can avoid a situationally determined sense of having sinned, which is not so easy to do in a change-oriented or complex society.

In Piri one can avoid transgressions. Knowledge of traditional laws, customs, and tabus is protective. It keeps one from blundering into trouble. If one does break the laws in an individual and culturally pathological act, guilt will be mobilized, but it is a sign of a breakdown of the ordinary controls and represents a private and poorly understood experience.

The value of a steady state is indicated in Piri, and to the *mā'ohi* of Roto, in a number of ways. The transformed Calvinistic God represents it. God, as I have noted, punishes people who become too proud, too ambitious, too innovative. He makes people sick who have too much property, who have come too far. He sends hurricanes into the world because westerners have tried to get to the moon. When things work out *better* than usual — in village affairs, in a family relationship, in fishing or farming — whereas a striving westerner might be tempted to set a new and higher goal, the villagers often consider it a matter of random good luck, a windfall, a kind of behavior which suggested either "childishness" or else "fatalism" to missionary minds.

To understand the missionary's wife, we may continue our ideal-type model building and ask what happens to problems of action when change in the goals and nature of the social system itself becomes an important personal goal. There are some *individuals* in Piri, like Tano, and more in Roto and other urban neighborhoods, who are striving, ambitious, future-oriented — who want to shift their group or some subsystem of it to new goals and new modes of relationship. They are "bad" within the terms of the steady-state ideal, and there are a variety of external and internal sanctions which tend to suppress their striving behaviors. But when change becomes a culturally approved and encouraged goal, individuals find themselves in paradoxical situations.

The situation in a change-oriented society, or in a society which emphasizes in any way the transcending of the given sociocultural situation, is given paradigmatic expression in Kierkegaard's discussion of the meaning of faith as expressed in Abraham's willingness to slay Isaac — to do what seems to be absurd evil in the service of some higher goal. "The ethical expression for what Abraham did is, that he would murder Isaac; the religious expression is, that he would sacrifice Isaac; but precisely in this contradiction consists the dread which can well make a man sleepless, and yet Abraham is not what he is without this dread" (Kierkegaard 1954; p. 41).

If one is involved in change, in making something new happen, one must be able to ignore the short-term balances and orientations related to shame and embarrassment and some of the regulators — laws, tabus, disapprovals, trouble, as well as empathy and pity — of peaceful system maintenance. Not completely, because there is, confusingly, a mixture of steady-state processes, of presentations of self as immediately acceptable, which are still maintained. It is never clear at which point these considerations *should* be violated. The moral emphasis now shifts from acts to intentions. For the consequences of the act cannot be judged solely by the ordinary and traditional concerns of hurt to others, or of respect for traditional goals and limits expressed in law and custom. The constant question now comes up whether an act is somehow good in terms of some other *potential* good. And it becomes important to know what it is that Abraham thinks he is doing.

In change-oriented groups[12] one must overcome the constrictions of embarrassment and shame; one must question the validity of clues for immediately adjustive behavior; one must be rebellious; one must do harm in relation to some aspects of the traditional system; one must have a special kind of internalized system for making judgments.

Now guilt comes to the fore, and the question becomes the *authenticity* of the feelings of guilt, feelings which are unavoidable. If I accept values of change I will violate old relationships; I will cause some suffering now for some future good. I will now *feel* guilty whatever I do, and must now decide which feelings of guilt are related to socially defined wrong — that is, are socially authentic — and which are unwarranted by social goals and realities and therefore "neurotic," or otherwise invalid. The question of authenticity of guilt feelings helps give Calvinistic sin its tone. That is, decisions are involved about authentic evildoing in a context of pervasive feelings of sinfulness.[13]

A change-oriented society seems to entail guilt feelings in those who involve themselves in that change. These guilt feelings must be brought into awareness and exposed to some sort of

12. In a complex but relatively static society those individuals who must operate in various subgroups of the society may, if the values and culture of the subgroups vary, face dilemmas similar to those of members of change-oriented groups.

13. In an attempt to separate guilt feelings into socioculturally warranted and unwarranted kinds, the "oedipal situation" takes on a special meaning. The sense of guilt generated by participating in change involves rebellion and detachment from family definitions, relationships, and authorities. By stressing analysis and awareness of the "oedipal situation" rather than repression, some of the guilt of change, movement, individuation, and seeking for new goals can be located and defined as "neurotic," as inauthentic, as invalid as a signal of wrongdoing.

This is, I think, related to the historic importance of psychoanalysis in the West and explains the sociocultural reasons for the centrality of the analysis of the oedipal complex. Its concern with authentic versus neurotic guilt is meaningless in a steady-state society.

systematic ordering. It is in this sense that western societies are "guilt societies" in a way that Tahiti is not.

Some Aspects of Personality
Related to Moral Behavior

I have argued that behavioral controls in Piri fall into two sets, one having to do with the presentation of the self as acceptable, the other having to do with action. The first set involves shame; the second involves guilt, but in ways which differ from the relation of guilt to moral decisions in complex or change-oriented societies. I have argued that these sets have to do with the integration of individuals into a particular kind of sociocultural system.

What has this to do with the more private aspects of individuals' personalities? The kinds of steady-state behavioral controls I have described seemed to be supported by tendencies to caution, gentleness, sensitivity to social contexts, and profound convictions about the impossibility of changing the eternal nature of things, which have something to do with prevalent qualities of people's personal organization.

Cautiousness and sensitivity to embarrassment pose a problem about the correct "quantity" for an individual. Overcautious individuals are regarded as pathologically shy and so labeled (*mā-mahu*). Even the "normal" degree of timidity and caution provides recurrent problems when some aggressiveness is called for, as in establishing sexual relationships.

Some overcoming of caution and timidity is necessary for the minimal socially adventurous behavior required by community life, but one who achieves a proper balance is still far from brash. Too *little* characterological timidity seemed less of a problem than too much. Redundant controls, involving first acceptance of behavioral norms or, if not, then sanctions of disapproval directed to the "swollen up" or "high" individual, would still keep such an individual's behavior within tolerable limits. If not, he might tend to leave the village for more modern urban life.

Various aspects of childhood and adolescent experience, of prevalent socialization patterns, which we will consider presently, seem related to timidity, to sensitivity to embarrassment and to the status of private guilt feelings in individuals. It may be useful here to describe schematically a few relevant features. (1) The encouragement of a generalized and diffuse fearfulness about the consequences of transgression is a conscious goal in socialization. (2) Between the ages of three and five, children, now culturally defined as being no longer "babies," are pushed away from close relations with succoring adults. At this time a good deal of affection is "withdrawn," and nothing in the child's real behavior causes the reversal. That is, much of the withdrawal of affection is not variably contingent on the parents' response to the child's moral behavior. Whatever moral responsibility the child may imagine he has for his changed status, it is no longer related to anything he may do, to his "goodness" or "badness." (3) Praise is rarely used to produce good behavior. The child may in general avoid punishment not by exceptional performance, but by not making mistakes. He is involved in a diffuse system of rules and management which is very difficult to manipulate, but which is nonintrusive. It does not punish a child unless he breaches fairly permissive boundaries of tolerable behavior.

Such aspects of socialization present in their very structure a reality constituting an unalterable system, in which proper fit and the maintenance of system variables are in the nature of things.

Most informants stress the protective aspects of sensitivity to shame and of laws and rules. Protection is from external and internal danger — other people are dangerous, and one is not able to control oneself. The feeling of the danger of other people seems very much a projection. I have argued that Piri and similar Tahitian communities have had comparatively little violence, crime, or destructive interpersonal behavior. It seems reasonable to assert at this point that guilt generated under the prevalent conditions of traditional psychological development remains diffuse, primitive, unfocused. The residues of separation from mothering adults cannot be worked through and given form, either in later experiences of separation and forgiveness or in the course of concrete "oedipal" interactions. One is left with diffuse primitive guilt traces and fear of aggression, very far from any differentiated patterning as a control bearing on specific behaviors, and generally far from awareness. This may explain some of the motivation toward cautiousness.

But one can be effectively cautious and effectively distance oneself from *situation-produced* feelings of guilt, which, as I have suggested, is difficult for people involved in social change.

Although people are sensitive to being shamed, this does not imply that they are "shame-ridden." Shaming and ridicule are sometimes directed toward children, but much less frequently than threats and hitting. They are applied in relation to a set of sphincter control and body mastery expectations that seem relaxed in comparison with various western standards.

Statements about sensitivity to embarrassment and shame are comparative in that they refer to western expectations of form and quantity in these matters. Much of the contrast is probably due to western attempts to modify, overcome, and suppress these shame/embarrassment controls, rather than something positive about the Tahitian situation. As Erik Erikson has remarked, "Shame is an infantile emotion insufficiently studied, because in our civilization it is so early and easily absorbed by guilt" (Erikson 1968; p. 110). It seems plausible that much of the form of the shame and embarrassment sensitivities in Piri, and among the *mā'ohi* of Roto, particularly those aspects related to discomfort involving problems of comfortable fit into familiar contexts, concerns phylogenetic dimensions, which may be amplified or played down in various psychocultural contexts.

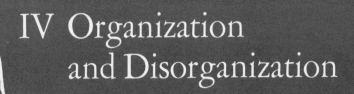

IV Organization
and Disorganization

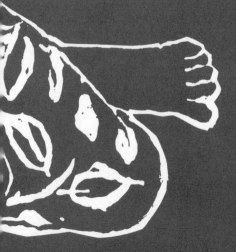

In these final chapters we turn to questions of organization and disorganization, of genesis and maintenance.

11

Fantasy

In a letter sent home from Tahiti in the early 1890s, Henry Adams complained, "I had a vague hope that somewhere in the round world, merely on the chances of the cards, I should sooner or later happen on some spot where a combination of attractions or amusements would detain me and give me interest or occupation; but the hope has almost vanished. The Polynesian is thin. The Melanesian is thick" (Adams 1930; p. 476).

Adams was responding to a variety of aspects of the situation and style of the Melanesians and Polynesians he had seen. I suspect that the Polynesian thinness had something to do with a comparative (this time with the Melanesians) lack of complexity and elaboration of symbolic forms.

I have repeatedly remarked on an emphasis on the daytime world, on casualness, on clean and fragrantly presented surfaces. Tahitian style lacks, to my aesthetic judgment, mystery — that is, a certain level of complexity and a wide use of symbolic forms suggesting meanings beyond common sense.

I noted in chapter 8 that if people in Piri and Roto were not involved in the culturally provided "institutionalized" fantasies of religion and the supernatural, they tend to inhabit a fairly literal, sense-bound, and thus commonsense world. They generate little new fantasy of their own.

In this chapter I will discuss some other aspects of public fantasy (besides the supernatural) and the major kind of private fantasy, dreaming, and I will return once more to the supercision operation (I hesitate to call it a rite in comparison with what have been called rites in Africa or Melanesia), which is the most important symbolic event for the men of the village.

One evening after supper at Teri'i Tui's house, Toni tells a tale. It is a *piri*, a "wonder." He directs it toward the children at the table, and his tone of voice and the rhythm of his speech indicate that it is an unusual narration. The story, as I paraphrased it afterward, went like this:

A certain man and his wife go out one day in their canoe into the lagoon to dive for clams. Letting the canoe drift, they both jump overboard. When the man comes back to the surface, he sees a woman swimming in the water, who seems to be his wife but who only has her appearance. This woman urges him to get into the canoe with her and to hurry off because she is pregnant. The man joins her and they paddle away. Now, his true wife returns to the surface of the water and sees him going off. She calls after him in a chanting song, begging him to return, but he does not hear her. The true wife, whose name we are told is Rori, the sea cucumber, is picked up by the sea and carried away to a far land. She too is pregnant, and in the far land she gives birth to twins, a boy and a girl. When they have grown from babies into children, they ask Rori who their father is. She answers that their father is one of the upright posts in the house. They do not accept this and continue to question her, and she finally tells them the true story. The children say that they will go to find their father. They begin to build a canoe. All the birds on the island come to help them, and it is soon built. Then a centipede takes the canoe on his back and carries it down to the seashore. Their mother tells them that they must paddle straight, and not let themselves drift, and that when they finally see red in the sky they will be near the land to which they must go. They follow her instructions and arrive there. When they get to the land, they ask a snail to conduct them to their father's house. The two children and the snail go to the house and hide underneath the elevated floor. When they hear their father inside, they knock on the floor of the house, and he calls out to them to ask what they want. They then tell him the true story. The father's false wife is still pregnant, she has not yet delivered the child. The children say to him that if he looks inside her belly, he will see a pig, not a baby. The father cuts into the false wife's abdomen, and it is indeed a pig. He throws the false wife into the fire and goes with his children back to their land to rejoin their true mother.

This tale was the only one I ever heard told at Teri'i Tui's house. As far as I could determine, such *piri* are now infrequently told, although they had more often been told to children in the childhood of the elder men in the village.

This little folktale has certain evident characteristics. It is a children's tale. Children are the "heroes," but, significantly, heroes who are able to act because of considerable help from "nature." The various animals help them freely out of their own will, their voyage is successful as a result of simply following directions, and their father gives easy assent to their version of the truth. For the children there is a problem, a quest, but no struggle.

The problem which is involved, the search for the true parent and the regularizing or completing of the family from the child's point of view, is, as we shall consider in the chapters on psychological development, one of the most poignant possible themes from the point of view of the experience of the village child.

There seems to be a certain simplicity in the symbolic transformations in this tale. Spirits take human forms but produce pig fetuses; animals act like people; time becomes dreamlike (so that a pregnancy spanning the time of a whole childhood is not surprising); and, in a "joke" within the tale, a house post stands for a father. These transformations are simple enough, close enough to reality, be it dream reality, to be "charming."

This tale stands out very much in my memory because it was the only tale or myth I heard told in Piri and Roto, except for some fragmentary references, as, for example, when features of the landscape were explained: "Here is where Maui's javelin broke off a piece of the cliff." Some of the old stories are kept precariously alive by the folklore programs of Radio Tahiti. Somebody in the village would occasionally go out of his way to explain to me how the breadfruit, for example, really derived from the head of an ancient hero who agreed to let his body be planted in order to yield food in a time of famine — a story which I, and presumably my informant, had heard for the first time just the night before on the radio.

Fragments of legends are also kept alive in the complex contrapuntal chants, the *himene tārava*, which are sung by groups from various villages and islands during the annual July festival. The secular and legendary type of *himene tārava*,[1] the *paripari fenua*, is, as the missionary dictionary has it, "a song about the transactions and qualities of a place." These songs about ancient heroes and chiefs of various districts would undoubtedly rapidly die out, as would the residues of the old storytelling dances and war dances, except for the stimulus of the July folk festival, which is strongly supported by the territorial government. The *paripari fenua*, first passed along orally, are now laboriously handwritten into copybooks, to be memorized by singers in the *himene* group. They are full of evident poetic devices — marked rhythms, a liberal use of archaic terms, idealized sentiments, and tensions produced by rearranging ordinary grammar. A fairly direct translation of a verse of a *paripari fenua* gives the idea:

On the sand, just standing
In the shade of a Pandanus tree
Then I gazed up at two birds in the sky,
Then I mused on my "love" [*arōfa*] for my homeland.

In contrast to the archaic *paripari fenua*, and other equally archaic storytelling dance forms, are various kinds of popular songs known throughout the territory. They belong to a generalized South Pacific neo-Polynesian music, in which musical forms from all the Polynesian groups and residues from songs brought into the islands by sailors and visitors have produced a vigorous popular form, which deserves study. In Piri popular songs are mostly a *taure'are'a* concern. There are sentimental and comic songs, songs of lost loves, of days spent in jail. There are also songs derived from old *'ārearea* songs, of less westernized form, which are fairly literal descriptions of sexual intercourse, in comic form.

Noteworthy among the neo-Polynesian songs are a few whose sweet or gay melody is at variance with shocking content. There is the song about Pinoi:

It is a truly frightening death.
Your death, O Pinoi.

1. The form is also used for some church hymns.

Your body has become
Like ashes from a fire.

When will you answer me. O woe,
O mother, I am destroyed with pain.

Pinoi had fled her father, who wanted to have intercourse with her. She hid in a grove of trees, to which her father set fire. And she was being burned to death. There are a fair number of similar sweetly sung ballads of incest, drowning, being eaten by sharks, and the like.

The plastic arts are almost nonexistent. Aside from the women's quilting and occasional slightly innovative house decoration, there are no plastic forms in Piri[2] for the expression of fantasy.[3]

If, in a quest for fantasy and symbolic expression, we turn to the symbolic action of ritual, we are still faced with "thinness." There are a variety of events in Piri which have something "ceremonious" about them. They are separated from the ordinary flow of life, have some special feeling associated with them, have at least minimal formal structures, and seem to be primarily concerned with a blending of social and psychological meanings. These are the rare formal weddings, funerals, birthday parties for very young children, the New Year's celebration (when people return to the village and villagers visit one another's houses), and the supercision operation.[4] These events, except for supercision based on western models, have rather less formality and use of symbolic forms than their western originals.

This impoverishment is due in part to cultural involution. Pre-Christian Tahiti had fairly elaborate ceremonies for events having to do with political events, the accession to chiefly titles, preparation for warfare, and the worship of important high gods.

2. Two or three men in Roto do entirely conventional painting on black velvet and pearl shell carving for sale to tourists and *demis*.
3. It is my impression that traditional (pre-Christian) Tahitian plastic arts were symbolically and expressively shallow in contrast to some of the art elsewhere in Polynesia and to much Melanesian art.
4. The July festival, introduced by the French, is a carnival-like festival which takes place outside of the villages and seems to have minimal meaning for village patterns, except as a welcome and useful escape from them.

There are some descriptions of the pre-Christian ceremonies related to important events in the lives of ordinary people. In previous chapters I have noted wounding rituals related to death and something about the form of the supercision operation. Pre-Christian Tahiti had a series of ceremonies which were rites of passage, markers of change in an individual's social status. These included tattooing, supercision, fattening procedures,[5] death ceremonies, and a series of related ceremonies called āmo'a, which had to do with the progressive differentiation and decreasing "sacredness"[6] of individuals through the life cycle.

Morrison described one of these āmo'a ceremonies:

The Amoa [āmo'a] we saw thus performed at a marriage ceremony, and differs very little from that performed through the different degrees of childhood. The friends of both parties being assembled at the morai [marae, sacred enclosure], the young man and his wife were placed on a large quantity of cloth spread for the purpose near the morai, alongside of each other, the man on the right of his wife. Opposite them at the distance of 30 or 40 yards and at the other end of the cloth sat the father, mother, uncles, and aunts of the bride. A priest then having furnished the mother with several pieces of sugar cane and some leaves from the rowavva (or sacred tree) she takes a shark's tooth and cutting her head on the forepart, lets a drop of blood fall on each piece of the sugar cane and placing a piece on a leaf give[s] two to the father and each of the uncles and aunts and keeps two for herself. These they place on the palms of their hands and holding them up to their foreheads rise up and proceed slowly along the cloth till they arrive where the young couple sit, keeping their bodies half bent all the way; and having deposited the leaves and sugar cane at the feet of the young pair, they retire without speaking in the same manner to their seats.

5. Douglas Oliver collates and analyzes the materials on pre-Christian ceremonies in Ancient Tahitian Society, part 2, chapter 10 (forthcoming). He believes that the fattening of adolescents may have been a more or less ritualized episode in the maturation process.

6. In pre-Christian Tahitian theory an infant was most "sacred," involved with tabus, and potentially contaminating. As he matured, an individual passed through various ceremonial stages which made him progressively less sacred and contaminating. See Oliver (forthcoming; part 2, chap. 10).

The priest then advances with a branch of the rowavva in his hand and makes a long prayer; which having finished, he goes to the young couple and bidding "God bless them in their union" (or as they express it, in their sleeping together), he takes up the leaves and pieces of sugar cane and proceeds to the morai, where he buries them with prayers and makes an offering to the Deity of a hog, etc. And in the meantime the couple rise and go to their parents and they embrace them and bestow their blessings on them. The cloth is then gathered up, and presented to the son-in-law, who generally throws part of it out for the young people present to scramble for, and they are proud that they can get a narrow strip of it to put on in honor to the rite and wear it till it is expended, telling all they know how they obtained it. The company then return to the bridegroom's house and he sends three or four hogs to his father-in-law, who has them immediately killed, and a feast made, of which all the males of both families partake; a feast is also prepared for the women and all partake of the festivity. The father of the bride then delivers her portion to her husband, as before described, and an exchange of names takes place. When a man adopts a friend for his son, the ceremony is the same, only placing the boy in the place of the woman, the ceremony is ratified, and the boy and his friends exchange names and are ever after looked as one of the family, the new friend becoming the adopted son of the boy's father. (Morrison 1935; pp. 188-89)

Supercision

In chapter 4 I described aspects of the supercision operation and suggested some meaningful features. Let me review these features here. The operation stands out as a bit of violence against a low-key and tranquil background.[7] The operation, a longitudinal cutting of the dorsal foreskin,[8] is a part of the transition to the *taure'are'a* period. Pressures of shaming, with their implications of lack of presentability and adequacy, are directed at

7. As I have noted, the other comparatively violent themes of pre-Christian Tahiti — tattoo, warfare, infanticide, self-wounding, human sacrifice — were given up quickly after the acceptance of Christianity.

8. In comparison with operations of penile "mutilation" in other cultures, this is perhaps the least mutilating and traumatic operation.

boys, who finally decide to have the operation. Cutting will increase the cleanliness of the head of the penis, will make it more sensitive sexually, will allow it to expand, and will prevent the danger of splitting of the foreskin. It has something quite overtly to do with castration, as indicated by terminological relationships and in joking remarks that one must not confuse supercision (*tehe*) and castration (*pātehe*).

The boys frequently go as a group, and they feel some sentimental attachment to that group afterward. The operation is done by an adult who "knows how to do it." In Piri he is a humble, hard-drinking man (by village drinking standards), who is one of the "grown-up *taure'are'a*."

After the operation the boys feel pleasure and pride. Everything has been more or less secret up until this point, but now a boy will exaggerate an awkward gait on the village path, so that it becomes known that he has been cut.

The individual symbolic elements of the supercision seem to form "words" in a larger symbolic "sentence." Let us examine this by considering how men recall the operation:

According to Poria, "Ah, well we went to be cut. We were five *taure'are'a*, we went to the seaside. Some went first to be cut, three had gone, and there were two left. No, there were two children who had finished being cut, and there were three left. Now one of the three went to be cut and he began to cry out [*āue*, the actual sound made in this kind of woeful crying out]. He began to *āue* in order to stir up fear, to stir up fear in the two who were left. He was only fooling, it was playful carrying on. Ah, '*Āue, āue*,' it was playful behavior. Those two, they became afraid."

("And you, were you one of those two?") "Yes, I was one of them, and I was afraid at that time. Afterward the others laughed. We hadn't gone to look, we were rather distant, and there was a laugh, they had tried to frighten us. But afterward, one of them called out, 'Ah, don't worry, we were fooling.' At that time I went to be cut, and *there wasn't any pain* [the italicized phrase is delivered with emphasis]." ("There wasn't any pain?") "My ears were being pressed, there wasn't any pain. It

was a lie, those people who had said it was very painful. There
was no pain. And when it was finished, we went into the sea,
and afterward, we treated it with Tahitian medicine and we
wrapped it in a cloth, and when it was finished, that was that,
we returned to the house, and we didn't go and work, but we
went to the house to eat. And that afternoon, we went and
heated [their penises] over the fire. We heated, we heated it,
then placed rocks [in the fire], then covered the rocks with
nono [*Morinda citrifolia*] leaves. And then put it on that skin,
put it in that place, and then we put on the medicine. And when
it was finished, wrapped it up, and returned to the house. We
had fun, that bunch of *taure'are'a*. The thing that was fun, indeed, was the medicine, the treatment. We treated each other.
We put on coconut water, we put it [the penis] over the fire,
and then stopped and put on medicine and there wasn't any
shame."

Poria has gone excitedly through this entire description with
few remarks and an occasional affirmative grunt from me. He
has managed to describe the healing procedures without mentioning the word for penis [*ure*] or any of the euphemisms for
it.

I ask him, "There wasn't any shame?" He answers, "This one
looked. That one looked." ("Looked at each other's penises?")
"I look at yours, you look at mine, at others, like that. Some
had great swelling. Great swelling. Others, just a little. It was
very agreeable [*au*], very much fun [*'arearea*], that activity."

Hiro approaches the description of the operation. "We did not
tell our parents. No, we did not tell. But when it was all over,
then we told. The reason [we didn't tell], if we had told then
the mothers would have been afraid, they would have been
afraid. The father, he would not have been afraid, because he
knew that it was not harmful. The mother though, she was
afraid, and she would tell her child, 'Don't.' Therefore, we did
not tell. When we were cut, ah, then we went and told, it was
finished. That's what we all did." ("How did your parents react
when they were told?") "Nothing special. And they said, 'Watch
carefully, treat it carefully.' Our treatment wasn't a foreign

medicine, but it was a true Tahitian medicine, leaves and flowers, the leaves and the leaf bud of the *pūrau* tree [*Hibiscus tiliaceus*]. We bit it into little pieces and put it on top, and for that place below, that place that was blistered by the urine, we put a warm stone. In the morning, then, we went into the beach, and we washed ourselves, and then warmed a stone, and then we took the stone and put it underneath. Brought it to that place that was blistered and all the blisters disappeared, and there was no water anymore. [The blisters became] *very very small.* [He says all this with a dramatic emphatic voice.] And then we put on the *pūrau* leaf because there was a lot of *pūrau* which we had gotten, and bit off the bud, and when it was ready, we put it on, and warmed it, and when it was finished, ah, then we tied it up. We tied it up, we didn't just bandage it in one place, but this day we tied it up like this, and the next day we moved it back, and then moved it back further, and then moved it back further, because if one ties it up in only one place, then it swells up very much, it swells up very much, that thing, that's the way we did it."

I then ask him what else happened that day. "There was fear . . . fear." I ask him, "You?" "No, all of us, because the first person that went, the first that went, he lied to us, the first person that went, he lied to us like this, '*Āue, āue, āue, āue.*' Now, we heard that sound, and there was fear. But one couldn't go back to the house, because one would then be mocked, there was nothing one could do, but when he went into the sea, when he went to wash, then he laughed. Now we were surprised, that he had lied to us in order to stir up our fear. It was like that, only. It was painful indeed, it was painful, but there was nothing to do. But it was a short pain, a short pain. They tear [only] one thing, it is like that."

And Teiva. He has been talking about the transition from childhood to the *taure'are'a* period. "One thing, the children want to be supercised. Supercised. Boys. That is the custom, for the children to change themselves from being children. He goes . . . and follows his desire to be a *taure'are'a.*"

After some other remarks, I ask him to tell me about it. He starts by describing contemporary Piri. "The boys go, and Tama [the man who is doing the cutting at this time], and one other fellow to cover the ears. [Teiva laughs.] Tahitians are different, that's how they give injections. [He is referring to the ear-holding's being equivalent to local anesthetics given by the French doctor and the island nurse.] [He laughs again.] ("He holds the ears?") "[So that there is] no pain. At that time of cutting, they [the children] also clench their jaws. At the time of cutting there is no pain, because they are firmly pressed, the ears, that place. [He demonstrates on his own ears.] The grownups, there is one to cut, one to cover [the ears]."

He goes on immediately, "Ah, it is finished. They go into the sea, to make the blood run off. And when they are finished in the sea, they take a bud of the guava, a young bud. Bite it off in the mouth, chew it. [He laughs.] And when it is ready, spread it on that torn place as medicine. Tie it up. When that is finished, put on some other medicine. Heat it over the fire, over the hot stones. Then wrap some hot stones in *nono* leaves and put them in a coconut shell. Then warm [the penis] over it. So that the swelling will go away. Like that. Then after a while put on some *amo'a* leaves [a fern, *Nephrodium exaltatum*]. Then you throw away the leaves . . . there is left a fine substance. Scrape it off with the hand. Spread it on that cut place."

Teiva then goes on to contrast the circumcision done by the French doctor or island nurse with the village supercision. I interrupt him and ask him whether there are any prayers connected with the supercision. "In the beginning, maybe. In Abraham's time. [He believes, like others, that supercision is a Christian custom.] Now, no, it has become a thing without value. You think about being cut, and you go and get cut. [And he laughs again.]"

He has been using the elegant word for supercision, the missionary-introduced *peritome*. I ask him whether it has another Tahitian name. "*Tehe*. And the pig, one *pātehes* [castrates] the pig. For a man, *tehe*. Not *pātehe* [but] *tehe*." ("It is different?")

"For the *pātehe* of the pig, the testicles are cut off. . . . Like the people in the Bible called *enuta* [eunuchs]."

And so forth.

One may make an inventory of the meaningful elements in a symbolic event such as supercision by adding up various interpretations and implications, or by getting the intellectual assistance of a native expert who has given the event much thought. The reminiscences of people who have experienced it give another dimension of meaning. It gives some idea of what they made of the symbolic elements, or at the very least, the use they are making of them in a particular kind of discourse.

I have mentioned some of the meanings ascribed to the cutting. But in the sequence, at least as it is remembered by most informants, the emphasis is on healing. The particular plants used in treatment vary in different descriptions. They belong to the large armamentarium of medicinal plants known to the Tahitians and have, as far as I could find out, no special symbolism of their own. For therapeutic plants, see Papy and L'Herbier (1957).

The sequence, as it is recounted and apparently as it is practiced, emphasizes negation. It is all done casually, secularly, by an unimportant man. Pain is commented on, called to the boys' attention, and then denied.[9] Healing is obsessively emphasized. The emphasis in the operation sequence is on mastery. Look, it seems to say, here is an injury ("not castration") and now see how you can get over it. It is a mastery not through bravery or self-control[10] but through healing in alliance with the resources of nature.

---

9. We have been told that the operation "is not castration." In nonverbal analogical statements such as ritual, there is no logical form for "not." It is necessary to present the form to be "negated," and then to show by the context that the form has a meaning other than its "usual" one. I will return to this in chapter 14.

10. A description of pre-Christian tattooing by Morrison illustrates some similarity in regard to casualness: "Everyone pleases their own fancy in the number of lines or the fashion of them, some making only one broad one while others have five or six small ones ornamented with stars and sprigs, etc." He describes the operation: "The tattooing is performed at the pleas-

Other messages are conveyed: within the operation event is peer solidarity, mutual exhibition, overcoming of shame and fear about penises (which is also part of the broader meaning of the sequence). There are various more covert body meanings — the penis which becomes clean may have something to do with eating and feeding.[11] The penile marking, and later reassurances, are reinforcers of sexual differentiation.

The larger sequence of events indicates separation from the household and transition to *taure'are'a*. (Recall that it is a symbolic sequence in a gradual transition.) It is a peer activity, initiated by the boys themselves (albeit in response to pressures from older *taure'are'a*). Informants disagree on whether it is better to tell parents before going, but most did not. (The issue whether to tell the parents or not came up in most of the interviews as part of the recounting of the events leading up to the cutting.) The boys go secretly and then return to the village to make it known that they have been cut. They are now presentable sexually to village girls.

The main private message in this small culturally provided phantasmagoria is "masculinity is safe."

---

ure of the parties who have it done. . . . [They] will not suffer the performer to leave off while they can bear a stroke, though they make such lamentation while they endure the pain that a stranger would suppose it was done against their will and that they were forced to suffer contrary to their inclination. The young females are more remarkable for bearing it than the males, though they cannot suffer more than one side to be done at a time, and the other may remain perhaps for twelve months after before it is finished, till which time they never conceive themselves company for women, being only counted as children till they have their tattooing done. While the girls are having it done they are always attended by some of their female relations who hold them while they struggle with the pain and keep their clothes from being kicked off, and should they from their tears draw pity on themselves and the person who holds them should persuade them to leave off, they are often in such a passion as to strike even their mother if she should happen to be performing that office" (Morrison 1935; pp. 221-22).

11. Recall that fellatio is common in homosexual and some heterosexual activities, and that there are some traditional references to being eaten as purification, that palatable presentation of the self seems to be an important metaphor in relation to shame and embarrassment.

Dreams

Whatever restraints individuals in Piri and Roto may have on personal fantasy during waking hours, they are, as they would say, taken with dreams from time to time.

Most dreams are considered due to either the influence of a troubling spirit, a *tūpapa'u*, or the wanderings of one's own soul (*vārua*). There is also a kind of dream which, according to some people, is not a true dream; it is caused by one's own thoughts, often when one is fatigued or troubled. This, it is said, is just like thinking during the day. The ordinary true dream is caused by the wandering of one's soul during the night. The soul observes things and meets other wandering souls. I did not find in Piri or Roto the logical inference, prevalent elsewhere in Oceania, that it would be dangerous to wake a sleeper because his soul was away from his body, although Manu, for example, said that it sometimes took a long time to awaken a sleeper because his *vārua* was far away. The explanation of dreaming by a wandering self or intelligence, a detachable personal element, blends with the theory of the spirit or *tūpapa'u*. The connection between dream and the deduction of soul and ghost has been anthropological common sense at least since Tylor's *Primitive Culture* in 1871.

Troubled dreams are often ascribed to the influence of *tūpapa'u* in the vicinity of the sleeper, and people very commonly explain their motives for praying before going to sleep as an attempt to keep such troubling and dream-disturbing *tūpapa'u* at a distance. The *tūpapa'u* who cause dreams can also cause hypnoid hallucinations (see chapter 12). Such *tūpapa'u* also come disguised as a person of the opposite sex to produce sexual orgastic dreams.

There are two common words for dreams, *moemoeā* and *ta'oto'otoā*. These two terms are largely equivalent, but many speakers use them with some differentiation. When they are contrasted, *moemoeā* tends to mean a disturbed dream, in which one talks or laughs out loud, or a dream made up of many shifting and confused scenes. *Ta'oto'otoā* tends to imply a dream in which there is less externally visible disturbance and in which a long and sequential story takes place. Those who make these differentiations say that the *moemoeā* is more likely to take place in the first part of the night, and the *ta'oto'otoā* in the later hours of the night. It is the *ta'oto'otoā*, the late night or early morning dream, that is more likely to be a prophetic dream, to contain a message.[12]

After childhood people often tell dreams to each other. Taere told me that he and Rahera often did so. I mentioned to him that *pōpa'a* did not usually tell their dreams. He asked me, unusually for him, "Why not?" *Taure'are'a* tell dreams to each other, older women tell theirs to their gossiping companions. The dreams are often told with considerable dramatic emphasis, as are accounts of movies and tales of the supernatural.

In Roto one day a *taure'are'a* girl, who had been living for some years with a considerably older European man who was soon to leave for work in Europe, told him a dream. She had dreamed that her father had gotten lost in the mountains in the center of the island, and she was seeking for him everywhere, unable to find him. The girl had been very casual about her *tāne*'s leaving, although she seemed attached to him. Men leave, and she would get another. But it was important that she tell him that dream.

Dreams not only express, they communicate. Or at least they seem to be used for communication in Piri and Roto. They communicate about emotions and relationships which are not expressed, which may in fact be otherwise unexpressible.

A special kind of dream telling involves those dreams in which a person is troubled by a malevolent *tūpapa'u*, which bothers

---

12. Similar differentiations have been reported for other cultures. Guiseppe Tucci notes of Tibetan dreams, "Some of these are easily explained on the theory of Humours: they are caused by too much or too little to eat. Like those dreams which come in the early hours of the night they have no significance. But the dreams which come during the last hours of sleep can provide serious omens" (Tucci 1967; p. 134).

In her popularization of the Greek myths, Edith Hamilton remarks of a dream of Europa's, "Once awake from this strange vision which had come at dawn, the time when true dreams oftenest visit mortals" (Hamilton 1942; p. 100).

him either out of hostility or out of sexual desire. People recount these dreams in an attempt to make the secret behavior of the *tūpapa'u* public, and thus to shame it away.

The interpretation of dreams is relatively rare. In analogy to the *tahu'a*'s interpretation of symptoms and problems, the interpretation of dreams denies any private and personal message and takes the dream to be a comment on the external world. Interpretation, that is, further disguises the more private statements in the dream.

Many years ago dreams in Piri were interpreted by the *tahu'a*, but in the years since the village last had its own *tahu'a*, there has been nobody who was particularly skilled at dream interpretation. If somebody feels that a dream has a *tapa'o* or "sign" in it, he will talk with one of the older men or women in the village who might have some ideas about it, or he might talk to several people, often getting conflicting interpretations. Some people attempt to interpret their own dreams, particularly if they think there might be a "good luck" sign in them, such as a tip, given by some helpful deceased ancestor, on the outcome of a soccer match, where one can bet and win some money.

People, talking about dream interpretation, say that dreams most often concern *feti'i* and often predict potential illness or trouble, although they sometimes concern one's own possible future. Some people, including Tama, the *tahu'a*, say that dreams should be interpreted by reversing the thing that is dreamed about. What is meant by "reversing" is not quite so simple.

Some of the young women in Piri gave these examples of standard dream interpretation. If you dream of a wedding, this means that someone will die, but on the other hand if you dream of a body, dressed in white, lying apparently dead but unburied, this represents a wedding. If you dream of someone who is dead and who then comes back to life, this represents a real death, as it represents first the illness, and then, as indicated by the coming back to life, the spirit leaving the body. But if you dream of a dead person who does not come to life, this represents someone who has fainted or who is ill, but who has not died.

Other examples of interpretations do not show "reversals," but make a rather straightforward, direct symbolic transformation. Thus, according to Manu, if you dream of an outrigger canoe which sinks, this indicates death. The canoe represents a coffin, and the sinking represents the passing of the body into the earth. (Canoes were actually used as coffins occasionally in pre-Christian Tahiti.) If the person you see in this dream, who may also be yourself, escapes by swimming, this represents an illness from which the person recovers. "Message" dreams may refer to past (for example, a relative's death, still unknown to the dreamer), present, or future. Dreams may also be warnings rather than clear predictions of the future, and by taking diligent action one may be able to prevent the predicted event.

Dreams may be taken entirely at their face value, without any need for interpretation at all. Manu told how his *vahine*, Tetua, had been clearing some brush during the day. She was approaching an old tree stump when suddenly a swarm of wasps rose out of it, warning her in time not to approach. That night she dreamed of an aunt of Manu's who had been dead for five years. The aunt said to her, "If I had not had pity on you, you would have been stung by those wasps." The aunt told Tetua in her dream that she had thrown a stone at the wasps' nest to make them fly up so Tetua would be warned.

A very special kind of dream is a message directly from God. Tama, the *tahu'a*, felt that his *tahu'a* profession was validated by such a dream. In Piri, it was said that Teiva had such a dream, which gave him the authority to lead the dissident members out of the established village church. When asked some years after the event about this, Teiva said, "It is possible I had such a vision, but I don't remember anymore. I think probably yes, but I'm not sure." We are a long way from the vision quest of the Crow Indians.

The dream is a window opening on the supernatural world. As Manu once said in reporting a dream, "I woke up and was very happy to see that the event I dreamt of hadn't taken place in this world. It was a matter belonging to the *pō*."

During the psychological interviews, I asked people to tell me dreams they remembered. This matter of producing a dream to order is obviously different from telling a dream out of some spontaneous need. Everyone agreed in principle to tell me a dream "as soon as they remembered one," but Pua, Tano, and Teiva (the latter two had said they made a practice of not paying much attention to dreams) were never able to "remember" a dream during the interviews.

These are the dreams recounted in the interviews. They were told in relatively brief and summary form (sometimes I was given a generalized example of a *type* of dream), with little of the detail and emotion that were characteristic of the spontaneous telling of dreams. In the interviews there was not perhaps the same need to recount dreams.

Poria (first dream): "I dream frequently. . . . There are different kinds of things that one sees in one's sleep — the *pua'atoro*,[13] a dog, a person. Sometimes in some nights, I dream and see a *vahine*. I am 'taking' a *vahine*. We are caressing, we go to the house. Sometimes we go strolling. I see an old girl friend of mine. She has come back, we are going together again. We speak. We have a good conversation. It's just like in the 'day world,' our conversation. Just like the world now, the way it goes inside the dream. We talk together one to the other, that's the way it is."

Poria (second dream): "One kind, I am chased by a *pua'atoro*. One time I had gone over by Tāvana's house. And I was chased back this way by a *pua'atoro*." ("Was it a male or female *pua'atoro*?") "I don't know what kind of *pua'atoro* — but it was a *pua'atoro* that was chasing me. I got over there towards Moe's house and then I took off in flight [like a bird]. I flew up in the air, the same as if I had wings. The *pua'atoro* wanted to run [toward me]. But you made fun of that *pua'atoro*. You mocked him, because one wasn't caught by him. That *pua'atoro* came and you went up onto a tree. And you weren't caught by him.

13. *Pua'atoro* means either a cow or a bull without distinction, unless "male" or "female" is added to the word. As there is no convenient term for cow/bull in English, I will keep it in Tahitian.

And it was all over, and I woke up afraid. I was afraid at the time that I woke up. I woke up afraid because I had been chased by that *pua'atoro*. And I woke up. And I thought, well, all that belongs to the *pō*. I thought about it, and I thought I had been chased. I escaped, and the *pua'atoro* had been chasing me. But then I awoke and knew that it was [only] a dream."

Poria (third dream): "Another one? There were many kinds of dreams. One time, I saw a great number of people. It was as if it was a gathering, and people were singing. It was like that. And the pastor came to supervise the praying." ("Was the pastor Tano?") "No. It was as if it wasn't known who was that pastor. Then the people sang. Then there was a *tūāro'i* service in the night. Then it was over and the people went to their houses to sleep. And then you went among the *taure'are'a* to have a good time. And then when the good time was finished, then they went to the house to sleep. It was like that. That's a good kind of dreaming, that kind of dream."

Poria (fourth dream): "One dream, I saw these people up in the sky. All kinds of people up in the sky. Some people with beards. Some people who had come here, some people from here — men and women — up in the sky following each other, it was like a picture. Up in the sky, every place, rotating in a great circle. Now after a time there came an airplane and shot [at us] here. Shot at Piri — came here, there were three, or two,[14] that came here. And they shot. I ran. Ran and hid. All the people ran and hid. All kinds of airplanes came here. Many airplanes came here in order to shoot at Piri. And I thought I was wounded. I was dying. I was startled. Because of the fear. I woke up. I thought, ah no, it is dream business."

Poria recounted these dreams one after another during the same interview. In an interview some months later he began to talk about dreams again.

Poria (fifth dream): "Sometimes I am 'involved in a dream' [*moemoeā hia*, a passive form, signifying taken by a dream]. I

14. Estimating a quantity and then decreasing it is common in Piri and Roto.

see a *pua'atoro*, or else a Chinese man is chasing me to cut me with a knife. Now I run, like that. Sometimes I fly. I fly, and I'm not caught by that Chinese man. I fly, and afterward I stop. The *pua'atoro*, that *pua'atoro* chases, like that, and I run, and fly off afterward. Sometimes, I am caught, those times that I am caught, it is a very bad thing. It is as if I had been killed. I don't know what to do, I am afraid, I wake up, I think, what was that affair, it was a frightening thing."

The *taure'are'a* Oro, asked about dreams, said that he dreamed frequently, perhaps every other night. Characteristically for him, the first example he gave was sexual.

Oro (first dream): "I think of a *vahine*. I see a *vahine*, I don't know where she has come from. I think, oh my, that tempting *vahine* [literally, *mā'a vahine* or "*vahine* food"]. When it is night, she bursts into your awareness, it is just as though you were making love [*here here*]. When you wake up there is no one there. It is said, that sort of thing is a *vahine tūpapa'u* [a spirit woman]."

Sometimes Oro has an orgasm during these dreams, and sometimes he does not. He had told me previously that sometimes in such dreams the young woman turns into a frightening old woman before the dream is finished, and I ask him about that. "Yes, when you have finished, then you see her, and it is as though she has become extremely old. When you had seen her just coming to you, she had no clothes on, her hair was very long and light-colored. She comes to sleep beside you, and afterward, when you have taken her, then she has finished through you [had an orgasm because of you], then you look, she is old, and because of that you wake, you feel yourself and you are wet." Oro awakens angry, and uses bad language to frighten off the spirit.

Oro (second dream): "Those kind of dreams, taking place in your sleep, for example, you are sleeping like that, and you dream, you dream of a *pua'atoro*. In that kind [of dream] you are chased by a *pua'atoro* and afterward you arrive on top of a tree. And the *pua'atoro* gets there also [to the base of the tree]. And because of that you wake up, you wake up because of that kind of a dream. You are lying there, lying on your stomach, it was just as though you were flying about, as though you were flying over the mountain. . . . You have been chased by a *pua-'atoro*, and afterward you took off in flight. It's the sort of thing, in your sleep, you arrive up in the tree. And the *pua'atoro* is coming, a black *pua'atoro*, and then you wake up."

Oro (third dream): "Yes, that kind of thing, you think of your parents. It is night, you are dreaming, you see a person who is dying, it takes the form of your parent. And afterward you wake up, with uncanny fear [*mehameha*], you wake up, and there isn't any uncanny thing [*peu*] to be seen."

Asked about the significance of dreams, Oro gives a simple "reversed interpretation." "Well, it's like, if you see your parent, and the parent comes toward you being very happy and comes to meet you — and then the next morning, you hear that that parent has taken sick." By such an interpretation, dreams of parental death mean good health.

Uta (first dream): "Sometimes I am taken by a dream that is rather frightening. And sometimes it is rather nice. [Uta needs more prompting than some of the others, and I ask him whether he remembers one of the fearful dreams.] There is one collection of dreams, it is if I am going along, and it is as if there comes a Chinese man, like that, with a stick, or else with a knife to cut . . . it is like, he chases one and cuts, and at that time, I began to run. And [I] can't run, because at that time I just can't, and I wake up. And then I think about it, and I am very much afraid."

This kind of dream in which he cannot escape, as the others do by flying, is, he says, frequent.

After Uta gives this example, I ask him about "good dreams." He says that good dreams are dreams that have signs in them, and the interview goes off in another direction away from dreaming. In a later interview the matter of dreams comes up again, and I ask him what he had meant by "signs" in dreams, and how he interpreted them. "When I have a dream, I don't speak and ask people about it, but, I think about it, if it isn't clear to me what its meaning is." I then ask to give me an example of a dream with a sign in it.

Uta (second dream): "One time, I had a dream, and I saw three gourds. They were drifting, they were drifting, those gourds, on the sea, and I went to fetch them, and I had almost picked up the first gourd, and it burst. I saw another one, and I was almost next to it when it also burst. And then I went to the next one, and I took it, and I was able to get that one. And I carried it to the house. I got to the house, and I woke at that time. Then, I thought it over, and I thought, I have a gourd. I looked, and I saw that I did not have a gourd, now that I had woken up. And I thought, what is the significance of that thing. But, I didn't go and ask people, 'What is the meaning of all that.'"

But, he goes on, he wasn't sure what the meaning of the dream was. I pushed him to give his opinion. "This dream, it is sort of − one week afterward, we went to play soccer. And I thought, maybe that affair [the dream] was an affair concerning soccer. We went to play soccer, and it was very much different, the soccer business [i.e., the way it turned out]. We won five matches, and the Parea team won too. There was no connection with the dream, therefore I don't understand anymore what was the meaning of that dream."

I ask him to give me other examples of dreams with signs in them, and he goes back to the dream of being chased by a Chinese man, which he had given me in the initial interview some six months before. "There is one time, I am chased by a Chinese man and cut with a knife or beaten with a stick. That sort of thing, I run, but there isn't any means [of escape]. I am awakened." I ask him what that dream means. "I am not sure about that. It isn't perhaps a sign, but it has to do with some evil intention perhaps of yours, that you are chased by the Chinese." I urge him to explain further. "I'm not exactly certain, [he laughs] it's only a thought. You decide to beat up some man, to go and steal. . . . You think, 'I'll go maybe and beat up that man, or else I'll go steal,' and afterward you get a dream, of being chased by a Chinese man, stuck with a knife, hit by a stick." I ask him if the dream is kind of a punishment, and he says, "It's not sure. . . . I think, from the ancestors perhaps. I think perhaps they don't wish that you should go and do that sort of thing, and because of that they give you a large ["important"] dream inside of you, so that you won't do that sort of thing, to alert you, to give you fear, and it's a good thing that Chinese goes and chases you, hits you with the wood, sticks you with the knife, and when you wake up and remember that thing, then you won't go and steal, because you are sure that you will be stuck with the knife, or else beaten with a stick. It's not entirely sure, but that's what I think, it may be like that."

The intellectually dull and constricted Taere presents the now familiar dreams. He dreams frequently, he says. Sometimes they are good dreams, sometimes fearful dreams. Asked to tell about his dreams, he says, "One kind was a dream about a *vahine*. And one time, one dreams of a *pua'atoro*, one is being chased by a *pua'atoro*." At this time I interrupt him to ask whether it was a bull or a cow, and unlike Poria, he has an answer. "It was a bull. It was as if I was going through a field full of *pua'atoro*, and the one *pua'atoro* got angry at me. And he chased me." Taere laughs. I ask him what happened then. "It was as though I was being strangled. I was as if the *pua'atoro* had seized me and butted me with his horns." The interview now moves off to other subjects.

Tāvana, asked to present a dream, presents the same one. "One kind of a dream is a little frightening. You see a thing, a *pua-'atoro*. [Asked about this later, he says it is a bull.] The kind of thing sort of gives you an uncanny feeling, you are afraid. You see a *pua'atoro* in the *pō*." Tāvana explains it prosaically. "You see a *pua'atoro* in the daytime, indeed you don't want to go next to him. You are afraid. And because of that, when you see him in the night, you are also afraid. And because of that, you don't want him to come near you." Tāvana says he has had dreams of being chased by a bull five or six times. Tāvana goes on to say that sometimes he had bad dreams after seeing the movies that occasionally were brought to Piri. But he did not recall them now.

Teiva and Tano, men of action and of willful self-control, also were "not able" to think of any dreams during the course of the interviews.

Neither Pua nor Veve Vahine had (with one exception) dreams to recount. Pua talked a good deal about dreams and what she thought of them and made of them, but did not "recall" one to tell about. Veve Vahine seemed to be mildly indignant when I asked her if she dreamed very much, as though dreaming, perhaps for a woman of her age and good relations with the church, might have been a sign of some kind of weakness. She said that when she was young she used to dream, but she doesn't remember those dreams anymore. She laughed at them then, but not now. She then recalled one very detailed dream, elaborately related to problems she had had upon becoming Tāvana's second wife. It occurred while she was in Papeete, and while she was being treated with cortisone for severe asthma. It thus had some of the quality of a delirium. (Her willingness to describe this cortisone-produced dream is a possible indication that for her, at least, the lack of reported dreams was an inability to recall them rather than an unwillingness to recount a remembered dream to me.) In summary, she had a vision of a woman who appeared suddenly in her room and who had her back toward her so that she could not see her face. She awoke very much afraid. She sent for a *tahu'a*, who interpreted this woman as the cause of her sickness, saying that it was the spirit of Tāvana's first *vahine*, and that her asthma was the result of the anger of this spirit.

Hiro says that sometimes he does not remember the dreams, sometimes he does. Some dreams "went all the way into this world," meaning that the dreams made him talk in his sleep, thus causing an event in this world, or else caused him to wake up into this world. Asked to talk about his dreams, he is first general.

"One kind of dream, it's like I am 'taking' a *vahine*. Another kind, I see my *vahine* and some man, a new *tāne* for her. I beat him up, and it goes right into this world [that is, causes him to thrash about in bed]. It's just as though I was striking with my fist, and then I wake up and my *vahine* cries out, and she is bruised in various places, it's like that. And when I finally wake up and look, and my *vahine* cries out to me, 'What's going on with you.'"

"One kind, I see a man, who is really very large, and I become afraid, and I am unable to move. I stay just like that, without being able [to move]. And I want to shout, but I can't. I am all weak."

This last example, given by Hiro as an example of one of his kinds of dreams, is the common half-dream, half-waking, semi-hypnotic state called a "hypnoid hallucination." It is related to, and illuminates, the meanings of the reported dreams, but will be considered later. It is of interest here to note that Hiro went on from talking about a dream which was accompanied by hitting — that is, by active, aggressive behavior — to a report of a situation in which he was paralyzed and weak.

Hiro goes on to talk about his ideas about the nature of dreams, and then returns to another example. "There is a kind of dream that I see frequently, in which I am going rapidly . . . if I am going rapidly, I am not caught. It is because of that, that we, Tahitians, when one goes rapidly, one isn't caught by that thing."

He is referring now to the spirit, the *tūpapa'u*, that he had been talking about in an explanation of his hypnoid state, a spirit which came and tried to strangle him in his sleep. "It doesn't, the thing doesn't . . . you aren't caught and [your throat] squeezed. But if you are running, and if it is like a stone was tied to your feet, if it is like that inside your dream, then your legs are very heavy and you can't run. Sometimes it is like a wind, a wind is in front of you, if you run you can't go. Then you are caught by the thing. If you move rapidly, move rapidly like a "bird," then you aren't caught. [*Manu*, "bird," is also used in some contexts for insect or small animal. The extended meaning seems to apply here.] You see that person, you see that person, he sees you, but he cannot grab you, you aren't caught, you run. But that business, if you are going, and you cannot run, you are caught. . . ."

And then this dream passes into the hypnoid state, because he "wakes up" and sees an image of the man in the room, and he is unable to shout. He says that when in a dream he is able to run or to fly, this is a good thing, because then nothing happens to him.

In a discussion of occasional difficulties in sleeping, Manu said that sometimes he woke up because of a fearful dream, but that this was rare. I ask him what kind of fearful dream, and he says, "It is as if, inside the dream, [there are] times that I dream something rather bad, like you hit somebody, then you are startled, and I wake in the night. — Sometimes I am hit by someone, or else it is I who hits someone else. . . . It is like, in the dream, that person is unconscious/dead [*pohe*] because of me. That is the time I wake up, afraid because that person is unconscious/ dead because of me. And I have thought that it is in this world, my beating up of that man. But after a bit, when I wake up, ah, I see that it was a dream, that's that, and that's the end of that thing."

Later in the same interview he comes back to the question of dreams, this time describing them in terms of his spirit wandering during the night. He repeats the story of somehow getting involved in a fight through which he causes the injury or death of someone, of waking up, of finding out that it was only an affair of his spirit wandering in the *pō*, and of being deeply relieved. He then goes on, "And inside the dream, it is like your spirit goes and wanders, and it meets your relatives in the *pō*, people who are dead, those 'parents' who are dead. Now your spirit meets that *tūpapa'u*. That is the time, you understand, you know that this is a *tūpapa'u*, that is the time that you moan, and speak [in your sleep]. It is as if your spirit was afraid and now you speak, and you wake from out of your dream."

Manu, asked for other examples of dreams, does not remember any more.

Finally, Flora limits her example to a prophetic dream. She says it is rare that she dreams. "I dreamed of my mother. My mother was dead [in actuality]. My mother came and said to me, 'You must take the twenty-eight, the twenty-eight. You must take the number twenty-eight tomorrow morning.' When it was morning, I woke up, and I went and spoke to Tetua that I had dreamed, that my mother had come to say to me, that I must take twenty-eight. Tetua said to me, 'You should go and bet on that number.'" Flora went and bet on the number in the lottery [this was during the July festival] and won. Flora went on to say that her mother frequently gave her tips on betting during the July festival.

Flora gives other examples of her mother's coming to her in dreams with lucky tips. I then ask her if there are any other kinds of dreams, and she says, "No, that's my dream." And repeated questions get the same answer, "No, that's my only dream."

The few dreams and generalized descriptions of types of dreams reported to me during the interviews were a selection from the repertory of remembered dreams[15] influenced to unknown degree by the meanings of the interviews and of the individuals' relationship to me. I cannot be sure to what extent the content of the dreams is a narrow specific comment on the interview situations or an indication of a more general response to pervasive aspects of people's experience. For the most part, the dreams were dreamed before the interview series, and not concurrently. The recall of dreams of being chased, and of escape through flying into the air, may have indicated the special threat of being interviewed, and conveyed people's sense of how they coped with that threat. Similarly, the fact noted below that none of the chasing figures was a Tahitian might have had some referral to me as an alien persecutor. But I was being as gentle and tactful as I could and, insofar as the dreams were responses to the interviews, they tapped, I think, a generalized and significant anxiety about exposure, intimacy, visibility.

Let us note a few salient features here. The dreams reported from Piri showed no overtly aggressive behavior at all by the dreamer, in contrast with at least some aggression in the dreams of the two men in Roto. The nonsexual dreams were of being chased or of being attacked — not by a recognizable Tahitian man or woman, but by a *pua'atoro* (usually a bull, but sometimes undifferentiated) — by a Chinese, or, in one dream of

15. A reported dream is in itself a complex product of whatever the core dream event in itself might have been, plus selective factors of recall and translation into discursive language. To describe this complex communicative sequence as "a dream" is a potentially misleading shorthand.

Poria's, by an alien airplane. Assuming that one personal aspect of the meaning of the "chaser" had something to do with a family member, presumably one or more of the males who functioned as an effective father to the dreamer, the symbolic "disguise" not only eliminates recognizable family members, but it also eliminates villagers and Tahitians in general. The chaser becomes a complete outsider, a Chinese or an animal. This has some possible bearing on the question of the ways in which control procedures in "socialization" are generalized, something I will consider in chapter 13.

Chased by the cow/bull or by the Chinese with a knife or stick, men in Piri (and Hiro on occasion) escape by taking off into flight. The ability to fly, to perch in the top of a tree, represents safety. The escape is usually successful — if not, one wakes. Sometimes one's feet are bogged down, one has trouble escaping; and sometimes one passes into a state of half-waking paralysis. In this state an uncanny, humanlike figure comes to strangle, weigh down, or enter into the semisleeper. He cannot move or call out.

Hiro and Manu, in Roto, reported more dreams in which they were aggressors and "active." But in Piri one either flies away or is paralyzed.

12

Adjustment and Readjustment

"Their chief disorders," wrote James Morrison,

are madness or insanity, agues, coughs and colds, swelled legs and arms, swellings under their ears like the evil,[1] ruptures and some few others. The insanity is only temporary, and perhaps may proceed from too great a flow of blood and spirits and a want of exercise, as it generally commences when the bread-[fruit] begins to be ripe, at which season others are troubled with boils on their legs and thighs, this being the wet season and the sun overhead, when they are more confined to their houses by the rain. This generally leaves them when the sun returns to the northward, and it is not common for a man or woman to have it return, though during its stay with them they are very mischievous and go quite naked. With some it stays longer than others and they have it in different degrees from a heavy dull melancholy to raving mad. They never bind them but let them run, and some travel all round the island naked in the time of their madness, and none interrupts them unless they do some mischief, as they suppose them possessed with some evil spirit. This is common to women as well as men, who are not restrained but suffered to take their own course till the spirit leaves them, when they return home and wear their clothes as usual. (Morrison 1935; pp. 228-29)

The pre-Christian Tahitians, pace the partisans of the Noble Savage, did have something which Morrison recognized as "madness or insanity." But he thought, "The insanity is only temporary." Some studies of "mental illness" in intact, simple communities have, in fact, noted a more rapid recovery from various

1. "The King's Evil," or scrofula, enlargement of lymph glands caused by tuberculosis.

kinds of "mental disorder" than in more complex or disorganized societies.[2] Perhaps Morrison was being accurate.

Morrison's description suggests that "mad" people were not mistreated or persecuted. Nor, from the fragmentary indications in the literature of the first days of western contact, were they treated with any special respect. Even those people who occasionally became possessed by spirits or gods and were useful for divination were, as we have noted in the discussion of the *tahu'a*, not given any special status *between* episodes of possession, although they certainly attracted attention while possessed.

Some of the earliest accounts illustrate attitudes toward episodes of possession. One of the first close observers of Tahitian life, Rodriguez, noted in his journal,

One of the Indians who had [during the previous day] been paddling for me in the canoe began making motions as if terror-stricken, in the middle of the night, giving yells at the same time and meanwhile walking backwards towards the sea, pointing

2. In a careful study Hsien Rin and Tsung-Yi Lin compared "mental illness" in the Malayo-Polynesian aborigines and the Chinese populations of Taiwan. They found similar *incidence* rates of psychotic disorders, but significant differences in the course of the disorders. "One of the most interesting observations made in the present study concerns the evolution of psychotic disorders. A large number of cases [among the aborigines] had an acute onset, the duration of the psychotic episode tended to be short, relapse was not frequent, except in manic-depressive psychosis, and a very small number of cases became seriously deteriorated. In other words, the psychotic cases tend to follow a relatively favourable clinical course and prognosis, and schizophrenic reaction was no exception in this regard. . . . What accounts for the rather benign nature of the psychotic process among the aborigines is rather an academic question to present day psychiatry. It may be that they are basically and constitutionally more capable of restoring psychological equilibrium. Another hypothesis may be advanced from the fact that their village life is less complicated and therefore a sufficient level of recovery may not be too difficult to achieve. It may also be possible that the community itself is therapeutic: the absence of stigma attached to mental illness, the intimate and close emotional ties between members of a family and also a clan or village, and the abundance of opportunities for group and community participation in respect to daily life, farming and festivals. A practical point should not be overlooked: the small number of deteriorated patients may be simply the results of the 'natural selection of the fit'" (Rin and Lin 1962; p. 145).

with his hand and making very vivid signs that he saw the Tupa-pao [*tūpapa'u*] or apparition of the devil, according to his ex-planation. . . . I had to call out for the others to come to my assistance. Meanwhile I noticed a change come over my man, and when I called him by name he was unable to answer me, owing to the ecstatic condition into which the evil spirit had plunged him. Some of the natives who belonged to my follow-ing then came up, and when they saw what had happened, as I have just related, they yielded, though in some apprehension, to my efforts to make them understand that by being Christian believers they need have no fear. Nevertheless one of them came along with a plantain shoot and laid it at the feet of the one pos-sessed, submissively begging the Evil One not to work any injury on him, nor on the others. Soon after this the man possessed burst out with an announcement that one of his mates had just died, here at this place. (Corney 1918; 3:137-38)

Later investigation proved the clairoyant announcement to be false.[3]

In the journal of his third voyage, Captain Cook and a Tahi-tian, Omai,

went ashore to take leave of the young chief. While we were with him one of those enthusiastics, which they call Eatuas, that is a man that they think is possessed with the spirit of the God, came and stood before us, he had all the appearance of a man not in his right senses. His only dress was a large quantity of plantain leaves wrapped around his waist. He spoke in a low squeaking voice so as hardly to be understood, at least not by me, but Omai said he understood him very well. . . . He remained squeaking by us about half an hour and then retired, no one took any notice of what he said, some indeed laughed at him. . . . [The chief] said he was . . . a bad man. Yet notwithstanding this

3. The relation of the "ego" to at least some such possession states in pre-Christian Tahiti is suggested in another quote from Rodriguez: "Just then the inspired person came on the scene in a passionately excited state and they immediately provided a seat for him, that he might blurt out the tom-fooleries that came into his head . . . for to the natives these were as an oracle. . . . I told Vehiatua he should soon see how much power he had, and on my calling out in a loud voice to them to bring me the musket, the inspired one made signs to me not to kill him" (Corney 1918; 3:148-49).

and the little notice they took of the man, superstition has so far got the better of their reason that they firmly believe the man to be possessed with the spirit of the Eatua. (Cook 1955-67; 3:191-92)

The more or less traditional vocabulary gathered in the missionary dictionary has terms bearing on extreme fear responses (e.g., "manavataahia," "to void excrements through fear"), apparent depressive states (e.g., "faataii," "to yield to discouragement"), deprivation responses (e.g., "mairohe," "sickness produced by ungratified desire"; "oroio," "to give oneself to grief and death"), sleep disorders (e.g., "anaeneaie," "to be unable to sleep because of anxiety or uneasiness"), intoxication (e.g., "hinana," "a sot by drinking 'ava,' a common drunkard"). There are terms for what seem to be diffuse cognitive and intellectual disturbances (e.g., "aoaoa," "rambling, unsettled, silly, delirious, foolish"; "maamaa," "a fool, an idiot"). There are terms for possession, trances, and various miscellaneous, possibly hysterical and phobic phenomena such as "fear of heights," spasms, convulsions, and "to have the senses beclouded; to have a vision." And there are terms for headache, asthma, bowel and stomach disorders, and so forth, the various disorders which are thought to indicate responses to stress induced by the sociocultural environment as well as responses to organic factors.

Headaches, fear of heights, confusion, intoxication, possession — these terms refer to disparate matters. Perhaps their major unity is that they can be fitted into the *Diagnostic and Statistical Manual* of the American Psychiatric Association, that compendium of the historical preoccupations of western psychiatrists. There are at least two different kinds of ideas which are connected with such terms: one is "pathology," the disorganization of a system;[4] the other is "deviance," which has to

4. "Pathology" is, in principle, determinable from transcultural considerations of optimal system operation. One can empirically determine contradictions, costs, inefficiencies, and failures in sociocultural and psychological systems, whether or not such "pathologies" are known in some sense to the people involved, or, if known, disapproved by them. In practice, the idea of "pathology" can easily be misused in an attempt to give scientific basis to a stance of moral disapproval.

do with local cultural judgments about what is "abnormal" behavior. One may say about this list of terms, and the other matters gathered into this chapter, that they involve *problems*, as seen by western professionals, by Tahitians, or by both, and problems of a peculiar type, having something to do with personal "adjustment."

I am using adjustment in a special sense, following a useful terminological distinction suggested by Clyde Kluckhohn (1944). He proposed that problems of personal psychological organization be called problems of "adjustment" and distinguished from problems of the relation of an individual to his sociocultural environment, which he called "adaptation."

In the following pages I will emphasize problems of adjustment which, I think, are significant for the understanding of the private worlds of people in Piri and Roto. There are two things which make the discussion somewhat awkward. First, insofar as I am considering the problems of people of Piri and Roto in comparison with my impression of kinds and prevalences of problems of adjustment in other populations, I must refer to things which do *not* (or "rarely") happen, as well as those which do. Second, I am concerned here with frequencies as well as patterns. The meaning of a frequency — "unusual," "common" — has to do with the actual counts and with a "normal" reference of some kind. How many headaches a year make for frequent headaches? Words such as "frequent" are full of theoretical assumptions. I do not have the kind of quantitative data on the community populations which would help resolve these problems. I will use "rare," "frequent," and so on, frequently (i.e., more than I would like to) during the following. Sometimes I have numbers, sometimes I am reporting a "clinical impression" of my informant or myself. Usually the informant and I mean something similar by "rare," and so on, although there are some surprises, as when Manu says that he only rarely (*varavara*) has hypnoid hallucinations, by which he means only once a month or once every two months.[5]

---

5. The various Tahitian frequency terms are used most often to imply some sort of ratio, but there are occasional surprising usages. Toni once

Hypnoid Hallucinations

Poria, Tāvana, Tano, Pua, Uta, and Taere, in Piri, and Manu and Hiro, in Roto, described what Poria called "a kind of dream," which had many similar qualities.

As Poria put it, "[Something] comes and squeezes you . . . squeezes your throat like that. You haven't said your prayers. Your throat gets squeezed, and you can't move. You can't move, your body, everything. It's as though you were dead/unconscious [*pohe*] . . . and it is like you see a *tūpapa'u*. The way it is, I am sleeping/lying down [*ta'oto* means both sleeping and lying down]. But my eyes are not closed, I see you coming toward me. And I just stay there, and then I don't see you, and then you begin to squeeze my throat. . . . You can see him, although your eyes are closed. You can see him coming. And it's just as though your body were dead/unconscious. And that thing enters inside of you."

In a later interview, I introduce the subject again by asking Poria, who in his dream about being chased by the *pua'atoro* did not know whether it was a cow or a bull, whether the *tūpapa'u* that approached him to squeeze his neck and enter into his body was a male or female spirit. He answers, as he had in relation to the dream, "It's not sure. One doesn't see its image [clearly]." I then ask him what he would guess it to be, and he answers, "Some are female *tūpapa'u*. You see her in the *pō* and you think that she is a day-world *vahine*. She comes to tempt/seduce you. You think that she [the *tūpapa'u*] is that *vahine* [that you know in the ordinary world]. She comes and gets close to you and you have desire for her. And, through all that, she squeezes your throat, you become dead/unconscious, and you don't know what's going on. She takes you." [*Rave* means both to take sexually and to take in general. Further questioning shows that Poria is thinking mostly of a sexual act, in which the female *tūpapa'u* "takes" him.]

---

told me that masturbation was very frequent (*pinepine*) in Papeete. Expecting to find suggestions about some important trend, I asked him why. It was, he explained, because there were so many people there.

("She is able to *rave* you like that?") "Yes, she can take you, and then you finish [have an orgasm] . . . you don't know, when you wake up, your pants are wet. That's the way it is with a female *tūpapa'u*. [He goes on without interruption.] The male *tūpapa'u*, he comes as your enemy. He comes in the form of a man, and he comes to squeeze your throat. A male *tūpapa'u* is a frightening thing. And you just lie there [literally, *vai noa*, "just exist"] and you don't know what's going on. You just lie there. After a while, when that thing finishes, when it lifts [from you], it is then that you know that your neck has been squeezed."

Poria had said previously at one time that the *tūpapa'u* entered into his body, and at another that the *tūpapa'u* simply approached next to him to squeeze his throat. I ask him again whether there are *tūpapa'u* which enter into his body. He answers, "Surely. It enters into you, and you are very badly off and weak. You can't talk. You can't move." ("How does he enter? —") "— Inside you?" ("In what place?") "I don't know that. I don't know." The interview now goes off in another direction.

Tāvana, who did not give much time to talking about fanciful and uncanny things, answering some questions about his ideas about *tūpapa'u*, reported a similar experience. "Sometimes, you are sleeping, and then your throat gets held; [something] comes and holds it. The *tūpapa'u* holds you. You try to move. He holds on well. Some *tūpapa'u*, they don't quickly let go, they just hold on. You try to call out."

Pua, talking about the same sort of thing, makes some differentiation of the state from a dream. She has emphasized that some dreams are natural phenomena, a matter of thought "concerning the things you did during the day, just thought; and those things come up during your sleep, and they are a dream. But the Devil [she is using the biblical "Devil," *tiaporo*, for *tūpapa'u*] is something different, he comes and squeezes your throat, like that. And that is different." Since she had denied experiencing this sort of thing in an earlier interview, I ask her again if this happens to her, and now she says yes. "And you see, you see, it is some dead people, who are angry at you, and they come. It squeezes your throat, you thrash about, you thrash about on top of the bed, but when you awake, you have only been sleeping. And it is as if you haven't been moving around at all. While you were sleeping, when that thing comes, you can wrestle with it. As you observe yourself [in the "dream"], it is as if you were wrestling with it. But when you finally wake up, no. And you sit up and pray. It was a devil which had come to tempt you. They want to find out if they are powerful, if your strength is only a little."

Tano also said that he had experienced having his throat squeezed during the night; he, like Pua, stresses his activity, rather than the paralysis which Poria and most others emphasize. He says in answer to my question about his experience of such a state, "Yes [I had it], and I also punched. It was as if some man had come to take you, and now, I punched him. One punches and one's fist hits something, and then you wake up. I'm not saying that that is necessarily a *tūpapa'u*, it comes perhaps out of your dream." The contrast here is that if it came from a dream, it would involve one's spirit encountering another spirit or *tūpapa'u* in the *pō*. But if it "is a *tūpapa'u*," then the *tūpapa'u* has approached one's body in this world. Tano goes on to say that he has had the experience of seeing something, starting to fight it, and then waking up with a hurt hand from having hit something.

Manu says that "it is rare" that he had the experience. By rare, he says, he means once a month or once every two months. ". . . I am sleeping, I am dreaming, and through the dream, that sort of thing comes. I see a *tūpapa'u* in the *pō*. That *tūpapa'u* has come into my house, and it has come all the way onto the bed, and seizes the throat. And in that time, when it begins to do that on top of you, then you can't cry out. You want to cry out, but you can't. Your whole body becomes weak. And when, after a long struggle, that thing lets go of you, then that is the time that you wake up. And your body is weak, when you wake up. And when they squeeze your throat, you groan. . . . You wish that somebody would come and wake you. And that thing doesn't finish quickly, it is a bit of time that it is on top of you, before that thing finishes." I ask him how long, and he estimates "five minutes." He believes this involves a male *tūpapa'u*. Manu did not have these experiences until he was in his *taure'are'a* period.

Manu sums it up, "The Tahitians say that when that sort of thing happens to you, that is the spirit of a person, a *tūpapa'u*. They go throughout all the houses to bother people in the night."

Hiro brings up the subject of hypnoid phenomena in connection with flight dreams. I have quoted some of this. "There is a kind of dream that I see frequently, in which I am going rapidly . . . if I am going rapidly, I am not caught. It is because of that, that we, Tahitians, when one goes rapidly, one isn't caught by that thing. It doesn't, the thing doesn't . . . you aren't caught and [your throat] squeezed. But if you are running, and if it is like a stone was tied to your feet, if it is like that inside your dream, then your legs are very heavy and you can't run. Sometimes it is like a wind, a wind is in front of you, if you run you can't go. Then you are caught by the thing. If you move rapidly, move rapidly like a bird, then you aren't caught. You see that person, you see that person, he sees you, but he cannot grab you, you aren't caught, you run. But that business, if you are going, and you cannot run, you are caught, you see that person, you open your eyes, and you see the image of a person. It is like that, and you want to cry out, and you can't cry out, you can only whisper. You want to say something; you can't you are as if dead, as if paralyzed." He is chased by men, Hiro says in answer to my question, but never by women; he is also chased by animals, often a horse. The men who chase him are, in contrast with the people of Piri, Tahitian men, and not Chinese. He has such experiences "frequently," several times a month.

The states which have been described seem related to "hypnagogic" and "hypnopompic" hallucinations. As a standard psychiatric text has it, these are "normal hallucinatory experiences."

Hypnagogic hallucinations occur in the drowsy state preceding deep sleep. They may contain both auditory and visual elements with great clarity and intensity. At times they are associated with paresthesias in the mouth and hand, the sound of murmured voices, and vague visual images of large objects approaching and receding. The latter group of hypnagogic hallucinations has been called the Isakower phenomenon and seems to represent a reawakening of the memory of early nursing experiences. *Although it is said that hypnagogic hallucinations occur most often in individuals suffering from hysteria, they can also occur in normal individuals particularly during childhood and early adolescence* [my italics]. What has been said of hypnagogic hallucinations is also true of hypnopompic hallucinations, except that the latter occur during the drowsy state following deep sleep and preceding awakening. (Linn 1967; pp. 565-66)

In Piri and Roto such hallucinations occur, in what seems to be a culturally specific and conventionalized form, in adults. These states present us with two problems — what it is that is being symbolized, and why they take the form of hypnoid hallucinations. Such states "are said to occur most often in individuals suffering from hysteria." "Hysteria" indicates a kind of behavior which is held to be more prevalent in simple societies than in "the West," and to have been much more common in western societies through the first decades of this century than it is now. I will return to these problems in later sections.

Other Hysteria-like States

Other "hysteria-like" states are culturally important in Piri and Roto in that episodes are used to give form to some salient cultural message, but they seem quite rare in comparison with hypnoid hallucinations.

I have mentioned (chapter 4) the "filled-up sickness," *ma'i fa'a'i*, which involves choking sensations in the throat and possible insanity or death and is said to be caused by prolonged virginity or, sometimes, by chilling or some other source of menstrual disorder in a woman who is no longer a virgin. I have noted its resemblance to the western theory of the wandering uterus which gave hysteria its name. *Ma'i fa'a'i* is said to be "natural," not caused by spirits, but due to an accumulation of menstrual blood in the body.

All informants knew about *ma'i fa'a'i* and could describe its symptoms. I was unable to find any reference to a case within Piri and Roto, except for Veve Vahine, who had had a brief episode of something she interpreted as *ma'i fa'a'i* during one of her adolescent menstrual periods. "There was a time when I had the *vahine* monthly sickness. That time it was very bad and my throat was stuck, because of that thing, that blood, which came up in great quantities [into the body]. It was really blocked, that place [her throat], it came inside of my nose." (This possibly involved physiologically induced "vicarious menstruation.")

Like *ma'i fa'a'i*, "possession" phenomena are culturally important, but are rare in the experience of the people I interviewed, and, according to reports and my observations, are rare in the experience of people in Piri and Roto. Poria had mentioned the hypnoid experience of a *tūpapa'u*'s entering into his body. He actually experienced becoming possessed. But this is not the day-world phenomenon of becoming "inspired" by a malevolent or message-bearing spirit. Fragments of possession are, as I have discussed, reported in the histories of those people who go to the *tahu'a*, and seem to be commonly produced in the course of the *tahu'a*'s treatment. Sometimes the possessing spirit talks, but more often it simply produces spontaneous movements or curious sensations.

Tama, the *tahu'a* (chapter 5) who saw clients with *ma'i tāpiri* from all over the Society Islands, had seen people with mutism, paralysis, anesthesias, and tremors, as well as the more obvious signs of possession — talking with an altered voice and subject matter, and peculiar coordinated movements.

The word for the spirit's act of possessing a person is *uru*. In New Zealand Maori and in some Tuamotuan dialects *uru* also means "to enter, penetrate, or glide into," which suggests the etymology of the word. The missionary dictionary defined it as "to be inspired, as the pretended Tahitian prophets; to be under the influence of some uncommon feeling." The latter usage does not seem to exist in contemporary Piri and Roto. The Pukui and Elbert *Hawaiian-English Dictionary* gives "inspired by a spirit, god, ideal, person," suggesting the same range as the missionary definition. It also gives its use for a thought which "entered of its own accord, hence, fancy, impulse, imagination." In these definitions *uru* indicates an intriguing hesitation between the psychological and the divine.

Only one informant reported a fully waking experience of being possessed. Oro, after going to Papeete, had been drinking at a friend's house. He suddenly became *uru hia* ["possessed" — *hia* is a passive particle]. He suddenly had great strength and broke down a door. He began to cry, and then went to sleep. His friends just left him alone. When he awoke, he felt recovered and relieved. He and his friends assumed that he had been possessed by a spirit.

I saw, and heard about, only one episode in Piri. This occurred shortly after I arrived in the village. A girl of about seventeen from the inland end of the village was said to be possessed during a period of two days. I visited her house the first evening. She lay on a mat, slowly writhing. She was silent and vacant-looking. Her relatives from various village households sat around her, observing and discussing the possible causes of her possession. Tano was sent for, and came and prayed over her. By the second day she had recovered.

None of the interviewees had had, according to their reports, paralyses (aside from the hypnoid ones), anesthesias, involuntary movements, or any of the other gross symbolic motor or sensory expressive "symptoms" associated with western "hysteria." Several had had visions during serious childhood illnesses. These were classified by them as being spirit-caused, and thus similar to hypnoid hallucinations and possession states. They were treated by *tahu'a*, and later were recalled vividly as important experiences; but they seemed to have been organically caused toxic deliria.

Minor Stress Reactions

Hysteria-like reactions are in part responses to problems, but they are more or less effective ways of responding to those problems. They represent a special kind of expression, of communication, of symbolism, and their explanation, as I have noted, requires an explanation both of their *content* — what is being expressed — and of their *form* — why it is being expressed in this particular way.

When we consider symptoms of stress — anxiety, tension, and the variety of "psychophysiological reactions" — we are dealing with something else. We are dealing with the direct expression of disorder.[6] If there is meaning and symbolism involved, it is a phylogenetically learned language, and not a cultural one. The *interpretation* of a given situation as stressful, and the meaning of the kind of stress involved (attack, deprivation) may have important cultural components, but the *response* is not symbolic in the same way as hysterial responses.

In comparison with reports on stress-related reactions in some other communities,[7] such symptoms seemed quite rare among my informants, and, from what I could judge of Piri at least, rare in the population. (In Piri I served as a combined drugstore and clinic, and I saw at least those disorders which people in the village thought serious enough to bring to my attention.)

Let us consider such minor symptoms as they are reported in the interviews.

I am not sure how to classify *mehameha*, the sense of the uncanny, among "symptoms." It seems to be a way of response shared by many people and a response to situations of a certain

6. Stress reactions, with psychophysiological responses (headaches, insomnia, sweating palms, digestive disturbances, and so forth), are characteristic of disordered sociocultural situations. The work of Alexander Leighton et al. (e.g., *Psychiatric disorder among the Yoruba* [1963]) and Dorothea Leighton et al. (e.g., *The character of danger: Psychiatric symptoms in selected communities* [1963]), among many others, has clearly documented this.

There seem to be specific pathologies (psychophysiological reactions, identity problems) for *all disordered societies. Ordered societies,* on the other hand, have different kinds of pathologies, depending on the kind of order.

7. Alexander Leighton reports that in Nigerian villages 40 percent of the people have "certain" or "probable" psychiatric disorder, and in "Stirling County" in Nova Scotia, 57 percent do (Leighton 1969). In disorganized communities, such as "midtown Manhattan," 23.4 percent of the people are said to have marked to serious disorders, 21.8 percent moderate disorders, and another 36.3 percent mild disorders (Srole et al. 1962; p. 138).

type. There is a peculiarity which should be remarked on here —
all nine of the men had had experiences of *mehameha*, and none
of the three women had.[8]

I asked the interviewees questions to elicit information on the
usual psychiatric array of "minor" symptoms — fear, anxiety,
depression, irritability, sleeping difficulties, physical symptoms
(inventorying the various "systems": respiratory, cardiovascular,
etc.), hypochondriasis, altered consciousness, confusion, and a
residual category of "troubles." I also looked for signs of tension or anxiety during the interviews.

During the interviews I saw little manifest anxiety and few
signs of personal disorder. Although people were often guarded
and "defensive," they were comfortably in control of themselves
and the situation.

A remark of Teiva's suggests the overall impression. I had
asked him, and others, about any experience of fear which
seemed either causeless or exaggerated. "It is very rare — and it
doesn't last long, perhaps two hours. . . . I would think that it
happens once or perhaps twice a year. . . . It isn't a frequent
thing. Now if I were in a foreign country or [on the island of]
Tahiti, where people are wounded by automobiles, ah, that
might be the time [to have fear], but here no."

Aside from Tano, who denies having fear in recent years,[9] the
others described occasional episodes. With the exception of Oro,
who frequently felt afraid in Papeete, they reported frequencies
ranging from once a month to once or twice a year. People reported such feelings as lasting for a half hour or an hour and
then disappearing. For some, the fear seemed related to their
concerns about others. Tāvana would sometimes get anxious
when one of his children was diving in the lagoon. Manu would

8. Veve Vahine had had one "uncanny" experience while she was being
treated with cortisone. It is noted in the section on dreams. I was not
aware of these differences while in the field and did not follow them with
further questions. I do not know if they indicate a valid contrast.

9. Tano is probably lying. He is uncertain of his church leadership and
is playing the role of a confident pastor who has ample *mana*. He was evidently very distressed when I first arrived in Piri.

worry about the health of Tetua. Some others, Uta, Teiva, Pua, and Veve Vahine, would feel briefly afraid without knowing why. Often they would pray and feel relieved.

Reports of tension-related physical symptoms also seemed uncommon by my "psychiatric" standards. All informants had occasional (perhaps two or three times a year) headaches and low back pain, upset stomachs, and diarrhea. (Obviously such symptoms can have causes other than stress.) People denied having sweaty palms, tremulousness, and most other signs of tension given in standard inventories.

Two of the people interviewed, Tano and Veve Vahine, had histories of asthma. Tano had developed asthma as a child, and it had disappeared in his twenties. Veve Vahine, who suffered considerably from it, had developed it in her twenties. Both Tano and Poria (the latter did not have a history of asthma) showed occasional breathing difficulty during the interviews.

Asthma, *aho pau*, or literally "used up breath," is listed in the missionary dictionary and is presumably a disorder of long standing. Although I did not do a general disease survey, asthma seemed, in Piri, the most common chronic illness of children and young people, among whom I noted at least eight cases. Insofar as asthma may have a psychological element, the particular dynamics which have been suggested for it are precisely those I would have expected to be psychopathologically salient for Piri, as later chapters will indicate. Thus,

Much of the recent emphasis on the psychological genesis of asthma has been concerned with the view that the significant psychodynamic process in asthma is unconscious fear of loss of the mother or mother figure. . . . French and Alexander reported a study of 27 asthmatic patients undergoing psychoanalytic treatment. They described the central emotional problem in asthma as a fear of separation from the mother and concluded that the asthmatic attack is equivalent to a repressed cry for the lost mother. Many investigators, including the authors, have come to the position that one of the most frequent psychodynamic themes in perennial asthmatic patients is an exaggerated need for a bond with the mother or mother figure. This need is accompanied by an acute fear of loss of the mother's love, which may be mobilized by an actual physical separation or by situations that threaten estrangement from the mother. (Stein and Schiavi 1967; pp. 1070-71)

Most of the informants reported occasional difficulty in falling asleep at night. They usually explained this as due to thoughts about the day's activities or about what had to be done the following day. Sometimes they remained awake thinking about problems, such as arguments with a spouse or worries about a child's sickness. On the other hand, waking up during the night or in the very early morning and then being unable to get back to sleep again (commonly reported in western depressive states) was said to be very unusual. People did wake up with occasional bad dreams or nightmares, but then they were usually able to get back to sleep quickly. In spite of occasional difficulty in falling asleep, informants said that fatigue on awakening in the morning was very rare. People said that even when they did have trouble falling asleep, they usually felt rested in the morning.

Overtly expressed hypochondriasis, anxious concern with body functions and their possible disorder, is generally absent. Oro is an exception. He is considerably concerned with fear of death, as has been noted, and with his own body integrity. Poria is also worried about possible illnesses and is concerned over a variety of minor symptoms. Part of this, at least, is because he lives alone and is particularly dependent on his own competence for his day-to-day living. All the other informants deny being anxiously concerned about body sensations or about serious consequences of ordinary illness. Some of this is related to the common magic "defense" that only things you are worried about can hurt you. Hypochondriasis in itself would produce the illness you feared. For some, the lack of concern was connected with an attitude of resignation. Teiva expressed this clearly. "All the sicknesses that I get, I don't worry about them. Because, even if one goes to the doctor, and one is cured that time, well then next year, you'll get sick anyhow. But if you go to the doctor, and he could cut out that disease and take it out of you, and then you wouldn't get sick any more, then you might go to

the doctor [and concern yourself about your illnesses].... We're
going to die anyhow, there's no use being concerned about it."
But in general the lack of concern seemed to be an expression
of a conviction that there was nothing to be concerned about.

Teiva's statement has a tone of "depression," as do statements
such as Oro's (chapter 9) about a lack of enthusiasm or drive
when there is nothing to do. The idea of depression as a "mental
illness" provides problems for any cross-cultural comparison. A
number of different kinds of symptoms are usually considered
to be part of the "depressive syndrome." By these criteria none
of the informants in Piri or Roto, or to my knowledge other
inhabitants, had "depressions." If depression is characterized by
overt guilt, self-accusation, and suicidal ideas, it was not present;
nor was it if defined by marked retardation or sadness. If depression is defined more subtly as "a decrease in self-esteem; a sense
of helplessness; the inhibition of ego functions to varying degrees; and a subjective feeling of sadness or loss of varying intensity" (Mack and Semrad 1967; p. 311), then there is a suggestion
of "depressive tone" for most of the informants.

Finally, in this catalog of things which do not characterize
people, none of the informants exhibited any symptoms or signs
of the type thought to be associated with the diagnosis of schizophrenia in western individuals.

"Major Mental Illness"

Although I found no people with major mental illness or psychosis (with the exception of senility) in either Piri or Roto,
there were such people elsewhere who were known to informants. There was, for example, a woman from one of the other
villages in Huahine who was described to me as having "a bad
head," *upo'o 'ino*, one of the terms for mental derangement. I
saw her occasionally in the port town on boat day. She usually
wore a white dress, with militarylike epaulets which she had devised for the shoulders, a bright red sash around her waist, and a
bizarre, very broad-brimmed flat hat — a caricatured uniform.
She carried a Bible and from time to time orated to the crowd.
At other times she would talk at people in imaginary conversa-

tions. People said she believed that the French gendarme at Fare was in love with her and that she would become his *vahine*. She was jealous of any other woman she believed had anything to do with the gendarme. Talking about her, Tino, in Teri'i Tui's household, said that she often made sense when he talked to her and that she had an excellent memory for things that have happened. However, he went on, often he cannot understand what she is saying — she seems to start one thing and then mix it up with something else.

The woman was in her forties. It was said that she had previously not been strange, had lived for many years with the same *tāne*, and had had many children. After the death of the *tāne*, however, she began to act peculiar and to dress strangely. On a return visit to Piri in 1970 I was told that she had completely recovered and was living quietly in her village.

I heard of two other people on Huahine described as seriously disturbed. One was a woman who, according to the gendarme, had been acting strangely and "having illusions" and who had disappeared from the island a year or two before. The other person, described by some people in Piri, had died some years ago. The man, who had a club foot, had had periodic episodes of peculiar behavior. Once he came to Piri late at night and began to ring the church bell. Everybody came running to see what had happened. People verbally criticized him, but they were not severe with him, because, as Toni said, "He was *upo'o 'ino*."

Manu, in Roto, remembered only one person who was *upo'o 'ino* in Roto. He had lived there twenty or thirty years ago. The children were afraid of him. He had a strange laugh and was dangerous if you teased him. Sometimes he chased the children.

In Huahine, with its 3,214 inhabitants, I heard of 3 persons whose behavior was strange enough to be specially categorized by villagers as something like "crazy." It was impossible just from the stories, or from my observation of the woman that I saw at Fare, to make a "diagnosis" (schizophrenia? mania? hysterical psychosis?), but these cases and the case in Roto were bizarre enough to attract some attention.

There is a mental asylum, essentially a custodial institution, at Papeete, which in August 1961 had twenty patients. Three were non-Polynesians, and the others came from all over French Polynesia, including the non-Tahitian islands. There were varying degrees of information available about the patients, not enough, generally, to understand either their social background or their case histories. Of the thirteen "permanent patients," who had the most adequate files, seven were from Tahitian areas (one of these seven was a Chinese of Tahitian birth), two came from the Australs, and two were from the Tuamotus. The other two were born outside French Polynesia. The birthplaces of the seven patients who were "under observation" were mostly not known, although they were all Polynesians. The patients seemed to have various degrees and types of disturbances. For many of the most seriously disturbed, those people who sat silently and apparently were out of all contact, it was impossible to know what kind of disorder they might have.

There were others, however, who fit easily into western diagnostic categories. There was a man in his forties, a Tahitian born in Papeete, who in 1961 had been in the hospital for ten years. According to his history, he had been more or less all right until he was fourteen years old. He learned to read and write and was doing adequately at school. At about the age of fourteen he began to isolate himself from other children and to stay with older people, talking seriously about adult concerns and "problems of the world." His behavior seemed strange to the people around him, and he was brought to the hospital, where he was diagnosed as psychotic and put into the asylum. When I saw him, he seemed friendly and childlike and would frequently burst into strange, mirthless laughter. Occasionally he would repeat a word or phrase over and over again. He knew where he was and that he was considered *upo'o 'ino*. He closely resembled western hospitalized "hebephrenic schizophrenics."

There were other patients who had delusions or paranoid ideas, and still others who seemed to have only moderate hysterical difficulties.

Because of the inadequate study of the people confined at the asylum and the unknown relationship of the number of people admitted to the total number of "cases" in the territory, there was no way of knowing the amount and kind of serious mental disorder in the territory or the possible differential sociocultural factors contributing to such disorders. But the people in the hospital indicated the by now familiar finding for other cultures, that there were at least some cases of "schizophrenia," recognizable because they had some formal similarity to western cases.

Drinking

One of the most salient activities in Piri and Roto having to do with "adjustment" is the drinking of alcoholic beverages. It is illuminating for many of the problems of this study, and I will consider it at some length.

The Society Islanders, like other Polynesian peoples, did not have alcoholic beverages at the time of first western contact. They used the mildly narcotic *kava*, or *'ava* as it was called in Tahitian, prepared from the root of the *Piper methysticum* plant. As James Morrison described its pre-Christian use,

Yava, or intoxicating pepper, is cultivated here with much care and pains; with the root of this, they intoxicate themselves. They always drink it before they eat and it is prepared thus — several hands have each a proportion of the root given them to chew, which, when they have done sufficiently, they spit it into a large platter. Some of the leaves are then infused and squeezed to pieces in it. And in the meantime another prepares a strainer from the stems of coarse grass called mo'oo, something like hemp, and the whole being well mixed is wrung through the strainer, and the leaves and chewings thrown away. The juice is then divided according to the number who are to drink it by dipping the strainer into the platter and wringing into each man's cup his share. They now drink their dose which as it is of a tolerable thick consistency and smells something like a mixture of rhubarb and jalap can be little better to take. [This] almost immediately deprives them of the use of their limbs and speech, but does not touch the mental faculty, and they appear in a thoughtful mood and frequently fall backwards before they have finished eating. Some of their attendants then attend to chafe their limbs all over till they fall asleep, and the rest retire and no noise is suffered to be made near them. After a few hours they are as fresh as if nothing had happened, and are ready for another dose. A jill of this juice is a sufficient dose, but if they eat anything immediately before it, it has no effect. . . . It is common to all but is more used by the chiefs and their families, servants, etc., than by the common people. . . . It is in much request among the people of rank, but even some of them never taste it. (Morrison 1935; p. 151)

If some people did not taste 'ava, others may have overused it by early Tahitian standards. According to Lieutenant William Bligh's journal for 5 November 1788, "Tynah's[10] youngest brother, Whydooah, came on board today with his wife, a very pretty woman. I have before described this man as a person much addicted to the use of the 'ava, and he was at this time so drunk with it, that he could scarce stand or speak. Tynah saw him and said he was a drunkard and would not speak to him" (Bligh 1937; 1:388). 'Ava drinking apparently was not related to ritual contexts as it was in other parts of Polynesia, such as Samoa and Tonga and the more closely related Tuamotu Islands.

Alcoholic drinks were offered by the first explorers to their guests. Joseph Banks, on Cook's first voyage to Tahiti in 1769, wrote, "Some there were who drank pretty freely of our liquors and in a few instances became very drunk but seemed far from pleased with their intoxication, the individuals afterwards shunning a repetition of it instead of greedily desiring it as most Indians are said to do" (Beaglehole 1962; 1:346).

Visitors to Tahiti after Cook noted occasional episodes of drunkenness among men and women of the "chiefly class," both on 'ava and on alcoholic beverages given by the Europeans. Alcoholic spirits were named 'ava no peritane, or "British 'ava," and 'ava has persisted as the name for strong liquor. The English language later provided the words for beer, pia, and wine, uaina.

10. "Tynah" was the chief of a district in Tahiti.

William Ellis, who worked in the Society Islands between 1817 and 1824, summarized his predecessors' reports for the years around 1815, when Tahitian society had become disorganized.

Intemperance at this time prevailed to an awful and unprecedented degree. By the Sandwich Islanders, who had arrived some years before, the natives had been taught to distill ardent spirits from the saccharine ti root, which they now practiced to a great extent, and exhibited, in a proportionate degree, all the demoralizing and debasing influence of drunkenness. Whole districts frequently united, to erect what might be termed a public still. . . . When the materials were prepared, the men and boys of the district assembled in a kind of temporary house, erected over the still, in order to drink the ava, as they called the spirit. The first that issued from the still being the strongest, they called the ao; it was carefully received, and given to the chief; that subsequently procured, was drunk by the people in general. In this employment they were sometimes engaged for several days together, drinking the spirit as it issued from the still, sinking into a state of indescribable wretchedness, and often practising the most ferocious barbarities. Under the unrestrained influence of their intoxicating draught, in their appearance and actions they resembled demons more than human beings. Sometimes, in a deserted still-house might be seen the fragments of the rude boiler, and the other appendages of the still, scattered in confusion on the ground; and among them the dead and mangled bodies of those who had been murdered with axes or billets of wood in the quarrels that had terminated their dissipation. (Ellis 1830; 1:229-31)

Drinking continued in Tahiti, particularly around Papeete, the center of chaotic western influence. Moerenhout noted for about 1830 that when there were a number of ships in port at Papeete, "the excesses of these foreigners had a bad effect on the Indians, who, like all the nations in their state, are only too easily given to drunkenness; thus one soon saw, everywhere, only drunks, at any time, on all sides, day and night, women and men" (Moerenhout 1837; 1:312). Moerenhout believed "that such an order of things, constantly getting worse, would have finished by ruining the islands, if a remedy had not been brought" (Moerenhout 1837; 1:234). The remedy was an attempt by the missionary-influenced native government to control the distribution of alcohol.

In 1849 a French observer who had lived in Tahiti from 1846 to 1848 noted: "[The Tahitian] likes strong liquors and in excess; not for themselves, but for the drunkenness that they produce. Therefore, he prefers brandy to the best wine. His goal is instantly to lose his reason. He wishes to drown it at once" (Lecucq 1849; p. 66). Henry Adams, writing from Tahiti in 1891 about Tahitian melancholy, hopelessness, and premature decay, added: "They are allowed all the rum they want, and they drink wildly." And the significant, "They are forbidden to dance or to keep any of their old warlike habits" (Adams 1930; p. 467).

In spite of these references to continued drinking, there is no further reference to violent, destructive behavior when drinking, of the type reported by Ellis. Most reports stressed, as we have noticed, the gentleness and peaceableness of the Tahitians, both drunk and sober.

There is little information on the nature and extent of drinking in the past on the outer islands. William Ellis, who worked in Huahine between 1817 and 1824, wrote of the awful intemperance of the previous decade as though it were over with. The missionary John Williams, returning from the Cook Islands to Raiatea in 1832, recorded:

On arriving at Raiatea, I was perfectly astounded at beholding the scenes of drunkenness which prevailed in my formerly flourishing station. There were scarcely a hundred people who had not disgraced themselves; and persons who had made a consistent profession of religion for years had been drawn into the vortex. The son and successor of old Tamatoa was a very dissipated young man, and when he succeeded to the government, instead of following his father's good example, he sanctioned the introduction of ardent spirits. Encouraged by him, and taking advantage of my absence, a trading captain brought a small cask on shore, and sold it to the natives. This revived their dormant appetite, and, like pent-up waters, the disposition burst forth, and with the impetuosity of a resistless torrent carried the people before it, so that they appeared maddened with infatuation. I could scarcely imagine that they were the same persons among whom I had lived so long, and of whom I had thought so highly. As the small cask which had been imported was sufficient only to awaken the desire for more, they had actually prepared nearly twenty stills, which were in active operation when I arrived.

Williams quickly restored order and soon had reports from his supporters that "every still was demolished, and every still-house burnt to the ground." And then, "having accomplished at Raiatea the destruction of the stills, and the re-establishment of law and order, we prepared to depart for Rarotonga" (Williams 1837; pp. 403-7).

There are other dim glimpses of outer island drinking, such as E. H. Lamont's mention of a trip to Huahine in the 1860s, when he "resided at the house of the old native teacher . . . [whose] sons . . . were wild scamps addicted to the bottle" (Lamont 1867; p. 70).

The drinking suggested by these brief descriptions differs markedly from the more restrained and integrated contemporary drinking practices. It is tempting to interpret it as the sort of socially and personally destructive drinking thought to be related to conditions of stressful culture change in which most nonpathological paths of adaptation have been psychologically or socially blocked. This is the explanation often given for the destructive drinking practices of some American Indians: "Among all those who drink to excess, whether Indian or non-Indian, there is a background of emotional troubles, frustrations and disappointments. Alcohol under these circumstances temporarily gives a sense of superiority and confidence, while dulling the senses so that the unpleasantness of life may be forgotten. Since drinking and criminality seem highest among Indians of all groups in the United States, it is pertinent to ask whether conditions of deprivation are, or have been, more severe among these people. . . . An examination of Indian-White relations through time gives some support to such a hypothesis" (Dozier 1966).

Contemporary experience, however, suggests that the historical reports on the severity of native drinking should be taken
with a certain caution. French officials in French Polynesia, visitors, and *demis*, commenting on "natives" or *indigènes*, tend to
present a distorted picture of *mā'ohi* drinking behavior. One
hears repeatedly that "natives drink to excess, they don't know
how to control their drinking, they should be protected." This
is so out of line with the actual behavior that it suggests stereo-
types related to the paternalism and anxieties of the colonial
stratified situation. It is probable that these and similar psychological sets — missionary puritanism, nostalgia for the undis-
turbed "noble savages" of the romantics, fears of primitivism
ready to resurge — affected, as they still affect, evaluations of
the severity of drinking.

But even with the necessary grain of salt added, there seem to
have been throughout the nineteenth century evidences of demoralization and extensive drunkenness which were not evident
during the early 1960s.

Edwin Lemert has contrasted contemporary drinking patterns
in the Society Islands, Cook Islands, and Samoa. He considered
Tahitian drinking to be predominantly "festive," rather than
"ritual" (i.e., under the control of fairly strict rules and supervision) as in the Cook Islands, or "secular" as in Samoa, where
"drinking lacks all but the basic elements of patterning, is without ritual, and seldom if ever has . . . been the basis of village or
district wide festive behavior." He believed that Tahitian drinking was integrated with Tahitian values, in contrast to Samoa,
where "drinking practices are unintegrated culturally and disruptive in extreme." Lemert felt that Tahitian festive drinking was
"contrary to the demands of a wage-work economy, and, as they
are more drawn into such economy, the form of their drinking
can be expected to change, presumably in a more secular direction." He also noted for Tahiti the pattern of plateau drinking,
the "long slow drunk." He noted that Tahitian males "when
sober, are quiet, shy and almost timid [which] also suggests one
of the main motivations for male drinking — to overcome shyness sufficiently to make sexual approaches to their women."
For Polynesia in general he stated, "Alcoholism in the sense of

addictive drinking, with complex personality changes and serious organic pathology, such as cirrhosis of the liver, is nowhere found among full-blooded Polynesians." He also noted "the large number of heavy drinkers who have successfully stopped their drinking" and that "guilt over drinking or drunkenness does not seem to develop in Polynesian society" (Lemert 1964). My observations in Piri and Roto confirm Lemert's generalizations.

The *mā'ohi* population of the Society Islands drinks mostly beer (made in the early 1960s by one local brewery), red Algerian wine, and, in the more rural areas, illegal, home-brewed orange "beer," which was the standard drink of twenty or thirty years ago in the outer islands. The beer, Hinano, is 5 percent alcohol by volume, and the wine varies between 10 percent and 12 percent. According to brewery officials, beer has become more popular than wine in recent years. In Piri orange beer is now much more rarely used than either wine or beer. Its illegality and "traditional" history give it some special meanings and uses reminiscent of prohibition drinking in the United States. Brewery officials[11] believe that beer has become popular because it is less expensive than wine and because "the Tahitians say that it makes them feel less heavy and tired than wine drinking does."

The amount of beer and wine consumed varies closely with local economic conditions, which in most parts of the Society Islands in the recent past have been dependent on fluctuations in the world vanilla market. People on the island of Huahine, for example, consumed about five thousand cases of beer (each case containing fifteen sixty-five-centiliter bottles) in 1961 and an average of about three thousand cases a year in 1962 and 1963, when the vanilla price had fallen.

Beer and wine are sold at bars and restaurants and licensed retail outlets in the small port towns in the outer islands. Before 1930 the sale of alcohol in the territory was controlled by "racial origin." These laws have been successively modified. The

11. For information on the consumption of beer I am indebted to M. F. Fourcade and to M. Albert Montaron of Papeete.

present laws regulating the distribution of alcoholic beverages largely date from 1959.[12] Distribution is now controlled by a system of licenses. Those licenses which permit the sale of all kinds of alcoholic beverages are more expensive and difficult to get. The classes of licenses permitting only beer and wine sales ("liquids of less than 14 percent alcohol") are those which are applied for and granted in the rural areas. There is also some control over the private shipment of hard spirits in any quantity from Tahiti to the outer islands. There is no indication that these controls are a hardship on rural Society Island drinkers. Those who drink seem to prefer mild alcoholic beverages.[13] And those *mā'ohi* Tahitians who live in or visit Papeete, where hard liquor is available, nevertheless drink beer or wine.

Drinking now is socially integrated in Piri, in the sense that it is an accepted part of community life and that there are community patterns of use and shared attitudes and norms concerning it. The relation of drinking to social structure may be said to be of a "dedifferentiating" kind. The historical pattern of intoxication as primarily a behavior of higher-status people does not exist now. Drinking tends to be connected with those occasions when people are associating who would not ordinarily do so. Most activities, as I have noted, are performed by small, relatively stable groups of people (household, kin group segments, small work groups) who are "accustomed," *mātau*, to one another, and therefore not embarrassed, *ha'amā*, within the range of the conventional tasks of the group. When out-of-group, pan-village, or intervillage activities do occur, drinking tends to be associated with them. It helps, it is generally said, overcome people's *ha'amā*.

12. The 1959 law, and a listing of previous related legislation, are published in the *Journal officiel de la Polynésie française*, 31 October 1959, pp. 711-17.

13. In a study of the comparative drinking practices of Polynesian Hawaiians and other ethnic groups in a Hawaiian plantation setting, Lemert notes that Hawaiians, in answering questions about the type of beverage usually consumed, "indicate an ethnic preference for beverages of moderate rather than high alcoholic content" (Lemert 1964a).

Drinking now represents one of the complex of "traditional" *mā'ohi* behaviors, about which, as we have noted, people are ambivalent: drinking is a little simple and regressive, reminiscent of the dimly conceived old "heathen" days; yet *mā'ohi* behavior is the kind of behavior people feel most comfortable with.

Adults in the village of Piri can be sorted roughly into three groups on the basis of village discussions of drinking behavior. There are "heavy drinkers," "normal drinkers," and a residue of people who do not drink. This last group includes people who had drunk heavily and then given it up (Uta, for example), or who had never drunk (or, at most, had drunk briefly during the *taure'are'a* period), such as Veve Vahine and Tano. Some of the people who "don't drink," such as Pua, take an occasional glass of beer or wine on festive occasions.

There are probably no adults in Piri who have never tasted beer or wine; many had their first sample as children. But most women had not gone beyond occasional tasting. There are two women in Piri who drank and got drunk occasionally during the year, and several others who drank moderately during festivals and on special occasions, but in Piri drinking is mostly a man's affair.

What I am calling "normal drinking," the kind of drinking done by people who are not specially characterized as "powerful drinkers" or some other special term in the village, is the way most of the men in the village drink.[14] They may drink an occasional glass of beer or wine, and they will drink more heavily during the major festival occasions. But they do not drink, or drink lightly, on all the other occasions when "heavy drinkers" drink regularly — on weekly trips into Fare or during minor special events in the village, such as the finishing of some group

14. Even though I am discussing Piri here, Roto is not visibly very much different. Manu and Hiro are "moderate drinkers." There are no evident western-type "alcoholics" in the area. Hiro drinks somewhat heavily by Piri standards, and Manu's *vahine* would be labeled a deviant drinker in Piri. Drinking, however, in the bars outside of Roto is an important activity for some men who are past what would be their *taure'are'a* period in Piri. It is easy to go outside of Roto to drink. There are thus fewer controls and probably more drinking. Most of it is still "festive drinking."

work project, the birthday party of a small child, or a marriage. Nor do they get together at someone's house solely for the purpose of drinking, as many of the "heavy drinkers" do.

There are at least five men in the village who had been "heavy drinkers" and who had given it up. Four of them (including Uta) had stopped entirely, and one (Tāvana) had cut down to two or three moderate one-day episodes a year. Three village men stopped by signing the "Blue Cross," a pledge which is felt to carry supernatural sanctions and is encouraged by the pastors of the Protestant church. Uta stopped when he joined the Mormons. There are "ex-heavy drinkers" in other villages in Huahine who reportedly stopped drinking without any religious reinforcement; they became *fiu*. [15]

There are six men in Piri who are "heavy drinkers." The youngest is in his thirties; the oldest, in his early sixties. Five of them, including Poria, are considered, in spite of their ages, "grown-up *taure'are'a*." Three of them have established families, and although the men are perhaps the least active in working their fields, they do provide for their families at least minimally. The other two "old adolescent" drinkers are bachelors. Poria lives alone; his friend Pana lives with relatives. The "grown-up *taure-'are'a*" drink together and have done so for many years. They gather every week or two in the evening at the house of one of them. Sometimes they make and drink orange beer. They often drink through the night, joking, singing, and occasionally fighting. The fights are not at all violent, and it is rare for anyone to be bruised. The next morning after a drinking bout they often sleep late. Occasionally, if they feel sick, they take a morning medicinal drink, but by the afternoon they are fishing or at work in the gardens, and it will be a week or two before they drink again.

15. Lemert, in his Hawaiian plantation study, notes, "It is of interest to note that the high percentage of nondrinkers in the [Polynesian] Hawaiian group is largely due to the relatively large number, 28%, who had drunk at one time but later gave it up. . . . Caucasians are unique among the groups in having no persons who had given up drinking" (Lemert 1964a; p. 693).

The sixth "heavy drinker" does not drink with the other drinking group. This is Teri'i Tui. He alternates between "dry" periods of several days, periods when he drinks a water glass or two of beer or wine with his meals, and occasions when by himself or with friends he drinks several bottles of wine or beer. During trips to Fare and during any gathering at his house he also drinks. What makes him different from others who drink on such occasions is that he looks very drunk after he has been drinking; he staggers, his head rolls around, he falls off his chair onto the floor. He then goes off to lie down and sleep. Later the same night he is often up working on some task around the house, and the next morning he is at work. On several occasions I saw him looking dramatically and uncoordinately drunk when suddenly, in response to some development of interest, he "pulled himself together" and acted in a relatively coordinated way.

The few drinkers who show uncoordinated drunken behavior often seems to be dramatizing and exaggerating, apparently out of proportion to the amount of alcohol they have taken. Albert T'Serstevens gives examples of this kind of behavior: "They often put a childlike imagination into their drunkenness. They walk straight before entering the village, but begin to stagger when they reach the first houses" (T'Serstevens 1950; p. 301).

In Huahine twenty or thirty years ago, drinking during the later *taure'are'a* period, between perhaps eighteen and twenty-three or twenty-four, was very much more common than it is now. At that period orange beer was brewed in a barrel in the brush outside the village, and some young men and women, joined by older village "heavy drinkers," would drink around the barrel, dance, sing, fight, and initiate sexual affairs. The details of this kind of drinking are obscured by sentiment or retrospective moral indignation on the part of villagers today. The drinking was festive and occasional and did not involve most of the adult villagers. Older *taure'are'a* now do not have any special drinking patterns and are among the village's "normal drinkers."

"Heavy drinkers" drink more frequently and more copiously than "normal drinkers." But the difference between "heavy" and "normal" is much less than in groups where pathological drinking exists in contrast to normal drinking. There are certain behaviors and interpretations which are generally characteristic of drinking, including most "heavy drinking." Let us consider them in summary form.

Drinking is usually kept at controlled levels or plateaus. Levels are reached, maintained, and not overshot. The heavier drinkers reach a somewhat higher level, but they can usually maintain this without getting very drunk. People's desire and ability to maintain a level, and the *particular* level, the depth of drunkenness, that is sought, are significant problems here.

The minor celebrations, which are one type of reward to a work group when a joint task is completed, provide good examples of plateau drinking. A large quantity of beer or wine is provided by the host, for whom the work was done. The participants keep drinking until the wine or beer is gone, which may take an afternoon, a night, and most of the following day. The drinkers eat from time to time and occasionally take a short nap. Occasionally a participant leaves for a brief period to do some task at his house and then returns. Most of the drinkers look dulled and bleary in the later stages of this sort of drinking, but they keep their drunkenness below a staggering level; others show some unsteadiness. But greatly uncoordinated drunkenness, with marked physical and verbal incoherence, is extraordinarily rare.

Similarly, in the New Year's festival at Piri or the July festival at Fare, I saw very few visibly "drunk" people, although many people were drinking.

There are, in addition to control of levels of intoxication, controls on the length of drinking. Even "heavy drinkers" stop in time to keep up with their tasks, and well before they become seriously ill. During the two major yearly festivals, people declare that they will drink until they are *fiu*, "fed up," until the desire has disappeared. The desire is sure to disappear, sometimes within a day, sometimes after three or four days. Many will drink, stop, and then start again three or four times during a festival, but the festivals are no bacchanalia. After several days of festival, people in Huahine seem eager to stop "enjoying themselves" and are ready to get back to their usual routines.

At festivals and special occasions in which drinking does occur the host or a village official often formally urges people to drink. For those who are not "heavy drinkers" there is a hesitancy which must be overcome.

The major visible effect of drinking is that drinkers seem more relaxed and at ease. There is more talking, joking, and laughing. While drinking at home gatherings older men occasionally sing the old courting and humorous sexual songs and dance the erotic *tāmure*. There is often a good deal of male homoerotic play. Two men may dance the *tāmure* together, or affectionately embrace each other, in ways characteristic of young male adolescents, but never of sober adults.

Affectionate or sexual behavior cross-sexually is rarely displayed in public drinking behavior in Piri or at Fare. (This is in contrast to the bars and streets of Papeete, where drinking is more often connected with visible heterosexual affectionate behavior.) This heterosexual restraint is a response to the public setting. For some of the young men, drinking gives them more courage, after they leave the public amusement area, to approach a girl in the hope of arranging sexual intercourse. Some types of foreplay, such as kissing and cunnilingus, are said to be more common after drinking.

Public aggressive behavior is very rare, even in crowds of people who have been drinking for two or three days. There is more aggression associated with drinking in the household, but this is generally limited violence. Some young men, after drinking, engage in the thrill-motivated semisport of sneaking into someone's house in the dark to steal some food.

Nondrinkers, or light drinkers, interact with relatively drunken people in a normal fashion. Even in those episodes of uncoordinated drunkenness, people will continue in close discussion and interaction with the drinker. However, if the drinker begins to act in a hostile fashion, and if joking with him does not stop him, people disengage from him and try not to provoke him or react to him.

Nondrinkers or light drinkers simply do not like the effect of alcohol. Taere, for example, drinks only during the festivals, and has an occasional glass of beer or wine when he eats. He started drinking a little at sixteen, and somewhat more heavily at seventeen. He never drank enough, he says, to stagger or "not know what was going on" or to be sick. When he drinks more than a little, he feels weak in his arms and legs, and he does not like it. He thinks about the money he is wasting, and he stops.

Drinking is an important activity for Oro. He started drinking at fourteen. "Not every day . . . two months [would go by] and I would feel enthusiasm [*'ana'anatae*] about drinking . . . orange beer, wine. . . . It wasn't a fixed habit." ("Before fourteen, when you were a child, did you taste wine or beer?") "Rarely. A taste [literally, *tāmata*, to "try out"]." ("It wasn't a fixed habit . . . and then afterward?") "Afterward, it got frequent, although not very frequent. It was those times when you were *fiu*. You wanted to drink." ("When you were *fiu*?") "When you were weary/bored [*haumani*]. You want fresh thoughts [*mana'o*], you drink to make that thing [the boredom] go away." ("How often [did you drink] in those days?") "Once a week . . . Sundays, I'd go and drink." ("Did you drink till you were drunk?") [*Ta'ero*, "drunk," also means "poison" or "poisoned."] ". . . Yes, each time I drank and become drunk. . . ." ("How many glasses of [western-style] beer?") "Those things go — three glasses, and then one's head begins to be woozy . . . [glasses] of Hinano beer. You start to feel woozy. . . . You want to drink again, to make it more, and then you are drunk." I then ask him what then happens inside him. After a little grammatically induced confusion, in which he answers that it is the beer, of course, which is happening inside of him, he says, "Then I feel happy [*'oa'oa*] and want to go and have a good time [*'ārearea*]. You don't feel embarrassed [*ha'amā*] or worried [*pe'ape'a*] anymore; you don't feel fear anymore — you just want to go and enjoy yourself." ("It is a fitting/nice [*au*] thing to be drunk?") "It is nice, but the next morning it isn't nice anymore. You still have that woozy feeling in your head. All you want is some cold water to drink."

Later I ask Oro what else changes when he drinks. "If you have been feeling angry, you drink and the anger goes completely away. You just want to enjoy yourself, you don't concern yourself [with the things which made you angry] anymore. . . . If you want a woman, if you are drunk it is easy. You don't have *ha'amā*. You go and talk to her. Even if she speaks unpleasantly to you, you don't pay any attention. . . . When I'm sober I have *ha'amā* about talking. I can't talk. When you are drunk, you can respond to what she says. If you are not drunk, it is very difficult."

After some further discussion he says, "Sometimes you remember [the next morning]. You are ashamed at the things you did when you were drunk. Those people who saw you, you are ashamed because of them. They mock, 'That *taure'are'a*, he is not worth anything.'"

Asked if he thought he would keep on drinking in the same way all his life, he said, "No. When you get older, you don't have the desire to do that sort of thing any more. You want to sometimes, but not frequently. When you are a *taure'are'a*, you don't trouble yourself. If you want to drink, you drink. But when you settle down with a woman, when you are mature, and when you have children, if you keep drinking, that is shameful. The children don't eat, they don't have clothes to wear."

Statements by Oro and others about drinking agreed in several aspects:

1. Drinking, within clear limits, is natural. It is not unusual, forbidden, or rebellious behavior. It does not set one off from others.

2. Not only is it natural but, again with set limits, it is a good thing. It is good for the body, good for the enjoyment of life. According to Tāvana, "Drinking is good, if you don't get very drunk. It is good for the body, especially orange beer. . . . It makes people energetic and well nourished."

The evaluation of moderate drinking as a good thing is not shared by everyone. Many women feel that drinking beyond a glass or two is always bad and can lead to dangerous consequences. As Pua says, "Some people say that drinking is a good thing, that it brings good ways of thinking. I don't think it is a good thing. It causes people to steal, to have bad thoughts. They want to commit adultery, to beat up their own parents, to beat up their own children." Drinking will cause loss of control. For such women, it is any drinking; for the drinkers themselves, it is "too much" drinking.

3. Describing the effects of drinking on themselves, people agree with Oro that it increases their sense of energy and liveliness, decreases feelings of boredom, decreases embarrassment and social and interpersonal timidity. "When I used to drink," says Uta, "I wasn't afraid of people." Poria feels that he would become weak and ill if he stopped his once-a-week "heavy" drinking. When he drinks, he says, his food does him more good.

Oro says that his feelings of anger disappear when he drinks. Others, and Oro himself at other times, say that when they drink they are able to express anger (or disappointment or other negative feelings) toward someone verbally — which they cannot easily do otherwise.

4. The limits within which drinking is natural and good are, I have asserted, clear. It is wrong if it makes you sick, or if it makes you feel bad — if you drink too much and lose your sense of well-being. The hangover is often stressed in discussions of drinking. As Tāvana remarks, "People are changed when they drink, the body is changed. It is as if it gets more powerful. . . . It is an agreeable feeling, of course, but a little while afterward it isn't anymore, because it goes back to its old state. There isn't any place without pain after one has been very drunk. The body is full of pain the next morning."

Drinking is wrong if one's behavior gets "out of control." Some informants, such as Uta, found their first experiences of relatively heavy drinking unpleasant because they did things, such as stealing food, which they remembered with anxiety the next morning. Some drank tentatively and lightly for years before they began to drink more heavily.

Drinking is also wrong, as Oro notes, if it causes adults to neglect their responsibilities.

When "heavy drinkers" stop after many years of drinking, the explanation for the decision is usually that they were *fiu*, that they did not want to drink any more. Illness or a family crisis may influence the timing of the decision, and the signing of the Blue Cross might reinforce and strengthen it, but the major explanation is a change in one's inner state. It is this change that young "heavy drinkers" expect will happen to them to cause them to become lighter drinkers as they mature.

If, from a cross-cultural viewpoint, *heavy* drinking includes frequent drinking to unconsciousness or to marked degrees of uncoordination, and *pathological* drinking involves significant rates of physical pathology (gastritis, delerium tremens, neuritis, hepatitis), compulsive drinking (long binges, round-the-clock drinking), and seriously disruptive interpersonal acts, then drinking in Piri, and from all indications throughout the Society Islands in general, is neither very heavy nor pathological. How might this be explained?

The form and severity of drinking behavior in a community is related both to the community regulation and integration of drinking behavior and to prevalent private psychological forms. Various balances of control between public community forces and private, more or less "internalized" ones are conceivable. For Piri, I believe that the most effective aspects of drinking regulation are the internalized ones. People in Piri and Roto, and Society Islanders in general, drink without becoming alcoholics. I would approach an explanation as follows.

1. Prevalent personal motives for drinking are served by low-level intoxication.[16] People in many situations (chapter 10) feel constricted, embarrassed, self-conscious, timid, and bored. When they drink, these feelings are quickly altered, and they feel stronger, more comfortable, livelier, and able to do things which they felt timid about before. Most of these things are socially useful and approved. For such shifts, moderate drinking is sufficient. Heavy drinking obliterates the social effectiveness and sense of well-being produced by moderate drinking.

16. This discussion is based on the idea that the use of alcohol fulfills a variety of diverse psychological and social functions. See, for example, Levy (1958), Chafetz and Demone (1962), Washburne (1961), and many of the articles in Pittman and Snyder (1962).

2. Conversely, motives for drinking for which high and prolonged levels of intoxication would be necessary are not prevalent: a desire for forgetfulness — related to identity confusion,
low self-esteem, stress, and frustration (all of which entered into
nineteenth-century Tahitian drinking patterns) — or a guilt-ridden
desire for alcohol-induced illness and purification or for simple
annihilation.

There is no indication that the people of Piri or Tahitians in
general struggle to control the expression of poorly inhibited,
pressing, and socially dangerous actions. (The emphasis is on
poorly inhibited.) There is no indication that people avoid drinking for fear of an uncontrolled explosion,[17] or drink deeply to
permit the explosion, or drink more deeply still to reach some
narcotic safety.

3. If people drink to relieve feelings of constriction and social
anxiety, why don't they overshoot? Why don't they get involved
with the formula supposedly associated with much pathological
drinking, "If a little drinking makes me happy, why shouldn't
more drinking make me happier?" To some degree they do
sometimes overshoot moderately and lose their sense of well-
being, lose some control, and later feel ashamed; and they suffer
from mild hangovers. But this mild overshooting acts as corrective "negative feedback," as some reinforcement for maintaining
moderate levels in subsequent drinking.

There are, I think, positive factors operating against overshooting, which are related to the effects of certain values and pervasive socialization practices. There is, as I will discuss, marked
discouragement during the "socialization" of young children of
close attachment to parents, of overt dependency behavior, and
of "regressive behavior." The young children learn that they
must become emotionally "self-sufficient" and that helpless

17. For example, for the Alorese, "The whole system of organized aggression or self-assertion becomes blocked, and the individual has a life-long
struggle to contain these impulses within limits. He thus lives in constant
fear that they will spill over and then get completely out of hand. Hence
he must avoid all intoxicants which diminish the powers of control" (Kardiner 1945; pp. 165-66).

babyish behavior will only be ignored or punished. Self-sufficiency, the early, abrupt transition from baby to independent child, is perhaps the major crisis that children have to surmount in growing up. I have suggested that the sense of the danger of becoming deeply involved emotionally in dependent relations, or any other relationships in which one does not maintain some ability to escape, is reinforced in various ways in the culture.

If dependency, helplessness, and regression to childlike behavior are perceived as profoundly disturbing, dangerous, and valueless (i.e., they do not pay off in the response of others), then in the absence of any other pervasive motives for drinking severe enough to produce such states, one would expect that helplessness-producing drinking would be avoided.[18]

4. If there is little need to seek high levels or prolonged periods of intoxication and, in fact, there are needs not to do so, it must be assumed that individuals have enough understanding of the effects and tempo of intoxication to prevent the undesired levels. Villagers have the opportunity to learn to drink (which, since it starts in the family, also diminishes the meaning of moderate drinking as rebellion) and to come to understand the meaning of clues to levels of intoxication.

Disruptive drinking was more severe in the nineteenth century during a period of major cultural readaptation, and it may soon become a problem again as a consequence of new social changes. But for the present a complex, integrated balance has been achieved.

Aspects of Attitude and Definition

At the beginning of the chapter I noted some of the traditional terms for talking about "maladjustment." There are several

18. This is related to the finding of Peter Field, in a cross-cultural survey of some variables associated with drunkenness, that *indulgent* behavior of parents toward children between five and twelve years old is *positively* and significantly correlated with severe drunkenness. Field notes in a footnote, "It is probably relevant in this connection that Parker [1959] has found fifteen articles reporting a close mother-son attachment in alcoholics, and several authors have reported that youngest children in a family are both relatively indulged and overrepresented among alcoholics" (Field 1962; p. 66).

words used now to indicate that one is "troubled" — that one is either involved in external disturbances or suffering from a troubling inner feeling. By far the most frequently used term for troubles, either external or internal, is *pe'ape'a*. (Judging from other Polynesian languages, the root meaning was something like "entangled.") For internal disturbance, *pe'ape'a* has the sense of "disturbed," "worried," "upset."

There are terms which have to do with intelligence and the separate matter of what and how well one has learned. *Ma'ūa* is used for very stupid or feeble-minded people. *Mā'au* is also used for dull or "dumb" people, but it is also used for "foolish action" in the sense of someone who is acting more childishly and less dignified than he should. *Pōiri*, which literally means "dark" or "obscure," is used to emphasize "ignorant," rather than fundamentally stupid (although a person who is *ma'ūa* will also be *pōiri*).

People who cannot concentrate, whose thoughts go from one thing to another, are *nevaneva* (there are other terms). One can be *nevaneva*, as children and adolescents are, as a "natural" quality or as a symptom, for example, of a head injury. People who are seriously confused and rambling or delirious are *āoaoa*.

A regular propensity to peculiar talk and behavior will get a person referred to as *upo'o 'ino*, literally "bad head." *Upo'o 'ino* refers to various "deranged" behaviors. Hiro talked of his father who had become confused after long exposure to the hot sun. He had been fishing and did not have his usual hat. He was *upo'o 'ino*, but not *ma'ama'a* ("crazy"), said Hiro. When people are *ma'ama'a*, they say strange and unununderstandable things. But his father simply did not answer correctly. You would ask him one thing, and he would answer as if it were another question. He didn't seem to understand where he was and what was going on.

Ma'ama'a is the most commonly used term for "strange" behavior. It refers to wild, bizarre, hard to understand communications, to something more than confusion. (One may be *ma'ama'a* and not confused.) The woman in her uniform preaching at Fare was *upo'o 'ino*, and she was also *ma'ama'a*. Tore, in Piri, with his dark glasses, knotted handkerchief hat, and frightening mannerisms, was *ma'ama'a*. *Ma'ama'a* is also used in various metaphorical ways. Falling in love is said to be *ma'ama'a* about someone. (I don't know if this is an adaptation from French or English. I prefer to think it is an independent invention.) Behavior which is disapproved is sometimes labeled *ma'ama'a*. A child in Teri'i Tui's household, acting in certain disapproved ways, would be asked, "What is the matter with you? Have you become *ma'ama'a*?"[19] "Crazy" seems to gloss *ma'ama'a* very well.

There are various causes of *upo'o 'ino*. Many of them are entirely natural. Senility, which makes people act like infants and makes their speech confused and rambling, is just something that happens. People who become confused or rambling after exposure to too much sun or after too much deep diving for pearl oysters are considered to be suffering from a naturally caused disorder – although something in the chain of events leading up to the precipitating event may have been supernaturally influenced.

Spirit explanations as immanent causes were mostly applied to a subcategory of *ma'ama'a* behavior. Such explanations were given, as in *ma'i tāpiri* in general, where the disorder followed immediately on a supernatural encounter or the violation of some supernaturally protected rule, or else they were given when the *ma'ama'a* behavior seemed to indicate that the person was "taken over" by some other personality. This might be indicated in behavior resembling possessed behavior or in visions, ideas, or speech of an uncanny, demonlike quality.

Neither of these two categories of derangement – those due to immediate natural causes or those due to immediate spirit causes – reflected directly on the essential character, on the essence, of the individual. (Stupidity is taken as a quality of the person.) The first is a matter of natural accident or disease. The second is a matter of spirit influence or possession, and once it was removed the individual would again be the kind of person

19. *Ma'ama'a*, in its application to children's behavior, seemed to be applied as a label to a different order of deviation than *ha'amā*. *Ma'ama'a* implied the derangement of a mode of orientation; *ha'amā* labeled a particular behavior as unpresentable.

he had been before his altered behavior. Thus, in significant contrast with attitudes in many other societies, being *upo'o 'ino* does not entail an irreversible stigma bearing on one's general and essential worth.

People with both kinds of *upo'o 'ino* were considered not responsible for their actions. They had to be looked after, like the senile and people suffering from the results of sunstroke, or attempts had to be made to treat them through magical means. If they were untreatable, people avoided them, teased them, and joked uneasily about them. (And some people, from other places at least, were exiled to the asylum in Papeete.) While affected, they were no longer ordinary citizens.

Although the terms for varieties of a "bad head" are sometimes used as epithets for socially disapproved behaviors, their core meanings imply that individuals while affected are altered in such a way that ordinary social controls — shaming, disapproval, reasoning, fear-based sanctions — do not apply. Faced with this problem, the people in Piri and Roto are, in general, tolerant.

13

Aspects of Growing Up

If the child is not born radically defective, which is seldom the case, they will mould it into proper shape.

Early Reports

The first European reports of Tahiti contain only a few scattered comments on how caretakers dealt with children. The report of the first missionary expedition in 1797 remarks, with some sentiment, of Tahitian women that "as wives, in private life, they are affectionate, tender, and obedient to their husbands and uncommonly fond of their children. They nurse them with the utmost care, and are particularly attentive to keep the infant's limbs supple and straight. A cripple is hardly ever seen among them in early life. A ricketty child is never known; anything resembling it would reflect the highest disgrace on the mother. If an utter stranger discovers the least defect in a child, he makes no scruple to blame the mother, and imputes it to her want of sense and experience in nursing, so that if the child is not born radically defective, which is seldom the case, they will mould it into proper shape" (Wilson 1799; p. 328).

Ellis has some notes bearing on the experience of infants and babies reconstructed for the years before his ministry. "The mother [following childbirth] bathed in the sea immediately after a profuse perspiration had been induced, and the infant was taken to the water almost as soon as it entered the world" (Ellis 1830; 1:342).

Moerenhout records bathing babies in cold water as a persisting practice in Tahiti: "It is a fact that few Polynesian woman die in childbirth; and that in spite of a habit which would seem not to be salutary, that of leading the woman and her baby to

.the river, and washing them both in cold water, as soon as the infant is delivered" (Moerenhout 1837; 2:160).

In his reconstruction of pre-Christian daily life in Tahiti, Moerenhout adds, "The mothers went there [to the river] with their children and washed them from their tenderest infancy with cold water, which is extremely cold in the mornings in Tahiti" (Moerenhout 1837; 2:75).

Ellis notes other experiences which may have been unpleasant for babies.

The Tahitian parents and nurses were careful in observing the features of the countenance and the shape of the child's head during the period of infancy, and often pressed or spread out the nostrils of the females, as a flat nose was considered by them a mark of beauty. The forehead and the back of the head of the boys were pressed upwards, so that the upper part of the skull appeared in the shape of a wedge. This, they said, was done to add to the terror of their aspect when they should become warriors. They were very careful to haune, or shave, the child's head with a shark's tooth. This must have been a tedious, and sometimes a painful operation, yet it was frequently repeated; and although every idolatrous ceremony connected with the treatment of their children has been discontinued for a number of years, the mothers are still very fond of shaving the heads, or cutting the hair of their infants as close as possible. This often gives them a very singular appearance. The children are in general large, and finely formed. (Ellis 1830; 1:343-44)[1]

Aside from cold baths and cosmetic manipulations, the infants and young children seem to have had indulged and easy lives. "The children were frequently nursed at the breast till they were able to walk, although they were fed with other food. . . . During the period of infancy, the children were seldom clothed, and were generally laid or carried in a horizontal position. They were never confined in bandages, or wrapped in tight clothing,

1. Based on animal experiments, it has been suggested that such culturally standard "stress induction" in infancy may facilitate growth and resistance to later stress. See, for example, Landauer and Whiting (1964).

but though remarkably plump and healthy in appearance, they were generally very weak until nearly twelve months old" (Ellis 1830; 1:343).

Bligh, echoing the missionaries' report, remarked that the Tahitians "are kind and human to one the other beyond a doubt and are tender parents" (Bligh 1937; 1:395). "Tenderness" included "permissiveness." Ellis, erroneously claiming that these characteristics were a result of conversion to Christianity, wrote, "The most civilized and Christian parts of the world do not furnish more affectionate parents than the Society Islanders now are. In general, they are too tender towards their children and do not exercise that discipline and control over them which the well-being of the child, and the happiness of the parent, requires" (Ellis 1830; 1:341).

The lack of discipline and control necessary for the child's well-being and the parents' happiness had been described for pre-Christian Tahiti, and ascribed by Morrison and others to the belief that a child, by virtue of combining the *mana* of both parents' lineages, had, in high-status families, at least, more *mana* than either of its parents.[2] I have already quoted (in connection with masturbation) Morrison's "They lay no restraint on their children because they are the head of their family and therefore do as they please" (Morrison 1935; p. 236).

Bligh, on his second voyage to Tahiti, remarked that these restraints on parental power applied particularly to high-status families. "It is not extraordinary that Tynah is not remarkably fond of his children, for he is in some degree weaned from them by the accursed custom of their becoming superior in rank. On that account no one approaches them except the mother to give them suck, and the man who is nurse. When the father speaks to the child it is at a distance of ten yards. Thus until the chil-

2. "The reason of all these ceremonies [the *amoa*, noted previously] are that as soon as the child is born, it being the fruit of the father and mother is superior to either as much as the fruit is to the tree for food, for which reason the child is as soon as born the head of the family and the honor and dignity of the father is transferred to the first-born child whether male or female" (Morrison 1935; p. 187).

dren become men and women they do not mix together like other people. Happily it is different with the lower orders. The fathers and mothers have mostly their little flock of children about them. They nurse them with great care and tenderness and receive returns of affection and respect." And, he adds, "few more engaging children are to be met with could we divest ourselves of the dislike to the colour" (Lee 1920; p. 110).

Ellis did not specify that the insufficiently controlled children were only of high-status families. If one may judge from contemporary Tahiti, what the early European observers interpreted as tenderness and permissiveness was pervasive. The problem with the children's being able to do as they pleased was to control what they pleased to do. We are not told how the early Tahitians managed this.[3]

3. John Forster has a windy passage dimly suggesting that there were limits, even in Eden: "The mildness of the climate, the happiness of organization, and the kind and benevolent temper of this people, together with their more enlightened intellects [he is contrasting them with "more degenerated nations"] contribute very much to refine and to ennoble that soft passion which is the first beginning of this congenial harmony; and hence the brutish instincts, which were wants of the same low rank with hunger and thirst, are raised to a lasting, virtuous passion. This refinement of mutual love and matrimonial complacency produces those tender regards with which this happy passion inspires its votaries for the beloved object, and it creates that mutual happiness, which is the result of all the more refined manners, and of their more polished behavior towards one another. The offspring of such a happy couple early imbibe by the examples of their parents that kindness and benevolence and those refined sentiments of love and happiness which contribute so much to confirm the felicity of their parents, and wish to reduce them to practice as soon as they feel the call of nature and find a partner whose sentiments are in unison with their own; so that these simple, but more exalted ideas of matrimonial union are thus propagated and perpetuated in the progeny of a virtuous and tender couple. But before they attain that age of discretion and maturity, the fond parents take peculiar care of their education. They frequently check the wild flights of their unruly passions, and instill order, moderate industry and the principles of benevolence and gratitude into their tender minds. I have seen mothers punishing obstinacy and disobedience, and though extremely fond of their children, they nevertheless are sensible enough thus far to do violence to their own feelings, that their children may not acquire a habit of ingratitude, obstinacy and immorality. I have likewise heard them expostulating with their unruly little ones, and

Contemporary Childhood

As we turn to a consideration of aspects of "growing up" in contemporary Piri and Roto, cautions are necessary. I am interested here in infancy and childhood not for their own sakes but, a very different matter, for the illumination they throw on adults' worlds. My speculations on the significant aspects of developmental experience are based on an unsystematic and peculiar mixture of my impressions of adults' organization, on adults' reminiscences of their childhoods, on village rules and reports about dealing with children, and on random observations of children's behavior and the reactions of others toward them,[4] all guided by sundry assumptions about how children learn.

With this mixture as a basis I will present some speculations on learning. But this is much further from systematic observations than most other generalizations in this book. Bits and pieces are easily assembled into apparent meaning, and the reader should be cautious.

And I am considering only a bit of learning, that which seems to have bearing on the themes of this book. Matters bearing on specific skills, on directly taught values, on direct instruction in reality — which one may call first-order learning — are not considered. Much is neglected, and conversely a few things are considered (inadequately) mainly because they are part of the traditional "notes and queries" about child development.

Much of what follows is generalized in the form, "The Tierra del Fuegans are awfully fond of their children." All children? Always? All Tierra del Fuegans? What does "fond" mean? But something must be said. This is a prolegomenon to a study of growing up in Piri and Roto.

---

expressing their displeasure at their conduct; all which proves that they have ideas of moral rectitude, of order and filial subordination, and of the necessity of instilling these principles early into the minds of their children" (J. Forster 1778; pp. 350-51).

4. I used a preliminary version (1953) of the *Field guide for a study of socialization* (Whiting, Child, and Lambert 1966) as a guide to systematic interviewing and observation, to supplement my own sense of significant areas. But for my purposes in this chapter I am only presenting remarks on forms which I judge to have some significance for the data and interpretations of this book.

I always had the strong conviction that children's experiences in Piri and Roto were shaped, that lessons were being offered and learned repeatedly. Such lessons were often apparent to me because they seemed strange — they were not what I had learned or would teach.

They are lessons which may help explain some action tendencies and some private meanings in adults. They influence adults toward a disposition, a potentiality, which is brought to culturally structured situations — situations which, as I will argue in the next chapter, are in themselves of considerable importance for maintaining private organization.

Consider the following. One evening in Teri'i Tui's house, I showed Tara (then ten years old) and Ari (eight) how to make birds by folding paper. Ari quickly lost interest, but Tara was intrigued by hers. She carried it around with her, placed it under her mat at night, and brought it to breakfast the next day. At lunch she had it with her again and put it on the table. In the eating room were her mother, Mari; her sisters Rui (sixteen) and Ari; her nephew, now brother by adoption, Etienne (five); and I. Mari and Rui seemed tense and restrained. Rui, who had been cooking and whose hands were dirty, walked over to Tara and roughly picked up the paper bird, asking, "What is this thing?" Tara began to cry. She continued for three or four minutes. Then her mother, who had been watching all this, began to yell at Tara. "Stop crying. What is the matter with you? Are you crazy?" A few days later Tara's relative situation was different. This time Ari came running into the house chased by Tara, holding a branch of a bush as a switch. Ari ran to their mother, who put her arm about her but in no way interfered with Tara, who hit Ari on the legs. Ari sat down on the floor and began to cry. Then Tara explained to their mother what Ari had done wrong. After a few minutes the mother told Ari to stop crying.

Or this. Tinomana, the twenty-seven-month-old son of a family living at the inland part of the village, one morning was busily trying to fill a small tin pail with water at a pathside tap which had been left open. The bucket had a hole in it, and the water kept running out. Tinomana patiently and seriously kept at his task. He would place the pail on the ground under the tap; when it was full he would lift it and start for the house; then, the water having run out, he would return to the tap and start again. His mother was out of sight in their nearby house. After he had repeated his attempts for ten minutes, his mother called him to come to the house. He ignored her and continued to try to fill his pail. Five minutes later, having called out to him three times, the last time threatening to beat him, his mother sent his next older brother, Philippe, five, to fetch Tinomana. Philippe turned off the tap and stood guard over it. Tinomana became red-faced and furious, began to cry, and threw the empty pail into the ditch. Philippe mimicked and mocked his crying. The mother, now watching, said nothing. Finally Tinomana, still crying, returned to the house.

What were these children learning? This depends in part on what they had already learned before these experiences. Let us consider some other experiences by which they might have been influenced before considering the implications of these episodes.

Early Experience

Except for one or two reports concerning women who were extremely unhappy in their relationship with their *tāne* (for example, Pua's story about Maote's first *vahine* who, because of her anger at Maote, had willfully caused the death of her child and her own death during childbirth), reports and observations suggest that most parents look forward to the birth of children and are not anxious about the delivery or the prospect of a new child. This is true even of many girls who are not in a settled relationship, for there is always the option of giving the child for adoption if the mother or the father does not want to keep it.

Intercourse is resumed shortly after delivery, when the *ma'i fānau*, the birth injuries, have healed, which, in contrast to other cultures where postpartum tabus on intercourse exist, suggests a relative lack of emphasis on the disruptive meaning of a new baby to the parents.

A first baby who is kept rather than given for adoption does, nevertheless, represent an important change for its parents. It

symbolizes some commitment to the relationship and some further relinquishing of *taure'are'a* hopes. As the new baby's parents have most likely been living with the parents of one or the
other and will remain with them for a while longer, the baby's
arrival does not, however, mean a major shift in its parents'
opportunities for intimacy.

The infant is referred to as an *'āiū*, or milk eater, and addressed
as *'āiū* until roughly the time he[5] begins to crawl, when he is referred to as *tamāri'i*, "child," and addressed by his given name.

The *'āiū* in its first two months or so is said to be in its *'aru-
'aru ra'a*, its feebleness. During this "feeble" period the child is
considered to be fragile. It is not given to other children for
care, and it is not usually taken outside. In some households it
is not washed with water during this period, but only with coconut oil. (The early custom of washing the infant with cold water
does not exist now.) People say that if a child dies during this
stage, one does not mourn so much; it is when it gets to be a
little bigger and smiles and recognizes you that people will begin
to really grieve if it dies. It is also during these *'aru'aru* months
that a child is likely to be given up for adoption, "before the
parents have become attached to it." Similarly, the early literature reports that pre-Christian infanticide (mostly female), which
had had among its declared purposes population control, was
only done immediately after delivery of the child, before it
cried, for otherwise the mother began to become attached to it.

This first stage, during which there seems to be some caution
about investing too much emotional concern in the infant, passes
when the baby is some two or two and a half months old. Mothers say that now it may be taken outside. It is now handed
around to a wide variety of caretakers other than the mother,
including young children. But the mother, biological or adop-

5. Faced with the dilemma of using the depersonalizing "it" or the mas-
culinizing "he" to refer to infants and children of both sexes, I will follow
Tahitian impersonality in referring to infants, but use "he" and "his" generally in referring to older boys and girls. The Tahitian third person singular pronoun does not distinguish "he" from "she," and this should be
remembered in reading quotations from Tahitian.

tive, is the main caretaker, and the baby is returned to her after frequent but brief excursions.

I almost never heard young babies crying in Piri. The houses along the village path, full of babies, were quiet in the evenings. Judging from the contented look of babies at this stage, things were going well for them.

As a baby becomes active, the people around it begin to respond to it as an amusing small adult, with an individuality and will of its own. This is suggested, in a playful way, even during pregnancy. Pregnant women, reacting to kicking and movements of the fetus, sometimes slap their abdomens and joke, "Be careful not to hit too hard, or I'll get even with you when you grow bigger."

The most common way of holding the baby now is with two hands, one underneath its buttocks and the other supporting its upper back and head. It is held as a separate individual, often at some distance from the mother's body, and clinging, blending, and cuddling are infrequently seen. When a young baby is being held this way, the holder is not able to do much except interact with the baby or talk with others. The baby will be put on the ground or handed to an older child if there is something to be done. Occasionally a caretaker may hold a baby straddling her hip, supported by a hand at its back, thus freeing her other hand. This method of holding was described for nineteenth-century Tahiti.[6] It is said now that it is bad for the baby and deforms the growth of its legs. When the baby gets older and is taken by older children, they will carry it on their backs, piggyback fashion, and it will actively hold on as they run around the village and play.

6. According to the notes of the Reverend John Orsmond (based on residence in Tahiti between 1817 and 1856), "The nurses are careful not to strain the spine of the infant. After three or four months, as it gets strong, it is kept much of the time upon a mat on the floor instead of the bed, and then it soon turns and learns to crawl. When the child is first carried in a sitting posture the nurse carefully props its back with one hand, called fa'ati'ati'a (raising), and continues to do so until the child can sit up alone. When it can crawl and walk it is carried sitting astride upon the hip of the nurse, who passes one arm under the child's arm and around its waist to hold it in position, a mode called tuta" (Henry 1928; p. 274).

The baby enters a period of considerable stimulation. It is the center of attention and of attraction in the household. People are fascinated and amused by it, but they seem to respond mostly to the imperfect fragments of adult behavior that it shows. Clinging, cuddling, caressing, and encouragement of its more infantlike behavior are little done. This is in contrast with the local Chinese families and some of the *demi* families in Papeete, who treat their several-month-old babies more like infants or dolls. A Tahitian woman, born in a rural village, who worked as a maid with European families, commented that European women played with dolls when they were children, in contrast with Tahitian women, who had played with babies. She said that she thought that European women, when they grew up, treated their own babies as if they were dolls.

The young child is understood to be an interesting, active, self-developing thing. One must watch over its feeding and appearance, be sure that child caretakers are competent to hold and carry it, and then observe with interest as it grows.

What do people expect, or say they expect, of young children? People do not express marked preference for either boys or girls, unless they have only one or the other among their previous children, a situation which can be remedied by adoption. The sex of a very young infant is not particularly salient in village reports; the several times that somebody reported to me that so-and-so had a new baby, the newsbearer frequently did not know whether it was a boy or a girl.

Questions about what kind of a child parents want are answered with a shrug or else "a good child," indicating, as we will see, one who will be relatively docile. People, pushed to say what they want of their children when they grow up, answer, typically, "whatever they want" or "that they should not be ignorant." Children are interpreted as natural, as given, with their own characteristics. They have to be dealt with and managed, but they will grow essentially in their own way.

And they will grow through natural stages. The nature of the infant, the nature of the child, the nature of the adolescent — commonly heard phrases indicate that each of these life stages has its own characteristics, which are in the nature of things. There is little, at the level of conscious planning, to be done.

Dealing with Children's Bodies

It is customary to note ways in which the problems presented by children's bodies are dealt with by caretakers. Fundamental cognitive and emotional orientations are thought to be learned here. It is in these stages, as the psychoanalysts[7] have suggested, that body becomes inextricably interwoven with many modes of meaning. We cannot be sure in culturally integrated settings about what is learned at these early stages and what is learned later. (The importance of very early learning in "neurotic" people is peculiar in that it is often discontinuous with, and in fact antithetical to, later learning and therefore has specially important explanatory force.) It seems likely that later learning will determine to a considerable degree how the residues of earlier experience will resonate in the adult mind.

Let us look rather grossly at some ways of dealing with babies as bodies.[8] As the work of William Caudill, for example, on the form and consequences of mother-infant reactions in Japan indicates (Caudill and Weinstein 1969), babies must be learning much in the fine patterning of their relations with caretakers that my methods miss.

Babies, placed on a small mat, sleep next to their mothers. Occasionally they are put under the same cover as the mother, but most often they have their own covers. Sometimes they are put between the mother and father. Occasionally, on the arrival of a baby, the father may move off to the other end of the room to sleep.

When another child is born, it will also be placed next to the mother. The older child continues to sleep near her, although it may find itself separated by one sleeping space. At about four or five years, children move off to sleep by themselves, although

7. Most notably summarized and developed in Erik Erikson's work, e.g., *Childhood and society* (1950).

8. Some aspects of parents' responses to children's sexual behavior are noted in chapter 4.

some children sleep next to their mothers until they are six or seven. Moving off is considered a decision to be made by the child himself. Sometimes young children, both girls and boys, will decide to sleep next to their fathers rather than their mothers.

The child's mat is covered with oilcloth to protect it from urine and feces. A generation ago banana leaves, which were first treated by passing them over a fire, were used for this purpose. From shortly after birth, the infant is diapered, and it is kept diapered until it starts to crawl. After that, it is often allowed to go naked, although it will still be kept diapered at night until it begins to be able to control its sphincters.

Parents' and older children's reaction to the urination and defecation of babies is low-key and matter-of-fact. Babies are routinely wiped up and cleaned without any demonstration of emotion or interruption of conversation or ordinary activity.

Sphincter control "training" often proceeds under the ideology which applies to most learning — "the child teaches himself." Thus Teiva, who guessed that he had stopped wetting the bed at three or four, says that he thought his own children stopped at two and one-half or three. I then ask him what he did to make the children stop bed-wetting. "Nothing. They stop urinating. There is no medicine [for it]." ("Do you yell at them, or hit them. . . .") "No. I don't tease them, or yell. . . . You can't yell because this is a child's nature. He doesn't know good behavior. Defecate, urinate — he doesn't know he should go outside. . . . [But] it will go away."

Such ideas about the child's natural development affect the pressures applied to it, but they do not mean that the child is really let to achieve sphincter control entirely in its own time. There are certainly caretakers' reactions of disapproval as they clean up messes, and in time they will assume that the child could stop if it wanted to.

When the child "can understand what is going on," which for this purpose is about one and one-half years of age, caretakers, particularly the mother, say such things as "that is dirty, go outside to do it." Critical remarks of increasing strength, mixed with shaming, continue for two or three years. Children of three to four years still urinate or defecate occasionally in the house and are increasingly threatened with being hit, which, like such threats generally, is most often not carried out.

By two, children tend to go outside to urinate and defecate. First they do it in the yard near the house, the mother or an older sibling cleaning up after them, and soon they learn to use the outhouse built over the lagoon. Children are supposed to wipe themselves with leaves and wash with water, but caretakers' supervision of this is relatively perfunctory, and two- and three-year-old children will sometimes smell of feces.

People say that children often continue to wet the bed until five or six and occasionally longer. Children are frequently awakened before elders go to sleep and asked if they have to urinate or, if they are still bed-wetters, told to go outside.

Etienne in Teri'i Tui's household still wet the bed at five, and there were frequent moderately shaming comments about it by his mother or siblings in the morning.

Children are not praised for control of excretion, but when they are considered old enough for self-control, they are criticized, mocked, or shamed for deviation. When they finally achieve control, it is said that it is because they are fearful.

Children are also taught early to keep their noses clean. They are punished for spitting in the house. They are criticized for passing flatus if it occurs at the table, but not elsewhere, even though it is considered somewhat shameful. Parents generally require children to bathe daily, and more frequently if they become particularly dirty.

These first lessons in presentability will have a peculiar force, because they will not be contradicted by later teaching that inner worth or achievement or some other quality of the self is more important than proper presentation.

Patterns of nursing are complex. Women credit themselves and village women generally with letting a child nurse as much as it wants to. There are many stories and examples of children nursing for five or more years. Flora claims that she nursed until she was nine. Women stop nursing, they say, when they have another baby or when the child wants to stop. A *demi* schoolteacher who had worked in Huahine told me that it is rare for mothers to say no to a child that wants to nurse. She had urged mothers to cut down on nursing and substitute other foods, but the mothers would say, "What can one do? It wants to nurse." Even after another child comes, an older child may continue to suckle occasionally at the mother's breast. People say that children stop eventually because older children and adults begin to tease them and make fun of them.

But in spite of verbal emphasis on permissiveness and stories of long nursing, earlier weaning is not uncommon, and there are subtle resistances to the child's "will to nurse." I saw frequent examples of a baby who wanted to nurse being brought to the mother by an older child, then being allowed to sit for several moments, either crying or making efforts to get at the breast, before it was fed. Sometimes a mother would take a child straining to nurse and give it an impatient shake before nursing it. Sometimes a child would be held and frustrated until it seemed to lose interest in nursing, and only then was the breast offered to it. Sometimes a mother would mock an infant's cries with a show of impatience, and then after a few minutes begin to feed it. The child who was gratified in terms of being able to nurse as much and as long as he wanted to was given a number of more or less subtle signals that his will was not to be gratified so simply.

Mothers reported that children waked and cried two or three or four times during the night, when they were "hungry for the breast."[9] Tano's *vahine*, talking about nursing practices, said, "Each time the child cries the mother feeds it at once. They are not like European mothers who [she has heard] let the baby cry." But Uta and other *tāne* expressed annoyance that often their *vahine* let the children wait while they finish other tasks, ignoring the children's cries.

---

9. Terms referring to nursing are related to hunger and eating, rather than to thirst and drinking.

Yet it is apparently rare for the mother to frustrate the child more than briefly. The child's crying is annoying to the parents, and any obvious or prolonged frustration of the child's nursing would be contrary to ideal behavior.

The usual time of weaning seems to be from one and a half to three years. The mother begins to show impatience, saying that she is *fiu*, "fed up," with nursing the baby. The child begins to get teased by mother and others. Eventually it "stops by itself." And those people who remember nursing recall "stopping by themselves" rather than being forced to stop.

Sometimes, as with Uta's children, when the mother wants to wean a child she sends it away to relatives for three or four days. But there were no reports in Piri of the direct forbidding of nursing in an encounter of mother and child, or of the use of unpleasant tasting substances on the breast to make the child stop nursing. Such substances are reported for Papeete, where there are changes in attitudes about nursing and other aspects of child management.

After weaning, some sucking behavior continues in older children. In Piri three or four children of seven or eight years of age suck their thumbs. There is no public criticism of this by the parents, or any public attempt to make them stop. In some households, however, children are reportedly told not to put their fingers in their mouths because "their fingers are dirty."

Psychological feeding disturbances, or children who are very fat or thin as a result of eating habits, are not apparent in Piri or in the life histories. Uta, asked about this, said that if one of his children were not hungry, elders would simply leave the food for him, and he could eat it when he wanted. Eating is not an area of particular conflict between children and parents, nor does it entail special problems. (In the interviews, with the exception of Tano, there are no obvious eating-related anxieties or fantasies. Village theories of illness do not emphasize orally introduced contaminants; the mode of influence or entrance of harmful forces is, significantly, unclear.)

Village children are active, energetic, and graceful. Their play involves much running and clearly exuberant body motion. The same children are able to sit still for long periods of time, when, for example, they are in a canoe or waiting with their families for the arrival of a boat at Fare.

Young children climb trees, play in the lagoon, and play with bush knives at a size when to my sense of children's abilities they are incompetent to do so. I was often tempted to grab a child and save him from dangers which no one else perceived. It seemed to me that village children were conceived as having more neuromuscular competency, and thus were allowed to practice more skills without interference or "help" from others, than middle-class western children of the same apparent age and size.

I do not have any systematic observation of the development of motility. Some villagers estimate that children crawl at about seven months and start walking at nine months to one year. People say that parents do not worry if children are delayed in learning to walk or talk. On the other hand, according to some, people do boast about children who begin to walk or talk at an early age, in the same way that they will boast about a young child who is particularly active or mischievous. Children are allowed to crawl and toddle when they will, with the help of an occasional hand, but there is no visible attempt to teach children walking or other motor skills. Some of the *demi* families in Roto use walkers or make other attempts to teach their children to walk, but as Tivini's wife puts it, "Tahitians let children learn to walk for themselves."

In Piri motor skills are often learned in the context of unsupervised encounters between children. A description from my field notes illustrates the flavor of such interactions. I had been watching the unsupervised play of two of Taere's children, Roger, four years and six months, and Simone, three years and three months:

There is a sense of strangeness about it, as though they were psychotic children. Very little of their play is verbal; screeches, laughter, and grunts make up 95 percent of the vocal communication. Their vigorous running, throwing, and pulling at trees has a great velocity, and seems to be an expression of relatively greater strength and motor skill than that of middle-class American children of similar ages. A great deal of the activity is mock aggressive. One of them, usually but not always the boy, picks up a heavy branch and first chases the other and then throws the branch, which is always aimed at the feet from a short distance. The accuracy is constant; it always misses, but barely. Adults pay no attention at all. Occasionally Simone starts to cry when too frightened or apparently overstimulated by Roger. She cries vigorously for thirty seconds, and then stops crying abruptly and completely and continues with their play.

Techniques of Control

Babies and young children appear to be happy, active, flourishing creatures. They are in intense interaction with the people around them, stimulated, bounced, handled, joggled, thrown around, told "look at this, look at that." They are not, I have said, commonly caressed or stroked or treated as fragile, but are the center of an active, adoring, delighted attention.

People are pleased and amused as a baby develops motor and verbal skills. As he gets to be about three, some serious behavior begins to be expected from him, such as picking up light trash around the house. As he does such tasks, people order him about and react to him in adult ways. The people around the child have been "reacting" to him in ways from which the child has, presumably, been learning. But now they will begin to expect something from him and more consciously try to mold him.

Sometimes people's response is to do nothing. Children who have temper tantrums outside the house are often allowed to kick and scream until they get tired of it. Matters which might well seem to a western observer to call for some response sometimes seem invisible to Tahitian caretakers.

One day, for example, in Teri'i Tui's household, Etienne discovered that his sisters had been given gifts by a visiting European, but that none had been given to him. He began acting "unusually," became irritable, made himself a nuisance, and got in the way of the play of the other children. He began to knock over small pieces of wood and toys that the girls were playing with. He then picked up a pair of scissors and began making stabbing motions at his sisters. He then began to cut off pieces of his own hair with the scissors. None of the older siblings or adults sitting around paid any visible attention at all to Etienne's behavior. Such a failure to respond is in itself a message.

When the people around a child decide that they must alter its behavior, they use "techniques." The word "technique" implies a conscious action informed by a goal. One sees a great variety of responses to children in Piri — approval, gift giving, withdrawal of love, threatening, and so forth. But much of this does not seem to be systematically related to "training" sequences, although such behaviors may have covert teaching functions. Parents, for example, may disguise their responses of pride and love for a child and offer them erratically in relation to a child's behavior. They urge more food to a child, grumbling, "You certainly are a nuisance, what will you want next." Praising or rewarding children, people say, will make them too hard to manage.

The important systematically and consciously used techniques for managing children in Piri and *mā'ohi* Roto are negative ones — verbal threatening, mild physical punishment, mild mocking and shaming — the purpose of which is to make children avoid error. Praise and reward are very rarely used as techniques; nor is the special negative sanction "withdrawal of love" systematically used for overt purposes of behavioral modification.

The usual term for actively dealing with children is *fa'atere*, literally "to steer." The overt goal of management of children is to produce docility and "fear." By fear is meant a fear of trouble, a fear of something going wrong. People hope that children will obey because they are "afraid" not to. The purpose of hitting a child, for example, is said to be so that he will become "afraid," and then he will not have to be hit anymore; and in fact in time this will happen.

It is better, if it is avoidable, not to tell the child what specific behaviors he must *not* do, a point of contrast noted by those villagers who have watched European parents interacting with their children. "A child who is told what he must not do is sure to go ahead and do that very thing." It is hoped that children will learn to stay out of trouble; what trouble is depends on the situation. Thus caretakers desire not so much fear about particular actions but a generalized disposition to be fearful, and thus docile. When a recalcitrant child suddenly yields, parents say with pride, "He is afraid." When children get hurt, people say, "It is a good thing, that will teach him to be more careful" — not just about climbing trees, but about everything.

The most common fear-producing techniques are verbal threats. Children are constantly told they will be beaten in one way or another if they continue to act badly. Sometimes a child is threatened that a foreigner will take him away or that a ghost will get him on the village path in the evening.[10] I heard occasional examples of other kinds of threats, such as "be careful or I won't feed you anymore" or threats to chase a child out of the house.

Another fear-producing technique is a capitalizing on accidents. Sometimes a young child will act aggressively and nothing will be said about it. But if he happens to fall down a while later, his parents and older siblings may yell at him, "Stop crying, it serves you right." There are several ways of saying "it serves you right," and one hears it frequently.

Fear-encouraging behavior can be quite cruel. One evening in Teri'i Tui's house, one of the children, Tara, discovered that a newly adopted baby at the house, a boy twenty-six months old, was afraid of a small doll. For thirty minutes the whole family — Teri'i Tui, Mari, and the older children — joined in with intense interest, laughing heartily, as one or another frightened the child with the doll. They kept bringing the doll near him, rubbing him with it, suddenly bringing it into his view. At first he would point to it, or turn away, or cry out. But after fifteen or twenty minutes he began to get more and more fretful, and began a continued sobbing. They kept up for another ten minutes before

10. There are no ghosts which are specifically involved with children in Piri. As I have noted, in the context of spirit-produced illnesses, children are thought to be less vulnerable to harmful spirits than are taure'are'a or adults.

they stopped. At other times the older children would try to frighten the baby by calling his attention to lizards.

Although children are threatened with being severely beaten, *taparahi*, hitting is done relatively rarely, when compared with the constant verbal threats of injuries and when compared with reported hitting practices in other Polynesian groups. Veve Vahine, asked to evaluate hitting as punishment for children, stated the ideal case. "Hitting [*tā'iri*] is not good. The [proper] hitting is with the mouth. That business, hitting with a stick, [they] don't listen/obey [*fa'aro'o*].[11] But your mouth, if you advise [*a'o*] him well, that is the good thing. . . . I tell you, that a child who is habitually hit, that is a very deaf child. It doesn't listen/obey if he is habitually hit. It is hit, and it isn't afraid [*mata'u*] anymore. But if your mouth speaks, if you show your irritation . . . then it listens/obeys."

There are various named kinds of hitting. *Taparahi* means to seriously beat or kill someone, and is something that one threatens but does not do unless one really wants to do someone grievous physical harm. The usual type of hitting is *tā'iri*. This is any blow with a stick or noncutting instrument, or a fairly light blow with an open hand. If it is the face or head that is slapped, it is called *pō'ara*. A blow with a closed fist is *tūpa'i* (also used to refer to the slaughter of an animal). The ordinary way of hitting a child is on the body, either with an open hand or with a switch, usually a light branch of a bush. A blow by the hand to the head or face, *pō'ara*, is considered to be particularly serious and insulting. (In traditional Tahitian culture the head was the most sacred part of the body.) Children are commonly hit on the legs with a switch, which is the least insulting kind of blow.

Some people in the interviews said they were never hit as children; others said they had been hit almost every day, usually by their mothers or, less frequently, by other household caretakers. Caretakers also yell angrily at their children. This is called *tama'i*, which refers to any verbal quarrel and also means war or battle. Generally, as children grow older yelling unaccompanied by hit-

11. *Fa'aro'o* means both to listen and to obey.

ting becomes the usual way displeasure is expressed, and a blow would be a serious insult to an adolescent.

Although verbal shaming and ridicule are used to express disapproval and to coerce proper behavior, they seem less frequently used than fear-inducing behaviors. Shaming, as has been noted, is directed toward breaches of self-control, such as bed-wetting, or to mark generally inadequate behavior. Such shaming does not seem in itself, as I have remarked in the discussion on moral controls, adequate to explain fully the later sensitivity of adults to shame and embarrassment. As I have suggested in chapter 10, it is more a question of shame's not being overcome through education in brashness, rather than specific methods of inducing shame feelings, which may be significant here.

When asked about withdrawal of love or affection or emotional closeness as a technique for managing children, villagers deny using it. However, any observation of village parents when they are angry or displeased indicates that they are more "distant" from the child than they ordinarily are. But parental withdrawal is not an effective socializing technique in Piri because it has to a large degree, as we shall see, already taken place as a routine response to the child's growing up. Parental withdrawal has, so to speak, been used for other purposes and cannot be (or at least is not) used for child management and for moral and behavioral training.

Positive techniques, rewards, are seldom used. Children are given gifts on birthdays and at Christmas, but these are not particularly related to activities of the child. In general failures are blamed, but good performance, being considered "natural," is not praised. Rewards are occasionally given, in the form of a gift such as a piece of candy. Pua will sometimes give a piece of candy to her children for helping to clean the yard and occasionally to induce a child to stop crying. But generally it is expected that there is natural proper behavior. One must attend to deviations.

Aspects of Later Teaching

Most of the patterns of teaching I have sketched occur when children are young, and are patterned in ways that are difficult for children to understand verbally. But when children get older and have to learn new tasks, they begin to have theories about how they are learning. Now we can use the interviews for illustrations.

Thus Manu discusses the learning of skills. "I can make and cook in an earth oven because I saw my 'grandfather' make them every day. I would sit next to him, and I understood how to do it. Sometimes in the large house of my 'grandfather,' in those times, he [the "grandfather"] would see that there was a fire in the cookhouse [i.e., Manu had made it]. He would come and look, and the earth oven was ready." I ask Manu what he learned from his adoptive father as he grew older and they went to work on the plantation at Flint Island. "I just looked at the way things were done, and when I got to be thirteen years old, I understood how to do the work." His adoptive father also instructed him. "When I would help him in the work, then he would teach me, 'Gather together the dried coconuts. Don't take many. Take the proper amount.' He taught me because I was little, and I could not take a heavy load. He bawled me out [*tama'i*] at those times. 'Here is how to do it, make it light.' He taught me a little bit, but most of the time, it was by my own eyes that I would see how to do the work."

A few minutes later I ask Manu if other families are different about actively teaching their children. "It isn't all the same. . . . Some parents direct [*fa'atere*] their children even though the child knows how to do the work. For example, if the child is doing work he knows how to do, the parent yells at him, 'It's not like that, but like that, like that, like that.'" Manu mimics the parents' interference in an angry, irritated tone of voice. "The parent wants the child to obey him."

In his first example the parents' correction of mistakes is unnecessary, even disruptive to the task. It is angrily given — mistakes are corrected when the mistake irritates someone. That is, in fact, what the mistake is.

Manu proceeds to another kind of family. "Some parents prefer to leave their children alone. Not to teach them anything. And then when that child grows up, that is the time they want to teach them. The child doesn't listen anymore. . . . He has grown up, and does as he wants. There is very little the parent has taught him." Utter neglect is equally bad.

And now comes the golden mean. "Some parents, at the time they see that a child begins to know how to do a task, that's enough, they don't trouble you anymore. Only at the one time that the parent sees you have made a mistake in doing the task, that is the time he counsels you, 'Not like that, but like this.'" Manu's various adoptive parents were, he says, like this. "I knew how to do things. That was the time they didn't teach anymore. They didn't counsel me. . . . I didn't make mistakes in my work, because I knew how to do it, how to finish the work skillfully. Now they couldn't cause complications for me about my work."

With the exception of Teiva, who contrasts himself explicitly with Tahitian upbringing, in that his Chinese father taught him to work, all the men believe that they learned their skills by themselves, by watching, with occasional corrective comments from an elder. As Poria said when asked how he learned to garden, to fish, to build houses, "By thinking it out [feruri]."

Uta, asked if his children are taught to walk, says, "We don't instruct children in walking, we just let a child alone and he walks." Asked if he teaches his boys gardening techniques, he says, "Rarely. I just let them watch. When they are ready, they do the work." He will correct mistakes, but doesn't spend much time on positive verbal instructions. The children learn by watching and by correction.

When adults do volunteer a list of things they teach children, it comprises such matters as "they shouldn't sleep during the day," "they should earn money," "they shouldn't steal," "they should wash their face in the morning, comb their hair, and fold the bedclothes." These lists emphasize general behaviors and goals, not the instrumental means to achieve them.

When Pua and Veve Vahine described how they had learned household skills from their "mothers," there was much less emphasis on self-teaching. "If they [mother, aunts] didn't teach me," said Pua, "I wouldn't know how to do those things." And, "My mother taught me. . . . It was because I stayed near her. I would go to school and return to her. 'Do that thing, that thing, that thing, that thing.' And I would do it. If not, I would be hit. Therefore, I learned to do things."

The Child's Autonomy

Manu's and Uta's arguments for minimal parental interference in the teaching of skills and Teiva's remarks, quoted earlier, about a child's self-control of his sphincters[12] have to do with a theme of a child's autonomy, which explains caretakers' concerns that a child be docile. For there is an underlying assumption that only if a child cooperates can he be made to obey, for he has an inviolable will of his own. If the child decides no, there will be little one can do about it. "Docility" means that he has agreed to say yes. If, for example, a parent wants to take a sick child to the nurse in Fare and the child refuses, the parent will say, "Well, we would like to take him, but there is nothing we can do about it, he doesn't want to go." I have seen people wait until a child was almost unconscious and therefore unable to protest before they would bring him.

People often avoid encounters with their children, so that they do not have to resist a child's will. Maote, the *tāne* of Pua, is trying one day to paint the hull of a canoe. One of his small daughters, still a young baby, begins to pull at his hands. Pua and Maote's adoptive mother, who are watching, try to distract her, but when this does not work they leave her alone in the hope that she will stop by herself and without any conflict, without becoming angry or crying.

Another man carves a canoe with a sharp ax, while a small boy crawls back and forth along the side of the canoe. Repeatedly the child passes the place where he is working. The man pauses until the child has passed by. He does not interfere with the child's freedom of movement, nor does he show any signals

---

12. Lest we forget, recall Arnold Gesell writing in 1940, "The former tendency to train a baby for elimination as early as 3 weeks of age is rapidly giving way to a new understanding of the manner in which a child achieves control. The 'successes' of early training were often transient and superficial, and they overlooked the excessive amount of time spent at the toilet!" (*The first five years of life*, p. 246).

of impatience or anger. Later the same child begins to play near a sharp bush knife. A man sitting nearby quietly removes the knife, but nothing is said to the child.

A child is thought to have considerable will and autonomy. If you do interfere directly with him, things may well get worse.

Withdrawal

If a child decides to rebel, there are problems. But one does not see many conflicts of will; usually children are docile. They are docile, I presume, because much of the system of controls comes to seem inevitable, in the nature of things. They learn to obey it as one learns not to try to walk through walls.

Inevitability of limits is conveyed, I think, in various ways. One is the message, "some of the things you want are unavailable." This is what children are learning when they are not being "spoiled." Such learning probably starts in such microexperiences as not getting breast-fed exactly at the moment or in the way the child wants, and is dramatically continued in an experience which children in Piri and Roto share with children throughout Polynesia and Micronesia and many other traditional cultures. As they begin to become more and more children rather than babies, and begin to be a bit irritating and willful because they are "thinking for themselves," people begin to find children less amusing. Instead of being the center of the household stage, the child whose bids for attention were responded to, encouraged, and, in fact, taught becomes annoying. He is now too old to show off, to "inflate" himself. The child is now, perhaps, between three and five years old. "He wants to play more outside the house," one is told, and he is encouraged to do so. Often another baby is born or adopted about this time, but even if it is not, the child is now defined as something different. This has been described for other Polynesian and Micronesian cultures as "rejection." More accurately, the child's desire for certain kinds of interactions is now no longer "indulged." This involves for the most part two kinds of activities: those involving showing off, being cocky, amusing, and exhibitionist, and those related to dependency and clinging. Dependent and clinging activities have been discouraged in subtle ways even before this period, but now the pressure against them is increased. Exhibitionist activities, however, have been encouraged. The child is now to be relatively ignored.

When I first came to Piri, Etienne was three years and eight months, and a spirited, comical performer. Before I left he was six, compressed, crying easily, sulking, and given to occasional falling-down, fist-pounding tantrums on the village path. A new baby had come, and Etienne played with him roughly enough to make him cry.

Children, pushed away from exhibitionism and from household attention in general, are now expected to spend more of their time outside with other children. They look moody and depressed and have temper tantrums which are either ignored or shouted at.

Children try to cling in a babyish way during this period, and are sometimes tolerated, sometimes brushed off. They are also particularly mischievous, contrary, and "difficult" with adults and older siblings, a kind of behavior which seems to combine anger and a testing of whether elders are still concerned with them. The irritation of their elders mounts.

And then, within a few months, one begins to see the sweet, polite, self-sufficient children who are the precursors of adult *mā'ohi* Tahitians.

The Form of the Socialization Network

Now we can return to the question of what the children were learning in the three episodes briefly described earlier in the chapter. I have suggested some of the kinds of experiences Tara, Ari, Etienne, Tinomana, and Philippe most likely had in the years before these episodes, episodes in which their education was proceeding.

In the first episode, Tara was learning a very important first-order lesson about not investing emotions in possessions. Rui dirtied the paper bird, and Mari supported Rui, telling Tara, furthermore, not to protest and that her crying was "crazy." I do not know what first order lesson Tara was teaching Ari a few days later. And Tinomana was simply being fetched. But these episodes illustrate some larger patterns of learning. They illustrate some typical features of what we might call "household socialization networks." These include the following.

1. There are a number of people who have the right and obligation to chastise and correct children, and who should also watch over them, protect them, and take care of them. This includes ideally parents, grandparents, brothers and sisters of parents and grandparents, and siblings and cousins. Siblings, cousins, aunts, and uncles have management and caretaking rights and duties only if they are older than the child. Spouses of uncles, aunts, siblings, and cousins have much more restrained rights and duties. They would be considered intrusive if they hit a child or scolded him severely, except under unusual circumstances.

In actuality the great majority of households in Piri are restricted to parents, siblings (both biological and adopted), and an occasional spouse and, perhaps, child of an older sibling.

2. Each person in the household with management rights and duties tends to manage all the children younger than he or she. When a child reaches adolescence there is much less management directed at him.

3. The older people in the family, particularly the mother, who has a central overseer position, do not interfere in acts of punishment initiated by junior members unless the punishment, or neglect, is considered grossly out of line. Older people will punish directly if they are the first to see a breach. But as overseers they make sure that older children are properly active about managing younger children and that the younger children accept punishment from the older ones without prolonged protest.

4. Most of the day-by-day training and caretaking interactions are between children who are close to each other in age. They play together more, and are generally more often in each other's company.

The amount of authority a small child has over a still smaller one is limited to some degree if they are in the household and older people are around. In Teri'i Tui's household Ari is as likely to report Etienne to Mari as to take direct action. When she does chastise him directly, older people in the household sometimes laugh. This is still considered partially as "playing at" authority. As children grow older they have more and more independent authority, and by eleven or so it is fairly complete. Outside the house Ari has somewhat more control over Etienne and more responsibility for him.

5. People's roles in the child management system shift depending on circumstances. In Teri'i Tui's household, when, for example, the mother and the oldest daughter are away, the second oldest daughter, Rui, takes over the mother's role of coordinator and even takes her mother's usual seat at the dining table. A more usual shift involves the younger children, who at one moment might be the recipient of orders or punishment and at the next the stern rebuker of a still younger child. This is Tara's experience in the two present examples.

6. Although, ideally, older siblings of both sexes should manage younger children, by the time boys reach ten or eleven they begin to spend most of their time out of the house with the other male adolescents in the village. They also spend time away from the house, fishing and helping with the garden work. Their sisters remain in the house until they are sixteen or older and ready to begin staying with a man. Even if they do stay with a *tāne*, they may bring him to their house. Thus at the age when children are moving into full responsibility for dealing with younger children, at ten or eleven boys are less likely than girls to be in or near the house.

7. People say that when children reach adolescence it is the mother's responsibility to manage the girls and the father's to manage the boys. But the boys need very little managing by this age in rural Society Island villages and have shifted to the male peer group for their next set of lessons about life. Although adolescent girls are exposed to more intense household supervision from their mothers and older sisters, they are interfered with less and less as they approach sixteen or seventeen.

8. The father is out of most of the management of children even when he is present in the household. He usually ignores

most of the punishing, correcting, and caretaking of children that goes on. If he interferes it is mainly when he is feeling particularly irritable.

But many mothers in the village use the father as a threat. He is someone who will really punish the children if they do not obey, but from whom the mother usually "protects" them by not telling him about their bad behavior. The father may actually be brought in by the mother if there is some particularly serious rebellion. Ordinarily, however, he does not punish, nor does he have any particularly tender, affectionate relations with the children after they pass early childhood. His tenderness for them is muted and hidden. But he backs up the mother, as she in turn backs up the younger authorities.

In summary, the household system for the management of children tends to be diffuse; children play a large part as managers of other children; many of the system's members have pivotal positions — at one moment they are the recipients of management, at another managers; and the system is sexually asymmetrical in terms of who is doing the managing.

What Is Being Learned

As children interact with others, or as people try to cope with children to bring them into some sort of basic acceptability or to teach them basic skills, children learn. They learn more than bowel control, how to clean up the yard, and how to plant taro, matters we may call first-order learning. (For a discussion of levels or orders of learning, see Bateson 1972; pp. 279-308.)

Much of the learning that is of interest for psychological organization comes from the forms and contexts in which first-order lessons are presented. These forms and contexts are influenced by caretakers' ideas and fantasies about what children are and what they should be, by qualities of the caretakers' personalities (e.g., consistency, harshness), by strategies available for dealing with children under the guidance of caretakers' conceptions about them, by the visibility and nature of other behaviors available as models for children, and by the structure of the communication network in which the child finds himself.[13]

Any attempt to understand the effect of culturally influenced learning on psychological development and organization is further complicated by the probability that the effect or meaning of any experience is dependent on what has been learned from previous experiences. In a study such as this one, where the life of children has only been glimpsed as a background for understanding adults — a method which is full of seductions to tautology — one can only present some (I hope) plausible sequences. I would suppose that some of the effects of the regularities of child experience I have indicated are as follows.

The establishment of a strong "core." Infants and young babies, who are most likely to be physically healthy and well nourished, are gestated, delivered, and cared for with little parental anxiety. They are treated with attention and indulgence, and presumably develop something which is a precursor of trust and optimism. Their core experiences and the echoes of these experiences in adult minds are strengthening ones. They will be able to endure later frustrations and corrections without fearing that they are being pushed back toward chaos or some other fearful state.

Training for latent capabilities. During the first three or four years certain behaviors are encouraged which will be discouraged later. These include exhibitionist behavior of all kinds, including playful (and even serious) aggressive and fighting behavior. These are behaviors which will be encouraged only in special contexts in adult life. The latent, but organized, system of ex-

13. Although these various aspects are closely interrelated in the learning experience of the child, in situations of social change they may change independently. Ideas, fantasies, and strategies of parents moving from a rural, traditional village to a more modern town may be similar to those of their peers and ancestors, but family membership and roles may be disturbed enough to markedly alter the psychological orientations of their children. Or new values and goals for education reaching the village adults may be skewed as attempts are made to pass them on to children through traditional strategies and communication networks.

hibitionism and aggressive competence will later prevent the pressures for conformity and gentleness from being crushing.

Pretraining for dominant tendencies. Lessons which will be repeated in various ways and in increasing force are prefigured in the first three years. Although babies are indulged, there is some early suppression of tenderness and of enveloping, infantilizing behavior such as cuddling. Babies are given kinesthetic messages of body separateness. Such messages are precursors for the development of autonomy and separateness which precedes and underlies patterns of yielding and cooperation.

Effects of early training. As caretakers cope with problems of hunger, excretion, and motility, they are permissive. The pressures for conformity with caretakers' expectations are subtle and are guided by the ideology that the child will do things when he is ready. The infant/child must get some sense that although there are pressures to conform, he will achieve what has to be achieved in his own time. The pressures to conform in early training are disguised. They consist of signals of disapproval and impatience, submerged in a general doctrine and approach of tolerance. The child will come to believe that he himself has decided to conform for his own purposes.

But at an early age the child must learn to coordinate and maneuver himself in relatively unprotected environments. This is associated with other pressures to grow away from dependence on adults. In concert they lead to an early self-sufficiency and, perhaps, to the closing of some possibilities of learning, those which depend on a more prolonged openness.

Training directed to body behaviors, as well as early teaching of skills, is by correction of mistakes. The child uses developing muscular assemblages and imitates the behavior of others. He is encouraged by being found cute. He is not often coached "positively" — "Do it this way." But his errors are corrected — "You are doing it wrong." He begins to learn that both learning and proper performance consist of scanning for and avoiding errors. Behind this is the assumption that there are natural and reliable systems into which one can fit by avoiding mistakes. The world can be depended upon to correct in a useful way. But it is annoying to be corrected. One will try to avoid corrections by doing what caretakers consider adequate. One learns to adapt to a given system by modifying one's immediate behavior to its conditions.

As the child grows older, he is taught to be cautious. He is frightened, threatened, and sometimes hit. This is done in part to make him avoid particular acts (e.g., dirtiness, protest against punishment) and partially to make the child sensitive to the disapproval of others. He is learning to be sensitive to the mobile, context-determined situation of his community, which at this stage is his household.

Effects of maternal distancing. After the child is three (or a year or two older, depending on family variables) he is old enough to learn new lessons.[14] The child is no longer "adored" much in the family. The child must begin to learn to quiet down, to "grow up," and to interact in very serious ways with other children.

What else does the child learn from this distancing? He learns, I think, as children and adults learn from the practice of adoption (chapter 14), that he will be separated from maternal closeness whatever he does, as a natural condition of life. There is no going back. He gets angry, mourns, and adjusts. He will go on with his quest for self-sufficiency. He will not believe that a great love or a great passion or a great deed will win love or salvation. He will learn to live quietly within the limits of what is given. He will also be less amenable to later threats of withdrawal of love for bad behavior.

14. John Bowlby has suggested that the third year involves a shift in a child's vital attachment behavior to maternal figures. "Since in the human child ontogeny of these systems [relating child and mother] is slow and complex, and their rate of development varies greatly from child to child, no simple statement about progress during the first year of life can be made. Once a child has entered his second year, however, and he is mobile, fairly typical attachment behavior is almost always seen. By that age in most children the integrate of behavioral systems concerned is readily activated especially by mother's departure or by anything frightening, and the stimuli that most effectively terminate the systems are sound, sight, or touch of mother. Until about the time a child reaches his third birthday the systems continue to be very readily activated" (Bowlby 1969; 1:179).

Now the child, pushed away from a close dependence on his mother or an equivalent, finds himself in a household network of management. And he learns from this too.

Diffuseness of supervision. What are the implications of the characteristics of this management system? Consider its diffuseness. Between the mother and father and the child are the other caretakers.

One cannot cope by manipulation of one or two key figures. There is always someone to correct you. One must obey, at least at the minimum level necessary to stay out of trouble. One becomes adapted to a system which cannot be changed by one's actions. And if there is no one person to manipulate, there is also no one person to blame.

John Whiting has argued that the distribution of power in the family, as it impinges on a child, influences whom the child pays closest attention to, not only as somebody to respond to and cope with, but as a model. The nature of this involvement seems to have consequences for the child's identity formation, for the ideals he holds for himself, and for the nature of his conscience.

Whiting suggests: "Cultural arrangements regarding the degree to which resource mediation ["resources" are things a child wants, including freedom from punishment] is focused on one member of the family or distributed among many, and customs regarding the differential mediation of different resources should have important effects on both the strength and content of the roles learned by identification. We would assume that where there is a high concentration of resource-control and mediation in one socialising agent, there will be a stronger and more generalised identification with that person than when resource-control is distributed among many agents" (Whiting 1960; p. 122).

Diffuseness of power control would, insofar as such theories of identification are correct, imply a diffusion of models for identification. This set of power-controlling models for a child in a typical household would be mostly female, and would include older children and young adolescents.

Even though power is relatively diffusely mediated, parents still have, ultimately, the most important power positions. But between them and their impact on a given child over a period of time is the system.

Children as managers. A child must cope with and learn from somewhat older children in contexts in which this learning is prominent and in which adults' guidance or control of the older child is relatively limited. What are the consequences of being socialized during childhood by immature members of the group?

Punishment by children for the transgression of a rule is sporadic, arbitrary, and related to mood. (This is also true to a somewhat lesser extent of punishment by adults, who were themselves raised by children.) Adults, as we have noted, are suspicious of authority, of anyone "having power over them." It is possible to see one element in such an attitude as a residue of experience with oppressive childish authorities.

Although the transmission of rules and values by children is arbitrary and mood-related, it is also based on simplified perceptions of the rules. James Ritchie, in a consideration of the implications of children's management of children among the New Zealand Maoris, believes that a certain psychological rigidity results from this:

the Maori child is typing himself against an older sibling's concept of the adult world. His perceptions of adult behaviour and adult roles are being strained through the perceptions of his older sib. The latter will only be approximately varying in their degree of conformity according to the age, sex, intelligence and experience variables of the older child. In this transmission of percepts from a child's view of the adult world to a child's view of a child's view of the world, the value structure is thrown into sharp relief. The limited comprehension of the older child requires that the values he sees around him be used in modifying the behaviour of younger children; he cannot therefore make do with a tentative approximation but must resolve his percepts into a formal structure from which he is able to direct and instruct younger children. Originality departs. The value-structure sets hard, prematurely, and the child enters onto a plateau in value-learning. (Ritchie 1956; p. 47)

The child learns something not only from being taught by other children (a learning derived from the content and form of the older child's teaching, from learning to cope with and respond to him, and from using him directly as a model for behavior), but also by having to teach and manage somewhat younger children.

Children in the middle positions in the family age structure are at one moment the recipients of management, at another the managers. Punishers not only are close to one in age, they are also punished. It would be difficult to idealize such authorities.

What is the effect of the child's having to take a socializer's role in a serious action situation, rather than only in fantasy or play as western children do? As the quotation above from Ritchie suggests, the type of early, active mastery needed for serious, minimally supervised management of other children implies some early closure and hardening of social learning.

Sexual asymmetry. A final structural aspect of the village system for managing children is that most of the managers in a household are usually women or girls. The father, although he is often physically present in the household, is related only in a vague way to most of the ordinary family socialization interactions in which preadolescent children are involved. Whiting's theory of modeling would predict that in such circumstances both boys and girls would tend to take female models for identification.

Images of parents. Behind the system of ordinary controls, parents do their own disciplining. The mother punishes disruptions of the system and anything that annoys her. "The mother and father are different [about disciplining]," reports Teiva. "The father hits [*tā'iri*] children, [as I do] myself, only through careful reflection that a child has made a mistake.... You aren't satisfied with what he did. [But] mothers, it isn't for important matters that they hit children.... The children come into the house with muddy feet, they hit. Clothes are torn somewhere, they hit. Something gets a little dirty, they hit." Mothers, he goes on, are easily irritated by disturbances, but fathers are different. They punish "when they are heavily fatigued from work or when the child has made a big mistake." The big mistake is usually a marked act of hostility or destruction, or of overt disrespect or rebellion.

And Tano, authority on proper discipline, describes his present household. "She [his *vahine*] often hits the children, I seldom." ("What makes you hit the children?") "For example, if the child argues about doing something I have forbidden him to do. If he doesn't listen to/obey words, I hit him. But hitting children, that is the responsibility of the mother. The mother manages all the children. I stay outside to oversee how things go. Ah, if the mother makes a mistake, at that time I tell her, 'Not like that but like this.' She [in contrast to Tano] hits them almost every day."

Mothers hit and yell and threaten because of "disorder," fathers for rebellion against the lower-order system of controls. But fathers, in principle, also prevent mothers from being unfairly severe, and some people remember their fathers as trying to be helpful to the children as well as reinforcing the household caretakers.

Although adults emphasize that women keep order in the household by hitting and threatening, they sometimes remember their own childhood experience in ways that indicate something of the way the order is achieved, and how it is perceived by children.

Thus, I ask Teiva if as a child he got angry when his adoptive mother hit him. "What would have been the use? Even if you were angry, there would be no way out, you would be hit anyway. You might get angry, because sometimes you hadn't made any mistake. But your reasoning wasn't accepted. There was nothing to do. You accepted. Sometimes she was easygoing. But if she were angry only she knew what made her decide to hit. I didn't know. It was *her* anger. I didn't know that she had become angry. She knew why. But I accepted. I didn't know what had made her angry." Young Teiva was learning to be cautious and, perhaps, to be generally anxious about powerful and erratic women.

Mother and the household system envelop one. One can get out and away when one is with one's friends, and for boys this escape will become emphasized in their *taure'are'a* period.[15] And because, I think, children have learned not to care too deeply about the mother or her equivalents in earlier learning, one can escape by doing what is necessary to get by without feeling that one's self is too importantly involved.

But in fears of contamination by menstrual blood, in dreams of spirit lovers turning into old women, in anxieties about vaginas, and in what I take to be compensatory and obsessive doctrines of women's similarity to men, there are suggestions that for men, at least, anxieties about women persist.

Fathers are reported sometimes as helping in household tasks, sometimes as threatened supporters of mother and siblings, sometimes as sporadic protectors, and sometimes as ineffectual. Mostly they are perceived as distant, on the periphery of things. They are not seen consciously as sources of restraint, as responsible for a child's problems, nor are they idealized or made bases for conscious (or, as far as I could determine, covert) modeling. (Although men may be remote to most ordinary household training sequences, their informal behavior is evident to children, which prevents idealization based on distance.)

In dreams and hypnoid hallucinations there are threats. But they are diffuse and disguised. Something is pursuing to punish, to hurt. But who? Why? It would not even occur to the Tahitian Oedipus to try to get to Thebes.

Redundancy

I have suggested some of the forms and regularities of the experience of children in Piri and the more traditional families of

15. Although in theory children may move to the household of a relative, and even become adopted there, this does not in fact provide a real escape from household authority, for the situation in the other household would be similar. In fact, except where an adopted child returns to his biological parents from a household in which he has been unusually mistreated, I heard of no examples of changing households. The possibility of escape is not used by children to negotiate with the household. Margaret Mead reported that in Samoa the possibility of changing households prevents children from feeling trapped. "The minute that the mildest annoyance grows up at home, the possibility of flight moderates the discipline and alleviates the child's sense of dependency" (*Coming of age in Samoa* [1928]; p. 36).

Roto which may have important consequences for the later psychological organization of adults. But these are only relatively probable experiences. There are some people who lived in two- or three-member households, or who were spoiled and indulged even after age three, or whose mothers were anxious about them as infants, or who never had to take care of smaller children. Such variations explain, I think, some of the differences between the principal subjects of this study. But for prevalent modes of behavior such as those presented here, there are many redundant influences. If a child is not affected by one shaping form, he will most likely be affected by another with a similar import.

Consider "gentleness." (1) The distancing experience produces a conviction that aggression cannot reverse frustrating situations. (2) So does the diffuseness of the socialization network. (3) There is specific training associated with aggression control. Although short, acute, "cathartic" expressions of anger are reacted to with amusement in younger children and tolerated in older ones, prolonged, severe, and reverberation-causing[16] angry behavior is strongly discouraged. (4) Punishment in general is through threats, with sporadic reinforcement through hitting. The threats seem to work, without the necessity of severe punishment. This diminishes the learning of hostile behavior by observing and mimicking aggressively acting parents.[17] Nor do parents provide aggressive models in their ordinary behavior. (5) Accidents are used and interpreted as punishment for aggressiveness. This seems to be strongly inhibiting.[18] (6) There are doctrines that

16. That is, interpersonal behavior which will not let a conflict cease after its first acute expression.

17. As Sears, Maccoby, and Levin (1957; p. 266) put it, "When the parents punish — particularly when they employ physical punishment — they are providing a living example of the use of aggression at the very moment they are trying to teach the child not to be aggressive. The child, who copies his parents in many ways, is likely to learn as much from this example of successful aggression on his parents' part as he is from the pain of punishment."

18. According to Albert Bandura, "Ordinarily the inhibiting effects of verbal threats rapidly extinguish through repeated disconfirmation, but the parents intermittently reinforce the threats by capitalizing on accidental contingencies. Impersonal agents rather than parents are the aggressors. Since they are omnipresent, fear of punishment by impersonal agents is

serious aggressive behavior will bring magical retaliation. Whatever one's other psychological orientations, one would be careful about being aggressive, as one would be about drinking a
bottle marked poison. (7) To show violent and prolonged anger
is a shame-producing sign of lack of control, which reflects on
one's general competence.

Such a set of convergent influences insures that most people
will be, or at least will act, reasonably gentle for one reason or
another. I imagine that such redundancies of control are a necessary feature of most culturally determined behavior.

Taure'are'a

"The *taure'are'a* period," says Oro, "is the happiest time. . . . In
my childhood, one was hit. You went to school and were mischievous and you were hit. You returned to the house and you
were ordered to do things. If you didn't go [and do them] you
were hit. Now, no. It is you alone."

And Poria, asked if his childhood was a good period. "No. In
my childhood there were many commands. . . . The parents
would order you to do this and that, and if you didn't obey you
were hit. Therefore it wasn't very happy. . . . Children, people
can command you, 'Fetch this. Fetch that.' If you don't go and
fetch it, you are hit. And other children come and disturb you;
and if he is angry he hits you. It's not happy. All the time one
cries. . . . Those people, those children, hit you, because you are
very small. . . ." ("And when you get to be a *taure'are'a*?") "You
are strong. He can't come and hit you, because you are a *taure-
'are'a*." ("And the orders?") ". . . they can't keep ordering you
about. If they order you around you say, 'Go fetch it yourself.'"

Poria's bravado is probably exaggerated in retrospect, but it
indicates, as did all the men's interviews, that the *taure'are'a*
period was, in part, an escape from childhood and from the
household.

---

likely to produce generalized inhibition, whereas punishment by socialization agents tends to establish specific inhibitory effects and often only in
the presence of the punitive agent" (personal communication, 1966).

Having learned to be docile as children, to have the proper amount of timidity, to avoid trouble, boys must now learn some extra lessons. They have to learn some daring. Boys separate from the household and first sit and listen to the older boys' songs and tales of derring-do. They become supercised, with its messages of freeing the bound penis, of overcoming dangers, and of passing into a new, larger relationship to the world in which there is still, but at a new level, safety, healing, and solidarity. One may now be sexually aggressive with girls, have adventures, steal for thrills, boast, travel to other villages. One can expand to a new set of limits.

Parents will indulge *taure'are'a* boys' behavior, older men will exaggerate their exploits in fantasy, and fathers will be secretly proud of their violation of proprieties. The boys have learned their earlier lessons well, and to an outsider they still seem polite and very well behaved. But by the standards of the village they are living their free, their wild years. When, having learned the necessary lessons of the period, they settle into the constraints of adulthood, their memories of the *taure'are'a* period will be an important consolation.[19]

When they are ready, people choose to become grown up, *pa'āri*. They will still be taught. But now the burden of the message will be on maintenance, rather than on growth. I will consider something of this in the next chapter.

19. The activities of the male *taure'are'a* have many parallels with an interesting organization in pre-Christian Tahiti called the *'arioi*, whose members were characterized by Morrison as a "set of young men of wild, amorous and volatile dispositions who from their infancy devote the youthful part of their lives to roving, pleasure and debauchery" (1935; p. 234). They seemed to represent in some ways a privileged, institutionalized "antistructure," which violated many of the tabus and proprieties of old Tahiti. According to Henri Lavondes (1968), the Marquesan term for *taure'are'a* is *ka'ioi*, and is derived from the Tahitian *'arioi*.

14

The Question of Maintenance

*It would seem . . . that not only are there critical problems of
the development of adequate models of the environment and
adequate coping strategies, but that there are also maintenance
problems of an order of delicacy that were not even imagined
before the pioneering experiments of Hebb and his associates at
McGill. . . . What is this maintenance problem? I would like to
suggest that it perhaps relates to a kind of continuing feedback-
evaluation process by which organisms guide their correction
strategies in perceiving, cognizing, and manipulating their
environments* (Bruner 1961; pp. 204-5).

*I suggest that the delimitation of an individual mind must always
depend upon what phenomena we wish to understand or explain.
Obviously there are lots of message pathways outside the skin,
and these and the messages which they carry must be included
as part of the mental system whenever they are relevant* (Bateson 1972; p. 458).

We are accustomed to thinking about sociocultural forms influencing the ontogenesis of individual psychological organization,
of conscience and cognition mediating between personal and
public worlds, and of individuals using cultural resources to pro-
mote their peace of mind.

But we tend, perhaps, to make a priori and covert assumptions
as we parse behavior into inside-the-skin and outside-the-skin
processes,[1] into "personality" and "culture," concerning the nature of the boundaries and transactions of the two systems.

1. "'Inner' and 'outer' are ever present distinctions, however camou-
flaged, in philosophical procedure as well as in conventional speech-forms
and in the traditional terminology of psychology. What holds 'inner' and

I have already commented on features of conscience and thinking which are presumably related to membership in a small, unified "communication system" such as Piri. Suppose that other aspects of "psychodynamic organization," of "personality" are in some ways more immediately and openly involved with environing sociocultural forms than may be the situation for people in complex urban settings. Would the import of "personality" and of "culture" be different in the two kinds of setting?

We assume that babies and children are open to the sociocultural forms about them in ways which affect their psychological growth. If adults are open in similar ways, we may, if we are emphasizing the individual, follow Bruner and wonder about sociocultural systems and their "maintenance" effects; or, if we are interested in "mind" in Bateson's sense, we may ask if the elementary units of mind tend to differ to some degree in the locus of the circuits in which "ideas" exist. (For Bateson, "The elementary cybernetic system with its messages in circuit is, in fact, the simplest unit of mind; and the transform of a difference traveling in a circuit is the elementary idea" [Bateson 1972; p. 459].)

It may be that in traditional communities a relatively few, but compelling, institutions focus and condense important maintenance information. Perhaps this was the case, for example, for the forms and tabus involved with eating in pre-Christian Tahiti, and of the series of rites of passage.

I propose, with some tentativeness in spite of the declarative prose, to consider two striking cultural forms in Piri and Roto as possible maintenance systems.

The Māhū

I have discussed the *māhū*, homosexuality, and the question of sexual identity in earlier chapters. I suggested that there seems to be, compared with western expectations, relatively less sexual

---

'outer' apart? . . . Bluntly the separator is skin; no other appears. . . . Psyches, minds, personalities, all belong in this class; skin is what holds them 'in'" (Bentley 1941).

differentiation, and I indicated in the last chapter some possible factors associated with this in children's development.

Whereas the development of girls' sexual identity may be simpler, because of the continuity of their adult roles and the household models to which they are exposed, boys seem to have to go through some extra steps to establish that aspect of their sexual identity which is based on contrast and complementarity to women.

The various meanings of the supercision event, part of the boys' passage from childhood to the larger community, are focused on the penis. The head of the penis is freed. Boys' independence from childhood becomes associated with their masculinity. But now the boys will enter a time of erotically tinged solidarity with other boys. And in turn they will have to free themselves from one another and, with some hesitation and regret, establish families.

It is, it may be recalled, a common supposition in Piri that there is at least one *māhū* and only one *māhū* in all villages. "When one dies then another substitutes. . . . God arranges it like this. It isn't allowed [that there should be] two *māhū* in one place." From the inquiries I made about the other villages on Huahine, although there were periods without a *māhū*, as there had been in Piri itself, and occasional brief periods when there were two, the supposition of "at least one, and no more than one to a community" seemed to report an actual tendency. All but one of the villages on Huahine reportedly had one *māhū* at the time of my study. The *māhū* appears to be a village role like the *tāvana* or the Protestant pastor.

Let us recall some aspects of the role and the community response to it. (1) It is said to be exclusive. (2) There is some compulsion about filling it. (3) Its essential defining characteristic is "doing woman's work," that is, a role reversal which is *publicly demonstrated* — either through clothes or through other public aspects of woman's role playing. Most villagers approve of, and are pleased by, the role reversal. But homosexual behavior is a covert part of the role, and it is disapproved by many villagers. Some villagers, in fact, believe that *māhū* do not generally engage in homosexual intercourse. (4) Several other men in Piri who are quite effeminate establish ordinary-seeming households. They may be described as *huru māhū*, "*māhū*ish," but they are not *māhū*. (5) Men who have sexual relations with the *māhū*, as did Oro, do not consider themselves abnormal. Villagers who know of such activities may disapprove, but they do not label the partners as unmanly. The *māhū* is considered as a substitute woman for the partner. (6) No one in Piri knows of *mā'ohi* men engaging in homosexual intercourse unless one of them is a *māhū*. (7) A new word, *raerae*, which reportedly originated in Papeete, is used by some to designate nontraditional types of homosexual behavior.

I would propose that in the relative absence of internalized structures organizing masculine identity, in the sense of contrast of manhood to womanhood, there have been developed various external forms which help clarify masculine definition. Thus it may be that the *māhū* role, with its clear-cut rules, its high visibility, its limited incumbency, and its preempting of homosexual behavior, carries essential information — is part of men's minds. It states, "There, clearly out in the open, is the *māhū*, the one man who has taken a female role. I am a non*māhū*. Whatever feelings I have about men and about being a man are no threat to me and to my eventual role as family head. I can see exactly what *he* is, and I am clear about myself in that I am not he."[2]

Adoption

I did not discuss adoption in the chapter on growing up, because I suspect that when considered in terms of its psychological import it has more to do with adults than with children.

Adoption in Piri is a frequent practice. In November 1962, Piri had 284 persons living in 54 households. There were 42 children living in households other than those of their biological

2. George Devereux, in an article on institutionalized homosexuality of the Mohave Indians, suggested that one of the functions of the practice was to create "an 'abscess of fixation' and [to localize] the disorder in a small area of the body social" (Devereux 1937; p. 520).

parents. Thirty-four of these children were identified by others in the household as *fa'a'amu*,[3] adopted, children. Three of the 42 were grandchildren with neither parent living in the household. Five were borderline cases, children who were living in the household for indefinite periods, but who were identified as a relative's child, rather than as a *fa'a'amu* child.

The oldest individual identified as a *fa'a'amu* child in a household was nineteen years old. There were, in all, 166 individuals nineteen years old or younger living as children in households. Thus 25 percent of this group in Piri did not live in the household of a biological parent.

The forty-two children lived in twenty-five households. One household had four, four had three, five had two, and the remaining sixteen households each had one child who was not biologically related. Of the twenty-nine households which did not have adopted children, some had had them in the past, and many had given children for adoption by other households. Thus the majority of households in Piri have been involved in adoption in one way or another.

According to studies by Paul Kay, 25 percent of the children in Roto in 1960 were adopted.[4]

3. *Fa'a'amu* means "to feed." It may be noted, as an apparent exception to the usual Polynesian metaphor of "feeding" for adoption, that the Davies missionary dictionary of terms collected in the 1830s also lists the now obsolete *fa'atāvai*, "to adopt another's child," which is derived from *tāvai*, "to tend, to look after, to look out for."

4. Kay studied Roto and one other community on the island of Tahiti. Both had adoption rates of about 25 percent. It is of interest to compare some reports on the frequency of adoption elsewhere in Polynesia and Micronesia. Early ethnographic statements about Polynesian and Micronesian adoption do not give exact frequencies, and often not even impressionistic ones. The lowest frequencies reported in early literature are for Futuna and Tikopia, both of which had elaborate norms and rules for adoption. Edwin Burrows, in a four-month stay in Futuna, wrote, "In spite of the various ways in which adoption may take place, it is not very frequent. In a census of two villages involving 474 individuals, only one was specifically labeled as an adopted child" (Burrows 1936; p. 60). Raymond Firth for Tikopia found 18 cases of "adhering children" and some borderline cases among 587 children and adolescents in a population of 1,281 persons divided into 218 households (Firth 1936; p. 204).

Adoption is an important practice throughout Polynesia and Micronesia. (For various data and approaches to the problem, see Carroll [1970].) As Robert Lowie remarked, "In some regions of the globe . . . adoption is practised on a scale wholly disproportionate to any rational grounds therefor. . . . Oceania as a whole represents a main center for adoption carried to unusual lengths" (Lowie 1962; p. 460).

Anthropologists have tried to provide "rational grounds" for the practice. Let us review some of them. In an early review of Polynesian adoption Raymond Firth wrote: "It is obvious that the custom is common in practically every Polynesian community and that the adoption most frequently practiced is that of kinsfolk. But within this general pattern there are many variations. I think it could be shown, if material were available, that such variations are not merely haphazard but each fits into the institutional configuration of the particular society" (Firth 1936; pp. 594-95).

A few years later Ernest Beaglehole summarized the usages of adoption in Polynesia: "Adoption was . . . a common practice in Polynesia, sometimes for the purpose of securing an heir, sometimes to cement an alliance between two lineages, sometimes to adjust matters of property-inheritance or to secure a share of a limited food supply; and at all times, probably because

---

Alan Howard found that 22 percent of Rotuman households in Fiji and 23 percent in Rotuma had adopted children. Twelve percent of all children in Rotuma were adopted, as were 13 percent of the Rotuman children living in Fiji. These figures refer to a child's status at the time of the census. Cumulative adoption rates are higher (Howard 1970; pp. 353-54).

J. E. Weckler, on the basis of genealogies, concluded that nearly one-third of all the children born on Mokil since 1775 had been adopted (Weckler 1953; p. 556).

Bengt Danielsson found that 40 percent of the children on Raroia in the Tuamotus were adopted. Danielsson enumerates both the number of adopting households and the number of donating households. Out of thirty-five households and subhouseholds (relatively distinct nuclear units in a household), eighteen had adopted children and twelve had donated children. Four households had both given and taken children, so that twenty-six of the thirty-five households in Raroia had been directly involved in adoption (Danielsson 1956b; p. 218).

Reports of frequencies for other communities are given in Carroll (1970).

children were always welcome in a Polynesian household that knew not the terrors of family budgets, the slavery of a standard of living, nor the slow disintegration of unemployment and starvation" (Beaglehole 1940; p. 54).

Similar factors have been emphasized in later work. Bengt Danielsson, for example, considering the very frequent adoption in Raroia in the Tuamotu Archipelago, stresses economic functions. The static economy "naturally makes it difficult for parents with many children to provide for them, and the natural way out is to give them away to couples with few children and plenty of land. On the other hand childless couples are pleased to adopt other people's children . . . since . . . the older generations are dependent on the younger. . . . Adoption is the Raroians' special form of life insurance" (Danielsson 1956*b*; p. 219).

Bernd Lambert, in an article on adoption in the Gilbert Islands in Micronesia, stresses kin bonds: "The majority of fosterage relationships grow out of long-standing friendships between the natural parents and the future foster-grandparents. . . . Fosterage is a means of transforming the tenuous link that ordinarily connects distant kinsmen into a far stronger and more significant one" (Lambert 1964; p. 238).

J. E. Weckler (1953), writing about adoption on Mokil in the Eastern Caroline Islands of Micronesia, suggests various motives. These include ideals of completed nuclear family membership ("without concern for and sometimes contrary to the adoptor's personal economic advantage" [p. 577]); the formation of bonds with unrelated people on or from other islands; the manipulation of land and the hope of economic gain for the child or for its patrilineal extended family.

There are instances in which the adoptors are seeking "social security" from the services of the child. But Weckler suggests that such emphases on economic uses of adoption in Mokil are recent and are due to economic acculturation. "Ancient cultural ideals and expectations still motivate people to participate in adoptions. But the economic facts of life on Mokil today often counteract traditional values. There is more jockeying for advantage by participants, and more concern about the economic aspects of adoption, than there used to be" (Weckler 1953; p. 567).

Adoption persists in some quite modernized Polynesian communities long after political, social, or economic uses of the types described for more traditional communities seem relevant. In studies of suburban Hawaiian "homestead" communities on Oahu, it has been found that adoption is prevalent. In the four Hawaiian communities studied, the percentages of households with adopted children were 32.5, 19.1, 31.6, and 25.5. The community with the lowest rate was a relatively newly established community with demographic peculiarities (Howard et al. 1970; p. 31). Howard and his associates ask, "Why, among a people whose culture seems to have been otherwise completely shattered, has the prevalence of adoption so dramatically survived? . . . Our evidence strongly suggests that most adoptions occur in spite of economic considerations rather than because of them." They suggest that "the answer appears to lie in the continued significance of nurturance as a motivational force among Hawaiians" (Howard et al. 1970; p. 46). They continue, "The act of adopting combines personal gratification with social reward in a compelling fashion for most Hawaiians" (p. 50).

Adoption, then, exists in a great variety of Micronesian and Polynesian settings, and persists in the face of marked political and socioeconomic changes. It serves, or has been thought to serve, a variety of functions.

Let us take another look at adoption in Piri. Children in Piri are transferred in two situations. First are those cases where the main pressure for transfer is the biological parents', usually the mother's, wish to give the child away. Second are those cases where the impetus comes from the adopting parents' wish to take the child. Many cases involve some combination of these two. Rarely, a mother who wishes to give a child away may have some temporary trouble placing him. This may be resolved by "temporarily" leaving a baby with a relative in another village and never taking it back. (The five "borderline" cases in Piri may be cases of this kind.) A more frequent asymmetry involves those transfers where the child is taken against the parents', again usually the mother's, will. This is the situation where, as Raymond Firth described it for Tikopia, "some member of the wider group of relatives . . . bears off a child from the married pair and brings it up in his own household" (Firth 1936; p. 204).

The expressed motives for giving children away are unambiguous. Mothers wish to give away children if they are still in the period of *taure'are'a* experimental and shifting sexual relations; if they do not want to settle down with the father of the child; if they are in an early *fa'aea* relationship but do not wish to become committed to it; if they have been in a more permanent relationship, which may include previous children, but at the time of the birth of the new child have had an argument with the father or have separated from him.

The expressed motives for seeking a *fa'a'amu* child (which should be distinguished from accepting a child that someone else wants to give) are not as clear, or as clearly articulated, by people in the village. Common explanations given are, "They liked the parents of the child, and therefore wanted to have one of their children"; "they did not have any children of their own"; "their children were growing up, and they wanted a new baby in the house." The latter explanations were supported by the household census. In twenty-two of the twenty-five households with adopted children in Piri, the adopted children were either the only children living in the household at the time (thirteen households) or the youngest child or children (nine households).

It is frequently said (particularly by men) that it is not difficult or particularly troubling for a biological mother (in those cases where she has not initiated the adoption) to give up a child. But some women, Pua for example, who have given up children express some cautious resentment and tell of ineffectual attempts to hold onto the child. Sometimes the demanding couple have to repeat their request over a period of months. But, if they are adamant enough, in time the mother yields. The common statement is, "So and so asked me for the baby. I gave it. I don't think about it anymore." As Homer Barnett writes for Palau, "Parents are expected . . . to take the changes of status [of their children given for adoption] as a matter of course. This is the ideal attitude and the one which is normally in evidence. There are, however, suggestions that although people acquiesce to the demands of custom, they are not always happy about it. These contrary sentiments are never overtly expressed except in individual cases and in unguarded moments" (Barnett 1960; p. 55).

The exchange is usually arranged during the mother's pregnancy. If the mother dies in childbirth or is ill, the infant is transferred at birth. Otherwise, infants are given either after they are five or six days old ("strong enough to leave the mother"), or sometimes after five or six months ("when they can be taken away from the breast").

Most statements about the relative treatment of adopted and biological children stress equality of treatment. As the schoolteacher, Tivini, put it, "After all, they took the children because they wanted them and because they love children." The great majority of adoptions are among *feti'i*. It is said that in the rare cases in which the adopted child is not a relative it might be more likely to be mistreated.

Village observation shows no gross differences in parents' treatment of adopted and biological children. There are probably some subtle differences. Thus biological children sometimes confront the adopted child with its special position. Veve Vahine, talking about her childhood, says, "We had an adopted child in our house then. She was older than I. My father loved her very much. When we would fight and she would say, 'I'll beat you up,' I'd say, 'Oh yes? Does this father belong to you?' . . . It made me angry; my father really loved her." She laughs in recounting this. But people seem to treat biological and *fa'a'amu* children very much alike.

A frequently reported aspect of Polynesian and Micronesian adoption is that it is not a complete transfer. The child has various residual relationships to his biological family. In the Tokelaus "in the simple village life, where the children roamed in and out of every house, the separation from parents was not absolute. A child always knew who his true parents were and understood his relationship to his foster parents" (Macgregor

1937; p. 38). In Palau "adopted children always know who their real parents are, for there is no effort made to conceal this fact from them. Indeed, concealment would not be feasible because the real father retains the privilege of using the patrimony of his children that comes from their foster father" (Barnett 1960; p. 54). Firth sums up for Polynesia, "Actual severance is usually fairly complete as far as residence is concerned, but a number of social contacts are usually maintained with the true parents" (Firth 1936; p. 595).

In Piri there are various degrees of transfer in the foster relationship. In some cases the biological parents are particularly cool toward a child they have given for adoption when they have casual contacts with it. Such a child is relatively cut off from his biological parents, although in some cases after the death of the adoptive parents the child will return to them. In the majority of cases where the biological parents live in the same village or one nearby, the child maintains contact with them. In some cases the child occasionally moves back and forth between the two families; but this is very rare. When a child is given for adoption, the biological parents theoretically relinquish their rights of control or influence over the child. But if the child is badly mistreated by the adoptive parents, the biological parents may try to take it back.

There are no discernible differences in the village status, in behavior, or in psychological characteristics as revealed in life history interviews between adults who had been adopted as children and those who had not. Adoption does not have any obvious differentiating effects.

In an article on adoption on Mokil, J. E. Weckler argues, "The adoption of children is a major means by which adults can alter the membership of that basic social unit, the elementary family. We may consequently expect that, where adoption is frequently resorted to, it will have important effects on the structure of the society and on the personality dynamics of the people involved" (Weckler 1953; p. 555). But who might it affect, and how? There do not seem to be socially important specific effects on the adopted individual.

The question of the locus of the effect of the practice of adoption arises in relation to Firth's treatment of "the adhering child," the *tama fakapiki*, in Tikopia:

This institution of the *tama fakapiki* has the effect of providing a child in a house where otherwise there is none to help in the work, but the natives do not always regard it primarily as a device for assisting barren couples or increasing the household strength. This is shown by the fact that though a man's eldest child is often taken by his younger brother who has as yet no offspring of his own, in other cases the child is added to an already existing set. It has no inferiority in the family to the real children. . . . [The practice is] a mark of respect to it and its parents. [If a man is generous] his children are sought by his kinfolk. At the back of this is the idea, quite clearly expressed in frequent statements to me by natives, that it is bad for a child to adhere only to its parents; it belongs to the larger group, the *kano a paito*, and must stand in an equal relation to all therein. . . .

Two mechanisms are employed to part the child from its parents. . . . The child may be severed from the household of its father and mother at an early age and attached to another; failing this, or supplemented by this, its interest is attracted by other members of its family circle who thus seduce its budding affections. The parents, it may be noted, regard this with approval. . . .

The basic social motive in this is to preserve as far as possible uniformity of conduct and attitudes within the larger social group and not allow the bonds of the individual family to become so strong as to threaten the wider harmony. This idea is put in practical form by the Tikopia in such statements as that it is bad for the child to be attached to its parents alone, since when they are away from the house — in the cultivations or out on the reef — it cries and will not be comforted by anyone else. This is a nuisance to the relatives, and to the parents themselves, who are always liable to be disturbed at their work or rest. They approve then that the child shall undergo a *social weaning* [original italics] as well as a physiological one. (Firth 1936; pp. 205-6)

Firth only found 18 cases of "adhering children" and some borderline cases among 587 children and adolescents. If the im-

portance of the practice for "not allowing the bonds of the individual family to become so strong as to threaten the wider
harmony" had been limited to the families involved, or to the
children directly involved, it would have been quite limited.

The Message of Adoption

Tāvana has been talking about his adoptive mother and her
methods of discipline. I ask him if he got angry with her when
she punished him. "I never got angry at her, even if she whipped
me, because I was aware that she had taken me. She took me.
So I thought I was the one who was at fault, that is why she hit
me. I wasn't angry at her." ("Explain that to me. . . .") "She
took me in my infancy . . . —" ("And, therefore . . .") "Therefore, I loved her although she may have been wrong in punishing
me. . . . I didn't get upset. I didn't get angry at her, because she
took me from my infancy and kept me. So, I thought, it wasn't
right to be angry with her." (". . . Suppose she had been your
biological mother, would that have been different? Is one more
grateful to an adoptive mother than to a biological mother?")
"There are two different situations. If you are not adopted, you
are grateful to your biological mother, because she gave birth
to you. On the other hand, when you are taken in your infancy
by somebody, it isn't worthwhile to think anymore about your
mother. The woman who took you is just the same as your biological mother. Your gratitude is great because you were an infant, and you were taken."

Teiva has a similar comment: "I'm not like some children,
when they are grown up they reject their parents . . . because I
came to realize if it weren't for her, who would have taken me
in my infancy?"

Biological parentage does not imply a fixed commitment.
There is a complex decision to be made by parents and relatives.

Tāvana remarks that children who are not given for adoption
are, or should be, grateful to their mother because she had given
birth to them. The covert formula may be assumed to be "she
gave birth to me, *and* she kept me." It seems that if there are a
number of adopted children in a community, particularly if

these seem to a village observer to have been transferred more or less randomly, then a social reality may be created which implies that children are kept by their parents not because of the natural, given order of things, but because (1) the parents happen to wish to and (2) they are allowed to by others in the community. That is, *all* parent/children relationships will tend to be seen as contingent on choices, as not categorically necessary consequences of biological parenthood.

It is useful to contrast some features of modern European and American adoption with the Polynesian and Micronesian cases. Distinctive features are associated with nonrelative adoption, which, for the United States, represents about 50 percent of adoptions. Adoption by "relatives" usually involves a stepparent in remarriages or, presumably, close relatives where one or both parents have died or become incapacitated (American Academy of Pediatrics 1959; p. 2).

According to H. David Kirk, "Considering the total stream of family behavior, the phenomenon of adoption is indeed numerically rather insignificant. The best available evidence suggests that about 2.5 percent of the child population of the United States is adopted" (Kirk 1964; pp. 1-2). As the Fischers noted in an American village study, "Adoption is a very rare phenomenon in North Village. It happened once during our year of residence, and no other cases were recorded by us. Legal adoption, however, is such a long and difficult process that it is only undertaken by those who are truly desperate to have children" (Fischer and Fischer 1963; p. 889).

As Kirk has stated, "In modern industrial societies, adoption is practiced as an emergency measure. Courts and agencies generally take the view that the original family relationship should be preserved for the child whenever possible. The practice is thus encircled by protective steps that signify the official reluctance to tamper with bonds of consanguinity" (Kirk 1964; p. 1).

In a United Nations study on the adoption of children in various western nations, one finds the statement, "Involving as it does a breaking of the ties which bind a child to his natural parents and substituting new ties with the adoptive parents, adoption has been deeply influenced in law and in practice by the more or less sacred character attributed to family bonds by society" (United Nations, Department of Social Affairs 1953; p. 9).

Consonant with the "sacred character" of the family bonds is an emphasis on secrecy of transfer: "Although all adoption workers are convinced of the necessity that the child himself should know he is adopted, it is also his right, as well as that of his natural and adoptive parents, that the adoption should not be advertised through public proceedings, but heard in camera, and that the records should be treated as strictly confidential. Such safeguards enable the child to be more closely identified with the adoptive family" (United Nations, Department of Social Affairs 1953; p. 24). The ideal of secrecy was limited by the requirement in every country in the United Nations study that incest between the child and a member of its biological family be avoided.

Ideals of western adoption, then, as reflected in these reports, are that it should be limited and relatively secret, and that it should involve a complete transfer (limited by incest rules) from one family to another.

According to a World Health Organization study, "The object in adoption is to establish between the adopting parents and the child relationships which coincide as nearly as possible with those between parents and natural children" (World Health Organization 1953; p. 4).

One may invert this and argue that an object of Polynesian and Micronesian adoption is to establish between parents and *natural* children relationships which coincide as nearly as possible with those between parents and adopted children.

Let us contrast Polynesian and Micronesian adoption and western adoption in terms of *form*, of the *meaning* or *message* contained in the form, and in terms of the *psychological implications* that may be supposed to follow from the impact of the message.

In *form*, Polynesian and Micronesian adoption is relatively frequent, public, and casual and involves only partial transfer of the adopted child to the new family. Western adoption is relatively infrequent, private, and formal and involves an almost complete transfer, limited in principle only by incest considerations.

The *message* in Polynesian and Micronesian adoption is "relationships between parents and children are fragile and conditional." The form of western adoption mutes the impact of the breaking of the biological relationship from community awareness and thus negatively, but actively, protects the essential western orientation that "relationships between parents and children are categorical."

What *implications* may follow from statements about the fixity of the parent/child, and more particularly the mother/child, bond? They may well be the familiar themes of Piri and Roto — there is nothing that belongs to you by right, so don't swagger, demand, or protest. But this granted, we will now determine the conditions under which whatever you need will be provided. People who give up children can later take others. Children lose one parent, but gain another.

The implications of western adoption seem to be for quests and passions, most clearly portrayed in romantic symbols, seeking to transcend the limits and restrictions of the larger community.

It is plausible that the nature of the parent/child bond is one of the most powerful statements available to members of a group as to the nature and possibilities of person/other (including nonhuman objects) bonds. It is hard to imagine a more potent way of delivering the message that there is no relationship which is not conditional (the community will explain the conditions) than Polynesian and Micronesian adoption.

The impact of this message is on adults and older children. When they are tempted to hold on, to become inflated, or ambitious, or disorganizingly innovative, it reminds them of where the power really lies. Westerners have a haunting feeling that it is, or should be, otherwise.

Foci of Control

The *māhū*, adoption, and supercision are three dramatic themes which stand with some visibility against the everyday flow of

life in Piri and *mā'ohi* Roto. Supercision makes its detailed statement to a small group of boys[5] — the *māhū* and adoption, I have
argued, to the community at large.

The *māhū*, the argument goes, helps stabilize men's identities
by contrast and negation. As the kinds of communication which
are involved are analogical, and as analogical language can express the negative only by expressing the feature to be negated
in a positive form and indicating by the context that the positive
form does not apply,[6] the *māhū* is grammatically necessary.

In the case of adoption the analogical forms serve as affirma-
tions and rehearsals of conflicted[7] or otherwise unstable major
orientations. The main form of the message is congruent with
the personal orientation it supports.

We know that any cultural form comes to serve a variety of
purposes; the discussion of Micronesian and Polynesian adoption
illustrates this. But some cultural forms may come to serve as
essential foci of psychocultural control, whatever other purposes they may serve. When the *māhū* becomes the *raerae*, when
supercision becomes circumcision done by a doctor or the village nurse, when Polynesian adoption becomes inverted into
western adoption, we have a structural transformation of Tahitian psychocultural organization into something new.

5. The larger community knows that "something has happened," they
have the simple "digital" statement that there has been a change of status.
The boys involved are receiving complex symbolic messages.
6. "All such [analogical] communication [in animals] is necessarily positive. To show the fangs is to mention combat, and to mention combat is to
propose it. There can be no simple iconic representation of a negative: no
simple way for an animal to say 'I will not bite you.' It is easy, however, to
imagine ways of communicating negative commands if (and *only* [original
italics] if) the other organism will first propose the pattern of action which
is to be forbidden" (Bateson 1972; p. 424).
7. That is, sharing and casual orientations require the suppression and
overcoming of evident tendencies to hold on, to be selfish, to set oneself
against the community.

15

Aspects of Personal Organization

There lives the dearest freshness deep down things.
Gerard Manley Hopkins, *God's Grandeur*

The behavior of each person in Piri and Roto is shaped by his participation in the structured environment in which he finds himself. But he does not simply respond in some generalized human manner to that environment; he brings to it qualities of psychological organization which influence his response.

Throughout this book I have discussed aspects of identity, of conscience, of thought, of emotion, and of meanings derived from prevalent childhood experiences, which seem to be characteristic of my informants and of many other people in the two communities. If we think of these psychological matters in relation to a particular individual we may consider them as "elements," as "traits," organized in some larger patterning, a patterning which in itself has some explanatory force for a person's actions.

But when we consider this most general psychological organization a specter arises, the idea of "personality."

" 'Personality,' " Ernest Hilgard reminds us, "is one of the most difficult concepts in psychology." He chooses to have the term mean "the configuration of individual characteristics and ways of behaving which determines an individual's unique adjustments to his environment." "The term 'personality,' " he continues, "is thus a very inclusive one. It is saved from being synonymous with all of psychology, because its reference is to the single individual and to the unique organization of the traits that characterize him and his activities" (Hilgard 1962; p. 447).

The difficulties of the concept are greatly compounded when it is used in anthropological analysis, for now it must be brought into juxtaposition with the equally problematic idea of "culture." In anthropological contexts "personality" is sometimes used in some sense akin to Hilgard's "configuration of individual characteristics," but it is also used sometimes as a *residual* concept, to explain behaviors, or aspects of behaviors, which are not explained by "culture." In this usage, rather different from the first, various attempts may be made to distinguish psychological elements which are more immediately and directly related to cultural forms and which may be trivial in regard to the organization of personality (e.g., the public aspects of the semantics of "chair" as known to a given individual) from psychological elements which are more distantly and convolutedly related to cultural forms (e.g., the shared covert meanings of a ritual symbol) or which, even if directly related to a cultural form, have importance for personal organization (e.g., culturally given classification of feeling states).

One attempt to combine the ideas of "the configuration of individual characteristics" and "psychological aspects which are not directly equivalent to 'culture'" into one model is to consider a "peripheral personality," a set of learned roles and of orientations which are the immediate internal representation of culture, versus a somehow more personally significant "central" aspect of personality. This central aspect of personality is supposed to be largely a matter of "motives" which are "deep, inner, hidden, basic, central, genotypic, resistant to change, and originating early in the life of the individual" (N. Sanford, quoted by Kaplan 1968; p. 334). Kaplan adds, "We might suggest that the 'orientation' aspects of personality may be characterized as peripheral while the 'motivational' aspects are central."

This approach, and related ones which restrict "personality" to "central" aspects, found support in the assumptions of early psychoanalytic theory. The first people studied in psychoanalysis were people who tended to have a maximal separation of public and private worlds in their personal organization, and they were people for whom infantile motives were of considerable force (and explanatory usefulness) in adult life.

There are two different questions about "central motives," so conceived, and about understandings derived from infantile experience and from the biological aspects of personality development. The first is how such motives and understandings color, tone, and shape later learning and behavior. Second, having located such influences, we must determine what explanatory *force* they have for the interpretation of adults' behavior or experience.

These are empirical questions. One can conceive of a spectrum of individuals — ranging from those for whom infantile experiences simply give some symbolic resonance to later organization to those for whom the residues of early experience provide dominating motivational pressures and bases for interpretation of a variety of situations.

Most of the people of Piri and Roto are not "neurotic." Early experiences, as I have argued in previous chapters, strongly shape later development and animate a vocabulary of symbols. But the effects of these earlier experiences are integrated, modified, and sometimes amplified by later forms. They tend to disappear into the larger fabric, as does the precursor of an organ in a successful embryo.

My essential question about personal psychological traits and about personal organization has been a limited one: What, if anything, do people bring to the repeated and ongoing situations in Piri and Roto by virtue of the *commonalities* of their private experience *as Tahitians* which influences the meaning of the situations for them and the action they make take?

Such a question does not consider "the unique organization of traits" characterizing an individual. Manu, Hiro, Poria, Pua, and the others are individuals and have unique personalities in Hilgard's sense. I have suggested that they share a variety of psychological features. The final question here is whether they have any shared qualities of more general psychological organization by virtue of being *mā'ohi* Tahitians.

Most of the traits I have considered are directly involved with mediations between people and the sociocultural situation. Features of general organization are more remotely involved. One might expect less tendency for uniformity in the details of these more remote features.

Psychoanalytic theory has provided us with constructs for making very elegant personality models. When I began my study I hoped that I would be able to organize my most general understanding of private internal organization by means of such constructs. Unfortunately, elegant psychodynamic models may be constructed from little data or, more properly, from masses of observations generated by prolonged, classical, and closely studied psychoanalytic dialogues.

Note that there are bits and pieces of many kinds in the behaviors, fantasies, pathologies, and so forth of the people of Piri and Roto. There are examples of a variety of defense mechanisms and conflicts, and indications of a wide spectrum of unconscious, infantile themes. One can, if one is so minded, take these fragments and present them as clues for one or another model of psychodynamic organization.

But these fragments are, more or less, human universals. To select out of the mass those behaviors which seem most plausibly and systematically related to the special and shared aspects of personality of the people of Piri and Roto requires some methodological restraint.

It would be valuable to work with a sufficient number of Tahitians over a sufficient number of months or years, meanwhile keeping one's own idiosyncratic personality sufficiently hidden, to approximate something like a western psychoanalytic situation. It seems unlikely that it could be done, since most of the understandings and situations which incline westerners to play this particular game seem lacking in the rural Tahitian world. But if one could, one would learn much more of the unique aspects of the personality of various Tahitians and of the ways in which such unique aspects, as well as panhuman aspects of personality, are related to public life. And one would be able to justify more detailed models of shared personality.

In previous chapters I have described subaspects of organization — aspects of conscience, of thought, and of meanings and constraints derived from childhood experience. Here, restricting myself to fairly ordinary language, I will suggest some possibly plausible features of shared organization and some traits (e.g., "distancing mechanisms") related to this organization.

I propose that people in Piri and *mā'ohi* Roto have these shared general features of personality organization. (1) People's personalities are smoothly integrated. (2) Successful integration is helped, in part, by the dissociation of organized aspects of the self. (3) There is a similarity of the "content" of dissociated forms. (4) Dissociation is aided by various devices for distancing and securing separation. (5) To compensate for the cost of dissociation and the devices for maintaining it, typical reconstructive devices are used.

Integration

I take it that gracefulness of behavior, infrequency of anxiety and symptoms of stress, and an ability to be comfortable within the usual and expectable range of situations in the community imply a smooth integration of ideas, feelings, motives, self-images, and whatever else may be taken as aspects of personality for people in Piri and Roto. I suppose that this smoothness of integration has something to do with the relation of individuals to community forms (adaptation) and to the internal adjustment of aspects of personality.

Adjusted systems can be structured in various ways. Consider first a strain, a tension, in the system. Hiro states what he thinks is the essential *mā'ohi* "psychological problem," and I agree. "A basic problem for Tahitians is that they are divided between their desire for liberty and their desire for security." In one form or another this is a concern for most of the informants. One needs other people. Being alone is abnormal, troublesome, dangerous. But being involved is restricting and entangling. One must find ways of establishing relations and somehow keeping some freedom, some distance, within them.

One must keep some freedom, but one cannot fight for it. In sleep one runs, one flies like a bird, or else one is paralyzed. Then one cannot move or fight or cry out. How does one avoid paralysis?

Dissociation

In shared themes in dreams, in hypnoid phenomena, in the possession treated and encouraged by the *tahu'a*, in the world of the *pō*,[1] and in the small obsessions, rigidities, and avoidances indicated in people's behaviors there seems to be an indication of a latent set of fears, wishes, impulses, and perceptions.

There are many ways, as psychoanalytic writings have argued, of dealing with aspects of personality and experience which are not congenial to the conscious self. Everyone uses "mechanisms of defense," but there are different ways in which matters are suppressed and repressed, and these have different costs and consequences.

The latent aspects of people's personalities in Piri and *mā'ohi* Roto are distinguished in that they seem to have some organization and autonomy as alternate systems of mind rather than being repressed "tendencies." They are, to use a psychiatric technical term, dissociated.

People in Piri and Roto have an "unconscious" which is organized in ways which seem to be disappearing in western settings along with the expression of this organization as "hysteria."[2]

---

1. Myths collected in Tahiti in the decades after European contact provide interesting suggestions on the implications of the separation of realms of reality. "The night [*pō*] was for the gods and the day [*ao*] was for man. It was only in the night [*pō*] that the gods were born after the world was made clear" (Henry 1928; p. 412).

   In a myth of war between the god Tumu "against men and the sky eternal of Tane," Tumu caused "constant heavy mists," famine, death, and suicide, and "drowsiness to exist by day and night in the world." Tane, "god of the beautiful things," countered with dry weather and clearness, overflowing plenty and shoals of live fish, and "wakefulness for the day and sleep for the night. The world was illuminated with the sun burning below in the daytime, and sleep fell upon man at nighttime" (Henry 1928; p. 353).

2. I would think that "dissociation" is a necessary consequence of simple, integrated cultural systems which (1) encourage the development throughout the life cycle of organized systems of meaning; (2) select among them in a limited way for acceptable everyday adult "selves"; and (3) support the culturally prevalent dissociated systems by giving them expression and interpretation in special, bounded contexts.

What Is Dissociated

From a variety of small clues — slips of the tongue, associations of content, symbols in dreams and fantasy,[3] one can make, as Freud taught us, inferences about personal orientations which are often covert or unconscious, in that they must be corrected and altered for sensible and acceptable community discourse, including its internal representation in "worked out" thought.

Inference about symbols and unconscious themes based on such data is a diffuse and personal matter, involving a sense of relevant context. The reader may concur that 'tis like a camel indeed, or not, as he will.

The shared covert aspects of personality have much to do, I think, with the discontinuities of child development. They include the following. (1) Wishes having to do with clinging, with possession, with "regressive dependency," that is, with being taken care of because one is weak, or needful, or special in some sense. (2) Traces of anger and depression having to do with separation from a single mothering individual. (3) Traces of fear of destructive consequences in relation to the anger. These traces of fear of punishment are reinforced by other experiences bearing on aggression training and conscience formation. (4) Fears that desires for clinging, for intimacy, for dependency will result in loss of autonomy.

Distancing Mechanisms

Tahitians, I suppose, use all the defensive and coping mechanisms described in the psychoanalytic literature, but the most salient ones are in aid of "liberty," a liberty which entails some distance from one's own passions and dissociated self, on the one hand, and emotion-laden entanglements with others on the

3. Some examples: Poria, explaining why anger is a bad thing, says, "It destroys the ba— ['in–, for 'ino], the good." And, "My father, they — he was far away." And Pua, "Now as to God, they protect you." ("You called God they?") "It was a mistake." And Hiro, asked if he ever thinks of committing suicide, "No. But I think sometimes that it would be better if I weren't staying with a *vahine*. Just myself alone." And Tāvana, "I'm not afraid of Paitia, even if he is bigger than I am." Paitia isn't bigger.

other. There are various ways in which people I observed do this. These are sometimes conscious strategies, sometimes habitual and automatic reactions. They may be loosely grouped as "distancing mechanisms."

Thus Tāvana is explaining to me his theory of thought and emotion — the eye sees something, and then fear begins. I choose an example. "The eye sees a cow/bull, and then what happens?" Tāvana answers, "Don't look." ("Don't look?") "Don't look any more and the fear will disappear." ("The fear will disappear? The good thing to do is not to look again? Turn away?") "That's it. Turn away so that the fear will disappear." I show my surprise. ("That is how to cure that fear?") Tāvana breaks into a hearty laugh.

Tāvana's joke is significant. He knows himself and his fellow villagers.

There are gross but effective ways of getting some room, some privacy, some distance in the crowded space of Piri and Roto. One can try to be self-sufficient, one can not talk (for a while) to people who anger or disturb one, one can be careful about exposing one's private thoughts or one's problems.

As Manu says, "When I encounter some trouble, I strengthen my courage. I don't want everyone to know that trouble has grown up. I make myself energetic and enthusiastic. I don't want other people to know. I want that only I should know about my troubles. . . . Because, Tahitians, when they know the kind of trouble you have, they go to someone else and build and build and build and twist. They rearrange your difficulties so that they don't have a good appearance. . . . They don't tell it correctly, they lie. . . . People believe them, and they think that that is, indeed, the cause of your trouble."

Nor does he tell problems to his *vahine*. "It is rare that I tell her. When I have trouble, it is for me alone. And when it's finished, that's that. It's rare that I tell Tetua, because a *vahine*, she is like those other people. When you tell your *vahine* the nature of the affair, now, all the time, she goes and meets her friends and says, 'We have trouble' and 'We are in difficulty' and so forth. And now, after a bit, everybody hears. . . . Now, that word spreads far, it doesn't stop anymore. So it is rare that I tell Tetua about troubles. When I have trouble, I carry it alone."

Tāvana's "don't look at it" and Manu's "don't talk about it" are backed up by miscellaneous subtler devices for distancing the self from various inconveniences. For example:

1. *Sleep.* In Teri'i Tui's household, during periods of particular tension one or more of the people involved would often go to sleep. The children sometimes did this when they had been severely yelled at, and adults did the same after a serious argument. Oro, who sometimes had episodes of fear in the evening, would "return quickly to the house . . . and get into bed. . . . You wanted to quickly fall asleep so that you would forget that thing. To fall asleep, and that's all, and the next morning you wouldn't remember it anymore."

2. *Conventionality.* A convenient way of protecting oneself from exposure in Piri and Roto is to use conventional forms of discourse and explanation which convey little except that one is, for whatever purposes, conforming. Many of the statements by Taere, Veve Vahine, and Uta seemed to be of this kind. They were stated in a rote manner and were predictable from some knowledge of the roles each was playing. These kinds of statements, frequent in the early stages of interviews, came in contexts where I had the impression that the speaker was being careful and defensive. For some people, such as Taere, restriction to conventional statements seems to be partially an indication of limited intelligence; the conventional statement is both a safe and an easily available reply.

3. *Calculation.* I have often emphasized the special status of *feruri*, worked-out thought. Such thought, and the language and behavior which express it, is the kind of thought for which one is responsible in the social and supernatural worlds. The pauses which sometimes occur when someone is working out his thoughts give some glimpse of the kind of process which may be entailed. In an interview with Tāvana, after he had said that he did not believe that souls go to heaven or hell in an afterlife, I asked him why he continued to go to church. He was silent, looking thoughtful, for thirty-three seconds, and then gave his

thought-out answer to my question. People gained time to *feruri* by culturally expected silences (most saliently and conventionally in formal group settings) and by various time-gaining devices during the interview, including the familiar western response to a question such as "What do you feel about such and such?" — "Who me?" "Yes, you." "Oh . . . well. . . ."

4. *Not caring.* The ability not to care, not to become involved emotionally, not to be concerned is thought to be a controllable behavior, unless one is unusually weak. People adopted in their childhood say they then "no longer concerned themselves with their biological parents"; or if they had been troubled or teased by some older member of the household, decided "it would be better if I didn't pay any more attention to him." However it is done, people achieve a certain stoicism.

5. *Not knowing.* Tāvana's joke about "not looking" being a radical solution for a problem suggests a general theme of not knowing, not looking, which, as I have noted in the discussion of moral behavior, balances the high potential visibility of action in these small communities.[4] Limiting one's knowledge about others, in the face of behavioral controls geared to village acceptability, allows one to be more tolerant about one's own behavior. "I am no worse than anyone else." Where goals are equilibrium and not change, many kinds of knowing — those which would alter the conventional understandings — serve no purpose.

6. *Depersonalization.* There are various frequently used devices which in form serve to separate the "responsible" part of an individual from other aspects of himself. One is the separating of thought into more responsible and less responsible aspects, *feruri* and *mana'o.* I have noted others. There is the frequent

---

4. Some years ago Wilbert Moore and Melvin Tumin discussed "Some Social Functions of Ignorance." They argued that "ignorance is both inescapable and an intrinsic element in social organization generally, although there are marked differences in the specific forms, degrees, and functions of ignorance in known social organizations" (Moore and Tumin 1949; p. 788). In small communities like Piri, where people have opportunities to observe one another over long periods of time and in various roles, ignorance must be maintained by intrapersonal and interpersonal devices.

verbal shift from "I," *vau*, to "you" (singular), *'oe*, which generalizes and distances. Another verbal form which implies depersonalization is the designation of parts of the body as actors, rather than the "I." "My ear did not wish to listen." "If anger arises in my intestines, my leg will start to go and my hands will start to cause trouble." "From my anger there grew up bad thoughts."

The personal effectiveness of such verbal forms is unclear. Their differential use in apparently uncomfortable statements suggests that they provide some relief. They are in one sense related to those doctrines of behaviors due to the "nature of things," which reduce individual responsibility and susceptibility to guilt and shame.

7. *Deflating.* There are various attempts to make aspects of oneself less important and less powerful, and therefore less vulnerable to the dangers which people feel power entails. Stylistically related to this, as I have already noted, is that when guessing at numbers, distances, or other quantifiable items, people often make a first guess and then *decrease* the quantity. Tāvana guesses that he lived in his youth in a certain village seven or perhaps six years. People estimate that someone has twelve or eleven or perhaps ten children, that it takes five or perhaps four days to reach a certain place.

Deflating is related to a disinclination to "inflate oneself," to "make oneself proud," to "make oneself high," to "make oneself great." The opposite of inflation is being low or humble, *ha'eha'a*, which is considered to be a valuable *mā'ohi* trait and one of the things which separates the *mā'ohi* from the *demi.*

Related to self-deflation are certain maneuvers which characteristically end up by indicating that one does not really have anything to be upset about after all. Thus people would compare the ways of life of the Europeans in Papeete and the Tahitians, and say that the Europeans have a clean life, they work in offices, and have lots of money, whereas the Tahitians have to work in the dirt. But then, it isn't such a bad thing to work in the dirt, one gets one's food. If one doesn't work, one would be hungry. Both kinds of life are good, they are just different.

Deflation does not involve any overt self-disrespect or contempt. It is an attempt to return oneself to a comfortable and safe community average.

The Problem of Paranoia

In the examples of dreams I gave for Piri, people were chased by animals and by Chinese and, in one dream, bombed by "foreign" airplanes. Psychoanalytic theory suggests that this sort of thing involves a denial of hostile impulses and their "projection" on others, as well as the construction of a fantasy to explain fears of punishment and destruction. What is of interest in these dreams is that the projection (whatever its personal function) moves beyond the family group, beyond the village, beyond fellow Tahitians, to animals and Chinese. This blame exogamy seems clearly useful for personal and village comfort.

According to Poria, "It is better to elect [and to be governed by] the French. They do evil, it doesn't make any difference. They are French. We Tahitians aren't troubled about that. But [we don't want] Tahitians harming Tahitians." It is easier to blame and become angry at people the further you are from them. French, Chinese, demis (or perhaps demis, Chinese in some contexts), villagers, extended family, household are the progressively closer positions.

But these are dreams and hesitantly articulated political opinions.[5] There is little ascription of blame for evil behavior to others, including Chinese, or animals, or curse-causing relatives in waking life, and this is particularly interesting because of the magical doctrines and subjective cognitive styles which one would expect to facilitate "paranoid" constructions, identifying others as sources of evil. Even those fanciful figures, the spirit members of the pō, are not generally considered to be evil, although much of the gross misfortune that does occur in the village is ascribed to one or more of them.

---

5. In the years since my study it has become more conventionally acceptable, because of the development of some panterritorial political ideologies, to blame the French for local difficulties.

When things go wrong in Piri, there is usually thought to be a reason. If a piece of soap is missing, someone must have taken it; if two sections of a hose come apart, someone must have separated them; if a dog dies, someone must have poisoned it. In more serious matters the intervention of *tahu'a* and *tūpapa'u* is suspected.

Poria, talking about his anxiety about stealing food for thrills when he has been drinking, mentions briefly that he sometimes fears that the food may have been poisoned, and then dismisses this to go on to his "real" fear, which is that he might have been seen.

Most typically, there is a moment of blame, of projecting evil into the world, and then it is finished. After a fleeting moment — or in the case of the *tahu'a*, some moderately prolonged suspicion — the people involved become once again Morrison's people of unruffled temper, free of suspicion or revenge.

Other cultures seem to have significant contrasts in the matter of suspicion and blame. Melanesians, who are characterized by Theodore Schwartz as having a "paranoid ethos" (Schwartz, in preparation), are said to be suspicious of surface forms, to be concerned with underlying hidden meanings and evils, and this in intravillage and, sometimes, intrafamilial relationships.

Why do fragments of suspicion and blame not develop into a "paranoid ethos" in Piri and Roto? Historically the "nondevelopment" of potentials for paranoid blame, as well as other Tahitian characteristics, may have something to do with the lack of an impinging outgroup to serve as a traditional enemy. Each "tribal unit" was part of a larger Tahitian community which was integrated by strong cultural, linguistic, and kin ties. Only the very distant "savages" of the Tuamotus and the Marquesas reminded Society Islanders on rare occasions that there were other kinds of people who might be psychologically useful, but contacts with them were infrequent and of minor import.

The question of what aspects of values, definitions, controls, early experience and training, and psychological organization now limit in Tahiti, and facilitate in parts of Melanesia, the development of suspiciousness needs comparative study. How much of the difference is due to suppression in the one place, and to facilitation in the other, is unclear.

Some of the control in Piri and Roto may have to do with the sense that when things go wrong it is often one's own fault, because one wittingly or unwittingly violated some reasonable rule which activated the sequence. This is particularly true of supernaturally mediated events. This belief has one of the elements of paranoia, a feeling that the universe is intimately concerned with one, but it may, when associated with some confidence of control, result in bland carefulness rather than overt suspiciousness. Another restraining form may be that suspiciousness and blame justify and call forth anger and destructive reaction. These escalate one's problems. It is more useful to limit one's suspicions.

At any rate, paranoid projection is restrained to dreams, to bits of the supernatural, and to momentary behaviors. It is not much used in the ordinary coping of daily life.

Reconstruction

Having achieved some casualness, some distance from the immediate press of their own and others' passions, people reconstruct ways of relating which are under considerable self-control. The craft of the actor replaces a more innocent directness. Courtesy, politeness, charm, the dramatic use of controlled emotion seem to me to be reconstructions, mature engagement built on more fundamental orientations of disengagement and caution.

Similarly, in pre-Christian Tahiti sexual behavior was taught as a craft. (For a review of descriptions on sexual training, attitudes, and behavior in pre-Christian and subsequent times in Polynesia, see Bengt Danielsson, *Love in the South Seas* [1956].) Echoes of this in present emphases on sexual techniques and pleasure have something to do, I think, with a control and deemphasis of romantic, child/parent meanings through a craftlike practice of sex.

"Controlled" does not mean "false." Love and sympathy, anger and loneliness are expressed and understood by means of and in spite of this maze of conventions, in spite of the difficulties of being human and of being Tahitian.

Other Aspects of Organization

I have suggested (chapter 10) that feelings of guilt as shaped by the conditions of development in Piri and Roto are diffuse and unfocused. They act as cues to avoid situations which might possibly produce developed and conscious feelings of guilt. Personal aspects of conscience are oriented toward avoidance of transgression rather than toward accomplishment. If informants have images of people serving as "ego ideals," they are generally people whose behavior is to be avoided.

Aspects of conscience, of dissociation, and of defense are associated with some inhibition of one's "drives." I have argued that uncongenial aspects of the personality are repressed in a special way, which has become rare for us. They do not seem to press constantly into awareness, causing anxiety and doubt, or gain constant muscular expression, leading to aches, tension, or awkwardness. Like the spirits, they exist in an organized and alternate world with their own symbols and forms. They are the spirits.

But the very success of this has its costs for people of Piri and Roto. Since they are not passionate people, it often takes some urging, or the help of drinking, to get them engaged in nonroutine situations. They do not push into things, but must be invited in. My impression is that they do not feel much inner pressure and push; but as long as they have enough sense of drive to be *'ana'anatae*, alert and enthusiastic, that is enough. When, rarely, the feeling of *'ana'anatae* is not present, they become *fiu* and there is little to do but wait it out, or change the activity.[6]

---

6. The importance of felt drive may have something to do with some lack of auxiliary drive from conscience. There are some illuminating suggestions from clinical psychiatry. Samuel Irwin surveyed a number of studies on depression and called attention to different types of depression. There were "melancholic depressions" where specific antidepressant agents were useful; cases with heightened arousal and agitation where tranquilizers were useful; and a group of cases "where the depression is secondary to a lack of initiative, inability to concentrate, and to organize and sustain activity" (p. 13). In connection with this latter (Tahitian and post modern?) type he notes, "What is perhaps not fully understood is that some optimum level of behavioral and possibly EEG arousal is required for each individual

Things fit together. People are generally comfortable, find their lives meaningful, and feel that they are having good lives as judged by their idea of what is possible. To an outside observer there are costs in the suppression of some human possibilities. The pervasive quiet and acceptance, which to a believer in *ad astra per aspera* indicates resignation, and a shadow of sadness remind one that it is possible to have yet other illusions and other costs.

Reflections on Male and Female Personality

In Tahitian verbal usage a "person," *ta'ata*, is assumed to be a man unless specially qualified.

It is evident that many of the special cultural themes, sequences of development, and special problems I have been considering have more to do with the psychocultural situation of men than of women.

Women's lives in Piri and Roto seem culturally simpler than men's lives. Girls usually stay close to the household, and their adult role is in many ways a continuation of their childhood and adolescent life. Boys have more discontinuities. They break out of childhood into the *taure'are'a* life. They must achieve a sexual aggressiveness which in some ways runs counter to childhood adaptations. They must eventually play household and village roles which are more different from their childhood roles than is the case for women.

In most traditional cultures men carry most of the specializations of the culture which are particularly related to the culture's history and special ecological adaptations. I think that there is a sense in which women from various cultures are more like one another than are the men. Men, with their heads full of special cultural roles and discriminations, of tabus and differentiated techniques, sense women as sources of contamination, of entropy, of a (culturally) destructive, albeit fascinating, otherness.

––––––

to effectively organize his intellectual and physical resources to cope with the environment and that much individual activity is related to and directed toward this end" (Irwin 1968; p. 14).

Women's culturally specified anxieties are often related to maintaining men's roles and sensibility. Perhaps men must live out the specialized cultural dream, the cultural madness, more than women. The most central household maintenance and economic tasks are more generally human, and are less prone to the peculiarities and the sometimes Byzantine elaborations of other parts of the cultural life.

Women have a perspective, an understanding, which for some purposes is a danger to their men. "They are imbued with the superstition," as Rodriguez told us, "that by getting food for the woman and eating in company with her, the men would be struck blind or crippled" (Corney 1913-19; 3:111).

It is for such reasons, among others, that the study of psychological forms in relation to the variability of culture finds itself emphasizing the personality psychology of men, or of women in their relation to men.

Postscript: Time

On 6 August 1961, a few weeks after I first arrived in Piri, it was announced on the Tahitian-language broadcast of Radio Tahiti that the passage of the Vostok 2, with Cosmonaut Gherman Titov within, would be visible in the sky after sundown. The entire village went down to the wharf to wait. Suddenly a starlike light appeared at the horizon and slowly arched across the sky. The villagers of Piri watched in silence. No one spoke for several moments after the glowing satellite had disappeared. Then someone in the crowd broke the silence. "The Tahitians," he said, "could never make anything like that."

Perhaps not in the short run. But between that night and the summer of 1970 when I last returned much had happened to the people of Piri. Time was flowing toward them.[1]

By 1970 the Piri of thatched houses was gone. There were only four old-style houses left, and the owners planned to replace them as soon as possible with the cement-walled, tin-roofed houses which were everywhere along the now widened village path. The path was in fact now a road, and led to the port town. There were four small trucks in the village. Teri'i Tui had one,

---

1. The Tahitian verbal forms for dealing with the progression of time imply two different ways of looking at time and change. In one set there is the suggestion of a fixed and static space, in which all events past, present, and future can be arranged. Ancient events are at the front of this space, and subsequent events are placed farther and farther back. "In front Teri'i was born; Natana was born in back" — first Teri'i, then Natana. "The generations behind us" — the generations yet to be born. The observer watches as the present moves back over the landscape of existence. The other set of terms suggests that future events flow toward an individual from in front of him and drop off behind him as past events. "The things in front" — future events. "The time nearly here" — something about to happen. "The days fallen away now" — past days.

and Teiva had two others. They transported produce and people to town and back for a fee.

The village also had four gasoline-driven electric generators, and Teri'i Tui's house was well stocked with electric lights, refrigerator, phonograph, and radio.

The children in the village were noticeably less shy. Often they spoke French to each other, to the mystification of Teri'i Tui and many other older people.

The village was full of children. Pua, by birth and adoption, had accumulated ten, and other households were burgeoning. In Teri'i's household some had left. Toni, now married to his *vahine* and with five children, lived in Papeete in a neat and modern small house and worked as a truck driver. His older children were at school in the city schools. Tara was also living in Papeete, unmarried, with a *tāne*; she had one child and was again pregnant. Ari worked as a waitress in a modern new hotel which had been built at Fare in anticipation of a busy foreign tourist trade.

But the house was far from empty. Romana and Tino, Teri'i's son Tihoni, Etienne (now a *taure'are'a*), Ramses (the baby who had arrived just before I left), another adopted girl of four or five, Teri'i, and Mari kept the household as full and varied as ever.

The village was excited at the new changes, the money that was coming in, the opening up of the world.

There were no more Mormons. The Mormons inland had all left the church, and some had left the village. People said they had kept fighting over how to distribute the responsibilities and offices of the congregation. Uta was drinking again, and the Mormon church building was locked up.

Teiva's group was the biggest church group. They had built a fine new church house. Tano still had his church and his congregation. The village had not come together again.

But the village was not quite aware of what was happening to it. The masses of children obscured matters. At least seventy villagers had left. An economic boom in Papeete, set off by a major French nuclear weapons testing program in the territory, had attracted men and their families to Papeete. Oro and Taere, who had gone early, did not return, and they were joined by Poria, most of his old *taure'are'a* cronies, and scores more.[2]

The people who were left behind, including Tāvana and Veve Vahine (now Tāvana Vahine), Teiva, and Tano, had important things to do in the village. The marginal people had left, people without lands or special positions. Things were quieter, perhaps even more peaceful without them.

But a stroll up the new Village road revealed that many of the older children and young *taure'are'a* were just waiting. As soon as they were old enough, they planned to leave too.

The others will certainly come back, people said. The ones I talked to in Papeete had no such intention.

Some of the people who had left Piri were scattered. Tore, the frightening man with the handkerchief cap (chapter 9), who had long before gone to Papeete, was in jail, I was told, for "molesting" a fourteen-year-old girl. Taere and his family had gone, as had many other Tahitians, to work in New Caledonia, a French territory in Melanesia.

Most of the people who had left Piri, though, lived together in an enclave at the outskirts of Papeete, along the Fa'ataua River. The men worked and had some money. The children went to school and learned French. Some of the houses had television sets, and in the evening they were crowded with people inside, while groups of neighbors stood outside the open windows to watch.

Poria, living among them, still had not found a *fa'aea vahine*. He looked happy and involved in his new life. He had adopted a son. They lived in a small, comfortable composition-board house. Poria worked on the roads, digging and carrying. He had money for movies and drinking with his friends. He said he

2. Census figures for 1962 and 1967 show that the Leeward Islands, which had been increasing in population at the rate of about 3 percent a year between 1956 and 1962 (owing to excess of births over deaths), lost 4.2 percent of their population between 1962 and 1967. Huahine as a whole lost 12.2 percent (Fages 1972).

would never go back to Piri except for the New Year's holidays.

Roto was slowly being replaced with expensive houses, and people were being driven out. Manu and Tetua had replaced their shack with a somewhat neater one. They did not know how long they would be able to stay there.

Flora had had a second baby by Hans, and then married him. Shortly afterward, he was killed by a car. She was living off the insurance settlement from the accident.

Hiro had an automobile and one thousand dollars in the bank. But, he said, with all the increase in salary he hadn't profited. His money bought less than before. Some Tahitians had made money selling their lands, but they wouldn't keep it, he said. It was the French and Chinese who had profited. Hiro was becoming very interested in practical politics. Hiro and Meri spoke French, as they understood it, to their children. "The children can always learn Tahitian from their friends." This was to help them prepare for school and jobs. But the children spoke French to their friends.

At a meeting of the Reformed Church of Jesus Christ of the Latter-Day Saints in Papeete the parishioners are troubled. They are for the most part middle-aged and older. They are worried about their children. The children wander everywhere and see how others live. They want such lives for themselves. They want money and clothes and motorbikes. They laugh at the *himene tarava* and the old customs. They do not respect or listen to their parents. But when they do ask questions, for example about schoolwork, the parents cannot help them. The people at the meeting ask what they should do. No one seems to know.

Appendix 1

Check Sheet of Topics for Psychodynamic Interviews

1. Locating data: name; birth date; birthplace; description of childhood house; childhood eating customs; languages and literacy; movements; schooling; travel.
2. Childhood household: members at various ages; sibling pattern; sleeping arrangement; caretaking agents for subject; time spent in and out of household; alternate households.
3. Nature of household relations (adult-adult, adult-children, children-children); leadership, quarrels, conflict resolution.
4. Data on significant caretakers: family background; where born; movements; occupation; education; languages; special statuses; illnesses; involvement and special roles in religion; death.
5. Responses to significant caretakers: evaluation, interaction pattern.
6. Patterns of identification: self compared to significant adults; special qualities of family; special qualities of ancestors; heroes; negative role models.
7. Early learning in family: nursing, weaning, excretion training; discipline and teaching patterns; familial values.
8. Childhood play: with whom; how chosen; activities; conflicts; special roles in play group; solitary play.
9. Evaluation of childhood.
10. Special circumstances of childhood, including illnesses.
11. Adolescence: age at beginning; signs of transition; nature of transition; associations; special roles; relations with household; major concerns; ideas about the future; sexual life; religious life; formal and informal learning; transition to adulthood; evaluation.
12. History of occupations and special roles.

13. Present associations: with whom; length; activities; nature of the relationship; quality of relations with neighbors, relatives, villagers; enemies.

14. Stress: illnesses; theory of illness; energy/fatigue; headaches; eating problems; hypochondriasis; sleep difficulties; irritability; depression; caused fear; anxiety; altered consciousness; suicidal ideas; use of alcohol; possession phenomena; experience with healers; major mental illness.

15. Aggression: causes, objects, frequency of anger; associated feelings; actions taken; evaluation and interpretation.

16. Moral controls: nature of forbidden desires; why not acted on; results of wrongdoing; moral principles.

17. Religion and the supernatural: present involvement; development of involvement; private uses of religion and the supernatural.

18. Death: interpretations of and reactions to own death and death of others.

19. Dreams: frequency; examples of significant, recurring, and recent dreams; interpretation; theory of dreaming.

20. Time sense: changes in time sense; generalization from private sense of duration to public time.

21. Spouse relationship: history; why chosen; evaluation; nature of the relationship; personal meanings of the relationship; conflict resolution.

22. Attitudes about sex roles: evaluation of male/female roles; interpretation of male/female role differences; jealousy; romantic love.

23. Homosexuality: wish to change sex; overt homosexual experience; attitudes about homosexuals.

24. Physical sexuality:
    a. (Women): reactions, interpretations, and evaluations of menarche, menstruation, menopause, childbirth.
    b. (General): play intercourse; onset of sexual feelings; masturbation; nocturnal dreams and nocturnal orgasms; partners; frequencies; impotent/frigid; idea of orgasm; evaluations and meanings.

25. Own children: meanings and evaluations, socialization goals and techniques.
26. Self: self-evaluation; self-disapproval; things to change; shifting selves; qualities of identity.
27. Past: evaluation of past, of ancestors, of the Tahitian past.
28. Future: plans and expectations for the future; proposed actions; attitudes and expectations about aging.
29. Community identity: evaluations and interpretations of Tahitians, of other groups.

Appendix 2

Interview Sample: Oro's Second Dream
(See chapter 11. The interviewer's remarks are in parentheses.)

Terā   mau   moemoeā,   tī   tā   'oe   pa'i   ta'oto   pa'i
Those [plural] dreams,   in   of you indeed sleep   indeed,

hō'e huru   e   ta'oto   ana'e   'oe   mī   terā
one kind [ongoing] sleeping finally   you   like   that

moemoeā   hia   e   moemoeā   pua'atoro. (Mm.) Terā
dream-taken [passive] by   dream   cow/bull.   (Mm.) That

huru   e   a'ua'u   hia   pa'i   'oe   e   te
kind [ongoing] chased [passive] indeed you by the

pua'atoro. (Mm.) 'A, i muri iho   ho'i,   tae   ra'a
cow/bull.   (Mm.) Ah, afterward indeed,   arrive   [process]

vau i ni'a i   te   tumu ra'au. (Mm.)   Tae   ato'a
I   on   the   tree.   (Mm.) Arrives also

mai   te   pua'atoro. (Mm.)   Nō ria,   hō'i,
toward me the   cow/bull.   (Mm.) Therefore, indeed,

e   ara,   e ara mai   pa'i   'oe.   Nō ria
[ongoing] awake,   awake   indeed you. Therefore

te vai ra   te   tahi   huru   ta'oto tā   'oe.   Mea
there exists the certain   kind   dream of you. Thing

tīpapa pa'i   'oe.   Ho'e huru teria,   e
prone   indeed you. As though this, [ongoing]

ma'urere   pa'i   'oe   e   ma'urere   'oe
flying around indeed you and flying around you

nā ni'a i   te   mou'a. (Pinepine mi   tera, 'oe?) 'Ae,
on   the mountain. (Often   like that, you?) Yes,

pinepine mi   tera,   ma'urere.   ('Ua
often   like that, flying around. ([Completed]

a'ua'u   hia   nā mua   'oe   e   ma'urere
Came to be chased [passive]   first   you and flying around

'oe i muri iho, mi   tera?)   'Ae, a'ua'u   ihoā   'oe   e
you afterward, like that?) Yes, chased indeed you by

te   pua'atoro (mm),   muri iho   ma'urere   'oe   (e
the cow/bull   (mm),   afterward flying around you (and

ora   ai?).   'Ae,   tetahi   huru,   tera   mea,
escaped   [resultant]?) Yes, one other kind, that thing,

nā'o ta'oto   ra.   (Mm.)   Ho'e huru, e tae   ana'e   'oe
from sleep there. (Mm.) For example, arrive finally you

i ni'a i   te   tumu ra'au. (Mm.) Hare ato'a   mai
on   the   tree.   (Mm.) Goes also   toward you

te   pua'atoro, (mm) pua'atoro 'ere'ere pa'i.   (Mm.)
the cow/bull, (mm) cow/bull   black   indeed. (Mm.)

Ho'e a huru, e ara   pa'i   'oe
For example wake indeed you.

Glossary

This glossary lists terms which are used repeatedly or which have some special importance. Some terms used in restricted contexts in the text and defined there are not listed. Many of the terms listed have other uses not considered in the text; sometimes their most literal sense is given in quotation marks. The exact transcription of Tahitian terms provides problems. Different speakers and communities have dialectical variations. It is also difficult to determine vowel length in some phonetic contexts, such as double vowels, after *h*, and after the glottal stop. The transcriptions in the glossary and in the text are based on the linguistic studies of Ralph White, and attempt to represent Tahitian as most of the informants used it.

'ā'au	intestines, the seat of the emotions
'āfa	half, culturally or racially mixed people
'āfaro	straight, correct
aho pau	asthma, "used up breath"
'ai ta'ata	incest; cannibalism; "to eat people"
'aiaru	transformation of an evil person into an evil ghost
'aito	ancient heroes or men of eminence
amo'a	fern, *Nephrodium exaltatum*
'amu	to eat
'amu ta'ata	incest; cannibalism; "to eat people"
'ana'anatae	a sense of inner push; enthusiasm
ao	daytime world; daylight part of the twenty-four-hour day
a'o	to advise
āoaoa	seriously confused, rambling, delirious
'ārearea	fun

515

ari'i	person of chiefly status
arōfa	empathy, pity
'aru'aru	weak and helpless
au	fittingness, relationship
āue	woeful crying out
'ava	alcoholic spirits; traditionally *Piper methysticum*
'etaretia	a communicant of the Protestant church
'ētene	heathen
fa'a'amu	"to feed"; adoption
fa'aea	to stay, to remain; to discontinue; to stay with a *tāne* or *vahine*
fa'a'ipo'ipo	"to make somebody one's darling," to marry
fa'a'oroma'i	to endure or bear an unpleasant situation
fa'aro'o	to listen, obey
fa'aru'e	to cast off
fa'atere	"to steer"; management of children
fa'atūri	adultery
faito	measurement, weight
fānau	to deliver a child
faufau	nauseated; nauseating
feruri	to articulate and work out thoughts
feti'i	all people who have some kind of cognatic or adoptive kinship relation to an individual or household; literally, "to tie or bind together"
fiu	the felt disappearance of the motivation for a task, annoyance
ha'amā	embarrassment, shame
ha'avare	lie, intentional falsehood
ha'eha'a	low, humble
hape	error, minor mistake
hāra	sin
haru	to rape, seize
haumani	fatigue
ha'uti	play
here	love

hia	passive particle
himene	chants and songs
hina	second-generation descendants
hina rere	third-generation descendants
hīna'āro	to want or desire something
hoa	friend
ho'i	traditional Tahitian "kiss"
hua	male and female genitalia
hua'ai	descendants
huahua	smegma
huru	kind, nature, essence
huru ē	strange, "of a different kind"
'ino	bad
i'oa pi'i	the "name by which one is called"
'ite	knowledge or understanding, to see
itoito	energy about doing things
mā	clean
ma'ama'a	"crazy"
mā'au	intellectually dull, foolish
maha	satisfaction, in the sense of relieving a desire
māhū	male transvestite or taker of female roles
ma'i	illness
ma'i 'āva'e	monthly sickness (menstruation)
ma'i fa'a'ī	illness caused by accumulation of menstrual blood
ma'i mau	illness caused by natural causes; nonspirit illness
ma'i tāpiri	illness caused by spirits
ma'i vahine	female sickness (menstruation)
maita'i	good
māmae	pain
māmahu	shy
mana	secular or supernatural power
mana'o	a thought, or the process of thinking
mana'o feruri	a worked-out thought
mā'ohi	traditional
marae	pre-Christian sacred enclosure

māramārama	enlightenment; introduced Christian knowledge, intelligence
marū	gentle
mata'u	apprehension of being in a fear-producing situation
mātau	accustomed, unembarrassed
mau	fixed, unchanging
ma'ūa	stupid or feeble-minded
māuiui	pain
mea	thing
mehameha	uncanny feelings
metua	relative of parental or ascending generation
metua tāne	"male parent"
metua vahine	"female parent"
mihi	grief
mo'emo'e	unpleasant feeling caused by being alone
moemoeā	dream
motoro	to enter a house secretly to try to have intercourse with a woman
muto'i	district native policeman
navenave	feelings of pleasure, particularly sexual pleasure
nevaneva	intellectually flighty, not concentrating
nī'au	braided coconut-palm leaves, used for thatching
noa	ordinary
nono	plant, *Morinda citrifolia*
'oa'oa	happy or content
'oe	second person singular
'ohure	buttocks
'ōna	third person singular
oni	male, of animals
ora	to live, to flourish
ori	to stroll, wander
'orometua a'o	a pastor
'ote	suck
'oto	grief
pa'ari	adult, wise, hard

pape	water
parau	speech, word
parau mau	true speech; truth
pareu	a cloth, worn as a dress or skirt by both men and women
paruparu	weak
pātehe	to castrate
pe'ape'a	troubled feelings; internal or external disturbances; guilt
pēpē	baby
peritome/piritome	polite term for supercision
peu	event involving a creature or influence from the spirit world; also customs
pia	beer
pīfa'o	curse
pinepine	frequent
piri	narrow or confined; curious or wondrous occurrence
pō	night; night world, land of spirits, gods, souls, and the dead
pō'ara	a blow to the head or face
pohe	death, unconsciousness
po'ipo'i	morning, the period after dawn
pōiri	ignorant; literally, "dark" or "obscure"
pōpa'a	white foreigners
pūai	strong
pūrau	tree, *Hibiscus tiliaceus*
raerae	inverted overt physical sexual behavior of either males or females
rave	to take, to take sexually
ri'ari'a	fear; mild revulsion about certain kinds of food
riri	anger
roa	long
rohirohi	exhausted
roto	within
rū'au	old
ta'ata	a person

ta'ata ha'eha'a	"humble" person
ta'ata tahiti	a Tahitian
ta'ero	drunk; poison, poisoned
tāho'o	a kind of curse
tahu'a	spirit doctor; expert practitioner
tai	seaward direction
ta'i	to weep or cry; the sound of a musical instrument
taiā	anticipation of mildly frightening events
taime	time
taiō	a formal bond-friend
tai'o	the enumeration of items in a series
taioro	white fermented coconut sauce; as an insult, smegma under uncut foreskin
tā'iri	light blow
tamāhine	girl child, "daughter"
tama'i	verbal quarrel; war, battle
tamaiti	a "son"
tamāri'i	a child
tamāroa	boy child
tāmata	to taste, try out
tāmure	erotic dance
tāne	a man; a woman's heterosexual partner
tano	to hit a target or mark, correct
ta'oto	sleeping, lying down
ta'oto'otoā	dream
tapa'o	a sign, mark
taparahi	to beat up or thrash; also, to kill
tapu	sacred; prohibited
tārēna	calendar
taruā	edible root, *Xanthosoma sagittifolium*
tātara	to untangle or unsnare
tātara hapa	regret; repent
tātea	seminal fluid
tau'a	a formal bond-friend
taure'are'a	life stage of "adolescence"

tāvana	village chief
tehe	supercision operation
teina	a man's younger brothers and male cousins; a woman's younger sisters and female cousins
teo	clitoris
tere	to sail, to journey
tiaporo	Devil
ti'aturi	to become emotionally concerned with; to trust, believe
tiho	anus
Tinito	Chinese
titi'o	defecation
tīto'i	to retract the foreskin of the penis
tīto'ito'i	masturbation
tōiaha	heavy
toto	blood
tōtōa	pranks
tua'ana	a man's older brothers and male cousins; a woman's older sisters and female cousins
tuahine	a man's sisters and female cousins
tū'āne	a woman's brothers and male cousins
tūāro'i	a type of religious meeting
tumu	basic; "trunk"
tūpa'i	a blow with a closed fist
tūpapa'u	ghosts, spirits
tupuna	ancestors
ture	law
tutae	feces
uaina	wine
ūfa	female, of animals
u'i	generation
upo'o 'ino	"bad head," a term for mental or behavioral derangement
ure hore	penis with the foreskin stripped back
uta	inland direction
vahine	woman, a man's partner

varavara	rare
vare	to be deceived
vari	menstrual blood; mud
vārua	soul
vārua 'ino	malevolent spirit
vārua maita'i	good spirit
vau	I, first person singular pronoun
veve	poverty, poor

References

Adams, Henry. 1930. *Letters of Henry Adams, 1858-1891*, ed. Worthington C. Ford. Boston and New York: Houghton Mifflin Co.
——. 1947. *Memoirs of Ari'i Taimai.* Originally published 1893. New York: Scholar's Facsimiles and Reprints.
American Academy of Pediatrics. 1959. *Adoption of children.* Evanston, Ill.: American Academy of Pediatrics.
Ashby, William Ross. 1956. *An introduction to cybernetics.* New York: John Wiley.
Barnett, Homer G. 1960. *Being a Palauan.* New York: Holt, Rinehart and Winston.
Bateson, Gregory. 1958. *Naven.* 2d ed. Stanford: Stanford University Press.
——. 1972. *Steps to an ecology of mind.* San Francisco: Chandler Publishing Co.
Beaglehole, Ernest. 1940. The Polynesian Maori. *Journal of the Polynesian Society* 49:39-68.
——.1957. *Social change in the South Pacific.* New York: Macmillan Co.
Beaglehole, John C., ed. 1962. *The Endeavour journal of Joseph Banks, 1768-1771.* 2 vols. Sydney: August and Robertson.
Benedict, Ruth. 1946. *The chrysanthemum and the sword.* Boston: Houghton Mifflin.
Bentley, Arthur F. 1941. The human skin: Philosophy's last line of defense. *Philosophy of Science* 8 (January):1-19.
Biggs, Bruce. 1960. *Maori marriage.* Polynesian Society Monographs, no. 1. Wellington, New Zealand: The Polynesian Society.
Bligh, William. 1937. *The log of the Bounty,* ed. Owen Rutter. 2 vols. London: Golden Cockerel Press.
Boas, Franz. 1911. *The mind of primitive man.* New York: Macmillan Co.
Bougainville, Louis Antoine de. 1958. *Voyage autour du monde.* Saverne, France: Club des libraires de France.
Bouvet (no initials). 1962. *Rapport sur la criminalité en Polynesie française.* Papeete, Tahiti: Gendarmerie nationale.
Bouvet and Iorsch (no initials). 1960. *Etude sommaire sur l'evolution de la criminalité à Tahiti et en Polynesie entre 1870 et 1959.* Papeete, Tahiti: Gendarmerie nationale.
Bowlby, John. 1969. *Attachment and loss.* Vol. 1. New York: Basic Books.
Bruner, Jerome. 1961. The cognitive consequences of early sensory deprivation. In *Sensory deprivation,* ed. Philip Solomon, Philip E. Kubzansky, P. Herbert Leiderman, Jack H. Meldelson, Richard Trumbull, and Donald Wexler. Cambridge: Harvard University Press.

Bruner, Jerome; Goodnow, Jacqueline; and Austin, George. 1956. *A study of thinking.* New York: John Wiley.

Bruner, Jerome; Olver, Rose; and Greenfield, Patricia. 1966. *Studies in cognitive growth.* New York: John Wiley.

Burrows, Edwin G. 1936. *Ethnology of Futuna.* Bernice P. Bishop Museum Bulletins, no. 138. Honolulu: Bishop Museum Press.

Carroll, Vern, ed. 1970. *Adoption in eastern Oceania.* Honolulu: University of Hawaii Press.

Caudill, William, and Weinstein, Helen. 1969. Maternal care and infant behavior in Japan and America. *Psychiatry* 32:12-43.

Chafetz, Morris E., and Demone, Harold W., Jr. 1962. *Alcoholism and society.* New York: Oxford University Press.

Cook, James. 1784. *A voyage to the Pacific Ocean . . . for making discoveries in the northern hemisphere.* 4 vols. London: Stockdale et al.

———. 1955-67. *The journals of Captain James Cook,* ed. John C. Beaglehole. 3 vols. Cambridge: At the University Press, Hakluyt Society.

Coppenrath, Gérald. 1967. *Les Chinois de Tahiti.* Publications de la Société des Océanistes, no. 21. Paris: Musée de l'homme.

Corney, Bolton G., ed. 1913-19. *The quest and occupation of Tahiti by the emissaries of Spain in 1772-1776.* 3 vols. Cambridge: At the University Press, Hakluyt Society.

Danielsson, Bengt. 1956*a. Love in the South Seas.* New York: Reynal.

———. 1956*b. Work and life on Raroia.* London: Allen and Unwin.

Davies, John. 1851. *A Tahitian and English dictionary.* Tahiti: London Missionary Society Press.

De Bovis, Edmond. 1909. *Etat de la Société taitienne à l'arrivée des Européens.* Papeete, Tahiti: Imprimerie du gouvernement.

Devereux, George. 1937. Institutionalized homosexuality of the Mohave Indians. *Human Biology* 9:498-527.

Doumenge, François. 1966. *L'homme dans le Pacifique Sud.* Publications de la Société des Océanistes, no. 19. Paris: Musée de l'homme.

Dozier, Edward P. 1966. Problem drinking among American Indians. *Quarterly Journal of Studies on Alcohol* 27:72-87.

Ekman, Paul, and Friesen, Wallace. 1969. Nonverbal leakage and clues to deception. *Psychiatry* 32 (February):88-106.

Ellis, William. 1830. *Polynesian researches.* 2 vols. London: Fisher, Son, and Jackson.

Erikson, Erik H. 1950. *Childhood and society.* New York: W. W. Norton.

———. 1968. *Identity: Youth and crisis.* New York: W. W. Norton.

Fages, Jean. 1972. Dénombrement de la population de 1967 dans la circonscription des Iles sous le Vent. *Journal de la Société des Océanistes* 34 (March):67-73.

Field, Peter B. 1962. A new cross-cultural study of drunkenness. In *Society, culture, and drinking patterns,* ed. David J. Pittman and Charles R. Snyder. New York: John Wiley.

Finney, Ben. 1964. Notes on bond-friendship. *Journal of the Polynesian Society* 73 (December):431-35.

Firth, Raymond. 1936. *We the Tikopia.* London: Allen and Unwin.

————. 1940. The analysis of *mana*: An empirical approach. *Journal of the Polynesian Society* 49:483-510.

Fischer, John, and Fischer, Ann. 1963. The New Englanders of Orchard Town, U.S.A. In *Six cultures: Studies of child rearing*, ed. Beatrice Whiting. New York: John Wiley.

Forster, George. 1777. *A voyage round the world . . . in the years 1772, 1773, 1774, 1775.* 2 vols. London: B. White.

Forster, John. 1778. *Observations made during a voyage round the world.* London: G. Robinson.

Freeman, Otis W., ed. 1951. *Geography of the Pacific.* New York: John Wiley.

Gauguin, Paul. 1957. *Noa Noa.* New York: Noonday Press.

Gesell, Arnold; Halverson, Henry; Thompson, Helen; Ilg, Frances; Castner, Burton; Ames, Louise; and Amatruda, Catherine. 1940. *The first five years of life.* New York: Harper and Brothers.

Gladwin, Thomas, and Sarason, Seymour B. 1953. *Truk: Man in paradise.* Viking Fund Publications in Anthropology, no. 20. New York: Wenner-Gren Foundation for Anthropological Research.

Gunson, W. N. 1959. Evangelical missionaries in the South Seas: 1797-1860. Ph.D. diss., Research School of Pacific Studies, Australian National University.

Hamilton, Edith. 1942. *Mythology.* Boston: Little, Brown.

Handy, E. S. Craighill. 1927. *Polynesian religion.* Bernice P. Bishop Museum Bulletins, no. 34. Honolulu: Bishop Museum Press.

Henry, Teuira. 1928. *Ancient Tahiti.* Bernice P. Bishop Museum Bulletins, no. 48. Honolulu: Bishop Museum Press.

Hilgard, Ernest. 1962. *Introduction to psychology.* 3d ed. New York: Harcourt, Brace and World.

Howard, Alan. 1970. Adoption on Rotuma. In *Adoption in eastern Oceania*, ed. Vern Carroll. Honolulu: University of Hawaii Press.

Howard, Alan; Heighton, Robert H., Jr.; Jordan, Cathie E.; and Gallimore, Ronald. 1970. Traditional and modern adoption patterns in Hawaii. In *Adoption in eastern Oceania*, ed. Vern Carroll. Honolulu: University of Hawaii Press.

Howard, Alan, and Scott, Robert A. 1965-66. Cultural values and attitudes toward death. *Journal of Existentialism* 6:161-74.

Inkeles, Alex; Hanfmann, Eugenia; and Beier, Helen. 1958. Modal personality and adjustment to the Soviet socio-political system. *Human Relations* 11 (February):3-22.

Inkeles, Alex, and Levinson, Daniel J. 1954. National character. In *Handbook of social psychology*, ed. Gardner Lindzey. Reading, Mass.: Addison-Wesley.

Irwin, Samuel. 1968. A rational framework for the development, evaluation, and use of psychoactive drugs. *American Journal of Psychiatry* 124 (February supplement):1-19.

Jullien, Michel. 1963. Aspects de la configuration ethnique et socio-economique de Papeete. In *Pacific port towns and cities*, ed. Alexander Spoehr. Honolulu: Bishop Museum Press.

Kaplan, Bert. 1968. Personality and social structure. In *Theory in anthropology*, ed. Robert Manners and David Kaplan. Chicago: Aldine.

Kardiner, Abram. 1945. *The psychological frontiers of society*. New York: Columbia University Press.

Kay, Paul. 1963. Aspects of social structure in Manuhoe. Ph.D. diss., Harvard University.

Kierkegaard, Søren. 1954. *Fear and trembling*. Rev. ed. New York: Doubleday.

Kirk, H. David. 1964. *Shared fate: A theory of adoption and mental health*. New York: Free Press.

Kluckhohn, Clyde. 1944. *Navaho witchcraft*. Boston: Beacon Press.

Kluckhohn, Florence, and Strodtbeck, Fred. 1961. *Variations in value orientations*. Evanston, Ill.: Row, Peterson.

Kroeber, Alfred L. 1948. *Anthropology*. Rev. ed. New York: Harcourt, Brace and World.

Lambert, Bernd. 1964. Fosterage in the northern Gilbert Islands. *Ethnology* 3:232-58.

Lamont, E. H. 1867. *Wild life among the Pacific islanders*. London: Hurst and Blackett.

Landauer, Thomas, and Whiting, John. 1964. Infantile stimulation and adult stature of human males. *American Anthropologist* 66 (October): 1007-28.

Lavondes, Henri. 1968. Le vocabulaire des valeurs culturelles dans la littérature orale des Iles Marquises. Mimeographed. Papeete: ORSTOM.

Lecucq, H. 1849. *Question de Tahiti*. Paris: Librairie militaire de Blot.

Lee, Ida, ed. 1920. *Captain Bligh's second voyage to the South Sea*. London: Longmans, Green.

Leighton, Alexander H. 1969. A comparative study of psychiatric disorder in Nigeria and rural North America. In *Changing perspectives in mental illness*, ed. Stanley Plog and Robert Edgerton. New York: Holt, Rinehart and Winston.

Leighton, Alexander H.; Lambo, T. Adeoye; Hughes, Charles C.; Leighton, Dorothea C.; Murphy, Jane M.; and Macklin, David B. 1963. *Psychiatric disorder among the Yoruba*. Ithaca: Cornell University Press.

Leighton, Dorothea C.; Harding, John S.; Macklin, David B.; Macmillan, Allister M.; and Leighton, Alexander H. 1963. *The character of danger: Psychiatric symptoms in selected communities*. The Stirling County Study of Psychiatric Disorder and Sociocultural Environment, vol. 3. New York: Basic Books.

Lemert, Edwin M. 1964a. Drinking in Hawaiian plantation society. *Quarterly Journal of Studies on Alcohol* 25:689-713.

———. 1964b. Forms and pathology of drinking in three Polynesian societies. *American Anthropologist* 66:361-74.

Levy, Robert I. 1958. The psychodynamic functions of alcohol. *Quarterly Journal of Studies on Alcohol* 19:649-59.

———. 1969. *Personality studies in Polynesia and Micronesia: Stability and change*. Working Papers, no. 8. Honolulu: University of Hawaii, Social Science Research Institute.

———. 1970. Teaching of the Tahitian language in the schools of French Polynesia. *Journal de la Société des Océanistes* 26 (March):79-83.

Lewis, C. S. 1961. *The Screwtape letters.* New York: Macmillan Co.

Linn, Louis. 1967. Clinical manifestations of psychiatric disorders. In *Comprehensive textbook of psychiatry,* ed. Alfred M. Freedman and Harold I. Kaplan. Baltimore: Williams and Wilkins Co.

London Missionary Society Archives. Letters and journals of missionaries.

Lowie, Robert. 1962. Primitive adoption. In *Encyclopaedia of the social sciences,* ed. Edwin Seligman and Alvin Johnson, vol. 1. New York: Macmillan Co.

McArthur, Norma. 1968. *Island populations of the Pacific.* Honolulu: University of Hawaii Press.

Macgregor, Gordon. 1937. *Ethnology of Tokelau Islands.* Bernice P. Bishop Museum Bulletin, no. 146. Honolulu: Bishop Museum Press.

Mack, John E., and Semrad, Elvin V. 1967. Classical psychoanalysis. In *Comprehensive textbook of psychiatry,* ed. Alfred M. Freedman and Harold I. Kaplan. Baltimore: Williams and Wilkins Co.

Mead, Margaret. 1949. *Coming of age in Samoa.* Originally published 1928. New York: William Morrow.

Moench, Richard U. 1963. Economic relations of Chinese in the Society Islands. Ph.D. diss., Harvard University.

Moerenhout, Jacques A. 1837. *Voyage aux îles du grand ocean.* 2 vols. Paris: Bertrand.

Monberg, Torben. 1966. The sacred and the profane: A survey of some Bellonese concepts. Appendix in *The religion of Bellona Island.* Copenhagen: National Museum of Denmark.

Moore, Wilbert, and Tumin, Melvin. 1949. Some social functions of ignorance. *American Sociological Review* 14:787-97.

Morrison, James. 1935. *The journal of James Morrison.* London: Golden Cockerel Press.

Newbury, Colin W., ed. 1961. *The history of the Tahitian mission, 1799-1830.* Cambridge: At the University Press, Hakluyt Society.

Oliver, Douglas. Forthcoming. *Ancient Tahitian society.* Honolulu: University Press of Hawaii.

Papy, H. Rene, and L'Herbier, Leon. 1957. *Nouveau catalogue des plantes medicinales de Tahiti.* Vol. 5, section 2, part 1. Toulouse: Travaux du Laboratoire forestier de Toulouse.

Parker, Frederick B. 1959. A comparison of the sex temperament of alcoholics and moderate drinkers. *American Sociological Review* 24:366-74.

Petrie, Asenath. 1967. *Individuality in pain and suffering.* Chicago: University of Chicago Press.

Piers, Gerhart, and Singer, Milton B. 1971. *Shame and guilt.* Originally published 1953. New York: W. W. Norton.

Pittenger, Robert E.; Hockett, Charles F.; and Danehy, John J. 1960. *The first five minutes.* Ithaca: Paul Martineau.

Pittman, David J., and Snyder, Charles R. 1962. *Society, culture, and drinking patterns.* New York: John Wiley.

Pukui, Mary K., and Elbert, Samuel. 1957. *Hawaiian-English dictionary.* Honolulu: University of Hawaii Press.

Rin, Hsien, and Lin, Tsung-Yi. 1962. Mental illness among Formosan aborigines as compared with the Chinese in Taiwan. *Journal of Mental Science* 108 (March):134-46.

Ritchie, James. 1956. *Basic personality in Rakau.* Wellington, New Zealand: Department of Psychology, Victoria University.

Robertson, George. 1948. *The discovery of Tahiti: A journal of the second voyage of H.M.S. Dolphin . . . in the years 1776, 1767, and 1768,* ed. Hugh Carrington. London: Hakluyt Society.

Schachtel, Ernest. 1949. On memory and childhood amnesia. In *A study of interpersonal relations,* ed. Patrick Mullahy. New York: Hermitage Press.

Schwartz, Theodore. In preparation. The cargo cult: A Melanesian type-response to culture contact. In *Responses to change,* ed. George DeVos.

Sears, Robert R.; Maccoby, Eleanor E.; and Levin, Harry. 1957. *Patterns of child rearing.* Evanston, Ill.: Row, Peterson.

Srole, Leo; Langner, Thomas S.; Michael, Stanley T.; Opler, Marvin K.; and Rennie, Thomas A. C. 1962. *Mental health in the metropolis: The Midtown Manhattan study.* Thomas A. C. Rennie Series in Social Psychiatry, vol. 1. New York: McGraw-Hill, Blakiston Division.

Stein, Marvin, and Schiavi, Raul. 1967. Respiratory disorders. In *Comprehensive textbook of psychiatry,* ed. Alfred Freedman and Harold Kaplan. Baltimore: Williams and Wilkins Co.

Sternbach, Richard A. 1968. *Pain.* New York: Academic Press.

Stimson, J. Frank, and Marshall, Donald S. 1964. *A Dictionary of some Tuamotuan dialects of the Polynesian language.* The Hague: Martinus Nijhoff.

Stocking, George W., Jr. 1968. *Race, culture, and evolution.* New York: Free Press.

Tahiti. 1967. *Bulletin de statistique.* Section d'études statistiques, Service du plan. Papeete, Tahiti. No. 1.

T'Serstevens, Albert. 1950. *Tahiti et sa couronne.* Paris: Albin Michel.

Tucci, Guiseppe. 1967. *Tibet.* Calcutta: Oxford and Ibh.

Turnbull, John. 1812. *A voyage round the world in the years 1800, 1801, 1802, 1803 and 1804.* London: A. Maxwell.

United Nations, Department of Social Affairs. 1953. *Study of adoption of children.*

Wallis, Samuel. 1766-68. Journal of his voyage round the world in the *Dolphin.* Fair copy. Wellington, New Zealand: Alexander Turnbull Library.

Washburne, Chandler. 1961. *Primitive drinking: A study of the uses and functions of alcohol in preliterate societies.* New York: College and University Press.

Weckler, J. E. 1953. Adoption on Mokil. *American Anthropologist* 55: 555-69.

Werner, Heinz. 1948. *The comparative psychology of mental development.* New York: International Universities Press.

White, Ralph G., ed. 1948. *E parau teie no roto mai i te moemoea no te pō mai* [The story of a dream from out of the *pō*]. Bakerfield, Conn.: Te Fare Vāna'a Press.

Whiting, John. 1960. Resource mediation and learning by identification. In *Personality development in children*, ed. Ira Iscoe and Harold W. Stevenson. Austin: University of Texas Press.

Whiting, John; Child, Irvin; and Lambert, William. 1966. *Field guide for a study of socialization*. Six Cultures Series, vol. 1. New York: John Wiley.

Williams, John. 1837. *Missionary enterprises in the South Sea Islands*. London: Snow.

Williams, John S. 1960. *Maori achievement motivation*. Victoria University of Wellington Publications in Psychology, no. 13. Wellington, New Zealand: Victoria University.

Wilson, James. 1799. *A missionary voyage to the Southern Pacific Ocean . . . in 1796, 1797, 1798*. London: T. Chapman.

Wolff, Harold, and Wolf, Stewart. 1948. *Pain*. American Lectures in Physiology, no. 5. Springfield, Ill.: Charles C. Thomas.

Wood, Arthur Lewis. 1961. *Crime and aggression in changing Ceylon*. Transactions of the American Philosophical Society, new series, vol. 51, part 8. Philadelphia: American Philosophical Society.

World Health Organization. 1953. *Joint UN/WHO meeting of experts on the mental health aspects of adoption*. WHO Technical Report Series, no. 70.

Wright, Louis, and Fry, Mary. 1936. *Puritans in the South Seas*. New York: Henry Holt.

Index

Abortion, 142
Abraham, 352-53
Absolutes, 263-64
Abstractions, cultural, 263-66
Acceptability, 348, 349, 350, 352
Accidents: death from, 226, 227n, 229; interpreted as punishment, 309, 311-12, 448, 467
"Acculturation," definition of, 33n
Accumulation, and security, 223, 230-31. *See also* Ambition
Action: evaluation of, 349, 350; importance of, 183-86, 320, 332-33, 339, 346, 347, 350; reason for, 322, 350, 353. *See also* Behavior, external
Adams, Henry, 23, 232, 361, 411
Adequacy, personal, 335-39, 347-48
Adjustment, meaning of, 392-93. *See also* "Maladjustment"; Mental illness
Adolescents. See *Taure'are'a*; *Taure'are'a* period
Adoption: against parents' will, 193, 477-79; as cultural form, 473-77, 481-86; economic aspects of, 476-77; frequency of, 27, 473-76, 483, 484; incomplete separation in, 479-80, 484; reasons for, 475-79, 483; by relatives, 474, 476, 478, 479, 483; in short-term relationships, 193-94; as symbol of contingency, 483, 484-85; terminology for, 474n; throughout Oceania, 474n, 475-77, 478-81; time of, 437; treatment of adopted children, 479, 480-81; western ideals of, 483-85
Adultery, 195-96, 330-33
Adulthood: activities of, 202; disadvantages of, 196-97; effect of socialization on, 176, 324, 434-35, 440, 459-62; friendships during, 202; and marriage, 194; transition to, 194, 196-97, 201-2, 436-37, 469, 472

Aggression: control of, 280-82, 467-68; mock, 280, 446. *See also* Anger; Fighting; Hostility; Violence
Aging, 207-8, 314
Agriculture. *See* Gardening
Airplanes, pursuit by, 379, 388, 498
Alcohol. *See* Drinking
Aloha, meaning of, 343n
Ambition: danger of, 181-82, 185, 186, 230, 288, 351, 497-98; disapproval of, 174, 185, 186, 288, 354, 497-98
Amusements, 22-25, 127
Ancestors: as agents in curses, 158-59, 160, 172; attitude toward, 87, 184-85, 208, 218-19; and dreams, 154, 376, 377, 382-83, 386-87; as guardians, 181; knowledge of, 87, 218-19. *See also* Past; Relatives; Spirits
Anger: attitude toward, 284-85; as cause of suicide, 225, 278-79, 286; control of, 224, 280-82, 287, 467-68; and curses, 158-59, 172, 286-87; expression of, 279-80, 282-83, 285-87; fear of, 287, 467-68; historical accounts of, 273-75; projection of, 498-99; at self, 224; terminology for, 284-85. *See also* Aggression; Violence
Animals: in dreams, 378, 380-81, 383, 387-88, 498; in Piri, 10-11, 30
"Anthropologist's friend," definition of, 39, 76. *See also* Manu; Poria
Anthropology, view of thinking, 242-45, 248-49
Anxiety: frequency of, 402-3; types of, 307-8; about women, 466. *See also* Fear; Timidity
Ao (daylight world), 149, 161, 492n
Approval, of self, 222-25. *See also* Acceptability
Architecture, 10, 11, 28-29, 35
Arguments: in settled relationships, 158-59, 199, 286-87; in short-term relation-